Understanding Operating Systems

Systems

Sixth Edition

Ann McIver McHoes
Ida M. Flynn

COURSE TECHNOLOGY
CENGAGE Learning™

Australia • Canada • Mexico • Singapore • Spain • United Kingdom • United States

COURSE TECHNOLOGY
CENGAGE Learning

Understanding Operating Systems, Sixth Edition

Ann McIver McHoes and Ida M. Flynn

Executive Editor: Marie Lee

Acquisitions Editor: Amy Jollymore

Senior Product Manager: Alyssa Pratt

Editorial Assistant: Zina Kresin

Content Project Manager: Jennifer Feltri

Art Director: Faith Brosnan

Print Buyer: Julio Esperas

Cover Designer: Night & Day Design

Cover Photos: iStockphoto

Proofreader: Suzanne Huizenga

Indexer: Ann McIver McHoes

Compositor: Integra

For product information and technology assistance, contact us at
Cengage Learning Customer & Sales Support, 1-800-354-9706

For permission to use material from this text or product, submit all requests online at **www.cengage.com/permissions**
Further permissions questions can be e-mailed to
permissionrequest@cengage.com

Library of Congress Control Number: 2010920344

ISBN-13: 978-0-5384-7004-9

ISBN-10: 0-5384-7004-6

Course Technology
20 Channel Center Street
Boston, MA 02210
USA

Some of the product names and company names used in this book have been used for identification purposes only and may be trademarks or registered trademarks of their respective manufacturers and sellers.

Any fictional data related to persons, or companies or URLs used throughout this book is intended for instructional purposes only. At the time this book was printed, any such data was fictional and not belonging to any real persons or companies.

Course Technology, a part of Cengage Learning, reserves the right to revise this publication and make changes from time to time in its content without notice.

Cengage Learning is a leading provider of customized learning solutions with office locations around the globe, including Singapore, the United Kingdom, Australia, Mexico, Brazil and Japan. Locate your local office at: **www.cengage.com/global**

Cengage Learning products are represented in Canada by Nelson Education, Ltd.

To learn more about Course Technology, visit
www.cengage.com/coursetechnology

Purchase any of our products at your local college store or at our preferred online store **www.CengageBrain.com**

Printed in the United States of America
1 2 3 4 5 6 7 16 15 14 13 12 11 10

Chapter 3   Memory Management: Virtual Memory   63

Chapter 4   Processor Management   107

Chapter 7 Device Management 203

Chapter 8	File Management	249

Part Two   Operating Systems in Practice   **397**

Chapter 13   UNIX Operating System   401

Chapter 16   Linux Operating System   499

Appendix

Glossary   529

Bibliography   559

Index   563

Preface

This book explains a very technical subject in a not-so-technical manner, putting the concepts of operating systems into a format that students can quickly grasp.

For those new to the subject, this text demonstrates what operating systems are, what they do, how they do it, how their performance can be evaluated, and how they compare with each other. Throughout the text we describe the overall function and tell readers where to find more detailed information, if they so desire.

For those with more technical backgrounds, this text introduces the subject concisely, describing the complexities of operating systems without going into intricate detail. One might say this book leaves off where other operating system textbooks begin.

To do so, we've made some assumptions about our audiences. First, we assume the readers have some familiarity with computing systems. Second, we assume they have a working knowledge of an operating system and how it interacts with them. We recommend (although we don't require) that readers be familiar with at least one operating system. In a few places, we found it necessary to include examples using Java or pseudocode to illustrate the inner workings of the operating systems; but, for readers who are unfamiliar with computer languages, we've added a prose description to each example that explains the events in more familiar terms.

Organization and Features

This book is structured to explain the functions of an operating system regardless of the hardware that houses it. The organization addresses a recurring problem with textbooks about technologies that continue to change—that is, the constant advances in evolving subject matter can make textbooks immediately outdated. To address this problem, we've divided the material into two parts: first, the concepts—which do not change quickly—and second, the specifics of operating systems—which change dramatically over the course of years and even months. Our goal is to give readers the ability to apply the topics intelligently, realizing that, although a command, or series of commands, used by one operating system may be different from another, their goals are the same and the functions of the operating systems are also the same.

Although it is more difficult to understand how operating systems work than to memorize the details of a single operating system, understanding general operating system concepts is a longer-lasting achievement. Such understanding also pays off in the long run because it allows one to adapt as technology changes—as, inevitably, it does. Therefore, the purpose of this book is to give computer users a solid background in the basics of operating systems, their functions and goals, and how they interact and interrelate.

Part One, the first 12 chapters, describes the theory of operating systems. It concentrates on each of the "managers" in turn and shows how they work together. Then it introduces network organization concepts, security, ethics, and management of network functions. Part Two examines actual operating systems, how they apply the theories presented in Part One, and how they compare with each other.

Chapter 1 gives a brief introduction to the subject. The meat of the text begins in Chapters 2 and 3 with memory management because it is the simplest component of the operating system to explain and has historically been tied to the advances from one operating system to the next. We explain the role of the Processor Manager in Chapters 4, 5, and 6, first discussing simple systems and then expanding the discussion to include multiprocessing systems. By the time we reach device management in Chapter 7 and file management in Chapter 8, readers will have been introduced to the four main managers found in every operating system. Chapters 9 and 10 introduce basic concepts related to networking, and Chapters 11 and 12 discuss security, ethics, and some of the tradeoffs that designers consider when attempting to satisfy the needs of their user population.

Each chapter includes learning objectives, key terms, and research topics. For technically oriented readers, the exercises at the end of each chapter include problems for advanced students. Please note that some advanced exercises assume knowledge of matters not presented in the book, but they're good for those who enjoy a challenge. We expect some readers from a more general background will cheerfully pass them by.

In an attempt to bring the concepts closer to home, throughout the book we've added real-life examples to illustrate abstract concepts. However, let no one confuse our conversational style with our considerable respect for the subject matter. The subject of operating systems is a complex one and it cannot be covered completely in these few pages. Therefore, this textbook does not attempt to give an in-depth treatise of operating systems theory and applications. This is the overall view.

Part Two introduces four operating systems in the order of their first release: UNIX, MS-DOS, Windows, and Linux. Here, each chapter discusses how one operating system applies the concepts discussed in Part One and how it compares with the others. Again, we must stress that this is a general discussion—an in-depth examination of an operating system would require details based on its current standard version, which can't be done here. We strongly suggest that readers use our discussion as a guide, a base to work from, when comparing the pros and cons of a specific operating system and supplement our work with research that's as current as possible.

The text concludes with several reference aids. Terms that are important within a chapter are listed at its conclusion as key terms. The extensive end-of-book Glossary includes brief definitions for hundreds of terms used in these pages. The Bibliography can guide the reader to basic research on the subject. Finally, the Appendix features the ACM Code of Ethics.

Not included in this text is a discussion of databases and data structures, except as examples of process synchronization problems, because they only tangentially relate to operating systems and are frequently the subject of other courses. We suggest that readers begin by learning the basics as presented in the following pages before pursuing these complex subjects.

Changes to the Sixth Edition

This edition has been thoroughly updated and features many improvements over the fifth edition:

- New references to Macintosh OS X, which is based on UNIX
- Numerous new homework exercises in every chapter
- Updated references to the expanding influence of wireless technology
- More networking information throughout the text
- Continuing emphasis on system security and patch management
- More discussion describing the management of multiple processors
- Updated detail in the chapters that discuss UNIX, Windows, and Linux
- New research topics and student exercises for the chapters on UNIX, MS-DOS, Windows, and Linux

Other changes throughout the text are editorial clarifications, expanded captions, and improved illustrations.

A Note for Instructors

The following supplements are available when this text is used in a classroom setting:

Electronic Instructor's Manual. The Instructor's Manual that accompanies this textbook includes additional instructional material to assist in class preparation, including Sample Syllabi, Chapter Outlines, Technical Notes, Lecture Notes, Quick Quizzes, Teaching Tips, and Discussion Topics.

Distance Learning. Course Technology is proud to present online test banks in WebCT and Blackboard to provide the most complete and dynamic learning experience possible. Instructors are encouraged to make the most of the course, both online and offline. For more information on how to access the online test bank, contact your local Course Technology sales representative.

PowerPoint Presentations. This book comes with Microsoft PowerPoint slides for each chapter. These are included as a teaching aid for classroom presentations, either to make available to students on the network for chapter review, or to be printed for classroom distribution. Instructors can add their own slides for additional topics that they introduce to the class.

Solutions. Selected solutions to Review Questions and Exercises are provided on the Instructor Resources CD-ROM and may also be found on the Cengage Course Technology Web site at *www.cengage.com/coursetechnology*. The solutions are password protected.

Order of Presentation. We have built this text with a modular construction to accommodate several presentation options, depending on the instructor's preference. For example, the syllabus can follow the chapters as listed in Chapter 1 through Chapter 12 to present the core concepts that all operating systems have in common. Using this path, students will learn about the management of memory, processors, devices, files, and networks, in that order. An alternative path might begin with Chapter 1, move next to processor management in Chapters 4 through 6, then to memory management in Chapters 2 and 3, touch on systems security and management in Chapters 11 and 12, and finally move to device and file management in Chapters 7 and 8. Because networking is often the subject of another course, instructors may choose to bypass Chapters 9 and 10, or include them for a more thorough treatment of operating systems.

We hope you find our discussion of ethics helpful in Chapter 11, which is included in response to requests by university adopters of the text who want to discuss this subject in their lectures.

In Part Two, we examine details about four specific operating systems in an attempt to show how the concepts in the first 12 chapters are applied by a specific operating system. In each case, the chapter is structured in a similar manner as the chapters in Part One. That is, they discuss the management of memory, processors, files, devices, networks, and systems. In addition, each includes an introduction to one or more user interfaces for that operating system. With this edition, we added exercises and research topics to each of these chapters to help students explore issues discussed in the preceding pages.

For the first time, we included references to the Macintosh OS X operating system in the UNIX chapter.

We continue to include MS-DOS in spite of its age because faculty reviewers and adopters have specifically requested it, presumably so students can learn the basics of this command-driven interface using a Windows emulator.

If you have suggestions for inclusion in this text, please send them along. Although we are squeezed for space, we are pleased to consider all possibilities.

Acknowledgments

Our gratitude goes to all of our friends and colleagues, who were so generous with their encouragement, advice, and support. Special thanks go to Robert Kleinmann, Eleanor Irwin, Charles R. Woratschek, Terri Lennox, and Roger Flynn for their assistance.

Special thanks also to those at Course Technology, Brooks/Cole, and PWS Publishing who made significant contributions to all six editions of this text, especially Alyssa Pratt, Kallie Swanson, Mike Sugarman, and Mary Thomas Stone. In addition, the following individuals made key contributions to this edition: Jennifer Feltri, Content Project Manager, and Sreejith Govindan, Integra.

We deeply appreciate the comments of the reviewers who helped us refine this edition:

Proposal Reviewers:
Nisheeth Agrawal: Calhoun Community College
Brian Arthur: Mary Baldwin College
Margaret Moore: University of Phoenix

Chapter Reviewers:
Kent Einspahr: Concordia University
Gary Heisler: Lansing Community College
Paul Hemler: Hampden-Sydney College

And to the many students and instructors who have sent helpful comments and suggestions since publication of the first edition in 1991, we thank you. Please keep them coming.

Ann McIver McHoes, mchoesa@duq.edu

Ida M. Flynn

Operating Systems Concepts

> *"So work the honey-bees,*
> *Creatures that by a rule in nature teach*
> *The act of order to a peopled kingdom.* *"*

—William Shakespeare (1564–1616; in Henry V)

All operating systems have certain core items in common: each must manage memory, processing capability, devices and peripherals, files, and networks. In Part One of this text we present an overview of these operating systems essentials.

- Chapter 1 introduces the subject.
- Chapters 2–3 discuss main memory management.
- Chapters 4–6 cover processor management.
- Chapter 7 concentrates on device management.
- Chapter 8 is devoted to file management.
- Chapters 9–10 briefly review networks.
- Chapter 11 discusses system security issues.
- Chapter 12 explores system management and the interaction of the operating system's components.

Then, in Part Two of the text (Chapters 13–16), we look at specific operating systems and how they apply the theory presented here in Part One.

Throughout our discussion of this very technical subject, we try to include definitions of terms that might be unfamiliar to you. However, it isn't always possible to describe a function and define the technical terms while keeping the explanation clear. Therefore, we've put the key terms with definitions at the end of each chapter, and at the end of the text is an extensive glossary for your reference. Items listed in the Key Terms are shown in boldface the first time they appear.

Throughout the book we keep our descriptions and examples as simple as possible to introduce you to the system's complexities without getting bogged down in technical detail. Therefore, be aware that for almost every topic explained in the following pages, there's much more information that can be studied. Our goal is to introduce you to the subject, and to encourage you to pursue your interest using other texts or primary sources if you need more detail.

Chapter 1

Introducing Operating Systems

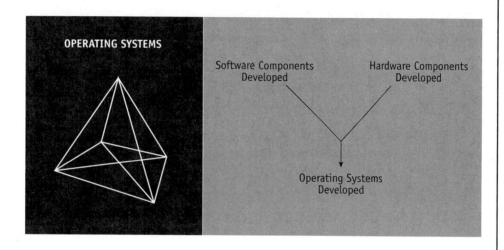

" I think there is a world market for maybe five computers. "

—Thomas J. Watson (1874–1956; chairman of IBM 1949–1956)

Learning Objectives

After completing this chapter, you should be able to describe:

- Innovations in operating system development
- The basic role of an operating system
- The major operating system software subsystem managers and their functions
- The types of machine hardware on which operating systems run
- The differences among batch, interactive, real-time, hybrid, and embedded operating systems
- Multiprocessing and its impact on the evolution of operating system software
- Virtualization and core architecture trends in new operating systems

Introduction

To understand an operating system is to understand the workings of an entire computer system, because the operating system manages each and every piece of hardware and software. This text explores what operating systems are, how they work, what they do, and why.

This chapter briefly describes how simple operating systems work and how, in general, they've evolved. The following chapters explore each component in more depth and show how its function relates to the other parts of the operating system. In other words, you see how the pieces work harmoniously to keep the computer system working smoothly.

What Is an Operating System?

A computer system consists of **software** (programs) and **hardware** (the physical machine and its electronic components). The **operating system** software is the chief piece of software, the portion of the computing system that manages all of the hardware and all of the other software. To be specific, it controls every file, every device, every section of main memory, and every nanosecond of processing time. It controls who can use the system and how. In short, it's the boss.

Therefore, each time the user sends a command, the operating system must make sure that the command is executed; or, if it's not executed, it must arrange for the user to get a message explaining the error. Remember: This doesn't necessarily mean that the operating system executes the command or sends the error message—but it does control the parts of the system that do.

Operating System Software

The pyramid shown in Figure 1.1 is an abstract representation of an operating system and demonstrates how its major components work together.

At the base of the pyramid are the four essential managers of every operating system: the **Memory Manager**, the **Processor Manager**, the **Device Manager**, and the **File Manager**. In fact, these managers are the basis of all operating systems and each is discussed in detail throughout the first part of this book. Each manager works closely with the other managers and performs its unique role regardless of which specific operating system is being discussed. At the top of the pyramid is the User Interface, from which users issue commands to the operating system. This is the component that's unique to each operating system—sometimes even between different versions of the same operating system.

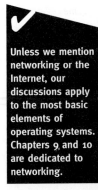

Unless we mention networking or the Internet, our discussions apply to the most basic elements of operating systems. Chapters 9 and 10 are dedicated to networking.

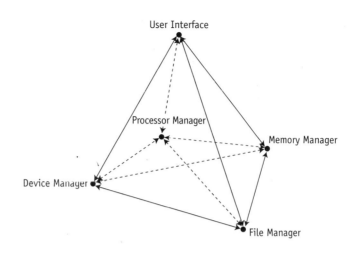

(figure 1.1)

This model of a non-networked operating system shows four subsystem managers supporting the User Interface.

A **network** was not always an integral part of operating systems; early systems were self-contained with all network capability added on top of existing operating systems. Now most operating systems routinely incorporate a **Network Manager**. The base of a pyramid for a networked operating system is shown in Figure 1.2.

Regardless of the size or configuration of the system, each of the subsystem managers, shown in Figure 1.3, must perform the following tasks:

- Monitor its resources continuously
- Enforce the policies that determine who gets what, when, and how much
- Allocate the resource when appropriate
- Deallocate the resource when appropriate

(figure 1.2)

Networked systems have a Network Manager that assumes responsibility for networking tasks while working harmoniously with every other manager.

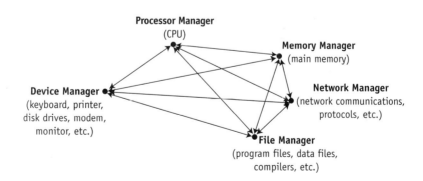

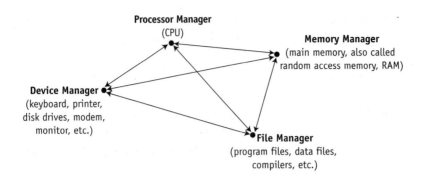

(figure 1.3)

Each subsystem manager at the base of the pyramid takes responsibility for its own tasks while working harmoniously with every other manager.

Main Memory Management

The Memory Manager (the subject of Chapters 2–3) is in charge of main memory, also known as RAM, short for Random Access Memory. The Memory Manager checks the validity of each request for memory space and, if it is a legal request, it allocates a portion of memory that isn't already in use. In a multiuser environment, the Memory Manager sets up a table to keep track of who is using which section of memory. Finally, when the time comes to reclaim the memory, the Memory Manager deallocates memory.

A primary responsibility of the Memory Manager is to protect the space in main memory occupied by the operating system itself—it can't allow any part of it to be accidentally or intentionally altered.

> ✔ **RAM is the computer's main memory and was called "primary storage" in early systems.**

Processor Management

The Processor Manager (the subject of Chapters 4–6) decides how to allocate the central processing unit (CPU). An important function of the Processor Manager is to keep track of the status of each process. A process is defined here as an instance of execution of a program.

The Processor Manager monitors whether the CPU is executing a process or waiting for a READ or WRITE command to finish execution. Because it handles the processes' transitions from one state of execution to another, it can be compared to a traffic controller. Once the Processor Manager allocates the processor, it sets up the necessary registers and tables and, when the job is finished or the maximum amount of time has expired, it reclaims the processor.

Think of it this way: The Processor Manager has two levels of responsibility. One is to handle jobs as they enter the system and the other is to manage each process within those jobs. The first part is handled by the Job Scheduler, the high-level portion of the Processor Manager, which accepts or rejects the incoming jobs. The second part is handled by the Process Scheduler, the low-level portion of the Processor Manager, which is responsible for deciding which process gets the CPU and for how long.

Device Management

The Device Manager (the subject of Chapter 7) monitors every device, channel, and control unit. Its job is to choose the most efficient way to allocate all of the system's devices, printers, ports, disk drives, and so forth, based on a scheduling policy chosen by the system's designers.

The Device Manager does this by allocating each resource, starting its operation, and, finally, deallocating the device, making it available to the next process or job.

File Management

The File Manager (the subject of Chapter 8) keeps track of every file in the system, including data files, program files, compilers, and applications. By using predetermined access policies, it enforces restrictions on who has access to which files. The File Manager also controls what users are allowed to do with files once they access them. For example, a user might have read-only access, read-and-write access, or the authority to create and delete files. Managing access control is a key part of file management. Finally, the File Manager allocates the necessary resources and later deallocates them.

Network Management

Operating systems with Internet or networking capability have a fifth essential manager called the Network Manager (the subject of Chapters 9–10) that provides a convenient way for users to share resources while controlling users' access to them. These resources include hardware (such as CPUs, memory areas, printers, tape drives, modems, and disk drives) and software (such as compilers, application programs, and data files).

User Interface

The user interface is the portion of the operating system that users interact with directly. In the old days, the user interface consisted of commands typed on a keyboard and displayed on a monitor, as shown in Figure 1.4. Now most systems allow users to choose a menu option from a list. The user interface, desktops, and formats vary widely from one operating system to another, as shown in Chapters 13–16 in Part Two of this text.

(figure 1.4)

Two user interfaces from Linux: a command-driven interface (left) and a menu-driven interface (right).

Cooperation Issues

However, it is not enough for each manager to perform its individual tasks. It must also be able to work harmoniously with every other manager. Here is a simplified example. Let's say someone chooses an option from a menu to execute a program. The following major steps must occur in sequence:

1. The Device Manager must receive the electrical impulses from the mouse or keyboard, form the command, and send the command to the User Interface, where the Processor Manager validates the command.

2. The Processor Manager then sends an acknowledgment message to be displayed on the monitor so the user realizes the command has been sent.

3. When the Processor Manager receives the command, it determines whether the program must be retrieved from storage or is already in memory, and then notifies the appropriate manager.

4. If the program is in storage, the File Manager must calculate its exact location on the disk and pass this information to the Device Manager, which retrieves the program and sends it to the Memory Manager.

5. The Memory Manager then finds space for it and records its exact location in memory. Once the program is in memory, the Memory Manager must track its location in memory (even if it's moved) as well as its progress as it's executed by the Processor Manager.

6. When the program has finished executing, it must send a finished message to the Processor Manager so that the processor can be assigned to the next program waiting in line.

7. Finally, the Processor Manager must forward the finished message to the Device Manager, so that it can notify the user and refresh the screen.

Although this is a vastly oversimplified demonstration of a complex operation, it illustrates some of the incredible precision required for the operating system to work smoothly. So although we'll be discussing each manager in isolation for much of this text, no single manager could perform its tasks without the active cooperation of every other part.

A Brief History of Machine Hardware

To appreciate the role of the operating system (which is software), we need to discuss the essential aspects of the computer system's hardware, the physical machine and its electronic components, including memory chips, input/output devices, **storage** devices, and the central processing unit (CPU).

- **Main memory** (random access memory, RAM) is where the data and instructions must reside to be processed.
- I/O devices, short for input/output devices, include every peripheral unit in the system such as printers, disk drives, CD/DVD drives, flash memory, keyboards, and so on.
- The **central processing unit** (CPU) is the brains with the circuitry (sometimes called the chip) to control the interpretation and execution of instructions. In essence, it controls the operation of the entire computer system, as illustrated in Figure 1.5. All storage references, data manipulations, and I/O operations are initiated or performed by the CPU.

Until the mid-1970s, computers were classified by capacity and price. A **mainframe** was a large machine—in size and in internal memory capacity. The IBM 360, introduced in

(figure 1.5)

A logical view of a typical computer system hardware configuration. The tower holds the central processing unit, the arithmetic and logic unit, registers, cache, and main memory, as well as controllers and interfaces shown within the dotted lines.

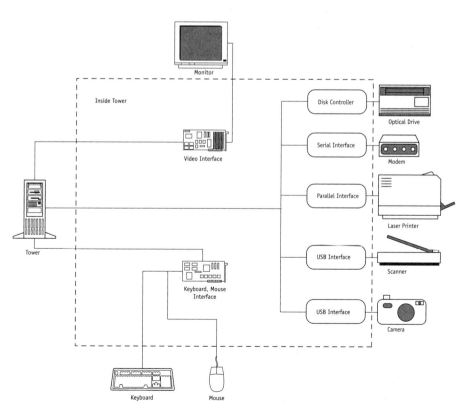

1964, is a classic example of an early mainframe. The IBM 360 model 30 required an air-conditioned room about 18 feet square to house the CPU, the operator's console, a printer, a card reader, and a keypunch machine. The CPU was 5 feet high and 6 feet wide, had an internal memory of 64K (considered large at that time), and a price tag of $200,000 in 1964 dollars. Because of its size and price at the time, its applications were generally limited to large computer centers belonging to the federal government, universities, and very large businesses.

The **minicomputer** was developed to meet the needs of smaller institutions, those with only a few dozen users. One of the early minicomputers was marketed by Digital Equipment Corporation to satisfy the needs of large schools and small colleges that began offering computer science courses in the early 1970s. (The price of its PDP-8 was less than $18,000.) Minicomputers are smaller in size and memory capacity and cheaper than mainframes. Today, computers that fall between microcomputers and mainframes in capacity are often called midrange computers.

The **supercomputer** was developed primarily for government applications needing massive and fast number-crunching ability to carry out military operations and weather forecasting. Business and industry became interested in the technology when the massive computers became faster and less expensive. A Cray supercomputer is a typical example with six to thousands of processors performing up to 2.4 trillion floating point operations per second (2.4 teraflops). Supercomputers are used for a wide range of tasks from scientific research to customer support and product development. They're often used to perform the intricate calculations required to create animated motion pictures. And they help oil companies in their search for oil by analyzing massive amounts of data (Stair, 1999).

The **microcomputer** was developed to offer inexpensive computation capability to individual users in the late 1970s. Early models featured a revolutionary amount of memory: 64K. Their physical size was smaller than the minicomputers of that time, though larger than the microcomputers of today. Eventually, microcomputers grew to accommodate software with larger capacity and greater speed. The distinguishing characteristic of the first microcomputer was its single-user status.

Powerful microcomputers developed for use by commercial, educational, and government enterprises are called **workstations**. Typically, workstations are networked together and are used to support engineering and technical users who perform massive mathematical computations or computer-aided design (CAD), or use other applications requiring very powerful CPUs, large amounts of main memory, and extremely high-resolution graphic displays to meet their needs.

Servers are powerful computers that provide specialized services to other computers on client/server networks. Examples can include print servers, Internet servers, e-mail servers, etc. Each performs critical network tasks. For instance, a file server, usually a

HP-UX, Sun Solaris, and Macintosh OS X are only three of many operating systems based on UNIX.

powerful computer with substantial file storage capacity (such as a large collection of hard drives), manages file storage and retrieval for other computers, called clients, on the network.

Platform	Operating System
Microcomputers	Linux, UNIX (includes Mac), Windows
Mainframe computers	IBM z/390, Linux, UNIX
Supercomputers	IRIX, Linux, UNICOS
Workstations, servers	Linux, UNIX, Windows
Networks	Linux, NetWare, UNIX, Windows
Personal digital assistants	BlackBerry, Linux, Palm OS, Windows Mobile

Some typical operating systems for a wide variety of platforms are shown in Table 1.1. Since the mid-1970s, rapid advances in computer technology have blurred the distinguishing characteristics of early machines: physical size, cost, and memory capacity. The most powerful mainframes today have multiple processors coordinated by the Processor Manager. Simple mainframes still have a large main memory, but now they're available in desk-sized cabinets.

Networking is an integral part of modern computer systems because it can connect workstations, servers, and peripheral devices into integrated computing systems. Networking capability has become a standard feature in many computing devices: personal organizers, personal digital assistants (PDAs), cell phones, and handheld Web browsers.

At one time, computers were classified by memory capacity; now they're distinguished by processor capacity. We must emphasize that these are relative categories and what is large today will become medium-sized and then small sometime in the near future.

In 1965, Intel executive Gordon Moore observed that each new processor chip contained roughly twice as much capacity as its predecessor, and each chip was released within 18–24 months of the previous chip. He predicted that the trend would cause computing power to rise exponentially over relatively brief periods of time. Now known as Moore's Law, shown in Figure 1.6, the trend has continued and is still remarkably accurate. The Intel 4004 chip in 1971 had 2,300 transistors while the Pentium II chip 20 years later had 7.5 million, and the Pentium 4 Extreme Edition processor introduced in 2004 had 178 million transistors. Moore's Law is often used by industry observers to make their chip capacity forecasts.

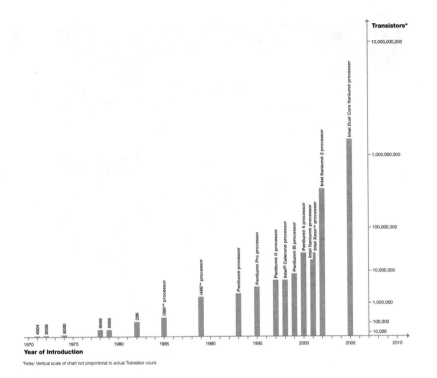

Types of Operating Systems

Operating systems for computers large and small fall into five categories distinguished by response time and how data is entered into the system: batch, interactive, real-time, hybrid, and embedded systems.

Batch systems date from the earliest computers, when they relied on stacks of punched cards or reels of magnetic tape for input. Jobs were entered by assembling the cards into a deck and running the entire deck of cards through a card reader as a group—a batch. The efficiency of a batch system is measured in **throughput**—the number of jobs completed in a given amount of time (for example, 550 jobs per hour).

Interactive systems give a faster turnaround than batch systems but are slower than the real-time systems we talk about next. They were introduced to satisfy the demands of users who needed fast turnaround when debugging their programs. The operating system required the development of time-sharing software, which would allow each user to interact directly with the computer system via commands entered from a typewriter-like terminal. The operating system provides immediate feedback to the user and response time can be measured in fractions of a second.

Real-time systems are used in time-critical environments where reliability is key and data must be processed within a strict time limit. The time limit need not be ultra-fast

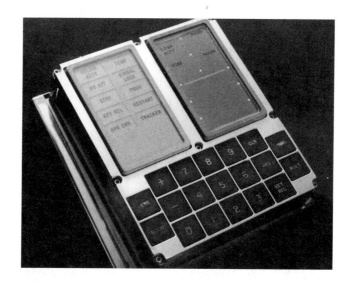

(figure 1.7)

The state-of-the art computer interface box for the Apollo spacecraft in 1968. The guidance computer had few moving parts and no vacuum tubes, making it both rugged and compact.

Courtesy of NASA

(though it often is), but system response time must meet the deadline or risk significant consequences. These systems also need to provide contingencies to fail gracefully—that is, preserve as much of the system's capabilities and data as possible to facilitate recovery. For example, real-time systems are used for space flights (as shown in Figure 1.7), airport traffic control, fly-by-wire aircraft, critical industrial processes, certain medical equipment, and telephone switching, to name a few.

There are two types of real-time systems depending on the consequences of missing the deadline:

- Hard real-time systems risk total system failure if the predicted time deadline is missed.
- Soft real-time systems suffer performance degradation, but not total system failure, as a consequence of a missed deadline.

Although it's theoretically possible to convert a general-purpose operating system into a real-time system by merely establishing a deadline, the unpredictability of these systems can't provide the guaranteed response times that real-time performance requires (Dougherty, 1995). Therefore, most embedded systems and real-time environments require operating systems that are specially designed to meet real-time needs.

Hybrid systems are a combination of batch and interactive. They appear to be interactive because individual users can access the system and get fast responses, but such a system actually accepts and runs batch programs in the background when the interactive load is light. A hybrid system takes advantage of the free time between high-demand usage of the system and low-demand times. Many large computer systems are hybrids.

Embedded systems are computers placed inside other products to add features and capabilities. For example, you find embedded computers in household appliances, automobiles, digital music players, elevators, and pacemakers. In the case of automobiles, embedded computers can help with engine performance, braking, and navigation. For example, several projects are under way to implement "smart roads," which would alert drivers in cars equipped with embedded computers to choose alternate routes when traffic becomes congested.

Operating systems for embedded computers are very different from those for general computer systems. Each one is designed to perform a set of specific programs, which are not interchangeable among systems. This permits the designers to make the operating system more efficient and take advantage of the computer's limited resources, such as memory, to their maximum.

Before a general-purpose operating system, such as Linux, UNIX, or Windows, can be used in an embedded system, the system designers must select which components, from the entire operating system, are needed in that particular environment. The final version of this operating system will include only the necessary elements; any unneeded features or functions will be dropped. Therefore, operating systems with a small **kernel** (the core portion of the software) and other functions that can be mixed and matched to meet the embedded system requirements will have potential in this market.

One example of a software product to help developers build an embedded system is Windows Automotive.

Brief History of Operating System Development

The evolution of operating system software parallels the evolution of the computer hardware it was designed to control. Here's a very brief overview of this evolution.

1940s

The first generation of computers (1940–1955) was a time of vacuum tube technology and computers the size of classrooms. Each computer was unique in structure and purpose. There was little need for standard operating system software because each computer's use was restricted to a few professionals working on mathematical, scientific, or military applications, all of whom were familiar with the idiosyncrasies of their hardware.

A typical program would include every instruction needed by the computer to perform the tasks requested. It would give explicit directions to the card reader (when to begin, how to interpret the data on the cards, when to end), the CPU (how and where to store the instructions in memory, what to calculate, where to find the data, where to send

(figure 1.8)

Dr. Grace Hopper's research journal from her work on Harvard's Mark I computer in 1945 included the remains of the first computer "bug," a moth that had become trapped in the computer's relays causing the system to crash. Today's use of the term "bug" stems from that first moth.

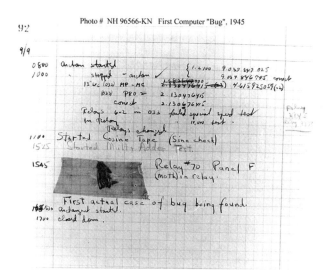

Photo # NH 96566-KN First Computer "Bug", 1945

the output), and the output device (when to begin, how to print out the finished product, how to format the page, and when to end).

The machines were operated by the programmers from the main console—it was a hands-on process. In fact, to debug a program, the programmer would stop the processor, read the contents of each register, make the corrections in memory locations, and then resume operation. The first bug was a moth trapped in a Harvard computer that caused it to fail, as shown in Figure 1.8.

To run programs, the programmers would have to reserve the machine for the length of time they estimated it would take the computer to execute the program. As a result, the machine was poorly utilized. The CPU processed data and made calculations for only a fraction of the available time and, in fact, the entire system sat idle between reservations.

In time, computer hardware and software became more standard and the execution of a program required fewer steps and less knowledge of the internal workings of the computer. Compilers and assemblers were developed to translate into binary code the English-like commands of the evolving high-level languages.

Rudimentary operating systems started to take shape with the creation of macros, library programs, standard subroutines, and utility programs. And they included device driver subroutines—prewritten programs that standardized the way input and output devices were used.

These early programs were at a significant disadvantage because they were designed to use their resources conservatively at the expense of understandability. That meant that many programs used convoluted logic that only the original programmer could understand, so it was nearly impossible for anyone else to debug or change the program later on.

1950s

Second-generation computers (1955–1965) were developed to meet the needs of new markets—government and business researchers. The business environment placed much more importance on the cost effectiveness of the system. Computers were still very expensive, especially when compared to other office equipment (the IBM 7094 was priced at $200,000). Therefore, throughput had to be maximized to make such an investment worthwhile for business use, which meant dramatically increasing the usage of the system.

Two improvements were widely adopted: Computer operators were hired to facilitate each machine's operation, and job scheduling was instituted. Job scheduling is a productivity improvement scheme that groups together programs with similar requirements. For example, several FORTRAN programs would be run together while the FORTRAN compiler was still resident in memory. Or all of the jobs using the card reader for input might be run together, and those using the tape drive would be run later. Some operators found that a mix of I/O device requirements was the most efficient combination. That is, by mixing tape-input programs with card-input programs, the tapes could be mounted or rewound while the card reader was busy. A typical punch card is shown in Figure 1.9.

Job scheduling introduced the need for control cards, which defined the exact nature of each program and its requirements, illustrated in Figure 1.10. This was one of the first uses of a job control language, which helped the operating system coordinate and manage the system resources by identifying the users and their jobs and specifying the resources required to execute each job.

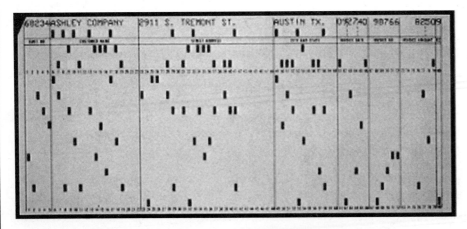

(figure 1.9)

Each letter or number printed along the top of the punch card is represented by a unique combination of holes beneath it.

From ibm.com

(figure 1.10)

The Job Control Language (called JCL) program structure and the order of punch cards for the DEC-10 computer.

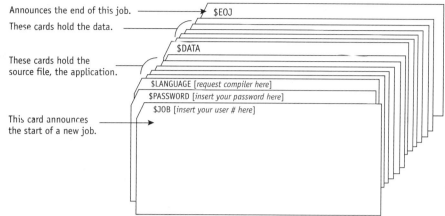

Announces the end of this job. ──────▶ $EOJ

These cards hold the data. ──────

$DATA

These cards hold the source file, the application. ──────

$LANGUAGE [*request compiler here*]

$PASSWORD [*insert your password here*]

$JOB [*insert your user # here*]

This card announces the start of a new job. ──────▶

But even with batching techniques, the faster second-generation computers allowed expensive time lags between the CPU and the I/O devices. For example, a job with 1600 cards could take 79 seconds to be read by the card reader and only 5 seconds of CPU time to assemble or compile. That meant the CPU was idle 94 percent of the time and busy only 6 percent of the time it was dedicated to that job—an inefficiency that resulted in poor overall system use.

Eventually, several factors helped improve the performance of the CPU:

• First, the speeds of I/O devices such as drums, tape drives, and disks gradually increased.

• Second, to use more of the available storage area in these devices, records were grouped into blocks before they were retrieved or stored. (This is called blocking, meaning that several logical records are grouped within one physical record, and is discussed in detail in Chapter 7.)

• Third, to reduce the discrepancy in speed between the I/O and the CPU, an interface called the control unit was placed between them to act as a buffer. A buffer is an interim storage area that works as a temporary holding place. As the slow input device reads one record, the control unit places each character of the record into the buffer. When the buffer is full, the entire record is quickly transmitted to the CPU. The process is just the opposite for output devices: The CPU places the entire record into the buffer, which is then passed on by the control unit at the slower rate required by the output device.

The buffers of this generation were conceptually similar to those now used routinely by Internet browsers to make video and audio playback smoother, as shown in Figure 1.11.

If a control unit had more than one buffer, the I/O process could be made even faster. For example, if the control unit had two buffers, the second buffer could be loaded while the first buffer was transmitting its contents to or from the CPU. Ideally, by the time the first was transmitted, the second was ready to go, and so on. In this way, input or output time was cut in half.

- Fourth, in addition to buffering, an early form of spooling was developed by moving offline the operations of card reading, printing, and "punching." For example, incoming jobs would be transferred from card decks to reels of magnetic tape offline. Then they could be read into the CPU from the tape at a speed much faster than that of the card reader. The spooler worked the same way as a buffer but, in this example, it was a separate offline device while a buffer was part of the main computer hardware.

Also during the second generation, techniques were developed to manage program libraries, create and maintain each data direct access address, and create and check file labels. Timer interrupts were developed to allow job sharing and to prevent infinite loops on programs that were mistakenly instructed to execute a single series of commands forever. Because a fixed amount of execution time was allocated to each program when it entered the system, and was monitored by the operating system, programs that were still running when the time expired were terminated.

During the second generation, programs were still assigned to the processor one at a time. The next step toward better use of the system's resources was the move to shared processing.

1960s

Third-generation computers date from the mid-1960s. They were designed with faster CPUs, but their speed still caused problems when they interacted with printers and other I/O devices that ran at slower speeds. The solution was **multiprogramming**, which introduced the concept of loading many programs at one time and sharing the attention of a single CPU.

The first multiprogramming systems allowed each program to be serviced in turn, one after another. The most common mechanism for implementing multiprogramming was the introduction of the concept of the interrupt, whereby the CPU was notified of events needing operating system services. For example, when a program issued a print command (called an input/output command or an I/O command), it generated an interrupt requesting the services of the I/O processor and the CPU was released to begin execution of the next job. This was called *passive multiprogramming* because the operating system didn't control the interrupts but waited for each job to end an execution sequence. It was less than ideal because if a job was CPU-bound (meaning that it performed a great deal of nonstop CPU processing before issuing an interrupt), it could tie up the CPU for a long time while all other jobs had to wait.

To counteract this effect, the operating system was soon given a more active role with the advent of *active multiprogramming*, which allowed each program to use only a preset slice of CPU time, which is discussed in Chapter 4. When time expired, the job was interrupted and another job was allowed to begin execution. The interrupted job had to wait until it was allowed to resume execution later. The idea of time slicing soon became common in many time-sharing systems.

Program scheduling, which was begun with second-generation systems, continued at this time but was complicated by the fact that main memory was occupied by many jobs. To solve this problem, the jobs were sorted into groups and then loaded into memory according to a preset rotation formula. The sorting was often determined by priority or memory requirements—whichever was found to be the most efficient use of the available resources. In addition to scheduling jobs, handling interrupts, and allocating memory, the operating systems also had to resolve conflicts whenever two jobs requested the same device at the same time, something we will explore in Chapter 5.

Even though there was progress in processor management, few major advances were made in data management.

1970S

After the third generation, during the late 1970s, computers had faster CPUs, creating an even greater disparity between their rapid processing speed and slower I/O access time. The first Cray supercomputer was released in 1976. Multiprogramming schemes to increase CPU use were limited by the physical capacity of the main memory, which was a limited resource and very expensive.

A solution to this physical limitation was the development of virtual memory, which took advantage of the fact that the CPU could process only one instruction at a time. With virtual memory, the entire program didn't need to reside in memory before execution could begin. A system with virtual memory would divide the programs into parts and keep them in secondary storage, bringing each part into memory only as it was needed. (Programmers of second-generation computers had used this concept with the roll in/roll out programming method, also called overlay, to execute programs that exceeded the physical memory of those computers.)

At this time there was also growing attention to the need for data resource conservation. Database management software became a popular tool because it organized data in an integrated manner, minimized redundancy, and simplified updating and access of data. A number of query systems were introduced that allowed even the novice user to retrieve specific pieces of the database. These queries were usually made via a terminal, which in turn mandated a growth in terminal support and data communication software.

Programmers soon became more removed from the intricacies of the computer, and application programs started using English-like words, modular structures, and standard operations. This trend toward the use of standards improved program management because program maintenance became faster and easier.

1980s

Development in the 1980s dramatically improved the cost/performance ratio of computer components. Hardware was more flexible, with logical functions built on easily replaceable circuit boards. And because it was less costly to create these circuit boards, more operating system functions were made part of the hardware itself, giving rise to a new concept—**firmware,** a word used to indicate that a program is permanently held in read-only memory (ROM), as opposed to being held in secondary storage. The job of the programmer, as it had been defined in previous years, changed dramatically because many programming functions were being carried out by the system's software, hence making the programmer's task simpler and less hardware dependent.

Eventually the industry moved to **multiprocessing** (having more than one processor), and more complex languages were designed to coordinate the activities of the multiple processors servicing a single job. As a result, it became possible to execute programs in parallel, and eventually operating systems for computers of every size were routinely expected to accommodate multiprocessing.

The evolution of personal computers and high-speed communications sparked the move to networked systems and distributed processing, enabling users in remote locations to share hardware and software resources. These systems required a new kind of operating system—one capable of managing multiple sets of subsystem managers, as well as hardware that might reside half a world away.

With network operating systems, users generally became aware of the existence of many networked resources, could log in to remote locations, and could manipulate files on networked computers distributed over a wide geographical area. Network operating systems were similar to single-processor operating systems in that each machine ran its own local operating system and had its own users. The difference was in the addition of a network interface controller with low-level software to drive the local operating system, as well as programs to allow remote login and remote file access. Still, even with these additions, the basic structure of the network operating system was quite close to that of a standalone system.

On the other hand, with distributed operating systems, users could think they were working with a typical uniprocessor system when in fact they were connected to a cluster of many processors working closely together. With these systems, users didn't need to know which processor was running their applications or which devices were storing their files. These details were all handled transparently by the operating system—something that required more than just adding a few lines of code to a uniprocessor operating system. The disadvantage of such a complex operating system was the requirement for more complex processor-scheduling algorithms. In addition, communications delays within the network sometimes meant that scheduling algorithms had to operate with incomplete or outdated information.

1990s

The overwhelming demand for Internet capability in the mid-1990s sparked the proliferation of networking capability. The World Wide Web, conceived in a paper, shown in Figure 1.12, by Tim Berners-Lee made the Internet accessible by computer users

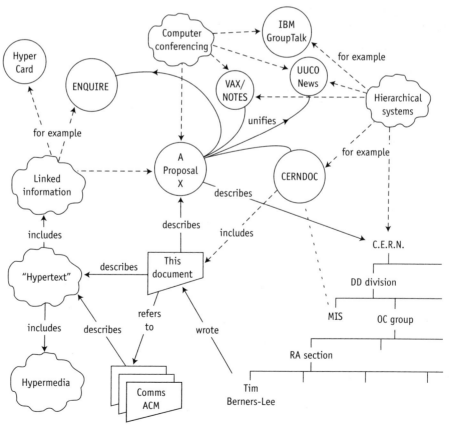

(figure 1.12)

Illustration from the first page of the 1989 proposal by Tim Berners-Lee describing his revolutionary "linked information system." Based on this research, he designed the first World Wide Web server and browser, making it available to the general public in 1991.

worldwide, not just the researchers who had come to depend on it for global communications. Web accessibility and e-mail became standard features of almost every operating system. However, increased networking also sparked increased demand for tighter security to protect hardware and software.

The decade also introduced a proliferation of multimedia applications demanding additional power, flexibility, and device compatibility for most operating systems. A typical multimedia computer houses devices to perform audio, video, and graphic creation and editing. Those functions can require many specialized devices such as a microphone, digital piano, Musical Instrument Digital Interface (MIDI), digital camera, digital video disc (DVD) drive, optical disc (CD) drives, speakers, additional monitors, projection devices, color printers, and high-speed Internet connections. These computers also require specialized hardware (such as controllers, cards, busses) and software to make them work together properly.

Multimedia applications need large amounts of storage capability that must be managed gracefully by the operating system. For example, each second of a 30-frame-per-minute full-screen video requires 27MB of storage unless the data is compressed in some way. To meet the demand for compressed video, special-purpose chips and video boards have been developed by hardware companies.

What's the effect of these technological advances on the operating system? Each advance requires a parallel advance in the software's management capabilities.

2000S

The new century emphasized the need for operating systems to offer improved flexibility, reliability, and speed. To meet the need for computers that could accommodate multiple operating systems running at the same time and sharing resources, the concept of virtual machines, shown in Figure 1.13, was developed and became commercially viable.

Virtualization is the creation of partitions on a single server, with each partition supporting a different operating system. In other words, it turns a single physical server into multiple virtual servers, often with multiple operating systems. Virtualization requires the operating system to have an intermediate manager to oversee each operating system's access to the server's physical resources. For example, with virtualization, a single processor can run 64 independent operating systems on workstations using a processor capable of allowing 64 separate threads (instruction sequences) to run at the same time.

(figure 1.13)

With virtualization, different operating systems can run on a single computer.

Courtesy of Parallels, Inc.

Processing speed has enjoyed a similar advancement with the development of multi-core processors, shown in Figure 1.14. Until recent years, the silicon wafer that forms the base of the computer chip circuitry held only a single CPU. However, with the introduction of dual-core processors, a single chip can hold multiple processor **cores**. Thus, a dual-core chip allows two sets of calculations to run at the same time, which sometimes leads to faster completion of the job. It's as if the user has two separate computers, and two processors, cooperating on a single task. As of this writing, designers have created chips that can hold 80 simple cores.

Does this hardware innovation affect the operating system software? Absolutely, because it must now manage the work of these multiple processors and be able to schedule and manage the processing of their multiple tasks. We'll explore some of the complexities of this in Chapter 6.

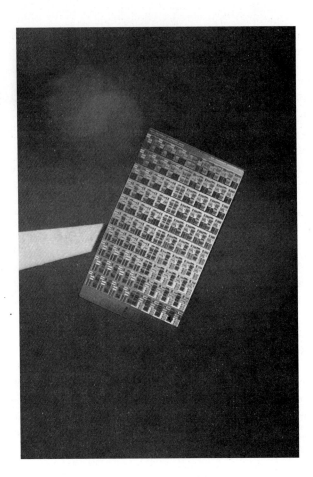

(Figure 1.14)

A single piece of silicon can hold 80 cores, which (to put it in simplest terms) can perform 80 calculations at one time.

Courtesy of Intel Corporation

Threads

Multi-core technology helps the operating system handle threads, multiple actions that can be executed at the same time. First, an explanation: The Processor Manager is responsible for processing each job submitted by a user. Jobs are made up of processes (sometimes called tasks in other textbooks), and processes consist of multiple threads.

A process has two characteristics:

• It requires space in main memory where it resides during its execution; although, from time to time, it requires other resources such as data files or I/O devices.

• It passes through several states (such as running, waiting, ready) from its initial arrival into the computer system to its completion.

Multiprogramming and virtual memory dictate that processes be swapped between main memory and secondary storage during their execution. With conventional processes (also known as heavyweight processes), this swapping results in a lot of overhead. That's because each time a swap takes place, all process information must be saved to preserve the process's integrity.

A **thread** (or lightweight process) can be defined as a unit smaller than a process, which can be scheduled and executed. Using this technique, the heavyweight process, which owns the resources, becomes a more passive element, while a thread becomes the element that uses the CPU and is scheduled for execution. Manipulating threads is less time consuming than manipulating processes, which are more complex. Some operating systems support multiple processes with a single thread, while others support multiple processes with multiple threads.

Multithreading allows applications to manage a separate process with several threads of control. Web browsers use multithreading routinely. For instance, one thread can retrieve images while another sends and retrieves e-mail. Multithreading is also used to increase responsiveness in a time-sharing system to increase resource sharing and decrease overhead.

Web browsers routinely use multithreading to allow users to explore multiple areas of interest on the Internet at the same time.

Object-Oriented Design

An important area of research that resulted in substantial efficiencies was that of the system architecture of operating systems—the way their components are programmed and organized, specifically the use of **object-oriented** design and the reorganization of the operating system's nucleus, the kernel. The kernel is the part of the operating system that resides in memory at all times, performs the most essential operating system tasks, and is protected by hardware from user tampering.

The first operating systems were designed as a comprehensive single unit, as shown in Figure 1.15 (a). They stored all required elements of the operating system in memory such as memory allocation, process scheduling, device allocation, and file management. This type of architecture made it cumbersome and time consuming for programmers to add new components to the operating system, or to modify existing ones.

Most recently, the part of the operating system that resides in memory has been limited to a few essential functions, such as process scheduling and memory allocation, while all other functions, such as device allocation, are provided by special modules, which are treated as regular applications, as shown in Figure 1.15 (b). This approach makes it easier to add new components or modify existing ones.

Object-oriented design was the driving force behind this new organization. Objects are self-contained modules (units of software) that provide models of the real world and can be reused in different applications. By working on objects, programmers can modify and customize pieces of an operating system without disrupting the integrity of the remainder of the system. In addition, using a modular, object-oriented approach can

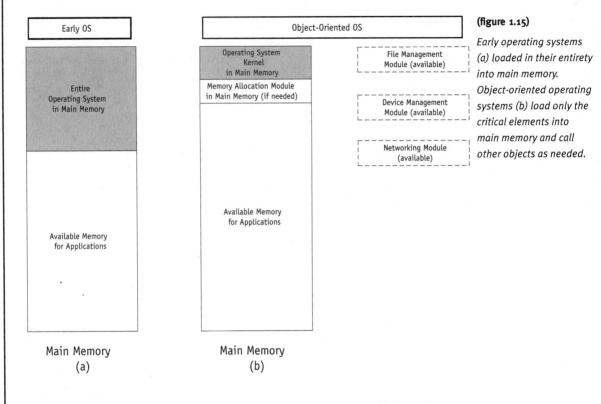

Early OS	Object-Oriented OS

Early OS

Entire
Operating System
in Main Memory

Available Memory
for Applications

Main Memory
(a)

Object-Oriented OS

Operating System
Kernel
in Main Memory

Memory Allocation Module
in Main Memory (if needed)

Available Memory
for Applications

Main Memory
(b)

File Management
Module (available)

Device Management
Module (available)

Networking Module
(available)

(figure 1.15)

Early operating systems (a) loaded in their entirety into main memory. Object-oriented operating systems (b) load only the critical elements into main memory and call other objects as needed.

make software development groups more productive than was possible with procedural structured programming.

Conclusion

In this chapter, we looked at the overall function of operating systems and how they have evolved to run increasingly complex computers and computer systems; but like any complex subject, there's much more detail to explore. As we'll see in the remainder of this text, there are many ways to perform every task and it's up to the designer of the operating system to choose the policies that best match the system's environment.

In the following chapters, we'll explore in detail how each portion of the operating system works, as well as its features, functions, benefits, and costs. We'll begin with the part of the operating system that's the heart of every computer: the module that manages main memory.

Key Terms

batch system: a type of system developed for the earliest computers that used punched cards or tape for input, which were entered in a batch.

central processing unit (CPU): the component with the circuitry, the "chips," to control the interpretation and execution of instructions.

core: the processing part of a CPU chip made up of the control unit and the arithmetic logic unit (ALU).

Device Manager: the section of the operating system responsible for controlling the use of devices. It monitors every device, channel, and control unit and chooses the most efficient way to allocate all of the system's devices.

embedded system: a dedicated computer system, often small and fast, that resides in a larger physical system such as jet aircraft or ships.

File Manager: the section of the operating system responsible for controlling the use of files.

firmware: software instructions or data that are stored in a fixed or "firm" way, usually implemented on read-only memory (ROM).

hardware: the physical machine and its components, including main memory, I/O devices, I/O channels, direct access storage devices, and the central processing unit.

hybrid system: a computer system that supports both batch and interactive processes.

interactive system: a system that allows each user to interact directly with the operating system via commands entered from a keyboard.

kernel: the primary part of the operating system that remains in random access memory (RAM) and is charged with performing the system's most essential tasks, such as managing main memory and disk access.

main memory: the memory unit that works directly with the CPU and in which the data and instructions must reside in order to be processed. Also called primary storage or internal memory.

mainframe: the historical name given to a large computer system characterized by its large size, high cost, and high performance.

Memory Manager: the section of the operating system responsible for controlling the use of memory. It checks the validity of each request for memory space and, if it's a legal request, allocates the amount needed to execute the job.

microcomputer: a small computer equipped with all the hardware and software necessary to perform one or more tasks.

minicomputer: a small to medium-sized computer system, also called a midrange computer.

multiprocessing: when two or more CPUs share the same main memory, most I/O devices, and the same control program routines. They service the same job stream and execute distinct processing programs concurrently.

multiprogramming: a technique that allows a single processor to process several programs residing simultaneously in main memory and interleaving their execution by overlapping I/O requests with CPU requests.

network: a system of interconnected computer systems and peripheral devices that exchange information with one another.

Network Manager: the section of the operating system responsible for controlling access to and the use of networked resources.

object-oriented: a programming philosophy whereby programs consist of self-contained, reusable modules called objects, each of which supports a specific function, but which are categorized into classes of objects that share the same function.

operating system: the software that manages all the resources of a computer system.

Processor Manager: a composite of two submanagers, the Job Scheduler and the Process Scheduler, which decides how to allocate the CPU.

real-time system: a computing system used in time-critical environments that require guaranteed response times, such as navigation systems, rapid transit systems, and industrial control systems.

server: a node that provides to clients various network services, such as file retrieval, printing, or database access services.

software: a collection of programs used to perform certain tasks. Software falls into three main categories: operating system programs, compilers and assemblers, and application programs.

storage: a place where data is stored in the computer system. Primary storage is main memory and secondary storage is nonvolatile media.

supercomputer: the fastest, most sophisticated computers made, used for complex calculations.

thread: a portion of a program that can run independently of other portions. Multithreaded application programs can have several threads running at one time with the same or different priorities.

throughput: a composite measure of a system's efficiency that counts the number of jobs served in a given unit of time.

virtualization: the creation of a virtual version of hardware or software. Operating system virtualization allows a single CPU to run multiple operating system images at the same time.

workstation: a desktop computer attached to a local area network that serves as an access point to that network.

Interesting Searches

For more background on a few of the topics discussed in this chapter, begin a search with these terms:

- Computer History Museum
- NASA - Computers Aboard the Space Shuttle
- IBM Computer History Archive
- History of the UNIX Operating System
- History of Microsoft Windows Products

Exercises

Research Topics

Whenever you research computer technology, make sure your resources are timely. Notice the date when the research was published. Also be sure to validate the authenticity of your sources. Avoid any that might be questionable, such as blogs and publicly edited online (wiki) sources.

A. Write a one-page review of an article about operating systems that appeared in a recent computing magazine or academic journal. Be sure to cite your source. Give a summary of the article, including the primary topic, the information presented, and the author's conclusion. Give your personal evaluation of the article, including the author's writing style, inappropriate use of jargon, topics that made the article interesting to you, and its relevance to your own experiences.

B. Research the Internet or current literature to identify an operating system that runs a cell phone or handheld computer. (These are generally known as mobile operating systems.) List the key features of the operating system and the hardware it is designed to run. Cite your sources.

Exercises

1. Name five current operating systems (not mentioned in this chapter) and the computers or configurations each operates.
2. Name the five key concepts about an operating system that you think a novice user needs to know and understand.

3. Explain the impact of the evolution of computer hardware and the accompanying evolution of operating system software.

4. In your opinion, has Moore's Law been a mere predictor of chip design, or a motivator for chip designers? Explain your answer.

5. Explain the fundamental differences between interactive, batch, real-time, and embedded systems.

6. List three situations that might demand a real-time operating system and explain why.

7. Give an example of an organization that might find batch-mode processing useful and explain why.

8. List three tangible (physical) data storage resources of a typical computer system. Explain the advantages and disadvantages of each.

9. Briefly compare active and passive multiprogramming.

10. Give at least two reasons why a multi-state bank might decide to buy six server computers instead of one more powerful computer. Explain your answer.

11. Select one of the following professionals: an insurance adjuster, a delivery person for a courier service, a newspaper reporter, a doctor (general practitioner), or a manager in a supermarket. Suggest at least two ways that such a person might use a handheld computer to work more efficiently.

Advanced Exercises

12. Compare the design goals and evolution of two operating systems described in Chapters 13–16 of this text.

13. Draw a system flowchart illustrating the steps performed by an operating system as it executes the instruction to back up a disk on a single-user computer system. Begin with the user typing the command on the keyboard or clicking the mouse and conclude with the display of the result on the monitor.

14. Identify the clock rates of processors that use (or used) 8 bits, 16 bits, 32 bits, and 64 bits. Discuss several implications involved in scheduling the CPU in a multiprocessing system using these processors.

15. In a multiprogramming and time-sharing environment, several users share the system simultaneously. This situation can result in various security problems. Name two such problems. Can we ensure the same degree of security in a time-share machine as we can in a dedicated machine? Explain your answers.

16. Give an example of an application where multithreading gives improved performance over single-threading.

17. If a process terminates, will its threads also terminate or will they continue to run? Explain your answer.

18. If a process is suspended (put into the "wait" state by an interrupt), will its threads also be suspended? Explain your answer and give an example.

Chapter 2 | Memory Management: Early Systems

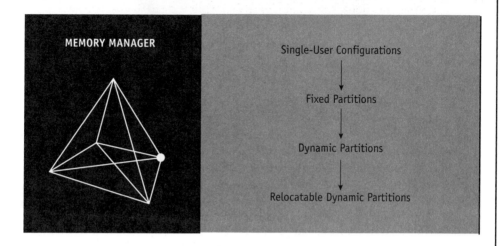

MEMORY MANAGER

Single-User Configurations

↓

Fixed Partitions

↓

Dynamic Partitions

↓

Relocatable Dynamic Partitions

> **"** *Memory is the primary and fundamental power, without which there could be no other intellectual operation.* **"**
>
> —Samuel Johnson *(1709–1784)*

Learning Objectives

After completing this chapter, you should be able to describe:

- The basic functionality of the three memory allocation schemes presented in this chapter: fixed partitions, dynamic partitions, relocatable dynamic partitions

- Best-fit memory allocation as well as first-fit memory allocation schemes

- How a memory list keeps track of available memory

- The importance of deallocation of memory in a dynamic partition system

- The importance of the bounds register in memory allocation schemes

- The role of compaction and how it improves memory allocation efficiency

(figure 2.1)

Main memory circuit from 1961 (before they became too small to see without magnification).

Courtesy of technikum29

The management of **main memory** is critical. In fact, from a historical perspective, the performance of the *entire* system has been directly dependent on two things: How much memory is available and how it is optimized while jobs are being processed. Pictured in Figure 2.1 is a main memory circuit from 1961. Since then, the physical size of memory units has become increasingly small and they are now available on small boards.

This chapter introduces the Memory Manager (also known as random access memory or RAM, core memory, or primary storage) and four types of memory allocation schemes: single-user systems, fixed partitions, dynamic partitions, and relocatable dynamic partitions.

These early memory management schemes are seldom used by today's operating systems, but they are important to study because each one introduced fundamental concepts that helped memory management evolve, as shown in Chapter 3, "Memory Management: Virtual Memory," which discusses memory allocation strategies for Linux. Information on how other operating systems manage memory is presented in the memory management sections in Part Two of the text.

Let's start with the simplest memory management scheme—the one used in the earliest generations of computer systems.

Single-User Contiguous Scheme

A single-user scheme supports one user on one computer running one job at a time. Sharing isn't possible.

The first memory allocation scheme worked like this: Each program to be processed was loaded in its entirety into memory and allocated as much contiguous space in memory as it needed, as shown in Figure 2.2. The key words here are *entirety* and *contiguous*. If the program was too large and didn't fit the available memory space, it couldn't be executed. And, although early computers were physically large, they had very little memory.

(figure 2.2)

*One program fit in memory
at a time. The remainder of
memory was unused.*

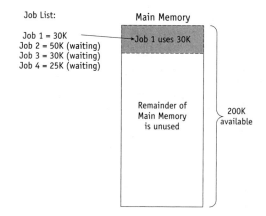

This demonstrates a significant limiting factor of all computers—they have only a finite amount of memory and if a program doesn't fit, then either the size of the main memory must be increased or the program must be modified. It's usually modified by making it smaller or by using methods that allow program segments (partitions made to the program) to be overlaid. (To overlay is to transfer segments of a program from secondary storage into main memory for execution, so that two or more segments take turns occupying the same memory locations.)

Single-user systems in a nonnetworked environment work the same way. Each user is given access to all available main memory for each job, and jobs are processed sequentially, one after the other. To allocate memory, the operating system uses a simple algorithm (step-by-step procedure to solve a problem):

Algorithm to Load a Job in a Single-User System

1 Store first memory location of program into base register (for memory protection)
2 Set program counter (it keeps track of memory space used by the program) equal to address of first memory location
3 Read first instruction of program
4 Increment program counter by number of bytes in instruction
5 Has the last instruction been reached?
    if yes, then stop loading program
    if no, then continue with step 6
6 Is program counter greater than memory size?
    if yes, then stop loading program
    if no, then continue with step 7
7 Load instruction in memory
8 Read next instruction of program
9 Go to step 4

Notice that the amount of work done by the operating system's Memory Manager is minimal, the code to perform the functions is straightforward, and the logic is quite simple. Only two hardware items are needed: a register to store the base **address** and an accumulator to keep track of the size of the program as it's being read into memory. Once the program is entirely loaded into memory, it remains there until execution is complete, either through normal termination or by intervention of the operating system.

One major problem with this type of memory allocation scheme is that it doesn't support multiprogramming or networking (both are discussed later in this text); it can handle only one job at a time. When these single-user configurations were first made available commercially in the late 1940s and early 1950s, they were used in research institutions but proved unacceptable for the business community—it wasn't cost effective to spend almost $200,000 for a piece of equipment that could be used by only one person at a time. Therefore, in the late 1950s and early 1960s a new scheme was needed to manage memory, which used partitions to take advantage of the computer system's resources by overlapping independent operations.

Fixed Partitions

The first attempt to allow for multiprogramming used **fixed partitions** (also called **static partitions**) within the main memory—one partition for each job. Because the size of each partition was designated when the system was powered on, each partition could only be reconfigured when the computer system was shut down, reconfigured, and restarted. Thus, once the system was in operation the partition sizes remained static.

A critical factor was introduced with this scheme: protection of the job's memory space. Once a partition was assigned to a job, no other job could be allowed to enter its boundaries, either accidentally or intentionally. This problem of partition intrusion didn't exist in single-user contiguous allocation schemes because only one job was present in main memory at any given time so only the portion of the operating system residing in main memory had to be protected. However, for the fixed partition allocation schemes, protection was mandatory for each partition present in main memory. Typically this was the joint responsibility of the hardware of the computer and the operating system.

The algorithm used to store jobs in memory requires a few more steps than the one used for a single-user system because the size of the job must be matched with the size of the partition to make sure it fits completely. Then, when a block of sufficient size is located, the status of the partition must be checked to see if it's available.

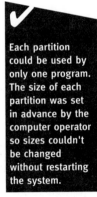

Each partition could be used by only one program. The size of each partition was set in advance by the computer operator so sizes couldn't be changed without restarting the system.

Algorithm to Load a Job in a Fixed Partition

1 Determine job's requested memory size
2 If job_size > size of largest partition
   Then reject the job
      print appropriate message to operator
      go to step 1 to handle next job in line
   Else
      continue with step 3
3 Set counter to 1
4 Do while counter <= number of partitions in memory
  If job_size > memory_partition_size(counter)
  Then counter = counter + 1
  Else
    If memory_partition_size(counter) = "free"
      Then load job into memory_partition(counter)
        change memory_partition_status(counter) to "busy"
        go to step 1 to handle next job in line
    Else
     counter = counter + 1
    End do
5 No partition available at this time, put job in waiting queue
6 Go to step 1 to handle next job in line

This partition scheme is more flexible than the single-user scheme because it allows several programs to be in memory at the same time. However, it still requires that the *entire* program be stored *contiguously* and *in memory* from the beginning to the end of its execution. In order to allocate memory spaces to jobs, the operating system's Memory Manager must keep a table, such as Table 2.1, which shows each memory partition size, its address, its access restrictions, and its current status (free or busy) for the system illustrated in Figure 2.3. (In Table 2.1 and the other tables in this chapter, K stands for kilobyte, which is 1,024 bytes. A more in-depth discussion of memory map tables is presented in Chapter 8, "File Management.")

(table 2.1)

A simplified fixed-partition memory table with the free partition shaded.

Partition Size	Memory Address	Access	Partition Status
100K	200K	Job 1	Busy
25K	300K	Job 4	Busy
25K	325K		Free
50K	350K	Job 2	Busy

As each job terminates, the status of its memory partition is changed from busy to free so an incoming job can be assigned to that partition.

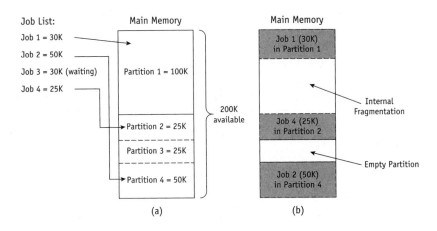

(figure 2.3)

Main memory use during fixed partition allocation of Table 2.1. Job 3 must wait even though 70K of free space is available in Partition 1, where Job 1 only occupies 30K of the 100K available. The jobs are allocated space on the basis of "first available partition of required size."

The fixed partition scheme works well if all of the jobs run on the system are of the same size or if the sizes are known ahead of time and don't vary between reconfigurations. Ideally, that would require accurate advance knowledge of all the jobs to be run on the system in the coming hours, days, or weeks. However, unless the operator can accurately predict the future, the sizes of the partitions are determined in an arbitrary fashion and they might be too small or too large for the jobs coming in.

There are significant consequences if the partition sizes are too small; larger jobs will be rejected if they're too big to fit into the largest partitions or will wait if the large partitions are busy. As a result, large jobs may have a longer turnaround time as they wait for free partitions of sufficient size or may never run.

On the other hand, if the partition sizes are too big, memory is wasted. If a job does not occupy the entire partition, the unused memory in the partition will remain idle; it can't be given to another job because each partition is allocated to only one job at a time. It's an indivisible unit. Figure 2.3 demonstrates one such circumstance.

This phenomenon of partial usage of fixed partitions and the coinciding creation of unused spaces within the partition is called **internal fragmentation**, and is a major drawback to the fixed partition memory allocation scheme.

✔

There are two types of fragmentation: internal and external. The type depends on the location of the wasted space.

Dynamic Partitions

With **dynamic partitions**, available memory is still kept in contiguous blocks but jobs are given only as much memory as they request when they are loaded for processing. Although this is a significant improvement over fixed partitions because memory isn't wasted within the partition, it doesn't entirely eliminate the problem.

As shown in Figure 2.4, a dynamic partition scheme fully utilizes memory when the first jobs are loaded. But as new jobs enter the system that are not the same size as those that

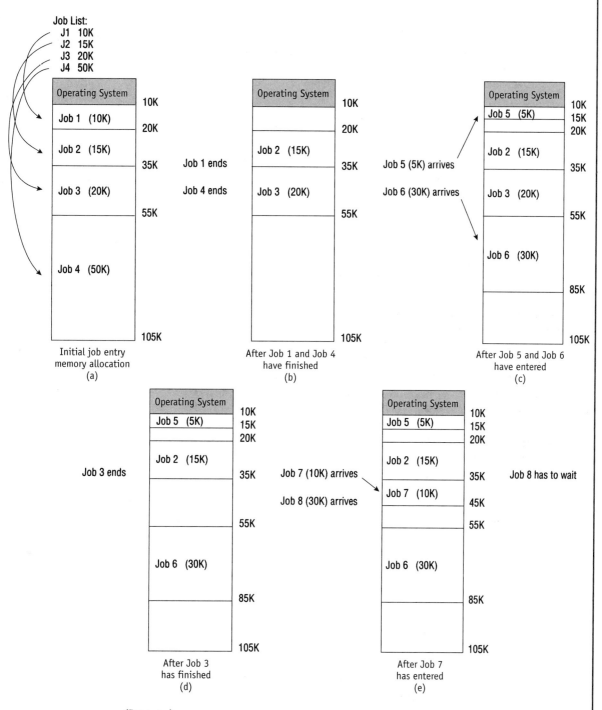

(figure 2.4)

Main memory use during dynamic partition allocation. Five snapshots (a-e) of main memory as eight jobs are submitted for processing and allocated space on the basis of "first come, first served." Job 8 has to wait (e) even though there's enough free memory between partitions to accommodate it.

just vacated memory, they are fit into the available spaces on a priority basis. Figure 2.4 demonstrates **first-come, first-served** priority. Therefore, the subsequent allocation of memory creates fragments of free memory between blocks of allocated memory. This problem is called **external fragmentation** and, like internal fragmentation, lets memory go to waste.

In the last snapshot, (e) in Figure 2.4, there are three free partitions of 5K, 10K, and 20K—35K in all—enough to accommodate Job 8, which only requires 30K. However they are not contiguous and, because the jobs are loaded in a contiguous manner, this scheme forces Job 8 to wait.

Before we go to the next allocation scheme, let's examine how the operating system keeps track of the free sections of memory.

Best-Fit Versus First-Fit Allocation

For both fixed and dynamic memory allocation schemes, the operating system must keep lists of each memory location noting which are free and which are busy. Then as new jobs come into the system, the free partitions must be allocated.

These partitions may be allocated on the basis of **first-fit memory allocation** (first partition fitting the requirements) or **best-fit memory allocation** (least wasted space, the smallest partition fitting the requirements). For both schemes, the Memory Manager organizes the memory lists of the free and used partitions (free/busy) either by size or by location. The best-fit allocation method keeps the free/busy lists in order by size, smallest to largest. The first-fit method keeps the free/busy lists organized by memory locations, low-order memory to high-order memory. Each has advantages depending on the needs of the particular allocation scheme— best-fit usually makes the best use of memory space; first-fit is faster in making the allocation.

To understand the trade-offs, imagine that you've turned your collection of books into a lending library. Let's say you have books of all shapes and sizes, and let's also say that there's a continuous stream of people taking books out and bringing them back— someone's always waiting. It's clear that you'll always be busy, and that's good, but you never have time to rearrange the bookshelves.

You need a system. Your shelves have fixed partitions with a few tall spaces for over-sized books, several shelves for paperbacks, and lots of room for textbooks. You'll need to keep track of which spaces on the shelves are full and where you have spaces for more. For the purposes of our example, we'll keep two lists: a free list showing all the available spaces, and a busy list showing all the occupied spaces. Each list will include the size and location of each space.

If you optimize speed, you may be wasting space. But if you optimize space, it may take longer.

So as each book is removed from its shelf, you'll update both lists by removing the space from the busy list and adding it to the free list. Then as your books are returned and placed back on a shelf, the two lists will be updated again.

There are two ways to organize your lists: by size or by location. If they're organized by size, the spaces for the smallest books are at the top of the list and those for the largest are at the bottom. When they're organized by location, the spaces closest to your lending desk are at the top of the list and the areas farthest away are at the bottom. Which option is best? It depends on what you want to optimize: space or speed of allocation.

If the lists are organized by size, you're optimizing your shelf space—as books arrive, you'll be able to put them in the spaces that fit them best. This is a best-fit scheme. If a paperback is returned, you'll place it on a shelf with the other paperbacks or at least with other small books. Similarly, oversized books will be shelved with other large books. Your lists make it easy to find the smallest available empty space where the book can fit. The disadvantage of this system is that you're wasting time looking for the best space. Your other customers have to wait for you to put each book away, so you won't be able to process as many customers as you could with the other kind of list.

In the second case, a list organized by shelf location, you're optimizing the time it takes you to put books back on the shelves. This is a first-fit scheme. This system ignores the size of the book that you're trying to put away. If the same paperback book arrives, you can quickly find it an empty space. In fact, any nearby empty space will suffice if it's large enough—even an encyclopedia rack can be used if it's close to your desk because you are optimizing the time it takes you to reshelve the books.

Of course, this is a fast method of shelving books, and if speed is important it's the best of the two alternatives. However, it isn't a good choice if your shelf space is limited or if many large books are returned, because large books must wait for the large spaces. If all of your large spaces are filled with small books, the customers returning large books must wait until a suitable space becomes available. (Eventually you'll need time to rearrange the books and compact your collection.)

Figure 2.5 shows how a large job can have problems with a first-fit memory allocation list. Jobs 1, 2, and 4 are able to enter the system and begin execution; Job 3 has to wait even though, if all of the fragments of memory were added together, there would be more than enough room to accommodate it. First-fit offers fast allocation, but it isn't always efficient.

On the other hand, the same job list using a best-fit scheme would use memory more efficiently, as shown in Figure 2.6. In this particular case, a best-fit scheme would yield better memory utilization.

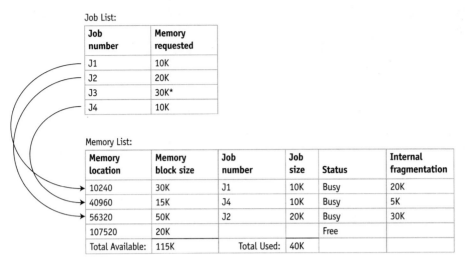

Job List:

Job number	Memory requested
J1	10K
J2	20K
J3	30K*
J4	10K

Memory List:

Memory location	Memory block size	Job number	Job size	Status	Internal fragmentation
10240	30K	J1	10K	Busy	20K
40960	15K	J4	10K	Busy	5K
56320	50K	J2	20K	Busy	30K
107520	20K			Free	
Total Available:	115K		Total Used:	40K	

(figure 2.5)

Using a first-fit scheme, Job 1 claims the first available space. Job 2 then claims the first partition large enough to accommodate it, but by doing so it takes the last block large enough to accommodate Job 3. Therefore, Job 3 (indicated by the asterisk) must wait until a large block becomes available, even though there's 75K of unused memory space (internal fragmentation). Notice that the memory list is ordered according to memory location.

Memory use has been increased but the memory allocation process takes more time. What's more, while internal fragmentation has been diminished, it hasn't been completely eliminated.

The first-fit algorithm assumes that the Memory Manager keeps two lists, one for free memory blocks and one for busy memory blocks. The operation consists of a simple loop that compares the size of each job to the size of each memory block until a block is found that's large enough to fit the job. Then the job is stored into that block of memory, and the Memory Manager moves out of the loop to fetch the next job from the entry queue. If the entire list is searched in vain, then the job is placed into a waiting queue. The Memory Manager then fetches the next job and repeats the process.

(figure 2.6)

Best-fit free scheme. Job 1 is allocated to the closest-fitting free partition, as are Job 2 and Job 3. Job 4 is allocated to the only available partition although it isn't the best-fitting one. In this scheme, all four jobs are served without waiting. Notice that the memory list is ordered according to memory size. This scheme uses memory more efficiently but it's slower to implement.

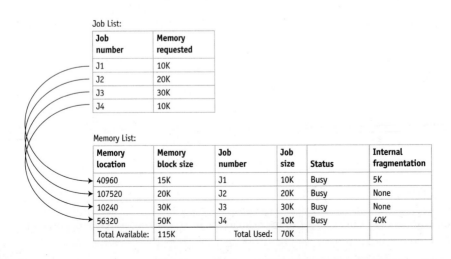

Job List:

Job number	Memory requested
J1	10K
J2	20K
J3	30K
J4	10K

Memory List:

Memory location	Memory block size	Job number	Job size	Status	Internal fragmentation
40960	15K	J1	10K	Busy	5K
107520	20K	J2	20K	Busy	None
10240	30K	J3	30K	Busy	None
56320	50K	J4	10K	Busy	40K
Total Available:	115K		Total Used:	70K	

The algorithms for best-fit and first-fit are very different. Here's how first-fit is implemented:

First-Fit Algorithm

1 Set counter to 1
2 Do while counter <= number of blocks in memory
   If job_size > memory_size(counter)
     Then counter = counter + 1
   Else
     load job into memory_size(counter)
     adjust free/busy memory lists
     go to step 4
   End do
3 Put job in waiting queue
4 Go fetch next job

In Table 2.2, a request for a block of 200 spaces has just been given to the Memory Manager. (The spaces may be words, bytes, or any other unit the system handles.) Using the first-fit algorithm and starting from the top of the list, the Memory Manager locates the first block of memory large enough to accommodate the job, which is at location 6785. The job is then loaded, starting at location 6785 and occupying the next 200 spaces. The next step is to adjust the free list to indicate that the block of free memory now starts at location 6985 (not 6785 as before) and that it contains only 400 spaces (not 600 as before).

(table 2.2)	Before Request		After Request	
	Beginning Address	**Memory Block Size**	**Beginning Address**	**Memory Block Size**
These two snapshots of memory show the status of each memory block before and after a request is made using the first-fit algorithm. (Note: All values are in decimal notation unless otherwise indicated.)	4075	105	4075	105
	5225	5	5225	5
	6785	600	*6985	400
	7560	20	7560	20
	7600	205	7600	205
	10250	4050	10250	4050
	15125	230	15125	230
	24500	1000	24500	1000

The algorithm for best-fit is slightly more complex because the goal is to find the smallest memory block into which the job will fit:

Best-Fit Algorithm

1 Initialize memory_block(o) = 99999

2 Compute initial_memory_waste = memory_block(o) − job_size

3 Initialize subscript = o

4 Set counter to 1

5 Do while counter <= number of blocks in memory

    If job_size > memory_size(counter)

      Then counter = counter + 1

    Else

      memory_waste = memory_size(counter) − job_size

    If initial_memory_waste > memory_waste

      Then subscript = counter

      initial_memory_waste = memory_waste

      counter = counter + 1

    End do

6 If subscript = o

    Then put job in waiting queue

    Else

      load job into memory_size(subscript)

      adjust free/busy memory lists

7 Go fetch next job

One of the problems with the best-fit algorithm is that the entire table must be searched before the allocation can be made because the memory blocks are physically stored in sequence according to their location in memory (and not by memory block sizes as shown in Figure 2.6). The system could execute an algorithm to continuously rearrange the list in ascending order by memory block size, but that would add more overhead and might not be an efficient use of processing time in the long run.

The best-fit algorithm is illustrated showing only the list of free memory blocks. Table 2.3 shows the free list before and after the best-fit block has been allocated to the same request presented in Table 2.2.

	Before Request		After Request	
Beginning Address	**Memory Block Size**		**Beginning Address**	**Memory Block Size**
4075	105		4075	105
5225	5		5225	5
6785	600		6785	600
7560	20		7560	20
7600	205		*7800	5
10250	4050		10250	4050
15125	230		15125	230
24500	1000		24500	1000

In Table 2.3, a request for a block of 200 spaces has just been given to the Memory Manager. Using the best-fit algorithm and starting from the top of the list, the Memory Manager searches the entire list and locates a block of memory starting at location 7600, which is the smallest block that's large enough to accommodate the job. The choice of this block minimizes the wasted space (only 5 spaces are wasted, which is less than in the four alternative blocks). The job is then stored, starting at location 7600 and occupying the next 200 spaces. Now the free list must be adjusted to show that the block of free memory starts at location 7800 (not 7600 as before) and that it contains only 5 spaces (not 205 as before).

Which is best—first-fit or best-fit? For many years there was no way to answer such a general question because performance depends on the job mix. Note that while the best-fit resulted in a better fit, it also resulted (and does so in the general case) in a smaller free space (5 spaces), which is known as a sliver.

In the exercises at the end of this chapter, two other hypothetical allocation schemes are explored: next-fit, which starts searching from the last allocated block for the next available block when a new job arrives; and worst-fit, which allocates the largest free available block to the new job. Worst-fit is the opposite of best-fit. Although it's a good way to explore the theory of memory allocation, it might not be the best choice for an actual system.

In recent years, access times have become so fast that the scheme that saves the more valuable resource, memory space, may be the best in some cases. Research continues to focus on finding the optimum allocation scheme. This includes optimum page size— a fixed allocation scheme we will cover in the next chapter, which is the key to improving the performance of the best-fit allocation scheme.

Deallocation

Until now, we've considered only the problem of how memory blocks are allocated, but eventually there comes a time when memory space must be released, or **deallocated**.

Whenever memory is deallocated, it creates an opportunity for external fragmentation.

For a fixed partition system, the process is quite straightforward. When the job is completed, the Memory Manager resets the status of the memory block where the job was stored to "free." Any code—for example, binary values with 0 indicating free and 1 indicating busy—may be used so the mechanical task of deallocating a block of memory is relatively simple.

A dynamic partition system uses a more complex algorithm because the algorithm tries to combine free areas of memory whenever possible. Therefore, the system must be prepared for three alternative situations:

- Case 1. When the block to be deallocated is adjacent to another free block
- Case 2. When the block to be deallocated is between two free blocks
- Case 3. When the block to be deallocated is isolated from other free blocks

The deallocation algorithm must be prepared for all three eventualities with a set of nested conditionals. The following algorithm is based on the fact that memory locations are listed using a lowest-to-highest address scheme. The algorithm would have to be modified to accommodate a different organization of memory locations. In this algorithm, *job_size* is the amount of memory being released by the terminating job, and *beginning_address* is the location of the first instruction for the job.

Algorithm to Deallocate Memory Blocks

```
If job_location is adjacent to one or more free blocks
    Then
    If job_location is between two free blocks
        Then merge all three blocks into one block
        memory_size(counter-1) = memory_size(counter-1) + job_size
        + memory_size(counter+1)
        set status of memory_size(counter+1) to null entry
    Else
        merge both blocks into one
        memory_size(counter-1) = memory_size(counter-1) + job_size
Else
        search for null entry in free memory list
        enter job_size and beginning_address in the entry slot
        set its status to "free"
```

Case 1: Joining Two Free Blocks

Table 2.4 shows how deallocation occurs in a dynamic memory allocation system when the job to be deallocated is next to one free memory block.

Beginning Address	Memory Block Size	Status
4075	105	Free
5225	5	Free
6785	600	Free
7560	20	Free
(7600)	(200)	(Busy)[1]
*7800	5	Free
10250	4050	Free
15125	230	Free
24500	1000	Free

[1]Although the numbers in parentheses don't appear in the free list, they've been inserted here for clarity. The job size is 200 and its beginning location is 7600.

After deallocation the free list looks like the one shown in Table 2.5.

Beginning Address	Memory Block Size	Status
4075	105	Free
5225	5	Free
6785	600	Free
7560	20	Free
*7600	205	Free
10250	4050	Free
15125	230	Free
24500	1000	Free

Using the deallocation algorithm, the system sees that the memory to be released is next to a free memory block, which starts at location 7800. Therefore, the list must be changed to reflect the starting address of the new free block, 7600, which was the address of the first instruction of the job that just released this block. In addition, the memory block size for this new free space must be changed to show its new size, which is the combined total of the two free partitions (200 + 5).

Case 2: Joining Three Free Blocks

When the deallocated memory space is between two free memory blocks, the process is similar, as shown in Table 2.6.

Using the deallocation algorithm, the system learns that the memory to be deallocated is between two free blocks of memory. Therefore, the sizes of the three free partitions (20 + 20 + 205) must be combined and the total stored with the smallest beginning address, 7560.

Beginning Address	Memory Block Size	Status
4075	105	Free
5225	5	Free
6785	600	Free
*7560	20	Free
(7580)	(20)	(Busy)[1]
*7600	205	Free
10250	4050	Free
15125	230	Free
24500	1000	Free

[1] Although the numbers in parentheses don't appear in the free list, they have been inserted here for clarity.

(table 2.6)

Case 2. This is the original free list before deallocation. The asterisks indicate the two free memory blocks that are adjacent to the soon-to-be-free memory block.

Because the entry at location 7600 has been combined with the previous entry, we must empty out this entry. We do that by changing the status to **null entry**, with no beginning address and no memory block size as indicated by an asterisk in Table 2.7. This negates the need to rearrange the list at the expense of memory.

Beginning Address	Memory Block Size	Status
4075	105	Free
5225	5	Free
6785	600	Free
7560	245	Free
*		(null entry)
10250	4050	Free
15125	230	Free
24500	1000	Free

(table 2.7)

Case 2. The free list after a job has released memory.

Case 3: Deallocating an Isolated Block

The third alternative is when the space to be deallocated is isolated from all other free areas.

For this example, we need to know more about how the busy memory list is configured. To simplify matters, let's look at the busy list for the memory area between locations 7560 and 10250. Remember that, starting at 7560, there's a free memory block of 245, so the busy memory area includes everything from location 7805 (7560 + 245) to 10250, which is the address of the next free block. The free list and busy list are shown in Table 2.8 and Table 2.9.

Beginning Address	Memory Block Size	Status
4075	105	Free
5225	5	Free
6785	600	Free
7560	245	Free
		(null entry)
10250	4050	Free
15125	230	Free
24500	1000	Free

Beginning Address	Memory Block Size	Status
7805	1000	Busy
*8805	445	Busy
9250	1000	Busy

Using the deallocation algorithm, the system learns that the memory block to be released is not adjacent to any free blocks of memory; instead it is between two other busy areas. Therefore, the system must search the table for a null entry.

The scheme presented in this example creates null entries in both the busy and the free lists during the process of allocation or deallocation of memory. An example of a null entry occurring as a result of deallocation was presented in Case 2. A null entry in the busy list occurs when a memory block between two other busy memory blocks is returned to the free list, as shown in Table 2.10. This mechanism ensures that all blocks are entered in the lists according to the beginning address of their memory location from smallest to largest.

Beginning Address	Memory Block Size	Status
7805	1000	Busy
*		(null entry)
9250	1000	Busy

(table 2.10)

Case 3. This is the busy list after the job has released its memory. The asterisk indicates the new null entry in the busy list.

When the null entry is found, the beginning memory location of the terminating job is entered in the beginning address column, the job size is entered under the memory block size column, and the status is changed from a null entry to free to indicate that a new block of memory is available, as shown in Table 2.11.

Beginning Address	Memory Block Size	Status
4075	105	Free
5225	5	Free
6785	600	Free
7560	245	Free
*8805	445	Free
10250	4050	Free
15125	230	Free
24500	1000	Free

(table 2.11)

Case 3. This is the free list after the job has released its memory. The asterisk indicates the new free block entry replacing the null entry.

Relocatable Dynamic Partitions

Both of the fixed and dynamic memory allocation schemes described thus far shared some unacceptable fragmentation characteristics that had to be resolved before the number of jobs waiting to be accepted became unwieldy. In addition, there was a growing need to use all the slivers of memory often left over.

The solution to both problems was the development of **relocatable dynamic partitions**. With this memory allocation scheme, the Memory Manager relocates programs to gather together all of the empty blocks and compact them to make one block of memory large enough to accommodate some or all of the jobs waiting to get in.

The **compaction** of memory, sometimes referred to as garbage collection or defragmentation, is performed by the operating system to reclaim fragmented sections of the memory space. Remember our earlier example of the makeshift lending library? If you stopped lending books for a few moments and rearranged the books in the most effective order, you would be compacting your collection. But this demonstrates its disad-

When you use a defragmentation utility, you are compacting memory and relocating file segments so they can be retrieved faster.

vantage—it's an overhead process, so that while compaction is being done everything else must wait.

Compaction isn't an easy task. First, every program in memory must be relocated so they're contiguous, and then every address, and every reference to an address, within each program must be adjusted to account for the program's new location in memory. However, all other values within the program (such as data values) must be left alone. In other words, the operating system must distinguish between addresses and data values, and the distinctions are not obvious once the program has been loaded into memory.

To appreciate the complexity of **relocation**, let's look at a typical program. Remember, all numbers are stored in memory as binary values, and in any given program instruction it's not uncommon to find addresses as well as data values. For example, an assembly language program might include the instruction to add the integer 1 to I. The source code instruction looks like this:

ADDI I, 1

However, after it has been translated into actual code it could look like this (for readability purposes the values are represented here in octal code, not binary code):

000007 271 01 0 00 000001

It's not immediately obvious which elements are addresses and which are instruction codes or data values. In fact, the address is the number on the left (000007). The instruction code is next (271), and the data value is on the right (000001).

The operating system can tell the function of each group of digits by its location in the line and the operation code. However, if the program is to be moved to another place in memory, each address must be identified, or flagged. So later the amount of memory locations by which the program has been displaced must be added to (or subtracted from) all of the original addresses in the program.

This becomes particularly important when the program includes loop sequences, decision sequences, and branching sequences, as well as data references. If, by chance, every address was not adjusted by the same value, the program would branch to the wrong section of the program or to a section of another program, or it would reference the wrong data.

The program in Figure 2.7 and Figure 2.8 shows how the operating system flags the addresses so that they can be adjusted if and when a program is relocated.

Internally, the addresses are marked with a special symbol (indicated in Figure 2.8 by apostrophes) so the Memory Manager will know to adjust them by the value stored in the relocation register. All of the other values (data values) are not marked and won't

```
A          EXP 132, 144, 125, 110      ;the data values
BEGIN:     MOVEI              1,0       ;initialize register 1
           MOVEI              2,0       ;initialize register 2
LOOP:      ADD                2,A(1)    ;add (A + reg 1) to reg 2
           ADDI               1,1       ;add 1 to reg 1
           CAIG               1,4-1     ;is register 1 > 4-1?
           JUMPA              LOOP      ;if not, go to Loop
           MOVE               3,2       ;if so, move reg 2 to reg 3
           IDIVI              3,4       ;divide reg 3 by 4,
                                        ;remainder to register 4
           EXIT                         ;end
           END
```

(figure 2.7)

An assembly language program that performs a simple incremental operation. This is what the programmer submits to the assembler. The commands are shown on the left and the comments explaining each command are shown on the right after the semicolons.

(addresses to be adjusted after relocation)

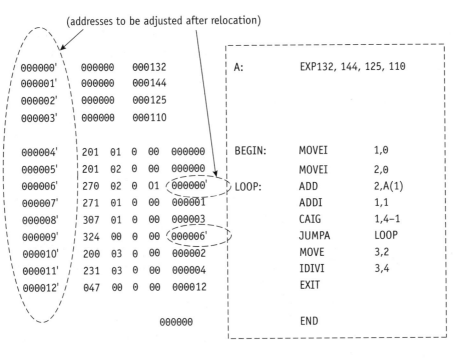

(figure 2.8)

The original assembly language program after it has been processed by the assembler, shown on the right (a). To run the program, the assembler translates it into machine readable code (b) with all addresses marked by a special symbol (shown here as an apostrophe) to distinguish addresses from data values. All addresses (and no data values) must be adjusted after relocation.

be changed after relocation. Other numbers in the program, those indicating instructions, registers, or constants used in the instruction, are also left alone.

Figure 2.9 illustrates what happens to a program in memory during compaction and relocation.

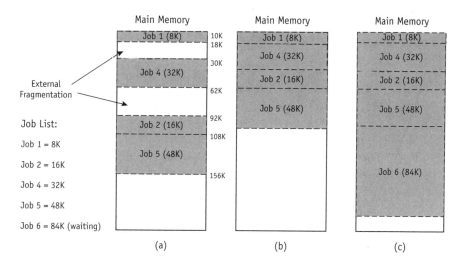

Main Memory | Main Memory | Main Memory

(a) (b) (c)

External Fragmentation

Job List:

Job 1 = 8K

Job 2 = 16K

Job 4 = 32K

Job 5 = 48K

Job 6 = 84K (waiting)

(figure 2.9)

Three snapshots of memory before and after compaction with the operating system occupying the first 10K of memory. When Job 6 arrives requiring 84K, the initial memory layout in (a) shows external fragmentation totaling 96K of space. Immediately after compaction (b), external fragmentation has been eliminated, making room for Job 6 which, after loading, is shown in (c).

This discussion of compaction raises three questions:

1. What goes on behind the scenes when relocation and compaction take place?
2. What keeps track of how far each job has moved from its original storage area?
3. What lists have to be updated?

The last question is easiest to answer. After relocation and compaction, both the free list and the busy list are updated. The free list is changed to show the partition for the new block of free memory: the one formed as a result of compaction that will be located in memory starting after the last location used by the last job. The busy list is changed to show the new locations for all of the jobs already in progress that were relocated. Each job will have a new address except for those that were already residing at the lowest memory locations.

To answer the other two questions we must learn more about the hardware components of a computer, specifically the registers. Special-purpose registers are used to help with the relocation. In some computers, two special registers are set aside for this purpose: the bounds register and the relocation register.

The **bounds register** is used to store the highest (or lowest, depending on the specific system) location in memory accessible by each program. This ensures that during execution, a program won't try to access memory locations that don't belong to it—that is, those that are out of bounds. The **relocation register** contains the value that must be added to each address referenced in the program so that the system will be able to access the correct memory addresses after relocation. If the program isn't relocated, the value stored in the program's relocation register is zero.

Figure 2.10 illustrates what happens during relocation by using the relocation register (all values are shown in decimal form).

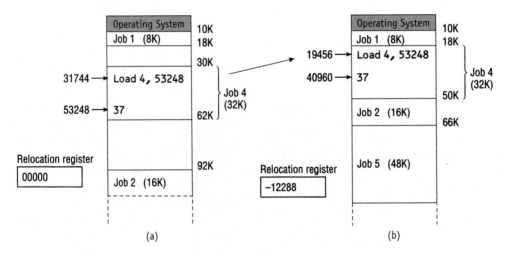

(figure 2.10)

Contents of relocation register and close-up of Job 4 memory area (a) before relocation and (b) after relocation and compaction.

Originally, Job 4 was loaded into memory starting at memory location 30K. (1K equals 1,024 bytes. Therefore, the exact starting address is: 30 * 1024 = 30,720.) It required a block of memory of 32K (or 32 * 1024 = 32,768) addressable locations. Therefore, when it was originally loaded, the job occupied the space from memory location 30720 to memory location 63488-1. Now, suppose that within the program, at memory location 31744, there's an instruction that looks like this:

```
LOAD 4, ANSWER
```

This assembly language command asks that the data value known as ANSWER be loaded into Register 4 for later computation. ANSWER, the value 37, is stored at memory location 53248. (In this example, Register 4 is a working/computation register, which is distinct from either the relocation or the bounds register.)

After relocation, Job 4 has been moved to a new starting memory address of 18K (actually 18 * 1024 = 18,432). Of course, the job still has its 32K addressable locations, so it now occupies memory from location 18432 to location 51200-1 and, thanks to the relocation register, all of the addresses will be adjusted accordingly.

What does the relocation register contain? In this example, it contains the value −12288. As calculated previously, 12288 is the size of the free block that has been moved forward toward the high addressable end of memory. The sign is negative because Job 4 has been moved back, closer to the low addressable end of memory, as shown at the top of Figure 2.10(b).

However, the program instruction (LOAD 4, ANSWER) has not been changed. The original address 53248 where ANSWER had been stored remains the same in the program no matter how many times it is relocated. Before the instruction is executed, however, the true address must be computed by adding the value stored in the relocation register to the address found at that instruction. If the addresses are not adjusted by the value stored in the relocation register, then even though memory location 31744 is still part of the job's accessible set of memory locations, it would not contain the LOAD command. Not only that, but location 53248 is now out of bounds. The instruction that was originally at 31744 has been moved to location 19456. That's because all of the instructions in this program have been moved back by 12K (12 * 1024 = 12,288), which is the size of the free block. Therefore, location 53248 has been displaced by −12288 and ANSWER, the data value 37, is now located at address 40960.

In effect, by compacting and relocating, the Memory Manager optimizes the use of memory and thus improves throughput—one of the measures of system performance. An unfortunate side effect is that more overhead is incurred than with the two previous memory allocation schemes. The crucial factor here is the timing of the compaction—when and how often it should be done. There are three options.

One approach is to do it when a certain percentage of memory becomes busy, say 75 percent. The disadvantage of this approach is that the system would incur unnecessary overhead if no jobs were waiting to use the remaining 25 percent.

A second approach is to compact memory only when there are jobs waiting to get in. This would entail constant checking of the entry queue, which might result in unnecessary overhead and slow down the processing of jobs already in the system.

A third approach is to do it after a prescribed amount of time has elapsed. If the amount of time chosen is too small, however, then the system will spend more time on compaction than on processing. If it's too large, too many jobs will congregate in the waiting queue and the advantages of compaction are lost.

As you can see, each option has its good and bad points. The best choice for any system is decided by the operating system designer who, based on the job mix and other factors, tries to optimize both processing time and memory use while keeping overhead as low as possible.

Conclusion

Four memory management techniques were presented in this chapter: single-user systems, fixed partitions, dynamic partitions, and relocatable dynamic partitions. They have three things in common: They all require that the entire program (1) be loaded into memory, (2) be stored contiguously, and (3) remain in memory until the job is completed.

Consequently, each puts severe restrictions on the size of the jobs because they can only be as large as the biggest partitions in memory.

These schemes were sufficient for the first three generations of computers, which processed jobs in batch mode. Turnaround time was measured in hours, or sometimes days, but that was a period when users expected such delays between the submission of their jobs and pick up of output. As you'll see in the next chapter, a new trend emerged during the third-generation computers of the late 1960s and early 1970s: Users were able to connect directly with the central processing unit via remote job entry stations, loading their jobs from online terminals that could interact more directly with the system. New methods of memory management were needed to accommodate them.

We'll see that the memory allocation schemes that followed had two new things in common. First, programs didn't have to be stored in contiguous memory locations— they could be divided into segments of variable sizes or pages of equal size. Each page, or segment, could be stored wherever there was an empty block big enough to hold it. Second, not all the pages, or segments, had to reside in memory during the execution of the job. These were significant advances for system designers, operators, and users alike.

Key Terms

address: a number that designates a particular memory location.

best-fit memory allocation: a main memory allocation scheme that considers all free blocks and selects for allocation the one that will result in the least amount of wasted space.

bounds register: a register used to store the highest location in memory legally accessible by each program.

compaction: the process of collecting fragments of available memory space into contiguous blocks by moving programs and data in a computer's memory or disk. Also called *garbage collection.*

deallocation: the process of freeing an allocated resource, whether memory space, a device, a file, or a CPU.

dynamic partitions: a memory allocation scheme in which jobs are given as much memory as they request when they are loaded for processing, thus creating their own partitions in main memory.

external fragmentation: a situation in which the dynamic allocation of memory creates unusable fragments of free memory between blocks of busy, or allocated, memory.

first come first served (FCFS): a nonpreemptive process scheduling policy that handles jobs according to their arrival time; the first job in the READY queue is processed first.

first-fit memory allocation: a main memory allocation scheme that searches from the beginning of the free block list and selects for allocation the first block of memory large enough to fulfill the request.

fixed partitions: a memory allocation scheme in which main memory is sectioned off, with portions assigned to each job.

internal fragmentation: a situation in which a fixed partition is only partially used by the program; the remaining space within the partition is unavailable to any other job and is therefore wasted.

kilobyte (K): a unit of memory or storage space equal to 1,024 bytes or 2^{10} bytes.

main memory: the unit that works directly with the CPU and in which the data and instructions must reside in order to be processed. Also called *random access memory (RAM), primary storage,* or *internal memory.*

null entry: an empty entry in a list.

relocatable dynamic partitions: a memory allocation scheme in which the system relocates programs in memory to gather together all of the empty blocks and compact them to make one block of memory that's large enough to accommodate some or all of the jobs waiting for memory.

relocation: (1) the process of moving a program from one area of memory to another; or (2) the process of adjusting address references in a program, by either software or hardware means, to allow the program to execute correctly when loaded in different sections of memory.

relocation register: a register that contains the value that must be added to each address referenced in the program so that it will be able to access the correct memory addresses after relocation.

static partitions: another term for *fixed partitions.*

Interesting Searches

- Core Memory Technology
- technikum29 Museum of Computer and Communication Technology
- How RAM Memory Works
- First Come First Served Algorithm
- Static vs. Dynamic Partitions
- Internal vs. External Fragmentation

Exercises

Research Topics

A. Three different number systems (in addition to the familiar base-10 system) are commonly used in computer science. Create a column of integers 1 through 30. In the next three columns show how each value is represented using the binary, octal, and hex number systems. Identify when and why each of the each three numbering systems is used. Cite your sources.

B. For a platform of your choice, investigate the growth in the size of main memory (RAM) from the time the platform was developed to the present day. Create a chart showing milestones in memory growth and the approximate date. Choose from microcomputers, midrange computers, and mainframes. Be sure to mention the organization that performed the RAM research and development and cite your sources.

Exercises

1. Explain the fundamental differences between internal fragmentation and external fragmentation. For each of the four memory management systems explained in this chapter (single user, fixed, dynamic, and relocatable dynamic), identify which one causes each type of fragmentation.

2. Which type of fragmentation is reduced by compaction? Explain your answer.

3. How often should relocation be performed? Explain your answer.

4. Imagine an operating system that does not perform memory deallocation. Name at least three unfortunate outcomes that would result and explain your answer.

5. Compare and contrast a fixed partition system and a dynamic partition system.

6. Compare and contrast a dynamic partition system and a relocatable dynamic partition system.

7. Given the following information:

Job list:

Job Number	Memory Requested	Memory Block	Memory Block Size
Job 1	690 K	Block 1	900 K (low-order memory)
Job 2	275 K	Block 2	910 K
Job 3	760 K	Block 3	300 K (high-order memory)

  a. Use the best-fit algorithm to indicate which memory blocks are allocated to each of the three arriving jobs.

  b. Use the first-fit algorithm to indicate which memory blocks are allocated to each of the three arriving jobs.

8. Given the following information:

Job list:

Job Number	Memory Requested	Memory Block	Memory Block Size
Job 1	275 K	Block 1	900 K (low-order memory)
Job 2	920 K	Block 2	910 K
Job 3	690 K	Block 3	300 K (high-order memory)

  a. Use the best-fit algorithm to indicate which memory blocks are allocated to each of the three arriving jobs.

  b. Use the first-fit algorithm to indicate which memory blocks are allocated to each of the three arriving jobs.

9. Next-fit is an allocation algorithm that keeps track of the partition that was allocated previously (last) and starts searching from that point on when a new job arrives.

  a. Are there any advantages of the next-fit algorithm? If so, what are they?

  b. How would it compare to best-fit and first-fit for the conditions given in Exercise 7?

  c. How would it compare to best-fit and first-fit for the conditions given in Exercise 8?

10. Worst-fit is an allocation algorithm that allocates the largest free block to a new job. This is the opposite of the best-fit algorithm.

  a. Are there any advantages of the worst-fit algorithm? If so, what are they?

  b. How would it compare to best-fit and first-fit for the conditions given in Exercise 7?

  c. How would it compare to best-fit and first-fit for the conditions given in Exercise 8?

Advanced Exercises

11. The relocation example presented in the chapter implies that compaction is done entirely in memory, without secondary storage. Can all free sections of memory be merged into one contiguous block using this approach? Why or why not?

12. To compact memory in some systems, some people suggest that all jobs in memory be copied to a secondary storage device and then reloaded (and relocated) contiguously into main memory, thus creating one free block after all jobs have been recopied into memory. Is this viable? Could you devise a better way to compact memory? Write your algorithm and explain why it is better.

13. Given the memory configuration in Figure 2.11, answer the following questions. At this point, Job 4 arrives requesting a block of 100K.

    a. Can Job 4 be accommodated? Why or why not?

    b. If relocation is used, what are the contents of the relocation registers for Job 1, Job 2, and Job 3 after compaction?

    c. What are the contents of the relocation register for Job 4 after it has been loaded into memory?

    d. An instruction that is part of Job 1 was originally loaded into memory location 22K. What is its new location after compaction?

    e. An instruction that is part of Job 2 was originally loaded into memory location 55K. What is its new location after compaction?

    f. An instruction that is part of Job 3 was originally loaded into memory location 80K. What is its new location after compaction?

    g. If an instruction was originally loaded into memory location 110K, what is its new location after compaction?

(figure 2.11)

Memory configuration for Exercise 13.

Programming Exercises

14. Here is a long-term programming project. Use the information that follows to complete this exercise.

Job List				Memory List	
Job Stream Number	Time	Job Size		Memory Block	Size
1	5	5760		1	9500
2	4	4190		2	7000
3	8	3290		3	4500
4	2	2030		4	8500
5	2	2550		5	3000
6	6	6990		6	9000
7	8	8940		7	1000
8	10	740		8	5500
9	7	3930		9	1500
10	6	6890		10	500
11	5	6580			
12	8	3820			
13	9	9140			
14	10	420			
15	10	220			
16	7	7540			
17	3	3210			
18	1	1380			
19	9	9850			
20	3	3610			
21	7	7540			
22	2	2710			
23	8	8390			
24	5	5950			
25	10	760			

At one large batch-processing computer installation, the management wants to decide what storage placement strategy will yield the best possible performance. The installation runs a large real storage (as opposed to "virtual" storage, which will be covered in the following chapter) computer under fixed partition multiprogramming. Each user program runs in a single group of contiguous storage locations. Users state their storage requirements and time units for CPU usage on their Job Control Card (it used to, and still does, work this way, although cards may not be used). The operating system allocates to each user the appropriate partition and starts up the user's job. The job remains in memory until completion. A total of 50,000 memory locations are available, divided into blocks as indicated in the table on the previous page.

a. Write (or calculate) an event-driven simulation to help you decide which storage placement strategy should be used at this installation. Your program would use the job stream and memory partitioning as indicated previously. Run the program until all jobs have been executed with the memory as is (in order by address). This will give you the first-fit type performance results.

b. Sort the memory partitions by size and run the program a second time; this will give you the best-fit performance results. For both parts a. and b., you are investigating the performance of the system using a typical job stream by measuring:

1. Throughput (how many jobs are processed per given time unit)
2. Storage utilization (percentage of partitions never used, percentage of partitions heavily used, etc.)
3. Waiting queue length
4. Waiting time in queue
5. Internal fragmentation

Given that jobs are served on a first-come, first-served basis:

c. Explain how the system handles conflicts when jobs are put into a waiting queue and there are still jobs entering the system—who goes first?

d. Explain how the system handles the "job clocks," which keep track of the amount of time each job has run, and the "wait clocks," which keep track of how long each job in the waiting queue has to wait.

e. Since this is an event-driven system, explain how you define "event" and what happens in your system when the event occurs.

f. Look at the results from the best-fit run and compare them with the results from the first-fit run. Explain what the results indicate about the performance of the system for this job mix and memory organization. Is one method of partitioning better than the other? Why or why not? Could you recommend one method over the other given your sample run? Would this hold in all cases? Write some conclusions and recommendations.

15. Suppose your system (as explained in Exercise 14) now has a "spooler" (storage area in which to temporarily hold jobs) and the job scheduler can choose which will be served from among 25 resident jobs. Suppose also that the first-come, first-served policy is replaced with a "faster-job, first-served" policy. This would require that a sort by time be performed on the job list before running the program. Does this make a difference in the results? Does it make a difference in your analysis? Does it make a difference in your conclusions and recommendations? The program should be run twice to test this new policy with both best-fit and first-fit.

16. Suppose your spooler (as described in Exercise 14) replaces the previous policy with one of "smallest-job, first-served." This would require that a sort by job size be performed on the job list before running the program. How do the results compare to the previous two sets of results? Will your analysis change? Will your conclusions change? The program should be run twice to test this new policy with both best-fit and first-fit.

Chapter 3 | Memory Management: Virtual Memory

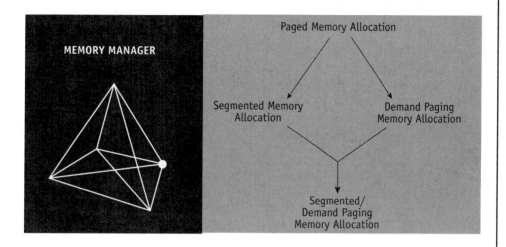

MEMORY MANAGER

Paged Memory Allocation

Segmented Memory Allocation

Demand Paging Memory Allocation

Segmented/ Demand Paging Memory Allocation

> ❝Nothing is so much strengthened by practice, or weakened by neglect, as memory. ❞
>
> —Quintillian *(A.D. 35–100)*

Learning Objectives

After completing this chapter, you should be able to describe:

- The basic functionality of the memory allocation methods covered in this chapter: paged, demand paging, segmented, and segmented/demand paged memory allocation
- The influence that these page allocation methods have had on virtual memory
- The difference between a first-in first-out page replacement policy, a least-recently-used page replacement policy, and a clock page replacement policy
- The mechanics of paging and how a memory allocation scheme determines which pages should be swapped out of memory
- The concept of the working set and how it is used in memory allocation schemes
- The impact that virtual memory had on multiprogramming
- Cache memory and its role in improving system response time

In the previous chapter we looked at simple memory allocation schemes. Each one required that the Memory Manager store the entire program in main memory in contiguous locations; and as we pointed out, each scheme solved some problems but created others, such as fragmentation or the overhead of relocation.

In this chapter we'll follow the evolution of virtual memory with four memory allocation schemes that first remove the restriction of storing the programs contiguously, and then eliminate the requirement that the entire program reside in memory during its execution. These schemes are paged, demand paging, segmented, and segmented/demand paged allocation, which form the foundation for our current virtual memory methods. Our discussion of cache memory will show how its use improves the performance of the Memory Manager.

Paged Memory Allocation

Before a job is loaded into memory, it is divided into parts called pages that will be loaded into memory locations called page frames. **Paged memory allocation** is based on the concept of dividing each incoming job into **pages** of equal size. Some operating systems choose a page size that is the same as the memory block size and that is also the same size as the sections of the disk on which the job is stored.

The sections of a disk are called **sectors** (or sometimes blocks), and the sections of main memory are called **page frames.** The scheme works quite efficiently when the pages, sectors, and page frames are all the same size. The exact size (the number of bytes that can be stored in each of them) is usually determined by the disk's sector size. Therefore, one sector will hold one page of job instructions and fit into one page frame of memory.

By working with page-sized pieces of the incoming job, memory can be used more efficiently.

Before executing a program, the Memory Manager prepares it by:

1. Determining the number of pages in the program
2. Locating enough empty page frames in main memory
3. Loading all of the program's pages into them

When the program is initially prepared for loading, its pages are in logical sequence—the first pages contain the first instructions of the program and the last page has the last instructions. We'll refer to the program's instructions as bytes or words.

The loading process is different from the schemes we studied in Chapter 2 because the pages do not have to be loaded in adjacent memory blocks. In fact, each page can be stored in any available page frame anywhere in main memory.

The primary advantage of storing programs in noncontiguous locations is that main memory is used more efficiently because an empty page frame can be used by any page of any job. In addition, the compaction scheme used for relocatable partitions is eliminated because there is no external fragmentation between page frames (and no internal fragmentation in most pages).

However, with every new solution comes a new problem. Because a job's pages can be located anywhere in main memory, the Memory Manager now needs a mechanism to keep track of them—and that means enlarging the size and complexity of the operating system software, which increases overhead.

The simplified example in Figure 3.1 shows how the Memory Manager keeps track of a program that is four pages long. To simplify the arithmetic, we've arbitrarily set the page size at 100 bytes. Job 1 is 350 bytes long and is being readied for execution.

Notice in Figure 3.1 that the last page (Page 3) is not fully utilized because the job is less than 400 bytes—the last page uses only 50 of the 100 bytes available. In fact, very few jobs perfectly fill all of the pages, so internal fragmentation is still a problem (but only in the last page of a job).

In Figure 3.1 (with seven free page frames), the operating system can accommodate jobs that vary in size from 1 to 700 bytes because they can be stored in the seven empty page frames. But a job that is larger than 700 bytes can't be accommodated until Job 1 ends its execution and releases the four page frames it occupies. And a job that is larger than 1100 bytes will never fit into the memory of this tiny system. Therefore, although

> **✔**
>
> In our examples, the first page is Page 0 and the second is Page 1, etc. Page frames are numbered the same way.

(figure 3.1)

Programs that are too long to fit on a single page are split into equal-sized pages that can be stored in free page frames. In this example, each page frame can hold 100 bytes. Job 1 is 350 bytes long and is divided among four page frames, leaving internal fragmentation in the last page frame. (The Page Map Table for this job is shown later in Table 3.2.)

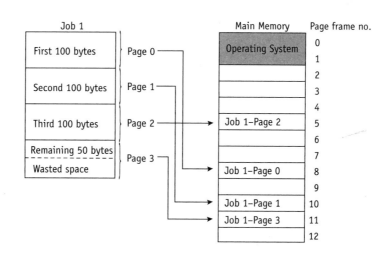

paged memory allocation offers the advantage of noncontiguous storage, it still requires that the entire job be stored in memory during its execution.

Figure 3.1 uses arrows and lines to show how a job's pages fit into page frames in memory, but the Memory Manager uses tables to keep track of them. There are essentially three tables that perform this function: the Job Table, Page Map Table, and Memory Map Table. Although different operating systems may have different names for them, the tables provide the same service regardless of the names they are given. All three tables reside in the part of main memory that is reserved for the operating system.

As shown in Table 3.1, the **Job Table (JT)** contains two values for each active job: the size of the job (shown on the left) and the memory location where its Page Map Table is stored (on the right). For example, the first job has a job size of 400 located at 3096 in memory. The Job Table is a dynamic list that grows as jobs are loaded into the system and shrinks, as shown in (b) in Table 3.1, as they are later completed.

Job Table		Job Table		Job Table	
Job Size	PMT Location	Job Size	PMT Location	Job Size	PMT Location
400	3096	400	3096	400	3096
200	3100			700	3100
500	3150	500	3150	500	3150
(a)		(b)		(c)	

(table 3.1)

This section of the Job Table (a) initially has three entries, one for each job in progress. When the second job ends (b), its entry in the table is released and it is replaced (c) by information about the next job that is to be processed.

Each active job has its own **Page Map Table (PMT)**, which contains the vital information for each page—the page number and its corresponding page frame memory address. Actually, the PMT includes only one entry per page. The page numbers are sequential (Page 0, Page 1, Page 2, through the last page), so it isn't necessary to list each page number in the PMT. The first entry in the PMT lists the page frame memory address for Page 0, the second entry is the address for Page 1, and so on.

The **Memory Map Table (MMT)** has one entry for each page frame listing its location and free/busy status.

At compilation time, every job is divided into pages. Using Job 1 from Figure 3.1, we can see how this works:

• Page 0 contains the first hundred bytes.

• Page 1 contains the second hundred bytes.

- Page 2 contains the third hundred bytes.
- Page 3 contains the last 50 bytes.

As you can see, the program has 350 bytes; but when they are stored, the system numbers them starting from 0 through 349. Therefore, the system refers to them as byte 0 through 349.

The **displacement**, or **offset**, of a byte (that is, how far away a byte is from the beginning of its page) is the factor used to locate that byte within its page frame. It is a relative factor.

In the simplified example shown in Figure 3.2, bytes 0, 100, 200, and 300 are the first bytes for pages 0, 1, 2, and 3, respectively, so each has a displacement of zero. Likewise, if the operating system needs to access byte 214, it can first go to page 2 and then go to byte 14 (the fifteenth line).

The first byte of each page has a displacement of zero, and the last byte, has a displacement of 99. So once the operating system finds the right page, it can access the correct bytes using its relative position within its page.

(figure 3.2)

Job 1 is 350 bytes long and is divided into four pages of 100 lines each.

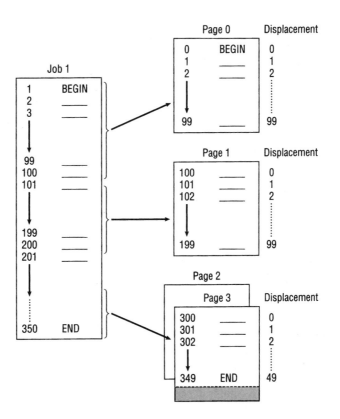

In this example, it is easy for us to see intuitively that all numbers less than 100 will be on Page 0, all numbers greater than or equal to 100 but less than 200 will be on Page 1, and so on. (That is the advantage of choosing a fixed page size, such as 100 bytes.) The operating system uses an algorithm to calculate the page and displacement; it is a simple arithmetic calculation.

To find the address of a given program instruction, the byte number is divided by the page size, keeping the remainder as an integer. The resulting quotient is the page number, and the remainder is the displacement within that page. When it is set up as a long division problem, it looks like this:

$$
\begin{array}{r}
\text{page number} \\
\hline
\text{page size}\,)\overline{\text{byte number to be located}} \\
\text{xxx} \\
\text{xxx} \\
\text{xxx} \\
\text{displacement}
\end{array}
$$

For example, if we use 100 bytes as the page size, the page number and the displacement (the location within that page) of byte 214 can be calculated using long division like this:

$$
\begin{array}{r}
2 \\
100\,)\overline{214} \\
\underline{200} \\
14
\end{array}
$$

The quotient (2) is the page number, and the remainder (14) is the displacement. So the byte is located on Page 2, 15 lines (Line 14) from the top of the page.

Let's try another example with a more common page size of 256 bytes. Say we are seeking the location of byte 384. When we divide 384 by 256, the result is 1.5. Therefore, the byte is located at the midpoint on the second page (Page 1).

$$
\begin{array}{r}
1.5 \\
256\,)\overline{384}
\end{array}
$$

To find the line's exact location, multiply the page size (256) by the decimal (0.5) to discover that the line we're seeking is located on Line 129 of Page 1.

Using the concepts just presented, and using the same parameters from the first example, answer these questions:

1. Could the operating system (or the hardware) get a page number that is greater than 3 if the program was searching for byte 214?
2. If it did, what should the operating system do?
3. Could the operating system get a remainder of more than 99?
4. What is the smallest remainder possible?

Here are the answers:

1. No, not if the application program was written correctly.
2. Send an error message and stop processing the program (because the page is out of bounds).
3. No, not if it divides correctly.
4. Zero.

The computer hardware performs the division, but the operating system is responsible for maintaining the tables that track the allocation and de-allocation of storage.

This procedure gives the location of an instruction with respect to the job's pages. However, these pages are only relative; each page is actually stored in a page frame that can be located anywhere in available main memory. Therefore, the algorithm needs to be expanded to find the exact location of the byte in main memory. To do so, we need to correlate each of the job's pages with its page frame number using the Page Map Table.

For example, if we look at the PMT for Job 1 from Figure 3.1, we see that it looks like the data in Table 3.2.

(table 3.2)

Page Map Table for Job 1 in Figure 3.1.

Job Page Number	Page Frame Number
0	8
1	10
2	5
3	11

In the first division example, we were looking for an instruction with a displacement of 14 on Page 2. To find its exact location in memory, the operating system (or the hardware) has to perform the following four steps. (In actuality, the operating system identifies the lines, or data values and instructions, as addresses [bytes or words]. We refer to them here as lines to make it easier to explain.)

STEP 1 Do the arithmetic computation just described to determine the page number and displacement of the requested byte.

• Page number = the integer quotient from the division of the job space address by the page size

• Displacement = the remainder from the page number division

In this example, the computation shows that the page number is 2 and the displacement is 14.

STEP 2 Refer to this job's PMT (shown in Table 3.2) and find out which page frame contains Page 2. Page 2 is located in Page Frame 5.

STEP 3 Get the address of the beginning of the page frame by multiplying the page frame number (5) by the page frame size (100).

```
ADDR_PAGE_FRAME = PAGE_FRAME_NUM * PAGE_SIZE
ADDR_PAGE_FRAME = 5(100)
```

STEP 4 Now add the displacement (calculated in step 1) to the starting address of the page frame to compute the precise location in memory of the instruction:

```
INSTR_ADDR_IN_MEM = ADDR_PAGE_FRAME + DISPL
INSTR_ADDR_IN_MEM = 500 + 14
```

The result of this maneuver tells us exactly where byte 14 is located in main memory.

Figure 3.3 shows another example and follows the hardware (and the operating system) as it runs an assembly language program that instructs the system to load into Register 1 the value found at byte 518.

In Figure 3.3, the page frame sizes in main memory are set at 512 bytes each and the page size is 512 bytes for this system. From the PMT we can see that this job has been divided into two pages. To find the exact location of byte 518 (where the system will find the value to load into Register 1), the system will do the following:

1. Compute the page number and displacement—the page number is 1, and the displacement is 6.
2. Go to the Page Map Table and retrieve the appropriate page frame number for Page 1. It is Page Frame 3.
3. Compute the starting address of the page frame by multiplying the page frame number by the page frame size: (3 * 512 = 1536).
4. Calculate the exact address of the instruction in main memory by adding the displacement to the starting address: (1536 + 6 = 1542). Therefore, memory address 1542 holds the value that should be loaded into Register 1.

(figure 3.3)

Job 1 with its Page Map Table. This snapshot of main memory shows the allocation of page frames to Job 1.

Job 1

Byte no.	Instruction/Data
000	BEGIN
025	LOAD R1, 518
518	3792

Main Memory / Page frame no.

		Page frame no.
0		0
512		1
1024		2
1536	Job 1 - Page 1	3
2048		4
2560	Job 1 - Page 0	5
3072		6
3584		7
		8

PMT for Job 1

Page no.	Page frame number
0	5
1	3

As you can see, this is a lengthy operation. Every time an instruction is executed, or a data value is used, the operating system (or the hardware) must translate the job space address, which is relative, into its physical address, which is absolute. This is called resolving the address, also called **address resolution**, or address translation. Of course, all of this processing is overhead, which takes processing capability away from the jobs waiting to be completed. However, in most systems the hardware does the paging, although the operating system is involved in dynamic paging, which will be covered later.

The advantage of a paging scheme is that it allows jobs to be allocated in noncontiguous memory locations so that memory is used more efficiently and more jobs can fit in the main memory (which is synonymous). However, there are disadvantages—overhead is increased and internal fragmentation is still a problem, although only in the last page of each job. The key to the success of this scheme is the size of the page. A page size that is too small will generate very long PMTs while a page size that is too large will result in excessive internal fragmentation. Determining the best page size is an important policy decision—there are no hard and fast rules that will guarantee optimal use of resources—and it is a problem we'll see again as we examine other paging alternatives. The best size depends on the actual job environment, the nature of the jobs being processed, and the constraints placed on the system.

Demand Paging

Demand paging introduced the concept of loading only a part of the program into memory for processing. It was the first widely used scheme that removed the restriction of having the entire job in memory from the beginning to the end of its processing. With demand paging, jobs are still divided into equally sized pages that initially reside in secondary storage. When the job begins to run, its pages are brought into memory only as they are needed.

Demand paging takes advantage of the fact that programs are written sequentially so that while one section, or module, is processed all of the other modules are idle. Not all the pages are accessed at the same time, or even sequentially. For example:

With demand paging, the pages are loaded as each is requested. This requires high-speed access to the pages.

• User-written error handling modules are processed only when a specific error is detected during execution. (For instance, they can be used to indicate to the operator that input data was incorrect or that a computation resulted in an invalid answer). If no error occurs, and we hope this is generally the case, these instructions are never processed and never need to be loaded into memory.

- Many modules are mutually exclusive. For example, if the input module is active (such as while a worksheet is being loaded) then the processing module is inactive. Similarly, if the processing module is active then the output module (such as printing) is idle.

- Certain program options are either mutually exclusive or not always accessible. This is easiest to visualize in menu-driven programs. For example, an application program may give the user several menu choices as shown in Figure 3.4. The system allows the operator to make only one selection at a time. If the user selects the first option then the module with the program instructions to move records to the file is the only one that is being used, so that is the only module that needs to be in memory at this time. The other modules all remain in secondary storage until they are called from the menu.

- Many tables are assigned a large fixed amount of address space even though only a fraction of the table is actually used. For example, a symbol table for an assembler might be prepared to handle 100 symbols. If only 10 symbols are used then 90 percent of the table remains unused.

File   Edit   Object   Type   Select   Filter   Effect   View   Window   Help

(figure 3.4)

When you choose one option from the menu of an application program such as this one, the other modules that aren't currently required (such as Help) don't need to be moved into memory immediately.

One of the most important innovations of demand paging was that it made virtual memory feasible. (Virtual memory will be discussed later in this chapter.) The demand paging scheme allows the user to run jobs with less main memory than is required if the operating system is using the paged memory allocation scheme described earlier. In fact, a demand paging scheme can give the appearance of an almost-infinite or nonfinite amount of physical memory when, in reality, physical memory is significantly less than infinite.

The key to the successful implementation of this scheme is the use of a high-speed direct access storage device (such as hard drives or flash memory) that can work directly with the CPU. That is vital because pages must be passed quickly from secondary storage to main memory and back again.

How and when the pages are passed (also called swapped) depends on predefined policies that determine when to make room for needed pages and how to do so. The operating system relies on tables (such as the Job Table, the Page Map Table, and the Memory Map Table) to implement the algorithm. These tables are basically the same as for paged memory allocation but with the addition of three new fields for each page

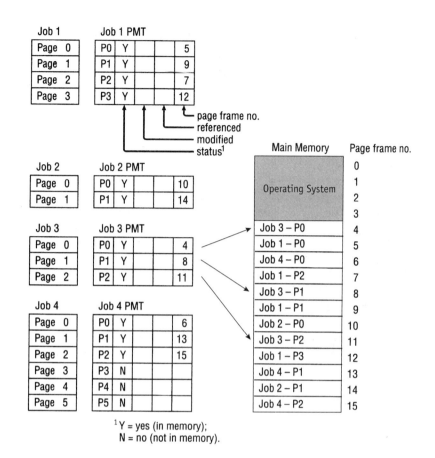

(figure 3.5)

Demand paging requires that the Page Map Table for each job keep track of each page as it is loaded or removed from main memory. Each PMT tracks the status of the page, whether it has been modified, whether it has been recently referenced, and the page frame number for each page currently in main memory. (Note: For this illustration, the Page Map Tables have been simplified. See Table 3.3 for more detail.)

in the PMT: one to determine if the page being requested is already in memory; a second to determine if the page contents have been modified; and a third to determine if the page has been referenced recently, as shown at the top of Figure 3.5.

The first field tells the system where to find each page. If it is already in memory, the system will be spared the time required to bring it from secondary storage. It is faster for the operating system to scan a table located in main memory than it is to retrieve a page from a disk.

The second field, noting if the page has been modified, is used to save time when pages are removed from main memory and returned to secondary storage. If the contents of the page haven't been modified then the page doesn't need to be rewritten to secondary storage. The original, already there, is correct.

The third field, which indicates any recent activity, is used to determine which pages show the most processing activity, and which are relatively inactive. This information is used by several page-swapping policy schemes to determine which pages should remain in main memory and which should be swapped out when the system needs to make room for other pages being requested.

For example, in Figure 3.5 the number of total job pages is 15, and the number of total available page frames is 12. (The operating system occupies the first four of the 16 page frames in main memory.)

Assuming the processing status illustrated in Figure 3.5, what happens when Job 4 requests that Page 3 be brought into memory if there are no empty page frames available?

A swap requires close interaction between hardware components, software algorithms, and policy schemes.

To move in a new page, a resident page must be swapped back into secondary storage. Specifically, that includes copying the resident page to the disk (if it was modified), and writing the new page into the empty page frame.

The hardware components generate the address of the required page, find the page number, and determine whether it is already in memory. The following algorithm makes up the hardware instruction processing cycle.

Hardware Instruction Processing Algorithm

1 Start processing instruction
2 Generate data address
3 Compute page number
4 If page is in memory
        Then
           get data and finish instruction
           advance to next instruction
           return to step 1
      Else
           generate page interrupt
           call page fault handler
      End if

The same process is followed when fetching an instruction.

When the test fails (meaning that the page is in secondary storage but not in memory), the operating system software takes over. The section of the operating system that resolves these problems is called the **page fault handler**. It determines whether there are empty page frames in memory so the requested page can be immediately copied from secondary storage. If all page frames are busy, the page fault handler must decide which page will be swapped out. (This decision is directly dependent on the predefined policy for page removal.) Then the swap is made.

Page Fault Handler Algorithm

1. If there is no free page frame
   Then
       select page to be swapped out using page removal algorithm
       update job's Page Map Table
       If content of page had been changed then
          write page to disk
       End if
   End if
2. Use page number from step 3 from the Hardware Instruction Processing Algorithm to get disk address where the requested page is stored (the File Manager, to be discussed in Chapter 8, uses the page number to get the disk address)
3. Read page into memory
4. Update job's Page Map Table
5. Update Memory Map Table
6. Restart interrupted instruction

Before continuing, three tables must be updated: the Page Map Tables for both jobs (the PMT with the page that was swapped out and the PMT with the page that was swapped in) and the Memory Map Table. Finally, the instruction that was interrupted is resumed and processing continues.

Although demand paging is a solution to inefficient memory utilization, it is not free of problems. When there is an excessive amount of **page swapping** between main memory and secondary storage, the operation becomes inefficient. This phenomenon is called **thrashing**. It uses a great deal of the computer's energy but accomplishes very little, and it is caused when a page is removed from memory but is called back shortly thereafter. Thrashing can occur across jobs, when a large number of jobs are vying for a relatively low number of free pages (the ratio of job pages to free memory page frames is high), or it can happen within a job—for example, in loops that cross page boundaries. We can demonstrate this with a simple example. Suppose the beginning of a loop falls at the bottom of a page and is completed at the top of the next page, as in the C program in Figure 3.6.

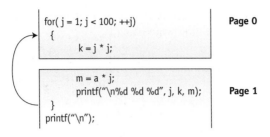

(figure 3.6)

An example of demand paging that causes a page swap each time the loop is executed and results in thrashing. If only a single page frame is available, this program will have one page fault each time the loop is executed.

The situation in Figure 3.6 assumes there is only one empty page frame available. The first page is loaded into memory and execution begins, but after executing the last command on Page 0, the page is swapped out to make room for Page 1. Now execution can continue with the first command on Page 1, but at the "}" symbol Page 1 must be swapped out so Page 0 can be brought back in to continue the loop. Before this program is completed, swapping will have occurred 100 times (unless another page frame becomes free so both pages can reside in memory at the same time). A failure to find a page in memory is often called a **page fault** and this example would generate 100 page faults (and swaps).

In such extreme cases, the rate of useful computation could be degraded by a factor of 100. Ideally, a demand paging scheme is most efficient when programmers are aware of the page size used by their operating system and are careful to design their programs to keep page faults to a minimum; but in reality, this is not often feasible.

Page Replacement Policies and Concepts

As we just learned, the policy that selects the page to be removed, the **page replacement policy**, is crucial to the efficiency of the system, and the algorithm to do that must be carefully selected.

Several such algorithms exist and it is a subject that enjoys a great deal of theoretical attention and research. Two of the most well-known are first-in first-out and least recently used. The **first-in first-out (FIFO) policy** is based on the theory that the best page to remove is the one that has been in memory the longest. The **least recently used (LRU) policy** chooses the page least recently accessed to be swapped out.

To illustrate the difference between FIFO and LRU, let us imagine a dresser drawer filled with your favorite sweaters. The drawer is full, but that didn't stop you from buying a new sweater. Now you have to put it away. Obviously it won't fit in your

Thrashing increases wear and tear on the hardware and slows data access.

sweater drawer unless you take something out, but which sweater should you move to the storage closet? Your decision will be based on a sweater removal policy.

You could take out your oldest sweater (the one that was first in), figuring that you probably won't use it again—hoping you won't discover in the following days that it is your most used, most treasured possession. Or, you could remove the sweater that you haven't worn recently and has been idle for the longest amount of time (the one that was least recently used). It is readily identifiable because it is at the bottom of the drawer. But just because it hasn't been used recently doesn't mean that a once-a-year occasion won't demand its appearance soon.

What guarantee do you have that once you have made your choice you won't be trekking to the storage closet to retrieve the sweater you stored yesterday? You could become a victim of thrashing.

Which is the best policy? It depends on the weather, the wearer, and the wardrobe. Of course, one option is to get another drawer. For an operating system (or a computer), this is the equivalent of adding more accessible memory, and we will explore that option after we discover how to more effectively use the memory we already have.

First-In First-Out

The first-in first-out (FIFO) page replacement policy will remove the pages that have been in memory the longest. The process of swapping pages is illustrated in Figure 3.7.

(figure 3.7)

The FIFO policy in action with only two page frames available. When the program calls for Page C, Page A must be moved out of the first page frame to make room for it, as shown by the solid lines. When Page A is needed again, it will replace Page B in the second page frame, as shown by the dotted lines. The entire sequence is shown in Figure 3.8.

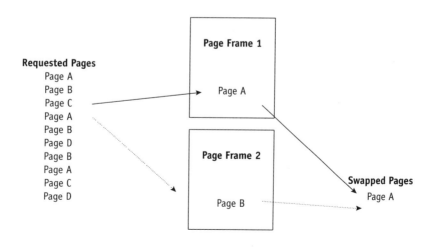

Requested Pages
Page A
Page B
Page C
Page A
Page B
Page D
Page B
Page A
Page C
Page D

Page Frame 1
Page A

Page Frame 2
Page B

Swapped Pages
Page A

Figure 3.8 shows how the FIFO algorithm works by following a job with four pages (A, B, C, D) as it is processed by a system with only two available page frames. Figure 3.8 displays how each page is swapped into and out of memory and marks each interrupt with an asterisk. We then count the number of page interrupts and compute the failure rate and the success rate. The job to be processed needs its pages in the following order: A, B, A, C, A, B, D, B, A, C, D.

When both page frames are occupied, each new page brought into memory will cause an existing one to be swapped out to secondary storage. A page interrupt, which we identify with an asterisk (*), is generated when a new page needs to be loaded into memory, whether a page is swapped out or not.

The efficiency of this configuration is dismal—there are 9 page interrupts out of 11 page requests due to the limited number of page frames available and the need for many new pages. To calculate the failure rate, we divide the number of interrupts by the number of page requests. The failure rate of this system is 9/11, which is 82 percent. Stated another way, the success rate is 2/11, or 18 percent. A failure rate this high is usually unacceptable.

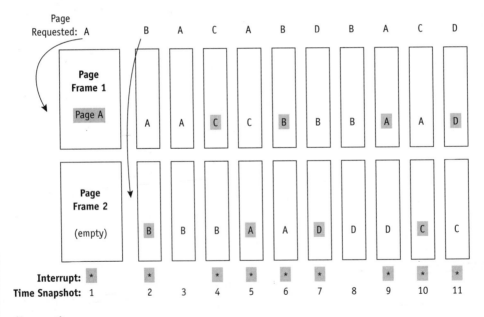

In Figure 3.8, using FIFO, Page A is swapped out when a newer page arrives even though it is used the most often.

(figure 3.8)

Using a FIFO policy, this page trace analysis shows how each page requested is swapped into the two available page frames. When the program is ready to be processed, all four pages are in secondary storage. When the program calls a page that isn't already in memory, a page interrupt is issued, as shown by the gray boxes and asterisks. This program resulted in nine page interrupts.

We are not saying FIFO is bad. We chose this example to show how FIFO works, not to diminish its appeal as a swapping policy. The high failure rate here is caused by both the limited amount of memory available and the order in which pages are requested by the program. The page order can't be changed by the system, although the size of main memory can be changed; but buying more memory may not always be the best solution—especially when you have many users and each one wants an unlimited amount of memory. There is no guarantee that buying more memory will always result in better performance; this is known as the **FIFO anomaly**, which is explained later in this chapter.

Least Recently Used

The least recently used (LRU) page replacement policy swaps out the pages that show the least amount of recent activity, figuring that these pages are the least likely to be used again in the immediate future. Conversely, if a page is used, it is likely to be used again soon; this is based on the theory of locality, which will be explained later in this chapter.

To see how it works, let us follow the same job in Figure 3.8 but using the LRU policy. The results are shown in Figure 3.9. To implement this policy, a queue of the requests is kept in FIFO order, a time stamp of when the job entered the system is saved, or a mark in the job's PMT is made periodically.

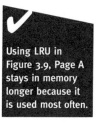

Using LRU in Figure 3.9, Page A stays in memory longer because it is used most often.

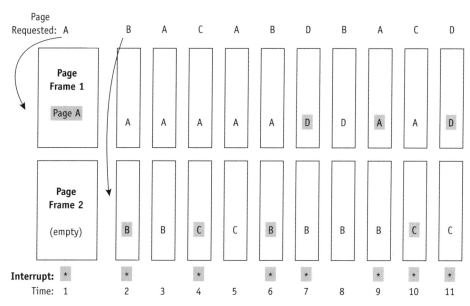

(figure 3.9)

Memory management using an LRU page removal policy for the program shown in Figure 3.8. Throughout the program, 11 page requests are issued, but they cause only 8 page interrupts.

The efficiency of this configuration is only slightly better than with FIFO. Here, there are 8 page interrupts out of 11 page requests, so the failure rate is 8/11, or 73 percent. In this example, an increase in main memory by one page frame would increase the success rate of both FIFO and LRU. However, we can't conclude on the basis of only one example that one policy is better than the others. In fact, LRU is a stack algorithm removal policy, which means that an increase in memory will never cause an increase in the number of page interrupts.

On the other hand, it has been shown that under certain circumstances adding more memory can, in rare cases, actually cause an increase in page interrupts when using a FIFO policy. As noted before, it is called the FIFO anomaly. But although it is an unusual occurrence, the fact that it exists coupled with the fact that pages are removed regardless of their activity (as was the case in Figure 3.8) has removed FIFO from the most favored policy position it held in some cases.

A variation of the LRU page replacement algorithm is known as the **clock page replacement policy** because it is implemented with a circular queue and uses a pointer to step through the reference bits of the active pages, simulating a clockwise motion. The algorithm is paced according to the computer's **clock cycle**, which is the time span between two ticks in its system clock. The algorithm checks the reference bit for each page. If the bit is one (indicating that it was recently referenced), the bit is reset to zero and the bit for the next page is checked. However, if the reference bit is zero (indicating that the page has not recently been referenced), that page is targeted for removal. If all the reference bits are set to one, then the pointer must cycle through the entire circular queue again giving each page a second and perhaps a third or fourth chance. Figure 3.10 shows a circular queue containing the reference bits for eight pages currently in memory. The pointer indicates the page that would be considered next for removal. Figure 3.10 shows what happens to the reference bits of the pages that have

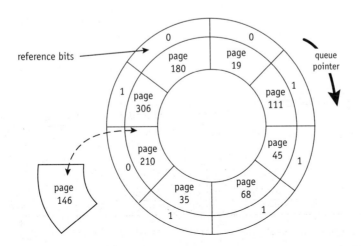

(figure 3.10)

A circular queue, which contains the page number and its reference bit. The pointer seeks the next candidate for removal and replaces page 210 with a new page, 146.

been given a second chance. When a new page, 146, has to be allocated to a page frame, it is assigned to the space that has a reference bit of zero, the space previously occupied by page 210.

A second variation of LRU uses an 8-bit reference byte and a bit-shifting technique to track the usage of each page currently in memory. When the page is first copied into memory, the leftmost bit of its reference byte is set to 1; and all bits to the right of the one are set to zero, as shown in Figure 3.11. At specific time intervals of the clock cycle, the Memory Manager shifts every page's reference bytes to the right by one bit, dropping their rightmost bit. Meanwhile, each time a page is referenced, the leftmost bit of its reference byte is set to 1.

This process of shifting bits to the right and resetting the leftmost bit to 1 when a page is referenced gives a history of each page's usage. For example, a page that has not been used for the last eight time ticks would have a reference byte of 00000000, while one that has been referenced once every time tick will have a reference byte of 11111111.

When a page fault occurs, the LRU policy selects the page with the smallest value in its reference byte because that would be the one least recently used. Figure 3.11 shows how the reference bytes for six active pages change during four snapshots of usage. In (a), the six pages have been initialized; this indicates that all of them have been referenced once. In (b), pages 1, 3, 5, and 6 have been referenced again (marked with 1), but pages 2 and 4 have not (now marked with 0 in the leftmost position). In (c), pages 1, 2, and 4 have been referenced. In (d), pages 1, 2, 4, and 6 have been referenced. In (e), pages 1 and 4 have been referenced.

As shown in Figure 3.11, the values stored in the reference bytes are not unique: page 3 and page 5 have the same value. In this case, the LRU policy may opt to swap out all of the pages with the smallest value, or may select one among them based on other criteria such as FIFO, priority, or whether the contents of the page have been modified.

Other page removal algorithms, MRU (most recently used) and LFU (least frequently used), are discussed in exercises at the end of this chapter.

(figure 3.11)

Notice how the reference bit for each page is updated with every time tick. Arrows (a) through (e) show how the initial bit shifts to the right with every tick of the clock.

Page Number	Time Snapshot 0	Time Snapshot 1	Time Snapshot 2	Time Snapshot 3	Time Snapshot 4
1	10000000	11000000	11100000	11110000	11111000
2	10000000	01000000	10100000	11010000	01101000
3	10000000	11000000	01100000	00110000	00011000
4	10000000	01000000	10100000	11010000	11101000
5	10000000	11000000	01100000	00110000	00011000
6	10000000	11000000	01100000	10110000	01011000
	(a)	(b)	(c)	(d)	(e)

The Mechanics of Paging

Before the Memory Manager can determine which pages will be swapped out, it needs specific information about each page in memory—information included in the Page Map Tables.

For example, in Figure 3.5, the Page Map Table for Job 1 included three bits: the status bit, the referenced bit, and the modified bit (these were the three middle columns: the two empty columns and the Y/N column representing "in memory"). But the representation of the table shown in Figure 3.5 was simplified for illustration purposes. It actually looks something like the one shown in Table 3.3.

✔

Each PMT must track each page's status, modifications, and references. It does so with three bits, each of which can be either 0 or 1.

Page	Status Bit	Referenced Bit	Modified Bit	Page Frame
0	1	1	1	5
1	1	0	0	9
2	1	0	0	7
3	1	1	0	12

(table 3.3)

Page Map Table for Job 1 shown in Figure 3.5.

As we said before, the status bit indicates whether the page is currently in memory. The referenced bit indicates whether the page has been called (referenced) recently. This bit is important because it is used by the LRU algorithm to determine which pages should be swapped out.

The modified bit indicates whether the contents of the page have been altered and, if so, the page must be rewritten to secondary storage when it is swapped out before its page frame is released. (A page frame with contents that have not been modified can be overwritten directly, thereby saving a step.) That is because when a page is swapped into memory it isn't removed from secondary storage. The page is merely copied—the original remains intact in secondary storage. Therefore, if the page isn't altered while it is in main memory (in which case the modified bit remains unchanged, zero), the page needn't be copied back to secondary storage when it is swapped out of memory—the page that is already there is correct. However, if modifications were made to the page, the new version of the page must be written over the older version—and that takes time.

Each bit can be either 0 or 1 as shown in Table 3.4.

(table 3.4)	Status Bit		Modified Bit		Referenced Bit	
	Value	Meaning	Value	Meaning	Value	Meaning
The meaning of the bits used in the Page Map Table.	0	not in memory	0	not modified	0	not called
	1	resides in memory	1	was modified	1	was called

The status bit for all pages in memory is 1. A page must be in memory before it can be swapped out so all of the candidates for swapping have a 1 in this column. The other two bits can be either 0 or 1, so there are four possible combinations of the referenced and modified bits as shown in Table 3.5.

(table 3.5)	Modified	Referenced	Meaning
Case 1	0	0	Not modified AND not referenced
Case 2	0	1	Not modified BUT was referenced
Case 3	1	0	Was modified BUT not referenced [impossible?]
Case 4	1	1	Was modified AND was referenced

Four possible combinations of modified and referenced bits and the meaning of each.

The FIFO algorithm uses only the modified and status bits when swapping pages, but the LRU looks at all three before deciding which pages to swap out.

Which page would the LRU policy choose first to swap? Of the four cases described in Table 3.5, it would choose pages in Case 1 as the ideal candidates for removal because they've been neither modified nor referenced. That means they wouldn't need to be rewritten to secondary storage, and they haven't been referenced recently. So the pages with zeros for these two bits would be the first to be swapped out.

What is the next most likely candidate? The LRU policy would choose Case 3 next because the other two, Case 2 and Case 4, were recently referenced. The bad news is that Case 3 pages have been modified, so it will take more time to swap them out. By process of elimination, then we can say that Case 2 is the third choice and Case 4 would be the pages least likely to be removed.

You may have noticed that Case 3 presents an interesting situation: apparently these pages have been modified without being referenced. How is that possible? The key lies in how the referenced bit is manipulated by the operating system. When the pages are brought into memory, they are all usually referenced at least once and that means that all of the pages soon have a referenced bit of 1. Of course the LRU algorithm would be defeated if every page indicated that it had been referenced. Therefore, to make sure the referenced bit actually indicates *recently* referenced, the operating system periodically resets it to 0. Then, as the pages are referenced during processing, the bit is changed from 0 to 1 and the LRU policy is able to identify which pages actually are frequently referenced. As you can imagine, there is one brief instant, just after the bits are reset, in which all of the pages (even the active pages) have reference bits of 0 and are vulnerable. But as processing continues, the most-referenced pages soon have their bits reset to 1, so the risk is minimized.

The Working Set

One innovation that improved the performance of demand paging schemes was the concept of the **working set**. A job's working set is the set of pages residing in memory that can be accessed directly without incurring a page fault.

When a user requests execution of a program, the first page is loaded into memory and execution continues as more pages are loaded: those containing variable declarations, others containing instructions, others containing data, and so on. After a while, most programs reach a fairly stable state and processing continues smoothly with very few additional page faults. At this point the job's working set is in memory, and the program won't generate many page faults until it gets to another phase requiring a different set of pages to do the work—a different working set.

Of course, it is possible that a poorly structured program could require that every one of its pages be in memory before processing can begin.

Fortunately, most programs are structured, and this leads to a **locality of reference** during the program's execution, meaning that during any phase of its execution the program references only a small fraction of its pages. For example, if a job is executing a loop then the instructions within the loop are referenced extensively while those outside the loop aren't used at all until the loop is completed—that is locality of reference. The same applies to sequential instructions, subroutine calls (within the subroutine), stack implementations, access to variables acting as counters or sums, or multidimensional variables such as arrays and tables (only a few of the pages are needed to handle the references).

It would be convenient if all of the pages in a job's working set were loaded into memory at one time to minimize the number of page faults and to speed up processing, but that is easier said than done. To do so, the system needs definitive answers to some difficult questions: How many pages comprise the working set? What is the maximum number of pages the operating system will allow for a working set?

The second question is particularly important in networked or time sharing systems, which regularly swap jobs (or pages of jobs) into memory and back to secondary storage to accommodate the needs of many users. The problem is this: every time a job is reloaded back into memory (or has pages swapped), it has to generate several page faults until its working set is back in memory and processing can continue. It is a time-consuming task for the CPU, which can't be processing jobs during the time it takes to process each page fault, as shown in Figure 3.12.

One solution adopted by many paging systems is to begin by identifying each job's working set and then loading it into memory in its entirety before allowing execution to begin. This is difficult to do before a job is executed but can be identified as its execution proceeds.

In a time-sharing or networked system, this means the operating system must keep track of the size and identity of every working set, making sure that the jobs destined for processing at any one time won't exceed the available memory. Some operating systems use a variable working set size and either increase it when necessary (the job requires more processing) or decrease it when necessary. This may mean that the number of jobs in memory will need to be reduced if, by doing so, the system can ensure the completion of each job and the subsequent release of its memory space.

We have looked at several examples of demand paging memory allocation schemes. Demand paging had two advantages. It was the first scheme in which a job was no

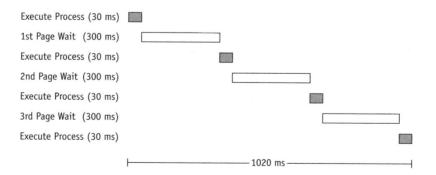

(figure 3.12)

Time line showing the amount of time required to process page faults for a single program. The program in this example takes 120 milliseconds (ms) to execute but an additional 900 ms to load the necessary pages into memory. Therefore, job turnaround is 1020 ms.

longer constrained by the size of physical memory and it introduced the concept of virtual memory. The second advantage was that it utilized memory more efficiently than the previous schemes because the sections of a job that were used seldom or not at all (such as error routines) weren't loaded into memory unless they were specifically requested. Its disadvantage was the increased overhead caused by the tables and the page interrupts. The next allocation scheme built on the advantages of both paging and dynamic partitions.

Segmented Memory Allocation

The concept of segmentation is based on the common practice by programmers of structuring their programs in modules—logical groupings of code. With **segmented memory allocation**, each job is divided into several **segments** of different sizes, one for each module that contains pieces that perform related functions. Segmented memory allocation was designed to reduce page faults that resulted from having a segment's loop split over two or more pages. A **subroutine** is an example of one such logical group. This is fundamentally different from a paging scheme, which divides the job into several pages all of the same size, each of which often contains pieces from more than one program module.

A second important difference is that main memory is no longer divided into page frames because the size of each segment is different—some are large and some are small. Therefore, as with the dynamic partitions discussed in Chapter 2, memory is allocated in a dynamic manner.

The Segment Map Table functions the same way as a Page Map Table but manages segments instead of pages.

When a program is compiled or assembled, the segments are set up according to the program's structural modules. Each segment is numbered and a **Segment Map Table (SMT)** is generated for each job; it contains the segment numbers, their lengths, access rights, status, and (when each is loaded into memory) its location in memory. Figures 3.13 and 3.14 show the same job, Job 1, composed of a main program and two subroutines, together with its Segment Map Table and actual main memory allocation.

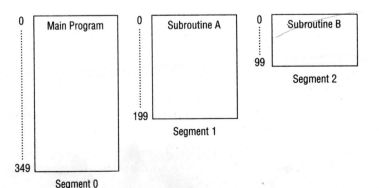

(figure 3.13)

Segmented memory allocation. Job 1 includes a main program, Subroutine A, and Subroutine B. It is one job divided into three segments.

As in demand paging, the referenced, modified, and status bits are used in segmentation and appear in the SMT but they aren't shown in Figures 3.13 and 3.14.

The Memory Manager needs to keep track of the segments in memory. This is done with three tables combining aspects of both dynamic partitions and demand paging memory management:

• The Job Table lists every job being processed (one for the whole system).

• The Segment Map Table lists details about each segment (one for each job).

• The Memory Map Table monitors the allocation of main memory (one for the whole system).

Like demand paging, the instructions within each segment are ordered sequentially, but the segments don't need to be stored contiguously in memory. We only need to know where each segment is stored. The contents of the segments themselves are contiguous in this scheme.

To access a specific location within a segment, we can perform an operation similar to the one used for paged memory management. The only difference is that we work with

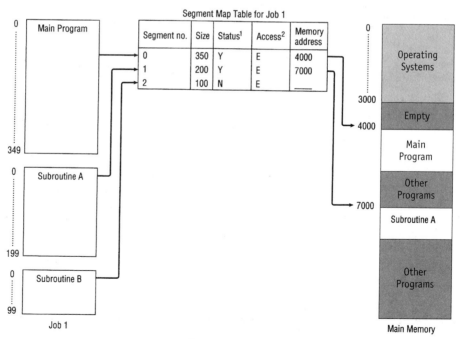

(figure 3.14)

The Segment Map Table tracks each segment for Job 1.

Segment Map Table for Job 1

Segment no.	Size	Status[1]	Access[2]	Memory address
0	350	Y	E	4000
1	200	Y	E	7000
2	100	N	E	___

[1] Y = in memory; N = not in memory.

[2] E = Execute only.

segments instead of pages. The addressing scheme requires the segment number and the displacement within that segment; and because the segments are of different sizes, the displacement must be verified to make sure it isn't outside of the segment's range.

In Figure 3.15, Segment 1 includes all of Subroutine A so the system finds the beginning address of Segment 1, address 7000, and it begins there.

If the instruction requested that processing begin at byte 100 of Subroutine A (which is possible in languages that support multiple entries into subroutines) then, to locate that item in memory, the Memory Manager would need to add 100 (the displacement) to 7000 (the beginning address of Segment 1). Its code could look like this:

```
ACTUAL_MEM_LOC = BEGIN_MEM_LOC + DISPLACEMENT
```

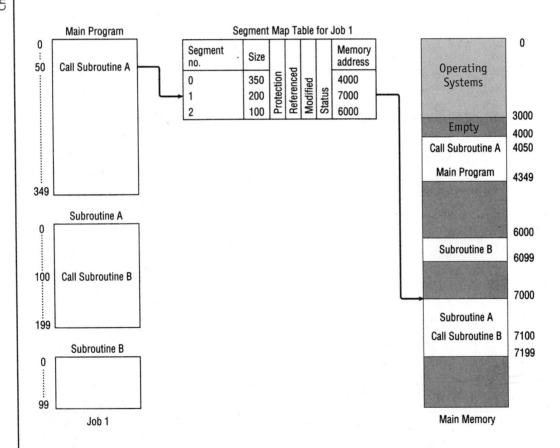

(figure 3.15)

During execution, the main program calls Subroutine A, which triggers the SMT to look up its location in memory.

Can the displacement be larger than the size of the segment? No, not if the program is coded correctly; however, accidents do happen and the Memory Manager must always guard against this possibility by checking the displacement against the size of the segment, verifying that it is not out of bounds.

To access a location in memory, when using either paged or segmented memory management, the address is composed of two values: the page or segment number and the displacement. Therefore, it is a two-dimensional addressing scheme:

SEGMENT_NUMBER & DISPLACEMENT

The disadvantage of any allocation scheme in which memory is partitioned dynamically is the return of external fragmentation. Therefore, recompaction of available memory is necessary from time to time (if that schema is used).

As you can see, there are many similarities between paging and segmentation, so they are often confused. The major difference is a conceptual one: pages are physical units that are invisible to the user's program and consist of fixed sizes; segments are logical units that are visible to the user's program and consist of variable sizes.

Segmented/Demand Paged Memory Allocation

The **segmented/demand paged memory allocation** scheme evolved from the two we have just discussed. It is a combination of segmentation and demand paging, and it offers the logical benefits of segmentation, as well as the physical benefits of paging. The logic isn't new. The algorithms used by the demand paging and segmented memory management schemes are applied here with only minor modifications.

This allocation scheme doesn't keep each segment as a single contiguous unit but subdivides it into pages of equal size, smaller than most segments, and more easily manipulated than whole segments. Therefore, many of the problems of segmentation (compaction, external fragmentation, and secondary storage handling) are removed because the pages are of fixed length.

This scheme, illustrated in Figure 3.16, requires four tables:
- The Job Table lists every job in process (one for the whole system).
- The Segment Map Table lists details about each segment (one for each job).
- The Page Map Table lists details about every page (one for each segment).
- The Memory Map Table monitors the allocation of the page frames in main memory (one for the whole system).

Note that the tables in Figure 3.16 have been simplified. The SMT actually includes additional information regarding protection (such as the authority to read, write, execute, and delete parts of the file), as well as which users have access to that segment (user only, group only, or everyone—some systems call these access categories owner, group, and world, respectively). In addition, the PMT includes the status, modified, and referenced bits.

To access a location in memory, the system must locate the address, which is composed of three entries: segment number, page number within that segment, and displacement within that page. It is a three-dimensional addressing scheme:

SEGMENT_NUMBER & PAGE_NUMBER & DISPLACEMENT

The major disadvantages of this memory allocation scheme are the overhead required for the extra tables and the time required to reference the segment table and the

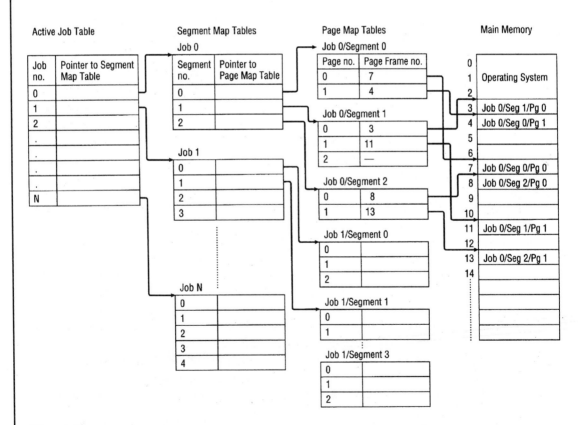

(figure 3.16)

How the Job Table, Segment Map Table, Page Map Table, and main memory interact in a segment/paging scheme.

page table. To minimize the number of references, many systems use associative memory to speed up the process.

Associative memory is a name given to several registers that are allocated to each job that is active. Their task is to associate several segment and page numbers belonging to the job being processed with their main memory addresses. These associative registers reside in main memory, and the exact number of registers varies from system to system.

To appreciate the role of associative memory, it is important to understand how the system works with segments and pages. In general, when a job is allocated to the CPU, its Segment Map Table is loaded into main memory while the Page Map Tables are loaded only as needed. As pages are swapped between main memory and secondary storage, all tables are updated.

Here is a typical procedure: when a page is first requested, the job's SMT is searched to locate its PMT; then the PMT is loaded and searched to determine the page's location in memory. If the page isn't in memory, then a page interrupt is issued, the page is brought into memory, and the table is updated. (As the example indicates, loading the PMT can cause a page interrupt, or fault, as well.) This process is just as tedious as it sounds, but it gets easier. Since this segment's PMT (or part of it) now resides in memory, any other requests for pages within this segment can be quickly accommodated because there is no need to bring the PMT into memory. However, accessing these tables (SMT and PMT) is time-consuming.

The two searches through associative memory and segment/page map tables take place at the same time.

That is the problem addressed by associative memory, which stores the information related to the most-recently-used pages. Then when a page request is issued, two searches begin—one through the segment and page tables and one through the contents of the associative registers.

If the search of the associative registers is successful, then the search through the tables is stopped (or eliminated) and the address translation is performed using the information in the associative registers. However, if the search of associative memory fails, no time is lost because the search through the SMTs and PMTs had already begun (in this schema). When this search is successful and the main memory address from the PMT has been determined, the address is used to continue execution of the program and the reference is also stored in one of the associative registers. If all of the associative registers are full, then an LRU (or other) algorithm is used and the least-recently-referenced associative register is used to hold the information on this requested page.

For example, a system with eight associative registers per job will use them to store the SMT and PMT for the last eight pages referenced by that job. When an address needs to be translated from segment and page numbers to a memory location, the system will look first in the eight associative registers. If a match is found, the memory location is taken from the associative register; if there is no match, then the SMTs and PMTs will continue to be searched and the new information will be stored in one of the eight registers as a result.

If a job is swapped out to secondary storage during its execution, then all of the information stored in its associative registers is saved, as well as the current PMT and SMT, so the displaced job can be resumed quickly when the CPU is reallocated to it. The primary advantage of a large associative memory is increased speed. The disadvantage is the high cost of the complex hardware required to perform the parallel searches. In some systems the searches do not run in parallel, but the search of the SMT and PMT follows the search of the associative registers.

Virtual Memory

Demand paging made it possible for a program to execute even though only a part of a program was loaded into main memory. In effect, virtual memory removed the restriction imposed on maximum program size. This capability of moving pages at will between main memory and secondary storage gave way to a new concept appropriately named **virtual memory**. Even though only a portion of each program is stored in memory, it gives users the appearance that their programs are being completely loaded in main memory during their entire processing time—a feat that would require an incredible amount of main memory.

With virtual memory, the amount of memory available for processing jobs can be much larger than available physical memory.

Until the implementation of virtual memory, the problem of making programs fit into available memory was left to the users. In the early days, programmers had to limit the size of their programs to make sure they fit into main memory; but sometimes that wasn't possible because the amount of memory allocated to them was too small to get the job done. Clever programmers solved the problem by writing tight programs wherever possible. It was the size of the program that counted most—and the instructions for these tight programs were nearly impossible for anyone but their authors to understand or maintain. The useful life of the program was limited to the employment of its programmer.

During the second generation, programmers started dividing their programs into sections that resembled working sets, really segments, originally called roll in/roll out and now called **overlays**. The program could begin with only the first overlay loaded into memory. As the first section neared completion, it would instruct the system to lay the second section of code over the first section already in memory. Then the second section would be processed. As that section finished, it would call in the third section to be overlaid, and so on until the program was finished. Some programs had multiple overlays in main memory at once.

Although the swapping of overlays between main memory and secondary storage was done by the system, the tedious task of dividing the program into sections was done by the programmer. It was the concept of overlays that suggested paging and segmentation and led to virtual memory, which was then implemented through demand paging and segmentation schemes. These schemes are compared in Table 3.6.

Virtual Memory with Paging	Virtual Memory with Segmentation
Allows internal fragmentation within page frames	Doesn't allow internal fragmentation
Doesn't allow external fragmentation	Allows external fragmentation
Programs are divided into equal-sized pages	Programs are divided into unequal-sized segments that contain logical groupings of code
The absolute address is calculated using page number and displacement	The absolute address is calculated using segment number and displacement
Requires PMT	Requires SMT

Segmentation allowed for sharing program code among users. This means that the shared segment contains: (1) an area where unchangeable code (called **reentrant code**) is stored, and (2) several data areas, one for each user. In this schema users share the code, which cannot be modified, and can modify the information stored in their own data areas as needed without affecting the data stored in other users' data areas.

Before virtual memory, sharing meant that copies of files were stored in each user's account. This allowed them to load their own copy and work on it at any time. This kind of sharing created a great deal of unnecessary system cost—the I/O overhead in loading the copies and the extra secondary storage needed. With virtual memory, those costs are substantially reduced because shared programs and subroutines are loaded on demand, satisfactorily reducing the storage requirements of main memory (although this is accomplished at the expense of the Memory Map Table).

The use of virtual memory requires cooperation between the Memory Manager (which tracks each page or segment) and the processor hardware (which issues the interrupt and resolves the virtual address). For example, when a page is needed that is not already in memory, a page fault is issued and the Memory Manager chooses a page frame, loads the page, and updates entries in the Memory Map Table and the Page Map Tables.

Virtual memory works well in a multiprogramming environment because most programs spend a lot of time waiting—they wait for I/O to be performed; they wait for pages to be swapped in or out; and in a time-sharing environment, they wait when their time slice is up (their turn to use the processor is expired). In a multiprogramming environment, the waiting time isn't lost, and the CPU simply moves to another job.

Virtual memory has increased the use of several programming techniques. For instance, it aids the development of large software systems because individual pieces can be developed independently and linked later on.

Virtual memory management has several advantages:

- A job's size is no longer restricted to the size of main memory (or the free space within main memory).
- Memory is used more efficiently because the only sections of a job stored in memory are those needed immediately, while those not needed remain in secondary storage.
- It allows an unlimited amount of multiprogramming, which can apply to many jobs, as in dynamic and static partitioning, or many users in a time-sharing environment.
- It eliminates external fragmentation and minimizes internal fragmentation by combining segmentation and paging (internal fragmentation occurs in the program).
- It allows the sharing of code and data.
- It facilitates dynamic linking of program segments.

The advantages far outweigh these disadvantages:

- Increased processor hardware costs.
- Increased overhead for handling paging interrupts.
- Increased software complexity to prevent thrashing.

Cache Memory

Caching is based on the idea that the system can use a small amount of expensive high-speed memory to make a large amount of slower, less-expensive memory work faster than main memory.

Because the cache is small in size (compared to main memory), it can use faster, more expensive memory chips and can be five to ten times faster than main memory and match the speed of the CPU. Therefore, when frequently used data or instructions are stored in cache memory, memory access time can be cut down significantly and the CPU can execute instructions faster, thus raising the overall performance of the computer system.

(figure 3.17)

Comparison of (a) the traditional path used by early computers between main memory and the CPU and (b) the path used by modern computers to connect the main memory and the CPU via cache memory.

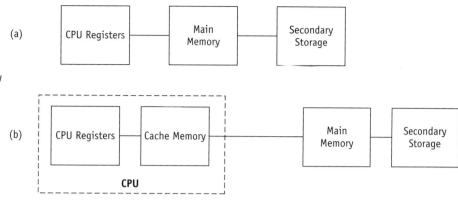

As shown in Figure 3.17(a), the original architecture of a computer was such that data and instructions were transferred from secondary storage to main memory and then to special-purpose registers for processing, increasing the amount of time needed to complete a program. However, because the same instructions are used repeatedly in most programs, computer system designers thought it would be more efficient if the system would not use a complete memory cycle every time an instruction or data value is required. Designers found that this could be done if they placed repeatedly used data in general-purpose registers instead of in main memory, but they found that this technique required extra work for the programmer. Moreover, from the point of view of the system, this use of general-purpose registers was not an optimal solution because those registers are often needed to store temporary results from other calculations, and because the amount of instructions used repeatedly often exceeds the capacity of the general-purpose registers.

To solve this problem, computer systems automatically store data in an intermediate memory unit called **cache memory**. This adds a middle layer to the original hierarchy. Cache memory can be thought of as an intermediary between main memory and the special-purpose registers, which are the domain of the CPU, as shown in Figure 3.17(b).

A typical microprocessor has two levels of caches: Level 1 (L1) and Level 2 (L2). Information enters the processor through the bus interface unit, which immediately sends one copy to the L2 cache, which is an integral part of the microprocessor and is directly connected to the CPU. A second copy is sent to a pair of L1 caches, which are built directly into the CPU. One of these L1 caches is designed to store instructions, while the other stores data to be used by the instructions. If an instruction needs more data, it is put on hold while the processor looks for it first in the data L1 cache, and then in the larger L2 cache before looking for it in main memory.

Because the L2 cache is an integral part of the microprocessor, data moves two to four times faster between the CPU and the L2 than between the CPU and main memory.

To understand the relationship between main memory and cache memory, consider the relationship between the size of the Web and the size of your private bookmark file. If main memory is the Web and cache memory is your private bookmark file where you collect your most frequently used Web addresses, then your bookmark file is small and may contain only 0.00001 percent of all the addresses in the Web; but the chance that you will soon visit a Web site that is in your bookmark file is high. Therefore, the purpose of your bookmark file is to keep your most recently accessed addresses so you can access them quickly, just as the purpose of cache memory is to keep handy the most recently accessed data and instructions so that the CPU can access them repeatedly without wasting time.

The movement of data, or instructions, from main memory to cache memory uses a method similar to that used in paging algorithms. First, cache memory is divided into blocks of equal size called slots. Then, when the CPU first requests an instruction or data from a location in main memory, the requested instruction and several others around it are transferred from main memory to cache memory where they are stored in one of the free slots. Moving a block at a time is based on the principle of locality of reference, which states that it is very likely that the next CPU request will be physically close to the one just requested. In addition to the block of data transferred, the slot also contains a label that indicates the main memory address from which the block was copied. When the CPU requests additional information from that location in main memory, cache memory is accessed first; and if the contents of one of the labels in a slot matches the address requested, then access to main memory is not required.

The algorithm to execute one of these "transfers from main memory" is simple to implement, as follows:

Main Memory Transfer Algorithm

1   CPU puts the address of a memory location in the Memory Address Register and requests data or an instruction to be retrieved from that address
2   A test is performed to determine if the block containing this address is already in a cache slot:

    If YES, transfer the information to the CPU register – DONE

    If NO: Access main memory for the block containing the requested address

        Allocate a free cache slot to the block

        Perform these in parallel: Transfer the information to CPU

                                     Load the block into slot

        DONE

This algorithm becomes more complicated if there aren't any free slots, which can occur because the size of cache memory is smaller than that of main memory, which means that individual slots cannot be permanently allocated to blocks. To address this contingency, the system needs a policy for block replacement, which could be one similar to those used in page replacement.

When designing cache memory, one must take into consideration the following four factors:

- *Cache size.* Studies have shown that having any cache, even a small one, can substantially improve the performance of the computer system.

- *Block size.* Because of the principle of locality of reference, as block size increases, the ratio of number of references found in the cache to the total number of references will be high.

- *Block replacement algorithm.* When all the slots are busy and a new block has to be brought into the cache, a block that is least likely to be used in the near future should be selected for replacement. However, as we saw in paging, this is nearly impossible to predict. A reasonable course of action is to select a block that has not been used for a long time. Therefore, LRU is the algorithm that is often chosen for block replacement, which requires a hardware mechanism to specify the least recently used slot.

- *Rewrite policy.* When the contents of a block residing in cache are changed, it must be written back to main memory before it is replaced by another block. A rewrite policy must be in place to determine when this writing will take place. On the one hand, it could be done every time that a change occurs, which would increase the number of memory writes, increasing overhead. On the other hand, it could be done only when the block is replaced or the process is finished, which would minimize overhead but would leave the block in main memory in an inconsistent state. This would create problems in multiprocessor environments and in cases where I/O modules can access main memory directly.

The optimal selection of cache size and replacement algorithm can result in 80 to 90 percent of all requests being in the cache, making for a very efficient memory system. This measure of efficiency, called the cache hit ratio (h), is used to determine the performance of cache memory and represents the percentage of total memory requests that are found in the cache:

$$\text{HitRatio} = \frac{\text{number of requests found in the cache}}{\text{total number of requests}} * 100$$

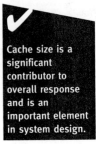

For example, if the total number of requests is 10, and 6 of those are found in cache memory, then the hit ratio is 60 percent.

```
HitRatio = (6 / 10) * 100 = 60%
```

On the other hand, if the total number of requests is 100, and 9 of those are found in cache memory, then the hit ratio is only 9 percent.

```
HitRatio = (9 / 100) * 100 = 9%
```

Another way to measure the efficiency of a system with cache memory, assuming that the system always checks the cache first, is to compute the average memory access time using the following formula:

```
AvgMemAccessTime = AvgCacheAccessTime + (1 - h) * AvgMainMemAccTime
```

For example, if we know that the average cache access time is 200 nanoseconds (nsec) and the average main memory access time is 1000 nsec, then a system with a hit ratio of 60 percent will have an average memory access time of 600 nsec:

```
AvgMemAccessTime = 200 + (1 - 0.60) * 1000 = 600 nsec
```

A system with a hit ratio of 9 percent will show an average memory access time of 1110 nsec:

```
AvgMemAccessTime = 200 + (1 - 0.09) * 1000 = 1110 nsec
```

Conclusion

The Memory Manager has the task of allocating memory to each job to be executed, and reclaiming it when execution is completed.

Each scheme we discussed in Chapters 2 and 3 was designed to address a different set of pressing problems; but, as we have seen, when some problems were solved, others were created. Table 3.7 shows how memory allocation schemes compare.

(table 3.7)

Comparison of the memory allocation schemes discussed in Chapters 2 and 3.

Scheme	Problem Solved	Problem Created	Changes in Software
Single-user contiguous		Job size limited to physical memory size; CPU often idle	None
Fixed partitions	Idle CPU time	Internal fragmentation; Job size limited to partition size	Add Processor Scheduler; Add protection handler
Dynamic partitions	Internal fragmentation	External fragmentation	None
Relocatable dynamic partitions	Internal fragmentation	Compaction overhead; Job size limited to physical memory size	Compaction algorithm
Paged	Need for compaction	Memory needed for tables; Job size limited to physical memory size; Internal fragmentation returns	Algorithms to handle Page Map Tables
Demand paged	Job size no longer limited to memory size; More efficient memory use; Allows large-scale multiprogramming and time-sharing	Larger number of tables; Possibility of thrashing; Overhead required by page interrupts; Necessary paging hardware	Page replacement algorithm; Search algorithm for pages in secondary storage
Segmented	Internal fragmentation	Difficulty managing variable-length segments in secondary storage; External fragmentation	Dynamic linking package; Two-dimensional addressing scheme
Segmented/ demand paged	Large virtual memory; Segment loaded on demand	Table handling overhead; Memory needed for page and segment tables	Three-dimensional addressing scheme

The Memory Manager is only one of several managers that make up the operating system. Once the jobs are loaded into memory using a memory allocation scheme, the Processor Manager must allocate the processor to process each job in the most efficient manner possible. We will see how that is done in the next chapter.

Key Terms

address resolution: the process of changing the address of an instruction or data item to the address in main memory at which it is to be loaded or relocated.

associative memory: the name given to several registers, allocated to each active process, whose contents associate several of the process segments and page numbers with their main memory addresses.

cache memory: a small, fast memory used to hold selected data and to provide faster access than would otherwise be possible.

clock cycle: the elapsed time between two ticks of the computer's system clock.

clock page replacement policy: a variation of the LRU policy that removes from main memory the pages that show the least amount of activity during recent clock cycles.

demand paging: a memory allocation scheme that loads a program's page into memory at the time it is needed for processing.

displacement: in a paged or segmented memory allocation environment, the difference between a page's relative address and the actual machine language address. Also called offset.

FIFO anomaly: an unusual circumstance through which adding more page frames causes an increase in page interrupts when using a FIFO page replacement policy.

first-in first-out (FIFO) policy: a page replacement policy that removes from main memory the pages that were brought in first.

Job Table (JT): a table in main memory that contains two values for each active job—the size of the job and the memory location where its page map table is stored.

least recently used (LRU) policy: a page-replacement policy that removes from main memory the pages that show the least amount of recent activity.

locality of reference: behavior observed in many executing programs in which memory locations recently referenced, and those near them, are likely to be referenced in the near future.

Memory Map Table (MMT): a table in main memory that contains as many entries as there are page frames and lists the location and free/busy status for each one.

offset: *see* displacement.

page: a fixed-size section of a user's job that corresponds in size to page frames in main memory.

page fault: a type of hardware interrupt caused by a reference to a page not residing in memory. The effect is to move a page out of main memory and into secondary storage so another page can be moved into memory.

page fault handler: the part of the Memory Manager that determines if there are empty page frames in memory so that the requested page can be immediately copied from secondary storage, or determines which page must be swapped out if all page frames are busy. Also known as a page interrupt handler.

page frame: an individual section of main memory of uniform size into which a single page may be loaded without causing external fragmentation.

Page Map Table (PMT): a table in main memory with the vital information for each page including the page number and its corresponding page frame memory address.

page replacement policy: an algorithm used by virtual memory systems to decide which page or segment to remove from main memory when a page frame is needed and memory is full.

page swapping: the process of moving a page out of main memory and into secondary storage so another page can be moved into memory in its place.

paged memory allocation: a memory allocation scheme based on the concept of dividing a user's job into sections of equal size to allow for noncontiguous program storage during execution.

reentrant code: code that can be used by two or more processes at the same time; each shares the same copy of the executable code but has separate data areas.

sector: a division in a disk's track, sometimes called a "block." The tracks are divided into sectors during the formatting process.

segment: a variable-size section of a user's job that contains a logical grouping of code.

Segment Map Table (SMT): a table in main memory with the vital information for each segment including the segment number and its corresponding memory address.

segmented/demand paged memory allocation: a memory allocation scheme based on the concept of dividing a user's job into logical groupings of code and loading them into memory as needed to minimize fragmentation.

segmented memory allocation: a memory allocation scheme based on the concept of dividing a user's job into logical groupings of code to allow for noncontiguous program storage during execution.

subroutine: also called a "subprogram," a segment of a program that can perform a specific function. Subroutines can reduce programming time when a specific function is required at more than one point in a program.

thrashing: a phenomenon in a virtual memory system where an excessive amount of page swapping back and forth between main memory and secondary storage results in higher overhead and little useful work.

virtual memory: a technique that allows programs to be executed even though they are not stored entirely in memory.

working set: a collection of pages to be kept in main memory for each active process in a virtual memory environment.

Interesting Searches

- Memory Card Suppliers
- Virtual Memory
- Working Set
- Cache Memory
- Thrashing

Exercises

Research Topics

A. The sizes of pages and page frames are often identical. Search academic sources to discover typical page sizes, what factors are considered by operating system developers when establishing these sizes, and whether or not hardware considerations are important. Cite your sources.

B. Core memory consists of the CPU and arithmetic logic unit but not the attached cache memory. On the Internet or using academic sources, research the design of multi-core memory and identify the roles played by cache memory Level 1 and Level 2. Does the implementation of cache memory on multi-core chips vary from one manufacturer to another? Explain and cite your sources.

Exercises

1. Compare and contrast internal fragmentation and external fragmentation. Explain the circumstances where one might be preferred over the other.

2. Describe how the function of the Page Map Table differs in paged vs. segmented/demand paging memory allocation.

3. Describe how the operating system detects thrashing. Once thrashing is detected, explain what the operating system can do to stop it.

4. Given that main memory is composed of three page frames for public use and

that a seven-page program (with pages a, b, c, d, e, f, g) requests pages in the following order:

a, b, a, c, d, a, e, f, g, c, b, g

a. Using the FIFO page removal algorithm, do a page trace analysis indicating page faults with asterisks (*). Then compute the failure and success ratios.

b. Increase the size of memory so it contains four page frames for public use. Using the same page requests as above and FIFO, do another page trace analysis and compute the failure and success ratios.

c. Did the result correspond with your intuition? Explain.

5. Given that main memory is composed of three page frames for public use and that a program requests pages in the following order:

a, d, b, a, f, b, e, c, g, f, b, g

a. Using the FIFO page removal algorithm, perform a page trace analysis indicating page faults with asterisks (*). Then compute the failure and success ratios.

b. Using the LRU page removal algorithm, perform a page trace analysis and compute the failure and success ratios.

c. Which is better? Why do you think it is better? Can you make general statements from this example? Why or why not?

6. Let us define "most-recently-used" (MRU) as a page removal algorithm that removes from memory the most recently used page. Perform a page trace analysis using three page frames and the page requests from the previous exercise. Compute the failure and success ratios and explain why you think MRU is, or is not, a viable memory allocation system.

7. By examining the reference bits for the six pages shown in Figure 3.11, identify which of the six pages was referenced most often as of the last time snapshot [shown in (e)]. Which page was referenced least often? Explain your answer.

8. To implement LRU, each page needs a referenced bit. If we wanted to implement a least frequently used (LFU) page removal algorithm, in which the page that was used the least would be removed from memory, what would we need to add to the tables? What software modifications would have to be made to support this new algorithm?

9. Calculate the cache Hit Ratio using the formula presented at the end of this chapter assuming that the total number of requests is 2056 and 1209 of those requests are found in the cache.

10. Assuming a hit ratio of 67 percent, calculate the Average Memory Access Time using the formula presented in this chapter if the Average Cache Access Time is 200 nsec and the Average Main Memory Access Time is 500 nsec.

11. Assuming a hit ratio of 31 percent, calculate the Average Memory Access Time using the formula presented in this chapter if the Average Cache Access Time is 125 nsec and the Average Main Memory Access Time is 300 nsec.

12. Using a paged memory allocation system with a page size of 2,048 bytes and an identical page frame size, and assuming the incoming data file is 25,600, calculate how many pages will be created by the file. Calculate the size of any resulting fragmentation. Explain whether this situation will result in internal fragmentation, external fragmentation, or both.

Advanced Exercises

13. Given that main memory is composed of four page frames for public use, use the following table to answer all parts of this problem:

Page Frame	Time When Loaded	Time When Last Referenced	Referenced Bit	Modified Bit
0	126	279	0	0
1	230	280	1	0
2	120	282	1	1
3	160	290	1	1

a. The contents of which page frame would be swapped out by FIFO?

b. The contents of which page frame would be swapped out by LRU?

c. The contents of which page frame would be swapped out by MRU?

d. The contents of which page frame would be swapped out by LFU?

14. Given three subroutines of 700, 200, and 500 words each, if segmentation is used then the total memory needed is the sum of the three sizes (if all three routines are loaded). However, if paging is used then some storage space is lost because subroutines rarely fill the last page completely, and that results in internal fragmentation. Determine the total amount of wasted memory due to internal fragmentation when the three subroutines are loaded into memory using each of the following page sizes:

a. 100 words

b. 600 words

c. 700 words

d. 900 words

15. Given the following Segment Map Tables for two jobs:

SMT for Job 1

Segment Number	Memory Location
0	4096
1	6144
2	9216
3	2048
4	7168

SMT for Job 2

Segment number	Memory location
0	2048
1	6144
2	9216

a. Which segments, if any, are shared between the two jobs?

b. If the segment now located at 7168 is swapped out and later reloaded at 8192, and the segment now at 2048 is swapped out and reloaded at 1024, what would the new segment tables look like?

Programming Exercises

16. This problem studies the effect of changing page sizes in a demand paging system.

The following sequence of requests for program words is taken from a 460-word program: 10, 11, 104, 170, 73, 309, 185, 245, 246, 434, 458, 364. Main memory can hold a total of 200 words for this program and the page frame size will match the size of the pages into which the program has been divided.

Calculate the page numbers according to the page size, divide by the page size, and the quotient gives the page number. The number of page frames in memory is the total number, 200, divided by the page size. For example, in problem (a) the page size is 100, which means that requests 10 and 11 are on Page 0, and requests 104 and 170 are on Page 1. The number of page frames is two.

a. Find the success frequency for the request list using a FIFO replacement algorithm and a page size of 100 words (there are two page frames).

b. Find the success frequency for the request list using a FIFO replacement algorithm and a page size of 20 words (10 pages, 0 through 9).

c. Find the success frequency for the request list using a FIFO replacement algorithm and a page size of 200 words.

d. What do your results indicate? Can you make any general statements about what happens when page sizes are halved or doubled?

e. Are there any overriding advantages in using smaller pages? What are the offsetting factors? Remember that transferring 200 words of information takes less than twice as long as transferring 100 words because of the way secondary storage devices operate (the transfer rate is higher than the access [search/find] rate).

f. Repeat (a) through (c) above, using a main memory of 400 words. The size of each page frame will again correspond to the size of the page.

g. What happened when more memory was given to the program? Can you make some general statements about this occurrence? What changes might you expect to see if the request list was much longer, as it would be in real life?

h. Could this request list happen during the execution of a real program? Explain.

i. Would you expect the success rate of an actual program under similar conditions to be higher or lower than the one in this problem?

17. Given the following information for an assembly language program:

Job size = 3126 bytes

Page size = 1024 bytes

instruction at memory location 532:	Load 1, 2098
instruction at memory location 1156:	Add 1, 2087
instruction at memory location 2086:	Sub 1, 1052
data at memory location 1052:	015672
data at memory location 2098:	114321
data at memory location 2087:	077435

a. How many pages are needed to store the entire job?

b. Compute the page number and displacement for each of the byte addresses where the data is stored. (Remember that page numbering starts at zero).

c. Determine whether the page number and displacements are legal for this job.

d. Explain why the page number and/or displacements may not be legal for this job.

e. Indicate what action the operating system might take when a page number or displacement is not legal.

Chapter 4

Processor Management

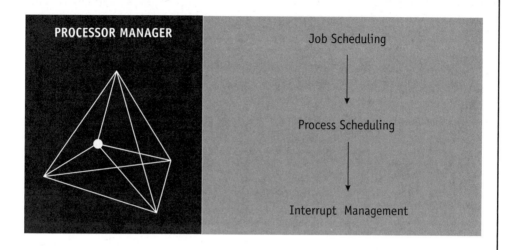

> 66 *Nature acts by progress . . . It goes and returns, then advances further, then twice as much backward, then more forward than ever.* 99

—Blaise Pascal *(1623–1662)*

Learning Objectives

After completing this chapter, you should be able to describe:

- The difference between job scheduling and process scheduling, and how they relate
- The advantages and disadvantages of process scheduling algorithms that are pre-emptive versus those that are nonpreemptive
- The goals of process scheduling policies in single-core CPUs
- Six different process scheduling algorithms
- The role of internal interrupts and the tasks performed by the interrupt handler

The Processor Manager is responsible for allocating the processor to execute the incoming jobs, and the tasks of those jobs. In this chapter, we'll see how a Processor Manager manages a single CPU to do so.

Overview

In a simple system, one with a single user and one processor, the process is busy only when it is executing the user's jobs. However, when there are many users, such as in a multiprogramming environment, or when there are multiple processes competing to be run by a single CPU, the processor must be allocated to each job in a fair and efficient manner. This can be a complex task as we'll see in this chapter, which is devoted to single processor systems. Those with multiple processors are discussed in Chapter 6.

Before we begin, let's clearly define some terms. A **program** is an inactive unit, such as a file stored on a disk. A program is not a process. To an operating system, a program or job is a unit of work that has been submitted by the user.

On the other hand, a **process** is an active entity that requires a set of resources, including a processor and special registers, to perform its function. A process, also called a **task,** is a single instance of a program in execution.

As mentioned in Chapter 1, a **thread** is a portion of a process that can run independently. For example, if your system allows processes to have a single thread of control and you want to see a series of pictures on a friend's Web site, you can instruct the browser to establish one connection between the two sites and download one picture at a time. However, if your system allows processes to have multiple threads of control, then you can request several pictures at the same time and the browser will set up multiple connections and download several pictures at once.

The **processor,** also known as the CPU (for central processing unit), is the part of the machine that performs the calculations and executes the programs.

Multiprogramming requires that the processor be allocated to each job or to each process for a period of time and deallocated at an appropriate moment. If the processor is deallocated during a program's execution, it must be done in such a way that it can be restarted later as easily as possible. It's a delicate procedure. To demonstrate, let's look at an everyday example.

Here you are, confident you can put together a toy despite the warning that some assembly is required. Armed with the instructions and lots of patience, you embark on your task—to read the directions, collect the necessary tools, follow each step in turn, and turn out the finished product.

The first step is to join Part A to Part B with a 2-inch screw, and as you complete that task you check off Step 1. Inspired by your success, you move on to Step 2 and then Step 3. You've only just completed the third step when a neighbor is injured while working with a power tool and cries for help.

Quickly you check off Step 3 in the directions so you know where you left off, then you drop your tools and race to your neighbor's side. After all, someone's immediate

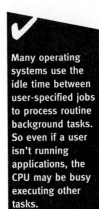

Many operating systems use the idle time between user-specified jobs to process routine background tasks. So even if a user isn't running applications, the CPU may be busy executing other tasks.

need is more important than your eventual success with the toy. Now you find yourself engaged in a very different task: following the instructions in a first-aid book and using bandages and antiseptic.

Once the injury has been successfully treated, you return to your previous job. As you pick up your tools, you refer to the instructions and see that you should begin with Step 4. You then continue with this project until it is finally completed.

In operating system terminology, you played the part of the *CPU* or *processor*. There were two *programs,* or *jobs*—one was the mission to assemble the toy and the second was to bandage the injury. When you were assembling the toy (Job A), each step you performed was a *process.* The call for help was an *interrupt;* and when you left the toy to treat your wounded friend, you left for a *higher priority program.* When you were interrupted, you performed a *context switch* when you marked Step 3 as the last completed instruction and put down your tools. Attending to the neighbor's injury became Job B. While you were executing the first-aid instructions, each of the steps you executed was again a *process.* And, of course, when each job was completed it was *finished* or terminated.

The Processor Manager would identify the series of events as follows:

`get the input for Job A`	(find the instructions in the box)
`identify resources`	(collect the necessary tools)
`execute the process`	(follow each step in turn)
`interrupt`	(neighbor calls)
`context switch to Job B`	(mark your place in the instructions)
`get the input for Job B`	(find your first-aid book)
`identify resources`	(collect the medical supplies)
`execute the process`	(follow each first-aid step)
`terminate Job B`	(return home)
`context switch to Job A`	(prepare to resume assembly)
`resume executing the interrupted process`	(follow remaining steps in turn)
`terminate Job A`	(turn out the finished toy)

As we've shown, a single processor can be shared by several jobs, or several processes—but if, and only if, the operating system has a scheduling policy, as well as a scheduling algorithm, to determine when to stop working on one job and proceed to another.

In this example, the scheduling algorithm was based on priority: you worked on the processes belonging to Job A until a higher priority job came along. Although this was a good algorithm in this case, a priority-based scheduling algorithm isn't always best, as we'll see later in this chapter.

About Multi-Core Technologies

A dual-core, quad-core, or other multi-core CPU has more than one processor (also called a core) on the computer chip. Multi-core engineering was driven by the problems caused by nano-sized transistors and their ultra-close placement on a computer chip. Although chips with millions of transistors that were very close together helped increase system performance dramatically, the close proximity of these transistors also increased current leakage and the amount of heat generated by the chip.

One solution was to create a single chip (one piece of silicon) with two or more processor cores. In other words, they replaced a single large processor with two half-sized processors, or four quarter-sized processors. This design allowed the same sized chip to produce less heat and offered the opportunity to permit multiple calculations to take place at the same time.

For the Processor Manager, multiple cores are more complex to manage than a single core. We'll discuss multiple core processing in Chapter 6.

Job Scheduling Versus Process Scheduling

The Processor Manager is a composite of two submanagers: one in charge of job scheduling and the other in charge of process scheduling. They're known as the **Job Scheduler** and the **Process Scheduler**.

Typically a user views a job either as a series of global job steps—compilation, loading, and execution—or as one all-encompassing step—execution. However, the scheduling of jobs is actually handled on two levels by most operating systems. If we return to the example presented earlier, we can see that a hierarchy exists between the Job Scheduler and the Process Scheduler.

The scheduling of the two jobs, to assemble the toy and to bandage the injury, was on a first-come, first-served and priority basis. Each job is initiated by the Job Scheduler based on certain criteria. Once a job is selected for execution, the Process Scheduler determines when each step, or set of steps, is executed—a decision that's also based on certain criteria. When you started assembling the toy, each step in the assembly instructions would have been selected for execution by the Process Scheduler.

Therefore, each job (or program) passes through a hierarchy of managers. Since the first one it encounters is the Job Scheduler, this is also called the **high-level scheduler**. It is only concerned with selecting jobs from a queue of incoming jobs and placing them in the process queue, whether batch or interactive, based on each job's characteristics. The Job Scheduler's goal is to put the jobs in a sequence that will use all of the system's resources as fully as possible.

This is an important function. For example, if the Job Scheduler selected several jobs to run consecutively and each had a lot of I/O, then the I/O devices would be kept very busy. The CPU might be busy handling the I/O (if an I/O controller were not used) so little computation might get done. On the other hand, if the Job Scheduler selected several consecutive jobs with a great deal of computation, then the CPU would be very busy doing that. The I/O devices would be idle waiting for I/O requests. Therefore, the Job Scheduler strives for a balanced mix of jobs that require large amounts of I/O interaction and jobs that require large amounts of computation. Its goal is to keep most components of the computer system busy most of the time.

Process Scheduler

Most of this chapter is dedicated to the Process Scheduler because after a job has been placed on the READY queue by the Job Scheduler, the Process Scheduler takes over. It determines which jobs will get the CPU, when, and for how long. It also decides when processing should be interrupted, determines which queues the job should be moved to during its execution, and recognizes when a job has concluded and should be terminated.

The Process Scheduler is the **low-level scheduler** that assigns the CPU to execute the processes of those jobs placed on the READY queue by the Job Scheduler. This becomes a crucial function when the processing of several jobs has to be orchestrated—just as when you had to set aside your assembly and rush to help your neighbor.

To schedule the CPU, the Process Scheduler takes advantage of a common trait among most computer programs: they alternate between CPU cycles and I/O cycles. Notice that the following job has one relatively long CPU cycle and two very brief I/O cycles:

> Data input (the first I/O cycle) and printing (the last I/O cycle) are brief compared to the time it takes to do the calculations (the CPU cycle).

```
{
printf("\nEnter the first integer: ");
scanf("%d", &a);
printf("\nEnter the second integer: ");      }  I/O cycle
scanf("%d", &b);

c = a+b
d = (a*b)-c                                   }  CPU cycle
e = a-b
f = d/e

printf("\n a+b= %d", c);
printf("\n (a*b)-c = %d", d);                 }  I/O cycle
printf("\n a-b = %d", e);
printf("\n d/e = %d", f);
}
```

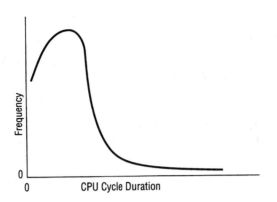

(figure 4.1)

Distribution of CPU cycle times. This distribution shows a greater number of jobs requesting short CPU cycles (the frequency peaks close to the low end of the CPU cycle axis), and fewer jobs requesting long CPU cycles.

Although the duration and frequency of CPU cycles vary from program to program, there are some general tendencies that can be exploited when selecting a scheduling algorithm. For example, **I/O-bound** jobs (such as printing a series of documents) have many brief CPU cycles and long I/O cycles, whereas **CPU-bound** jobs (such as finding the first 300 prime numbers) have long CPU cycles and shorter I/O cycles. The total effect of all CPU cycles, from both I/O-bound and CPU-bound jobs, approximates a Poisson distribution curve as shown in Figure 4.1.

In a highly interactive environment, there's also a third layer of the Processor Manager called the **middle-level scheduler**. In some cases, especially when the system is overloaded, the middle-level scheduler finds it is advantageous to remove active jobs from memory to reduce the degree of multiprogramming, which allows jobs to be completed faster. The jobs that are swapped out and eventually swapped back in are managed by the middle-level scheduler.

In a single-user environment, there's no distinction made between job and process scheduling because only one job is active in the system at any given time. So the CPU and all other resources are dedicated to that job, and to each of its processes in turn, until the job is completed.

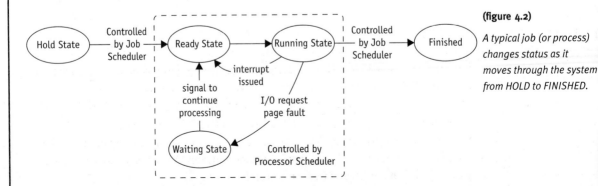

(figure 4.2)

A typical job (or process) changes status as it moves through the system from HOLD to FINISHED.

Job and Process Status

As a job moves through the system, it's always in one of five states (or at least three) as it changes from HOLD to READY to RUNNING to WAITING and eventually to FINISHED as shown in Figure 4.2. These are called the **job status** or the **process status**.

Here's how the job status changes when a user submits a job to the system via batch or interactive mode. When the job is accepted by the system, it's put on HOLD and placed in a queue. In some systems, the job spooler (or disk controller) creates a table with the characteristics of each job in the queue and notes the important features of the job, such as an estimate of CPU time, priority, special I/O devices required, and maximum memory required. This table is used by the Job Scheduler to decide which job is to be run next.

From HOLD, the job moves to READY when it's ready to run but is waiting for the CPU. In some systems, the job (or process) might be placed on the READY list directly. RUNNING, of course, means that the job is being processed. In a single processor system, this is one "job" or process. WAITING means that the job can't continue until a specific resource is allocated or an I/O operation has finished. Upon completion, the job is FINISHED and returned to the user.

The transition from one job or process status to another is initiated by either the Job Scheduler or the Process Scheduler:

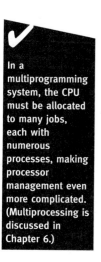

In a multiprogramming system, the CPU must be allocated to many jobs, each with numerous processes, making processor management even more complicated. (Multiprocessing is discussed in Chapter 6.)

- The transition from HOLD to READY is initiated by the Job Scheduler according to some predefined policy. At this point, the availability of enough main memory and any requested devices is checked.

- The transition from READY to RUNNING is handled by the Process Scheduler according to some predefined algorithm (i.e., FCFS, SJN, priority scheduling, SRT, or round robin—all of which will be discussed shortly).

- The transition from RUNNING back to READY is handled by the Process Scheduler according to some predefined time limit or other criterion, for example a priority interrupt.

- The transition from RUNNING to WAITING is handled by the Process Scheduler and is initiated by an instruction in the job such as a command to READ, WRITE, or other I/O request, or one that requires a page fetch.

- The transition from WAITING to READY is handled by the Process Scheduler and is initiated by a signal from the I/O device manager that the I/O request has been satisfied and the job can continue. In the case of a page fetch, the page fault handler will signal that the page is now in memory and the process can be placed on the READY queue.

- Eventually, the transition from RUNNING to FINISHED is initiated by the Process Scheduler or the Job Scheduler either when (1) the job is successfully completed and it ends execution or (2) the operating system indicates that an error has occurred and the job is being terminated prematurely.

Process Control Blocks

Each process in the system is represented by a data structure called a **Process Control Block (PCB)** that performs the same function as a traveler's passport. The PCB (illustrated in Figure 4.3) contains the basic information about the job, including what it is, where it's going, how much of its processing has been completed, where it's stored, and how much it has spent in using resources.

Process identification
Process status
Process state:
    Process status word
    Register contents
    Main memory
    Resources
    Process priority
Accounting

(figure 4.3)

Contents of each job's Process Control Block.

Process Identification

Each job is uniquely identified by the user's identification and a pointer connecting it to its descriptor (supplied by the Job Scheduler when the job first enters the system and is placed on HOLD).

Process Status

This indicates the current status of the job—HOLD, READY, RUNNING, or WAITING—and the resources responsible for that status.

Process State

This contains all of the information needed to indicate the current state of the job such as:

- *Process Status Word*—the current instruction counter and register contents when the job isn't running but is either on HOLD or is READY or WAITING. If the job is RUNNING, this information is left undefined.
- *Register Contents*—the contents of the register if the job has been interrupted and is waiting to resume processing.
- *Main Memory*—pertinent information, including the address where the job is stored and, in the case of virtual memory, the mapping between virtual and physical memory locations.

- *Resources*—information about all resources allocated to this job. Each resource has an identification field listing its type and a field describing details of its allocation, such as the sector address on a disk. These resources can be hardware units (disk drives or printers, for example) or files.

- *Process Priority*—used by systems using a priority scheduling algorithm to select which job will be run next.

Accounting

This contains information used mainly for billing purposes and performance measurement. It indicates what kind of resources the job used and for how long. Typical charges include:

- Amount of CPU time used from beginning to end of its execution.

- Total time the job was in the system until it exited.

- Main storage occupancy—how long the job stayed in memory until it finished execution. This is usually a combination of time and space used; for example, in a paging system it may be recorded in units of page-seconds.

- Secondary storage used during execution. This, too, is recorded as a combination of time and space used.

- System programs used, such as compilers, editors, or utilities.

- Number and type of I/O operations, including I/O transmission time, that includes utilization of channels, control units, and devices.

- Time spent waiting for I/O completion.

- Number of input records read (specifically, those entered online or coming from optical scanners, card readers, or other input devices), and number of output records written.

PCBs and Queueing

A job's PCB is created when the Job Scheduler accepts the job and is updated as the job progresses from the beginning to the end of its execution.

Queues use PCBs to track jobs the same way customs officials use passports to track international visitors. The PCB contains all of the data about the job needed by the operating system to manage the processing of the job. As the job moves through the system, its progress is noted in the PCB.

The PCBs, not the jobs, are linked to form the queues as shown in Figure 4.4. Although each PCB is not drawn in detail, the reader should imagine each queue as a linked list of PCBs. The PCBs for every ready job are linked on the READY queue, and

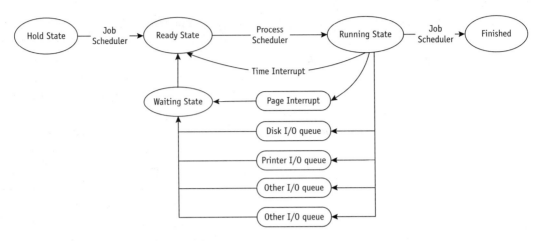

(figure 4.4)

Queuing paths from HOLD to FINISHED. The Job and Processor schedulers release the resources when the job leaves the RUNNING state.

all of the PCBs for the jobs just entering the system are linked on the HOLD queue. The jobs that are WAITING, however, are linked together by "reason for waiting," so the PCBs for the jobs in this category are linked into several queues. For example, the PCBs for jobs that are waiting for I/O on a specific disk drive are linked together, while those waiting for the printer are linked in a different queue. These queues need to be managed in an orderly fashion and that's determined by the process scheduling policies and algorithms.

Process Scheduling Policies

In a multiprogramming environment, there are usually more jobs to be executed than could possibly be run at one time. Before the operating system can schedule them, it needs to resolve three limitations of the system: (1) there are a finite number of resources (such as disk drives, printers, and tape drives); (2) some resources, once they're allocated, can't be shared with another job (e.g., printers); and (3) some resources require operator intervention—that is, they can't be reassigned automatically from job to job (such as tape drives).

What's a good **process scheduling policy**? Several criteria come to mind, but notice in the list below that some contradict each other:

• *Maximize throughput.* Run as many jobs as possible in a given amount of time. This could be accomplished easily by running only short jobs or by running jobs without interruptions.

- *Minimize response time.* Quickly turn around interactive requests. This could be done by running only interactive jobs and letting the batch jobs wait until the interactive load ceases.

- *Minimize turnaround time.* Move entire jobs in and out of the system quickly. This could be done by running all batch jobs first (because batch jobs can be grouped to run more efficiently than interactive jobs).

- *Minimize waiting time.* Move jobs out of the READY queue as quickly as possible. This could only be done by reducing the number of users allowed on the system so the CPU would be available immediately whenever a job entered the READY queue.

- *Maximize CPU efficiency.* Keep the CPU busy 100 percent of the time. This could be done by running only CPU-bound jobs (and not I/O-bound jobs).

- *Ensure fairness for all jobs.* Give everyone an equal amount of CPU and I/O time. This could be done by not giving special treatment to any job, regardless of its processing characteristics or priority.

As we can see from this list, if the system favors one type of user then it hurts another or doesn't efficiently use its resources. The final decision rests with the system designer, who must determine which criteria are most important for that specific system. For example, you might decide to "maximize CPU utilization while minimizing response time and balancing the use of all system components through a mix of I/O-bound and CPU-bound jobs." So you would select the scheduling policy that most closely satisfies your criteria.

Although the Job Scheduler selects jobs to ensure that the READY and I/O queues remain balanced, there are instances when a job claims the CPU for a very long time before issuing an I/O request. If I/O requests are being satisfied (this is done by an I/O controller and will be discussed later), this extensive use of the CPU will build up the READY queue while emptying out the I/O queues, which creates an unacceptable imbalance in the system.

To solve this problem, the Process Scheduler often uses a timing mechanism and periodically interrupts running processes when a predetermined slice of time has expired. When that happens, the scheduler suspends all activity on the job currently running and reschedules it into the READY queue; it will be continued later. The CPU is now allocated to another job that runs until one of three things happens: the timer goes off, the job issues an I/O command, or the job is finished. Then the job moves to the READY queue, the WAIT queue, or the FINISHED queue, respectively. An I/O request is called a **natural wait** in multiprogramming environments (it allows the processor to be allocated to another job).

A scheduling strategy that interrupts the processing of a job and transfers the CPU to another job is called a **preemptive scheduling policy**; it is widely used in time-sharing environments. The alternative, of course, is a **nonpreemptive scheduling policy**, which functions without external interrupts (interrupts external to the job). Therefore, once a job captures the processor and begins execution, it remains in the RUNNING state uninterrupted until it issues an I/O request (natural wait) or until it is finished (with exceptions made for infinite loops, which are interrupted by both preemptive and non-preemptive policies).

Process Scheduling Algorithms

The Process Scheduler relies on a **process scheduling algorithm,** based on a specific policy, to allocate the CPU and move jobs through the system. Early operating systems used nonpreemptive policies designed to move batch jobs through the system as efficiently as possible. Most current systems, with their emphasis on interactive use and **response time,** use an algorithm that takes care of the immediate requests of interactive users.

Here are six process scheduling algorithms that have been used extensively.

First-Come, First-Served

First-come, first-served (FCFS) is a nonpreemptive scheduling algorithm that handles jobs according to their arrival time: the earlier they arrive, the sooner they're served. It's a very simple algorithm to implement because it uses a FIFO queue. This algorithm is fine for most batch systems, but it is unacceptable for interactive systems because interactive users expect quick response times.

With FCFS, as a new job enters the system its PCB is linked to the end of the READY queue and it is removed from the front of the queue when the processor becomes available—that is, after it has processed all of the jobs before it in the queue.

In a strictly FCFS system there are no WAIT queues (each job is run to completion), although there may be systems in which control (context) is switched on a natural wait (I/O request) and then the job resumes on I/O completion.

The following examples presume a strictly FCFS environment (no multiprogramming). **Turnaround time** is unpredictable with the FCFS policy; consider the following three jobs:

• Job A has a CPU cycle of 15 milliseconds.
• Job B has a CPU cycle of 2 milliseconds.
• Job C has a CPU cycle of 1 millisecond.

For each job, the CPU cycle contains both the actual CPU usage and the I/O requests. That is, it is the total run time. Using an FCFS algorithm with an arrival sequence of A, B, C, the timeline is shown in Figure 4.5.

(figure 4.5)

Timeline for job sequence A, B, C using the FCFS algorithm.

If all three jobs arrive almost simultaneously, we can calculate that the turnaround time for Job A is 15, for Job B is 17, and for Job C is 18. So the average turnaround time is:

$$\frac{15 + 17 + 18}{3} = 16.67$$

However, if the jobs arrived in a different order, say C, B, A, then the results using the same FCFS algorithm would be as shown in Figure 4.6.

(figure 4.6)

Timeline for job sequence C, B, A using the FCFS algorithm.

Job C	Job B	Job A	
0	1	3	18

In this example the turnaround time for Job A is 18, for Job B is 3, and for Job C is 1 and the average turnaround time is:

$$\frac{18 + 3 + 1}{3} = 7.3$$

That's quite an improvement over the first sequence. Unfortunately, these two examples illustrate the primary disadvantage of using the FCFS concept—the average turnaround times vary widely and are seldom minimized. In fact, when there are three jobs in the READY queue, the system has only a 1 in 6 chance of running the jobs in the most advantageous sequence (C, B, A). With four jobs the odds fall to 1 in 24, and so on.

✔

FCFS is the only algorithm discussed in this chapter that includes an element of chance. The others do not.

If one job monopolizes the system, the extent of its overall effect on system performance depends on the scheduling policy and whether the job is CPU-bound or I/O-bound. While a job with a long CPU cycle (in this example, Job A) is using the CPU, the other jobs in the system are waiting for processing or finishing their I/O requests (if an I/O controller is used) and joining the READY queue to wait for their turn to use the processor. If the I/O requests are not being serviced, the I/O queues would remain stable while the READY list grew (with new arrivals). In extreme cases, the READY queue could fill to capacity while the I/O queues would be empty, or stable, and the I/O devices would sit idle.

On the other hand, if the job is processing a lengthy I/O cycle, the I/O queues quickly build to overflowing and the CPU could be sitting idle (if an I/O controller is used). This situation is eventually resolved when the I/O-bound job finishes its I/O cycle, the queues start moving again, and the system can recover from the bottleneck.

In a strictly FCFS algorithm, neither situation occurs. However, the turnaround time is variable (unpredictable). For this reason, FCFS is a less attractive algorithm than one that would serve the shortest job first, as the next scheduling algorithm does, even in a nonmultiprogramming environment.

Shortest Job Next

Shortest job next (SJN) is a nonpreemptive scheduling algorithm (also known as shortest job first, or SJF) that handles jobs based on the length of their CPU cycle time. It's easiest to implement in batch environments where the estimated CPU time required to run the job is given in advance by each user at the start of each job. However, it doesn't work in interactive systems because users don't estimate in advance the CPU time required to run their jobs.

For example, here are four batch jobs, all in the READY queue, for which the CPU cycle, or run time, is estimated as follows:

Job: A B C D
CPU cycle: 5 2 6 4

The SJN algorithm would review the four jobs and schedule them for processing in this order: B, D, A, C. The timeline is shown in Figure 4.7.

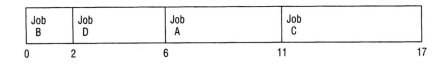

(figure 4.7)

Timeline for job sequence B, D, A, C using the SJN algorithm.

The average turnaround time is:

$$\frac{2 + 6 + 11 + 17}{4} = 9.0$$

Let's take a minute to see why this algorithm can be proved to be optimal and will consistently give the minimum average turnaround time. We'll use the previous example to derive a general formula.

If we look at Figure 4.7, we can see that Job B finishes in its given time (2), Job D finishes in its given time plus the time it waited for B to run (4 + 2), Job A finishes in its given time plus D's time plus B's time (5 + 4 + 2), and Job C finishes in its given time plus that of the previous three (6 + 5 + 4 + 2). So when calculating the average we have:

$$\frac{(2) + (4 + 2) + (5 + 4 + 2) + (6 + 5 + 4 + 2)}{4} = 9.0$$

As you can see, the time for the first job appears in the equation four times— once for each job. Similarly, the time for the second job appears three times (the number of jobs minus one). The time for the third job appears twice (number of jobs minus 2) and the time for the fourth job appears only once (number of jobs minus 3).

So the above equation can be rewritten as:

$$\frac{4 * 2 + 3 * 4 + 2 * 5 + 1 * 6}{4} = 9.0$$

Because the time for the first job appears in the equation four times, it has four times the effect on the average time than does the length of the fourth job, which appears only once. Therefore, if the first job requires the shortest computation time, followed in turn by the other jobs, ordered from shortest to longest, then the result will be the smallest possible average. The formula for the average is as follows

$$\frac{t_1(n) + t_2(n - 1) + t_3(n - 2) + \ ... \ + t_n(n(1))}{n}$$

where n is the number of jobs in the queue and $t_j (j = 1, 2, 3,...,n)$ is the length of the CPU cycle for each of the jobs.

However, the SJN algorithm is optimal only when all of the jobs are available at the same time and the CPU estimates are available and accurate.

Priority Scheduling

Priority scheduling is a nonpreemptive algorithm and one of the most common scheduling algorithms in batch systems, even though it may give slower turnaround to some users. This algorithm gives preferential treatment to important jobs. It allows the programs with the highest priority to be processed first, and they aren't interrupted until their CPU cycles (run times) are completed or a natural wait occurs. If two or more jobs with equal priority are present in the READY queue, the processor is allocated to the one that arrived first (first-come, first-served within priority).

Priorities can be assigned by a system administrator using characteristics extrinsic to the jobs. For example, they can be assigned based on the position of the user (researchers first, students last) or, in commercial environments, they can be purchased by the users who pay more for higher priority to guarantee the fastest possible processing of their jobs. With a priority algorithm, jobs are usually linked to one of several READY queues by the Job Scheduler based on their priority so the Process Scheduler manages multiple READY queues instead of just one. Details about multiple queues are presented later in this chapter.

Priorities can also be determined by the Processor Manager based on characteristics intrinsic to the jobs such as:

- *Memory requirements.* Jobs requiring large amounts of memory could be allocated lower priorities than those requesting small amounts of memory, or vice versa.
- *Number and type of peripheral devices.* Jobs requiring many peripheral devices would be allocated lower priorities than those requesting fewer devices.
- *Total CPU time.* Jobs having a long CPU cycle, or estimated run time, would be given lower priorities than those having a brief estimated run time.
- *Amount of time already spent in the system.* This is the total amount of elapsed time since the job was accepted for processing. Some systems increase the priority of jobs that have been in the system for an unusually long time to expedite their exit. This is known as **aging**.

These criteria are used to determine default priorities in many systems. The default priorities can be overruled by specific priorities named by users.

There are also preemptive priority schemes. These will be discussed later in this chapter in the section on multiple queues.

Shortest Remaining Time

Shortest remaining time (SRT) is the preemptive version of the SJN algorithm. The processor is allocated to the job closest to completion—but even this job can be preempted if a newer job in the READY queue has a time to completion that's shorter.

This algorithm can't be implemented in an interactive system because it requires advance knowledge of the CPU time required to finish each job. It is often used in batch environments, when it is desirable to give preference to short jobs, even though SRT involves more overhead than SJN because the operating system has to frequently monitor the CPU time for all the jobs in the READY queue and must perform context switching for the jobs being swapped (switched) at preemption time (not necessarily swapped out to the disk, although this might occur as well).

The example in Figure 4.8 shows how the SRT algorithm works with four jobs that arrived in quick succession (one CPU cycle apart).

If several jobs have the same amount of time remaining, the job that has been waiting the longest goes next. In other words, it uses the FCFS algorithm to break the tie.

Arrival time: 0 1 2 3
Job: A B C D
CPU cycle: 6 3 1 4

In this case, the turnaround time is the completion time of each job minus its arrival time:

Job: A B C D
Turnaround: 14 4 1 6

So the average turnaround time is:

$$\frac{14 + 4 + 1 + 6}{4} = 6.25$$

(figure 4.8)

Timeline for job sequence A, B, C, D using the preemptive SRT algorithm. Each job is interrupted after one CPU cycle if another job is waiting with less CPU time remaining.

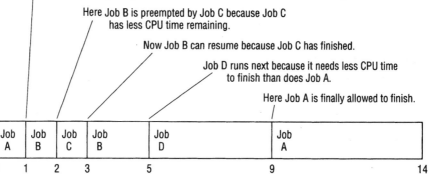

Here Job A is preempted by Job B because Job B has less CPU time remaining.

Here Job B is preempted by Job C because Job C has less CPU time remaining.

Now Job B can resume because Job C has finished.

Job D runs next because it needs less CPU time to finish than does Job A.

Here Job A is finally allowed to finish.

Job A	Job B	Job C	Job B	Job D	Job A

0   1   2   3   5   9   14

How does that compare to the same problem using the nonpreemptive SJN policy? Figure 4.9 shows the same situation using SJN.

In this case, the turnaround time is:

Job: A B C D
Turnaround: 6 9 5 11

So the average turnaround time is:

$$\frac{6 + 9 + 5 + 11}{4} = 7.75$$

(figure 4.9)

Timeline for the same job sequence A, B, C, D using the nonpreemptive SJN algorithm.

Job A	Job C	Job B	Job D

0   6   7   10   14

Note in Figure 4.9 that initially A is the only job in the READY queue so it runs first and continues until it's finished because SJN is a nonpreemptive algorithm. The next job to be run is C because when Job A is finished (at time 6), all of the other jobs (B, C, and D) have arrived. Of those three, C has the shortest CPU cycle, so it is the next one run, then B, and finally D.

Therefore, with this example, SRT at 6.25 is faster than SJN at 7.75. However, we neglected to include the time required by the SRT algorithm to do the context switching. **Context switching** is required by all preemptive algorithms. When Job A is preempted, all of its processing information must be saved in its PCB for later, when Job A's execution is to be continued, and the contents of Job B's PCB are loaded into the appropriate registers so it can start running again; this is a context switch. Later, when Job A is once again assigned to the processor, another context switch is performed. This time the information from the preempted job is stored in its PCB, and the contents of Job A's PCB are loaded into the appropriate registers.

How the context switching is actually done depends on the architecture of the CPU; in many systems, there are special instructions that provide quick saving and restoring of information. The switching is designed to be performed efficiently but, no matter how fast it is, it still takes valuable CPU time. So although SRT appears to be faster, in a real operating environment its advantages are diminished by the time spent in context switching. A precise comparison of SRT and SJN would have to include the time required to do the context switching.

Round Robin

Round robin is a preemptive process scheduling algorithm that is used extensively in interactive systems. It's easy to implement and isn't based on job characteristics but on a predetermined slice of time that's given to each job to ensure that the CPU is equally shared among all active processes and isn't monopolized by any one job.

This time slice is called a **time quantum** and its size is crucial to the performance of the system. It usually varies from 100 milliseconds to 1 or 2 seconds.

Jobs are placed in the READY queue using a first-come, first-served scheme and the Process Scheduler selects the first job from the front of the queue, sets the timer to the time quantum, and allocates the CPU to this job. If processing isn't finished when time expires, the job is preempted and put at the end of the READY queue and its information is saved in its PCB.

In the event that the job's CPU cycle is shorter than the time quantum, one of two actions will take place: (1) If this is the job's last CPU cycle and the job is finished, then all resources allocated to it are released and the completed job is returned to the user;

(2) if the CPU cycle has been interrupted by an I/O request, then information about the job is saved in its PCB and it is linked at the end of the appropriate I/O queue. Later, when the I/O request has been satisfied, it is returned to the end of the READY queue to await allocation of the CPU.

The example in Figure 4.10 illustrates a round robin algorithm with a time slice of 4 milliseconds (I/O requests are ignored):

Arrival time: 0   1   2   3
Job: A   B   C   D
CPU cycle: 8   4   9   5

(figure 4.10)

Timeline for job sequence A, B, C, D using the preemptive round robin algorithm with time slices of 4 ms.

Job A	Job B	Job C	Job D	Job A	Job C	Job D	Job C
0	4	8	12	16	20	24	25 26

The turnaround time is the completion time minus the arrival time:

Job: A   B   C   D
Turnaround: 20   7 24 22

So the average turnaround time is:

$$\frac{20 + 7 + 24 + 22}{4} = 18.25$$

Note that in Figure 4.10, Job A was preempted once because it needed 8 milliseconds to complete its CPU cycle, while Job B terminated in one time quantum. Job C was preempted twice because it needed 9 milliseconds to complete its CPU cycle, and Job D was preempted once because it needed 5 milliseconds. In their last execution or swap into memory, both Jobs D and C used the CPU for only 1 millisecond and terminated before their last time quantum expired, releasing the CPU sooner.

The efficiency of round robin depends on the size of the time quantum in relation to the average CPU cycle. If the quantum is too large—that is, if it's larger than most CPU cycles—then the algorithm reduces to the FCFS scheme. If the quantum is too small, then the amount of context switching slows down the execution of the jobs and the amount of overhead is dramatically increased, as the three examples in Figure 4.11 demonstrate. Job A has a CPU cycle of 8 milliseconds. The amount of context switching increases as the time quantum decreases in size.

In Figure 4.11, the first case (a) has a time quantum of 10 milliseconds and there is no context switching (and no overhead). The CPU cycle ends shortly before the time

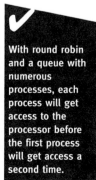

With round robin and a queue with numerous processes, each process will get access to the processor before the first process will get access a second time.

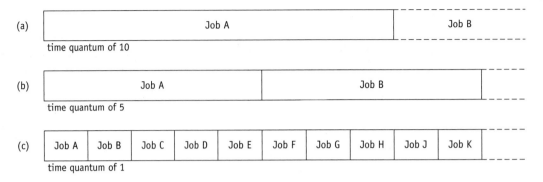

(figure 4.11)

Context switches for three different time quantums. In (a), Job A (which requires only 8 cycles to run to completion) finishes before the time quantum of 10 expires. In (b) and (c), the time quantum expires first, interrupting the jobs.

quantum expires and the job runs to completion. For this job with this time quantum, there is no difference between the round robin algorithm and the FCFS algorithm.

In the second case (b), with a time quantum of 5 milliseconds, there is one context switch. The job is preempted once when the time quantum expires, so there is some overhead for context switching and there would be a delayed turnaround based on the number of other jobs in the system.

In the third case (c), with a time quantum of 1 millisecond, there are 10 context switches because the job is preempted every time the time quantum expires; overhead becomes costly and turnaround time suffers accordingly.

What's the best time quantum size? The answer should be predictable by now: it depends on the system. If it's an interactive environment, the system is expected to respond quickly to its users, especially when they make simple requests. If it's a batch system, response time is not a factor (turnaround is) and overhead becomes very important.

Here are two general rules of thumb for selecting the proper time quantum: (1) it should be long enough to allow 80 percent of the CPU cycles to run to completion, and (2) it should be at least 100 times longer than the time required to perform one context switch. These rules are used in some systems, but they are not inflexible.

Multiple-Level Queues

Multiple-level queues isn't really a separate scheduling algorithm but works in conjunction with several of the schemes already discussed and is found in systems with jobs that can be grouped according to a common characteristic. We've already introduced at least one kind of multiple-level queue—that of a priority-based system with different queues for each priority level.

Another kind of system might gather all of the CPU-bound jobs in one queue and all I/O-bound jobs in another. The Process Scheduler then alternately selects jobs from each queue to keep the system balanced.

A third common example is one used in a hybrid environment that supports both batch and interactive jobs. The batch jobs are put in one queue called the background queue while the interactive jobs are put in a foreground queue and are treated more favorably than those on the background queue.

All of these examples have one thing in common: The scheduling policy is based on some predetermined scheme that allocates special treatment to the jobs in each queue. Within each queue, the jobs are served in FCFS fashion.

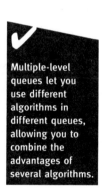

Multiple-level queues let you use different algorithms in different queues, allowing you to combine the advantages of several algorithms.

Multiple-level queues raise some interesting questions:

- Is the processor allocated to the jobs in the first queue until it is empty before moving to the next queue, or does it travel from queue to queue until the last job on the last queue has been served and then go back to serve the first job on the first queue, or something in between?
- Is this fair to those who have earned, or paid for, a higher priority?
- Is it fair to those in a low-priority queue?
- If the processor is allocated to the jobs on the first queue and it never empties out, when will the jobs in the last queues be served?
- Can the jobs in the last queues get "time off for good behavior" and eventually move to better queues?

The answers depend on the policy used by the system to service the queues. There are four primary methods to the movement: not allowing movement between queues, moving jobs from queue to queue, moving jobs from queue to queue and increasing the time quantums for lower queues, and giving special treatment to jobs that have been in the system for a long time (aging).

Case 1: No Movement Between Queues

No movement between queues is a very simple policy that rewards those who have high-priority jobs. The processor is allocated to the jobs in the high-priority queue in FCFS fashion and it is allocated to jobs in low-priority queues only when the high-priority queues are empty. This policy can be justified if there are relatively few users with high-priority jobs so the top queues quickly empty out, allowing the processor to spend a fair amount of time running the low-priority jobs.

Case 2: Movement Between Queues

Movement between queues is a policy that adjusts the priorities assigned to each job: High-priority jobs are treated like all the others once they are in the system. (Their initial priority may be favorable.) When a time quantum interrupt occurs, the job is preempted and moved to the end of the next lower queue. A job may also have its priority increased; for example, when it issues an I/O request before its time quantum has expired.

This policy is fairest in a system in which the jobs are handled according to their computing cycle characteristics: CPU-bound or I/O-bound. This assumes that a job that exceeds its time quantum is CPU-bound and will require more CPU allocation than one that requests I/O before the time quantum expires. Therefore, the CPU-bound jobs are placed at the end of the next lower-level queue when they're preempted because of the expiration of the time quantum, while I/O-bound jobs are returned to the end of the next higher-level queue once their I/O request has finished. This facilitates I/O-bound jobs and is good in interactive systems.

Case 3: Variable Time Quantum Per Queue

Variable time quantum per queue is a variation of the movement between queues policy, and it allows for faster turnaround of CPU-bound jobs.

In this scheme, each of the queues is given a time quantum twice as long as the previous queue. The highest queue might have a time quantum of 100 milliseconds. So the second-highest queue would have a time quantum of 200 milliseconds, the third would have 400 milliseconds, and so on. If there are enough queues, the lowest one might have a relatively long time quantum of 3 seconds or more.

If a job doesn't finish its CPU cycle in the first time quantum, it is moved to the end of the next lower-level queue; and when the processor is next allocated to it, the job executes for twice as long as before. With this scheme a CPU-bound job can execute for longer and longer periods of time, thus improving its chances of finishing faster.

Case 4: Aging

Aging is used to ensure that jobs in the lower-level queues will eventually complete their execution. The operating system keeps track of each job's waiting time and when a job gets too old—that is, when it reaches a certain time limit—the system moves the job to the next highest queue, and so on until it reaches the top queue. A more drastic aging policy is one that moves the old job directly from the lowest queue to the end of the top queue. Regardless of its actual implementation, an aging policy guards against the indefinite postponement of unwieldy jobs. As you might expect, **indefinite postponement** means that a job's execution is delayed for an undefined amount of time because it is repeatedly pre-empted so other jobs can be processed. (We all know examples of an unpleasant task that's been indefinitely postponed to make time for a more appealing pastime). Eventually the situation could lead to the old job's starvation. Indefinite postponement is a major problem when allocating resources and one that will be discussed in detail in Chapter 5.

A Word About Interrupts

We first encountered **interrupts** in Chapter 3 when the Memory Manager issued page interrupts to accommodate job requests. In this chapter we examined another type of interrupt that occurs when the time quantum expires and the processor is deallocated from the running job and allocated to another one.

There are other interrupts that are caused by events internal to the process. I/O interrupts are issued when a READ or WRITE command is issued. (We'll explain them in detail in Chapter 7.) Internal interrupts, or synchronous interrupts, also occur as a direct result of the arithmetic operation or job instruction currently being processed.

Illegal arithmetic operations, such as the following, can generate interrupts:
• Attempts to divide by zero
• Floating-point operations generating an overflow or underflow
• Fixed-point addition or subtraction that causes an arithmetic overflow

Illegal job instructions, such as the following, can also generate interrupts:
• Attempts to access protected or nonexistent storage locations
• Attempts to use an undefined operation code
• Operating on invalid data
• Attempts to make system changes, such as trying to change the size of the time quantum

The control program that handles the interruption sequence of events is called the **interrupt handler**. When the operating system detects a nonrecoverable error, the interrupt handler typically follows this sequence:

1. The type of interrupt is described and stored—to be passed on to the user as an error message.

2. The state of the interrupted process is saved, including the value of the program counter, the mode specification, and the contents of all registers.

3. The interrupt is processed: The error message and state of the interrupted process are sent to the user; program execution is halted; any resources allocated to the job are released; and the job exits the system.

4. The processor resumes normal operation.

If we're dealing with internal interrupts only, which are nonrecoverable, the job is terminated in Step 3. However, when the interrupt handler is working with an I/O interrupt, time quantum, or other recoverable interrupt, Step 3 simply halts the job and moves it to the appropriate I/O device queue, or READY queue (on time out). Later, when the I/O request is finished, the job is returned to the READY queue. If it was a time out (quantum interrupt), the job (or process) is already on the READY queue.

Conclusion

The Processor Manager must allocate the CPU among all the system's users. In this chapter we've made the distinction between job scheduling, the selection of incoming jobs based on their characteristics, and process scheduling, the instant-by-instant allocation of the CPU. We've also described how interrupts are generated and resolved by the interrupt handler.

Each scheduling algorithm presented in this chapter has unique characteristics, objectives, and applications. A system designer can choose the best policy and algorithm only after carefully evaluating their strengths and weaknesses. Table 4.1 shows how the algorithms presented in this chapter compare.

In the next chapter we'll explore the demands placed on the Processor Manager as it attempts to synchronize execution of all the jobs in the system.

Algorithm	Policy Type	Best for	Disadvantages	Advantages
FCFS	Nonpreemptive	Batch	Unpredictable turnaround times	Easy to implement
SJN	Nonpreemptive	Batch	Indefinite postponement of some jobs	Minimizes average waiting time
Priority scheduling	Nonpreemptive	Batch	Indefinite postponement of some jobs	Ensures fast completion of important jobs
SRT	Preemptive	Batch	Overhead incurred by context switching	Ensures fast completion of short jobs
Round robin	Preemptive	Interactive	Requires selection of good time quantum	Provides reasonable response times to interactive users; provides fair CPU allocation
Multiple-level queues	Preemptive/ Nonpreemptive	Batch/ interactive	Overhead incurred by monitoring of queues	Flexible scheme; counteracts indefinite postponement with aging or other queue movement; gives fair treatment to CPU-bound jobs by incrementing time quantums on lower-priority queues or other queue movement

(table 4.1)

Comparison of the scheduling algorithms discussed in this chapter.

Key Terms

aging: a policy used to ensure that jobs that have been in the system for a long time in the lower-level queues will eventually complete their execution.

context switching: the acts of saving a job's processing information in its PCB so the job can be swapped out of memory and of loading the processing information from the PCB of another job into the appropriate registers so the CPU can process it. Context switching occurs in all preemptive policies.

CPU-bound: a job that will perform a great deal of nonstop processing before issuing an interrupt.

first-come, first-served (FCFS): a nonpreemptive process scheduling policy (or algorithm) that handles jobs according to their arrival time.

high-level scheduler: a synonym for the Job Scheduler.

I/O-bound: a job that requires a large number of input/output operations, resulting in too much free time for the CPU.

indefinite postponement: signifies that a job's execution is delayed indefinitely because it is repeatedly preempted so other jobs can be processed.

interrupt: a hardware signal that suspends execution of a program and activates the execution of a special program known as the interrupt handler.

interrupt handler: the program that controls what action should be taken by the operating system when a sequence of events is interrupted.

Job Scheduler: the high-level scheduler of the Processor Manager that selects jobs from a queue of incoming jobs based on each job's characteristics.

job status: the condition of a job as it moves through the system from the beginning to the end of its execution.

low-level scheduler: a synonym for the Process Scheduler.

middle-level scheduler: a scheduler used by the Processor Manager when the system to remove active processes from memory becomes overloaded. The middle-level scheduler swaps these processes back into memory when the system overload has cleared.

multiple-level queues: a process scheduling scheme (used with other scheduling algorithms) that groups jobs according to a common characteristic.

multiprogramming: a technique that allows a single processor to process several programs residing simultaneously in main memory and interleaving their execution by overlapping I/O requests with CPU requests.

natural wait: a common term used to identify an I/O request from a program in a multiprogramming environment that would cause a process to wait "naturally" before resuming execution.

nonpreemptive scheduling policy: a job scheduling strategy that functions without external interrupts so that once a job captures the processor and begins execution, it remains in the running state uninterrupted until it issues an I/O request or it's finished.

preemptive scheduling policy: any process scheduling strategy that, based on predetermined policies, interrupts the processing of a job and transfers the CPU to another job. It is widely used in time-sharing environments.

priority scheduling: a nonpreemptive process scheduling policy (or algorithm) that allows for the execution of high-priority jobs before low-priority jobs.

process: an instance of execution of a program that is identifiable and controllable by the operating system.

Process Control Block (PCB): a data structure that contains information about the current status and characteristics of a process.

Process Scheduler: the low-level scheduler of the Processor Manager that establishes the order in which processes in the READY queue will be served by the CPU.

process scheduling algorithm: an algorithm used by the Job Scheduler to allocate the CPU and move jobs through the system.

process scheduling policy: any policy used by the Processor Manager to select the order in which incoming jobs will be executed.

process status: information stored in the job's PCB that indicates the current position of the job and the resources responsible for that status.

processor: (1) a synonym for the CPU, or (2) any component in a computing system capable of performing a sequence of activities.

program: an interactive unit, such as a file stored on a disk.

queue: a linked list of PCBs that indicates the order in which jobs or processes will be serviced.

response time: a measure of the efficiency of an interactive system that tracks the speed with which the system will respond to a user's command.

round robin: a preemptive process scheduling policy (or algorithm) that allocates to each job one unit of processing time per turn to ensure that the CPU is equally shared among all active processes and isn't monopolized by any one job.

shortest job next (SJN): a nonpreemptive process scheduling policy (or algorithm) that selects the waiting job with the shortest CPU cycle time.

shortest remaining time (SRT): a preemptive process scheduling policy (or algorithm) similar to the SJN algorithm that allocates the processor to the job closest to completion.

task: (1) the term used to describe a process, or (2) the basic unit of concurrent programming languages that defines a sequence of instructions that may be executed in parallel with other similar units.

thread: a portion of a program that can run independently of other portions. Multithreaded applications programs can have several threads running at one time with the same or different priorities.

time quantum: a period of time assigned to a process for execution before it is pre-empted.

turnaround time: a measure of a system's efficiency that tracks the time required to execute a job and return output to the user.

Interesting Searches

- CPU Cycle Time
- Task Control Block (TCB)
- Processor Bottleneck
- Processor Queue Length
- I/O Interrupts

Exercises

Research Topics

A. Multi-core technology can often, but not necessarily always, make applications run faster. Research some real-life computing environments that are expected to benefit from multi-core chips and briefly explain why. Cite your academic sources.

B. Compare two processors currently being produced for personal computers. Use standard industry benchmarks for your comparison and briefly list the advantages and disadvantages of each. You can compare different processors from the same manufacturer (such as two Intel processors) or different processors from different manufacturers (such as Intel and AMD).

Exercises

1. Figure 4.12 is a simplified process model of you, in which there are only two states: sleeping and waking. You make the transition from waking to sleeping when you are tired, and from sleeping to waking when the alarm clock goes off.

   a. Add three more states to the diagram (for example, one might be eating).

   b. State all of the possible transitions among the five states.

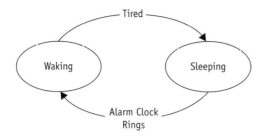

(figure 4.12)

Process model of two states.

2. Describe context switching in lay terms and identify the process information that needs to be saved, changed, or updated when context switching takes place.

3. Five jobs (A, B, C, D, E) are already in the READY queue waiting to be processed. Their estimated CPU cycles are respectively: 2, 10, 15, 6, and 8. Using SJN, in what order should they be processed?

4. A job running in a system, with variable time quantums per queue, needs 30 milliseconds to run to completion. If the first queue has a time quantum of 5 milliseconds and each queue thereafter has a time quantum that is twice as large as the previous one, how many times will the job be interrupted and on which queue will it finish its execution?

5. Describe the advantages of having a separate queue for Print I/O and for Disk I/O as illustrated in Figure 4.4.

6. Given the following information:

Job	Arrival Time	CPU Cycle
A	0	2
B	1	12
C	2	4
D	4	1
E	5	8
F	7	5
G	8	3

Using SJN, draw a timeline showing the time that each job arrives and the order that each is processed. Calculate the finish time for each job.

7. Given the following information:

Job	Arrival Time	CPU Cycle
A	0	10
B	2	12
C	3	3
D	6	1
E	9	15

Draw a timeline for each of the following scheduling algorithms. (It may be helpful to first compute a start and finish time for each job.)

a. FCFS

b. SJN

c. SRT

d. Round robin (using a time quantum of 5, ignore context switching and natural wait)

8. Using the same information from Exercise 7, calculate which jobs will have arrived ready for processing by the time the first job is finished or interrupted using each of the following scheduling algorithms.

a. FCFS

b. SJN

c. SRT

d. Round robin (using a time quantum of 5, ignore context switching and natural wait)

9. Using the same information given for Exercise 7, compute the waiting time and turnaround time for every job for each of the following scheduling algorithms (ignoring context switching overhead).

a. FCFS

b. SJN

c. SRT

d. Round robin (using a time quantum of 2)

Advanced Exercises

10. Consider a variation of round robin in which a process that has used its full time quantum is returned to the end of the READY queue, while one that has used half of its time quantum is returned to the middle of the queue and one

that has used one-fourth of its time quantum goes to a place one-fourth of the distance away from the beginning of the queue.

a. What is the objective of this scheduling policy?

b. Discuss the advantage and disadvantage of its implementation.

11. In a single-user dedicated system, such as a personal computer, it's easy for the user to determine when a job is caught in an infinite loop. The typical solution to this problem is for the user to manually intervene and terminate the job. What mechanism would you implement in the Process Scheduler to automate the termination of a job that's in an infinite loop? Take into account jobs that legitimately use large amounts of CPU time; for example, one "finding the first 10,000 prime numbers."

12. Some guidelines for selecting the right time quantum were given in this chapter. As a system designer, how would you know when you have chosen the best time quantum? What factors would make this time quantum best from the user's point of view? What factors would make this time quantum best from the system's point of view?

13. Using the process state diagrams of Figure 4.2, explain why there's no transition:

a. From the READY state to the WAITING state

b. From the WAITING state to the RUNNING state

Programming Exercises

14. Write a program that will simulate FCFS, SJN, SRT, and round robin scheduling algorithms. For each algorithm, the program should compute waiting time and turnaround time of every job as well as the average waiting time and average turnaround time. The average values should be consolidated in a table for easy comparison. You may use the following data to test your program. The time quantum for round robin is 4 milliseconds and the context switching time is 0.

Arrival Time	CPU Cycle (in milliseconds)
0	6
3	2
5	1
9	7
10	5
12	3

14	4
16	5
17	7
19	2

15. Using your program from Exercise 14, change the context switching time to 0.4 milliseconds. Compare outputs from both runs and discuss which would be the better policy. Describe any drastic changes encountered or a lack of changes and why.

Process Management

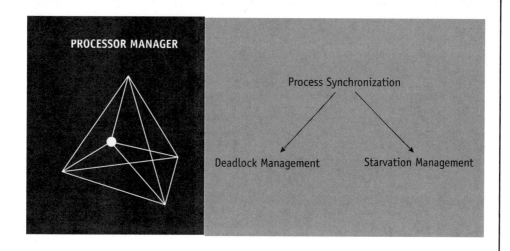

PROCESSOR MANAGER

Process Synchronization

Deadlock Management   Starvation Management

We have all heard the story of the animal standing in doubt between two stacks of hay and starving to death.

—Abraham Lincoln (*1809–1865*)

Learning Objectives

After completing this chapter, you should be able to describe:

- Several causes of system deadlock and livelock
- The difference between preventing and avoiding deadlocks
- How to detect and recover from deadlocks
- The concept of process starvation and how to detect and recover from it
- The concept of a race and how to prevent it
- The difference between deadlock, starvation, and race

We've already looked at resource sharing from two perspectives, that of sharing memory and sharing one processor, but the processor sharing described thus far was the best case scenario, free of conflicts and complications. In this chapter, we address the problems caused when many processes compete for relatively few resources and the system stops responding as it should and is unable to service all of the processes in the system.

Let's look at how a lack of **process synchronization** can result in two extreme conditions: deadlock or starvation.

In early operating systems, deadlock was known by the more descriptive phrase "deadly embrace" and that's exactly what happens when the system freezes. It's a system-wide tangle of resource requests that begins when two or more jobs are put on hold, each waiting for a vital resource to become available. The problem builds when the resources needed by those jobs are the resources held by other jobs that are also waiting to run but cannot because they're waiting for other unavailable resources. The tangled jobs come to a standstill. The deadlock is complete if the remainder of the system comes to a standstill as well. When the situation can't be resolved by the operating system, then intervention is required.

A **deadlock** is most easily described with an example—a narrow staircase in a building (we'll return to this example throughout this chapter). The staircase was built as a fire escape route, but people working in the building often take the stairs instead of waiting for the slow elevators. Traffic on the staircase moves well unless two people, traveling in opposite directions, need to pass on the stairs—there's room for only one person on each step. In this example, the staircase is the system and the steps and landings are the resources. There's a landing between each floor and it's wide enough for people to share it, but the stairs are not and can be allocated to only one person at a time. Problems occur when someone going up the stairs meets someone coming down, and each refuses to retreat to a wider place. This creates a deadlock, which is the subject of much of our discussion on process synchronization.

Similarly, if two people on the landing try to pass each other but cannot do so because as one steps to the right, the other steps to the left, and vice versa, then the step-climbers will continue moving but neither will ever move forward. This is called **livelock**.

On the other hand, if a few patient people wait on the landing for a break in the opposing traffic, and that break never comes, they could wait there forever. That results in **starvation**, an extreme case of indefinite postponement, and is discussed at the end of this chapter.

Deadlock

Deadlock is more serious than indefinite postponement or starvation because it affects more than one job. Because resources are being tied up, the entire system (not just a few programs) is affected. The example most often used to illustrate deadlock is a traffic jam.

As shown in Figure 5.1, there's no simple and immediate solution to a deadlock; no one can move forward until someone moves out of the way, but no one can move out of the way until either someone advances or the rear of a line moves back. Obviously it requires outside intervention to remove one of the four vehicles from an intersection or to make a line move back. Only then can the deadlock be resolved.

Deadlocks became prevalent with the introduction of interactive systems, which generally improve the use of resources through dynamic resource sharing, but this capability also increases the possibility of deadlocks.

(figure 5.1)

A classic case of traffic deadlock on four one-way streets. This is "gridlock," where no vehicles can move forward to clear the traffic jam.

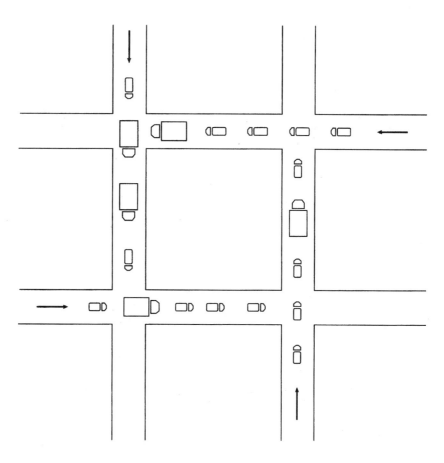

In some computer systems, deadlocks are regarded as a mere inconvenience that causes delays. But for real-time systems, deadlocks cause critical situations. For example, a deadlock in a hospital's life support system or in the guidance system aboard an aircraft could endanger lives. Regardless of the environment, the operating system must either prevent deadlocks or resolve them when they happen. In Chapter 12, we'll learn how to calculate system reliability and availability, which can be affected by processor conflicts.

Seven Cases of Deadlock

A deadlock usually occurs when nonsharable, nonpreemptable resources, such as files, printers, or scanners, are allocated to jobs that eventually require other nonsharable, nonpreemptive resources—resources that have been locked by other jobs. However, deadlocks aren't restricted to files, printers, and scanners. They can also occur on sharable resources that are locked, such as disks and databases.

Directed graphs visually represent the system's resources and processes, and show how they are deadlocked. Using a series of squares (for resources) and circles (for processes), and connectors with arrows (for requests), directed graphs can be manipulated to understand how deadlocks occur.

Case 1: Deadlocks on File Requests

If jobs are allowed to request and hold files for the duration of their execution, a deadlock can occur as the simplified directed graph shown in Figure 5.2 graphically illustrates.

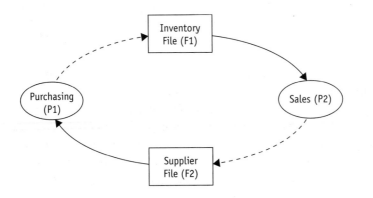

(figure 5.2)

Case 1. These two processes, shown as circles, are each waiting for a resource, shown as rectangles, that has already been allocated to the other process, thus creating a deadlock.

For example, consider the case of a home construction company with two application programs, purchasing (P1) and sales (P2), which are active at the same time. Both need to access two files, inventory (F1) and suppliers (F2), to read and write transactions. One day the system deadlocks when the following sequence of events takes place:

1. Purchasing (P1) accesses the supplier file (F2) to place an order for more lumber.
2. Sales (P2) accesses the inventory file (F1) to reserve the parts that will be required to build the home ordered that day.
3. Purchasing (P1) doesn't release the supplier file (F2) but requests the inventory file (F1) to verify the quantity of lumber on hand before placing its order for more, but P1 is blocked because F1 is being held by P2.
4. Meanwhile, sales (P2) doesn't release the inventory file (F1) but requests the supplier file (F2) to check the schedule of a subcontractor. At this point, P2 is also blocked because F2 is being held by P1.

Any other programs that require F1 or F2 will be put on hold as long as this situation continues. This deadlock will remain until one of the two programs is closed or forcibly removed and its file is released. Only then can the other program continue and the system return to normal.

Case 2: Deadlocks in Databases

A deadlock can also occur if two processes access and lock records in a database.

To appreciate the following scenario, remember that database queries and transactions are often relatively brief processes that either search or modify parts of a database. Requests usually arrive at random and may be interleaved arbitrarily.

Locking is a technique used to guarantee the integrity of the data through which the user locks out all other users while working with the database. Locking can be done at three different levels: the entire database can be locked for the duration of the request; a subsection of the database can be locked; or only the individual record can be locked until the process is completed. Locking the entire database (the most extreme and most successful solution) prevents a deadlock from occurring but it restricts access to the database to one user at a time and, in a multiuser environment, response times are significantly slowed; this is normally an unacceptable solution. When the locking is performed on only one part of the database, access time is improved but the possibility of a deadlock is increased because different processes sometimes need to work with several parts of the database at the same time.

Here's a system that locks each record when it is accessed until the process is completed. There are two processes (P1 and P2), each of which needs to update two records (R1 and R2), and the following sequence leads to a deadlock:

1. P1 accesses R1 and locks it.
2. P2 accesses R2 and locks it.
3. P1 requests R2, which is locked by P2.
4. P2 requests R1, which is locked by P1.

An alternative, of course, is to avoid the use of locks—but that leads to other difficulties. If locks are not used to preserve their integrity, the updated records in the database might include only some of the data—and their contents would depend on the order in which each process finishes its execution. This is known as a **race** between processes and is illustrated in the following example and Figure 5.3.

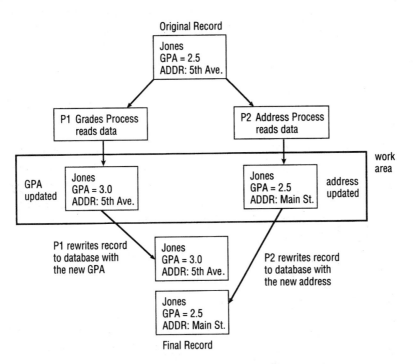

(figure 5.3)

Case 2. P1 finishes first and wins the race but its version of the record will soon be overwritten by P2. Regardless of which process wins the race, the final version of the data will be incorrect.

Let's say you are a student of a university that maintains most of its files on a database that can be accessed by several different programs, including one for grades and another listing home addresses. You've just moved so you send the university a change of address form at the end of the fall term, shortly after grades are submitted. And one fateful day, both programs race to access your record in the database:

1. The grades process (P1) is the first to access your record (R1), and it copies the record to its work area.

2. The address process (P2) accesses your record (R1) and copies it to its work area.

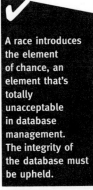

A race introduces the element of chance, an element that's totally unacceptable in database management. The integrity of the database must be upheld.

3. P1 changes your student record (R1) by entering your grades for the fall term and calculating your new grade average.

4. P2 changes your record (R1) by updating the address field.

5. P1 finishes its work first and rewrites its version of your record back to the database. Your grades have been updated, but your address hasn't.

6. P2 finishes and rewrites its updated record back to the database. Your address has been changed, but your grades haven't. According to the database, you didn't attend school this term.

If we reverse the order and say that P2 won the race, your grades will be updated but not your address. Depending on your success in the classroom, you might prefer one mishap over the other; but from the operating system's point of view, either alternative is unacceptable because incorrect data is allowed to corrupt the database. The system can't allow the integrity of the database to depend on a random sequence of events.

Case 3: Deadlocks in Dedicated Device Allocation

The use of a group of dedicated devices, such as a cluster of DVD read/write drives, can also deadlock the system.

Let's say two users from the local board of education are each running a program (P1 and P2), and both programs will eventually need two DVD drivers to copy files from one disc to another. The system is small, however, and when the two programs are begun, only two DVD-R drives are available and they're allocated on an "as requested" basis. Soon the following sequence transpires:

1. P1 requests drive 1 and gets it.

2. P2 requests drive 2 and gets it.

3. P1 requests drive 2 but is blocked.

4. P2 requests drive 1 but is blocked.

Neither job can continue because each is waiting for the other to finish and release its drive—an event that will never occur. A similar series of events could deadlock any group of dedicated devices.

Case 4: Deadlocks in Multiple Device Allocation

Deadlocks aren't restricted to processes contending for the same type of device; they can happen when several processes request, and hold on to, several dedicated devices while other processes act in a similar manner as shown in Figure 5.4.

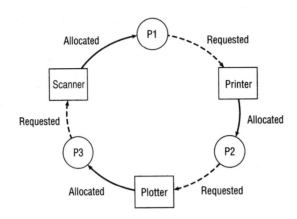

(figure 5.4)

Case 4. Three processes, shown as circles, are each waiting for a device that has already been allocated to another process, thus creating a deadlock.

Consider the case of an engineering design firm with three programs (P1, P2, and P3) and three dedicated devices: scanner, printer, and plotter. The following sequence of events will result in deadlock:

1. P1 requests and gets the scanner.
2. P2 requests and gets the printer.
3. P3 requests and gets the plotter.
4. P1 requests the printer but is blocked.
5. P2 requests the plotter but is blocked.
6. P3 requests the scanner but is blocked.

As in the earlier examples, none of the jobs can continue because each is waiting for a resource being held by another.

Case 5: Deadlocks in Spooling

Although in the previous example the printer was a dedicated device, printers are usually sharable devices, called virtual devices, that use high-speed storage to transfer data between it and the CPU. The spooler accepts output from several users and acts as a temporary storage area for all output until the printer is ready to accept it. This process is called **spooling**. If the printer needs all of a job's output before it will begin printing, but the spooling system fills the available space with only partially completed output, then a deadlock can occur. It happens like this.

Let's say it's one hour before the big project is due for a computer class. Twenty-six frantic programmers key in their final changes and, with only minutes to spare, all issue print commands. The spooler receives the pages one at a time from each of the students but the pages are received separately, several page ones, page twos, etc. The printer is ready to print the first completed document it gets, but as the spooler canvasses its files it has the first page for many programs but the last page for none of them. Alas, the spooler is full of partially completed output so no other pages can be accepted, but none of the jobs can be printed out (which would release their disk space) because the printer only accepts completed output files. It's an unfortunate state of affairs.

This scenario isn't limited to printers. Any part of the system that relies on spooling, such as one that handles incoming jobs or transfers files over a network, is vulnerable to such a deadlock.

Case 6: Deadlocks in a Network

A network that's congested or has filled a large percentage of its I/O buffer space can become deadlocked if it doesn't have protocols to control the flow of messages through the network as shown in Figure 5.5.

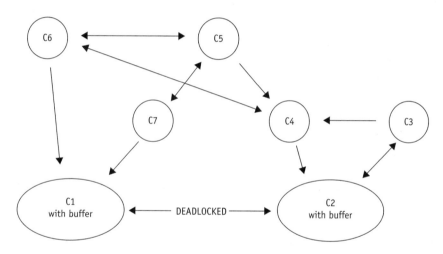

(figure 5.5)

Case 6, deadlocked network flow. Notice that only two nodes, C1 and C2, have buffers. Each circle represents a node and each line represents a communication path. The arrows indicate the direction of data flow.

For example, a medium-sized word-processing center has seven computers on a network, each on different nodes. C1 receives messages from nodes C2, C6, and C7 and sends messages to only one: C2. C2 receives messages from nodes C1, C3, and C4 and sends messages to only C1 and C3. The direction of the arrows in Figure 5.5 indicates the flow of messages.

Messages received by C1 from C6 and C7 and destined for C2 are buffered in an output queue. Messages received by C2 from C3 and C4 and destined for C1 are buffered in an output queue. As the traffic increases, the length of each output queue increases until all of the available buffer space is filled. At this point C1 can't accept any more messages (from C2 or any other computer) because there's no more buffer space available to store them. For the same reason, C2 can't accept any messages from C1 or any other computer, not even a request to send. The communication path between C1 and C2 becomes deadlocked; and because C1 can't send messages to any other computer except C2 and can only receive messages from C6 and C7, those routes also become deadlocked. C1 can't send word to C2 about the problem and so the deadlock can't be resolved without outside intervention.

Case 7: Deadlocks in Disk Sharing

Disks are designed to be shared, so it's not uncommon for two processes to be accessing different areas of the same disk. This ability to share creates an active type of deadlock, known as livelock. Processes use a form of busy-waiting that's different from a natural wait. In this case, it's waiting to share a resource but never actually gains control of it. In Figure 5.6, two competing processes are sending conflicting commands, causing livelock. Notice that neither process is blocked, which would cause a deadlock. Instead, each is active but never reaches fulfillment.

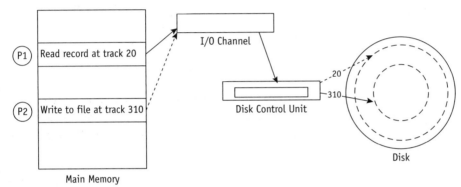

(figure 5.6)

Case 7. Two processes are each waiting for an I/O request to be filled: one at track 20 and one at track 310. But by the time the read/write arm reaches one track, a competing command for the other track has been issued, so neither command is satisfied and livelock occurs.

For example, at an insurance company the system performs many daily transactions. One day the following series of events ties up the system:

1. Customer Service (P1) wishes to show a payment so it issues a command to read the balance, which is stored on track 20 of a disk.

2. While the control unit is moving the arm to track 20, P1 is put on hold and the I/O channel is free to process the next I/O request.

3. While the arm is moving into position, Accounts Payable (P2) gains control of the I/O channel and issues a command to write someone else's payment to a record stored on track 310. If the command is not "locked out," P2 will be put on hold while the control unit moves the arm to track 310.

4. Because P2 is "on hold" while the arm is moving, the channel can be captured again by P1, which reconfirms its command to "read from track 20."

5. Because the last command from P2 had forced the arm mechanism to track 310, the disk control unit begins to reposition the arm to track 20 to satisfy P1. The I/O channel would be released because P1 is once again put on hold, so it could be captured by P2, which issues a WRITE command only to discover that the arm mechanism needs to be repositioned.

As a result, the arm is in a constant state of motion, moving back and forth between tracks 20 and 310 as it responds to the two competing commands, but satisfies neither.

Conditions for Deadlock

In each of these seven cases, the deadlock (or livelock) involved the interaction of several processes and resources, but each deadlock was preceded by the simultaneous occurrence of four conditions that the operating system (or other systems) could have recognized: mutual exclusion, resource holding, no preemption, and circular wait. It's important to remember that each of these four conditions is necessary for the operating system to work smoothly. None of them can be removed easily without causing the system's overall functioning to suffer. Therefore, the system needs to recognize the combination of conditions before they occur and threaten to cause the system to lock up.

To illustrate these four conditions, let's revisit the staircase example from the beginning of the chapter to identify the four conditions required for a deadlock.

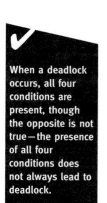

When a deadlock occurs, all four conditions are present, though the opposite is not true—the presence of all four conditions does not always lead to deadlock.

When two people meet between landings, they can't pass because the steps can hold only one person at a time. **Mutual exclusion**, the act of allowing only one person (or process) to have access to a step (a dedicated resource), is the first condition for deadlock.

When two people meet on the stairs and each one holds ground and waits for the other to retreat, that is an example of **resource holding** (as opposed to resource sharing), the second condition for deadlock.

In this example, each step is dedicated to the climber (or the descender); it is allocated to the holder for as long as needed. This is called **no preemption**, the lack of temporary reallocation of resources, and is the third condition for deadlock.

These three lead to the fourth condition of **circular wait** in which each person (or process) involved in the impasse is waiting for another to voluntarily release the step (or resource) so that at least one will be able to continue on and eventually arrive at the destination.

All four conditions are required for the deadlock to occur, and as long as all four conditions are present the deadlock will continue; but if one condition can be removed, the deadlock will be resolved. In fact, if the four conditions can be prevented from ever occurring at the same time, deadlocks can be prevented. Although this concept is obvious, it isn't easy to implement.

Modeling Deadlocks

Holt showed how the four conditions can be modeled using **directed graphs**. (We used modified directed graphs in Figure 5.2 and Figure 5.4.) These graphs use two kinds of symbols: processes represented by circles and resources represented by squares. A solid arrow from a resource to a process, shown in Figure 5.7(a), means that the process is holding that resource. A dashed line with an arrow from a process to a resource, shown in Figure 5.7(b), means that the process is waiting for that resource. The direction of the arrow indicates the flow. If there's a cycle in the graph then there's a deadlock involving the processes and the resources in the cycle.

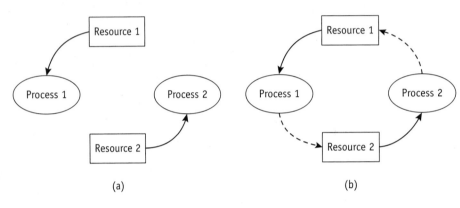

(a) (b)

(figure 5.7)

In (a), Resource 1 is being held by Process 1 and Resource 2 is held by Process 2 in a system that is not deadlocked. In (b), Process 1 requests Resource 2 but doesn't release Resource 1, and Process 2 does the same — creating a deadlock. (If one process released its resource, the deadlock would be resolved.)

The following system has three processes—P1, P2, P3—and three resources—R1, R2, R3—each of a different type: printer, disk drive, and plotter. Because there is no specified order in which the requests are handled, we'll look at three different possible scenarios using graphs to help us detect any deadlocks.

Scenario 1

The first scenario's sequence of events is shown in Table 5.1. The directed graph is shown in Figure 5.8.

Event	Action
1	P1 requests and is allocated the printer R1.
2	P1 releases the printer R1.
3	P2 requests and is allocated the disk drive R2.
4	P2 releases the disk R2.
5	P3 requests and is allocated the plotter R3.
6	P3 releases the plotter R3.

(table 5.1)

First scenario's sequence of events is shown in the directed graph in Figure 5.8.

Notice in the directed graph that there are no cycles. Therefore, we can safely conclude that a deadlock can't occur even if each process requests every resource *if* the resources are released before the next process requests them.

(figure 5.8)

First scenario. The system will stay free of deadlocks if each resource is released before it is requested by the next process.

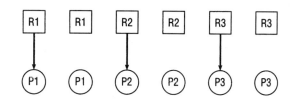

Scenario 2

Now, consider a second scenario's sequence of events shown in Table 5.2.

(table 5.2)

The second scenario's sequence of events is shown in the two directed graphs shown in Figure 5.9.

Event	Action
1	P1 requests and is allocated R1.
2	P2 requests and is allocated R2.
3	P3 requests and is allocated R3.
4	P1 requests R2.
5	P2 requests R3.
6	P3 requests R1.

The progression of the directed graph is shown in Figure 5.9. A deadlock occurs because every process is waiting for a resource that is being held by another process, but none will be released without intervention.

(figure 5.9)

Second scenario. The system (a) becomes deadlocked (b) when P3 requests R1. Notice the circular wait.

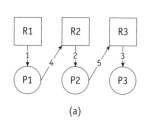
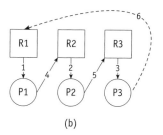

(a) (b)

Scenario 3

The third scenario is shown in Table 5.3. As shown in Figure 5.10, the resources are released before deadlock can occur.

Event	Action
1	P1 requests and is allocated R1.
2	P1 requests and is allocated R2.
3	P2 requests R1.
4	P3 requests and is allocated R3.
5	P1 releases R1, which is allocated to P2.
6	P3 requests R2.
7	P1 releases R2, which is allocated to P3.

(table 5.3)

The third scenario's sequence of events is shown in the directed graph in Figure 5.10.

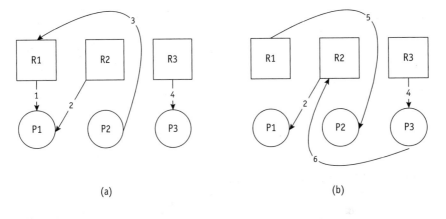

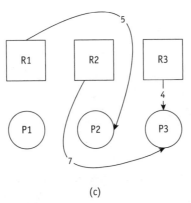

(figure 5.10)

The third scenario. After event 4, the directed graph looks like (a) and P2 is blocked because P1 is holding on to R1. However, event 5 breaks the deadlock and the graph soon looks like (b). Again there is a blocked process, P3, which must wait for the release of R2 in event 7 when the graph looks like (c).

Another Example

The examples presented so far have examined cases in which one or more resources of different types were allocated to a process. However, the graphs can be expanded to include several resources of the same type, such as tape drives, which can be allocated individually or in groups to the same process. These graphs cluster the devices of the same type into one entity, shown in Figure 5.11 as a rectangle, and the arrows show the links between the single resource and the processes using it.

Figure 5.11 gives an example of a cluster with three resources of the same type, such as three disk drives, each allocated to a different process. Although Figure 5.11(a) seems to be stable (no deadlock can occur), this is not the case because if all three processes request one more resource without releasing the one they are using, then deadlock will occur as shown in Figure 5.11(b).

(figure 5.11)

(a): A fully allocated cluster of resources. There are as many lines coming out of it as there are resources, units, in it. The state of (a) is uncertain because a request for another unit by all three processes would create a deadlock as shown in (b).

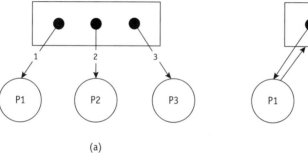

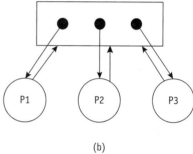

(a)   (b)

Strategies for Handling Deadlocks

As these examples show, the requests and releases are received in an unpredictable order, which makes it very difficult to design a foolproof preventive policy. In general, operating systems use one of three strategies to deal with deadlocks:

• Prevent one of the four conditions from occurring (**prevention**).

• Avoid the deadlock if it becomes probable (**avoidance**).

• Detect the deadlock when it occurs and recover from it gracefully (**detection**).

Prevention

To prevent a deadlock, the operating system must eliminate one of the four necessary conditions, a task complicated by the fact that the same condition can't be eliminated from every resource.

Mutual exclusion is necessary in any computer system because some resources such as memory, CPU, and dedicated devices must be exclusively allocated to one user at a time. In the case of I/O devices, such as printers, the mutual exclusion may be bypassed by spooling, which allows the output from many jobs to be stored in separate temporary spool files at the same time, and each complete output file is then selected for printing when the device is ready. However, we may be trading one type of deadlock (Case 3: Deadlocks in Dedicated Device Allocation) for another (Case 5: Deadlocks in Spooling).

Resource holding, where a job holds on to one resource while waiting for another one that's not yet available, could be sidestepped by forcing each job to request, at creation time, every resource it will need to run to completion. For example, if every job in a batch system is given as much memory as it needs, then the number of active jobs will be dictated by how many can fit in memory—a policy that would significantly decrease the degree of multiprogramming. In addition, peripheral devices would be idle because they would be allocated to a job even though they wouldn't be used all the time. As we've said before, this was used successfully in batch environments although it reduced the effective use of resources and restricted the amount of multiprogramming. But it doesn't work as well in interactive systems.

No preemption could be bypassed by allowing the operating system to deallocate resources from jobs. This can be done if the state of the job can be easily saved and restored, as when a job is preempted in a round robin environment or a page is swapped to secondary storage in a virtual memory system. On the other hand, preemption of a dedicated I/O device (printer, plotter, tape drive, and so on), or of files during the modification process, can require some extremely unpleasant recovery tasks.

Circular wait can be bypassed if the operating system prevents the formation of a circle. One such solution was proposed by Havender and is based on a numbering system for the resources such as: printer = 1, disk = 2, tape = 3, plotter = 4, and so on. The system forces each job to request its resources in ascending order: any "number one" devices required by the job would be requested first; any "number two" devices would be requested next; and so on. So if a job needed a printer and then a plotter, it would request them in this order: printer (#1) first and then the plotter (#4). If the job required the plotter first and then the printer, it would still request the printer first (which is a #1) even though it wouldn't be used right away. A job could request a printer (#1) and then a disk (#2) and then a tape (#3); but if it needed another printer (#1) late in its processing, it would still have to anticipate that need when it requested the first one, and before it requested the disk.

This scheme of "hierarchical ordering" removes the possibility of a circular wait and therefore guarantees the removal of deadlocks. It doesn't require that jobs state their maximum needs in advance, but it does require that the jobs anticipate the order in which they will request resources. From the perspective of a system designer, one of the difficulties of this scheme is discovering the best order for the resources so that the needs of the majority of the users are satisfied. Another difficulty is that of assigning a ranking to nonphysical resources such as files or locked database records where there is no basis for assigning a higher number to one over another.

Avoidance

Even if the operating system can't remove one of the conditions for deadlock, it can avoid one if the system knows ahead of time the sequence of requests associated with each of the active processes. As was illustrated in the graphs presented in Figure 5.7 through Figure 5.11, there exists at least one allocation of resources sequence that will allow jobs to continue without becoming deadlocked.

One such algorithm was proposed by Dijkstra in 1965 to regulate resource allocation to avoid deadlocks. The Banker's Algorithm is based on a bank with a fixed amount of capital that operates on the following principles:

• No customer will be granted a loan exceeding the bank's total capital.

• All customers will be given a maximum credit limit when opening an account.

• No customer will be allowed to borrow over the limit.

• The sum of all loans won't exceed the bank's total capital.

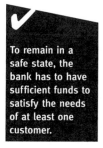

To remain in a safe state, the bank has to have sufficient funds to satisfy the needs of at least one customer.

Under these conditions, the bank isn't required to have on hand the total of all maximum lending quotas before it can open up for business (we'll assume the bank will always have the same fixed total and we'll disregard interest charged on loans). For our example, the bank has a total capital fund of $10,000 and has three customers, C1, C2, and C3, who have maximum credit limits of $4,000, $5,000, and $8,000, respectively. Table 5.4 illustrates the state of affairs of the bank after some loans have been granted to C2 and C3. This is called a **safe state** because the bank still has enough money left to satisfy the maximum requests of C1, C2, or C3.

(table 5.4)

The bank started with $10,000 and has remaining capital of $4,000 after these loans. Therefore, it's in a "safe state."

Customer	Loan Amount	Maximum Credit	Remaining Credit
C1	0	4,000	4,000
C2	2,000	5,000	3,000
C3	4,000	8,000	4,000

Total loaned: $6,000

Total capital fund: $10,000

A few weeks later after more loans have been made, and some have been repaid, the bank is in the **unsafe state** represented in Table 5.5.

Customer	Loan Amount	Maximum Credit	Remaining Credit
C1	2,000	4,000	2,000
C2	3,000	5,000	2,000
C3	4,000	8,000	4,000

Total loaned: $9,000

Total capital fund: $10,000

(table 5.5)

The bank only has remaining capital of $1,000 after these loans and therefore is in an "unsafe state."

This is an unsafe state because with only $1,000 left, the bank can't satisfy anyone's maximum request; and if the bank lent the $1,000 to anyone, then it would be deadlocked (it can't make a loan). An unsafe state doesn't necessarily lead to deadlock, but it does indicate that the system is an excellent candidate for one. After all, none of the customers is required to request the maximum, but the bank doesn't know the exact amount that will eventually be requested; and as long as the bank's capital is less than the maximum amount available for individual loans, it can't guarantee that it will be able to fill every loan request.

If we substitute jobs for customers and dedicated devices for dollars, we can apply the same banking principles to an operating system. In this example the system has 10 devices.

Table 5.6 shows our system in a safe state and Table 5.7 depicts the same system in an unsafe state. As before, a safe state is one in which at least one job can finish because there are enough available resources to satisfy its maximum needs. Then, using the resources released by the finished job, the maximum needs of another job can be filled and that job can be finished, and so on until all jobs are done.

Job No.	Devices Allocated	Maximum Required	Remaining Needs
1	0	4	4
2	2	5	3
3	4	8	4

Total number of devices allocated: 6

Total number of devices in system: 10

(table 5.6)

Resource assignments after initial allocations. A safe state: Six devices are allocated and four units are still available.

(table 5.7)	Job No.	Devices Allocated	Maximum Required	Remaining Needs
	1	2	4	2
	2	3	5	2
	3	4	8	4

Resource assignments after later allocations. An unsafe state: Only one unit is available but every job requires at least two to complete its execution.

Total number of devices allocated: 9

Total number of devices in system: 10

The operating system must be sure never to satisfy a request that moves it from a safe state to an unsafe one. Therefore, as users' requests are satisfied, the operating system must identify the job with the smallest number of remaining resources and make sure that the number of available resources is always equal to, or greater than, the number needed for this job to run to completion. Requests that would place the safe state in jeopardy must be blocked by the operating system until they can be safely accommodated.

If this elegant solution is expanded to work with several classes of resources, the system sets up a "resource assignment table" for each type of resource and tracks each table to keep the system in a safe state.

If the system is always kept in a safe state, all requests will eventually be satisfied and a deadlock will be avoided.

Although the Banker's Algorithm has been used to avoid deadlocks in systems with a few resources, it isn't always practical for most systems for several reasons:

• As they enter the system, jobs must predict the maximum number of resources needed. As we've said before, this isn't practical in interactive systems.

• The number of total resources for each class must remain constant. If a device breaks and becomes suddenly unavailable, the algorithm won't work (the system may already be in an unsafe state).

• The number of jobs must remain fixed, something that isn't possible in interactive systems where the number of active jobs is constantly changing.

• The overhead cost incurred by running the avoidance algorithm can be quite high when there are many active jobs and many devices because it has to be invoked for every request.

• Resources aren't well utilized because the algorithm assumes the worst case and, as a result, keeps vital resources unavailable to guard against unsafe states.

• Scheduling suffers as a result of the poor utilization and jobs are kept waiting for resource allocation. A steady stream of jobs asking for a few resources can cause the indefinite postponement of a more complex job requiring many resources.

Detection

The directed graphs presented earlier in this chapter showed how the existence of a circular wait indicated a deadlock, so it's reasonable to conclude that deadlocks can be detected by building directed resource graphs and looking for cycles. Unlike the avoidance algorithm, which must be performed every time there is a request, the algorithm used to detect circularity can be executed whenever it is appropriate: every hour, once a day, only when the operator notices that throughput has deteriorated, or when an angry user complains.

The detection algorithm can be explained by using directed resource graphs and "reducing" them. Begin with a system that is in use, as shown in Figure 5.12(a). The steps to reduce a graph are these:

1. Find a process that is currently using a resource and *not waiting* for one. This process can be removed from the graph (by disconnecting the link tying the resource to the process, such as P3 in Figure 5.12(b)), and the resource can be returned to the "available list." This is possible because the process would eventually finish and return the resource.

2. Find a process that's waiting only for resource classes that aren't fully allocated (such as P2 in Figure 5.12(c)). This process isn't contributing to deadlock since it would eventually get the resource it's waiting for, finish its work, and return the resource to the "available list" as shown in Figure 5.12(c)."

3. Go back to step 1 and continue with steps 1 and 2 until all lines connecting resources to processes have been removed, eventually reaching the stage shown in Figure 5.12(d).

If there are any lines left, this indicates that the request of the process in question can't be satisfied and that a deadlock exists. Figure 5.12 illustrates a system in which three processes—P1, P2, and P3—and three resources—R1, R2, and R3—aren't deadlocked.

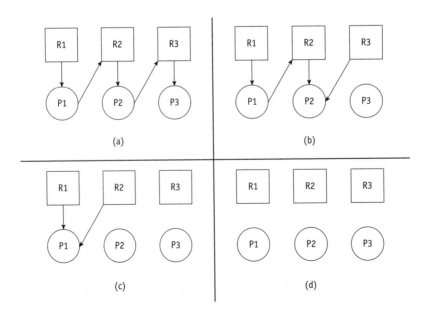

(figure 5.12)

This system is deadlock-free because the graph can be completely reduced, as shown in (d).

Figure 5.12 shows the stages of a graph reduction from (a), the original state. In (b), the link between P3 and R3 can be removed because P3 isn't waiting for any other resources to finish, so R3 is released and allocated to P2 (step 1). In (c), the links between P2 and R3 and between P2 and R2 can be removed because P2 has all of its requested resources and can run to completion—and then R2 can be allocated to P1. Finally, in (d), the links between P1 and R2 and between P1 and R1 can be removed because P1 has all of its requested resources and can finish successfully. Therefore, the graph is completely resolved. However, Figure 5.13 shows a very similar situation that is deadlocked because of a key difference: P2 is linked to R1.

(figure 5.13)

Even after this graph (a) is reduced as much as possible (by removing the request from P3), it is still deadlocked (b).

(a) (b)

The deadlocked system in Figure 5.13 can't be reduced. In (a), the link between P3 and R3 can be removed because P3 isn't waiting for any other resource, so R3 is released and allocated to P2. But in (b), P2 has only two of the three resources it needs to finish and it is waiting for R1. But R1 can't be released by P1 because P1 is waiting for R2, which is held by P2; moreover, P1 can't finish because it is waiting for P2 to finish (and release R2), and P2 can't finish because it's waiting for R1. This is a circular wait.

Recovery

Once a deadlock has been detected, it must be untangled and the system returned to normal as quickly as possible. There are several **recovery** algorithms, but they all have one feature in common: They all require at least one **victim**, an expendable job, which, when removed from the deadlock, will free the system. Unfortunately for the victim, removal generally requires that the job be restarted from the beginning or from a convenient midpoint.

The first and simplest recovery method, and the most drastic, is to terminate every job that's active in the system and restart them from the beginning.

The second method is to terminate only the jobs involved in the deadlock and ask their users to resubmit them.

The third method is to identify which jobs are involved in the deadlock and terminate them one at a time, checking to see if the deadlock is eliminated after each removal, until the deadlock has been resolved. Once the system is freed, the remaining jobs are allowed to complete their processing and later the halted jobs are started again from the beginning.

The fourth method can be put into effect only if the job keeps a record, a snapshot, of its progress so it can be interrupted and then continued without starting again from the beginning of its execution. The snapshot is like the landing in our staircase example: Instead of forcing the deadlocked stair climbers to return to the bottom of the stairs, they need to retreat only to the nearest landing and wait until the others have passed. Then the climb can be resumed. In general, this method is favored for long-running jobs to help them make a speedy recovery.

Until now we've offered solutions involving the jobs caught in the deadlock. The next two methods concentrate on the nondeadlocked jobs and the resources they hold. One of them, the fifth method in our list, selects a nondeadlocked job, preempts the resources it's holding, and allocates them to a deadlocked process so it can resume execution, thus breaking the deadlock. The sixth method stops new jobs from entering the system, which allows the nondeadlocked jobs to run to completion so they'll release their resources. Eventually, with fewer jobs in the system, competition for resources is curtailed so the deadlocked processes get the resources they need to run to completion. This method is the only one listed here that doesn't rely on a victim, and it's not guaranteed to work unless the number of available resources surpasses that needed by at least one of the deadlocked jobs to run (this is possible with multiple resources).

Several factors must be considered to select the victim that will have the least-negative effect on the system. The most common are:
- The priority of the job under consideration—high-priority jobs are usually untouched
- CPU time used by the job—jobs close to completion are usually left alone
- The number of other jobs that would be affected if this job were selected as the victim

In addition, programs working with databases also deserve special treatment because a database that is only partially updated is only partially correct. Therefore, jobs that are modifying data shouldn't be selected for termination because the consistency and validity of the database would be jeopardized. Fortunately, designers of many database systems have included sophisticated recovery mechanisms so damage to the database is minimized if a transaction is interrupted or terminated before completion.

Starvation

So far we have concentrated on deadlocks, the result of liberal allocation of resources. At the opposite end is starvation, the result of conservative allocation of resources where a single job is prevented from execution because it's kept waiting for resources that never become available. To illustrate this, the case of the dining philosophers problem was introduced by Dijkstra in 1968.

Five philosophers are sitting at a round table, each deep in thought, and in the center lies a bowl of spaghetti that is accessible to everyone. There are forks on the table—one between each philosopher, as illustrated in Figure 5.14. Local custom dictates that each philosopher must use two forks, the forks on either side of the plate, to eat the spaghetti, but there are only five forks—not the 10 it would require for all five thinkers to eat at once—and that's unfortunate for Philosopher 2.

When they sit down to dinner, Philosopher 1 (P1) is the first to take the two forks (F1 and F5) on either side of the plate and begins to eat. Inspired by his colleague,

(figure 5.14)

The dining philosophers' table, before the meal begins.

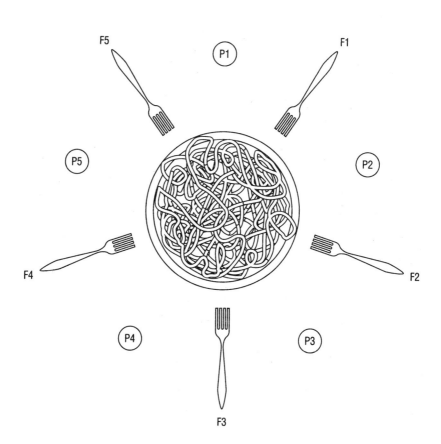

Philosopher 3 (P3) does likewise, using F2 and F3. Now Philosopher 2 (P2) decides to begin the meal but is unable to start because no forks are available: F1 has been allocated to P1, and F2 has been allocated to P3, and the only remaining fork can be used only by P4 or P5. So (P2) must wait.

Soon, P3 finishes eating, puts down his two forks, and resumes his pondering. Should the fork beside him (F2), that's now free, be allocated to the hungry philosopher (P2)? Although it's tempting, such a move would be a bad precedent because if the philosophers are allowed to tie up resources with only the hope that the other required resource will become available, the dinner could easily slip into an unsafe state; it would be only a matter of time before each philosopher held a single fork—and nobody could eat. So the resources are allocated to the philosophers only when both forks are available at the same time. The status of the "system" is illustrated in Figure 5.15.

P4 and P5 are quietly thinking and P1 is still eating when P3 (who should be full) decides to eat some more; and because the resources are free, he is able to take F2 and F3 once again. Soon thereafter, P1 finishes and releases F1 and F5, but P2 is still not

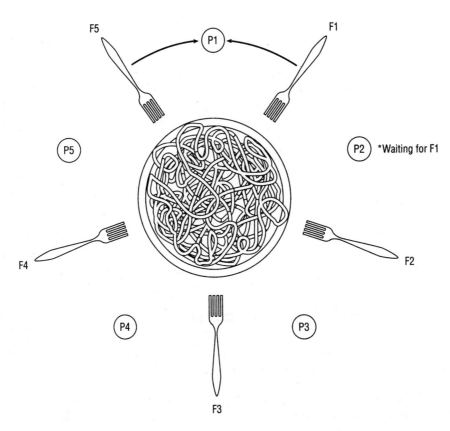

(figure 5.15)

Each philosopher must have both forks to begin eating, the one on the right and the one on the left. Unless the resources, the forks, are allocated fairly, some philosophers may starve.

able to eat because F2 is now allocated. This scenario could continue forever; and as long as P1 and P3 alternate their use of the available resources, P2 must wait. P1 and P3 can eat any time they wish while P2 starves—only inches from nourishment.

In a computer environment, the resources are like forks and the competing processes are like dining philosophers. If the resource manager doesn't watch for starving processes and jobs, and plan for their eventual completion, they could remain in the system forever waiting for the right combination of resources.

To address this problem, an algorithm designed to detect starving jobs can be implemented, which tracks how long each job has been waiting for resources (this is the same as aging, described in Chapter 4). Once starvation has been detected, the system can block new jobs until the starving jobs have been satisfied. This algorithm must be monitored closely: If monitoring is done too often, then new jobs will be blocked too frequently and throughput will be diminished. If it's not done often enough, then starving jobs will remain in the system for an unacceptably long period of time.

Conclusion

Every operating system must dynamically allocate a limited number of resources while avoiding the two extremes of deadlock and starvation.

In this chapter we discussed several methods of dealing with livelocks and deadlocks: prevention, avoidance, and detection and recovery. Deadlocks can be prevented by not allowing the four conditions of a deadlock to occur in the system at the same time. By eliminating at least one of the four conditions (mutual exclusion, resource holding, no preemption, and circular wait), the system can be kept deadlock-free. As we've seen, the disadvantage of a preventive policy is that each of these conditions is vital to different parts of the system at least some of the time, so prevention algorithms are complex and to routinely execute them involves high overhead.

Deadlocks can be avoided by clearly identifying safe states and unsafe states and requiring the system to keep enough resources in reserve to guarantee that all jobs active in the system can run to completion. The disadvantage of an avoidance policy is that the system's resources aren't allocated to their fullest potential.

If a system doesn't support prevention or avoidance, then it must be prepared to detect and recover from the deadlocks that occur. Unfortunately, this option usually relies on the selection of at least one "victim"—a job that must be terminated before it finishes execution and restarted from the beginning.

In the next chapter, we'll look at problems related to the synchronization of processes in a multiprocessing environment.

Key Terms

avoidance: the dynamic strategy of deadlock avoidance that attempts to ensure that resources are never allocated in such a way as to place a system in an unsafe state.

circular wait: one of four conditions for deadlock through which each process involved is waiting for a resource being held by another; each process is blocked and can't continue, resulting in deadlock.

deadlock: a problem occurring when the resources needed by some jobs to finish execution are held by other jobs, which, in turn, are waiting for other resources to become available. Also called *deadly embrace.*

detection: the process of examining the state of an operating system to determine whether a deadlock exists.

directed graphs: a graphic model representing various states of resource allocations.

livelock: a locked system whereby two (or more) processes continually block the forward progress of the others without making any forward progress themselves. It is similar to a deadlock except that neither process is blocked or obviously waiting; both are in a continuous state of change.

locking: a technique used to guarantee the integrity of the data in a database through which the user locks out all other users while working with the database.

mutual exclusion: one of four conditions for deadlock in which only one process is allowed to have access to a resource.

no preemption: one of four conditions for deadlock in which a process is allowed to hold on to resources while it is waiting for other resources to finish execution.

prevention: a design strategy for an operating system where resources are managed in such a way that some of the necessary conditions for deadlock do not hold.

process synchronization: (1) the need for algorithms to resolve conflicts between processors in a multiprocessing environment; or (2) the need to ensure that events occur in the proper order even if they are carried out by several processes.

race: a synchronization problem between two processes vying for the same resource.

recovery: the steps that must be taken, when deadlock is detected, by breaking the circle of waiting processes.

resource holding: one of four conditions for deadlock in which each process refuses to relinquish the resources it holds until its execution is completed even though it isn't using them because it's waiting for other resources.

safe state: the situation in which the system has enough available resources to guarantee the completion of at least one job running on the system.

spooling: a technique developed to speed I/O by collecting in a disk file either input received from slow input devices or output going to slow output devices, such as printers.

starvation: the result of conservative allocation of resources in which a single job is prevented from execution because it's kept waiting for resources that never become available.

unsafe state: a situation in which the system has too few available resources to guarantee the completion of at least one job running on the system. It can lead to deadlock.

victim: an expendable job that is selected for removal from a deadlocked system to provide more resources to the waiting jobs and resolve the deadlock.

Interesting Searches

- False Deadlock Detection
- Starvation and Livelock Detection
- Distributed Deadlock Detection
- Deadlock Resolution Algorithms
- Operating System Freeze

Exercises

Research Topics

A. In Chapter 3 we discussed the problem of thrashing. Research current literature to investigate the role of deadlock and any resulting thrashing. Discuss how you would begin to quantify the cost to the system (in terms of throughput and performance) of deadlock-caused thrashing. Cite your sources.

B. Research the problem of livelock in a networked environment. Describe how it differs from deadlock and give an example of the problem. Identify at least two different methods the operating system could use to detect and resolve livelock. Cite your sources.

Exercises

1. Give a computer system example (different from the one described in this chapter) of a race that would yield a different result depending on the order of processing.

2. Give at least two "real life" examples (not related to a computer system environment) of each of these concepts: deadlock, starvation, and race. Describe how the deadlocks can be resolved.

3. Select one example of deadlock from Exercise 2 and identify which elements of the deadlock represent the four necessary conditions for all deadlocks.

4. Describe the fate of the "victim" in deadlock resolution. Describe the actions required to complete the victim's tasks.

5. Using the narrow staircase example from the beginning of this chapter, create a list of actions or tasks that would allow people to use the staircase without causing deadlock or starvation.

6. Figure 5.16 shows a tunnel going through a mountain and two streets parallel to each other—one at each end of the tunnel. Traffic lights are located at each end of the tunnel to control the cross flow of traffic through each intersection. Based on this figure, answer the following questions:

   a. How can deadlock occur and under what circumstances?

   b. How can deadlock be detected?

   c. Give a solution to prevent deadlock and starvation.

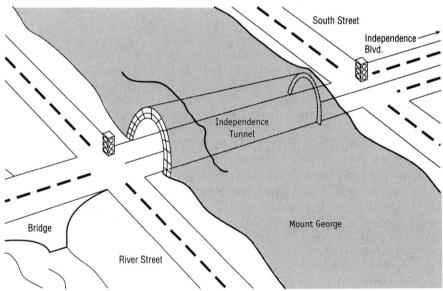

(Figure 5.16)

Traffic flow diagram for Exercise 6.

7. Consider the directed resource graph shown in Figure 5.17 and answer the following questions:

   a. Are there any blocked processes?

   b. Is this system deadlocked?

   c. What is the resulting graph after reduction by P1?

   d. What is the resulting graph after reduction by P2?

e. If Both P1 and P2 have requested R2, answer these questions:

1. What is the status of the system if the request by P2 is granted before that of P1?

2. What is the status of the system if the request by P1 is granted before that of P2?

(Figure 5.17)

Directed resource graph for Exercise 7.

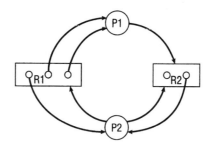

8. Consider the directed resource graph shown in Figure 5.18, and answer the following questions:

a. Identify all of the deadlocked processes.

b. Can the directed graph be reduced, partially or totally?

c. Can the deadlock be resolved without selecting a victim?

d. Which requests by the three processes for resources from R2 would you satisfy to *minimize* the number of processes involved in the deadlock?

e. Conversely, which requests by the three processes for resources from R2 would you satisfy to *maximize* the number of processes involved in deadlock?

(Figure 5.18)

Directed resource graph for Exercise 8.

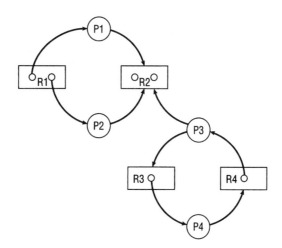

9. Consider an archival system with 13 dedicated devices. All jobs currently running on this system require a maximum of five drives to complete but they each run for long periods of time with just four drives and request the fifth one only at the very end of the run. Assume that the job stream is endless.

a. Suppose your operating system supports a very conservative device allocation policy so that no job will be started unless all the required drives have been allocated to it for the entire duration of its run.

1. What is the maximum number of jobs that can be active at once? Explain your answer.

2. What are the minimum and maximum number of tape drives that may be idle as a result of this policy? Explain your answer.

b. Suppose your operating system supports the Banker's Algorithm.

1. What is the maximum number of jobs that can be in progress at once? Explain your answer.

2. What are the minimum and maximum number of drives that may be idle as a result of this policy? Explain your answer.

10-12. For the three systems described below, given that all of the devices are of the same type, and using the definitions presented in the discussion of the Banker's Algorithm, answer these questions:

a. Determine the remaining needs for each job in each system.

b. Determine whether each system is safe or unsafe.

c. If the system is in a safe state, list the sequence of requests and releases that will make it possible for all processes to run to completion.

d. If the system is in an unsafe state, show how it's possible for deadlock to occur.

10. System A has 12 devices; only one is available.

Job No.	Devices Allocated	Maximum Required	Remaining Needs
1	5	6	
2	4	7	
3	2	6	
4	0	2	

11. System B has 14 devices; only two are available.

Job No.	Devices Allocated	Maximum Required	Remaining Needs
1	5	8	
2	3	9	
3	4	8	

12. System C has 12 devices; only two are available.

Job No.	Devices Allocated	Maximum Required	Remaining Needs
1	5	8	
2	4	6	
3	1	4	

Advanced Exercises

13. Suppose you are an operating system designer and have been approached by the system administrator to help solve the recurring deadlock problem in your installation's spooling system. What features might you incorporate into the operating system so that deadlocks in the spooling system can be resolved without losing the work (the system processing) already performed by the deadlocked processes?

14. As we discussed in this chapter, a system that is in an unsafe state is not necessarily deadlocked. Explain why this is true. Give an example of such a system (in an unsafe state) and describe how all the processes could be completed without causing deadlock to occur.

15. Explain how you would design and implement a mechanism to allow the operating system to detect which, if any, processes are starving.

16. Given the four primary types of resources—CPU, memory, storage devices, and files—select for each one the most suitable technique described in this chapter to fight deadlock and briefly explain why it is your choice.

17. State the limitations imposed on programs (and on systems) that have to follow a hierarchical ordering of resources, such as disks, printers, and files.

18. Consider a banking system with 10 accounts. Funds may be transferred between two of those accounts by following these steps:

    lock A(i);   lock A(j);
    update A(i);   update A(j);
    unlock A(i);   unlock A(j);

    a. Can this system become deadlocked? If yes, show how. If no, explain why not.

    b. Could the numbering request policy (presented in the chapter discussion about detection) be implemented to prevent deadlock if the number of accounts is dynamic? Explain why or why not.

Chapter 6

Concurrent Processes

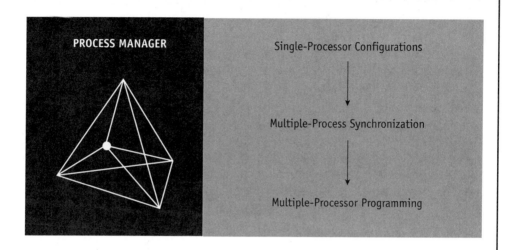

PROCESS MANAGER

Single-Processor Configurations

↓

Multiple-Process Synchronization

↓

Multiple-Processor Programming

Learning Objectives

After completing this chapter, you should be able to describe:

- The critical difference between processes and processors, and their connection
- The differences among common configurations of multiprocessing systems
- The basic concepts of multi-core processor technology
- The significance of a critical region in process synchronization
- The essential ideas behind process synchronization software
- The need for process cooperation when several processors work together
- The similarities and differences between processes and threads
- How processors cooperate when executing a job, process, or thread
- The significance of concurrent programming languages and their applications

In Chapters 4 and 5, we described multiprogramming systems that use only one CPU, one processor, which is shared by several jobs or processes. This is called *multiprogramming*. In this chapter we look at another common situation, *multiprocessing* systems, which have several processors working together in several distinctly different configurations.

Multiprocessing systems include single computers with multiple cores as well as linked computing systems with only one processor each to share processing among them.

What Is Parallel Processing?

Parallel processing, one form of **multiprocessing**, is a situation in which two or more processors operate in unison. That means two or more CPUs are executing instructions simultaneously. In multiprocessing systems, the Processor Manager has to coordinate the activity of each processor, as well as synchronize cooperative interaction among the CPUs.

There are two primary benefits to parallel processing systems: increased reliability and faster processing.

The reliability stems from the availability of more than one CPU: If one processor fails, then the others can continue to operate and absorb the load. This isn't simple to do; the system must be carefully designed so that, first, the failing processor can inform other processors to take over and, second, the operating system can restructure its resource allocation strategies so the remaining processors don't become overloaded.

The increased processing speed is often achieved because sometimes instructions can be processed in parallel, two or more at a time, in one of several ways. Some systems allocate a CPU to each program or job. Others allocate a CPU to each working set or parts of it. Still others subdivide individual instructions so that each subdivision can be processed simultaneously (which is called concurrent programming).

Increased flexibility brings increased complexity, however, and two major challenges remain: how to connect the processors into configurations and how to orchestrate their interaction, which applies to multiple interacting processes as well. (It might help if you think of each process as being run on a separate processor.)

The complexities of the Processor Manager's task when dealing with multiple processors or multiple processes are easily illustrated with an example: You're late for an early afternoon appointment and you're in danger of missing lunch, so you get in line for the drive-through window of the local fast-food shop. When you place your order, the order clerk confirms your request, tells you how much it will cost, and asks you to drive to the pickup window where a cashier collects your money and hands over your order. All's well and once again you're on your way—driving and thriving. You just witnessed a well-synchronized multiprocessing system. Although you came in contact with just two processors—the order clerk and the cashier—there were at least two other processors behind the scenes who cooperated to make the system work—the cook and the bagger.

A fast-food lunch spot is similar to the six-step information retrieval system below. It is described in a different way in Table 6.1.

a) Processor 1 (the order clerk) accepts the query, checks for errors, and passes the request on to Processor 2 (the bagger).

b) Processor 2 (the bagger) searches the database for the required information (the hamburger).

c) Processor 3 (the cook) retrieves the data from the database (the meat to cook for the hamburger) if it's kept off-line in secondary storage.

d) Once the data is gathered (the hamburger is cooked), it's placed where Processor 2 can get it (in the hamburger bin).

e) Processor 2 (the bagger) passes it on to Processor 4 (the cashier).

f) Processor 4 (the cashier) routes the response (your order) back to the originator of the request—you.

	Originator	Action	Receiver
(table 6.1) *The six steps of the fast-food lunch stop.*	Processor 1 (the order clerk)	Accepts the query, checks for errors, and passes the request on to =>	Processor 2 (the bagger)
	Processor 2 (the bagger)	Searches the database for the required information (the hamburger)	
	Processor 3 (the cook)	Retrieves the data from the database (the meat to cook for the hamburger) if it's kept off-line in secondary storage	
	Processor 3 (the cook)	Once the data is gathered (the hamburger is cooked), it's placed where the receiver => can get it (in the hamburger bin)	Processor 2 (the bagger)
	Processor 2 (the bagger)	Passes it on to =>	Processor 4 (the cashier)
	Processor 4 (the cashier)	Routes the response (your order) back to the originator of the request =>	You

Synchronization is the key to the system's success because many things can go wrong in a multiprocessing system. For example, what if the communications system broke down and you couldn't speak with the order clerk? What if the cook produced hamburgers at full speed all day, even during slow periods? What would happen to the extra hamburgers? What if the cook became badly burned and couldn't cook anymore? What would the bagger do if there were no hamburgers? What if the cashier decided to take your money but didn't give you any food? Obviously, the system can't work properly unless every processor communicates and cooperates with every other processor.

Evolution of Multiprocessors

Multiprocessing can take place at several different levels, each of which requires a different frequency of synchronization, as shown in Table 6.2. Notice that at the job level, multiprocessing is fairly benign. It's as if each job is running on its own workstation with shared system resources. On the other hand, when multiprocessing takes place at the thread level, a high degree of synchronization is required to disassemble each process, perform the thread's instructions, and then correctly reassemble the process. This may require additional work by the programmer, as we'll see later in this chapter.

✔

One single-core CPU chip in 2003 placed about 10 million transistors into one square millimeter, roughly the size of the tip of a ball point pen.

Parallelism Level	Process Assignments	Synchronization Required
Job Level	Each job has its own processor and all processes and threads are run by that same processor.	No explicit synchronization required.
Process Level	Unrelated processes, regardless of job, are assigned to any available processor.	Moderate amount of synchronization required to track processes.
Thread Level	Threads are assigned to available processors.	High degree of synchronization required, often requiring explicit instructions from the programmer.

(table 6.2)

Levels of parallelism and the required synchronization among processors.

Introduction to Multi-Core Processors

Multi-core processors have several processors on a single chip. As processors became smaller in size (as predicted by Moore's Law) and faster in processing speed, CPU designers began to use nanometer-sized transistors. Each transistor switches between two positions—0 and 1—as the computer conducts its binary arithmetic at increasingly fast speeds. However, as transistors reached nano-sized dimensions and the space between transistors became ever closer, the quantum physics of electrons got in the way.

In a nutshell, here's the problem. When transistors are placed extremely close together, electrons have the ability to spontaneously tunnel, at random, from one transistor to another, causing a tiny but measurable amount of current to leak. The smaller the transistor, the more significant the leak. (When an electron does this "tunneling," it seems to spontaneously disappear from one transistor and appear in another nearby transistor. It's as if a Star Trek voyager asked the electron to be "beamed aboard" the second transistor.)

A second problem was the heat generated by the chip. As processors became faster, the heat also climbed and became increasingly difficult to disperse. These heat and tunneling issues threatened to limit the ability of chip designers to make processors ever smaller.

One solution was to create a single chip (one piece of silicon) with two "processor cores" in the same amount of space. With this arrangement, two sets of calculations can take place at the same time. The two cores on the chip generate less heat than a single core of the same size and tunneling is reduced; however, the two cores each run more slowly than the single core chip. Therefore, to get improved performance from a dual-core chip, the software has to be structured to take advantage of the double calculation capability of the new chip design. Building on their success with two-core chips, designers have created multi-core processors with predictions, as of this writing, that 80 or more cores will be placed on a single chip, as shown in Chapter 1.

Does this hardware innovation affect the operating system? Yes, because it must manage multiple processors, multiple RAMs, and the processing of many tasks at once. However, a dual-core chip is not always faster than a single-core chip. It depends on the tasks being performed and whether they're multi-threaded or sequential.

Software that requires sequential calculations will run slower on a dual-core chip than on a single-core chip.

Typical Multiprocessing Configurations

Much depends on how the multiple processors are configured within the system. Three typical configurations are: master/slave, loosely coupled, and symmetric.

Master/Slave Configuration

The **master/slave** configuration is an asymmetric multiprocessing system. Think of it as a single-processor system with additional slave processors, each of which is managed by the primary master processor as shown in Figure 6.1.

The master processor is responsible for managing the entire system—all files, devices, memory, and processors. Therefore, it maintains the status of all processes in the system, performs storage management activities, schedules the work for the other processors, and executes all control programs. This configuration is well suited for computing environments in which processing time is divided between front-end and back-end processors; in these cases, the front-end processor takes care of the interactive users and quick jobs, and the back-end processor takes care of those with long jobs using the batch mode.

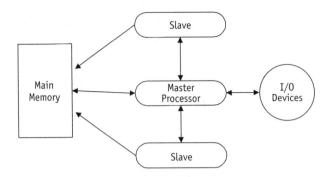

(figure 6.1)

In a master/slave multiprocessing configuration, slave processors can access main memory directly but they must send all I/O requests through the master processor.

The primary advantage of this configuration is its simplicity. However, it has three serious disadvantages:

• Its reliability is no higher than for a single-processor system because if the master processor fails, the entire system fails.

• It can lead to poor use of resources because if a slave processor should become free while the master processor is busy, the slave must wait until the master becomes free and can assign more work to it.

• It increases the number of interrupts because all slave processors must interrupt the master processor every time they need operating system intervention, such as for I/O requests. This creates long queues at the master processor level when there are many processors and many interrupts.

Loosely Coupled Configuration

The **loosely coupled configuration** features several complete computer systems, each with its own memory, I/O devices, CPU, and operating system, as shown in Figure 6.2. This configuration is called loosely coupled because each processor controls its own resources—its own files, access to memory, and its own I/O devices—and that means that each processor maintains its own commands and I/O management tables. The only

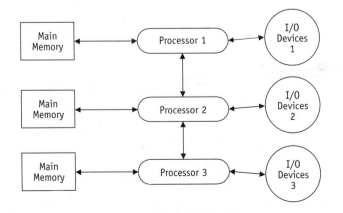

(figure 6.2)

In a loosely coupled multiprocessing configuration, each processor has its own dedicated resources.

difference between a loosely coupled multiprocessing system and a collection of independent single-processing systems is that each processor can communicate and cooperate with the others.

When a job arrives for the first time, it's assigned to one processor. Once allocated, the job remains with the same processor until it's finished. Therefore, each processor must have global tables that indicate to which processor each job has been allocated.

To keep the system well balanced and to ensure the best use of resources, job scheduling is based on several requirements and policies. For example, new jobs might be assigned to the processor with the lightest load or the best combination of output devices available.

This system isn't prone to catastrophic system failures because even when a single processor fails, the others can continue to work independently. However, it can be difficult to detect when a processor has failed.

Symmetric Configuration

The **symmetric configuration** (also called tightly coupled) has four advantages over loosely coupled configuration:

• It's more reliable.

• It uses resources effectively.

• It can balance loads well.

• It can degrade gracefully in the event of a failure.

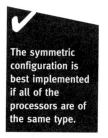

The symmetric configuration is best implemented if all of the processors are of the same type.

However, it is the most difficult configuration to implement because the processes must be well synchronized to avoid the problems of races and deadlocks that we discussed in Chapter 5.

In a symmetric configuration (as depicted in Figure 6.3), processor scheduling is decentralized. A single copy of the operating system and a global table listing each process and its status is stored in a common area of memory so every processor has access to it. Each processor uses the same scheduling algorithm to select which process it will run next.

(figure 6.3)

A symmetric multiprocessing configuration with homogeneous processors. Processes must be carefully synchronized to avoid deadlocks and starvation.

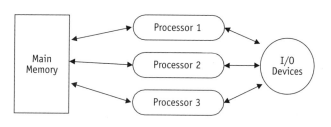

Whenever a process is interrupted, whether because of an I/O request or another type of interrupt, its processor updates the corresponding entry in the process list and finds another process to run. This means that the processors are kept quite busy. But it also means that any given job or task may be executed by several different processors during its run time. And because each processor has access to all I/O devices and can reference any storage unit, there are more conflicts as several processors try to access the same resource at the same time.

This presents the obvious need for algorithms to resolve conflicts between processors—that's called **process synchronization**.

Process Synchronization Software

The success of process synchronization hinges on the capability of the operating system to make a resource unavailable to other processes while it is being used by one of them. These "resources" can include printers and other I/O devices, a location in storage, or a data file. In essence, the used resource must be locked away from other processes until it is released. Only when it is released is a waiting process allowed to use the resource. This is where synchronization is critical. A mistake could leave a job waiting indefinitely (starvation) or, if it's a key resource, cause a deadlock.

It is the same thing that can happen in a crowded ice cream shop. Customers take a number to be served. The numbers on the wall are changed by the clerks who pull a chain to increment them as they attend to each customer. But what happens when there is no synchronization between serving the customers and changing the number? Chaos. This is the case of the missed waiting customer.

Let's say your number is 75. Clerk 1 is waiting on customer 73 and Clerk 2 is waiting on customer 74. The sign on the wall says "Now Serving #74" and you're ready with your order. Clerk 2 finishes with customer 74 and pulls the chain so the sign says "Now Serving #75." But just then the clerk is called to the telephone and leaves the building, never to return (an interrupt). Meanwhile, Clerk 1 pulls the chain and proceeds to wait on #76—and you've missed your turn. If you speak up quickly, you can correct the mistake gracefully; but when it happens in a computer system, the outcome isn't as easily remedied.

Consider the scenario in which Processor 1 and Processor 2 finish with their current jobs at the same time. To run the next job, each processor must:

1. Consult the list of jobs to see which one should be run next.
2. Retrieve the job for execution.
3. Increment the READY list to the next job.
4. Execute it.

Both go to the READY list to select a job. Processor 1 sees that Job 74 is the next job to be run and goes to retrieve it. A moment later, Processor 2 also selects Job 74 and goes to retrieve it. Shortly thereafter, Processor 1, having retrieved Job 74, returns to the READY list and increments it, moving Job 75 to the top. A moment later Processor 2 returns; it has also retrieved Job 74 and is ready to process it, so it increments the READY list and now Job 76 is moved to the top and becomes the next job in line to be processed. Job 75 has become the missed waiting customer and will never be processed, while Job 74 is being processed twice—an unacceptable state of affairs.

There are several other places where this problem can occur: memory and page allocation tables, I/O tables, application databases, and any shared resource.

Obviously, this situation calls for synchronization. Several synchronization mechanisms are available to provide cooperation and communication among processes. The common element in all synchronization schemes is to allow a process to finish work on a critical part of the program before other processes have access to it. This is applicable both to multiprocessors and to two or more processes in a single-processor (time-shared) processing system. It is called a **critical region** because it is a critical section and its execution must be handled as a unit. As we've seen, the processes within a critical region can't be interleaved without threatening the integrity of the operation.

The lock-and-key technique is conceptually the same one that's used to lock databases, as discussed in Chapter 5, so different users can access the same database without causing a deadlock.

Synchronization is sometimes implemented as a lock-and-key arrangement: Before a process can work on a critical region, it must get the key. And once it has the key, all other processes are locked out until it finishes, unlocks the entry to the critical region, and returns the key so that another process can get the key and begin work. This sequence consists of two actions: (1) the process must first see if the key is available and (2) if it is available, the process must pick it up and put it in the lock to make it unavailable to all other processes. For this scheme to work, both actions must be performed in a single machine cycle; otherwise it is conceivable that while the first process is ready to pick up the key, another one would find the key available and prepare to pick up the key—and each could block the other from proceeding any further.

Several locking mechanisms have been developed, including test-and-set, WAIT and SIGNAL, and semaphores.

Test-and-Set

Test-and-set is a single, indivisible machine instruction known simply as **TS** and was introduced by IBM for its multiprocessing System 360/370 computers. In a single machine cycle it tests to see if the key is available and, if it is, sets it to unavailable.

The actual key is a single bit in a storage location that can contain a 0 (if it's free) or a 1 (if busy). We can consider TS to be a function subprogram that has one parameter (the storage location) and returns one value (the condition code: busy/free), with the exception that it takes only one machine cycle.

Therefore, a process (Process 1) would test the condition code using the TS instruction before entering a critical region. If no other process was in this critical region, then Process 1 would be allowed to proceed and the condition code would be changed from 0 to 1. Later, when Process 1 exits the critical region, the condition code is reset to 0 so another process can enter. On the other hand, if Process 1 finds a busy condition code, then it's placed in a waiting loop where it continues to test the condition code and waits until it's free.

Although it's a simple procedure to implement, and it works well for a small number of processes, test-and-set has two major drawbacks. First, when many processes are waiting to enter a critical region, starvation could occur because the processes gain access in an arbitrary fashion. Unless a first-come, first-served policy were set up, some processes could be favored over others. A second drawback is that the waiting processes remain in unproductive, resource-consuming wait loops, requiring context switching. This is known as **busy waiting**—which not only consumes valuable processor time but also relies on the competing processes to test the key, something that is best handled by the operating system or the hardware.

WAIT and SIGNAL

WAIT and SIGNAL is a modification of test-and-set that's designed to remove busy waiting. Two new operations, which are mutually exclusive and become part of the process scheduler's set of operations, are WAIT and SIGNAL.

WAIT is activated when the process encounters a busy condition code. WAIT sets the process's process control block (PCB) to the blocked state and links it to the queue of processes waiting to enter this particular critical region. The Process Scheduler then selects another process for execution. SIGNAL is activated when a process exits the critical region and the condition code is set to "free." It checks the queue of processes waiting to enter this critical region and selects one, setting it to the READY state. Eventually the Process Scheduler will choose this process for running. The addition of the operations WAIT and SIGNAL frees the processes from the busy waiting dilemma and returns control to the operating system, which can then run other jobs while the waiting processes are idle (WAIT).

Semaphores

A **semaphore** is a non-negative integer variable that's used as a binary signal, a flag. One of the most well-known semaphores was the signaling device, shown in Figure 6.4, used by railroads to indicate whether a section of track was clear. When the arm of the semaphore was raised, the track was clear and the train was allowed to proceed. When the arm was lowered, the track was busy and the train had to wait until the arm was raised. It had only two positions, up or down (on or off).

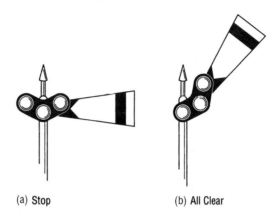

(a) **Stop**   (b) **All Clear**

In an operating system, a semaphore performs a similar function: It signals if and when a resource is free and can be used by a process. Dijkstra (1965) introduced two operations to overcome the process synchronization problem we've discussed. Dijkstra called them P and V, and that's how they're known today. The P stands for the Dutch word *proberen* (to test) and the V stands for *verhogen* (to increment). The P and V operations do just that: They test and increment.

Here's how they work. If we let s be a semaphore variable, then the V operation on s is simply to increment s by 1. The action can be stated as:

$$V(s): s: = s + 1$$

This in turn necessitates a fetch, increment, and store sequence. Like the test-and-set operation, the increment operation must be performed as a single indivisible action to avoid deadlocks. And that means that s cannot be accessed by any other process during the operation.

The operation P on s is to test the value of s and, if it's not 0, to decrement it by 1. The action can be stated as:

$$P(s): \text{If } s > 0 \text{ then } s: = s - 1$$

This involves a test, fetch, decrement, and store sequence. Again this sequence must be performed as an indivisible action in a single machine cycle or be arranged so that the process cannot take action until the operation (test or increment) is finished.

The operations to test or increment are executed by the operating system in response to calls issued by any one process naming a semaphore as parameter (this alleviates the process from having control). If $s = 0$, it means that the critical region is busy and the process calling on the test operation must wait until the operation can be executed and that's not until $s > 0$.

As shown in Table 6.3, P3 is placed in the WAIT state (for the semaphore) on State 4. As also shown in Table 6.3, for States 6 and 8, when a process exits the critical region, the value of s is reset to 1 indicating that the critical region is free. This, in turn, triggers the awakening of one of the blocked processes, its entry into the critical region, and the resetting of s to 0. In State 7, P1 and P2 are not trying to do processing in that critical region and P4 is still blocked.

State Number	Actions Calling Process	Operation	Running in Critical Region	Results Blocked on s	Value of s
0					1
1	P1	test(s)	P1		0
2	P1	increment(s)			1
3	P2	test(s)	P2		0
4	P3	test(s)	P2	P3	0
5	P4	test(s)	P2	P3, P4	0
6	P2	increment(s)	P3	P4	0
7			P3	P4	0
8	P3	increment(s)	P4		0
9	P4	increment(s)			1

(table 6.3)

The sequence of states for four processes calling test and increment (P and V) operations on the binary semaphore s. (Note: The value of the semaphore before the operation is shown on the line preceding the operation. The current value is on the same line.)

After State 5 of Table 6.3, the longest waiting process, P3, was the one selected to enter the critical region, but that isn't necessarily the case unless the system is using a first-in, first-out selection policy. In fact, the choice of which job will be processed next depends on the algorithm used by this portion of the Process Scheduler.

As you can see from Table 6.3, test and increment operations on semaphore s enforce the concept of mutual exclusion, which is necessary to avoid having two operations attempt to execute at the same time. The name traditionally given to this semaphore in the literature is **mutex** and it stands for MUTual EXclusion. So the operations become:

```
test(mutex): if mutex > 0 then mutex: = mutex - 1
increment(mutex): mutex: = mutex + 1
```

In Chapter 5 we talked about the requirement for mutual exclusion when several jobs were trying to access the same shared physical resources. The concept is the same here, but we have several processes trying to access the same shared critical region. The procedure can generalize to semaphores having values greater than 0 and 1.

Thus far we've looked at the problem of mutual exclusion presented by interacting parallel processes using the same shared data at different rates of execution. This can apply to several processes on more than one processor, or interacting (codependent) processes on a single processor. In this case, the concept of a critical region becomes necessary because it ensures that parallel processes will modify shared data only while in the critical region.

In sequential computations mutual exclusion is achieved automatically because each operation is handled in order, one at a time. However, in parallel computations the order of execution can change, so mutual exclusion must be explicitly stated and maintained. In fact, the entire premise of parallel processes hinges on the requirement that all operations on common variables consistently exclude one another over time.

Process Cooperation

There are occasions when several processes work directly together to complete a common task. Two famous examples are the problems of producers and consumers, and of readers and writers. Each case requires both mutual exclusion and synchronization, and each is implemented by using semaphores.

Producers and Consumers

The classic problem of **producers and consumers** is one in which one process produces some data that another process consumes later. Although we'll describe the case with one producer and one consumer, it can be expanded to several pairs of producers and consumers.

Let's return for a moment to the fast-food framework at the beginning of this chapter because the synchronization between two of the processors (the cook and the bagger) represents a significant problem in operating systems. The cook *produces* hamburgers that are sent to the bagger *(consumed)*. Both processors have access to one common area, the hamburger bin, which can hold only a finite number of hamburgers (this is called a buffer area). The bin is a necessary storage area because the speed at which hamburgers are produced is independent from the speed at which they are consumed.

Problems arise at two extremes: when the producer attempts to add to an already full bin (as when the cook tries to put one more hamburger into a full bin) and when the consumer attempts to draw from an empty bin (as when the bagger tries to take a hamburger that hasn't been made yet). In real life, the people watch the bin and if it's empty or too full the problem is recognized and quickly resolved. However, in a computer system such resolution is not so easy.

Consider the case of the prolific CPU. The CPU can generate output data much faster than a printer can print it. Therefore, since this involves a producer and a consumer of two different speeds, we need a buffer where the producer can temporarily store data that can be retrieved by the consumer at a more appropriate speed. Figure 6.5 shows three typical buffer states.

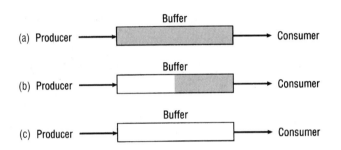

Because the buffer can hold only a finite amount of data, the synchronization process must delay the producer from generating more data when the buffer is full. It must also be prepared to delay the consumer from retrieving data when the buffer is empty. This task can be implemented by two counting semaphores—one to indicate the number of full positions in the buffer and the other to indicate the number of empty positions in the buffer.

A third semaphore, mutex, will ensure mutual exclusion between processes.

Producer	Consumer
produce data	P (full)
P (empty)	P (mutex)
P (mutex)	read data from buffer
write data into buffer	V (mutex)
V (mutex)	V (empty)
V (full)	consume data

(table 6.4)

Definitions of the Producers and Consumers processes.

(table 6.5)

Definitions of the elements in the Producers and Consumers Algorithm.

Variables, Functions	Definitions
full	defined as a semaphore
empty	defined as a semaphore
mutex	defined as a semaphore
n	the maximum number of positions in the buffer
V (x)	x: = x + 1 (x is any variable defined as a semaphore)
P (x)	if x > o then x: = x − 1
mutex = 1	means the process is allowed to enter the critical region
COBEGIN	the delimiter that indicates the *beginning* of concurrent processing
COEND	the delimiter that indicates the *end* of concurrent processing

Given the definitions in Table 6.4 and Table 6.5, the Producers and Consumers Algorithm shown below synchronizes the interaction between the producer and consumer.

Producers and Consumers Algorithm
```
empty:          = n
full:           = 0
mutex:          = 1
COBEGIN
   repeat until no more data PRODUCER
   repeat until buffer is empty CONSUMER
COEND
```

The processes (PRODUCER and CONSUMER) then execute as described. Try the code with n = 3 or try an alternate order of execution to see how it actually works.

The concept of producers and consumers can be extended to buffers that hold records or other data, as well as to other situations in which direct process-to-process communication of messages is required.

Readers and Writers

The problem of **readers and writers** was first formulated by Courtois, Heymans, and Parnas (1971) and arises when two types of processes need to access a shared resource such as a file or database. They called these processes readers and writers.

An airline reservation system is a good example. The readers are those who want flight information. They're called readers because they only read the existing data; they don't modify it. And because no one is changing the database, the system can allow many readers to be active at the same time—there's no need to enforce mutual exclusion among them.

The writers are those who are making reservations on a particular flight. Writers must be carefully accommodated because they are modifying existing data in the database. The system can't allow someone to be writing while someone else is reading (or writing). Therefore, it must enforce mutual exclusion if there are groups of readers and a writer, or if there are several writers, in the system. Of course the system must be fair when it enforces its policy to avoid indefinite postponement of readers or writers.

In the original paper, Courtois, Heymans, and Parnas offered two solutions using P and V operations. The first gives priority to readers over writers so readers are kept waiting only if a writer is actually modifying the data. However, this policy results in writer starvation if there is a continuous stream of readers. The second policy gives priority to the writers. In this case, as soon as a writer arrives, any readers that are already active are allowed to finish processing, but all additional readers are put on hold until the writer is done. Obviously this policy results in reader starvation if a continuous stream of writers is present. Either scenario is unacceptable.

To prevent either type of starvation, Hoare (1974) proposed the following combination priority policy. When a writer is finished, any and all readers who are waiting, or on hold, are allowed to read. Then, when that group of readers is finished, the writer who is on hold can begin, and any *new* readers who arrive in the meantime aren't allowed to start until the writer is finished.

The state of the system can be summarized by four counters initialized to 0:
- Number of readers who have *requested* a resource and haven't yet released it ($R1 = 0$)
- Number of readers who are *using* a resource and haven't yet released it ($R2 = 0$)
- Number of writers who have *requested* a resource and haven't yet released it ($W1 = 0$)
- Number of writers who are *using* a resource and haven't yet released it ($W2 = 0$)

This can be implemented using two semaphores to ensure mutual exclusion between readers and writers. A resource can be given to all readers, provided that no writers are processing ($W2 = 0$). A resource can be given to a writer, provided that no readers are reading ($R2 = 0$) and no writers are writing ($W2 = 0$).

Readers must always call two procedures: the first checks whether the resources can be immediately granted for reading; and then, when the resource is released, the second checks to see if there are any writers waiting. The same holds true for writers. The first procedure must determine if the resource can be immediately granted for writing, and then, upon releasing the resource, the second procedure will find out if any readers are waiting.

Concurrent Programming

Until now we've looked at multiprocessing as several jobs executing at the same time on a single processor (which interacts with I/O processors, for example) or on multiprocessors. Multiprocessing can also refer to one job using several processors to execute sets of instructions in parallel. The concept isn't new, but it requires a programming language and a computer system that can support this type of construct. This type of system is referred to as a **concurrent processing** system.

Applications of Concurrent Programming

Most programming languages are serial in nature—instructions are executed one at a time. Therefore, to resolve an arithmetic expression, every operation is done in sequence following the order prescribed by the programmer and compiler. Table 6.6 shows the steps to compute the following expression:

$$A = 3 * B * C + 4 / (D + E) ** (F - G)$$

	Step No.	Operation	Result
(table 6.6)	1	(F – G)	Store difference in T_1
The sequential	2	(D + E)	Store sum in T_2
computation of the	3	$(T_2) ** (T_1)$	Store power in T_1
expression requires	4	$4 / (T_1)$	Store quotient in T_2
several steps. (In this	5	3 * B	Store product in T_1
example, there are seven	6	$(T_1) * C$	Store product in T_1
steps, but each step may	7	$(T_1) + (T_2)$	Store sum in A
involve more than one			
machine operation.)			

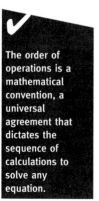

The order of operations is a mathematical convention, a universal agreement that dictates the sequence of calculations to solve any equation.

All equations follow a standard **order of operations**, which states that to solve an equation you first perform all calculations in parentheses. Second, you calculate all exponents. Third, you perform all multiplication and division. Fourth, you perform the addition and subtraction. For each step you go from left to right. If you were to perform the calculations in some other order, you would run the risk of finding the incorrect answer.

For many computational purposes, serial processing is sufficient; it's easy to implement and fast enough for most users.

However, arithmetic expressions can be processed differently if we use a language that allows for concurrent processing. Let's revisit two terms—**COBEGIN** and **COEND**—

that will indicate to the compiler which instructions can be processed concurrently. Then we'll rewrite our expression to take advantage of a concurrent processing compiler.

```
COBEGIN
    T1 = 3 * B
    T2 = D + E
    T3 = F - G
COEND
COBEGIN
    T4 = T1 * C
    T5 = T2 ** T3
COEND
    A = T4 + 4 / T5
```

As shown in Table 6.7, to solve $A = 3 * B * C + 4 / (D + E) ** (F - G)$, the first three operations can be done at the same time if our computer system has at least three processors. The next two operations are done at the same time, and the last expression is performed serially with the results of the first two steps.

Step No.	Processor	Operation	Result
1	1	3 * B	Store product in T_1
	2	(D + E)	Store sum in T_2
	3	(F – G)	Store difference in T_3
2	1	(T_1) * C	Store product in T_4
	2	(T_2) ** (T_3)	Store power in T_5
3	1	4 / (T_5)	Store quotient in T_1
4	1	(T_4) + (T_1)	Store sum in A

(table 6.7)

With concurrent processing, the seven-step procedure can be processed in only four steps, which reduces execution time.

With this system we've increased the computation speed, but we've also increased the complexity of the programming language and the hardware (both machinery and communication among machines). In fact, we've also placed a large burden on the programmer—to explicitly state which instructions can be executed in parallel. This is **explicit parallelism**.

The automatic detection by the *compiler* of instructions that can be performed in parallel is called **implicit parallelism**.

With a true concurrent processing system, the example presented in Table 6.6 and Table 6.7 is coded as a single expression. It is the compiler that translates the algebraic expression into separate instructions and decides which steps can be performed in parallel and which in serial mode.

For example, the equation $Y = A + B * C + D$ could be rearranged by the compiler as $A + D + B * C$ so that two operations $A + D$ and $B * C$ would be done in parallel, leaving the final addition to be calculated last.

As shown in the four cases that follow, concurrent processing can also dramatically reduce the complexity of working with array operations within loops, of performing matrix multiplication, of conducting parallel searches in databases, and of sorting or merging files. Some of these systems use parallel processors that execute the same type of tasks.

Case 1: Array Operations

To perform an array operation within a loop in three steps, the instruction might say:

```
for(j = 1; j <= 3; j++)
a(j) = b(j) + c(j);
```

If we use three processors, the instruction can be performed in a single step like this:

Processor #1:

$a(1) = b(1) + c(1)$

Processor #2:

$a(2) = b(2) + c(2)$

Processor #3:

$a(3) = b(3) + c(3)$

Case 2: Matrix Multiplication

Matrix multiplication requires many multiplication and addition operations that can take place concurrently, such as this equation: Matrix C = Matrix 1 * Matrix 2.

$$\text{Matrix C} = \text{Matrix 1} * \text{Matrix 2}$$

$$\begin{bmatrix} z & y & x \\ w & v & u \\ t & s & r \end{bmatrix} = \begin{bmatrix} A & B & C \\ D & E & F \end{bmatrix} * \begin{bmatrix} K & L \\ M & N \\ O & P \end{bmatrix}$$

To find z in Matrix C, you multiply the elements in the first *column* of Matrix 1 by the corresponding elements in the first *row* of Matrix 2 and then add the products. Therefore, one calculation is this: $z = (A * K) + (D * L)$. Likewise, $x = (C * K) + (F * L)$ and $r = (C * O) + (F * P)$.

Using one processor, the answer to this equation can be computed in 27 steps. By multiplying several elements of the first row of Matrix 1 by corresponding elements in Matrix 2, three processors could cooperate to resolve this equation in fewer steps. The actual number of products that could be computed at the same time would depend on the number of processors available. With two processors it takes only 18 steps to perform the calculations in parallel. With three, it would require even fewer. Notice that concurrent processing does not necessarily cut processing activity in direct proportion to the number of processors available. In this example, by doubling the number of processors from one to two, the number of calculations was reduced by one-third—not by one-half.

Case 3: Searching Databases

Database searching is a common non-mathematical application for concurrent processing systems. For example, if a word is sought from a dictionary database or a part number from an inventory listing, the entire file can be split into discrete sections with one processor allocated to each section. This results in a significant reduction in search time. Once the item is found, all processors can be deallocated and set to work on the next task. Even if the item sought is in the last record of the database, a concurrent search is faster than if a single processor was allocated to search the database.

Case 4: Sorting or Merging Files

By dividing a large file into sections, each with its own processor, every section can be sorted at the same time. Then pairs of sections can be merged together until the entire file is whole again—and sorted.

Threads and Concurrent Programming

So far we have considered the cooperation and synchronization of traditional processes, also known as heavyweight processes, which have the following characteristics:

- They pass through several states from their initial entry into the computer system to their completion: ready, running, waiting, delayed, and blocked.
- They require space in main memory where they reside during their execution.
- From time to time they require other resources such as data.

As we have seen in Chapters 3 and 4, these processes are often swapped between main memory and secondary storage during their execution to accommodate multiprogramming and to take advantage of virtual memory. Every time a swap occurs, overhead increases because of all the information that has to be saved.

To minimize this overhead time, most current operating systems support the implementation of threads, or lightweight processes, which have become part of numerous application packages. Threads are supported at both the kernel and user level and can be managed by either the operating system or the application that created them.

A thread, introduced in Chapter 1, is a smaller unit within a process, which can be scheduled and executed. Threads share the same resources as the process that created

✔

An example of Case 4 would be if you and a friend each had part of a deck of cards. Each of you (playing the part of a processor) would sort your own cards before you'd merge the two piles into one sorted deck.

them, which now becomes a more passive element because the thread is the unit that uses the CPU and is scheduled for execution. Processes might have from one to several active threads, which can be created, scheduled and synchronized more efficiently because the amount of information needed is reduced. When running a process with multiple threads in a computer system with a single CPU, the processor switches very quickly from one thread to another, giving the impression that the threads are executing in parallel. However, it is only in systems with multiple CPUs that the multiple threads in a process are actually executed in parallel.

Each active thread in a process has its own processor registers, program counter, stack and status, but shares the data area and the resources allocated to its process. Each thread has its own program counter and stack, which is used to store variables dynamically created by a process. For example, function calls in C might create variables that are local to the function. These variables are stored in the stack when the function is invoked and are destroyed when the function is exited. Since threads within a process share the same space and resources they can communicate more efficiently, increasing processing performance.

Consider how a Web server can improve performance and interactivity by using threads. When a Web server receives requests for images or pages, it serves each request with a different thread. For example, the process that receives all the requests may have one thread that accepts these requests and creates a new separate thread for each request received. This new thread retrieves the required information and sends it to the remote client. While this thread is doing its task, the original thread is free to accept more requests. Web servers are multiprocessor systems that allow for the concurrent completion of several requests, thus improving throughput and response time. Instead of creating and destroying threads to serve incoming requests, which would increase the overhead, Web servers keep a pool of threads that can be assigned to those requests. After a thread has completed its task, instead of being destroyed, it is returned to the pool to be assigned to another request.

Thread States

As a thread moves through the system it is in one of five states, not counting its creation and finished states, as shown in Figure 6.6. When an application creates a thread, it is made ready by allocating to it the needed resources and placing it in the READY queue. The thread state changes from READY to RUNNING when the Thread Scheduler, whose function is similar to that of the Process Scheduler, assigns it a processor.

A thread transitions from RUNNING to WAITING when it has to wait for an event outside its control to occur. For example, a mouse click can be the trigger event for a thread to change states, causing a transition from WAITING to READY. Alternatively, another thread, having completed its task, can send a signal indicating that the waiting thread can continue to execute. This is similar to the WAIT and SIGNAL process synchronization algorithm.

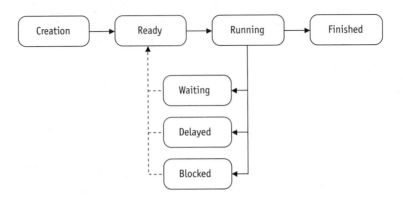

(figure 6.6)

A typical thread changes states from READY to FINISHED as it moves through the system.

When an application such as a word processor has the capability of delaying the processing of a thread by a specified amount of time, it causes the thread to transition from RUNNING to DELAYED. When the prescribed time has elapsed, the thread transitions from DELAYED to READY. For example, the thread that periodically backs up a current document to disk will be delayed for a period of time after it has completed the backup. After the time has expired, it performs the next backup and then is delayed again. If the delay was not built into the application, this thread would be forced into a loop that would continuously test to see if it was time to do a backup, wasting processor time and reducing system performance. Setting up a delay state avoids the problems of the test-and-set process synchronization algorithm.

A thread transitions from RUNNING to BLOCKED when an application issues an I/O request. After the I/O is completed, the thread returns to the READY state. When a thread transitions from RUNNING to FINISHED, all its resources are released and it can exit the system.

As you can see, the same operations are performed on both traditional processes and threads. Therefore, the operating system must be able to support:

- Creating new threads
- Setting up a thread so it is ready to execute
- Delaying, or putting to sleep, threads for a specified amount of time
- Blocking, or suspending, threads that are waiting for I/O to be completed
- Setting threads on a WAIT state until a specific event has occurred
- Scheduling threads for execution
- Synchronizing thread execution using semaphores, events, or conditional variables
- Terminating a thread and releasing its resources

To do so, the operating system needs to track the critical information for each thread.

Thread Control Block

Just as processes are represented by Process Control Blocks (PCBs), so threads are represented by **Thread Control Blocks** (TCBs), which contain basic information about a thread such as its ID, state, and a pointer to the process that created it. Figure 6.7 shows the contents of a typical TCB:

- A thread ID, a unique identifier assigned by the operating system when the thread is created
- The thread state, which changes as the thread progresses through its execution; state changes, as well as all other entries in the TCB, apply individually to each thread
- CPU information, which contains everything that the operating system needs to know about how far the thread has executed, which instruction is currently being performed, and what data is being used
- Thread priority, used to indicate the weight of this thread relative to other threads and used by the Thread Scheduler when determining which thread should be selected from the READY queue
- A **pointer** to the process that created the thread
- Pointers to other threads created by this thread

(figure 6.7)

Comparison of a typical Thread Control Block (TCB) vs. a Process Control Block (PCB) from Chapter 4.

```
Thread identification
Thread state
CPU information:
           Program counter
           Register contents
Thread priority
Pointer to process that created this thread
Pointers to all other threads created by this thread
```

```
Process identification
Process status
Process state:
           Process status word
           Register contents
           Main memory
           Resources
           Process priority
Accounting
```

Concurrent Programming Languages

Early programming languages did not support the creation of threads or the existence of concurrent processes. Typically, they gave programmers the possibility of creating a single process or thread of control. The Ada programming language, developed in the late 1970s, was one of the first languages to provide specific concurrency commands. Java, developed by Sun Microsystems, Inc., was designed as a universal software platform for Internet applications and has been widely adopted.

Java

Java was released in 1995 as the first software platform that allowed programmers to code an application with the capability to run on any computer. This type of universal software platform was an attempt to solve several issues: first, the high cost of developing software applications for each of the many incompatible computer architectures available; second, the needs of distributed client-server environments; and third, the growth of the Internet and the Web, which added more complexity to program development.

Java uses both a compiler and an interpreter. The source code of a Java program is first compiled into an intermediate language called Java bytecodes, which are platform-independent. This means that one can compile a Java program on any computer that has a Java compiler, and the bytecodes can then be run on any computer that has a Java interpreter.

The interpreter is designed to fit in with the hardware and operating system specifications of the computer that will run the Java bytecodes. Its function is to parse and run each bytecode instruction on that computer.

This combination of compiler and interpreter makes it easy to distribute Java applications because they don't have to be rewritten to accommodate the characteristics of every computer system. Once the program has been compiled it can be ported to, and run on, any system with a Java interpreter.

The Java Platform

Typically a computer platform contains the hardware and software where a program runs. The Java platform is a software-only platform that runs on top of other hardware-based platforms. It has two components: the Java Virtual Machine (Java VM), and the Java Application Programming Interface (Java API).

Java VM is the foundation for the Java platform and contains the Java interpreter, which runs the bytecodes provided by the compiler. Java VM sits on top of many different hardware-based platforms, as shown in Figure 6.8.

One of Java's great strengths is that a program can run on many different platforms from computers to telephones without requiring customization for each platform.

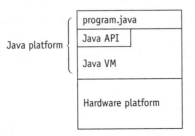

Java platform

| program.java |
| Java API |
| Java VM |

| Hardware platform |

(figure 6.8)

A process used by the Java platform to shield a Java program from a computer's hardware.

The Java API is a collection of software modules that programmers can use in their applications. The Java API is grouped into libraries of related classes and interfaces. These libraries, also known as packages, provide well-tested objects ranging from basic data types to I/O functions, from network interfaces to graphical user interface kits.

The Java Language Environment

Java was designed to make it easy for experienced programmers to learn. Its syntax is familiar because it looks and feels like C++. It is object-oriented, which means it takes advantage of modern software development methodologies and fits well into distributed client-server applications.

One of Java's features is that memory allocation is done at run time, unlike C and C++ where memory allocation is done at compilation time. Java's compiled code references memory via symbolic "handles" that are translated into real memory addresses at run time by the Java interpreter. This means that the memory allocation and referencing models are not visible to programmers, but are controlled entirely by the underlying run-time platform.

Because Java applications run in distributed environments, security is a very important built-in feature of the language and the run-time system. It provides compile-time checking and run-time checking, which helps programmers create very reliable software. For example, while a Java program is executing it can request particular classes to be loaded from anywhere in the network. In this case all incoming code is checked by a verifier, which ensures that the code is correct and can run safely without putting the Java interpreter at risk.

With its sophisticated synchronization capabilities, Java supports multithreading at the language level. The language library provides the *thread* class, and the run-time system provides monitor and condition lock primitives. The thread class is a collection of methods used to start, run, stop, and check the status of a thread. Java's threads are preemptive and, depending on the platform on which the Java interpreter executes, can also be time-sliced.

When a programmer declares some methods within a class to be synchronized, they are not run concurrently. These synchronized methods are under the control of monitors that ensure that variables remain in a consistent state. When a synchronized method begins to run it is given a monitor for the current object, which does not allow any other synchronized method in that object to execute. The monitor is released when a synchronized method exits, which allows other synchronized methods within the same object to run.

Java technology continues to be popular with programmers for several reasons:

- It offers the capability of running a single program on various platforms without having to make any changes.
- It offers a robust set of features such as run-time memory allocation, security, and multi-threading.
- It is used for many Web and Internet applications, and integrates well with browsers that can run Java applets with audio, video, and animation directly in a Web page.

Conclusion

Multiprocessing can occur in several configurations: in a single-processor system where interacting processes obtain control of the processor at different times, or in systems with multiple processors, where the work of each processor communicates and cooperates with the others and is synchronized by the Processor Manager. Three multiprocessing systems are described in this chapter: master/slave, loosely coupled, and symmetric. Each can be configured in a variety of ways.

The success of any multiprocessing system depends on the ability of the system to synchronize its processes with the system's other resources. The concept of mutual exclusion helps keep the processes with the allocated resources from becoming deadlocked. Mutual exclusion is maintained with a series of techniques, including test-and-set, WAIT and SIGNAL, and semaphores: test (P), increment (V), and mutex.

Hardware and software mechanisms are used to synchronize the many processes but care must be taken to avoid the typical problems of synchronization: missed waiting customers, the synchronization of producers and consumers, and the mutual exclusion of readers and writers.

Continuing innovations in concurrent processing, including threads and multi-core processors, are requiring fundamental changes to operating systems so they can take advantage of these new technologies. These innovations require retooling of the many applications that run on them as well as the operating system software. Research in this area is expected to grow significantly in the next few years.

In the next chapter we look at the module of the operating system that manages the printers, disk drives, tape drives, and terminals—the Device Manager.

Key Terms

busy waiting: a method by which processes, waiting for an event to occur, continuously test to see if the condition has changed and remain in unproductive, resource-consuming wait loops.

COBEGIN: command used with COEND to indicate to a multiprocessing compiler the beginning of a section where instructions can be processed concurrently.

COEND: command used with COBEGIN to indicate to a multiprocessing compiler the end of a section where instructions can be processed concurrently.

concurrent processing: execution by a single processor of a set of processes in such a way that they appear to be happening at the same time.

critical region: a part of a program that must complete execution before other processes can have access to the resources being used.

explicit parallelism: a type of concurrent programming that requires that the programmer explicitly state which instructions can be executed in parallel.

implicit parallelism: a type of concurrent programming in which the compiler automatically detects which instructions can be performed in parallel.

Java: a cross-platform programming language, developed by Sun Microsystems, that closely resembles C++ and runs on any computer capable of running the Java interpreter.

loosely coupled configuration: a multiprocessing configuration in which each processor has a copy of the operating system and controls its own resources.

master/slave: an asymmetric multiprocessing configuration consisting of a single processor system connected to "slave" processors each of which is managed by the primary "master" processor, which provides the scheduling functions and jobs.

multi-core processor: a computer chip that contains more than a single central processing unit (CPU).

multiprocessing: when two or more processors share system resources that may include some or all of the following: the same main memory, I/O devices, and control program routines.

mutex: a condition that specifies that only one process may update (modify) a shared resource at a time to ensure correct operation and results.

order of operations: the algebraic convention that dictates the order in which elements of a formula are calculated. Also called *precedence of operations* or *rules of precedence*.

parallel processing: the process of operating two or more CPUs in parallel, with more than one CPU executing instructions simultaneously.

pointer: an address or other indicator of location.

process synchronization: (1) the need for algorithms to resolve conflicts between processors in a multiprocessing environment; or (2) the need to ensure that events occur in the proper order even if they are carried out by several processes.

producers and consumers: a classic problem in which a process produces data that will be consumed, or used, by another process.

readers and writers: a problem that arises when two types of processes need to access a shared resource such as a file or a database.

semaphore: a type of shared data item that may contain either binary or nonnegative integer values and is used to provide mutual exclusion.

symmetric configuration: a multiprocessing configuration in which processor scheduling is decentralized and each processor is of the same type.

test-and-set (TS): an indivisible machine instruction, which is executed in a single machine cycle to determine whether the processor is available.

Thread Control Block (TCB): a data structure that contains information about the current status and characteristics of a thread.

WAIT and SIGNAL: a modification of the test-and-set synchronization mechanism that's designed to remove busy waiting.

Interesting Searches

- ADA Programming Language
- Multi-core CPU Speed
- Multithreaded Processing
- Real-time Processing
- Cluster Computing

Exercises

Research Topics

A. Research current literature to identify a computer model with exceptional parallel processing ability. Identify the manufacturer, the maximum number of processors the computer uses, how fast the machine can perform calculations, and typical applications for it. Cite your sources. If your answer includes terms not used in this chapter, be sure to define them.

B. Research current literature to identify a recent project that has combined the processing capacity of numerous small computers to address a problem. Identify the operating system used to coordinate the processors for this project and discuss the obstacles overcome to make the system work. If your answer includes terms not used in this chapter, be sure to define them. Cite your sources.

Exercises

1. Compare the processors' access to printers and other I/O devices for the master/slave and the symmetric multiprocessing configurations. Give a real-life example where the master/slave configuration might be preferred.

2. Compare the processors' access to main memory for the loosely coupled configuration and the symmetric multiprocessing configurations. Give a real-life example where the symmetric configuration might be preferred.

3. Describe the programmer's role when implementing explicit parallelism.

4. Describe the programmer's role when implementing implicit parallelism.

5. What steps does a well-designed multiprocessing system follow when it detects that a processor is failing? What is the central goal of most multiprocessing systems?

6. Give an example from real life of busy waiting.

7. In the last chapter, we discussed deadlocks. Describe in your own words why mutual exclusion is necessary for multiprogramming systems.

8. Compare and contrast multiprocessing and concurrent processing. Describe the role of process synchronization for both systems.

9. Describe the purpose of a buffer and give an example from your own experience where its use clearly benefits system response.

10. Consider this formula:

$$G = (A + C^2) * (E-1)^3 / D + B$$

   a. Show the order that a processor would follow to calculate G. To do so, break down the equation into the correct order of operations with one calculation per step. Show the formula for each step.

   b. Find the value of G: if A = 5, B = 10, C = 3, D = 8, and E = 5.

11. Consider this formula:

$$G = D + (A + C^2) * E / (D + B)^3$$

   a. Show the order that a processor would follow to calculate G. To do so, break down the equation into the correct order of operations with one calculation per step. Show the formula for each step.

   b. Find the value of G: if A = 5, B = 10, C = 3, D = 8, and E = 5.

12. Rewrite each of the following arithmetic expressions to take advantage of concurrent processing and then code each. Use the terms COBEGIN and COEND to delimit the sections of concurrent code.

    a. A+B*R*Z – N*M+C^2

    b. (X*(Y*Z*W*R)+M+N+P)

    c. ((J+K*L*M*N)*I)

13. Rewrite each of the following expressions for concurrent processing and then code each one. Use the terms COBEGIN and COEND to delimit the sections of concurrent code. Identify which expressions, if any, might NOT run faster in a concurrent processing environment.

    a. H^2*(O*(N+T))

    b. X*(Y*Z*W*R)

    c. M*T*R

Advanced Exercises

14. Use the test and increment (P and V) semaphore operations to simulate the traffic flow at the intersection of two one-way streets. The following rules should be satisfied:

    • Only one car can be crossing at any given time.

    • A car should be allowed to cross the intersection only if there are no cars coming from the other street.

    • When cars are coming from both streets, they should take turns to prevent indefinite postponements in either street.

15. Compare and contrast the critical region and working set.

16. Consider the following program segments for two different processes (P1, P2) executing concurrently and where B and A are not shared variables, but *x* starts at 0 and is a shared variable.

Processor #1:	Processor #2:
for(a = 1; a <= 3; a++) x = x + 1;	for(b = 1; b <= 3; b++) x = x + 1;

    If the processes P1 and P2 execute only once at any speed, what are the possible resulting values of *x*? Explain your answers.

17. Examine one of the programs you have written recently and indicate which operations could be executed concurrently. How long did it take you to do this? When might it be a good idea to write your programs in such a way that they can be run concurrently?

18. Consider the following segment taken from a C program:

```
for(j = 1; j <= 12; j++)
{
    printf("\nEnter an integer value:");
    scanf("%d", &x);
    if(x == 0)
    y(j)=0;
    if(x != 0)
    y(j)=10;
}
```

a. Recode it so it will run more efficiently in a single-processor system.

b. Given that a multiprocessing environment with four symmetrical processors is available, recode the segment as an efficient concurrent program that performs the same function as the original C program.

c. Given that all processors have identical capabilities, compare the execution speeds of the original C segment with the execution speeds of your segments for parts (a) and (b).

Programming Exercises

19. Dijkstra introduced the Sleeping Barber Problem (Dijkstra, 1965): A barbershop is divided into two rooms. The waiting room has *n* chairs and the work room only has the barber chair. When the waiting room is empty, the barber goes to sleep in the barber chair. If a customer comes in and the barber is asleep, he knows it's his turn to get his hair cut. So he wakes up the barber and takes his turn in the barber chair. But if the waiting room is not empty, the customer must take a seat in the waiting room and wait his turn. Write a program that will coordinate the barber and his customers.

20. Patil introduced the Cigarette Smokers Problem (Patil, 1971): Three smokers and a supplier make up this system. Each smoker wants to roll a cigarette and smoke it immediately. However, to smoke a cigarette the smoker needs three ingredients—paper, tobacco, and a match. To the great discomfort of everyone involved, each smoker has only one of the ingredients: Smoker 1 has lots of paper, Smoker 2 has lots of tobacco, and Smoker 3 has the matches. And, of course, the rules of the group don't allow hoarding, swapping, or sharing. The supplier, who doesn't smoke, provides all three ingredients and he has an infinite amount of all three items. But he only provides two of them at a time—and only when no one is smoking. Here's how it works. The supplier randomly selects and places two different items on the table (which is accessible to all three smokers), and the smoker with the remaining ingredient immediately

takes them, rolls, and smokes a cigarette. When he's finished smoking he signals the supplier, who then places another two randomly selected items on the table, and so on.

Write a program that will synchronize the supplier with the smokers. Keep track of how many cigarettes each smoker consumes. Is this a fair supplier? Why or why not?

Chapter 7

Device Management

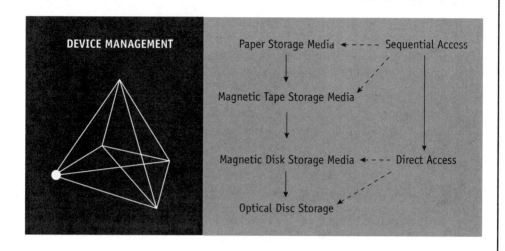

DEVICE MANAGEMENT

Paper Storage Media ← - - - - Sequential Access

Magnetic Tape Storage Media

Magnetic Disk Storage Media ← - - - Direct Access

Optical Disc Storage

"_Nothing endures but change._ **"**

—Heraclitus of Ephesus (*c. 540 B.C. – 480 B.C.*)

Learning Objectives

After completing this chapter, you should be able to describe:

- Features of dedicated, shared, and virtual devices
- Differences between sequential and direct access media
- Concepts of blocking and buffering, and how they improve I/O performance
- Roles of seek time, search time, and transfer time in calculating access time
- Differences in access times in several types of devices
- Critical components of the input/output subsystem, and how they interact
- Strengths and weaknesses of common seek strategies, including FCFS, SSTF, SCAN/LOOK, C-SCAN/C-LOOK, and how they compare
- Different levels of RAID and what sets each apart from the others

Despite the multitude of devices that appear (and disappear) in the marketplace and the swift rate of change in device technology, the Device Manager must manage every peripheral device of the system. To do so, it must maintain a delicate balance of supply and demand—balancing the system's finite supply of devices with users' almost-infinite demand for them.

Device management involves four basic functions:

- Monitoring the status of each device, such as storage drives, printers, and other peripheral devices
- Enforcing preset policies to determine which process will get a device and for how long
- Allocating the devices
- Deallocating them at two levels—at the process (or task) level when an I/O command has been executed and the device is temporarily released, and then at the job level when the job is finished and the device is permanently released

Types of Devices

The system's peripheral devices generally fall into one of three categories: dedicated, shared, and virtual. The differences are a function of the characteristics of the devices, as well as how they're managed by the Device Manager.

Dedicated devices are assigned to only one job at a time; they serve that job for the entire time it's active or until it releases them. Some devices, such as tape drives, printers, and plotters, demand this kind of allocation scheme, because it would be awkward to let several users share them. A shared plotter might produce half of one user's graph and half of another. The disadvantage of dedicated devices is that they must be allocated to a single user for the duration of a job's execution, which can be quite inefficient, especially when the device isn't used 100 percent of the time. And some devices can be shared or virtual.

Shared devices can be assigned to several processes. For instance, a disk, or any other direct access **storage** device (often shortened to DASD), can be shared by several processes at the same time by interleaving their requests, but this interleaving must be carefully controlled by the Device Manager. All conflicts—such as when Process A and Process B each need to read from the same disk—must be resolved based on predetermined policies to decide which request will be handled first.

Virtual devices are a combination of the first two: They're dedicated devices that have been transformed into shared devices. For example, printers (which are dedicated devices) are converted into sharable devices through a spooling program that reroutes all print requests to a disk. Only when all of a job's output is complete, and the printer is ready to print out the entire document, is the output sent to the printer for printing.

(This procedure has to be managed carefully to prevent deadlock, as we explained in Chapter 5.) Because disks are sharable devices, this technique can convert one printer into several virtual printers, thus improving both its performance and use. Spooling is a technique that is often used to speed up slow dedicated I/O devices.

For example, the **universal serial bus (USB) controller** acts as an interface between the operating system, device drivers, and applications and the devices that are attached via the USB host. One USB host (assisted by USB hubs) can accommodate up to 127 different devices, including flash memory, cameras, scanners, musical keyboards, etc. Each device is identified by the USB host controller with a unique identification number, which allows many devices to exchange data with the computer using the same USB connection.

The USB controller assigns bandwidth to each device depending on its priority:

- Highest priority is assigned to real-time exchanges where no interruption in the data flow is allowed, such as video or sound data.
- Medium priority is assigned to devices that can allow occasional interrupts without jeopardizing the use of the device, such as a keyboard or joystick.
- Lowest priority is assigned to bulk transfers or exchanges that can accommodate slower data flow, such as printers or scanners.

Regardless of the specific attributes of the device, the most important differences among them are speed and degree of sharability.

Storage media are divided into two groups: **sequential access media**, which store records sequentially, one after the other; and **direct access storage devices (DASD)**, which can store either sequential or direct access files. There are vast differences in their speed and sharability.

The first storage medium was paper in the form of printouts, punch cards, and paper tape.

Sequential Access Storage Media

Magnetic tape was developed for routine secondary storage in early computer systems and features records that are stored serially, one after the other.

The length of these records is usually determined by the application program and each record can be identified by its position on the tape. Therefore, to access a single record, the tape must be mounted and fast-forwarded from its beginning until the desired position is located. This can be a time-consuming process.

To appreciate just how long it takes, let's consider a hypothetical computer system that uses a reel of tape that is 2400 feet long (see Figure 7.1). Data is recorded on eight of the nine parallel tracks that run the length of the tape. (The ninth track, shown at the top of the figure, holds a parity bit that is used for routine error checking.)

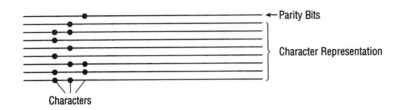

(figure 7.1)

*Nine-track magnetic tape
with three characters
recorded using odd parity.
A 1/2-inch wide reel of
tape, typically used to
back up a mainframe
computer, can store
thousands of characters,
or bytes, per inch.*

The number of characters that can be recorded per inch is determined by the density of the tape, such as 1600 bytes per inch (bpi). For example, if you had records of 160 characters each, and were storing them on a tape with a density of 1600 bpi, then theoretically you could store 10 records on one inch of tape. However, in actual practice, it would depend on how you decided to store the records: individually or grouped into blocks. If the records are stored individually, each record would need to be separated by a space to indicate its starting and ending places. If the records are stored in blocks, then the entire block is preceded by a space and followed by a space, but the individual records are stored sequentially within the block.

To appreciate the difference between storing individually or in blocks, let's look at the mechanics of reading and writing on magnetic tape. Magnetic tape moves under the read/write head only when there's a need to access a record; at all other times it's standing still. So the tape moves in jerks as it stops, reads, and moves on at high speed, or stops, writes, and starts again, and so on. Records would be written in the same way.

The tape needs time and space to stop, so a gap is inserted between each record. This **interrecord gap** (**IRG**) is about ½ inch long regardless of the sizes of the records it separates. Therefore, if 10 records are stored individually, there will be nine ½-inch IRGs between each record. (In this example we assume each record is only ⅒ inch.)

In Figure 7.2, 5.5 inches of tape are required to store 1 inch of data—not a very efficient way to use the storage medium.

(figure 7.2)

*IRGs in magnetic tape.
Each record requires only
1/10 inch of tape, for a
total of 1 inch. When 10
records are stored
individually on magnetic
tape, they are separated
by IRGs, which adds up to
4.5 inches of tape. This
totals 5.5 inches of tape.*

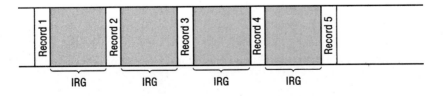

An alternative is to group the records into blocks before recording them on tape. This is called **blocking** and it's performed when the file is created. (Later, when you retrieve them, you must be sure to unblock them accurately.)

The number of records in a block is usually determined by the application program, and it's often set to take advantage of the **transfer rate,** which is the density of the tape (measured in bpi), multiplied by the tape drive speed, called transport speed, which is measured in inches per second (ips):

$$\text{transfer rate (ips)} = \text{density} * \text{transport speed}$$

Let's say that in our hypothetical system the transport speed is 200 ips. Therefore, at 1600 bpi, a total of 320,000 bytes can be transferred in one second, so theoretically the optimal size of a block is 320,000 bytes. But there's a catch: This technique requires that the *entire* block be read into a buffer, so the buffer must be at least as large as the block.

Notice in Figure 7.3 that the gap (now called an interblock gap or IBG) is still ½ inch long, but the data from each block of 10 records is now stored on only 1 inch of tape—so we've used only 1.5 inches of tape (instead of the 5.5 inches shown in Figure 7.2), and we've wasted only ½ inch of tape (instead of 4.5 inches).

(figure 7.3)

Two blocks of records stored on magnetic tape, each preceded by an IBG of 1/2 inch. Each block holds 10 records, each of which is still 1/10 inch. The block, however, is 1 inch, for a total of 1.5 inches.

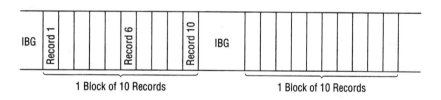

1 Block of 10 Records   1 Block of 10 Records

Blocking has two distinct advantages:

- Fewer I/O operations are needed because a single READ command can move an entire block, the physical record that includes several logical records, into main memory.
- Less tape is wasted because the size of the physical record exceeds the size of the gap.

The two disadvantages of blocking seem mild by comparison:

- Overhead and software routines are needed for blocking, deblocking, and recordkeeping.
- Buffer space may be wasted if you need only one logical record but must read an entire block to get it.

How long does it take to access a block or record on magnetic tape? It depends on where the record is located, but we can make some general calculations. For example, our 2400-foot reel of tape with a tape transport speed of 200 ips can be read without stopping in approximately 2.5 minutes. Therefore, it would take 2.5 minutes to access the last record on the tape. On the average, then, it would take 1.25 minutes to access a record. And to access one record after another sequentially would take as long as it takes to start and stop a tape—which is 0.003 seconds, or 3 milliseconds (ms).

As we can see from Table 7.1, **access times** can vary widely. That makes magnetic tape a poor medium for routine secondary storage except for files with very high sequential activity—that is, those requiring that 90 to 100 percent of the records be accessed sequentially during an application.

Benchmarks	Access Time
Maximum access	2.5 minutes
Average access	1.25 minutes
Sequential access	3 milliseconds

(table 7.1)

Access times for 2400-foot magnetic tape with a tape transport speed of 200 ips.

Direct Access Storage Devices

Direct access storage devices (DASDs) are devices that can directly read or write to a specific place. DASDs can be grouped into three categories: magnetic disks, optical discs, and flash memory. Although the variance in DASD access times isn't as wide as with magnetic tape, the location of the specific record still has a direct effect on the amount of time required to access it.

Fixed-Head Magnetic Disk Storage

A fixed-head magnetic disk looks like a large CD or DVD covered with magnetic film that has been formatted, usually on both sides, into concentric circles. Each circle is a **track**. Data is recorded serially on each track by the fixed read/write head positioned over it.

A fixed-head disk, shown in Figure 7.4, is also very fast—faster than the movable-head disks we'll talk about in the next section. However, its major disadvantages are its high cost and its reduced storage space compared to a movable-head disk (because the tracks must be positioned farther apart to accommodate the width of the read/write heads). These devices have been used when speed is of the utmost importance, such as space flight or aircraft applications.

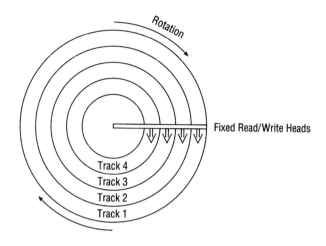

Movable-Head Magnetic Disk Storage

Movable-head magnetic disks, such as computer hard drives, have one read/write head
that floats over each surface of each disk. Disks can be a single platter, or part of a disk
pack, which is a stack of magnetic platters. Figure 7.5 shows a typical disk pack—several platters stacked on a common central spindle, separated by enough space to allow
the read/write heads to move between each pair of disks.

As shown in Figure 7.5, each platter (except those at the top and bottom of the stack)
has two surfaces for recording, and each surface is formatted with a specific number
of concentric tracks where the data is recorded. The number of tracks varies from
manufacturer to manufacturer, but typically there are a thousand or more on a high-
capacity hard disk. Each track on each surface is numbered: Track 0 identifies the outermost concentric circle on each surface; the highest-numbered track is in the center.

The arm, shown in Figure 7.6, moves two read/write heads between each pair of surfaces:
one for the surface above it and one for the surface below. The arm moves all of the heads
in unison, so if one head is on Track 36, then all of the heads are on Track 36—in other
words, they're all positioned on the same track but on their respective surfaces creating a
virtual cylinder.

This raises some interesting questions: Is it more efficient to write a series of records on
surface one and, when that surface is full, to continue writing on surface two, and then

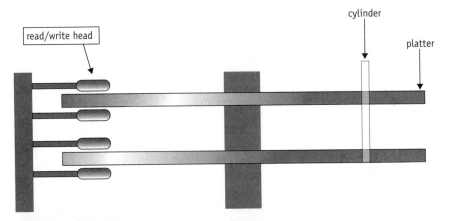

(figure 7.5)

A disk pack is a stack of magnetic platters. The read/write heads move between each pair of surfaces, and all of the heads are moved in unison by the arm.

(figure 7.6)

A typical hard drive from a PC showing the arm that floats over the surface of the disk.

© Courtesy Seagate Technology

on surface three, and so on? Or is it better to fill up every outside track of every surface before moving the heads inward to the next track position to continue writing?

It's slower to fill a disk pack surface-by-surface than it is to fill it up track-by-track—and this leads us to a valuable concept. If we fill Track 0 of all of the surfaces, we've got a virtual **cylinder** of data. There are as many cylinders as there are tracks, and the cylinders are as tall as the disk pack. You could visualize the cylinders as a series of smaller and smaller soup cans, each nested inside the larger ones.

To access any given record, the system needs three things: its cylinder number, so the arm can move the read/write heads to it; its surface number, so the proper read/write head is activated; and its sector number, as shown in Figure 7.7, so the read/write head knows the instant when it should begin reading or writing.

(figure 7.7)

On a magnetic disk, the sectors are of different sizes: bigger at the rim and smaller at the center. The disk spins at a constant angular velocity (CAV) to compensate for this difference. Some optical discs can read and write on multiple layers, greatly enhancing storage capacity.

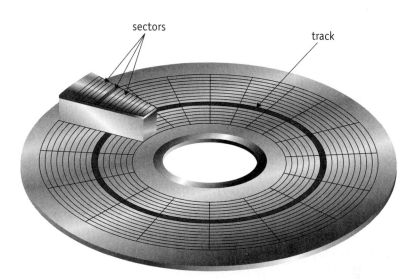

(figure 7.7)

On a magnetic disk, the sectors are of different sizes: bigger at the rim and smaller at the center. The disk spins at a constant angular velocity (CAV) to compensate for this difference. Some optical discs can read and write on multiple layers, greatly enhancing storage capacity.

One clarification: We've used the term *surface* in this discussion because it makes the concepts easier to understand. However, conventional literature generally uses the term *track* to identify both the surface and the concentric track. Therefore, our use of *surface/track* coincides with the term *track* or *head* used in some other texts.

Optical Disc Storage

The advent of optical disc storage was made possible by developments in laser technology. Among the many differences between an optical disc and a magnetic disk is the design of the disc track and sectors.

The spelling convention for an optical storage device is *disc*, to differentiate it from a magnetic storage *disk*.

A magnetic disk, which consists of concentric tracks of sectors, spins at a constant speed—this is called constant angular velocity (CAV). Because the sectors at the outside of the disk spin faster past the read/write head than the inner sectors, outside sectors are much larger than sectors located near the center of the disk. This format wastes storage space but maximizes the speed with which data can be retrieved.

On the other hand, an optical disc consists of a single spiraling track of same-sized sectors running from the center to the rim of the disc, as shown in Figure 7.8. This single track also has sectors, but all sectors are the same size regardless of their locations on the disc. This design allows many more sectors, and much more data, to fit on an optical disc compared to a magnetic disk of the same size. The disc drive adjusts the speed of the disc's spin to compensate for the sector's location on the disc—this is called constant linear velocity (CLV). Therefore, the disc spins faster to read sectors located at

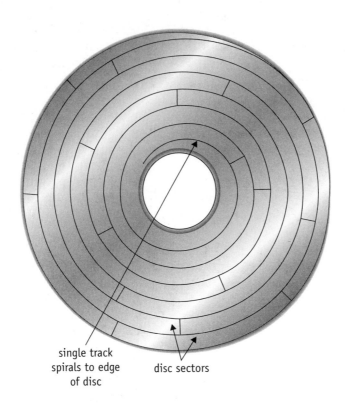

single track
spirals to edge
of disc

disc sectors

(figure 7.8)

On an optical disc, the sectors (not all sectors are shown here) are of the same size throughout the disc. The disc drive changes speed to compensate, but it spins at a constant linear velocity (CLV).

the center of the disc, and slower to read sectors near the outer edge. If you listen to a disc drive in action, you can hear it change speeds as it makes these adjustments.

Two of the most important measures of optical disc drive performance are sustained data transfer rate and average access time. The data transfer rate is measured in megabytes per second and refers to the speed at which massive amounts of data can be read from the disc. This factor is crucial for applications requiring sequential access, such as for audio and video playback. For example, a DVD with a fast data transfer rate will drop fewer frames when playing back a recorded video segment than will a unit with a slower transfer rate. This creates an image that's much smoother.

However, to retrieve data that is not stored sequentially, the drive's access time may be more important. Access time, which indicates the average time required to move the head to a specific place on the disc, is expressed in milliseconds (ms). The fastest units have the smallest average access time, which is the most important factor when searching for information randomly, such as in a database. Therefore, a fast data-transfer rate is most important for sequential disc access, such as for video playback, whereas fast access time is crucial when retrieving data that's widely dispersed on the disc.

A third important feature of optical disc drives is cache size. Although it's not a speed measurement, cache size has a substantial impact on perceived performance. A hardware cache acts as a buffer by transferring blocks of data from the disc, anticipating that the user may want to reread some recently retrieved information, which can be done quickly if the information remains in the cache. In some cases, the cache can also act as a read-ahead buffer, looking for the next block of information on the disc. Read-ahead caches might appear to be most useful for multimedia playback, where a continuous stream of data is flowing. However, because they fill up quickly, read-ahead caches actually become more useful when paging through a database or electronic book. In these cases, the cache has time to recover while the user is reading the current piece of information.

There are several types of optical-disc systems, depending on the medium and the capacity of the discs: CDs, DVDs, and Blu-ray as shown in Figure 7.9.

To put data on an optical disc, a high-intensity laser beam burns indentations on the disc that are called pits. These **pits,** which represent 0s, contrast with the unburned flat areas, called **lands,** which represent 1s. The first sectors are located in the center of the disc and the laser moves outward reading each sector in turn. If a disc has multiple layers, the laser's course is reversed to read the second layer with the arm moving from the outer edge to the inner.

(figure 7.9)

CD readable technology (left) uses a red laser to write on the bottom of the disc's substrate. DVDs (middle) use a smaller red laser to write on the disc's substrate so tracks can be layered, one on top of the other. Blu-ray (right) uses a finer blue laser to write on multiple layers with more tightly packed tracks. (from blu-raydisc.com)

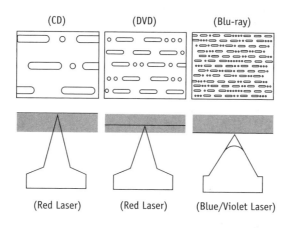

CD and DVD Technology

In the CD or DVD player, data is read back by focusing a low-powered red laser on it, which shines through the protective layer of the disc onto the CD track (or DVD tracks) where data is recorded. Light striking a land is reflected into a photodetector while light striking a pit is scattered and absorbed. The photodetector then converts the intensity of the light into a digital signal of 1s and 0s.

Recordable CD and DVD disc drives require more expensive disc controllers than the read-only disc players because they need to incorporate write mechanisms specific to each medium. For example, a CD consists of several layers, including a gold reflective layer and a dye layer, which is used to record the data. The write head uses a high-powered laser beam to record data. A permanent mark is made on the dye when the energy from the laser beam is absorbed into it and it cannot be erased after it is recorded. When it is read, the existence of a mark on the dye will cause the laser beam to scatter and light is not returned back to the read head. However, when there are no marks on the dye, the gold layer reflects the light right back to the read head. This is similar to the process of reading pits and lands. The software used to create a recordable CD (CD-R) uses a standard format, such as ISO 9096, which automatically checks for errors and creates a table of contents, used to keep track of each file's location.

Similarly, recordable and rewritable CDs (CD-RWs) use a process called phase change technology to write, change, and erase data. The disc's recording layer uses an alloy of silver, indium, antimony, and tellurium. The recording layer has two different phase states: amorphous and crystalline. In the amorphous state, light is not reflected as well as in the crystalline state.

To record data, a laser beam heats up the disc and changes the state from crystalline to amorphous. When data is read by means of a low-power laser beam, the amorphous state scatters the light that does not get picked up by the read head. This is interpreted as a 0 and is similar to what occurs when reading pits. On the other hand, when the light hits the crystalline areas, light is reflected back to the read head, and this is similar to what occurs when reading lands and is interpreted as a 1. To erase data, the CD-RW drive uses a low-energy beam to heat up the pits just enough to loosen the alloy and return it to its original crystalline state.

Although DVDs use the same design and are the same size and shape as CDs, they can store much more data. A dual-layer, single-sided DVD can hold the equivalent of 13 CDs; its red laser, with a shorter wavelength than the CD's red laser, makes smaller pits and allows the spiral to be wound tighter.

When the advantages of compression technology (discussed in the next chapter) are added to the high capacity of a DVD, such as MPEG video compression, a single-sided, double-layer DVD can hold 8.6GB, more than enough space to hold a two-hour movie with enhanced audio.

Blu-ray Disc Technology

A Blu-ray disc is the same physical size as a DVD or CD but the laser technology used to read and write data is quite different. As shown in Figure 7.9, the pits (each representing a 1) on a Blu-ray disc are much smaller and the tracks are wound much tighter than they are on a DVD or CD. Although Blu-ray products can be made backward compatible so they can accommodate the older CDs and DVDs, the Blu-ray's blue-violet laser (405nm) has a shorter wavelength than the CD/DVD's red laser (650nm). This allows data to be packed more tightly and stored in less space.

In addition, the blue-violet laser can write on a much thinner layer on the disc, allowing multiple layers to be written on top of each other and vastly increasing the amount of data that can be stored on a single disc. The disc's format was created to further the commercial prospects for high-definition video, and to store large amounts of data, particularly for games and interactive applications via the Java programming language. Blu-ray players execute Java programs for menus and user interaction.

As of this writing, each Blu-ray disc can hold much more data (50GB for a two-layer disc) than can a similar DVD (8.5GB for a two-layer disc). (Pioneer Electronics has reported that its new 20-layer discs can hold 500GB.) Reading speed is also much faster with the fastest Blu-ray players featuring 432 Mbps (comparable DVD players reach 168.75 Mbps). Like CDs and DVDs, Blu-ray discs are available in several formats: read-only (BD-ROM), recordable (BD-R), and rewritable (BD-RE).

Flash Memory Storage

Flash memory is a type of electrically erasable programmable read-only memory (EEP-ROM). It's a nonvolatile removable medium that emulates random access memory, but, unlike RAM, stores data securely even when it's removed from its power source. Historically, flash memory was primarily used to store startup (boot up) information for computers, but is now used to store data for cell phones, mobile devices, music players, cameras, and more.

Flash memory uses a phenomenon (known as Fowler-Nordheim tunneling) to send electrons through a floating gate transistor where they remain even after power is turned off. Flash memory allows users to store data. It is sold in a variety of configurations, including compact flash, smart cards, and memory sticks, and they often connect to the computer through the USB port.

Flash memory gets its name from the technique used to erase its data. To write data, an electric charge is sent through one transistor, called the floating gate, then through a metal oxide layer, and into a second transistor called the control gate where the charge is stored in a cell until it's erased. To reset all values, a strong electrical field, called a

Removable flash memory devices go by a variety of names: flash drives, memory cards, smart cards, thumb drives, camera cards, memory sticks, and more.

flash, is applied to the entire card. However, flash memory isn't indestructible. It has two limitations: The bits can be erased only by applying the flash to a large block of memory and, with each flash erasure, the block becomes less stable. In time (after 10,000 to 1,000,000 uses), a flash memory device will no longer reliably store data.

Magnetic Disk Drive Access Times

Depending on whether a disk has fixed or movable heads, there can be as many as three factors that contribute to the time required to access a file: seek time, search time, and transfer time.

To date, **seek time** has been the slowest of the three factors. This is the time required to position the read/write head on the proper track. Obviously, seek time doesn't apply to devices with fixed read/write heads because each track has its own read/write head. **Search time**, also known as rotational delay, is the time it takes to rotate the disk until the requested record is moved under the read/write head. **Transfer time** is the fastest of the three; that's when the data is actually transferred from secondary storage to main memory.

Fixed-Head Drives

Fixed-head disk drives are fast. The total amount of time required to access data depends on the rotational speed, which varies from device to device but is constant within each device, and the position of the record relative to the position of the read/write head. Therefore, total access time is the sum of search time plus transfer time.

> search time (rotational delay)
> + transfer time (data transfer)
> access time

Because the disk rotates continuously, there are three basic positions for the requested record in relation to the position of the read/write head. Figure 7.10(a) shows the best possible situation because the record is next to the read/write head when the I/O command is executed; this gives a rotational delay of zero. Figure 7.10(b) shows the average situation because the record is directly opposite the read/write head when the I/O command is executed; this gives a rotational delay of $t/2$ where t (time) is one full rotation. Figure 7.10(c) shows the worst situation because the record has just rotated past the read/write head when the I/O command is executed; this gives a rotational delay of t because it will take one full rotation for the record to reposition itself under the read/write head.

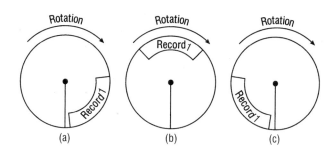

How long will it take to access a record? If one complete revolution takes 16.8 ms, then the average rotational delay, as shown in Figure 7.10(b), is 8.4 ms. The data-transfer time varies from device to device, but a typical value is 0.00094 ms per byte—the size of the record dictates this value. For example, if it takes 0.094 ms (almost 0.1 ms) to transfer a record with 100 bytes, then the resulting access times are shown in Table 7.2.

(table 7.2)

Access times for a
fixed-head disk drive at
16.8 ms/revolution.

Benchmarks	Access Time
Maximum access	16.8 ms + 0.00094 ms/byte
Average access	8.4 ms + 0.00094 ms/byte
Sequential access	Depends on the length of the record; generally less than 1 ms (known as the transfer rate)

Data recorded on fixed head drives may or may not be blocked at the discretion of the application programmer. Blocking isn't used to save space because there are no IRGs between records. Instead, blocking is used to save time.

To illustrate the advantages of blocking the records, let's use the same values shown in Table 7.2 for a record containing 100 bytes and blocks containing 10 records. If we were to read 10 records individually, we would multiply the access time for a single record by 10:

$$\text{access time} = 8.4 + 0.094 = 8.494 \text{ ms for one record}$$
$$\text{total access time} = 10(8.4 + 0.094) = 84.940 \text{ ms for 10 records}$$

On the other hand, to read one block of 10 records we would make a single access, so we'd compute the access time only once, multiplying the transfer rate by 10:

$$\text{access time} = 8.4 + (0.094 * 10)$$
$$= 8.4 + 0.94$$
$$= 9.34 \text{ ms for 10 records in one block}$$

Once the block is in memory, the software that handles blocking and deblocking takes over. But, the amount of time used in deblocking must be less than what you saved in access time (75.6 ms) for this to be a productive move.

Movable-Head Devices

Movable-head disk drives add a third time element to the computation of access time. Seek time is the time required to move the arm into position over the proper track. So now the formula for access time is:

$$\begin{array}{l} \text{seek time (arm movement)} \\ \text{search time (rotational delay)} \\ + \ \underline{\text{transfer time (data transfer)}} \\ \text{access time} \end{array}$$

Of the three components of access time in this equation, seek time is the longest. We'll examine several seek strategies in a moment.

The calculations to figure search time (rotational delay) and transfer time are the same as those presented for fixed-head drives. The maximum seek time, which is the maximum time required to move the arm, is typically 50 ms. Table 7.3 compares typical access times for movable-head drives.

Benchmarks	Access Time
Maximum access	50 ms + 16.8 ms + 0.00094 ms/byte
Average access	25 ms + 8.4 ms + 0.00094 ms/byte
Sequential access	Depends on the length of the record, generally less than 1 ms

(table 7.3)

Typical access times for a movable-head drive, such as the hard drive, shown in Figure 7.6.

The variance in access time has increased in comparison to that of the fixed-head drive but it's relatively small—especially when compared to tape access, which varies from milliseconds to minutes. Again, blocking is a good way to minimize access time. If we use the same example as for fixed-head disks and consider the average case with 10 seeks followed by 10 searches, we would get:

$$\begin{array}{ll} \text{access time} & = 25 + 8.4 + 0.094 = 33.494 \text{ ms for one record} \\ \text{total access time} & = 10 * 33.494 \\ & = 334.94 \text{ ms for 10 records} \\ & \quad \text{(about } \frac{1}{3} \text{ of a second)} \end{array}$$

But when we put the 10 records into one block, the access time is significantly decreased:

$$\text{total access time} = 25 + 8.4 + (0.094 * 10)$$
$$= 33.4 + 0.94$$
$$= 34.34 \text{ ms for 10 records}$$
$$(\text{about } \tfrac{1}{29} \text{ of a second})$$

We stress that these figures wouldn't apply in an actual operating environment. For instance, we haven't taken into consideration what else is happening in the system while I/O is taking place. Therefore, although we can show the comparable performance of these components of the system, we're not seeing the whole picture.

Components of the I/O Subsystem

The pieces of the I/O subsystem all have to work harmoniously, and they work in a manner similar to the mythical "Flynn Taxicab Company" shown in Figure 7.11.

Many requests come in from all over the city to the taxi company dispatcher. It's the dispatcher's job to handle the incoming calls as fast as they arrive and to find out who needs transportation, where they are, where they're going, and when. Then the dispatcher

(figure 7.11)

The taxicab company works in a manner similar to an I/O subsystem. One mechanic can service several vehicles just as an I/O control unit can operate several devices, as shown in Figure 7.12.

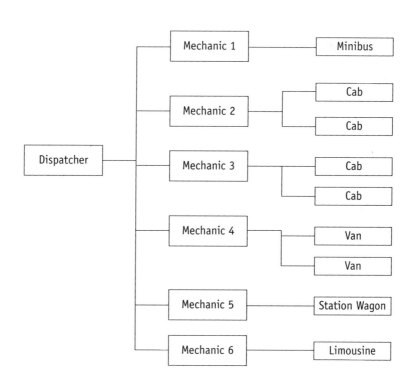

organizes the calls into an order that will use the company's resources as efficiently as possible. That's not easy, because the cab company has a variety of vehicles at its disposal: ordinary taxicabs, station wagons, vans, limos, and a minibus. These are serviced by specialized mechanics. A mechanic handles only one type of vehicle, which is made available to many drivers. Once the order is set, the dispatcher calls the mechanic who, ideally, has the vehicle ready for the driver who jumps into the appropriate vehicle, picks up the waiting passengers, and delivers them quickly to their respective destinations.

That's the ideal—but problems sometimes occur; rainy days mean too many phone calls to fulfill every request, vehicles are not mechanically sound, and sometimes the limo is already busy.

The **I/O subsystem**'s components perform similar functions. The channel plays the part of the dispatcher in this example. Its job is to keep up with the I/O requests from the CPU and pass them down the line to the appropriate control unit. The control units play the part of the mechanics. The I/O devices play the part of the vehicles.

I/O channels are programmable units placed between the CPU and the control units. Their job is to synchronize the fast speed of the CPU with the slow speed of the I/O device, and they make it possible to overlap I/O operations with processor operations so the CPU and I/O can process concurrently. Channels use **I/O channel programs**, which can range in size from one to many instructions. Each channel program specifies the action to be performed by the devices and controls the transmission of data between main memory and the control units.

The channel sends one signal for each function, and the **I/O control unit** interprets the signal, which might say "go to the top of the page" if the device is a printer or "rewind" if the device is a tape drive. Although a control unit is sometimes part of the device, in most systems a single control unit is attached to several similar devices, so we distinguish between the control unit and the device.

Some systems also have a disk controller, or disk drive interface, which is a special-purpose device used to link the disk drives with the system bus. Disk drive interfaces control the transfer of information between the disk drives and the rest of the computer system. The operating system normally deals with the controller, not the device.

At the start of an I/O command, the information passed from the CPU to the channel is this:

• I/O command (READ, WRITE, REWIND, etc.)

• Channel number

• Address of the physical record to be transferred (from or to secondary storage)

• Starting address of a memory buffer from which or into which the record is to be transferred

Because the channels are as fast as the CPU they work with, each channel can direct several control units by interleaving commands (just as we had several mechanics directed by a single dispatcher). In addition, each control unit can direct several devices (just as a single mechanic could repair several vehicles of the same type). A typical configuration might have one channel and up to eight control units, each of which communicates with up to eight I/O devices. Channels are often shared because they're the most expensive items in the entire I/O subsystem.

The system shown in Figure 7.12 requires that the entire path be available when an I/O command is initiated. However, there's some flexibility built into the system because each unit can end independently of the others, as will be explained in the next section. This figure also shows the hierarchical nature of the interconnection and the one-to-one correspondence between each device and its transmission path.

Additional flexibility can be built into the system by connecting more than one channel to a control unit or by connecting more than one control unit to a single device. That's the same as if the mechanics of the Flynn Taxicab Company could also make repairs for the ABC Taxicab Company, or if its vehicles could be used by ABC drivers (or if the drivers in the company could share vehicles).

These multiple paths increase the reliability of the I/O subsystem by keeping communication lines open even if a component malfunctions. Figure 7.13 shows the same system presented in Figure 7.12, but with one control unit connected to two channels and one device connected to two control units.

(figure 7.12)

Typical I/O subsystem configuration.

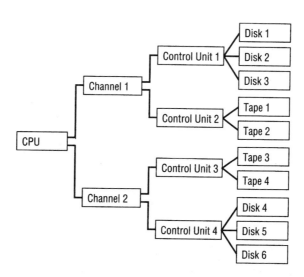

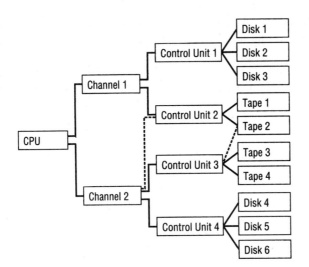

(figure 7.13)

I/O subsystem configuration with multiple paths, which increase both flexibility and reliability. With two additional paths, shown with dashed lines, if Control Unit 2 malfunctions, then Tape 2 can still be accessed via Control Unit 3.

Communication Among Devices

The Device Manager relies on several auxiliary features to keep running efficiently under the demanding conditions of a busy computer system, and there are three problems that must be resolved:

- It needs to know which components are busy and which are free.
- It must be able to accommodate the requests that come in during heavy I/O traffic.
- It must accommodate the disparity of speeds between the CPU and the I/O devices.

The first is solved by structuring the interaction between units. The last two problems are handled by buffering records and queuing requests.

As we mentioned previously, each unit in the I/O subsystem can finish its operation independently from the others. For example, after a device has begun writing a record, and before it has completed the task, the connection between the device and its control unit can be cut off so the control unit can initiate another I/O task with another device. Meanwhile, at the other end of the system, the CPU is free to process data while I/O is being performed, which allows for concurrent processing and I/O.

The success of the operation depends on the system's ability to know when a device has completed an operation. This is done with a hardware flag that must be tested by the CPU. This flag is made up of three bits and resides in the **Channel Status Word** (**CSW**), which is in a predefined location in main memory and contains information indicating the status of the channel. Each bit represents one of the components of the I/O subsystem, one each for the channel, control unit, and device. Each bit is changed from 0 to 1 to indicate that the unit has changed from free to busy. Each component has access to the flag, which can be tested before proceeding with the next I/O

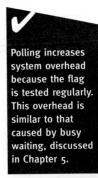

Polling increases system overhead because the flag is tested regularly. This overhead is similar to that caused by busy waiting, discussed in Chapter 5.

operation to ensure that the entire path is free and vice versa. There are two common ways to perform this test—polling and using interrupts.

Polling uses a special machine instruction to test the flag. For example, the CPU periodically tests the channel status bit (in the CSW). If the channel is still busy, the CPU performs some other processing task until the test shows that the channel is free; then the channel performs the I/O operation. The major disadvantage with this scheme is determining how often the flag should be polled. If polling is done too frequently, the CPU wastes time testing the flag just to find out that the channel is still busy. On the other hand, if polling is done too seldom, the channel could sit idle for long periods of time.

The use of **interrupts** is a more efficient way to test the flag. Instead of having the CPU test the flag, a hardware mechanism does the test as part of every machine instruction executed by the CPU. If the channel is busy, the flag is set so that execution of the current sequence of instructions is automatically interrupted and control is transferred to the interrupt handler, which is part of the operating system and resides in a predefined location in memory.

The interrupt handler's job is to determine the best course of action based on the current situation because it's not unusual for more than one unit to have caused the I/O interrupt. So the interrupt handler must find out which unit sent the signal, analyze its status, restart it when appropriate with the next operation, and finally return control to the interrupted process.

Some sophisticated systems are equipped with hardware that can distinguish between several types of interrupts. These interrupts are ordered by priority, and each one can transfer control to a corresponding location in memory. The memory locations are ranked in order according to the same priorities. So if the CPU is executing the interrupt-handler routine associated with a given priority, the hardware will automatically intercept all interrupts at the same or at lower priorities. This multiple-priority interrupt system helps improve resource utilization because each interrupt is handled according to its relative importance.

Direct memory access (DMA) is an I/O technique that allows a control unit to directly access main memory. This means that once reading or writing has begun, the remainder of the data can be transferred to and from memory without CPU intervention. However, it is possible that the DMA control unit and the CPU compete for the system bus if they happen to need it at the same time. To activate this process, the CPU sends enough information—such as the type of operation (read or write), the unit number of the I/O device needed, the location in memory where data is to be read from or written to, and the amount of data (bytes or words) to be transferred—to the DMA control unit to initiate the transfer of data; the CPU then can go on to another task while the control unit completes the transfer independently. The DMA controller sends an interrupt to the CPU to indicate that the operation is completed. This mode of data transfer is used for high-speed devices such as disks.

Without DMA, the CPU is responsible for the physical movement of data between main memory and the device—a time-consuming task that results in significant overhead and decreased CPU utilization.

Buffers are used extensively to better synchronize the movement of data between the relatively slow I/O devices and the very fast CPU. Buffers are temporary storage areas residing in three convenient locations throughout the system: main memory, channels, and control units. They're used to store data read from an input device before it's needed by the processor and to store data that will be written to an output device. A typical use of buffers (mentioned earlier in this chapter) occurs when blocked records are either read from, or written to, an I/O device. In this case, one physical record contains several logical records and must reside in memory while the processing of each individual record takes place. For example, if a block contains five records, then a physical READ occurs with every six READ commands; all other READ requests are directed to retrieve information from the buffer (this buffer may be set by the application program).

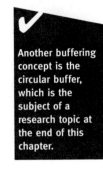

Another buffering concept is the circular buffer, which is the subject of a research topic at the end of this chapter.

To minimize the idle time for devices and, even more important, to maximize their throughput, the technique of double buffering is used, as shown in Figure 7.14. In this system, two buffers are present in main memory, channels, and control units. The objective is to have a record ready to be transferred to or from memory at any time to avoid any possible delay that might be caused by waiting for a buffer to fill up with data. Thus, while one record is being processed by the CPU, another can be read or written by the channel.

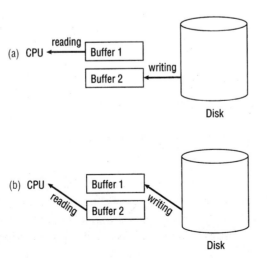

(figure 7.14)

Example of double buffering: (a) the CPU is reading from Buffer 1 as Buffer 2 is being filled; (b) once Buffer 2 is filled, it can be read quickly by the CPU while Buffer 1 is being filled again.

When using blocked records, upon receipt of the command to "READ last logical record," the channel can start reading the next physical record, which results in overlapped I/O and processing. When the first READ command is received, two records are transferred from the device to immediately fill both buffers. Then, as the data from one buffer has been processed, the second buffer is ready. As the second is being read, the first buffer is being filled with data from a third record, and so on.

Management of I/O Requests

Although most users think of an I/O request as an elementary machine action, the Device Manager actually divides the task into three parts with each one handled by a specific software component of the I/O subsystem. The I/O traffic controller watches the status of all devices, control units, and channels. The I/O scheduler implements the policies that determine the allocation of, and access to, the devices, control units, and channels. The I/O device handler performs the actual transfer of data and processes the device interrupts. Let's look at these in more detail.

The **I/O traffic controller** monitors the status of every device, control unit, and channel. It's a job that becomes more complex as the number of units in the I/O subsystem increases and as the number of paths between these units increases. The traffic controller has three main tasks: (1) it must determine if there's at least one path available; (2) if there's more than one path available, it must determine which to select; and (3) if the paths are all busy, it must determine when one will become available.

To do all this, the traffic controller maintains a database containing the status and connections for each unit in the I/O subsystem, grouped into Channel Control Blocks, Control Unit Control Blocks, and Device Control Blocks, as shown in Table 7.4.

	Channel Control Block	Control Unit Control Block	Device Control Block
(table 7.4) *Each control block contains the information it needs to manage its part of the I/O subsystem.*	• Channel identification • Status • List of control units connected to it • List of processes waiting for it	• Control unit identification • Status • List of channels connected to it • List of devices connected to it • List of processes waiting for it	• Device identification • Status • List of control units connected to it • List of processes waiting for it

To choose a free path to satisfy an I/O request, the traffic controller traces backward from the control block of the requested device through the control units to the channels. If a path is not available, a common occurrence under heavy load conditions, the process (actually its Process Control Block, or PCB, as described in Chapter 4) is linked to the queues kept in the control blocks of the requested device, control unit, and channel. This creates multiple wait queues with one queue per path. Later, when a path becomes available, the traffic controller quickly selects the first PCB from the queue for that path.

The **I/O scheduler** performs the same job as the Process Scheduler described in Chapter 4 on processor management—that is, it allocates the devices, control units, and channels. Under heavy loads, when the number of requests is greater than the number of available paths, the I/O scheduler must decide which request to satisfy first. Many of the criteria and objectives discussed in Chapter 4 also apply here. In many systems, the major difference between I/O scheduling and process scheduling is that I/O requests are not preempted. Once the channel program has started, it's allowed to continue to completion even though I/O requests with higher priorities may have entered the queue. This is feasible because channel programs are relatively short, 50 to 100 ms. Other systems subdivide an I/O request into several stages and allow preemption of the I/O request at any one of these stages.

Some systems allow the I/O scheduler to give preferential treatment to I/O requests from high-priority programs. In that case, if a process has high priority, then its I/O requests would also have high priority and would be satisfied before other I/O requests with lower priorities. The I/O scheduler must synchronize its work with the traffic controller to make sure that a path is available to satisfy the selected I/O requests.

The **I/O device handler** processes the I/O interrupts, handles error conditions, and provides detailed scheduling algorithms, which are extremely device dependent. Each type of I/O device has its own device handler algorithm.

Device Handler Seek Strategies

A **seek strategy** for the I/O device handler is the predetermined policy that the device handler uses to allocate access to the device among the many processes that may be waiting for it. It determines the order in which the processes get the device, and the goal is to keep seek time to a minimum. We'll look at some of the most commonly used seek strategies—first-come, first-served (FCFS); shortest seek time first (SSTF); and SCAN and its variations LOOK, N-Step SCAN, C-SCAN, and C-LOOK.

Every scheduling algorithm should do the following:
- Minimize arm movement
- Minimize mean response time
- Minimize the variance in response time

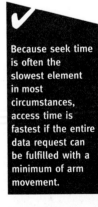

Because seek time is often the slowest element in most circumstances, access time is fastest if the entire data request can be fulfilled with a minimum of arm movement.

These goals are only a guide. In actual systems, the designer must choose the strategy that makes the system as fair as possible to the general user population while using the system's resources as efficiently as possible.

First-come, first-served (FCFS) is the simplest device-scheduling algorithm; it is easy to program and essentially fair to users. However, on average, it doesn't meet any of the three goals of a seek strategy. To illustrate, consider a single-sided disk with one record-able surface where the tracks are numbered from 0 to 49. It takes 1 ms to travel from one track to the next adjacent one. For this example, let's say that while retrieving data from Track 15, the following list of requests has arrived: Tracks 4, 40, 11, 35, 7, and 14. Let's also assume that once a requested track has been reached, the entire track is read into main memory. The path of the read/write head looks like the graph shown in Figure 7.15.

(figure 7.15)

The arm makes many time-consuming movements as it travels from track to track to satisfy all requests in FCFS order.

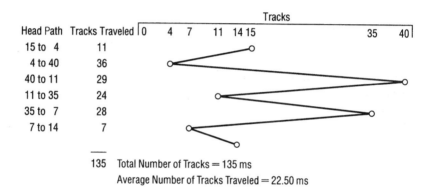

In Figure 7.15, it takes a long time, 135 ms, to satisfy the entire series of requests— and that's before considering the work to be done when the arm is finally in place—search time and data transfer.

FCFS has an obvious disadvantage of extreme arm movement: from 15 to 4, up to 40, back to 11, up to 35, back to 7, and, finally, up to 14. Remember, seek time is the most time-consuming of the three functions performed here, so any algorithm that can min-imize it is preferable to FCFS.

Shortest seek time first (SSTF) uses the same underlying philosophy as Shortest Job Next (described in Chapter 4), where the shortest jobs are processed first and longer jobs are made to wait. With SSTF, the request with the track closest to the one being served (that is, the one with the shortest distance to travel) is the next to be satisfied, thus minimizing overall seek time. Figure 7.16 shows what happens to the same track requests that took 135 ms to service using FCFS; in this example, all track requests are present and on the wait queue.

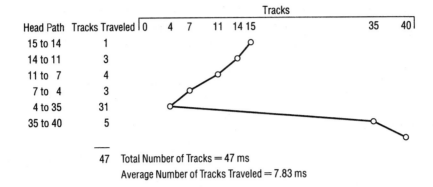

(figure 7.16)

Using the SSTF algorithm, with all track requests on the wait queue, arm movement is reduced by almost one third while satisfying the same requests shown in Figure 7.15 (using the FCFS algorithm).

Again, without considering search time and data transfer time, it took 47 ms to satisfy all requests—which is about one third of the time required by FCFS. That's a substantial improvement.

But SSTF has its disadvantages. Remember that the Shortest Job Next (SJN) process scheduling algorithm had a tendency to favor the short jobs and postpone the long, unwieldy jobs. The same holds true for SSTF. It favors easy-to-reach requests and postpones traveling to those that are out of the way.

For example, let's say that in the previous example, the arm is at Track 11 and is preparing to go to Track 7 when the system suddenly gets a deluge of requests, including requests for Tracks 22, 13, 16, 29, 1, and 21. With SSTF, the system notes that Track 13 is closer to the arm's present position (only two tracks away) than the older request for Track 7 (five tracks away), so Track 13 is handled first. Of the requests now waiting, the next closest is Track 16, so off it goes—moving farther and farther away from Tracks 7 and 1. In fact, during periods of heavy loads, the arm stays in the center of the disk, where it can satisfy the majority of requests easily and it ignores (or indefinitely postpones) those on the outer edges of the disk. Therefore, this algorithm meets the first goal of seek strategies but fails to meet the other two.

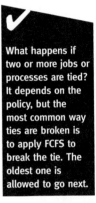

What happens if two or more jobs or processes are tied? It depends on the policy, but the most common way ties are broken is to apply FCFS to break the tie. The oldest one is allowed to go next.

SCAN uses a directional bit to indicate whether the arm is moving toward the center of the disk or away from it. The algorithm moves the arm methodically from the outer to the inner track, servicing every request in its path. When it reaches the innermost track, it reverses direction and moves toward the outer tracks, again servicing every request in its path. The most common variation of SCAN is **LOOK**, sometimes known as the elevator algorithm, in which the arm doesn't necessarily go all the way to either edge unless there are requests there. In effect, it "looks" ahead for a request before going to service it. In Figure 7.17, we assume that the arm is moving first toward the inner (higher-numbered) tracks before reversing direction. In this example, all track requests are present and on the wait queue.

Again, without adding search time and data transfer time, it took 61 ms to satisfy all requests, 14 ms more than with SSTF. Does this make SCAN a less attractive algorithm than SSTF? For this particular example, the answer is yes. But for the overall system, the answer is no because it eliminates the possibility of indefinite postponement of requests in out-of-the-way places—at either edge of the disk.

Also, as requests arrive, each is incorporated in its proper place in the queue and serviced when the arm reaches that track. Therefore, if Track 11 is being served when the request for Track 13 arrives, the arm continues on its way to Track 7 and then to Track 1. Track 13 must wait until the arm starts on its way back, as does the request for Track 16. This eliminates a great deal of arm movement and saves time in the end. In fact, SCAN meets all three goals for seek strategies.

Variations of SCAN, in addition to LOOK, are N-Step SCAN, C-SCAN, and C-LOOK.

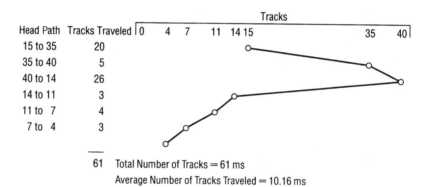

(figure 7.17)

The LOOK algorithm makes the arm move systematically from the first requested track at one edge of the disk to the last requested track at the other edge. In this example, all track requests are on the wait queue.

Head Path	Tracks Traveled
15 to 35	20
35 to 40	5
40 to 14	26
14 to 11	3
11 to 7	4
7 to 4	3
	61

Total Number of Tracks = 61 ms

Average Number of Tracks Traveled = 10.16 ms

N-Step SCAN holds all new requests until the arm starts on its way back. Any requests that arrive while the arm is in motion are grouped for the arm's next sweep.

With **C-SCAN** (an abbreviation for Circular SCAN), the arm picks up requests on its path during the inward sweep. When the innermost track has been reached, it immediately returns to the outermost track and starts servicing requests that arrived during its last inward sweep. With this modification, the system can provide quicker service to those requests that accumulated for the low-numbered tracks while the arm was moving inward. The theory here is that by the time the arm reaches the highest-numbered tracks, there are few requests immediately behind it. However, there are many requests at the far end of the disk and these have been waiting the longest. Therefore, C-SCAN is designed to provide a more uniform wait time.

C-LOOK is an optimization of C-SCAN, just as LOOK is an optimization of SCAN. In this algorithm, the sweep inward stops at the last high-numbered track request, so the arm doesn't move all the way to the last track unless it's required to do so. In addition, the arm doesn't necessarily return to the lowest-numbered track; it returns only to the lowest-numbered track that's requested.

Which strategy is best? It's up to the system designer to select the best algorithm for each environment. It's a job that's complicated because the day-to-day performance of any scheduling algorithm depends on the load it must handle; but some broad generalizations can be made based on simulation studies:

- FCFS works well with light loads; but as soon as the load grows, service time becomes unacceptably long.
- SSTF is quite popular and intuitively appealing. It works well with moderate loads but has the problem of localization under heavy loads.
- SCAN works well with light to moderate loads and eliminates the problem of indefinite postponement. SCAN is similar to SSTF in throughput and mean service times.
- C-SCAN works well with moderate to heavy loads and has a very small variance in service times.

The best scheduling algorithm for a specific computing system may be a combination of more than one scheme. For instance, it might be a combination of two schemes: SCAN or LOOK during light to moderate loads, and C-SCAN or C-LOOK during heavy load times.

Search Strategies: Rotational Ordering

So far we've only tried to optimize seek times. To complete the picture, we'll now look at a way to optimize search times by ordering the requests once the read/write heads have been positioned. This search strategy is called **rotational ordering**.

To help illustrate the abstract concept of rotational ordering, let's consider a virtual cylinder with a movable read/write head.

Figure 7.18 illustrates the list of requests arriving at this cylinder for different sectors on different tracks. For this example, we'll assume that the cylinder has only five tracks, numbered 0 through 4, and that each track contains five sectors, numbered 0 through 4. We'll take the requests in the order in which they arrive.

(figure 7.18)

This movable-head cylinder takes 5 ms to move the read/write head from one track to the next. The read/write head is initially positioned at Track 0, Sector 0. It takes 5 ms to rotate the cylinder from Sector 0 to Sector 4 and 1 ms to transfer one sector from the cylinder to main memory.

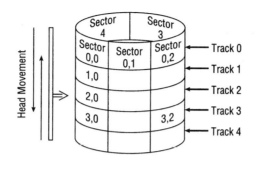

Request List	
Track	Sector
0	1
1	4
1	3
2	0
2	3
2	1
3	2
3	0

Each request is satisfied as it comes in. The results are shown in Table 7.5.

(table 7.5)

It takes 36 ms to fill the eight requests on the movable-head cylinder shown in Figure 7.18.

	Request (Track, Sector)	Seek Time	Search Time	Data Transfer	Total Time
1.	0,1	0	1	1	2
2.	1,4	5	2	1	8
3.	1,3	0	3	1	4
4.	2,0	5	1	1	7
5.	2,3	0	2	1	3
6.	2,4	0	0	1	1
7.	3,2	5	2	1	8
8.	3,0	0	2	1	3
	TOTALS	15 ms +	13 ms +	8 ms =	36 ms

Although nothing can be done to improve the time spent moving the read/write head because it's dependent on the hardware, the amount of time wasted due to rotational delay can be reduced. If the requests are ordered within each track so that the first sector requested on the second track is the next number higher than the one just served, rotational delay will be minimized, as shown in Table 7.6.

To properly implement this algorithm, the device controller must provide rotational sensing so the device driver can see which sector is currently under the read/write head. Under heavy I/O loads, this kind of ordering can significantly increase throughput, especially if the device has fixed read/write heads rather than movable heads.

Disk pack cylinders are an extension of the previous example. Once the heads are positioned on a cylinder, each surface has its own read/write head shown in Figure 7.5. So rotational ordering can be accomplished on a surface-by-surface basis, and the read/write heads can be activated in turn with no additional movement required.

Request (Track, Sector)		Seek Time	Search Time	Data Transfer	Total Time
1.	0,1	0	1	1	2
2.	1,3	5	1	1	7
3.	1,4	0	0	1	1
4.	2,0	5	0	1	6
5.	2,3	0	2	1	3
6.	2,4	0	0	1	1
7.	3,0	5	0	1	6
8.	3,2	0	1	1	2
	TOTALS	15 ms +	5 ms +	8 ms =	28 ms

(table 7.6)

It takes 28 ms to fill the same eight requests shown in Table 7.5 after the requests are ordered to minimize search time, reducing it from 13 ms to 5 ms.

Only one read/write head can be active at any one time, so the controller must be ready to handle mutually exclusive requests such as Request 2 and Request 5 in Table 7.6. They're mutually exclusive because both are requesting Sector 3, one at Track 1 and the other at Track 2, but only one of the two read/write heads can be transmitting at any given time. So the policy could state that the tracks will be processed from low-numbered to high-numbered and then from high-numbered to low-numbered in a sweeping motion such as that used in SCAN. Therefore, to handle requests on a disk pack, there would be two orderings of requests: one to handle the position of the read/write heads making up the cylinder and the other to handle the processing of each cylinder.

RAID

RAID is a set of physical disk drives that is viewed as a single logical unit by the operating system. It was introduced to close the widening gap between increasingly fast processors and slower disk drives. RAID assumes that several small-capacity disk drives are preferable to a few large-capacity disk drives because, by distributing the data among several smaller disks, the system can simultaneously access the requested data from the multiple drives, resulting in improved I/O performance and improved data recovery in the event of disk failure.

A typical disk array configuration may have five disk drives connected to a specialized controller, which houses the software that coordinates the transfer of data from the disks in the array to a large-capacity disk connected to the I/O subsystem, as shown in Figure 7.19. This configuration is viewed by the operating system as a single large-capacity disk, so that no software changes are needed.

(figure 7.19)

Data being transferred in parallel from a Level 0 RAID configuration to a large-capacity disk. The software in the controller ensures that the strips are stored in correct order.

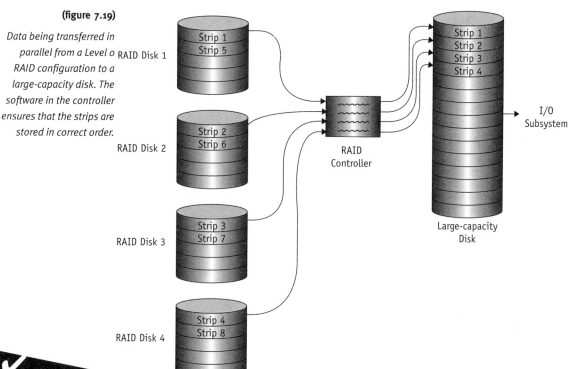

Data Transferred in Parallel

Data is divided into segments called strips, which are distributed across the disks in the array. A set of consecutive strips across disks is called a **stripe** and the whole process is called striping. Figure 7.19 shows how data strips are distributed in an array of four disks.

RAID technology was originally proposed by researchers at the University of California at Berkeley, who created the acronym to stand for Redundant Array of Inexpensive Disks. The industry has since amended the acronym to represent Redundant Array of Independent Disks to emphasize the scheme's improved disk performance and reliability.

There are seven primary levels of RAID, numbered from Level 0 through Level 6. It should be noted that the levels do not indicate a hierarchy but rather denote different

While RAID introduces the much-needed concept of redundancy to help systems recover from hardware failure, most RAID configurations require more disk drives, which increases hardware costs.

233

types of configurations and error correction capabilities. Table 7.7 provides a summary of the seven levels including how error correction is implemented and the perceived quality of performance.

RAID Level	Error Correction Method	I/O Request Rate	Data Transfer Rate
0	None	Excellent	Excellent
1	Mirroring	Read: Good Write: Fair	Read: Fair Write: Fair
2	Hamming code	Poor	Excellent
3	Word parity	Poor	Excellent
4	Strip parity	Read: Excellent Write: Fair	Read: Fair Write: Poor
5	Distributed strip parity	Read: Excellent Write: Fair	Read: Fair Write: Poor
6	Distributed strip parity and independent data check	Read: Excellent Write: Poor	Read: Fair Write: Poor

(table 7.7)

The seven standard levels of RAID provide various degrees of error correction. Cost, speed, and the system's applications are significant factors to consider when choosing a system.

Level Zero

RAID Level 0 uses data striping without parity, without error correction. It is the only level that does not provide error correction, or redundancy, and so it is not considered a true form of RAID because it cannot recover from hardware failure. However, it does offer the same significant benefit of all RAID systems—that this group of devices appears to the operating system as a single logical unit.

Raid Level 0 is well suited to transferring large quantities of non-critical data. In the configuration shown in Figure 7.20, when the operating system issues a read command for the first four strips, all four strips can be transferred in parallel, improving system performance. Level 0 works well in combination with other configurations as we'll see in our discussion about Nested RAID Levels.

Level One

RAID Level 1 also uses striping, and is called a mirrored configuration because it provides redundancy by having a duplicate set of all data in a mirror array of disks, which acts as a backup system in the event of hardware failure. If one drive should fail, the system would immediately retrieve the data from its backup disk, making this a very reliable system. Figure 7.21 shows a RAID Level 1 configuration with three disks on each identical array: main and mirror.

Using Level 1, read requests can be satisfied by either disk containing the requested data. The choice of disk could minimize seek time and rotational delay. The disadvantage is that write requests require twice as much *effort* because data must be written twice, once to each set of disks. However, this does not require twice the amount of *time* because both writes can be done in parallel.

Level 1 is an expensive system to construct because it requires at least twice the disk capacity of a Level 0 system, but its advantage of improved reliability makes it ideal for data-critical real-time systems.

(figure 7.20)

RAID Level 0 with four disks in the array. Strips 1, 2, 3, and 4 make up a stripe. Strips 5, 6, 7, and 8 make up another stripe, and so on.

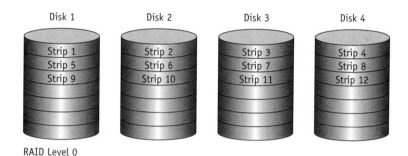

RAID Level 0

(figure 7.21)

RAID Level 1 with three disks in the main array and three corresponding disks in the backup array, the mirrored array.

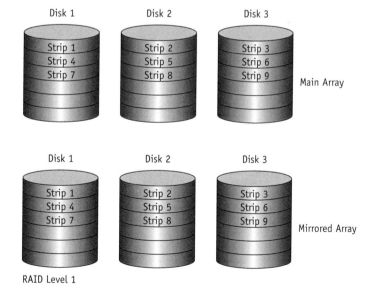

RAID Level 1

Level Two

RAID Level 2 uses very small strips (often the size of a word or a byte) and uses a Hamming code to provide error detection and correction, or redundancy. The **Hamming code** is an algorithm that adds extra, redundant bits to the data and is therefore able to correct single-bit errors and detect double-bit errors.

Level 2 is an expensive and complex configuration to implement because the number of disks in the array depends on the size of the strip, and all drives must be highly synchronized in both rotational movement and arm positioning. For example, if each strip is 4 bits, then the Hamming code adds three parity bits in positions 1, 2, and 4 of the newly created 7-bit data item. In the example of RAID Level 2 shown in Figure 7.22, the array has seven disks, one for each bit. Its advantage is that, if a drive should malfunction, only one bit would be affected and the data could be quickly corrected.

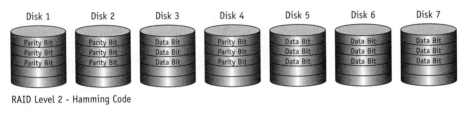

RAID Level 2 - Hamming Code

(figure 7.22)

RAID Level 2. Seven disks are needed in the array to store a 4-bit data item, one for each bit and three for the parity bits. Each disk stores either a bit or a parity bit based on the Hamming code used for redundancy.

Level Three

RAID Level 3 is a modification of Level 2 that requires only one disk for redundancy. Only one parity bit is computed for each strip, and it is stored in the designated redundant disk. Figure 7.23 shows a five-disk array that can store 4-bit strips and their parity bit. If a drive malfunctions, the RAID controller considers all bits coming from that drive to be 0 and notes the location of the damaged bit. Therefore, if a data item being read has a parity error, then the controller knows that the bit from the faulty drive should have been a 1 and corrects it. If data is written to an array that has a malfunctioning disk, the controller keeps the parity consistent so data can be regenerated when the array is restored. The system returns to normal when the failed disk is replaced and its contents are regenerated on the new disk.

Level Four

RAID Level 4 uses the same strip scheme found in Levels 0 and 1, but it computes a parity for each strip, and then it stores these parities in the corresponding strip in the designated parity disk. Figure 7.24 shows a Level 4 disk array with four disks; the first

(figure 7.23)

RAID Level 3. A 4-bit data item is stored in the first four disks of the array. The fifth disk is used to store the parity for the stored data item.

(figure 7.24)

RAID Level 4. The array contains four disks: the first three are used to store data strips, and the fourth is used to store the parity of those strips.

three hold data while the fourth stores the parities for the corresponding strips on the first three disks. The advantage of Level 4 is that if any one drive fails, data can be restored using the bits in the parity disk. Parity is computed every time a write command is executed. However, if data is rewritten, then the RAID controller must update both the data and parity strips. Therefore, the parity disk is accessed with every write, or rewrite, operation, sometimes causing a bottleneck in the system.

Level Five

RAID Level 5 is a modification of Level 4. Instead of designating one disk for storing parities, it distributes the parity strips across the disks, which avoids the bottleneck created in Level 4. Its disadvantage is that regenerating data from a failed drive is more complicated. Figure 7.25 shows a Level 5 disk array with four disks.

(figure 7.25)

RAID Level 5 with four disks. Notice how the parity strips are distributed among the disks.

Level Six

RAID Level 6 was introduced by the Berkeley research team in a paper that followed its original outline of RAID levels. This system provides an extra degree of error detection and correction because it requires two different parity calculations. One calculation is the same as that used in Levels 4 and 5; the other is an independent data-check algorithm. Both parities are distributed on separate disks across the array, and they are stored in the strip that corresponds to the data strips, as shown in Figure 7.26. The advantage is that the double parity allows for data restoration even if two disks fail.

However, the redundancy increases the time needed to write data because each write affects two parity strips. In addition, Level 6 requires that two disks become dedicated to parity strips and not data, which therefore reduces the number of data disks in the array.

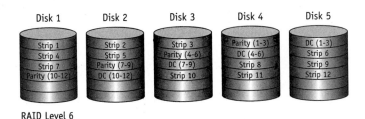

RAID Level 6

(figure 7.26)

RAID Level 6. Notice how parity strips and data check (DC) strips are distributed across the disks.

Nested RAID Levels

Additional complex configurations of RAID can be created by combining multiple levels. For example, a RAID Level 10 system consists of a Level 1 system mirrored to a second Level 1 system, both controlled by a single Level 0 system, as shown in Figure 7.27. Some RAID combinations are listed in Table 7.8.

RAID Level	Combinations
01 (or 0+1)	A Level 1 system consisting of multiple Level 0 systems
10 (or 1+0)	A Level 0 system consisting of multiple Level 1 systems
03 (or 0+3)	A Level 3 system consisting of multiple Level 0 systems
30 (or 3+0)	A Level 0 system consisting of multiple Level 3 systems
50 (or 5+0)	A Level 0 system consisting of multiple Level 5 systems
60 (or 6+0)	A Level 0 system consisting of multiple Level 6 systems

(table 7.8)

Some common nested RAID configurations. Important: RAID 01 and 03 are not to be confused with RAID Levels 1 and 3, respectively.

(figure 7.27)

A RAID Level 10 system.

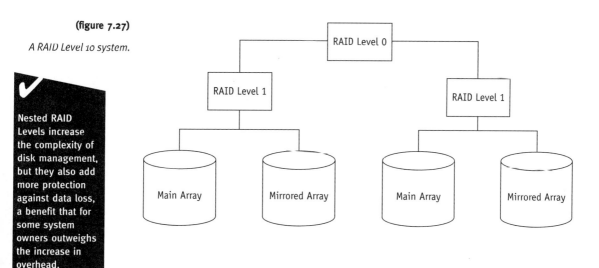

✔

Nested RAID Levels increase the complexity of disk management, but they also add more protection against data loss, a benefit that for some system owners outweighs the increase in overhead.

Conclusion

The Device Manager's job is to manage every system device as effectively as possible despite the unique characteristics of each. The devices have varying speeds and degrees of sharability; some can handle direct access and some only sequential access. For magnetic media, they can have one or many read/write heads, and the heads can be in a fixed position for optimum speed or able to move across the surface for optimum storage space. For optical media, the Device Manager tracks storage locations and adjusts the disc's speed accordingly so data is recorded and retrieved correctly. For flash memory, the Device Manager tracks every USB device and assures that data is sent and received correctly.

Balancing the demand for these devices is a complex task that's divided among several hardware components: channels, control units, and the devices themselves. The success of the I/O subsystem depends on the communications that link these parts.

In this chapter we reviewed several seek strategies, each with distinct advantages and disadvantages, as shown in Table 7.9.

Strategy	Advantages	Disadvantages
FCFS	• Easy to implement • Sufficient for light loads	• Doesn't provide best average service • Doesn't maximize throughput
SSTF	• Throughput better than FCFS • Tends to minimize arm movement • Tends to minimize response time	• May cause starvation of some requests • Localizes under heavy loads
SCAN/LOOK	• Eliminates starvation • Throughput similar to SSTF • Works well with light to moderate loads	• Needs directional bit • More complex algorithm to implement • Increased overhead
N-Step SCAN	• Easier to implement than SCAN	• The most recent requests wait longer than with SCAN
C-SCAN/C-LOOK	• Works well with moderate to heavy loads • No directional bit • Small variance in service time • C-LOOK doesn't travel to unused tracks	• May not be fair to recent requests for high-numbered tracks • More complex algorithm than N-Step SCAN, causing more overhead

(table 7.9)

Comparison of DASD seek strategies discussed in this chapter.

Our discussion of RAID included a comparison of the considerable strengths and weaknesses of each level, and combinations of levels, as well as the potential boost to system reliability and error correction that each represents.

Thus far in this text, we've reviewed three of the operating system's managers: the Memory Manager, the Processor Manager, and the Device Manager. In the next chapter, we'll meet the fourth, the File Manager, which is responsible for the health and well-being of every file used by the system, including the system's files, those submitted by users, and those generated as output.

Key Terms

access time: the total time required to access data in secondary storage.

blocking: a storage-saving and I/O-saving technique that groups individual records into a block that's stored and retrieved as a unit.

buffers: temporary storage areas residing in main memory, channels, and control units.

Channel Status Word (CSW): a data structure that contains information indicating the condition of the channel, including three bits for the three components of the I/O subsystem—one each for the channel, control unit, and device.

C-LOOK: a scheduling strategy for direct access storage devices that's an optimization of C-SCAN.

C-SCAN: a scheduling strategy for direct access storage devices that's used to optimize seek time. It's an abbreviation for circular-SCAN.

cylinder: a concept that describes a virtual tube that is formed when two or more read/write heads are positioned at the same track, at the same relative position, on their respective surfaces.

dedicated device: a device that can be assigned to only one job at a time; it serves that job for the entire time the job is active.

direct access storage device (DASD): any secondary storage device that can directly read or write to a specific place. Sometimes called a random access storage device.

direct memory access (DMA): an I/O technique that allows a control unit to access main memory directly and transfer data without the intervention of the CPU.

first-come, first-served (FCFS): the simplest scheduling algorithm for direct access storage devices that satisfies track requests in the order in which they are received.

flash memory: a type of nonvolatile memory used as a secondary storage device that can be erased and reprogrammed in blocks of data.

Hamming code: an error-detecting and error-correcting code that greatly improves the reliability of data, named after mathematician Richard Hamming, its inventor.

I/O channel: a specialized programmable unit placed between the CPU and the control units, which synchronizes the fast speed of the CPU with the slow speed of the I/O device and vice versa, making it possible to overlap I/O operations with CPU operations.

I/O channel program: the program that controls the channels.

I/O control unit: the hardware unit containing the electronic components common to one type of I/O device, such as a disk drive.

I/O device handler: the module that processes the I/O interrupts, handles error conditions, and provides detailed scheduling algorithms that are extremely device dependent.

I/O scheduler: one of the modules of the I/O subsystem that allocates the devices, control units, and channels.

I/O subsystem: a collection of modules within the operating system that controls all I/O requests.

I/O traffic controller: one of the modules of the I/O subsystem that monitors the status of every device, control unit, and channel.

interrecord gap (IRG): an unused space between records on a magnetic tape. It facilitates the tape's start/stop operations.

interrupt: a hardware signal that suspends execution of a program and activates the execution of a special program known as the interrupt handler.

lands: flat surface areas on the reflective layer of an optical disc. Each land is interpreted as a 1. Contrasts with pits, which are interpreted as 0s.

LOOK: a scheduling strategy for direct access storage devices that's used to optimize seek time. Sometimes known as the elevator algorithm.

N-step SCAN: a variation of the SCAN scheduling strategy for direct access storage devices that's used to optimize seek times.

pits: tiny depressions on the reflective layer of an optical disc. Each pit is interpreted as a 0. Contrasts with lands, which are interpreted as 1s.

RAID: acronym for redundant array of independent disks; a group of hard disks controlled in such a way that they speed read access of data on secondary storage devices and aid data recovery.

rotational ordering: an algorithm used to reorder record requests within tracks to optimize search time.

SCAN: a scheduling strategy for direct access storage devices that's used to optimize seek time. The most common variations are N-step SCAN and C-SCAN.

search time: the time it takes to rotate the disk from the moment an I/O command is issued until the requested record is moved under the read/write head. Also known as rotational delay.

seek strategy: a predetermined policy used by the I/O device handler to optimize seek times.

seek time: the time required to position the read/write head on the proper track from the time the I/O request is issued.

sequential access medium: any medium that stores records only in a sequential manner, one after the other, such as magnetic tape.

shared device: a device that can be assigned to several active processes at the same time.

shortest seek time first (SSTF): a scheduling strategy for direct access storage devices that's used to optimize seek time. The track requests are ordered so the one closest to the currently active track is satisfied first and the ones farthest away are made to wait.

storage: the place where data is stored in the computer system. Secondary storage is nonvolatile media, such as disks and flash memory. Primary storage is main memory.

stripe: a set of consecutive strips across disks; the strips contain data bits and sometimes parity bits depending on the RAID level.

track: a path on a storage medium along which data is recorded.

transfer rate: the rate at which data is transferred from sequential access media.

transfer time: the time required for data to be transferred between secondary storage and main memory.

universal serial bus (USB) controller: the interface between the operating system, device drivers, and applications that read and write to devices connected to the computer through the USB port.

virtual device: a dedicated device that has been transformed into a shared device through the use of spooling techniques.

Interesting Searches

- Solid State Hard Drive
- Circular Buffers
- Direct Memory Access
- RAID Level Performance
- Blu-ray Storage Media

Exercises

Research Topics

A. Conduct research to discover two of the fastest devices available today for desktop computers or workstations that can be used to copy important files from the computer to a medium (paper, disk, flash memory, tape, etc.), and that can be removed and stored in a safe place off-site. For both devices, explain in a short paragraph why you believe they are the best available. Include important benchmarks. Cite your sources and attach documentation from your research to substantiate your answer.

B. Consult current academic literature to research the concept of the circular buffer. Define it and compare and contrast it to a single buffer and double buffers. Explain why the circular buffer might be advantageous in multimedia applications. Cite your sources and the dates your source information was published.

Exercises

1. Name three examples of secondary storage media other than hard disks.
2. Describe how primary storage differs from secondary storage.

3. Explain the differences between buffering and blocking.

4. Given the following characteristics for a disk pack with 10 platters yielding 18 recordable surfaces:

Rotational speed = 10 ms

Transfer rate = 0.1 ms/track

Density per track = 19,000 bytes

Number of records to be stored = 200,000 records

Size of each record = 160 bytes

Block size = 10 logical records

Number of tracks per surface = 500

Find the following:

a. Number of blocks per track

b. Waste per track

c. Number of tracks required to store the entire file

d. Total waste to store the entire file

e. Time to write all of the blocks (Use rotational speed; ignore the time it takes to move to the next track.)

f. Time to write all of the records if they're not blocked. (Use rotational speed; ignore the time it takes to move to the next track.)

g. Optimal blocking factor to minimize waste

h. What would be the answer to (e) if the time it takes to move to the next track were 5 ms?

i. What would be the answer to (f) if the time it takes to move to the next track were 5 ms?

5. Given the following characteristics for a magnetic tape:

Density = 1600 bpi

Speed = 200 inches/second

Size = 2400 feet

Start/stop time = 3 ms

Number of records to be stored = 200,000 records

Size of each record = 160 bytes

Block size = 10 logical records

IBG = 0.5 inch

Find the following:

a. Number of blocks needed

b. Size of the block in bytes

c. Time required to read one block

    d. Time required to write all of the blocks

    e. Amount of tape used for data only, in inches

    f. Total amount of tape used (data + IBGs), in inches

6. Given that it takes 1 ms to travel from one track to the next, and that the arm is originally positioned at Track 15 moving toward the low-numbered tracks, and you are using the LOOK scheduling policy, compute how long it will take to satisfy the following requests—4, 40, 35, 11, 14, and 7. All requests are present in the wait queue. (Ignore rotational time and transfer time; just consider seek time.) Why do you think there is a difference between your result and the one in Figure 7.17?

7. Minimizing the variance of system response time is an important goal, but it does not always prevent an occasional user from suffering indefinite postponement. What mechanism would you incorporate into a disk scheduling policy to counteract this problem and still provide reasonable response time to the user population as a whole?

Advanced Exercises

8. What is the difference between buffering and spooling?

9. Under light loading conditions, every disk scheduling policy discussed in this chapter tends to behave like one of the policies discussed in this chapter. Which one is it and why?

10. Assume you have a file of 10 records (identified as A, B, C, . . . J) to be stored on a disk that holds 10 records per track. Once the file is stored, the records will be accessed sequentially: A, B, C, . . . J. It takes 2 ms to process each record once it has been transferred into memory. It takes 10 ms for the disk to complete one rotation. It takes 1 ms to transfer the record from the disk to main memory. Suppose you store the records in the order given: A, B, C, . . . J.

    Compute how long it will take to process all 10 records. Break up your computation into (1) the time to transfer a record, (2) the time to process a record, and (3) the time to access the next record.

11. Given the same situation described in the previous exercise.

    a. Organize the records so that they're stored in non-alphabetical order (not A, B, C, . . . J) to reduce the time it takes to process them sequentially in alphabetical order.

b. Compute how long it will take to process all 10 records using this new order. Break up your computation into (1) the time to transfer a record, (2) the time to process a record, and (3) the time to access the next record.

12. Track requests are not usually equally or evenly distributed. For example, the tracks where the disk directory resides are accessed more often than those where the user's files reside. Suppose that you know that 50 percent of the requests are for a small, fixed number of cylinders.

a. Which one of the scheduling policies presented in this chapter would be the best under these conditions?

b. Can you design one that would be better?

13. Complete the following chart for three optical storage devices. Cite your sources.

Type	Transfer Rate (bytes per second)	Storage Capacity	Average Access Time	Cost in Dollars
CD-RW				
DVD-RW				
Blu-ray				

14. Give an example of an environment or application that best matches the characteristics of each of the following RAID levels:

a. Level 0

b. Level 1

c. Level 3

d. Level 5

e. Level 6

Programming Exercise

15. Write a program that will simulate the FCFS, SSTF, LOOK, and C-LOOK seek optimization strategies. Assume that:

a. The disk's outer track is the 0 track and the disk contains 200 tracks per surface. Each track holds eight sectors numbered 0 through 7.

b. A seek takes $10 + 0.1 * T$ ms, where T is the number of tracks of motion from one request to the next, and 10 is a movement time constant.

c. One full rotation takes 8 ms.

d. Transfer time is 1 ms.

Use the following data to test your program:

Arrival Time	Track Requested	Sector Requested
0	45	0
23	132	6
25	20	2
29	23	1
35	198	7
45	170	5
57	180	3
83	78	4
88	73	5
95	150	7

For comparison purposes, compute the average, variance, and standard deviation of the time required to accommodate all requests under each of the strategies. Consolidate your results into a table.

Optional: Run your program again with different data and compare your results. Recommend the best policy and explain why.

Chapter 8

File Management

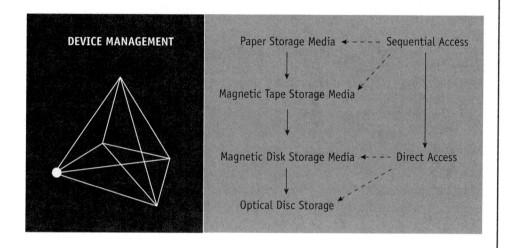

DEVICE MANAGEMENT

Paper Storage Media ◄ - - - - Sequential Access

Magnetic Tape Storage Media

Magnetic Disk Storage Media ◄ - - - Direct Access

Optical Disc Storage

> **"** *Knowledge is of two kinds. We know a subject ourselves, or we know where we can find information upon it.* **"**
>
> —Samuel Johnson *(1709–1784)*

Learning Objectives

After completing this chapter, you should be able to describe:

- The fundamentals of file management and the structure of the file management system
- File-naming conventions, including the role of extensions
- The difference between fixed-length and variable-length record format
- The advantages and disadvantages of contiguous, noncontiguous, and indexed file storage techniques
- Comparisons of sequential and direct file access
- Access control techniques and how they compare
- The role of data compression in file storage

The File Manager controls every file in the system. In this chapter we'll learn how files are organized logically, how they're stored physically, how they're accessed, and who is allowed to access them. We'll also study the interaction between the File Manager and the Device Manager.

The efficiency of the File Manager depends on how the system's files are organized (sequential, direct, or indexed sequential); how they're stored (contiguously, noncontiguously, or indexed); how each file's records are structured (fixed-length or variable-length); and how access to these files is controlled. We'll look at each of these variables in this chapter.

The File Manager

The File Manager (also called the file management system) is the software responsible for creating, deleting, modifying, and controlling access to files—as well as for managing the resources used by the files. The File Manager provides support for libraries of programs and data to online users, for spooling operations, and for interactive computing. These functions are performed in collaboration with the Device Manager.

Responsibilities of the File Manager

The File Manager has a complex job. It's in charge of the system's physical components, its information resources, and the policies used to store and distribute the files. To carry out its responsibilities, it must perform these four tasks:

1. Keep track of where each file is stored.
2. Use a policy that will determine where and how the files will be stored, making sure to efficiently use the available storage space and provide efficient access to the files.
3. Allocate each file when a user has been cleared for access to it, then record its use.
4. Deallocate the file when the file is to be returned to storage, and communicate its availability to others who may be waiting for it.

For example, the file system is like a library, with the File Manager playing the part of the librarian who performs the same four tasks:

1. A librarian uses the catalog to keep track of each item in the collection; each entry lists the call number and the details that help patrons find the books they want.
2. The library relies on a policy to store everything in the collection including oversized books, magazines, books-on-tape, DVDs, maps, and videos. And they must be physically arranged so people can find what they need.

3. When it's requested, the item is retrieved from its shelf and the borrower's name is noted in the circulation records.

4. When the item is returned, the librarian makes the appropriate notation in the circulation records and reshelves it.

In a computer system, the File Manager keeps track of its files with directories that contain the filename, its physical location in secondary storage, and important information about each file.

The File Manager's policy determines where each file is stored and how the system, and its users, will be able to access them simply—via commands that are independent from device details. In addition, the policy must determine who will have access to what material, and this involves two factors: flexibility of access to the information and its subsequent protection. The File Manager does this by allowing access to shared files, providing distributed access, and allowing users to browse through public directories. Meanwhile, the operating system must protect its files against system malfunctions and provide security checks via account numbers and passwords to preserve the integrity of the data and safeguard against tampering. These protection techniques are explained later in this chapter.

The computer system *allocates* a file by activating the appropriate secondary storage device and loading the file into memory while updating its records of who is using what file.

Finally, the File Manager *deallocates* a file by updating the file tables and rewriting the file (if revised) to the secondary storage device. Any processes waiting to access the file are then notified of its availability.

Definitions

Before we continue, let's take a minute to define some basic file elements, illustrated in Figure 8.1, that relate to our discussion of the File Manager.

(figure 8.1)

Files are made up of records. Records consist of fields.

Record 19 →	Field A	Field B	Field C	Field D
Record 20 →	Field A	Field B	Field C	Field D
Record 21 →	Field A	Field B	Field C	Field D
Record 22 →	Field A	Field B	Field C	Field D

A **field** is a group of related bytes that can be identified by the user with a name, type, and size. A **record** is a group of related fields.

A **file** is a group of related records that contains information to be used by specific application programs to generate reports. This type of file contains data and is sometimes called a flat file because it has no connections to other files; unlike databases, it has no dimensionality.

A **database** appears to the File Manager to be a type of file, but databases are more complex because they're actually groups of related files that are interconnected at various levels to give users flexibility of access to the data stored. If the user's database requires a specific structure, the File Manager must be able to support it.

Program files contain instructions and data files contain data; but as far as storage is concerned, the File Manager treats them exactly the same way.

Directories are special files with listings of filenames and their attributes. Data collected to monitor system performance and provide for system accounting is collected into files. In fact, every program and data file accessed by the computer system, as well as every piece of computer software, is treated as a file.

Interacting with the File Manager

The user communicates with the File Manager, which responds to specific commands.

Some examples displayed in Figure 8.2 are OPEN, DELETE, RENAME, and COPY. Actually, files can be created with other system-specific terms: for example, the first time a user gives the command to save a file, it's actually the CREATE command. In other operating systems, the OPEN NEW command within a program indicates to the File Manager that a file must be created.

These commands and many more were designed to be very simple to use, so they're devoid of the detailed instructions required to run the device (information in the device driver) where the file may be stored. That is, they're device independent. Therefore, to access a file, the user doesn't need to know its exact physical location on the disk pack (the cylinder, surface, and sector), the medium in which it's stored (archival tape, magnetic disk, optical disc, or flash storage), or the network specifics. That's fortunate because file access is a complex process. Each logical command is broken down into a sequence of signals that trigger the step-by-step actions performed by the device and supervise the progress of the operation by testing the device's status.

(figure 8.2)

Typical menu of file options.

For example, when a user's program issues a command to read a record from a disk the READ instruction has to be decomposed into the following steps:

1. Move the read/write heads to the cylinder or track where the record is to be found.
2. Wait for the rotational delay until the sector containing the desired record passes under the read/write head.
3. Activate the appropriate read/write head and read the record.
4. Transfer the record to main memory.
5. Set a flag to indicate that the device is free to satisfy another request.

While all of this is going on, the system must check for possible error conditions. The File Manager does all of this, freeing the user from including in each program the low-level instructions for every device to be used: the terminal, keyboard, printer, CD, disk drive, etc. Without the File Manager, every program would need to include instructions to operate all of the different types of devices and every model within each type. Considering the rapid development and increased sophistication of I/O devices, it would be impractical to require each program to include these minute operational details. That's the advantage of device independence.

Typical Volume Configuration

Network resources are typically given a logical volume label for easy identification, such as z, x, w, etc.

Normally the active files for a computer system reside on secondary storage units. Some devices accommodate removable storage units—such as CDs, DVDs, floppy disks, USB devices, and other removable media—so files that aren't frequently used can be stored offline and mounted only when the user specifically requests them. Other devices feature integrated storage units, such as hard disks and nonremovable disk packs.

Each storage unit, whether it's removable or not, is considered a **volume**, and each volume can contain several files, so they're called "multifile volumes." However, some files are extremely large and are contained in several volumes; not surprisingly, these are called "multivolume files."

Each volume in the system is given a name. The File Manager writes this name and other descriptive information, as shown in Figure 8.3, on an easy-to-access place on each unit: the innermost part of the CD or DVD, the beginning of the tape, or the first sector of the outermost track of the disk pack. Once identified, the operating system can interact with the storage unit.

Creation Date	◄─── Date when volume was created
Pointer to Directory Area	◄─── Indicates first sector where directory is stored
Pointer to File Area	◄─── Indicates first sector where file is stored
File System Code	◄─── Used to detect volumes with incorrect formats
Volume Name	◄─── User-allocated name

(figure 8.3)

The volume descriptor, which is stored at the beginning of each volume, includes this vital information about the storage unit.

The **master file directory (MFD)** is stored immediately after the volume descriptor and lists the names and characteristics of every file contained in that volume. The filenames in the MFD can refer to program files, data files, and/or system files. And if the File Manager supports subdirectories, they're listed in the MFD as well. The remainder of the volume is used for file storage.

The first operating systems supported only a single directory per volume. This directory was created by the File Manager and contained the names of files, usually organized in alphabetical, spatial, or chronological order. Although it was simple to implement and maintain, this scheme had some major disadvantages:

• It would take a long time to search for an individual file, especially if the MFD was organized in an arbitrary order.

• If the user had more than 256 small files stored in the volume, the directory space (with a 256 filename limit) would fill up before the disk storage space filled up. The user would then receive a message of "disk full" when only the directory itself was full.

• Users couldn't create subdirectories to group the files that were related.

• Multiple users couldn't safeguard their files from other users because the entire directory was freely made available to every user in the group on request.

• Each program in the entire directory needed a unique name, even those directories serving many users, so only one person using that directory could have a program named Program1.

This could cause havoc in an introductory computer science class. For example, what if the first person named the first programming assignment Program1? Then the rest of the class would have interesting choices: write a new program and give it a different name; write a new program and name it Program1 (which would erase the original version); or simply open Program1, modify it, and then save it with changes. With the latter option, the entire class could end up with a single, though perhaps terrific, program.

Introducing Subdirectories

File Managers create an MFD for each volume that can contain entries for both files and subdirectories. A **subdirectory** is created when a user opens an account to access the computer system. Although this user directory is treated as a file, its entry in the MFD is flagged to indicate to the File Manager that this file is really a subdirectory and has unique properties—in fact, its records are filenames pointing to files.

Although this was an improvement from the single directory scheme (now all of the students could name their first programs Program1), it didn't solve the problems encountered by prolific users who wanted to group their files in a logical order to improve the accessibility and efficiency of the system.

Today's File Managers encourage users to create their own subdirectories, so related files can be grouped together. Many computer users and some operating systems call these subdirectories "folders." This structure is an extension of the previous two-level directory organization, and it's implemented as an upside-down tree, as shown in Figure 8.4.

Tree structures allow the system to efficiently search individual directories because there are fewer entries in each directory. However, the path to the requested file may lead through several directories. For every file request, the MFD is the point of entry. Actually, the MFD is usually transparent to the user—it's accessible only by the operating system. When the user wants to access a specific file, the filename is sent to the File Manager. The File Manager first searches the MFD for the user's directory, and it then searches the user's directory and any subdirectories for the requested file and its location.

Regardless of the complexity of the directory structure, each file entry in every directory contains information describing the file; it's called the file descriptor. Information typically included in a file descriptor includes the following:

- Filename—within a single directory, filenames must be unique; in some operating systems, the filenames are case sensitive
- File type—the organization and usage that are dependent on the system (for example, files and directories)
- File size—although it could be computed from other information, the size is kept here for convenience
- File location—identification of the first physical block (or all blocks) where the file is stored

- Date and time of creation
- Owner
- Protection information—access restrictions, based on who is allowed to access the file and what type of access is allowed
- Record size—its fixed size or its maximum size, depending on the type of record

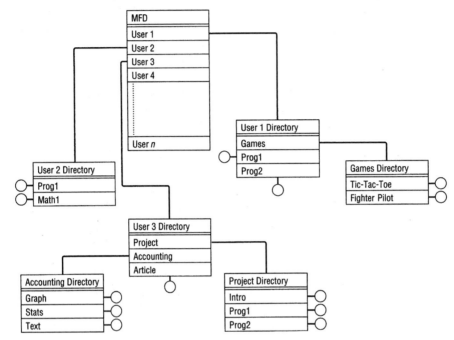

(figure 8.4)

File directory tree structure. The "root" is the MFD shown at the top, each node is a directory file, and each branch is a directory entry pointing to either another directory or to a real file. All program and data files subsequently added to the tree are the leaves, represented by circles.

File-Naming Conventions

A file's name can be much longer than it appears. Depending on the File Manager, it can have from two to many components. The two components common to many filenames are a **relative filename** and an **extension**.

To avoid confusion, in the following discussion we'll use the term "complete filename" to identify the file's **absolute filename** (that's the long name that includes all path information), and "relative filename" to indicate the name without **path** information that appears in directory listings and folders.

The relative filename is the name that differentiates it from other files in the same directory. Examples can include DEPARTMENT ADDRESSES, TAXES_PHOTOG, or AUTOEXEC. Generally, the relative filename can vary in length from one to many characters and can include letters of the alphabet, as well as digits. However, every operating system has specific rules that affect the length of the relative name and the types of

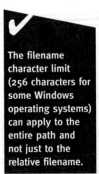

The filename character limit (256 characters for some Windows operating systems) can apply to the entire path and not just to the relative filename.

characters allowed. Most operating systems allow names with dozens of characters including spaces, hyphens, underlines, and certain other keyboard characters.

Some operating systems require an extension that's appended to the relative filename. It's usually two or three characters long and is separated from the relative name by a period, and its purpose is to identify the type of file or its contents. For example, in a Windows operating system, a typical relative filename with extension would be BASIA_TUNE.MP3. Similarly, TAKE OUT MENU.RTF and TAKE OUT MENU.DOC both indicate that they can be opened with a word processing application. What happens if an extension is incorrect or unknown? Most ask for guidance from the user, as shown in Figure 8.5.

(figure 8.5)

To open a file with an unrecognized extension, Windows asks the user to choose an application to associate with that type of file.

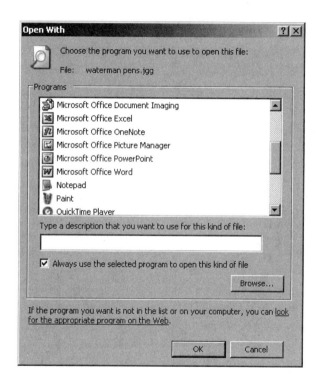

Some extensions (such as EXE, BAT, COB, and FOR) are restricted by certain operating systems because they serve as a signal to the system to use a specific compiler or program to run these files.

There may be other components required for a file's complete name. Here's how a file named INVENTORY_COST.DOC is identified by different operating systems:

1. Using a Windows operating system and a personal computer with three disk drives, the file's complete name is composed of its relative name and extension, preceded by the drive label and directory name:

   C:\IMFST\FLYNN\INVENTORY_COST.DOC

This indicates to the system that the file INVENTORY_COST.DOC requires a word processing application program, and it can be found in the directory; IMFST; subdirectory FLYNN in the volume residing on drive C.

2. A UNIX or Linux system might identify the file as:

```
/usr/imfst/flynn/inventory_cost.doc
```

The first entry is represented by the forward slash (/). This represents a special master directory called the *root*. Next is the name of the first subdirectory, usr/imfst, followed by a sub-subdirectory, /flynn, in this multiple directory system. The final entry is the file's relative name, inventory_cost.doc. (Notice that UNIX and Linux filenames are case sensitive and often expressed in lowercase.)

As you can see, the names tend to grow in length as the file manager grows in flexibility. The folders on a system with a graphical user interface, such as Windows or Macintosh, are actually directories or subdirectories. When someone creates a folder, the system creates a subdirectory in the current directory or folder.

Why don't users see the complete file name when accessing a file? First, the File Manager selects a directory for the user when the interactive session begins, so all file operations requested by that user start from this "home" or "base" directory. Second, from this home directory, the user selects a subdirectory, which is called a **current directory** or **working directory**. Thereafter, the files are presumed to be located in this current directory. Whenever a file is accessed, the user types in the relative name, and the File Manager adds the proper prefix. As long as users refer to files in the working directory, they can access their files without entering the complete name.

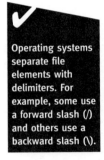

Operating systems separate file elements with delimiters. For example, some use a forward slash (/) and others use a backward slash (\).

The concept of a current directory is based on the underlying hierarchy of a tree structure, as shown in Figure 8.4, and allows programmers to retrieve a file by typing only its relative filename…

```
INVENTORY_COST.DOC
```

…and not its complete filename:

```
C:\IMFST\FLYNN\INVENTORY_COST.DOC
```

File Organization

When we discuss file organization, we are talking about the arrangement of records within a file because all files are composed of records. When a user gives a command to modify the contents of a file, it's actually a command to access records within the file.

Record Format

All files are composed of records. When a user gives a command to modify the contents of a file, it's actually a command to access records within the file. Within each file, the records are all presumed to have the same format: they can be of fixed length or of variable length, as shown in Figure 8.6. And these records, regardless of their format, can be blocked or not blocked.

(figure 8.6)

When data is stored in fixed-length fields (a), data that extends beyond the fixed size is truncated. When data is stored in a variable-length record format (b), the size expands to fit the contents, but it takes longer to access it.

(a) | Dan | Whitesto | 1243 Ele | Harrisbu | PA | | 412 683- |

(b) | Dan | Whitestone | 1243 Elementary Ave. | Harrisburg | PA |

Fixed-length records are the most common because they're the easiest to access directly. That's why they're ideal for data files. The critical aspect of fixed-length records is the size of the record. If it's too small—smaller than the number of characters to be stored in the record—the leftover characters are truncated. But if the record size is too large—larger than the number of characters to be stored—storage space is wasted.

Variable-length records don't leave empty storage space and don't truncate any characters, thus eliminating the two disadvantages of fixed-length records. But while they can easily be read (one after the other), they're difficult to access directly because it's hard to calculate exactly where the record is located. That's why they're used most frequently in files that are likely to be accessed sequentially, such as text files and program files or files that use an index to access their records. The record format, how it's blocked, and other related information is kept in the file descriptor.

The amount of space that's actually used to store the supplementary information varies from system to system and conforms to the physical limitations of the storage medium, as we'll see later in this chapter.

Physical File Organization

The physical organization of a file has to do with the way records are arranged and the characteristics of the medium used to store it.

On magnetic disks (hard drives), files can be organized in one of several ways: sequential, direct, or indexed sequential. To select the best of these file organizations, the programmer or analyst usually considers these practical characteristics:

- Volatility of the data—the frequency with which additions and deletions are made
- Activity of the file—the percentage of records processed during a given run
- Size of the file
- Response time—the amount of time the user is willing to wait before the requested operation is completed (This is especially crucial when doing time-sensitive searches)

Sequential record organization is by far the easiest to implement because records are stored and retrieved serially, one after the other. To find a specific record, the file is searched from its beginning until the requested record is found.

To speed the process, some optimization features may be built into the system. One is to select a key field from the record and then sort the records by that field before storing them. Later, when a user requests a specific record, the system searches only the key field of each record in the file. The search is ended when either an exact match is found or the key field for the requested record is smaller than the value of the record last compared, in which case the message "record not found" is sent to the user and the search is terminated.

Although this technique aids the search process, it complicates file maintenance because the original order must be preserved every time records are added or deleted. And to preserve the physical order, the file must be completely rewritten or maintained in a sorted fashion every time it's updated.

A **direct record organization** uses direct access files, which, of course, can be implemented only on direct access storage devices (discussed in Chapter 7). These files give users the flexibility of accessing any record in any order without having to begin a search from the beginning of the file to do so. It's also known as "random organization," and its files are called "random access files."

Records are identified by their **relative addresses**—their addresses relative to the beginning of the file. These **logical addresses** are computed when the records are stored and then again when the records are retrieved.

The method used is quite straightforward. The user identifies a field (or combination of fields) in the record format and designates it as the **key field** because it uniquely identifies each record. The program used to store the data follows a set of instructions, called a **hashing algorithm**, that transforms each key into a number: the record's logical address. This is given to the File Manager, which takes the necessary steps to translate the logical address into a physical address (cylinder, surface, and record numbers), preserving the file organization. The same procedure is used to retrieve a record.

A direct access file can also be accessed sequentially, by starting at the first relative address and going to each record down the line.

Direct access files can be updated more quickly than sequential files because records can be quickly rewritten to their original addresses after modifications have been made. And there's no need to preserve the order of the records so adding or deleting them takes very little time.

Databases use a hash table to speed up access to data records. Using a hashing algorithm, each record is uniquely identified, and the hash table contains pointers to each record.

For example, data for a telephone mail-order firm must be accessed quickly so customer information can be retrieved quickly. To do so, they can use hashing algorithms to directly access their data. Let's say you're placing an order, and you're asked for your postal code and street number (let's say they are 15213 and 2737). The program that retrieves information from the data file uses that key in a hashing algorithm to calculate the logical address where your record is stored. So when the order clerk types 152132737, the screen soon shows a list of all current customers whose customer numbers generated the same logical address. If you're in the database, the operator knows right away. If not, you will be soon.

The problem with hashing algorithms is that several records with unique keys (such as customer numbers) may generate the same logical address—and then there's a collision, as shown in Figure 8.7. When that happens, the program must generate another logical address before presenting it to the File Manager for storage. Records that collide are stored in an overflow area that was set aside when the file was created. Although the program does all the work of linking the records from the overflow area to their corresponding logical address, the File Manager must handle the physical allocation of space.

(figure 8.7)

The hashing algorithm causes a collision. Using a combination of street address and postal code, it generates the same logical address (152132737) for three different records.

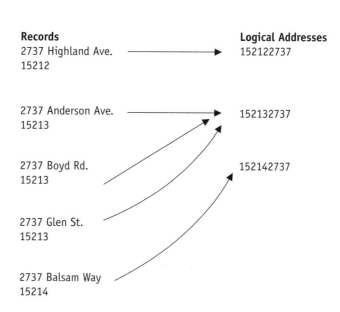

Records	Logical Addresses
2737 Highland Ave. 15212	152122737
2737 Anderson Ave. 15213	152132737
2737 Boyd Rd. 15213	152142737
2737 Glen St. 15213	
2737 Balsam Way 15214	

The maximum size of the file is established when it's created, and eventually either the file might become completely full or the number of records stored in the overflow area might become so large that the efficiency of retrieval is lost. At that time, the file must be reorganized and rewritten, which requires intervention by the File Manager.

Indexed sequential record organization combines the best of sequential and direct access. It's created and maintained through an Indexed Sequential Access Method (ISAM) application, which removes the burden of handling overflows and preserves record order from the shoulders of the programmer.

This type of organization doesn't create collisions because it doesn't use the result of the hashing algorithm to generate a record's address. Instead, it uses this information to generate an index file through which the records are retrieved. This organization divides an ordered sequential file into blocks of equal size. Their size is determined by the File Manager to take advantage of physical storage devices and to optimize retrieval strategies. Each entry in the index file contains the highest record key and the physical location of the data block where this record, and the records with smaller keys, are stored.

Therefore, to access any record in the file, the system begins by searching the index file and then goes to the physical location indicated at that entry. We can say, then, that the index file acts as a pointer to the data file. An indexed sequential file also has overflow areas, but they're spread throughout the file, perhaps every few records, so expansion of existing records can take place, and new records can be located in close physical sequence as well as in logical sequence. Another overflow area is located apart from the main data area but is used only when the other overflow areas are completely filled. We call it the overflow of last resort.

This last-resort overflow area can store records added during the lifetime of the file. The records are kept in logical order by the software package without much effort on the part of the programmer. Of course, when too many records have been added here, the retrieval process slows down because the search for a record has to go from the index to the main data area and eventually to the overflow area.

When retrieval time becomes too slow, the file has to be reorganized. That's a job that, although it's not as tedious as reorganizing direct access files, is usually performed by maintenance software.

For most dynamic files, indexed sequential is the organization of choice because it allows both direct access to a few requested records and sequential access to many.

Physical Storage Allocation

The File Manager must work with files not just as whole units but also as logical units or records. Records within a file must have the same format, but they can vary in length, as shown in Figure 8.8.

In turn, records are subdivided into fields. In most cases, their structure is managed by application programs and not the operating system. An exception is made for those systems that are heavily oriented to database applications, where the File Manager handles field structure.

So when we talk about file storage, we're actually referring to record storage. How are the records within a file stored? At this stage the File Manager and Device Manager have to cooperate to ensure successful storage and retrieval of records. In Chapter 7 on device management, we introduced the concept of logical versus physical records, and this theme recurs here from the point of view of the File Manager.

(figure 8.8)

Every record in a file must have the same format but can be of different sizes, as shown in these five examples of the most common record formats. The supplementary information in (b), (c), (d), and (e) is provided by the File Manager, when the record is stored.

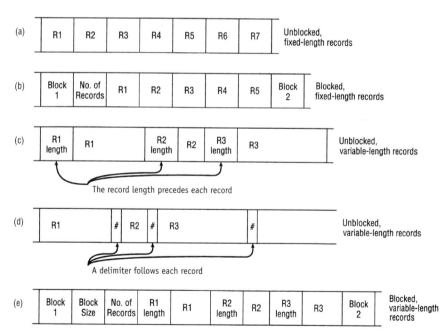

Contiguous Storage

When records use **contiguous storage**, they're stored one after the other. This was the scheme used in early operating systems. It's very simple to implement and manage. Any record can be found and read, once its starting address and size are known, so the directory is very streamlined. Its second advantage is ease of direct access because every part of the file is stored in the same compact area.

The primary disadvantage is that a file can't be expanded unless there's empty space available immediately following it, as shown in Figure 8.9. Therefore, room for expansion must be provided when the file is created. If there's not enough room, the entire file must be recopied to a larger section of the disk every time records are added. The second disadvantage is fragmentation (slivers of unused storage space), which can be overcome by compacting and rearranging files. And, of course, the files can't be accessed while compaction is taking place.

(figure 8.9)

With contiguous file storage, File A can't be expanded without being rewritten to a larger storage area. File B can be expanded, by only one record replacing the free space preceding File C.

Free Space	File A Record 1	File A Record 2	File A Record 3	File A Record 4	File A Record 5	File B Record 1	File B Record 2	File B Record 3	File B Record 4	Free Space	File C Record 1

The File Manager keeps track of the empty storage areas by treating them as files—they're entered in the directory but are flagged to differentiate them from real files. Usually the directory is kept in order by sector number, so adjacent empty areas can be combined into one large free space.

Noncontiguous Storage

Noncontiguous storage allocation allows files to use any storage space available on the disk. A file's records are stored in a contiguous manner, only if there's enough empty space. Any remaining records and all other additions to the file are stored in other sections of the disk. In some systems these are called the **extents** of the file and are linked together with pointers. The physical size of each extent is determined by the operating system and is usually 256—or another power of two—bytes.

File extents are usually linked in one of two ways. Linking can take place at the storage level, where each extent points to the next one in the sequence, as shown in Figure 8.10. The directory entry consists of the filename, the storage location of the first extent, the location of the last extent, and the total number of extents not counting the first.

(figure 8.10)

Noncontiguous file storage
with linking taking place at
the storage level. File 1
starts in address 2 and
continues in addresses 8,
20, and 18. The directory
lists the file's starting
address, ending address,
and the number of extents
it uses. Each block of
storage includes its
address and a pointer to
the next block for the file,
as well as the data itself.

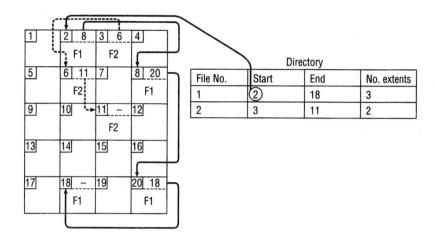

(figure 8.10)

Noncontiguous file storage with linking taking place at the storage level. File 1 starts in address 2 and continues in addresses 8, 20, and 18. The directory lists the file's starting address, ending address, and the number of extents it uses. Each block of storage includes its address and a pointer to the next block for the file, as well as the data itself.

The alternative is for the linking to take place at the directory level, as shown in Figure 8.11. Each extent is listed with its physical address, its size, and a pointer to the next extent. A null pointer, shown in Figure 8.11 as a hyphen (-), indicates that it's the last one.

Although both noncontiguous allocation schemes eliminate external storage fragmentation and the need for compaction, they don't support direct access because there's no easy way to determine the exact location of a specific record.

Files are usually declared to be either sequential or direct when they're created, so the File Manager can select the most efficient method of storage allocation: contiguous for direct files and noncontiguous for sequential. Operating systems must have the capability to support both storage allocation schemes.

Files can then be converted from one type to another by creating a file of the desired type and copying the contents of the old file into the new file, using a program designed for that specific purpose.

Indexed Storage

Indexed storage allocation allows direct record access by bringing together the pointers linking every extent of that file into an index block. Every file has its own index block, which consists of the addresses of each disk sector that make up the file. The index lists each entry in the same order in which the sectors are linked, as

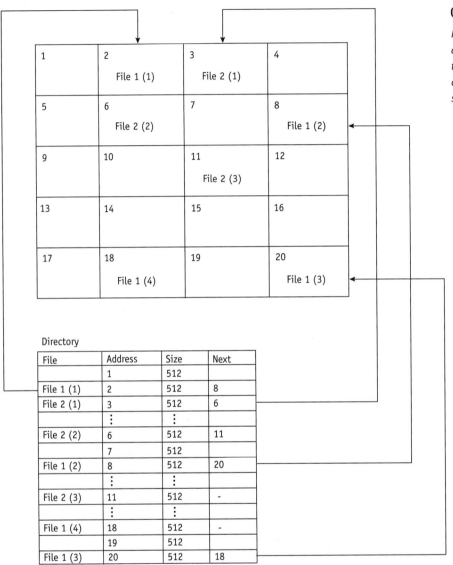

(figure 8.11)

Noncontiguous storage allocation with linking taking place at the directory level for the files shown in Figure 8.10.

shown in Figure 8.12. For example, the third entry in the index block corresponds to the third sector making up the file.

When a file is created, the pointers in the index block are all set to null. Then, as each sector is filled, the pointer is set to the appropriate sector address—to be precise, the address is removed from the empty space list and copied into its position in the index block.

This scheme supports both sequential and direct access, but it doesn't necessarily improve the use of storage space because each file must have an index block—usually the size of one disk sector. For larger files with more entries, several levels of indexes

(figure 8.12)

Indexed storage allocation with a one-level index, allowing direct access to each record for the files shown in Figures 8.10 and 8.11.

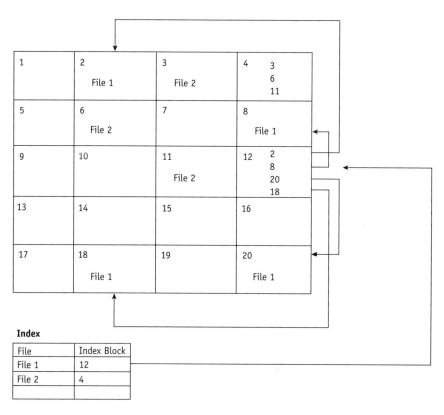

can be generated; in which case, to find a desired record, the File Manager accesses the first index (the highest level), which points to a second index (lower level), which points to an even lower-level index and eventually to the data record.

Access Methods

Access methods are dictated by a file's organization; the most flexibility is allowed with indexed sequential files and the least with sequential.

A file that has been organized in sequential fashion can support only sequential access to its records, and these records can be of either fixed or variable length, as shown in Figure 8.6. The File Manager uses the address of the last byte read to access the next sequential record. Therefore, the **current byte address (CBA)** must be updated every time a record is accessed, such as when the READ command is executed.

Figure 8.13 shows the difference between storage of fixed-length and of variable-length records.

(a)

Record 1	Record 2	Record 3	Record 4	Record 5
RL = x	RL = x	RL = x	RL = x	RL = x

(b)

m	Record 1	n	Record 2	p	Rec.3	q	Record 4
	RL = m		RL = n		RL = p		RL = q

(figure 8.13)

Fixed- versus variable-length records. (a) Fixed-length records have the same number of bytes, so record length (RL) is the constant x. (b) With variable-length records, RL isn't a constant. Therefore, it's recorded on the sequential media immediately preceding each record.

Sequential Access

For *sequential access of fixed-length records*, the CBA is updated simply by incrementing it by the record length (RL), which is a constant:

$$CBA = CBA + RL$$

For *sequential access of variable-length records*, the File Manager adds the length of the record (RL) plus the number of bytes used to hold the record length (N, which holds the constant shown as m, n, p, or q, in Figure 8.13) to the CBA.

$$CBA = CBA + N + RL$$

Direct Access

If a file is organized in direct fashion, it can be accessed easily in either direct or sequential order if the records are of fixed length. In the case of *direct access with fixed-length records*, the CBA can be computed directly from the record length and the desired record number RN (information provided through the READ command) minus 1:

$$CBA = (RN - 1) * RL$$

For example, if we're looking for the beginning of the eleventh record and the fixed record length is 25 bytes, the CBA would be:

$$(11 - 1) * 25 = 250$$

However, if the file is organized for *direct access with variable-length records*, it's virtually impossible to access a record directly because the address of the desired record

can't be easily computed. Therefore, to access a record, the File Manager must do a sequential search through the records. In fact, it becomes a half-sequential read through the file because the File Manager could save the address of the last record accessed, and when the next request arrives, it could search forward from the CBA—if the address of the desired record was between the CBA and the end of the file. Otherwise, the search would start from the beginning of the file. It could be said that this semi-sequential search is only semi-adequate.

An alternative is for the File Manager to keep a table of record numbers and their CBAs. Then, to fill a request, this table is searched for the exact storage location of the desired record, so the direct access reduces to a table lookup.

To avoid dealing with this problem, many systems force users to have their files organized for fixed-length records, if the records are to be accessed directly.

Records in an *indexed sequential file* can be accessed either sequentially or directly, so either of the procedures to compute the CBA presented in this section would apply but with one extra step: the index file must be searched for the pointer to the block where the data is stored. Because the index file is smaller than the data file, it can be kept in main memory, and a quick search can be performed to locate the block where the desired record is located. Then, the block can be retrieved from secondary storage, and the beginning byte address of the record can be calculated. In systems that support several levels of indexing to improve access to very large files, the index at each level must be searched before the computation of the CBA can be done. The entry point to this type of data file is usually through the index file.

As we've shown, a file's organization and the methods used to access its records are very closely intertwined; so when one talks about a specific type of organization, one is almost certainly implying a specific type of access.

Levels in a File Management System

The efficient management of files can't be separated from the efficient management of the devices that house them. This chapter and the previous one on device management have presented the wide range of functions that have to be organized for an I/O system to perform efficiently. In this section, we'll outline one of the many hierarchies used to perform those functions.

The highest level module is called the "basic file system," and it passes information through the access control verification module to the logical file system, which, in turn, notifies the physical file system, which works with the Device Manager. Figure 8.14 shows the hierarchy.

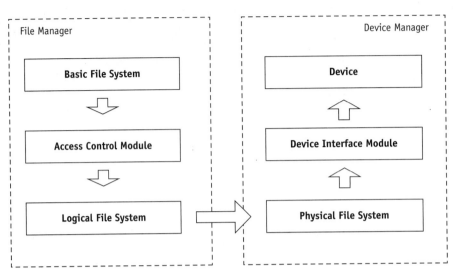

(figure 8.14)

Typical modules of a file management system showing how information is passed from the File Manager to the Device Manager.

Each level of the file management system is implemented using structured and modular programming techniques that also set up a hierarchy—that is, the higher positioned modules pass information to the lower modules, so that they, in turn, can perform the required service and continue the communication down the chain to the lowest module, which communicates with the physical device and interacts with the Device Manager. Only then is the record made available to the user's program.

Each of the modules can be further subdivided into more specific tasks, as we can see when we follow this I/O instruction through the file management system:

READ RECORD NUMBER 7 FROM FILE CLASSES INTO STUDENT

CLASSES is the name of a direct access file previously opened for input, and STUDENT is a data record previously defined within the program and occupying specific memory locations.

Because the file has already been opened, the file directory has already been searched to verify the existence of CLASSES, and pertinent information about the file has been brought into the operating system's active file table. This information includes its record size, the address of its first physical record, its protection, and access control information, as shown in the UNIX directory listing in Table 8.1.

Access Control	No. of Links	Group	Owner	No. of Bytes	Date	Time	Filename
drwxrwxr-x	2	journal	comp	12820	Jan 10	19:32	ArtWarehouse
drwxrwxr-x	2	journal	comp	12844	Dec 15	09:59	bus_transport
-rwxr-xr-x	1	journal	comp	2705221	Mar 6	11:38	CLASSES
-rwxr--r--	1	journal	comp	12556	Feb 20	18:08	PAYroll
-rwx------	1	journal	comp	8721	Jan 17	07:32	supplier

(table 8.1)

A typical list of files stored in the directory called journal.

This information is used by the basic file system, which activates the access control verification module to verify that this user is permitted to perform this operation with this file. If access is allowed, information and control are passed along to the logical file system. If not, a message saying "access denied" is sent to the user.

Using the information passed down by the basic file system, the logical file system transforms the record number to its byte address using the familiar formula:

$$CBA = (RN - 1) * RL$$

This result, together with the address of the first physical record and, in the case where records are blocked, the physical block size, is passed down to the physical file system, which computes the location where the desired record physically resides. If there's more than one record in that block, it computes the record's offset within that block using these formulas:

$$\text{block number} = \text{integers} \left[\frac{\text{byte address}}{\text{physical block size}} \right] + \text{address of the first physical record}$$

$$\text{offset} = \text{remainder} \left[\frac{\text{byte address}}{\text{physical block size}} \right]$$

This information is passed on to the device interface module, which, in turn, transforms the block number to the actual cylinder/surface/record combination needed to retrieve the information from the secondary storage device. Once retrieved, here's where the device-scheduling algorithms come into play, as the information is placed in a buffer and control returns to the physical file system, which copies the information into the desired memory location. Finally, when the operation is complete, the "all clear" message is passed on to all other modules.

Although we used a READ command for our example, a WRITE command is handled in exactly the same way until the process reaches the device handler. At that point, the portion of the device interface module that handles allocation of free space, the allocation module, is called into play because it's responsible for keeping track of unused areas in each storage device.

We need to note here that verification, the process of making sure that a request is valid, occurs at every level of the file management system. The first verification occurs at the directory level when the file system checks to see if the requested file exists. The second occurs when the access control verification module determines whether access is allowed. The third occurs when the logical file system checks to see if the requested byte address is within the file's limits. Finally, the device interface module checks to see whether the storage device exists.

Therefore, the correct operation of this simple user command requires the coordinated effort of every part of the file management system.

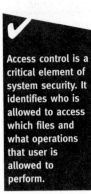

Access control is a critical element of system security. It identifies who is allowed to access which files and what operations that user is allowed to perform.

Access Control Verification Module

The first operating systems couldn't support file sharing among users. For instance, early systems needed 10 copies of a compiler to serve 10 users. Today's systems require only a single copy to serve everyone, regardless of the number of active programs in the system. In fact, any file can be shared—from data files and user-owned program files to system files. The advantages of file sharing are numerous. In addition to saving space, it allows for synchronization of data updates, as when two applications are updating the same data file. It also improves the efficiency of the system's resources because if files are shared in main memory, then there's a reduction of I/O operations.

However, as often happens, progress brings problems. The disadvantage of file sharing is that the integrity of each file must be safeguarded; that calls for control over who is allowed to access the file and what type of access is permitted. There are five possible actions that can be performed on a file—the ability to READ only, WRITE only, EXECUTE only, DELETE only, or some combination of the four. Each file management system has its own method to control file access.

Access Control Matrix

The **access control matrix** is intuitively appealing and easy to implement, but because of its size it only works well for systems with a few files and a few users. In the matrix, each column identifies a user and each row identifies a file. The intersection of the row and column contains the access rights for that user to that file, as Table 8.2 illustrates.

	User 1	User 2	User 3	User 4	User 5
File 1	RWED	R-E-	----	RWE-	--E-
File 2	----	R-E-	R-E-	--E-	----
File 3	----	RWED	----	--E-	----
File 4	R-E-	----	----	----	RWED
File 5	----	----	----	----	RWED

In the actual implementation, the letters RWED are represented by bits 1 and 0: a 1 indicates that access is allowed, and a 0 indicates access is denied. Therefore, as shown in Table 8.3, the code for User 2 for File 1 would read "1010" and not "R-E-".

Access	R	W	E	D	Resulting Code
R-E-	✓		✓		1010
R-E-	✓		✓		1010
RWED	✓	✓	✓	✓	1111
----					0000
----					0000

As you can see, the access control matrix is a simple method; but as the numbers of files and users increase, the matrix becomes extremely large—sometimes too large to store in main memory. Another disadvantage is that a lot of space is wasted because many of the entries are all null, such as in Table 8.2, where User 3 isn't allowed into most of the files, and File 5 is restricted to all but one user. A scheme that conserved space would have only one entry for User 3 or one for File 5, but that's incompatible with the matrix format.

Access Control Lists

The **access control list** is a modification of the access control matrix. Each file is entered in the list and contains the names of the users who are allowed to access it and the type of access each is permitted. To shorten the list, only those who may use the file are named; those denied any access are grouped under a global heading such as WORLD, as shown in Table 8.4.

File	Access
File 1	USER1 (RWED), USER2 (R-E-), USER4 (RWE-), USER5 (--E-), WORLD (----)
File 2	USER2 (R-E-), USER3 (R-E-), USER4 (--E-), WORLD (----)
File 3	USER2 (RWED), USER4 (--E-), WORLD (----)
File 4	USER1 (R-E-), USER5 (RWED), WORLD (----)
File 5	USER5 (RWED), WORLD (----)

(table 8.4)

An access control list showing which users are allowed to access each file. This method requires less storage space than an access control matrix.

Some systems shorten the access control list even more by putting every user into a category: system, owner, group, and world. SYSTEM or ADMIN is designated for system personnel who have unlimited access to all files in the system. The OWNER has absolute control over all files created in the owner's account. An owner may create a GROUP file so that all users belonging to the appropriate group have access to it. WORLD is composed of all other users in the system; that is, those who don't fall into any of the other three categories. In this system, the File Manager designates default types of access to all files at creation time, and it's the owner's responsibility to change them as needed.

Capability Lists

A **capability list** shows the access control information from a different perspective. It lists every user and the files to which each has access, as shown in Table 8.5.

User	Access
User 1	File 1 (RWED), File 4 (R-E-)
User 2	File 1 (R-E-), File 2 (R-E-), File 3 (RWED)
User 3	File 2 (R-E-)
User 4	File 1 (RWE-), File 2 (--E-), File 3 (--E-)
User 5	File 1 (--E-), File 4 (RWED), File 5 (RWED)

(table 8.5)

A capability list shows files for each user and requires less storage space than an access control matrix; and when users are added or deleted from the system, is easier to maintain than an access control list.

Of the three schemes described so far, the most commonly used is the access control list. However, capability lists are gaining in popularity because in operating systems such as Linux or UNIX, they control access to devices as well as to files.

Although both methods seem to be the same, there are some subtle differences best explained with an analogy. A capability list may be equated to specific concert tickets that are made available to only individuals whose names appear on the list. On the other hand, an access control list can be equated to the reservation list in a restaurant that has limited seating, with each seat assigned to a certain individual.

Data Compression

Data compression algorithms consist of two types: lossless algorithms typically used for text or arithmetic files, which retain all the data in the file throughout the compression-decompression process; and lossy algorithms, which are typically used for image and sound files and remove data permanently. At first glance, one wouldn't think that a loss of data would be tolerable; but when the deleted data is unwanted noise, tones beyond a human's ability to hear, or light spectrum that we can't see, deleting this data can be undetectable and therefore acceptable.

Text Compression

To compress text in a database, three methods are described briefly here: records with repeated characters, repeated terms, and front-end compression.

Records with repeated characters: Data in a fixed-length field might include a short name followed by many blank characters. This can be replaced with a variable-length field and a special code to indicate how many blanks were truncated.

For example, let's say the original string, ADAMS, looks like this when it's stored uncompressed in a field that's 15 characters wide (*b* stands for a blank character):

ADAMSbbbbbbbbbb

When it's encoded it looks like this:

ADAMSb10

Likewise, numbers with many zeros can be shortened, too, with a code (in this case, the pound sign #) to indicate how many zeros must be added to recreate the original number. For instance, if the original entry is this number:

300000000

the encoded entry is this:

3#8

Repeated terms can be compressed by using symbols to represent each of the most commonly used words in the database. For example, in a university's student database, common words like *student, course, teacher, classroom, grade,* and *department* could each be represented with a single character. Of course, the system must be able to distinguish between compressed and uncompressed data.

Front-end compression builds on the previous data element. For example, the student database where the students' names are kept in alphabetical order could be compressed, as shown in Table 8.6.

Original List	Compressed List
Smith, Betty	Smith, Betty
Smith, Donald	7Donald
Smith, Gino	7Gino
Smithberger, John	5berger, John
Smithbren, Ali	6ren, Ali
Smithco, Rachel	5co, Rachel
Smither, Kevin	5er, Kevin
Smithers, Renny	7s, Renny
Snyder, Katherine	1nyder, Katherine

(table 8.6)

Each entry takes a given number of characters from the previous entry that they have in common and adds the characters that make it unique. So "Smithbren, Ali" uses the first six characters from "Smithberger, John" and adds "ren, Ali." Therefore, the entry is "6ren, Ali."

There is a trade-off: storage space is gained, but processing time is lost. Remember, for all data compression schemes, the system must be able to distinguish between compressed and uncompressed data.

Other Compression Schemes

Lossy compression allows a loss of data from the original file to allow significant compression. This means the compression process is irreversible as the original file cannot be reconstructed. The specifics of the compression algorithm are highly dependent on the type of file being compressed, with JPEG a popular option for still images and MPEG for video images. For video and music files, the International Organization for Standardization (ISO) has issued MPEG standards that "are international standards dealing with the compression, decompression, processing, and coded representation of moving pictures, audio, and their combination."

ISO is the world's leading developer of international standards. For more information about current compression standards and other industry standards, we encourage you to visit *http://www.iso.org*.

Conclusion

The File Manager controls every file in the system and processes the user's commands (read, write, modify, create, delete, etc.) to interact with any file on the system. It also manages the access control procedures to maintain the integrity and security of the files under its control.

To achieve its goals, the File Manager must be able to accommodate a variety of file organizations, physical storage allocation schemes, record types, and access methods. And, as we've seen, this requires increasingly complex file management software.

In this chapter we discussed:
• Sequential, direct, and indexed sequential file organization
• Contiguous, noncontiguous, and indexed file storage allocation
• Fixed-length versus variable-length records
• Three methods of access control
• Data compression techniques

To get the most from a File Manager, it's important for users to realize the strengths and weaknesses of its segments—which access methods are allowed on which devices and with which record structures—and the advantages and disadvantages of each in overall efficiency.

Key Terms

absolute filename: a file's name, as given by the user, preceded by the directory (or directories) where the file is found and, when necessary, the specific device label.

access control list: an access control method that lists each file, the names of the users who are allowed to access it, and the type of access each is permitted.

access control matrix: an access control method that uses a matrix with every file, every user, and the type of access each user is permitted on each file.

capability list: an access control method that lists every user, the files to which each has access, and the type of access allowed to those files.

contiguous storage: a type of file storage in which all the information is stored in adjacent locations in a storage medium.

current byte address (CBA): the address of the last byte read. It is used by the File Manager to access records in secondary storage and must be updated every time a record is accessed.

current directory: the directory or subdirectory in which the user is working.

data compression: a procedure used to reduce the amount of space required to store data by reducing, encoding, or abbreviating repetitive terms or characters.

database: a group of related files that are interconnected at various levels to give users flexibility of access to the data stored.

direct record organization: files stored in a direct access storage device and organized to give users the flexibility of accessing any record at random, regardless of its position in the file.

directory: a storage area in a secondary storage volume (disk, disk pack, etc.) containing information about files stored in that volume.

extension: in some operating systems, it's the part of the filename that indicates which compiler or software package is needed to run the files. In UNIX and Linux, it is optional and called a *suffix*.

extents: any remaining records and all other additions to the file that are stored in other sections of the disk.

field: a group of related bytes that can be identified by the user with a name, type, and size. A record is made up of fields.

file: a group of related records that contains information to be used by specific application programs to generate reports.

file descriptor: information kept in the directory to describe a file or file extent.

fixed-length record: a record that always contains the same number of characters.

hashing algorithm: the set of instructions used to perform a key-to-address transformation in which a record's key field determines its location.

indexed sequential record organization: a way of organizing data in a direct access storage device. An index is created to show where the data records are stored. Any data record can be retrieved by consulting the index first.

key field: (1) a unique field or combination of fields in a record that uniquely identifies that record; or (2) the field that determines the position of a record in a sorted sequence.

logical address: the result of a key-to-address transformation.

master file directory (MFD): a file stored immediately after the volume descriptor. It lists the names and characteristics of every file contained in that volume.

noncontiguous storage: a type of file storage in which the information is stored in non-adjacent locations in a storage medium.

path: the sequence of directories and subdirectories the operating system must follow to find a specific file.

program file: a file that contains instructions for the computer.

record: a group of related fields treated as a unit. A file is a group of related records.

relative address: in a direct organization environment, it indicates the position of a record relative to the beginning of the file.

relative filename: a file's name and extension that differentiates it from other files in the same directory.

sequential record organization: the organization of records in a specific sequence. Records in a sequential file must be processed one after another.

subdirectory: a directory created by the user within the boundaries of an existing directory. Some operating systems call this a folder.

variable-length record: a record that isn't of uniform length, doesn't leave empty storage space, and doesn't truncate any characters.

volume: any secondary storage unit, such as hard disks, disk packs, CDs, DVDs, removable disks, flash memory, or tapes.

working directory: the directory or subdirectory in which the user is currently working.

Interesting Searches

- Cloud Computing File Storage
- File Backup Policies
- File Compression Techniques
- File Access Audits
- Filename Limitations
- Hash Function

Exercises

Research Topics

A. Research the size of operating system software by finding the amount of secondary storage (disk) space required by different versions of the same operating system or different operating systems. If their sizes are substantially different, explain why that may be the case, such as platform issues, features, etc. Cite your sources.

B. Consult current literature to research file-naming conventions for four different operating systems (not including UNIX, MS-DOS, Windows, or Linux). Note the acceptable range of characters, maximum length, case sensitivity, etc. Give examples of both acceptable and unacceptable filenames. For extra credit, explain how the File Managers for those operating systems shorten long filenames (if they do so) in their internal lists to make them easier to manipulate. Cite your sources.

Exercises

1. Explain in your own words why file deallocation is important and what would happen if it did not occur on a regular basis.

2. Describe how the File Manager allocates a file to a single user. List the steps that you think would be followed and explain your reasoning.

3. Is device independence important to the File Manager? Why or why not? Describe the consequences if that were not the case.

4. Do you think file retrieval is different on a menu-driven system and a command-driven system? Explain your answer and describe any differences between the two. Give an example of when each would be preferred over the other.

5. Imagine one real-life example of each: a multi-file volume and a multi-volume file. Include a description of the media used for storage and a general description of the data in the file.

6. As described in this chapter, files can be formatted with fixed-length fields or variable-length fields. In your opinion, would it be feasible to combine both formats in a single disk? Explain the reasons for your answer.

7. Explain why it's difficult to support direct access to files with variable-length records. Suggest a method for handling this type of file if direct access is required.

8. Give an example of the names of three files from your own computer that do not reside at the root or master directory. For each file, list both the relative filename and its complete filename.

9. In your own words, describe the purpose of the working directory and how it can speed or slow file access. In your opinion, should there be more than one working directory? Explain.

10. For each of the following entries in an access control matrix for User 2010, give the type of access allowed for each of the following files:

    a. File1   --E-

    b. File2   RWED

    c. File3   R-E-

    d. File4   R---

11. For each of the following entries in an access control list, give the type of access allowed for each user of File221 and describe who is included in the WORLD category:

    a. User2010   R-E-

    b. User2014   --E-

    c. User2017   RWED

    d. WORLD   R---

12. Devise a way to compress the following list of last names using a lossless technique similar to that shown in Table 8.6. Describe your method and show the compressed list. Explain why your technique is lossless (and not lossy).

    POWE

    POWELL

    POWER

    POWERS

    PORUN

Advanced Exercises

13. If you were designing the file access control system for a highly secure environment and were given a choice between the establishment of many access categories and just a few access categories, which would you select and why?

14. Compare and contrast dynamic memory allocation and the allocation of files in secondary storage.

15. When is compaction of secondary storage beneficial from the File Manager's perspective? Give several examples. List some problems that could be presented as a result of compaction and explain how they might be avoided.

16. While sophisticated File Managers implement file sharing by allowing several users to access a single copy of a file at the same time, others implement file sharing by providing a copy of the file to each user. List the advantages and disadvantages of each method.

Chapter 9

Network Organization Concepts

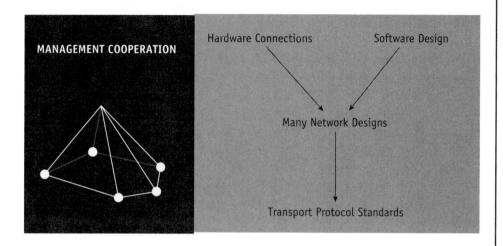

Learning Objectives

After completing this chapter, you should be able to describe:

• Several different network topologies—including the star, ring, bus, tree, and hybrid—and how they connect numerous hosts to the network

• Several types of networks: LAN, MAN, WAN, and wireless LAN

• The difference between circuit switching and packet switching, and examples of everyday use that favor each

• Conflict resolution procedures that allow a network to share common transmission hardware and software effectively

• The two transport protocol models (OSI and TCP/IP) and how the layers of each one compare

When computer facilities are connected together by data-communication components, they form a network of resources to support the many functions of the organization. Networks provide an essential infrastructure for members of the information-based society to process, manipulate, and distribute data and information to each other. This chapter introduces the terminology and basic concepts of networks.

Basic Terminology

In general, a **network** is a collection of loosely coupled processors interconnected by communication links using cables, wireless technology, or a combination of both.

A common goal of all networked systems is to provide a convenient way to share resources while controlling users' access to them. These resources include both hardware (such as a CPU, memory, printers, USB ports, and disk drives) and software (such as application programs and data files).

There are two general configurations for operating systems for networks. The oldest added a networking capability to a single-user operating system. This is called a **network operating system (NOS)**. With this configuration, users are aware of the specific assortment of computers and resources in the network and can access them by logging on to the appropriate remote host or by transferring data from the remote computer to their own.

With the second configuration, users don't need to know where and how each machine is connected to the system; they can access remote resources as if they were local resources. A **distributed operating system (D/OS)** provides good control for distributed computing systems and allows their resources to be accessed in a unified way. A distributed operating system represents a total view across multiple computer systems for controlling and managing resources without local dependencies. Management is a cooperative process that encompasses every resource and involves every site.

A distributed operating system is composed of the same four managers previously discussed but with a wider scope. At a minimum, it must provide the following components: process or object management, memory management, file management, device management, and network management, as shown in Figure 9.1. A distributed operating system offers several important advantages over older operating systems and NOSs including easy and reliable resource sharing, faster computation, adequate load balancing, good reliability, and dependable electronic communications among the network's users.

In a distributed system, each processor classifies the other processors and their resources as **remote** and considers its own resources **local**. The size, type, and

(figure 9.1)

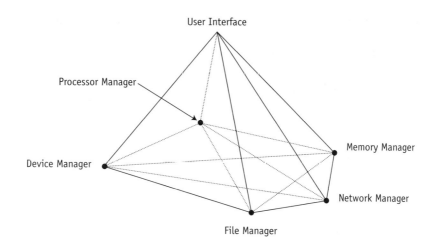

This five-sided pyramid graphically illustrates how the five managers in a networked system work together and support the user interface.

identification of processors vary. Processors are referred to as **sites**, **hosts**, and **nodes** depending on the context in which they're mentioned. Usually, the term "site" indicates a specific location in a network containing one or more computer systems, "host" indicates a specific computer system found at a site whose services and resources can be used from remote locations, and "node" (or, more formally, "node name") refers to the name assigned to a computer system connected to a network to identify it to other computers in the network, shown in Figure 9.2.

Typically, a host at one site, called the server, has resources that a host at another site, called the client, wants to use. But the assignments aren't static. Hosts can alternate between being clients or servers depending on their requirements.

(figure 9.2)

Clients request data or services from the host server and wait for the response. If the client host has resources needed by the server host, the roles can be reversed.

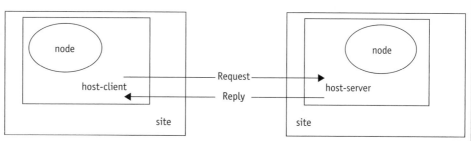

In this discussion, we've simplified the concept of client and server to represent static network software that's located at two different sites. That is, we've assumed that the host-client is a client all of the time, and that the host-server is always a server. However, the actual roles of client and server often alternate between two networked hosts, depending on the application and the network configuration. In this text, we've chosen to use the simplest configuration to make our explanation as clear as possible.

Network Topologies

Sites in any networked system can be physically or logically connected to one another in a certain **topology**, the geometric arrangement of connections (cables, wireless, or both) that link the nodes. The most common geometric arrangements are star, ring, bus, tree, and hybrid. In each topology there are trade-offs between the need for fast communication among all sites, the tolerance of failure at a site or communication link, the cost of long communication lines, and the difficulty of connecting one site to a large number of other sites. It's important to note that the physical topology of a network may not reflect its logical topology. For example, a network that is wired in a star configuration can be logically arranged to operate as if it is a ring. That is, it can be made to manipulate a token in a ring-like fashion even though its cables are arranged in a star topology. To keep our explanations in this chapter as simple as possible, whenever we discuss topologies, we are assuming that the logical structure of the network is identical to the physical structure.

For the network designer, there are many alternatives available, all of which will probably solve the customer's requirements. When deciding which configuration to use, designers should keep in mind four criteria:

- Basic cost—the expense required to link the various sites in the system
- Communications cost—the time required to send a message from one site to another
- Reliability—the assurance that many sites can still communicate with each other even if a link or site in the system fails
- User's environment—the critical parameters that the network must meet to be a successful business investment

It's quite possible that there are several possible solutions for each customer. The best choice would need to consider all four criteria. For example, an international data retrieval company might consider the fastest communications and the most flexible hardware configuration to be a cost-effective investment. But a neighborhood charity might put the most emphasis on having a low-cost networking solution. Over-engineering the neighborhood system could be just as big a mistake as under-engineering the international customer's network. The key to choosing the best design is to understand the available technology, as well as the customer's business requirements and budget.

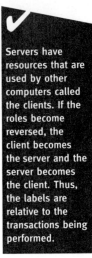

Servers have resources that are used by other computers called the clients. If the roles become reversed, the client becomes the server and the server becomes the client. Thus, the labels are relative to the transactions being performed.

Star

A **star topology**, sometimes called a hub or centralized topology, is a traditional approach to interconnecting devices in which all transmitted data must pass through a central controller when going from a sender to a receiver, as shown in Figure 9.3.

(figure 9.3)

Star topology. Hosts are connected to each other through a central controller, which assumes all responsibility for routing messages to the appropriate host. Data flow between the hosts and the central controller is represented by dotted lines. Direct host-to-host communication isn't permitted.

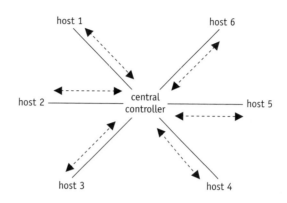

Star topology permits easy routing because the central station knows the path to all other sites and, because there is a central control point, access to the network can be controlled easily, and priority status can be given to selected sites. However, this centralization of control requires that the central site be extremely reliable and able to handle all network traffic, no matter how heavy.

Ring

In the **ring topology** all sites are connected in a closed loop, as shown in Figure 9.4, with the first site connected to the last.

(figure 9.4)

Ring topology. Hosts are connected to each other in a circular fashion with data flowing in one direction only, shown here as dotted lines. The network can be connected to other networks via a bridge or gateway.

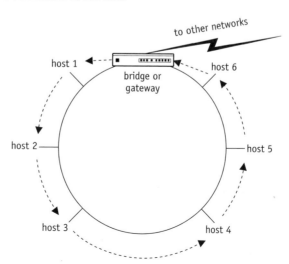

A ring network can connect to other networks via the bridge or gateway, depending on the **protocol** used by each network. (The protocol is the specific set of rules used to control the flow of messages through the network.) If the other network has the same protocol, then a bridge is used to connect the networks. If the other network has a different protocol, a gateway is used.

Data is transmitted in packets that also contain source and destination address fields. Each packet is passed from node to node in one direction only, and the destination station copies the data into a local buffer. Typically, the packet continues to circulate until it returns to the source station, where it's removed from the ring. There are some variations to this basic topology, such as the double loop network, shown in Figure 9.5, and a set of multiple rings bridged together, as shown in Figure 9.6. Both variations provide more flexibility, but at a cost.

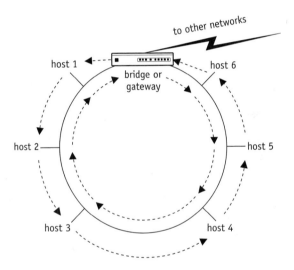

(figure 9.5)

Double loop computer network using a ring topology. Packets of data flow in both directions.

(figure 9.6)

Multiple rings bridged together. Three rings connected to each other by two bridges. This variation of ring topology allows several networks with the same protocol to be linked together.

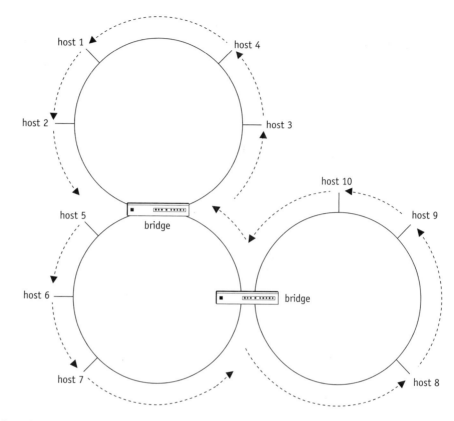

(figure 9.6)

Multiple rings bridged together. Three rings connected to each other by two bridges. This variation of ring topology allows several networks with the same protocol to be linked together.

Although ring topologies share the disadvantage that every node must be functional for the network to perform properly, rings can be designed that allow failed nodes to be bypassed—a critical consideration for network stability.

Bus

In the **bus topology** all sites are connected to a single communication line running the length of the network, as shown in Figure 9.7.

(figure 9.7)

Bus topology. Hosts are connected to one another in a linear fashion. Data flows in both directions from host to host and is turned around when it reaches an end point controller.

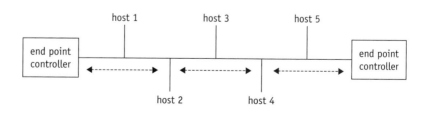

Devices are physically connected by means of cables that run between them, but the cables don't pass through a centralized controller mechanism. Messages from any site circulate in both directions through the entire communication line and can be received by all other sites.

Because all sites share a common communication line, only one of them can successfully send messages at any one time. Therefore, a control mechanism is needed to prevent collisions. In this environment, data may pass directly from one device to another, or it may be routed to an end point controller at the end of the line. In a bus, if the data reaches an end point controller without being accepted by a host, the end point controller turns it around and sends it back so the message can be accepted by the appropriate node on the way to the other end point controller. With some busses, each message must always go to the end of the line before going back down the communication line to the node to which it's addressed. However, other bus networks allow messages to be sent directly to the target node without reaching an end point controller.

Tree

The **tree topology** is a collection of busses. The communication line is a branching cable with no closed loops, as shown in Figure 9.8.

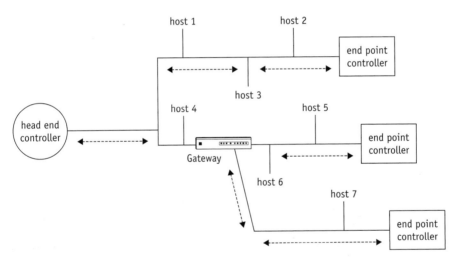

(figure 9.8)

Tree topology. Data flows up and down the branches of the trees and is absorbed by controllers at the end points. Gateways help minimize differences between the protocol used on one part of the network and the different protocol used on the branch with host 7.

The tree layout begins at the head end, where one or more cables start. Each cable may have branches that may, in turn, have additional branches, potentially resulting in quite complex arrangements. Using bridges as special fitters between busses of the same protocol and as translators to those with different protocols allows designers to create networks that can operate at speeds more responsive to the hosts in the network. In a tree configuration, a message from any site circulates through the communication line and can be received by all other sites, until it reaches the end points. If a message reaches an end point controller without being accepted by a host, the end point controller absorbs it—it isn't turned around as it is when using a bus topology. One advantage of bus and tree topologies is that even if a single node fails, message traffic can still flow through the network.

Hybrid

A **hybrid topology** is some combination of any of the four topologies discussed here. For example, a hybrid can be made by replacing a single host in a star configuration with a ring, as shown in Figure 9.9. Or a star configuration could have a bus topology as one of the communication lines feeding its hub, as shown in Figure 9.10.

(figure 9.9)

Hybrid topology, version 1. This network combines a star and a ring, connected by a bridge. Hosts 5, 6, 7, and 8 are located on the ring.

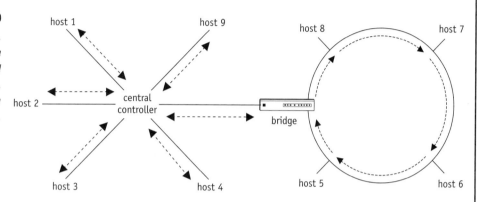

(figure 9.10)

Hybrid topology, version 2. This network combines star and bus topologies. Hosts 5, 6, 7, and 8 are located on the bus.

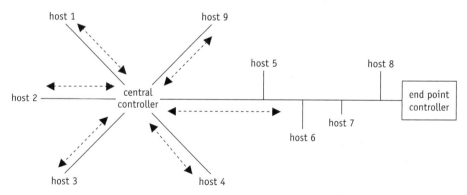

The objective of a hybrid configuration is to select among the strong points of each topology and combine them to meet that system's communications requirements most effectively.

Network Types

It's often useful to group networks according to the physical distances they cover. Although the characteristics that define each group are becoming increasingly blurred as communications technology advances, networks are generally divided into local area networks, metropolitan area networks, and wide area networks. In recent years, the wireless local area network has become ubiquitous.

Local Area Network

A **local area network** (**LAN**) defines a configuration found within a single office building, warehouse, campus, or similar computing environment. Such a network is generally owned, used, and operated by a single organization and allows computers to communicate directly through a common communication line. Typically, it's a cluster of personal computers or workstations located in the same general area. Although a LAN may be physically confined to a well-defined local area, its communications aren't limited to that area because the LAN can be a component of a larger communication network and can provide easy access to other networks through a bridge or a gateway.

A **bridge** is a device, and the software to operate it, that connects two or more geographically distant local area networks that use the same protocols. For example, a simple bridge could be used to connect two local area networks that use the Ethernet networking technology. (Ethernet is discussed later in this chapter.)

A **gateway,** on the other hand, is a more complex device and software used to connect two or more local area networks or systems that use different protocols. A gateway will translate one network's protocol into another, resolving hardware and software incompatibilities. For example, the systems network architecture (commonly called SNA) gateway can connect a microcomputer network to a mainframe host.

High-speed LANs have a data rate that varies from 100 megabits per second to more than 40 gigabits per second. Because the sites are close to each other, bandwidths are available to support very high-speed transmission for fully animated, full-color graphics and video, digital voice transmission, and other high data-rate signals. The previously described topologies—star, ring, bus, tree, and hybrid—are normally used to construct local area networks. The transmission medium used may vary from one topology to another. Factors to be considered when selecting a transmission medium are cost, data rate, reliability, number of devices that can be supported, distance between units, and technical limitations.

Metropolitan Area Network

A **metropolitan area network (MAN)** defines a configuration spanning an area larger than a LAN, ranging from several blocks of buildings to an entire city but not exceeding a circumference of 100 kilometers. In some instances MANs are owned and operated as public utilities, providing the means for internetworking several LANs.

A MAN is a high-speed network often configured as a logical ring. Depending on the protocol used, messages are either transmitted in one direction using only one ring, as illustrated in Figure 9.4, or in both directions using two counter-rotating rings, as illustrated in Figure 9.5. One ring always carries messages in one direction and the other always carries messages in the opposite direction.

Wide Area Network

The Internet is a wide area network that's accessible from LANs and MANs.

A **wide area network (WAN)** defines a configuration that interconnects communication facilities in different parts of the world, or that's operated as part of a public utility. WANs use the communications lines of common carriers, which are government-regulated private companies, such as telephone companies that already provide the general public with communication facilities. WANs use a broad range of communication media, including satellite and microwaves; in some cases, the speed of transmission is limited by the capabilities of the communication line. WANs are generally slower than LANs.

The first WAN, ARPANET, was developed in 1969 by the Advanced Research Projects Agency (ARPA); responsibility for its operation was transferred in 1975 to the Defense Communications Agency. Its successor, the **Internet**, is the most widely recognized WAN, but there exist other commercial WANs.

Wireless Local Area Network

A **wireless local area network (WLAN)** is a local area network that uses wireless technology to connect computers or workstations located within the range of the network. As shown in Table 9.1, the Institute of Electrical and Electronics Engineers (IEEE) has specified several standards for wireless networking, each with different ranges.

IEEE Standard	Net Bit Rate	Range Indoors	Frequency	Compatibility
802.11a	54 Mbps	25-75 feet	5 GHz	First IEEE wireless standard
802.11b	11 Mbps	100-150 feet	2.4 GHz	Not compatible with 802.11g
802.11g	54 Mbps	100-150 feet	2.4 GHz	Compatible with 802.11b
802.11n	600 Mbps	300 feet	5 GHz	Compatible with 802.11g

(table 9.1)

Comparison of three IEEE standards for wireless networks (IEEE, 2007). The fourth standard, 802.11n, is expected to be published in November 2009.

For wireless nodes (workstations, laptops, etc.), a WLAN can provide easy access to a larger network or the Internet, as shown in Figure 9.11. Keep in mind that a WLAN typically poses security vulnerabilities because of its open architecture and the inherent difficulty of keeping out unauthorized intruders.

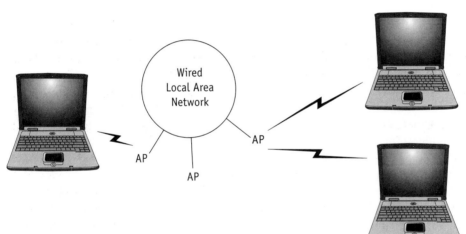

(figure 9.11)

In a WLAN, wireless-enabled nodes connect to the cabled LAN via access points (APs) if they are located within the range of the device sending the signal.

The IEEE mobile WiMAX standard (802.16), approved in 2005 by the Institute of Electrical and Electronics Engineers, promises to deliver high-bandwidth data over much longer distances (up to 10 miles) than the current Wi-Fi standard (IEEE, 2007). This is a fast-changing subject, so we encourage you to research current literature for the latest developments.

Software Design Issues

So far we've examined the configurations of a network's hardware components. In this section we'll examine four software issues that must be addressed by network designers:

- How do sites use addresses to locate other sites?
- How are messages routed and how are they sent?
- How do processes communicate with each other?
- How are conflicting demands for resources resolved?

Addressing Conventions

Network sites need to determine how to uniquely identify their users, so they can communicate with each other and access each other's resources. Names, addresses, and routes are required because sites aren't directly connected to each other except over point-to-point links; therefore, addressing protocols are closely related to the network topology and geographic location of each site. In some cases, a distinction is made between "local name," which refers to the name by which a unit is known within its own system, and "global name," the name by which a unit is known outside its own system. This distinction is useful because it allows each site the freedom to identify its units according to their own standards without imposing uniform naming rules, something that would be difficult to implement at the local level. On the other hand, a global name must follow standard name lengths, formats, and other global conventions.

Using an Internet address as a typical example, we can see that it follows a hierarchical organization, starting from left to right in the following sequence: from logical user to host machine, from host machine to net machine, from net machine to cluster, and from cluster to network. For example, in each Internet address—*someone@icarus.lis.pitt.edu* or *igss12@aber.ac.uk*—the periods are used to separate each component. These electronic mail addresses, which are fairly easy to remember, must be translated (or "resolved," using a concept similar to that described in Chapter 3) to corresponding hardware addresses. This conversion is done by the networking section of the computer's operating system.

The examples given above follow the **Domain Name Service (DNS)** protocol, a general-purpose distributed data query service whose principal function is the resolution of Internet addresses. If we dissect *someone@icarus.lis.pitt.edu* into its components, we have the following:

- *someone* is the logical user,
- *icarus* is the host for the user called someone,
- *lis* is the net machine for icarus,

- *pitt* is the cluster for lis, and
- *edu* is the network for the University of Pittsburgh.

Not all components need to be present in all Internet addresses. Nevertheless, the DNS is able to resolve them by examining each one in reverse order.

Routing Strategies

A **router** is an internetworking device, primarily software driven, which directs traffic between two different types of LANs or two network segments with different protocol addresses. It operates at the network layer, which is explained later in this chapter.

Routing allows data to get from one point on a network to another. To do so, each destination must be uniquely identified. Once the data is at the proper network, the router makes sure that the correct node in the network receives it. The role of routers changes as network designs change. Routers are used extensively for connecting sites to each other and to the Internet. They can be used for a variety of functions, including securing the information that is generated in predefined areas, choosing the fastest route from one point to another, and providing redundant network connections so that a problem in one area will not degrade network operations in other areas.

Routing protocols must consider addressing, address resolution, message format, and error reporting. Most routing protocols are based on an addressing format that uses a network and a node number to identify each node. When a network is powered on, each router records in a table the addresses of the networks that are directly connected. Because routing protocols permit interaction between routers, sharing network destinations that each router may have acquired as it performs its services becomes easy. At specified intervals each router in the internetwork broadcasts a copy of its entire routing table. Eventually, all of the routers know how to get to each of the different destination networks.

Although the addresses allow routers to send data from one network to another, they can't be used to get from one point in a network to another point in the *same* network. This must be done through address resolution, which allows a router to map the original address to a hardware address and store the mapping in a table to be used for future transmissions.

A variety of message formats are defined by routing protocols. These messages are used to allow the protocol to perform its functions, such as finding new nodes on a network, testing to determine whether they're working, reporting error conditions, exchanging routing information, establishing connections, and transmitting data.

Data transmission does not always run smoothly. For example, conditions may arise that cause errors such as inability to reach a destination because of a malfunctioning node or network. In cases such as this, routers and routing protocols would report the error condition, although they would not attempt to correct the error; error correction is left to protocols at other levels of the network's architecture.

Two of the most widely used routing protocols in the Internet are routing information protocol and open shortest path first.

Routing Information Protocol

In **routing information protocol (RIP)**, selection of a path to transfer data from one network to another is based on the number of intermediate nodes, or hops, between the source and the destination. The path with the smallest number of hops is always chosen. This distance vector algorithm is easy to implement, but it may not be the best in today's networking environment because it does not take into consideration other important factors such as bandwidth, data priority, or type of network. That is, it can exclude faster or more reliable paths from being selected just because they have more hops. Another limitation of RIP relates to routing tables. The entire table is updated and reissued every 30 seconds, whether or not changes have occurred; this increases internetwork traffic and negatively affects the delivery of messages. In addition, the tables propagate from one router to another. Thus, in the case of an internetwork with 15 hops, it would take more than seven minutes for a change to be known at the other end of the internetwork. Because not all routers would have the same information about the internetwork, a failure at any one of the hops could create an unstable environment for all message traffic.

Open Shortest Path First

In **open shortest path first (OSPF)**, selection of a transmission path is made only after the state of a network has been determined so that if an intermediate hop is malfunctioning, it's eliminated immediately from consideration until its services have been restored. Routing update messages are sent only when changes in the routing environment occur, thereby reducing the number of messages in the internetwork and reducing the size of the messages by not sending the entire routing table. However, memory usage is increased because OSPF keeps track of more information than RIP. In addition, the savings in bandwidth consumption are offset by the higher CPU usage needed for the calculation of the shortest path, which is based on Dijkstra's algorithm, simply stated as find the shortest paths from a given source to all other destinations by proceeding in stages and developing the path in increasing path lengths.

When a router uses Dijkstra's algorithm, it computes all the different paths to get to each destination in the internetwork, creating what is known as a topological database. This data structure is maintained by OSPF and is updated whenever failures occur. Therefore, a router would simply check its topological database to determine whether a path was available, and would then use Dijkstra's algorithm to generate a shortest-path tree to get around the failed link.

Connection Models

A communication network isn't concerned with the content of data being transmitted but with moving the data from one point to another. Because it would be prohibitive to connect each node in a network to all other nodes, the nodes are connected to a communication network designed to minimize transmission costs and to provide full connectivity among all attached devices. Data entering the network at one point is routed to its destination by being switched from node to node, whether by circuit switching or by packet switching.

Circuit Switching

Circuit switching is a communication model in which a dedicated communication path is established between two hosts. The path is a connected sequence of links and the connection between the two points exists until one of them is disconnected. The connection path must be set up before data transmission begins; therefore, if the entire path becomes unavailable, messages can't be transmitted because the circuit would not be complete. The telephone system is a good example of a circuit-switched network.

In terms of performance, there is a delay before signal transfer begins while the connection is set up. However, once the circuit is completed, the network is transparent to users and information is transmitted at a fixed rate of speed with insignificant delays at intermediate nodes.

Packet Switching

Packet switching is basically a store-and-forward technique in which a message is divided into multiple equal-sized units called **packets,** which are then sent through the network to their destination where they're reassembled into their original long format, as shown in Figure 9.12.

Packet switching is an effective technology for long-distance data transmission and provides more flexibility than circuit switching because it permits data transmission between devices that receive or transmit data at different rates. However, there is no guarantee that after a message has been divided into packets the packets will all travel along the same path to their destination or that they will arrive in their physical

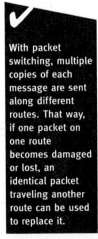

With packet switching, multiple copies of each message are sent along different routes. That way, if one packet on one route becomes damaged or lost, an identical packet traveling another route can be used to replace it.

(figure 9.12)

A packet switching network does not require a dedicated connection. It sends packets using a three-step procedure: (a) divide the data into addressed packets; (b) send each packet toward its destination; (c) and, at the destination, confirm receipt of all packets, place them in order, reassemble the data, and deliver it to the recipient.

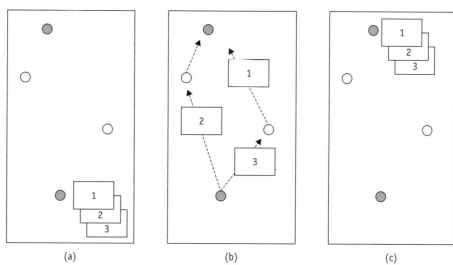

(a) (b) (c)

sequential order. In addition, packets from one message may be interspersed with those from other messages as they travel toward their destinations. Therefore, a header containing pertinent information about the packet is attached to each packet before it's transmitted. The information contained in the packet header varies according to the routing method used by the network.

The idea is similar to sending a series of 30 reference books through a package delivery system. Six boxes contain five volumes each, and each box is labeled with its sequence number (e.g., box 2 of 6), as well as its ultimate destination. As space on passing delivery trucks becomes available, each box is forwarded to a central switching center where it's stored until space becomes available to send it to the next switching center closer to its destination. Eventually, when all six boxes arrive, they're put in their original order, the 30 volumes are unpacked, and the original sequence is restored.

As shown in Table 9.2, packet switching is fundamentally different from circuit switching, also a store-and-forward technique, in which an entire message is accepted by a central switching node and forwarded to its destination when one of two events occurs: all circuits are free to send the entire message at once, or the receiving node requests its stored messages.

Circuit Switching	Packet Switching	(table 9.2)
• Transmits in real time	• Transmits in batches	*Comparison of circuit and packet switching.*
• Preferred in low-volume networks	• Preferred in high-volume networks	
• Reduced line efficiency	• High line efficiency	
• Dedicated to a single transmission	• Shared by many transmissions	
• Preferred for voice communications	• Not good for voice communications	
• Easily overloaded	• Accommodates varying priority among packets	

Packet switching provides greater line efficiency because a single node-to-node circuit can be shared by several packets and does not sit idle over long periods of time. Although delivery may be delayed as traffic increases, packets can still be accepted and transmitted.

That's also in contrast to circuit switching networks, which, when they become overloaded, refuse to accept new connections until the load decreases. Have you ever received a busy signal when trying to place a long-distance telephone call during a major holiday? That problem is similar to a circuit switching network's overload response.

Packet switching allows users to allocate priorities to their messages so that a router with several packets queued for transmission can send the higher priority packets first. In addition, packet switching networks are more reliable than other types because most nodes are connected by more than one link, so that if one circuit should fail, a completely different path may be established between nodes.

There are two different methods of selecting the path: datagrams and virtual circuits. In the datagram approach, the destination and sequence number of the packet are added to the information uniquely identifying the message to which the packet belongs; each packet is then handled independently and a route is selected as each packet is accepted into the network. This is similar to the shipping label that's added to each package in the book shipment example. At their destination, all packets belonging to the same message are then reassembled by sequence number into one continuous message and, finally, are delivered to the addressee. Because the message can't be delivered until all packets have been accounted for, it's up to the receiving node to request retransmission of lost or damaged packets. This routing method has two distinct advantages: It helps diminish congestion by sending incoming packets through less heavily used paths, and it provides more reliability because alternate paths may be set up when one node fails.

In the virtual circuit approach, the destination and packet sequence number aren't added to the information identifying the packet's message because a complete path from sender to receiver is established before transmission starts—all the packets belonging to that message use the same route. Although it's a similar concept, this is different from the dedicated path used in circuit switching because any node can have several virtual circuits to any other node. Its advantage over the datagram method is that its routing decision is made only once for all packets belonging to the same message—a feature that should speed up message transmission for long messages. On the other hand, it has a disadvantage in that if a node fails, all virtual circuits using that node become unavailable. In addition, when the circuit experiences heavy traffic, congestion is more difficult to resolve.

Conflict Resolution

Because a network consists of devices sharing a common transmission capability, some method to control usage of the medium is necessary to facilitate equal and fair access to this common resource. First we will describe some medium access control techniques: round robin, reservation, and contention. Then we will briefly examine three common medium access control protocols used to implement access to resources: carrier sense multiple access (CSMA); token passing; and distributed-queue, dual bus (DQDB).

Access Control Techniques

The round robin access control used here follows the same principles as round robin processor management, described in Chapter 4.

In networks, round robin allows each node on the network to use the communication medium. If the node has data to send, it's given a certain amount of time to complete the transmission, at the end of which, the opportunity is passed to the next node. If the node has no data to send, or if it completes transmission before the time is up, then the next node begins its turn. Round robin is an efficient technique when there are many nodes transmitting over long periods of time. However, when there are few nodes transmitting over long periods of time, the overhead incurred in passing turns from node to node can be substantial, making other techniques preferable depending on whether transmissions are short and intermittent, as in interactive terminal-host sessions, or lengthy and continuous, as in massive file transfer sessions.

The reservation technique is well-suited for lengthy and continuous traffic. Access time on the medium is divided into slots and a node can reserve future time slots for its use. The technique is similar to that found in synchronous time-division multiplexing, used for multiplexing digitized voice streams, where the time slots are fixed in length and preassigned to each node. This technique could be good for a configuration with several terminals connected to a host computer through a single I/O port.

The contention technique is better for short and intermittent traffic. No attempt is made to determine whose turn it is to transmit, so nodes compete for access to the medium. Therefore, it works well under light to moderate traffic, but performance tends to break down under heavy loads. This technique's major advantage is that it's easy to implement.

Access protocols currently in use are based on the previously mentioned techniques and are discussed here with regard to their role in LAN environments.

CSMA

Carrier sense multiple access (CSMA) is a contention-based protocol that's easy to implement. Carrier sense means that a node on the network will listen to or test the communication medium before transmitting any messages, thus preventing a collision with another node that's currently transmitting. Multiple access means that several nodes are connected to the same communication line as peers, on the same level, and with equal privileges.

Although a node will not transmit until the line is quiet, two or more nodes could come to that conclusion at the same instant. If more than one transmission is sent simultaneously, creating a collision, the data from all transmissions will be damaged and the line will remain unusable while the damaged messages are dissipated. When the receiving nodes fail to acknowledge receipt of their transmissions, the sending nodes will know that the messages did not reach their destinations successfully and both will be retransmitted. The probability of this happening increases if the nodes are farther apart, making CSMA a less appealing access protocol for large or complex networks.

Therefore, the original algorithm was modified to include collision detection and was named carrier sense multiple access with collision detection (CSMA/CD). **Ethernet** is the most widely known CSMA/CD protocol. Collision detection does not eliminate collisions, but it does reduce them. When a collision occurs, a jamming signal is sent immediately to both sending nodes, which then wait a random period before trying again. With this protocol, the amount of wasted transmission capacity is reduced to the time it takes to detect the collision.

A different modification is CSMA with collision avoidance (CSMA/CA). Collision avoidance means that the access method prevents multiple nodes from colliding during transmission. However, opinion on its efficiency is divided. Some claim it's more efficient than collision detection, whereas others contend that it lowers a network's performance when there are a large number of nodes. The CSMA/CA protocol is implemented in LocalTalk, Apple's cabling system, which uses a protocol called LocalTalk link access protocol. A terminal connected to an Apple CSMA/CA network would send out a three-byte packet to indicate that it wants to start transmitting. This packet tells all other terminals to wait until the first is finished transmitting before they initiate transmissions. If collisions do occur, they involve only the three-byte packets, not the actual data. This protocol does not guarantee the data will reach its destination, but it ensures that any data that's delivered will be error-free.

Token Passing

In a token passing network, a special electronic message, called a "token," is generated when the network is turned on and is then passed along from node to node. Only the node with the token is allowed to transmit, and after it has done so, it must pass the token on to another node. These networks typically have either a bus or ring topology and are popular because access is fast and collisions are nonexistent.

In a **token bus** network, the token is passed to each node in turn. Upon receipt of the token, a node attaches the data to it to be transmitted and sends the packet, containing both the token and the data, to its destination. The receiving node copies the data, adds the acknowledgment, and returns the packet to the sending node, which then passes the token on to the next node in logical sequence.

Initially, node order is determined by a cooperative decentralized algorithm. Once the network is up and running, turns are determined by priority based on node activity. A node requiring the token frequently will have a higher priority than one that seldom needs it. A table of node addresses is kept in priority order by the network. When a transmission is complete, the token passes from the node that just finished to the one having the next lower entry in the table. When the lowest priority node has been serviced, the token returns to the top of the table, and the process is repeated.

This process is similar to a train engine pulling into the station. If the stationmaster has a delivery to send, those cars are attached to the engine and the train is dispatched to its destination with no intermediate stops. When it arrives, the cars are detached, and the engine is sent back to the point of origin with the message that the shipment was successfully received. After delivering that message to the shipment's originator, the engine proceeds to the next station to pick up a delivery.

Implementation of this protocol dictates higher overhead at each node than does CSMA/CD, and nodes may have long waits under certain conditions before receiving the token.

The token ring network was originally developed by IBM in the 1970s.

Token ring is the most widely used protocol for ring topology; it became better known than token bus when IBM made its Token Ring Network commercially available. It's based on the use of a token that moves between the nodes in turn and in one direction only. When it's not carrying a message, the token is called a "free" token. If a node wants to send a message, it must wait for the free token to come by. It then changes the token from free to busy and sends its message immediately following the busy token. Meanwhile, all other nodes must wait for the token to become free and come to them again before they're able to transmit a message.

The receiving node copies the message in the packet and sets the copied bit to indicate it was successfully received; the packet then continues on its way, making a complete round trip back to the sending node, which then releases the new free token on the network. At this point, the next node down the line with data to send will be able to pick up the free token and repeat the process.

DQDB

The distributed-queue, dual bus (DQDB) protocol is intended for use with a dual-bus configuration, where each bus transports data in only one direction and has been standardized by one of the IEEE committees as part of its MAN standards. Transmission on each bus consists of a steady stream of fixed-size slots, as shown in Figure 9.13. Slots generated at one end of each bus are marked free and sent downstream, where they're marked busy and written to by nodes that are ready to transmit data. Nodes read and copy data from the slots, which then continue to travel toward the end of the bus, where they dissipate.

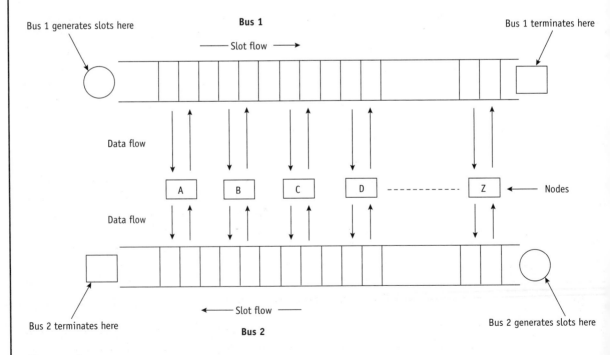

(figure 9.13)

Distributed-queue, dual bus protocol. Free slots are generated at one end of each bus and flow in only one direction. Using DQDB, if node C wants to send data to node D, it must wait for a free slot on Bus 1 because the slots are flowing toward node D on that bus.

The distributed access protocol is based on a distributed reservation scheme and can be summarized as follows. If node C in Figure 9.13 wants to send data to node D, it would use Bus 1 because the slots are flowing toward D on that bus. However, if the nodes before C monopolize the slots, then C would not be able to transmit its data to D. To solve the problem, C can use Bus 2 to send a reservation to its upstream neighbors. The protocol states that a node will allow free slots to go by until outstanding reservations from downstream nodes have been satisfied. Therefore, the protocol must provide a mechanism by which each station can keep track of the requests of its downstream peers.

This mechanism is handled by a pair of first-in, first-out queues and a pair of counters, one for each bus, at each of the nodes in the network. This is a very effective protocol providing negligible delays under light loads and predictable queuing under heavy loads. This combination makes the DQDB protocol suitable for MANs that manage large file transfers and are able to satisfy the needs of interactive users.

Transport Protocol Standards

During the 1980s, network usage began to grow at a fast pace, as did the need to integrate dissimilar network devices from different vendors—a task that became increasingly difficult as the number and complexity of network devices increased. Soon the user community pressured the industry to create a single universally adopted network architecture that would allow true multivendor interoperability. We'll review two models, OSI and TCP/IP.

OSI Reference Model

The **International Organization for Standardization (ISO)**, which makes technical recommendations about data communication interfaces, took on the task of creating such a network architecture. Its efforts resulted in the **open systems interconnection (OSI) reference model**, which serves as a framework for defining the services that a network should provide to its users. This model provides the basis for connecting open systems for distributed applications processing. The word "open" means that any two systems that conform to the reference model and the related standards can be connected, regardless of the vendor.

Once all services were identified, similar functions were collected together into seven logical clusters known as layers. One of the main reasons used to define the seven layers was to group easily localized functions so that each layer could be redesigned and its protocols changed in any way to take advantage of new advances in architecture, hardware, or software without changing the services expected from and provided to the adjacent layers. Boundaries between layers were selected at points that past experience had revealed to be effective. The resulting seven-layer OSI model handles data transmission from one terminal or application program to another. Figure 9.14 shows how data passes through the seven layers and how it's organized: from the application layer, the one closest to the user, to the physical layer, the one closest to the cables, modems, and circuits. A brief description of each layer's function follows.

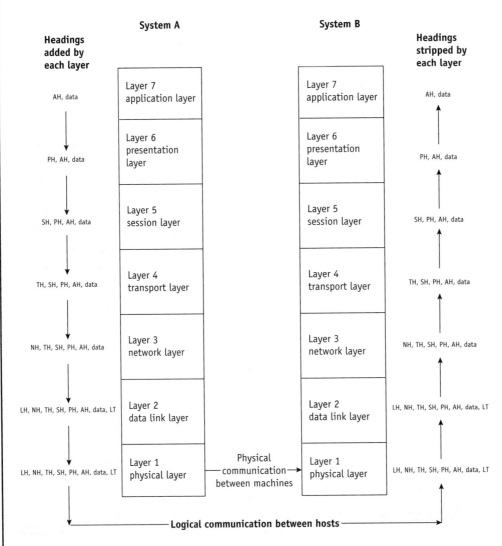

(figure 9.14)

The OSI transport protocol model. At every layer of the sending unit, System A, a new header is attached to the previous packet before it's passed on to the next lower layer. Finally, at the data link layer, a link trailer (LT) is added, completing the frame, which is passed to the physical layer for transmission. Then the receiving unit removes each header or trailer until it delivers the data to the application program at Layer 7 on System B.

Layer 1—The Physical Layer

Layer 1 is at the bottom of the model. This is where the mechanical, electrical, and functional specifications for connecting a device to a particular network are described. Layer 1 is primarily concerned with transmitting bits over communication lines, so voltages of electricity and timing factors are important. This is the only layer concerned with hardware, and all data must be passed down to it for actual data transfer between units to occur. (Layers 2 through 7 all are concerned with software, and communication between units at these levels is only virtual.) Examples of physical layer specifications are 100Base-T, RS449, and CCITT V.35.

Layer 2—The Data Link Layer

Because software is needed to implement Layer 2, this software must be stored in some type of programmable device such as a front-end processor, network node, or micro-computer. Bridging between two homogeneous networks occurs at this layer. On one side, the data link layer establishes and controls the physical path of communications before sending data to the physical layer below it. It takes the data, which has been divided into packets by the layers above it, and physically assembles the packet for trans-mission by completing its frame. Frames contain data combined with control and error detection characters so that Layer 1 can transmit a continuous stream of bits without concern for their format or meaning. On the other side, it checks for transmission errors and resolves problems caused by damaged, lost, or duplicate message frames so that Layer 3 can work with error-free messages. Typical data link level protocols are High-Level Data Link Control (HDLC) and Synchronous Data Link Control (SDLC).

Layer 3—The Network Layer

Layer 3 provides services, such as addressing and routing, that move data through the network to its destination. Basically, the software at this level accepts blocks of data from Layer 4, the transport layer, resizes them into shorter packets, and routes them to the proper destination. Addressing methods that allow a node and its network to be identified, as well as algorithms to handle address resolution, are specified in this layer. A database of routing tables keeps track of all possible routes a packet may take and determines how many different circuits exist between any two packet switching nodes. This database may be stored at this level to provide efficient packet routing and should be dynamically updated to include information about any failed circuit and the trans-mission volume present in the active circuits.

Layer 4—The Transport Layer

Layer 4 is also known as the host-to-host or end-to-end layer because it maintains reli-able data transmission between end users. A program at the source computer can send a virtual communication to a similar program at a destination machine by using message headers and control messages. However, the physical path still goes to Layer 1 and across to the destination computer. Software for this layer contains facilities that handle user addressing and ensures that all the packets of data have been received and that none have been lost. This software may be stored in front-end processors, packet switching nodes, or host computers. In addition, this layer has a mechanism that regulates the flow of information so a fast host can't overrun a slower terminal or an overloaded host. A well-known transport layer protocol is Transmission Control Protocol (TCP).

Layer 5—The Session Layer

Layer 5 is responsible for providing a user-oriented connection service and transferring data over the communication lines. The transport layer is responsible for creating and maintaining a logical connection between end points. The session layer provides a user interface that adds value to the transport layer in the form of dialogue management and error recovery. Sometimes the session layer is known as the "data flow control" layer because it establishes the connection between two applications or processes, enforces the regulations for carrying on the session, controls the flow of data, and resets the connection if it fails. This layer might also perform some accounting functions to ensure that users receive their bills. The functions of the transport layer and session layer are very similar and, because the operating system of the host computer generally handles the session layer, it would be natural to combine both layers into one, as does TCP/IP.

Layer 6—The Presentation Layer

Layer 6 is responsible for data manipulation functions common to many applications, such as formatting, compression, and encryption. Data conversion, syntax conversion, and protocol conversion are common tasks performed in this layer. Gateways connecting networks with different protocols are presentation layer devices; one of their functions is to accommodate totally different interfaces as seen by a terminal in one node and expected by the application program at the host computer. For example, IBM's Customer Information Control System (CICS) teleprocessing monitor is a presentation layer service located in a host mainframe, although it provides additional functions beyond the presentation layer.

Layer 7—The Application Layer

At Layer 7, application programs, terminals, and computers access the network. This layer provides the interface to users and is responsible for formatting user data before passing it to the lower layers for transmission to a remote host. It contains network management functions and tools to support distributed applications. File transfer and e-mail are two of the most common application protocols and functions.

Once the OSI model is assembled, it allows nodes to communicate with each other. Each layer provides a completely different array of functions to the network, but all the layers work in unison to ensure that the network provides reliable transparent service to the users.

TCP/IP Model

The **Transmission Control Protocol/Internet Protocol (TCP/IP) reference model** is probably the oldest transport protocol standard. It's the basis for Internet communications and is the most widely used network layer protocol in use today. It was developed for the U.S. Department of Defense's ARPANET and provides reasonably efficient and error-free transmission between different systems. Because it's a file-transfer protocol, large files can be sent across sometimes unreliable networks with a high probability that the data will arrive error free. Some differences between the TCP/IP model and the OSI reference model are the significance that TCP/IP places on internetworking and providing connectionless services, and its management of certain functions, such as accounting for use of resources.

The TCP/IP model organizes a communication system with three main components: processes, hosts, and networks. Processes execute on hosts, which can often support multiple simultaneous processes that are defined as primary units that need to communicate. These processes communicate across the networks to which hosts are connected. Based on this hierarchy, the model can be roughly partitioned into two major tasks: one that manages the transfer of information to the host in which the process resides, and one that ensures it gets to the correct process within the host. Therefore, a network needs to be concerned only with routing data between hosts, as long as the hosts can then direct the data to the appropriate processes. With this in mind, the TCP/IP model can be arranged into four layers instead of OSI's seven, as shown in Figure 9.15. A brief description of the layers' functions and how they relate to the OSI model follows.

Network Access Layer

The network access layer is equivalent to the physical, data link, and part of the network layers of the OSI model. Protocols at this layer provide access to a communication network. Some of the functions performed here are flow control, error control between hosts, security, and priority implementation.

Internet Layer

The Internet layer is equivalent to the portion of the network layer of the OSI model that isn't already included in the previous layer, specifically the mechanism that performs routing functions. Therefore, this protocol is usually implemented within gateways and hosts. An example of a standard set by the U.S. Department of Defense

OSI Model

TCP/IP Model

OSI Model	TCP/IP Model
Layer 7 application layer	Layer 4 process/ application layer
Layer 6 presentation layer	
Layer 5 session layer	Layer 3 host-host layer
Layer 4 transport layer	
Layer 3 network layer	Layer 2 Internet layer
Layer 2 data link layer	Layer 1 network access layer
Layer 1 physical layer	

(figure 9.15)

Comparison of OSI and TCP/IP models and their functional layers.

(DoD) is the Internet Protocol (IP), which provides connectionless service for end systems to communicate across one or more networks.

Host-Host Layer

The host-host layer is equivalent to the transport and session layers of the OSI model. As its name indicates, this layer supports mechanisms to transfer data between two processes on different host computers. Services provided in the host-host layer also include error checking, flow control, and an ability to manipulate connection control signals. An example of a standard set by the DoD is the Transmission Control Protocol (TCP), which provides a reliable end-to-end data transfer service.

Process/Application Layer

The process/application layer is equivalent to the presentation and application layers of the OSI model. It includes protocols for computer-to-computer resource sharing and terminal-to-computer remote access. Specific examples of standards set by the DoD for this layer are File Transfer Protocol (FTP), a simple application for transfer of ASCII, EBCDIC, and binary files; Simple Mail Transfer Protocol (SMTP), a simple electronic mail facility; and Telnet, a simple asynchronous terminal capability that provides remote log-on capabilities to users working at a terminal or a personal computer.

Conclusion

Although operating systems for networks necessarily include the functions of the four managers discussed so far in this textbook—the Memory Manager, Processor Manager, Device Manager, and File Manager—they also need to coordinate all those functions among the network's many varied pieces of hardware and software, no matter where they're physically located.

There is no single gauge by which we can measure the success of a network's operating system, but at a minimum it must meet the reliability requirements of its owners. That is, when a node fails—and all networks experience node failure from time to time—the operating system must detect the failure, change routing instructions to avoid that node, and make sure every lost message is retransmitted until it's successfully received.

In this chapter we've introduced the basic network organization concepts: common terminology, network topologies, types of networks, software design issues, and transport protocol standards. Bear in mind, however, that this is a complicated subject and we've only just touched the surface in these few pages. For more information about connecting topics discussed here, refer to the texts or references listed at the end of the book.

Key Terms

bridge: a data-link layer device used to interconnect multiple networks using the same protocol.

bus topology: network architecture to connect elements together along a single line.

circuit switching: a communication model in which a dedicated communication path is established between two hosts and on which all messages travel.

distributed operating system (D/OS): an operating system that provides control for a distributed computing system, allowing its resources to be accessed in a unified way.

Domain Name Service (DNS): a general-purpose, distributed, replicated data query service. Its principal function is the resolution of Internet addresses based on fully qualified domain names.

Ethernet: a popular LAN network technology in which nodes contend for access to a network. Inexpensive, easy to install and maintain.

gateway: a communications device or program that passes data between networks having similar functions but different protocols.

host: (1) the Internet term for a network node that is capable of communicating at the application layer. Each Internet host has a unique IP address. (2) a networked computer with centralized program or data files that makes those resources available to other computers on the network.

hybrid topology: a network architecture that combines other types of network topologies to accommodate particular operating characteristics or traffic volumes.

Internet: the largest collection of networks interconnected with routers. The Internet is a multi-protocol internetwork.

International Organization for Standardization (ISO): a voluntary, non-treaty organization responsible for creating international standards in many areas, including computers and communications.

local: pertaining to the network node to which a user is attached.

local area network (LAN): a data network intended to serve an area covering only a few square kilometers or less.

metropolitan area network (MAN): a data network intended to serve an area approximating that of a large city.

network: a collection of loosely coupled processors interconnected by communications links using cables, wireless technology, or a combination.

network operating system (NOS): the software that manages network resources for a node on a network and may provide security and access control.

node: a network-layer addressable device attached to a computer network.

open shortest path first (OSPF): a protocol designed for use in Internet Protocol (IP) networks, concerned with tracking the operational state of every network interface.

open systems interconnection (OSI) reference model: a seven-layer conceptual structure describing computer network architectures and the ways in which data passes through them.

packet: a unit of data sent across a network.

packet switching: a communication model in which messages are individually routed between hosts, with no previously established communication path.

protocol: a set of rules to control the flow of messages through a network.

remote: pertaining to a node at the distant end of a network connection.

ring topology: a network topology; each node is connected to two adjacent nodes.

router: a device that forwards traffic between networks.

routing information protocol (RIP): a routing protocol used by IP, based on a distance-vector algorithm.

site: a specific location on a network containing one or more computer systems.

star topology: a network topology in which multiple network nodes are connected through a single, central node.

token ring: a type of local area network with stations wired into a ring network.

token bus: a type of local area network with nodes connected to a common cable using a CSMA/CA protocol.

topology: in a network, the geometric arrangement of connections (cables, wireless, or both) that link the nodes.

Transmission Control Protocol/Internet Protocol (TCP/IP) reference model: a common acronym for the suite of transport-layer and application-layer protocols that operate over the Internet Protocol.

tree topology: a network architecture in which elements are connected in a hierarchical structure.

wide area network (WAN): a network usually constructed with long-distance, point-to-point lines, covering a large geographic area.

wireless local area network (WLAN): a local area network with wireless nodes.

Interesting Searches

- IEEE Wireless Standards
- WiMAX vs. Wi-Fi
- Voice Over Internet Protocol (VoIP)
- Network Topologies
- Routing Protocols

Exercises

Research Topics

A. Name several operating systems that run LANs today. Do not include different versions of a single operating system. For each operating system, list its name, the platform or network it operates on, and its distributor or manufacturer. Cite your sources.

B. In this chapter, we discussed the WiMAX standard. Consult current literature to further explore the status of WiMAX technology. Describe any barriers to commercial use and the applications that show the most promise. Explain which countries expect to benefit the most and why. Be sure to cite your sources. If your discussion includes terms not used in the text, define them.

Exercises

1. As mentioned in this chapter, sometimes clients and servers exchange roles with clients becoming servers at times. Give an example where a client always remains the client and never becomes the server.

2. Explain why network operating systems were phased out when distributed operating systems gained popularity.

3. An early network topology was the token bus. Describe how the role of the token c in the token bus network compares with the token ring network.

4. In your own words, describe the functional differences between a bridge and a gateway. Give an example of each.

5. Explain the major advantages and disadvantages of a star topology.

6. Explain the major advantages and disadvantages of a bus topology.

7. Describe how a network with a star topology can be manipulated to act as if it uses a ring topology.

8. Referring to Figure 9.9, describe the flow of data from host to host as it moves from host 1 to host 6 including each controller or bridge.

9. Referring to Figure 9.10, describe the flow of data from host to host as it moves from host 1 to host 6 including each controller or bridge.

10. Describe a hybrid topology and draw graphic illustrations of two examples.

11. Discuss at least three advantages of a hard-wired LAN compared to a wireless LAN and describe one situation where the wired LAN would be preferred.

12. Discuss the primary difference between a bridge and a gateway, and give a real-life example that uses each one.

13. Explain the role of routers when moving data from one host to another in the same network.

14. This chapter described packet routing. Give the two examples in which packets can be routed and explain how they differ.

15. Give two real-life examples where packet switching would be preferred over circuit switching and explain why.

16. Compare the virtual circuit approach to packet switching and describe its advantages.

17. Compare and contrast the two most widely used routing protocols: routing information protocol (RIP) and open shortest path first (OSFP).

18. Identify a network topology that would best suit each of the following environments and explain why:

    a. Dormitory floor

    b. University campus

    c. Airport

    d. State or province

Advanced Exercises

19. Although not explicitly discussed in the chapter, packet size would seem to have an impact on transmission time. Discuss whether or not this is true and explain why. Specifically compare the concept of the number of bits that constitute the *data* portion of the packet and the number of bits that constitute the *address* portion of the packet. Remember that the address is overhead and it has an impact on data transmission rates.

    Offer a comprehensive example comparing packet sizes and resulting transmission times. For example, look at some of your e-mail messages and compare the number of bytes that constitute the message with the number of bytes for the address. Compute the results for several e-mails and give your conclusions.

20. Discuss what is incorrect with the following logic: Packet switching requires control and address bits to be added to each packet, which causes considerable overhead in packet switching. In circuit switching, a dedicated circuit is set up and no extra bits are needed.

    a. Therefore, there is no overhead in circuit switching.

    b. Because there is no overhead in circuit switching, line utilization must be more efficient than in packet switching.

21. Describe the differences between CSMA/CD and CSMA/CA. Provide one real-life example where CSMA/CD is used. Provide one real-life example where CSMA/CA is used.

22. Explain the circumstances under which a token ring network is more effective than an Ethernet network.

23. Even though the OSI model of networking specifies seven layers of functionality, most computer systems use fewer layers to implement a network. Why do they use fewer layers? What problems could be caused by the use of fewer layers?

| # Management of Network Functions

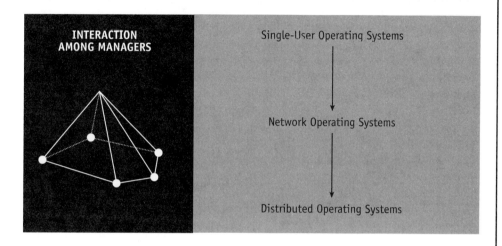

> **"** *As knowledge increases, wonder deepens.* **"**
>
> —Charles Morgan *(1894–1958)*

Learning Objectives

After completing this chapter, you should be able to describe:

- The complexities introduced to operating systems by network capabilities
- Network operating systems (NOSs) compared to distributed operating systems (DO/Ss)
- How a DO/S performs memory, process, device, and file management
- How a NOS performs memory, process, device, and file management
- Important features of DO/Ss and NOSs

When organizations move toward completely decentralized systems, more and more computing devices are linked through complex networks of wireless communications, teleconferencing equipment, host computers, and other digital technologies. But there are two problems with this expansion. First, a tremendous demand is placed on data communication networks by the staggering number of hardware interconnections. Second, the user community places increasing pressure on these networks to operate with greater reliability, security, and speed.

In this chapter we'll explore the differences between network operating systems and distributed operating systems. We'll explain process-based and object-based operating system models and use them to define the roles of the Memory, Processor, Device, File, and Network Managers in distributed operating systems, and we'll discuss the role of network operating systems.

History of Networks

Networks were created initially to share expensive hardware resources such as large mainframes, laser printers, and sizable hard disks. These physical networks, with their network operating systems, allowed organizations to increase the availability of these resources and spread the cost among many users. However, the focus of technology changed when system owners realized that a network's most prized resource wasn't the hardware—it was the information stored on it. Soon many operating systems were enhanced with network capabilities to give users throughout an organization easy access to centralized information resources. The network operating system was developed first, followed by the more powerful distributed operating system.

Today, applications collectively known as computer-supported cooperative work, or **groupware**, use a set of technologies called **distributed processing** to allow even greater access to centralized information and to allow users to work together to complete common tasks.

Comparison of Network and Distributed Operating Systems

The **network operating system** (NOS) evolved from the need to give users global access to resources, globally manage the network's processes, and make the network almost completely transparent for users and their sites' operating systems, known as local operating systems. A typical NOS is shown in Figure 10.1.

A network operating system gives local operating systems extended powers. That is, it gives the local system new ability to accept a request to perform processing or to access data that's not available locally. It starts by determining where the resources are located. Then it initiates the operation and returns the appropriate data or service to the requester.

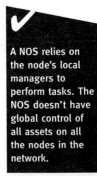

A NOS relies on the node's local managers to perform tasks. The NOS doesn't have global control of all assets on all the nodes in the network.

(figure 10.1)

In a NOS environment, each node, shown here as a circle, is managed by its own local operating system, shown here as triangles. Their respective network operating systems, shown here as squares, come into play only when one site's system needs to work with another site's system.

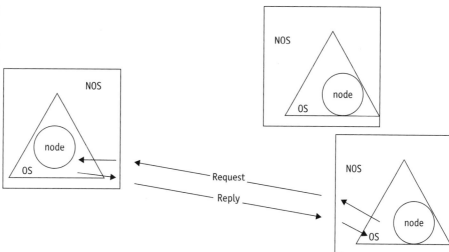

It's important that the NOS accomplish this transparently. The local operating system views the action as having been performed onsite. That's because the network operating system handles the interfacing details and coordinates the remote processing. It also coordinates communications between the local operating systems by tracking the status and location of all entities in the system.

The local operating systems are traditional operating systems designed to run a single computer. That means they can perform a task only if the process is part of their environment; otherwise, they must pass the request on to the network operating system to run it. To a local operating system, it appears that the NOS is the server performing the task, whereas in reality the NOS is only the facilitator.

The biggest limitation of a NOS is that it doesn't take global control over memory management, process management, device management, or file management. Rather, it sees them as autonomous *local* functions that must interact with each other. This limited view is problematic because an operating system can't achieve true distributed computing or processing functions without *global* control of all assets, not only assets at the network communication level. This need for global control led to the development of the **distributed operating system (DO/S)**. (Although they use a similar acronym, the DO/S described in this chapter must not be confused with the DOS [disk operating system] for microcomputers or MS-DOS, described in Chapter 14.)

Distributed operating systems provide a unified environment designed to optimize operations for the network as a whole, not just for local sites, as illustrated in Figure 10.2.

The major difference between a NOS and a DO/S is how each views and manages the local and global resources. A NOS builds on capabilities provided by the local

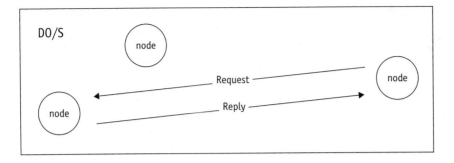

(figure 10.2)

In a DO/S environment, all nodes are part of a globally managed operating system designed to optimize all system resources. Requests between nodes are handled entirely by the DO/S as well as every operation at every node.

operating system and extends it to satisfy new needs. It accesses resources by using local mechanisms, and each system is controlled and managed locally based on that system's policy. On the other hand, the DO/S considers system resources to be globally owned and manages them as such. It accesses resources using *global* mechanisms rather than *local* mechanisms, with system control and management based on a single system-wide policy. A comparison of the two types of systems is shown in Table 10.1.

Network Operating System (NOS)	Distributed Operating System (DO/S)
Resources owned by local nodes	Resources owned by global system
Local resources managed by local operating system	Local resources managed by a global DO/S
Access performed by a local operating system	Access performed by the DO/S
Requests passed from one local operating system to another via the NOS	Requests passed directly from node to node via the DO/S

(table 10.1)

Comparison of a NOS and a DO/S, two types of operating systems used to manage networked resources.

For example, in a typical NOS environment, a user who wants to run a local process at a remote site must (1) log on to the local network, (2) instruct the local system to migrate the process or data to the remote site, and then (3) send a request to the remote site to schedule the process on its system. Thereafter, the remote site views the process as a newly created process within its local operating system's environment and manages it without outside intervention. If the process needs to be synchronized with processes at remote sites, the process needs to have embedded calls to initiate action by the NOS. These calls are typically added on top of the local operating system to provide the communications link between the two processes on the different devices. This complicates the task of synchronization, which is the responsibility of the user and is only partially supported by the operating system.

On the other hand, a system managed by a DO/S handles the same example differently. If one site has a process that requires resources at another site, then the task is presented to the DO/S as just another process. The user acquires no additional responsibility. The DO/S examines the process control block to determine the specific requirements for this process. Then, using its process scheduler, the DO/S determines how to best execute the process based on the site's current knowledge of the state of the total system. The process scheduler then takes this process, along with all other processes ready to run on the network, and calculates their order of execution on each node while optimizing global run time and maintaining process priorities. The emphasis is on maintaining the operating system's global functionality, policies, and goals.

To globally manage the network's entire suite of resources, a DO/S is typically constructed with a replicated **kernel** operating system—low-level, hardware-control software (firmware) with system-level software for resource management. This software may be unique or duplicated throughout the system. Its purpose is to allocate and manage the system's resources so that global system policies, not local policies, are maximized. The DO/S also has a layer that hides the network and its intricacies from users so they can use the network as a single logical system and not as a collection of independent cooperating entities.

A DO/S has global control of all assets on all the nodes in the network.

DO/S Development

Although the DO/S was developed after the NOS, its global management of network devices is the easiest to understand, so we'll explain it first.

Because a DO/S manages the entire group of resources within the network in a global fashion, resources are allocated based on negotiation and compromise among equally important peer sites in the distributed system. One advantage of this type of system is its ability to support file copying, electronic mail, and remote printing without requiring the user to install special server software on local machines. Here's how operating system management functions are performed by a DO/S.

Memory Management

For each node, the Memory Manager uses a kernel with a paging algorithm to track the amount of memory that's available. The algorithm is based on the goals of the local system but the policies and mechanisms that are used at the local sites are driven by the requirements of the global system. To accommodate both local and global needs, memory allocation and deallocation depend on scheduling and resource-sharing schemes that optimize the resources of the entire network.

The Memory Manager for a network works the same way as it does for a stand-alone operating system, but it's extended to accept requests for memory from both local and global sources. On a local level, the Memory Manager allocates pages based on the local policy. On a global level, it receives requests from the Process Manager to provide memory to new or expanding client or server processes. The Memory Manager also uses local resources to perform garbage collection in memory, perform compaction, decide which are the most and least active processes, and determine which processes to preempt to provide space for others.

To control the demand, the Memory Manager handles requests from the Process Manager to allocate and deallocate space based on the network's usage patterns. In a distributed environment, the combined memory for the entire network is made up of several subpools, one for each processor, and the Memory Manager has a subcomponent that exists on each processor.

When an application tries to access a page that's not in memory, a page fault occurs and the Memory Manager automatically brings that page into memory. If the page is changed while in memory, the Memory Manager writes the changed page back to the file when it's time to swap the page out of memory.

Before allocating space, the Memory Manager examines the total free memory table. If the request can be filled, the memory is allocated and the table is modified to show the location of the allocated space.

The Memory Manager also manages virtual memory. Specifically, it allocates and deallocates virtual memory, reads and writes to virtual memory, swaps virtual pages to disk, gets information about virtual pages, locks virtual pages in memory, and protects the pages that need to be protected.

Pages are protected using hardware or low-level memory management software in each site's kernel. This protection is summoned as pages are loaded into memory. Several protection checks are performed on the pages, as shown in Table 10.2.

Access Allowed	Protection
Read/write	Allows users to have full access to the page's contents, giving them the ability to read and write.
Read-only	Allows users to read the page but they're not allowed to modify it.
Execute-only	Allows users to use the page but they're not allowed to read or modify it. This means that although a user's process can't read or write to the page, it can jump to an address within the page and start executing. This is appropriate for shared application software, editors, and compilers.
Guard-page	Used to facilitate automatic bounds-checking on stacks and other types of data structures.
No access	Prevents users from gaining access to the page. This is typically used by debugging or virus protection software to prevent a process from reading from or writing to a particular page.

(table 10.2)

Protection checks are performed on pages as they're loaded into memory. The last three controls shown in this table are needed to make sure processes don't write to pages that should be read-only.

Process Management

In a network, the Processor Manager provides the policies and mechanisms to create, delete, abort, name, rename, find, schedule, block, run, and synchronize processes, and provides real-time priority execution if required. In addition, the Processor Manager manages the states of execution: READY, RUNNING, and WAIT as described in Chapter 4. To do this, each CPU in the network is required to have its own run-time kernel that manages the hardware—the lowest-level operation on the physical device, as shown in Figure 10.3.

(figure 10.3)

Each kernel controls each piece of hardware, including the CPU. Each kernel is operated by the DO/S, which, in turn, is directed by the application software running on the host computer. In this way, the most cumbersome functions are hidden from the user.

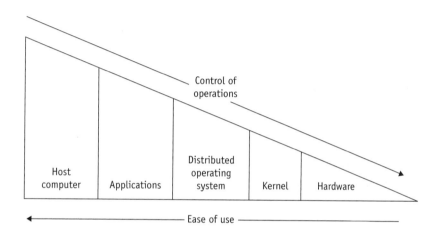

A kernel actually controls and operates the CPU and manages the queues used for states of execution, although upper-level system policies direct how process control blocks (PCBs) are stored in the queues and how they're selected to be run. Therefore, each kernel assumes the role of helping the system reach its operational goals.

The kernel's states are dependent on the global system's process scheduler and dispatcher, which organize the queues within the local CPU and choose the running policy that's used to execute the processes on those queues. Typically, the system's scheduling function has three parts: a decision mode, a priority function, and an arbitration rule.

The decision mode determines which policies are used when scheduling a resource. Options could include preemptive, nonpreemptive, round robin, etc.

The priority function gives the scheduling algorithm the policy that's used to assign an order to processes in the execution cycle. This priority is often determined using a calculation that's based on system characteristics such as occurrence of events, task recurrence, system loading levels, or program run time characteristics. Examples of these run-time characteristics are most time remaining (MTR), least time remaining (LTR), and so on.

323

The arbitration rule is a policy that's used to resolve conflicts between jobs of equal priority. That is, it typically dictates the order in which jobs of the same priority are to be executed. Two examples of arbitration rules are last-in first-out (LIFO) and first-in first-out (FIFO).

Most advances in job scheduling rely on one of three theories: queuing theory, statistical decision theory, or estimation theory. (These queuing and statistical decision theories are the same as those discussed in statistics courses.) An example of estimation theory is a scheduler based on process priorities and durations. It maximizes the system's throughput by using durations to compute and schedule the optimal way to interleave process chunks. Distributed scheduling is better achieved when migration of the scheduling function and policies considers all aspects of the system, including I/O, devices, processes, and communications.

Processes are created, located, synchronized, and deleted using specific procedures. To create a process, the Process Manager (which is part of the Processor Manager) starts by creating a process control block (PCB) with information similar to the PCBs discussed in Chapter 4, but with additional information identifying the process's location in the network. To locate a process, the Process Manager uses a system directory or process that searches all kernel queue spaces—this requires system support for inter-process communications. To synchronize processes, the Process Manager uses message passing or remote procedure calls. To delete or terminate a process, the Process Manager finds the PCB accesses it, and deletes it.

There are two ways to design a distributed operating system. The first is a **process-based DO/S** in which network resources are managed as a large heterogeneous collection. The second and more recent is an **object-based DO/S**, which clumps each type of hardware with its necessary operational software into discrete objects that are manipulated as a unit. Of the two, process-based DO/S most closely resembles the theory described in Chapter 4.

Process-Based DO/S

A process-based DO/S provides for process management through the use of client/server processes synchronized and linked together through messages and ports, also known as channels or pipes. The major emphasis is on processes and messages and how they provide the basic features essential to process management such as process creation, scheduling, pausing, communication, and identification, to name a few.

The issue of how to provide these features can be addressed in several ways. For example, the processes can be managed from a single copy of the operating system, from multiple cooperating peers, or from some combination of the two. Operating systems for distributed computers are typically configured as a kernel on each site. All other services that are dependent on particular devices are typically found on the sites where

Cooperation among managers is key to successful process management in a DO/S environment.

the devices are located. As users enter the system, they're given a unique process identifier and then assigned to a site for processing by the scheduling manager.

In a distributed system, there is a high level of cooperation and sharing of actions and data maintained by the sites when determining which process should be loaded and where it should be run. This is done by exchanging messages between site operating systems. Once a process is scheduled for service, it must be initiated at the assigned site by a dispatcher. The dispatcher takes directions from the operating system's scheduler, allocates the device to the process, and initiates its execution. This procedure may necessitate moving a process from memory in one site to memory at another site; reorganizing a site's memory allocation; reorganizing a site's READY, RUNNING, and WAIT queues; and initiating the scheduled process. The Processor Manager only recognizes processes and their demands for service. It responds to them based on the established scheduling policy, which determines what must be done to manage the processes. As mentioned in earlier chapters, policies for scheduling must consider issues such as load balancing, overhead minimization, memory loading minimization, and first-come first-served and least-time-remaining.

Synchronization is a key issue in network process management. For example, processes can coordinate their activities by passing messages to each other. In addition, processes can pass synchronization parameters from one port to another using **primitives**, well-defined low-level operating system mechanisms such as "send and receive," to carry out the proper logistics to synchronize actions within a process. For instance, when a process reaches a point at which it needs service from an external source, such as an I/O request, it sends a message searching for the service. While it waits for a response, the processor server puts the process in a WAIT state.

Interrupts, which cause a processor to be assigned to another process, also are represented as messages that are sent to the proper process for service. For example, an interrupt may cause the active process to be blocked and moved into a WAIT state. Later, when the cause for the interruption ends, the processor server unblocks the interrupted process and restores it to a READY state.

Object-Based DO/S

An object-based DO/S has a different way of looking at the computer system. Instead of viewing the system as a collection of individual resources and processes, the system is viewed as a collection of **objects**. An object can represent hardware (such as CPUs and memory), software (such as files, programs, semaphores, and data), or a combination of the two (printers, scanners, tape drives, and disks—each bundled with the software required to operate it). Each object in the system has a unique identifier to differentiate it from all other objects in the system.

Objects are viewed as abstract entities, data types that can go through a change of state, act according to set patterns, be manipulated, or exist in relation to other objects in a manner appropriate to the object's semantics in the system. This means that objects have a set of unchanging properties that defines them and their behavior within the context of their defined parameters. For example, a writable CD drive has unchanging properties that include the following: data can be written to a disc, data can be read from a disc, reading and writing can't take place concurrently, and the data's beginning and ending points can't be compromised. If we use these simple rules to construct a simulation of a CD-R drive, we have created an accurate representation of this object.

To determine an object's state, one must perform an appropriate operation on it, such as reading or writing to a hard disk, because the object is identified by the set of operations one can send it. The combination of the operations with their internally defined data structures and computations represents an object's instantiation. Typically, systems using this concept have a large number of objects but a small number of operations on the objects. For example, a printer can have three operations: one to advance a full page, one to advance one line, and one to advance one character.

Therefore, in an object-based DO/S, process management becomes object management, with processes acting as discrete objects. Process management, in this case, deals with the policies and mechanisms for controlling the operations and the creation and destruction of objects. Therefore, process management has two components: the kernel level and the Process Manager.

The Kernel Level

The **kernel level** provides the basic mechanisms for building the operating system by creating, managing, scheduling, synchronizing, and deleting objects, and it does so dynamically. For example, when an object is created, it's assigned all the resources needed for its operation and is given control until the task is completed. Then the object returns control to the kernel, which selects the next object to be executed.

The kernel also has ultimate responsibility for the network's capability lists, discussed in Chapter 8. Each site has both a capability manager that maintains the capability list for its objects and a directory listing the location for all capabilities in the system. This directory guides local requests for capabilities to other sites on which they're located.

For example, if a process requests access to a region in memory, the capability manager first determines whether the requesting process has been previously granted rights. If so, then it can proceed. If not, it processes the request for access rights. When the requester has access rights, the capability manager grants the requester access to the named object, in this case the region in memory. If the named object is at a remote site, the local capability manager directs the requester, using a new address computation and message, to the remote capability manager.

The kernel is also responsible for process synchronization mechanisms and communication support. Typically, synchronization is implemented as some form of shared variable, such as the WAIT and SIGNAL codes discussed in Chapter 6. Communication between distributed objects can be in the form of shared data objects, message objects, or control interactions. Most systems provide different communications primitives to their objects, which are either synchronous (either the sender and receiver are linked and ready to send and receive) or asynchronous (there is some shareable area such as a mailbox, queue, or stack to which the communicated information is sent). In some cases, the receiver periodically checks to see if anyone has sent anything. In other cases, the communicated information arrives at the receiver's workstation without any effort on the part of the receiver; it just waits. There can also be a combination of these. An example of this communication model might have a mechanism that signals the receiver whenever a communication arrives at the sharable area so the information can be fetched whenever it's convenient. The advantage of this system is that it eliminates unnecessary checking when no messages are waiting.

Finally, the kernel environment for distributed systems must have a scheduler with a consistent and robust mechanism for scheduling objects within the system according to its operation's goals.

The Process Manager

If the kernel doesn't already have primitives (test and set, P and V, etc.) to work with the hardware, then the Process Manager has to create its own primitives before going on with its job. The Process Manager has responsibility for the following tasks: creating objects, dispatching objects, scheduling objects, synchronizing operations on objects, communicating among objects, and deleting objects. To perform these tasks, the Process Manager uses the kernel environment, which provides the primitives it needs to capture the low-level hardware in the system.

For example, to run a database object, the Process Manager must do the following steps in order:

1. Determine whether or not the object is in memory. If so, go to step 3.
2. If it's not in memory, find the object on secondary storage, allocate space in memory for it, and log it into the proper locations.
3. Provide the proper scheduling information for the object.
4. Once the object has been scheduled, wait for the kernel dispatcher to pull it out and place it into the RUNNING state.

Thus far we've discussed the similarities between the object-based and process-based managers. The major difference between them is that objects contain all of their state information. That means that the information is stored *with* the object, not separately in another part of the system such as in a PCB or other data structure separate from the object.

Device Management

In all distributed systems, devices must be opened, read from, written to, and closed. In addition, device parameters must be initialized and status bits must be set or cleared—just as in stand-alone systems. All of this can be done on a global, cluster, or localized basis.

Usually users prefer to choose devices by name, and let the distributed operating system select and operate the best device from among those available. For example, if users need specific control of a device, then they should be able to call a device by name, such as DISK 12. When the choice is made, the DO/S takes control, allocating the unit when it's available, assigning it to the user when the OPEN command is issued, operating it, and then deallocating it when the job is finished.

The device can't be allocated until the Device Manager examines the device's status and, when it's free, sends the requesting process a unique device identifier—a name that's used for all communication between the process and the device. Later, when the process issues a CLOSE command, the device is released. That's when the DO/S resets the device's state information and returns its device control block to the device's READY queue. For example, when a user wants to print a file by executing a print command, the DO/S follows a process similar to this:

1. The user's File Manager places a copy of the file in the DO/S spooler directory.
2. The spooler selects the file from the spooler directory and initiates an open request to the DO/S File Manager.
3. When the open request is satisfied, the spooler initiates another open request to a networked line printer's device driver.
4. When the second open request is satisfied, the spooler sends the file to the printer's input buffer. This can be accomplished through a direct message transfer or a packet transfer, as described in Chapter 9.
5. When printing is complete, the DO/S File Manager deletes the copy of the file from the spooler.
6. Finally, the device is reset and closed.

This system works only if the DO/S keeps a global accounting of each network device and its availability, maintaining each device's status record and control block, and distributing this information to all sites. As shown in Figure 10.4, the DO/S Device Manager is a collection of remote device drivers connected to and associated with the devices, but controlled by status data that's provided by the DO/S Device Manager.

Process-Based DO/S

All resources in the process-based DO/S are controlled by servers called "guardians" or "administrators." These servers are responsible for accepting requests for service

(figure 10.4)

All devices are operated by their individual device managers or device drivers using specific status data that's controlled by the DO/S Device Manager. In this example, the network has three disk drives and three printers.

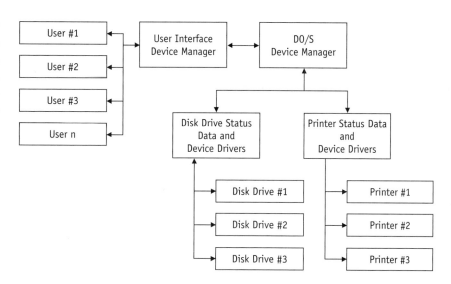

on the individual devices they control, processing each request fairly, providing service to the requestor, and returning to serve others, as shown in Figure 10.5.

However, not all systems have a simple collection of resources. Many have clusters of printers, disk drives, tapes, and so on. To control these clusters as a group, most process-based systems are configured around complex **server processes**, which manage multiple resources or divide the work among subordinate processes. The administrator process is configured as a Device Manager and includes the software needed to accept local and remote requests for service, decipher their meaning, and act on them. Typically a server process is made up of one or more device drivers, a Device Manager, and a network server component.

(figure 10.5)

In a process-based DO/S, requests move from the requestor to the process scheduler to the dispatcher to the server. Interrupt processing manages I/O or processing problems. The WAIT state is used to suspend and resume processing. It functions identically to the WAIT state described in Chapter 4.

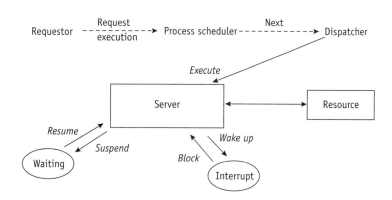

Object-Based DO/S

In an object-based DO/S, each device is managed the same way throughout the network. The physical device is considered an object, just like other network resources, and is surrounded by a layer of software that gives other objects a complete view of the device object.

The physical device is manipulated by a set of operations, explicit commands that mobilize the device to perform its designated functions. For example, an object to control a tape unit requires operations to rewind, fast forward, and scan. To use a tape drive, users issue an operation on a tape object such as this:

WITH TAPE 1 DO FAST FORWARD (N) RECORDS

This causes the tape drive to advance N records. This assumes, of course, that the operating system has already granted authorization to the user to use the tape object.

A disk drive works the same way. Users access the drive by sending operations to the Device Manager to create a new file, destroy an old file, open or close an existing file, read information from a file, or write to it. Users don't need to know the underlying mechanisms that implement the operations—they just need to know which operations work.

The details required to operate each disk drive are contained in device driver software.

One advantage of object-based DO/S is that the objects can be assembled to communicate and synchronize with each other to provide a distributed network of resources, with each object knowing the location of its distributed peers. So, if the local device manager can't satisfy a user's request, the request is sent to another device manager, a peer. Again, users don't need to know if the network's resources are centralized or distributed—only that their requests are satisfied.

For this system to be successful, the Device Manager object at each site needs to maintain a current directory of device objects at all sites. Then, when a requesting object needs to use a printer, for example, the request is presented to its local device manager. If the local manager has the means and opportunity to provide the proper service, it prints the request. If it can't meet the request locally, it sends the request to a peer Device Manager that has the appropriate resources. It's this remote Device Manager that processes the request and performs the operation.

File Management

Distributed file management gives users the illusion that the network is a single logical file system that's implemented on an assortment of devices and computers. Therefore, the main function of a DO/S File Manager is to provide transparent mechanisms to find and open, read, write, close, create, and delete files, no matter where they're located in the network, as shown in Table 10.3.

(table 10.3)	Desired File Function	File Manager's Action
Typical file management functions and the necessary actions of the File Manager.	Find and Open	It uses a master directory with information about all files stored anywhere on the system and sets up a channel to the file.
	Read	It sets up a channel to the file and attempts to read it using simple file access schemes. However, a read operation won't work if the file is currently being created or modified.
	Write	It sets up a channel to the file and attempts to write to it using simple file access schemes. To write to a file, the requesting process must have exclusive access to it. This can be accomplished by locking the file, a technique frequently used in database systems. While a file is locked, all other requesting processes must wait until the file is unlocked before they can write to or read the file.
	Close	It sends a command to the remote server to unlock that file. This is typically accomplished by changing the information in the directory at the file's storage site.
	Create	It creates a unique file identifier in the network's master directory and assigns space for it on a storage device.
	Delete	It erases the unique file identifier in the master directory and deallocates the space reserved for it on the storage device.

File management systems are a subset of database managers, which provide more capabilities to user processes than file systems and are being implemented as distributed database management systems as part of local area network systems.

Therefore, the tasks required by a DO/S include those typically found in a distributed database environment. These involve a host of controls and mechanisms necessary to provide consistent, synchronized, and reliable management of system and user information assets, including the following:

• Concurrency control

• Data redundancy

• Location transparency and distributed directory

• Deadlock resolution or recovery

• Query processing

Concurrency Control

Concurrency control techniques give the system the ability to perform concurrent reads and writes, as long as the results of these actions don't jeopardize the contents of the database. That means that the results of all concurrent transactions are the same as if the transactions had been executed one at a time, in some arbitrary serial order, thereby providing the serial execution view on a database. The concurrency control mechanism keeps the database in a consistent state as the transactions are being processed.

For example, let's say a group of airline reservation agents are making flight arrangements for telephone callers. By using concurrency control techniques, the File Manager allows each agent to read and write to the airline's huge database if, and only if, each read and write doesn't interfere with another that's already taking place. These techniques provide a serial execution view on a database.

Data Redundancy

Data redundancy can make files much faster and easier to read. That's because the File Manager can allow a process to read the copy that's closest or easiest to access. Or, if the file is very large, the read request can be split into several different requests, each of which is fulfilled at a different file location. For example, if an airline reservation system received a request for information about passengers on a certain flight, and the database was stored in three different locations, then one read request could search the passengers with last names beginning with A–K, the second read request could search L–R, and the third read request could search S–Z. The results of all three requests are combined before returning the results to the requester.

Data redundancy also has beneficial aspects from a disaster recovery standpoint because if one site fails, operations can be restarted at another site with the same resources. Later, the failed site can be reinstated by copying all files that were updated since the failure. The disadvantage of redundant data is the task of keeping multiple copies of the same file up-to-date at all times. Every time a file is updated, every other copy of the file must be updated in the identical way and the update must be performed according to the system's reliability standards.

Based on the algorithm used and the method of recovery, the system can require that updates be performed at all sites before any reads occur to a master site or to a majority of sites. Some typically used update algorithms are: unanimous agreement, primary site copy, moving primary site, and majority site agreement.

Location Transparency and Distributed Directory

Location transparency means that users aren't concerned with the physical location of their files. Instead, they deal with the network as a single system. Location transparency is provided by mechanisms and directories that map logical data items to physical locations. The mechanisms usually use information about data that's stored at all sites in the form of directories.

The distributed directory manages transparency of data location and enhances data recovery for users. The directory contains definitions dealing with the physical and logical structure for the stored data, as well as the policies and mechanisms for mapping between the two. In addition, it contains the systemwide names of all resources and the addressing mechanisms for locating and accessing them.

✔ Locking (such as at a database's field or record levels) is one form of concurrency control.

Deadlock Resolution or Recovery

Deadlock detection and recovery, described in Chapter 5, are critical issues in distributed systems. The most important function is to detect and recover from a circular wait. This occurs when one process requests a resource (such as a file, disk drive, modem, or tape unit), which we'll call Resource B, while it keeps exclusive control over another resource, which we'll call Resource A. Meanwhile, a second process requests use of Resource A while it keeps exclusive control over Resource B. A directed graph for this example is shown in Figure 10.6 (the solid lines represent resources allocated to processes, and the dotted lines represent resource requests by processes).

However, most real-life examples of circular wait are much more complex and difficult to detect because they involve multiple processes and multiple resources—all waiting for a resource that's held exclusively by another process.

(figure 10.6)

This example of circular wait was created when Process 1 requested Resource B without releasing its exclusive control over Resource A. Likewise, Process 2 requested Resource A without releasing Resource B.

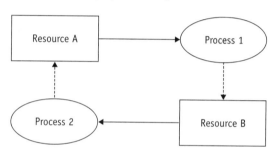

Detection, prevention, avoidance, and recovery are all strategies used by a distributed system. To recognize circular waits, the system uses directed resource graphs and looks for cycles. To prevent circular waits, the system tries to delay the start of a transaction until it has all the resources it will request during its execution. To avoid circular waits, the system tries to allow execution only when it knows that the transaction can run to completion. To recover from a deadlock caused by circular waits, the system selects the best victim—one that can be restarted without much difficulty and one that, when terminated, will free enough resources so the others can finish. Then the system kills the victim, forces that process to restart from the beginning, and reallocates its resources to the waiting processes.

Query Processing

Query processing is the function of processing requests for information. Query processing techniques try to increase the effectiveness of global query execution sequences, local site processing sequences, and device processing sequences. All of these relate directly to the network's global process scheduling problem. Therefore, to ensure consistency of the entire system's scheduling scheme, the query processing strategy must be an integral part of the processing scheduling strategy.

Network Management

The network management function is a communications function that's unique to networked systems because stand-alone operating systems don't need to communicate with other systems. For a DO/S, the Network Manager provides the policies and mechanisms necessary to provide intrasite and intersite communication among concurrent processes. For intrasite processes within the network, the Network Manager provides process identifiers and logical paths to other processes—in a one-to-one, one-to-few, one-to-many, or one-to-all manner—while dynamically managing these paths.

The Network Manager has many diverse responsibilities. It must be able to locate processes in the network, send messages throughout the network, and track media use. In addition, it must be able to reliably transfer data, code and decode messages, retransmit errors, perform parity checking, do cyclic redundancy checks, establish redundant links, and acknowledge messages and replies, if necessary.

The Network Manager begins by registering each network process as soon as it has been assigned a unique physical designator. It then sends this identifier to all other sites in the network. From that moment, the process is logged with all sites in the network.

When processes—or objects—need to communicate with each other, the Network Manager links them together through a port—a logical door on one process that can be linked with a port on another process, thus establishing a logical path for the two to communicate. Ports usually have physical buffers and I/O channels, and represent physical assets that must be used wisely by the Network Manager. Ports can be assigned to one process or to many.

Processes require routing because of the underlying network topology and the processes' location. Routing can be as simple as a process-device pair address that associates one logical process with one physical site. Or it can incorporate many levels traversing multiple links in either a direct or a hop count form, as described in Chapter 9.

In addition to routing, other functions required from the Network Manager are keeping statistics on network use (for use in message scheduling, fault localizations, and rerouting) and providing mechanisms to aid process time synchronization. This standardization mechanism is commonly known as a systemwide clock, a device that allows system components at various sites to compensate for time variations because of delays caused by the distributed communication system.

Process-Based DO/S

In a process-based DO/S, interprocess communication is transparent to users. The Network Manager assumes full responsibility for allocating ports to the processes that request them, identifying every process in the network, controlling the flow of messages, and guaranteeing the transmission and acceptance of messages without errors.

The Network Manager routinely acts as the interfacing mechanism for every process in the system and handles message traffic, relieving users of the need to know where their processes are physically located in the network. As traffic operator, the Network Manager accepts and interprets each process's commands to send and receive. Then it transforms those commands into low-level actions that actually transmit the messages over network communications links.

Object-Based DO/S

A Network Manager object makes both intermode and intramode communications among cooperative objects easy. A process, the active code elements within objects, can begin an operation at a specific instance of an object by sending a request message. The user doesn't need to know the location of the receiver. The user only needs to know the receiver's name and the Network Manager takes over, providing the message's proper routing to the receiver. A process can also invoke an operation that's part of its local object environment.

Generally, network communications allow some level of the following functions: send, receive, request, and reply, as described in Table 10.4.

Function	Purpose
Send	Allows objects to send a message with operations to any object in the system.
Receive	Warns objects of incoming communications from an object in the system.
Request	Provides a mechanism for objects to ask for particular services. For example, they can request that a message be sent.
Reply	Allows objects to do one of three things: • Respond to requests for communications from another object • Respond to a send command that they aren't prepared for • Indicate that they're ready to accept a send command; a message can now be sent knowing that the receiver is awaiting it

(table 10.4)

Communications sent by the Network Manager allow objects to perform at least one of four functions.

Network Manager services are usually provided at the kernel level to better accommodate the many objects that use them and to offer efficient service. However, depending on the system, the Network Manager may be a simple utility that handles only send and receive primitives. Or perhaps it's constructed using ports, or channels. A simple send-and-receive utility requires that users know the name of the objects they need to communicate with, whereas the port or channel system requires users to know only the name of the port or channel with which the object is associated. For example, if a communications facility is supported by a port-object type mechanism, then objects are grouped as senders, receivers, ports, and messages, and are linked together using capability lists.

NOS Development

A NOS typically runs on a computer called a **server** and performs services for network workstations called **clients**. Although computers can assume the role of clients most or all of the time, any given computer can assume the role of server (or client), depending on the requirements of the network. Client and server are not hardware-specific terms. Instead, they are role-specific terms.

Many modern network operating systems are true operating systems that include the four management functions: memory management, process scheduling, file management, and device management including disk and I/O operations. In addition, they have a network management function with responsibility for network communications, protocols, etc. In a NOS, the network management functions come into play only when the system needs to use the network, as shown in Figure 10.7. At all other times, the Network Manager is dormant and the operating system operates as if it's a stand-alone system.

Although NOSs can run applications as well as other operating systems, their focus is on sharing resources instead of running programs. For example, a single-user operating system such as early versions of Windows, or even a multiuser system such as

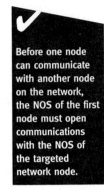

Before one node can communicate with another node on the network, the NOS of the first node must open communications with the NOS of the targeted network node.

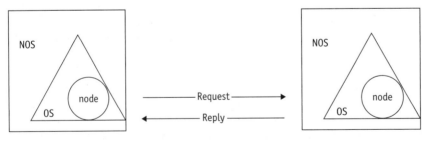

(figure 10.7)

In a NOS environment, the four managers of the operating system manage all system resources at that site unless and until the node needs to communicate with another node on the network.

UNIX or Linux, focuses on the user's ability to run applications. On the other hand, network operating systems focus on the workstations' ability to share the server's resources including applications and data as well as expensive shared resources such as printers and high-speed modems.

In the following pages we describe some of the features commonly found in a network operating system without focusing on any one in particular. The best NOS choice depends on many factors including the applications to be run on the server, the technical support required, the user's level of training, and the compatibility of the hardware with other networking systems.

Important NOS Features

Most network operating systems are implemented as early versions of 32-bit or 64-bit software. However, more important than the processor is the support a NOS provides for standard local area network technologies and client desktop operating systems.

Networks are becoming increasingly heterogeneous. That is, they support workstations running a wide variety of operating systems. For example, a single network might include workstations running Windows, the Macintosh operating system, and Linux. For a NOS to serve as the networking glue, it must provide strong support for every operating system in the corporate information network, sustaining as many current standards as necessary. Therefore, it must have a robust architecture that adapts easily to new technologies.

For example, a NOS should preserve the user's expectations for a desktop system. That means that the network's resources should appear as simple extensions of that user's existing system. For example, on a Windows computer, a network drive should appear as just another hard disk but with a different volume name and a different drive letter. On a Macintosh computer, the network drive should appear as an icon for a volume on the desktop. And on a Linux system, the drive should appear as a mountable file system.

A NOS is designed to operate a wide range of third-party software applications and hardware devices including hard drives, modems, CD-ROM drives, and network interface cards. A NOS also supports software for multiuser network applications, such as electronic messaging, as well as networking expansions such as new protocol stacks.

Finally, the NOS must blend efficiency with security. Its constant goal is to provide network clients with quick and easy access to the network's data and resources without compromising network security. A compromised network instantly loses data integrity and the confidence of its users.

Major NOS Functions

An important NOS function is to let users transfer files from one computer to another. In this case, each system controls and manages its own file system. For example, the Internet provides the **File Transfer Protocol (FTP)** program. So, if students in a UNIX programming class need to copy a data file from the university computer to their home computers to complete an assignment, then each student begins by issuing the following command to create the FTP connection:

```
ftp unixs.cis.pitt.edu
```

This opens the FTP program, which then asks the student for a login name and password. Once this information has been verified by the UNIX operating system, each student is allowed to copy the file from the host computer by using this command:

```
get filename.ext
```

In this example, *filename.ext* is the absolute filename and extension of the required data file. That means the user must know *exactly* where the file is located—in which directory and subdirectory the file is stored. That's because the file location isn't transparent to the user.

This find-and-copy technique isn't considered true file sharing because all users wanting access to the data file must copy the file onto their own systems, thereby duplicating the code and wasting space. This practice also adds **version control** difficulties because when one user modifies the file in any way, those changes aren't reflected on other copies already stored in other directories unless each user replaces the old version with the new version.

For a collection of files to be available to the general public, the files must be placed in a public FTP directory on an FTP server. Then, anyone with an FTP client or a Web browser can download copies of the files on demand using a process called **anonymous FTP**. The advantage of an FTP connection is that it doesn't force files to pass through mail programs that might encode or decode the document. Therefore, all FTP documents usually download faster while retaining their necessary characteristics, including templates, formatting, fonts, and graphics.

Web visitors don't usually visit the FTP server until they want to download a file. When they click on the download link, they're transferred to the FTP server. These FTP sites aren't usually designed for easy browsing but Web browsers can be used to handle FTP files with some limitations. Most Web browsers display FTP directories using graphical icons to represent available files and directories. Typical Web browser commands and features can be used to download FTP files just as they do other Web objects. The advantage of using the Web for FTP is that most users already know how the Web browser works and don't need to learn new software.

Conclusion

The first operating systems for networks were NOSs. Although they were adequate, they didn't take full advantage of the global resources available to all connected sites. The development of DO/Ss specifically addressed that need.

Every networked system, whether a NOS or a DO/S, has specific requirements. Each must be secure from unauthorized access yet accessible to authorized users. Each must monitor its available system resources, including memory, processors, devices, and files (as described in Chapters 2 through 8), as well as its communications links. In addition, because it's a networking operating system, it must perform the required networking tasks described in Chapter 9.

Each of the technological advances we've discussed thus far have created security vulnerabilities. System security experts like to say that the only secure computer is one that is unplugged from its power source. In the next chapter we'll look at key elements of system security and ethics, and the role of the system administrator in safeguarding the network's most valuable resource—its data.

Key Terms

anonymous FTP: a use of File Transfer Protocol that allows a user to retrieve documents, files, programs, and other data from anywhere in the Internet without having to establish a user ID and password.

client: a user node that requests and makes use of various network services.

distributed operating system (DO/S): an operating system that provides control for a distributed computing system, allowing its resources to be accessed in a unified way.

distributed processing: a method of data processing in which files are stored at many different locations and in which processing takes place at different sites.

File Transfer Protocol (FTP): a protocol that allows a user on one host to access and transfer files to or from another host over a TCP/IP network.

groupware: software applications that support cooperative work over a network.

kernel: the part of the operating system that resides in main memory at all times and performs the most essential tasks, such as managing memory and handling disk input and output.

kernel level: in an object-based distributed operating system, it provides the basic mechanisms for dynamically building parts of the operating system by creating, managing, scheduling, synchronizing, and deleting objects.

network operating system (NOS): the software that manages network resources for a node on a network and may provide security and access control.

object: any one of the many entities that constitute a computer system, such as CPUs, terminals, disk drives, files, or databases.

object-based DO/S: a view of distributed operating systems where each hardware unit is bundled with its required operational software, forming a discrete object to be handled as an entity.

primitives: well-defined, predictable, low-level operating system mechanisms that allow higher-level operating system components to perform their functions without considering direct hardware manipulation.

process-based DO/S: a view of distributed operating systems that encompasses all the system's processes and resources.

server: a node that provides to clients various network services such as file retrieval, printing, or database access services.

server process: a logical unit composed of one or more device drivers, a device manager, and a network server module needed to control clusters or similar devices in a process-based, distributed operating system environment.

version control: the tracking and updating of a specific release of a piece of hardware or software.

Interesting Searches

- Concurrency Control
- Network Processing
- Network Process Synchronization
- Operating Systems Kernel
- File Transfer Protocol (FTP)

Exercises

Research Topics

A. Research the concept of query processing in distributed systems. Build on the brief description provided in this chapter and explain what it is and (in simple terms) how it works in a distributed network. Is it a necessary tool? Does query processing increase network processing speed ? Why or Why not? What effect does the size of the network have on query processing speed? Cite your sources.

B. Identify four early operating systems for networks and explain which group each belonged to (as defined in this chapter)—NOS or DO/S. State the reasons for your answer and cite your sources.

Exercises

1. Briefly compare the advantages of a NOS with a DO/S and explain which you would prefer to operate and why.

2. If your DO/S had four nodes, how many operating systems would it have? Explain your answer.

3. If your NOS had four nodes, how many operating systems would it have? Explain your answer.

4. We discussed several levels of file access in this chapter including read/write, read-only, execute-only, guard-page, and no access. If you are maintaining a database containing confidential patient information and need to restrict UPDATE access to five individuals, restrict READ access to only 15 others, and disallow access to any other users, then which access level would you assign to the individuals in each of the three groups: the chosen five, the other 15, and everyone else? Explain your answer.

5. Explain in your own words the steps a DO/S File Manager uses to open a file, read data from it, update that data, and close the file. Do those steps change if the data is not changed? Explain the reasons for your answer.

6. List three benefits of data redundancy as described in this chapter.

7. Describe in detail how a DO/S protects a file from access or modification by an unauthorized user. Compare it to NOS file protection.

8. Process control blocks (PCBs) were discussed in Chapter 4 in the context of non-networked systems. In a distributed operating system, what additional information needs to be noted in the PCB in order for the Processor Manager to successfully manage processes correctly?

9. Describe how the DO/S Processor Manager attempts to prevent deadlocks in the network. Then describe how it tries to avoid them and, if necessary, recover from a deadlock.

10. Explain in your own words why process synchronization is critical in network process management.

Advanced Exercises

11. Which kind of network structure (NOS or DO/S) do you believe is less likely to crash or freeze if a spooler malfunction should deadlock a node? Explain your conclusion and suggest whether or not system robustness in this instance is reason enough to choose one structure over the other.

12. Compare and contrast the two varieties of distributed operating systems discussed in this chapter: a process-based DO/S and an object-based DO/S.

13. If you were managing a hospital's network, what policies would you implement to protect your system? Keep in mind that as system administrator, your job is to provide the correct level of accessibility to authorized users while denying access to those who lack authorization.

14. Remembering our discussion of deadlocks in Chapter 5, if you were designing a networked system, how would you manage the threat of deadlocks in your network? Consider all of the following: prevention, detection, avoidance, and recovery.

15. Describe the top 10 critical duties of a network administrator for a distributed operating system. Identify the level of access needed by the administrator and explain why. Describe in your own words how you would manage access control for a network with multiple system administrators.

Chapter 11

Security and Ethics

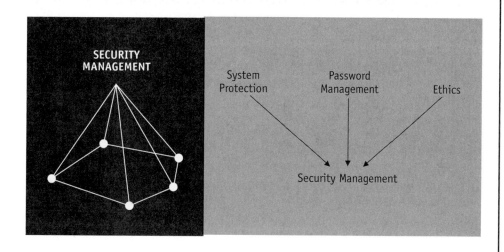

"Perfection of means and confusion of goals seem, in my opinion, to characterize our age."

—Albert Einstein *(1879–1955)*

Learning Objectives

After completing this chapter, you should be able to describe:

- The role of the operating system with regard to system security
- The effects of system security practices on overall system performance
- The levels of system security that can be implemented and the threats posed by evolving technologies
- The differences among computer viruses, worms, and blended threats
- The role of education and ethical practices in system security

Every computing system has conflicting needs: to share resources and to protect them. In the early days, security consisted of a secure lock and a few keys. That is, the system was physically guarded and only authorized users were allowed in its vicinity, and that was sufficient when the user group was limited to several dozen individuals. However, with the advent of data communication, networking, the proliferation of personal computers, telecommunications software, Web sites, and e-mail, the user community has grown to include millions of people, making computer security much more difficult.

System security is a vast and complex subject worthy of its own text. While we cannot do justice to the subject in a single chapter, we introduce the important concepts here and encourage the reader to review current research about the subject. Keep in mind that this subject changes with lightning speed and is well worth constant monitoring by system owners, operators, and users.

> ✔
> An integral part of both system security and system management is the timely application of patches. This topic is discussed in detail in the next chapter.

Role of the Operating System in Security

The operating system plays a key role in computer system security because it has access to every part of the system. Any vulnerability at the operating system level opens the entire system to attack. The more complex and powerful the operating system, the more likely it is to have vulnerabilities to attack. As a result, system administrators must be on guard to arm their operating systems with all available defenses against attack and possible failure.

System Survivability

System survivability is defined as "the capability of a system to fulfill its mission, in a timely manner, in the presence of attacks, failures, or accidents (Linger, 2002)."

- The term *system* refers to any system. It's used here in the broadest possible sense from laptop to distributed system to supercomputer.
- A *mission* is a very high-level set of requirements or goals.
- *In a timely manner* refers to system response time, a critical factor for most systems.
- The terms *attack*, *failure*, and *accident* refer to any potentially damaging incident, regardless of the cause, whether intentional or not.

Before a system can be considered survivable, it must meet all of these requirements, especially with respect to services that are considered essential to the organization in the face of adverse challenges. The four key properties of survivable systems are resistance to attacks, recognition of attacks and resulting damage, recovery of essential services after an attack, and adaptation and evolution of system defense mechanisms to mitigate future attacks.

With the elevated risks in recent years of system intrusion and compromise, system designers have recognized the critical need for system survivability that's incorporated into system development. It's no longer satisfactory to add survivability factors to the system only as an afterthought. Examples of sample strategies that can be built into systems to enhance their survivability are shown in Table 11.1.

Key Property	Description	Example Strategies
Resistance to attacks	Strategies for repelling attacks	Authentication Access controls Encryption Message filtering System diversification Functional isolation
Recognition of attacks and damage	Strategies for detecting attacks and evaluating damage	Intrusion detection Integrity checking
Recovery of essential and full services after attack	Strategies for limiting damage, restoring compromised information or functionality, maintaining or restoring essential services within mission time constraints, restoring full services	Redundant components Data replication System backup and restoration Contingency planning
Adaptation and evolution to reduce effectiveness of future attacks	Strategies for improving system survivability based on knowledge gained from intrusions	Intrusion recognition patterns

Levels of Protection

Once a system is breached, the integrity of every file on the system and the data in those files can no longer be trusted. For each computer configuration, the system administrator must evaluate the risk of intrusion, which, in turn, depends on the level of connectivity given to the system, as shown in Table 11.2.

Configuration	Ease of Protection	Relative Risk	Vulnerabilities
Single computer (without e-mail or Internet)	High	Low	Compromised passwords, viruses
LAN connected (without Internet)	Medium	Medium	Sniffers, spoofing (+password, viruses)
LAN connected (with Internet)	Low	High	E-mail, Web servers, FTP, Telnet (+sniffers, spoofing, password, viruses)

All of the vulnerabilities shown in Table 11.2 are discussed later in this chapter.

Backup and Recovery

Having sufficient **backup** and **recovery** policies in place and performing other archiving techniques are standard operating procedure for most computing systems. Many system managers use a layered backup schedule. That is, they back up the entire system once a week and only back up daily the files that were changed that day. As an extra measure of safety, copies of complete system backups are stored for three to six months in a safe off-site location.

Backups become essential when the system becomes unavailable because of a natural disaster or when a computer virus infects your system. If you discover it early, you can run eradication software and reload damaged files from your backup copies. Of course, any changes made since the files were backed up will have to be regenerated.

Backups, with one set stored off-site, are also crucial to disaster recovery. The disaster could come from anywhere. Here are just a few of the threats:

- water from a fire upstairs
- fire from an electrical connection
- malfunctioning server
- corrupted archival media
- intrusion from unauthorized users

The importance of adequate backups is illustrated in an example from a 2005 CERT report about a system administrator angry about employment decisions at the defense manufacturing firm where he worked. Upon learning that he would be given a smaller role managing the computer network that he alone had developed and managed, he took the initiative to centralize the software supporting the company's manufacturing processes on a single server. Then he intimidated a coworker into giving him the only backup tapes for that software. When the system administrator was terminated, a logic bomb that he had previously planted detonated and deleted the only remaining copy of the critical software from the company's server. The cost? The company estimated that the damage exceeded $10 million, which led, in turn, to the layoff of some 80 employees. More case stories can be found at *www.cert.org*.

Written policies and procedures and regular user training are essential elements of system management. Most system failures are caused by honest mistakes made by well-intentioned users—not by malicious intruders. Written security procedures should recommend frequent password changes, reliable backup procedures, guidelines for loading new software, compliance with software licenses, network safeguards, guidelines for monitoring network activity, and rules for terminal access.

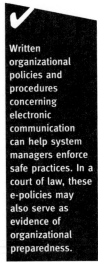

Written organizational policies and procedures concerning electronic communication can help system managers enforce safe practices. In a court of law, these e-policies may also serve as evidence of organizational preparedness.

Security Breaches

A gap in system security can be malicious or not. For instance, some intrusions are the result of an uneducated user and the unauthorized access to system resources. But others stem from the purposeful disruption of the system's operation, and still others are purely accidental such as hardware malfunctions, undetected errors in the operating system or applications, or natural disasters. Malicious or not, a breach of security severely damages the system's credibility. Following are some types of security breaks that can occur.

Unintentional Intrusions

An unintentional attack is defined as any breach of security or modification of data that was not the result of a planned intrusion.

When nonsynchronized processes access data records and modify some of a record's fields, it's called accidental incomplete modification of data. An example was given in Chapter 5 when we discussed the topic of a race in a database with two processes working on the same student record and writing different versions of it to the database.

Errors can occur when data values are incorrectly stored because the field isn't large enough to hold the numeric value stored there. For example, when a field is too small to hold a numeric value, FORTRAN replaces the number with a string of asterisks, and COBOL simply truncates the higher-order digits, as shown in Figure 11.1.

(figure 11.1)

The original data value is shown (a) in a field large enough to hold it. If the field is too small, FORTRAN (b) replaces the data with asterisks. COBOL (c) truncates the higher-order digits (values to the left of the dotted line) and stores only the digits that remain.

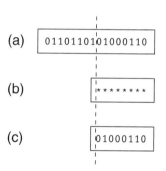

Neither error would be flagged or trigger an error message at the time of storage—they would be discovered only when the value is retrieved. Needless to say, that's an inconvenient time to make such an unpleasant discovery.

Intentional Attacks

Intentional unauthorized access includes denial of service attacks, browsing, wiretapping, repeated trials, trapdoors, and trash collection. These attacks are fundamentally different from viruses and worms and the like (covered shortly), which inflict widespread damage to numerous companies and organizations—without specifying certain ones as targets.

This example comes from a 2005 CERT report on insider threats. An application developer, who lost his IT sector job as a result of company downsizing, expressed his displeasure at being laid off just prior to the Christmas holiday by launching a systematic attack on his former employer's computer network. Three weeks following his termination, the insider used the username and password of one of his former coworkers to gain remote access to the network and modify several of the company's Web pages, changing text and inserting pornographic images. He also sent each of the company's customers an e-mail message advising that the Web site had been hacked. Each e-mail message also contained that customer's usernames and passwords for the Web site. An investigation was initiated, but it failed to identify the insider as the perpetrator. A month and a half later, he again remotely accessed the network, executed a script to reset all network passwords and changed 4,000 pricing records to reflect bogus information. This former employee ultimately was identified as the perpetrator and prosecuted. He was sentenced to serve five months in prison and two years on supervised probation, and ordered to pay $48,600 restitution to his former employer.

Intentional Unauthorized Access

Denial of service (DoS) attacks are synchronized attempts to deny service to authorized users by causing a computer (usually a Web server) to perform a task (often an unproductive task) over and over, thereby making the system unavailable to perform the work it is designed to do. For example, if a Web server designed to accept orders from customers over the Internet is diverted from its appointed task with repeated commands to identify itself, then the computer becomes unavailable to serve the customers online.

Browsing is when unauthorized users gain the capability to search through storage, directories, or files for information they aren't privileged to read. The term storage refers to main memory or to unallocated space on disks or tapes. Sometimes the browsing occurs after the previous job has finished. When a section of main memory is allocated to a process, the data from a previous job often remains in memory—it isn't usually erased by the system—and so it's available to a browser. The same applies to data stored in secondary storage.

Wiretapping is nothing new. Just as telephone lines can be tapped, so can most data communication lines. When wiretapping is passive, the unauthorized user is just listening to the transmission but isn't changing the contents. There are two reasons for passive tapping: to copy data while bypassing any authorization procedures and to collect specific information (such as **passwords**) that will permit the tapper to enter the system at a later date. In an unsecured wireless network environment, wiretapping is not difficult.

Active wiretapping is when the data being sent is modified. Two methods of active wiretapping are "between lines transmission" and "piggyback entry." Between lines doesn't alter the messages sent by the legitimate user, but it inserts additional messages into the communication line while the legitimate user is pausing. Piggyback entry intercepts and modifies the original messages. This can be done by breaking the communication line and routing the message to another computer that acts as the host. For example, the tapper could intercept a logoff message, return the expected acknowledgment of the logoff to the user, and then continue the interactive session with all the privileges of the original user—without anyone knowing.

Repeated trials describes the method used to enter systems by guessing authentic passwords. If an intruder knows the basic scheme for creating passwords such as length of password and symbols allowed to create it, then the system can be compromised with a program that systematically goes through all possible combinations until a valid combination is found. This isn't as long a process as one might think if the passwords are short or if the intruder learns enough about the intended victim/user, as shown in Table 11.3. Because the intruder doesn't need to break a specific password, the guessing of any user's password allows entry to the system and access to its resources.

(table 11.3)	No. of Alphabetic Characters	Possible Combinations	Human Attempt avg. time to discovery at 1 try/second	Computer Attempt avg. time to discovery at 1 million tries/second
Average time required for a human and computer to guess passwords up to 10 alphabetic characters (A–Z) using brute force.	1	26	13 seconds	.000013 seconds
	2	$26^2 = 676$	6 minutes	.000338 seconds
	3	$26^3 = 17,576$	2.5 hours	.008788 seconds
	8	$26^8 = 208,827,064,576$	6,640 years	58 hours
	10	$26^{10} = (1.4 \times 10)^{14}$	4.5 million years	4.5 years

Trapdoors, including backdoor passwords, are defined as unspecified and undocumented entry points to the system. It's possible that trapdoors can be caused by a flaw in the system design. More likely, they are installed by a system diagnostician or programmer for future use. Or, they are incorporated into the system code by a destructive virus or by a Trojan—one that's seemingly innocuous but that executes hidden instructions. Regardless of the reason for its existence, a trapdoor leaves the system vulnerable to future intrusion.

Trash collection, also known as dumpster diving, is an evening pastime for those who enjoy perusing anything and everything thrown out by system users—the discarded disks, CDs, faxes, printer ribbons, as well as printouts of source code, programs, memory dumps, and notes. They all can yield important information that can be used to enter the system illegally. It's recommended that system administrators adopt a policy of routinely shredding all work that can conceivably contain data, code, passwords, access information, Web site development information, or clues to the organization's financial workings. The importance of this obvious precaution can't be overstated.

Legally, it's important to know that malicious attacks on computers may violate U.S. federal and state laws and invite penalties. Generally, those convicted in the United States have lost their computing systems and many have been sentenced to significant fines, jail terms, or both.

Viruses

A **virus** is defined as a small program written to alter the way a computer operates, without the permission or knowledge of the user. A virus must meet two criteria:

- It must be self-executing. Often, this means placing its own code in the path of another program.
- It must be self-replicating. Usually, this is accomplished by copying itself from infected files to clean files as shown in Figure 11.2. Viruses can infect desktop computers and network servers alike and spread each time the host file is executed.

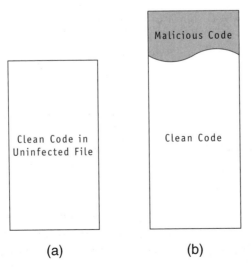

(a)   (b)

(figure 11.2)

A file infector virus attacks a clean file (a) by attaching a small program to it (b), which executes every time the infected file runs.

Viruses are usually written to attack a certain operating system. Therefore, it's unusual for the same virus code to successfully attack a Linux workstation and a Windows server. Writers of virus code usually exploit a known vulnerability in the operating system software, hence the need to keep it correctly updated with patches—something we discuss in Chapter 12.

Some viruses are designed to significantly damage the infected computer such as by deleting or corrupting files or reformatting the hard disk. Others are not so malicious but merely make their presence known by delivering text, video, or audio messages to the computer's user. However, no virus can be considered benign because all viruses confiscate valuable memory and storage space required by legitimate programs and often cause system failures and data loss. There are five recognized types of viruses, as shown in Table 11.4.

(table 11.4)	Type of Virus	Description
Five types of viruses.	File infector virus	Infects files on the computer, normally executable files such as .exe and .com files commonly found on Microsoft operating systems. These viruses commonly become resident in memory and then infect any clean executable program that runs on that computer.
	Boot sector virus	Infects the boot record, the system area of a floppy disk or hard drive. These viruses activate whenever the user starts up (powers on) the computer. Most boot sector viruses were written for MS-DOS, but other operating systems are potential targets.
	Master boot record virus	Infects the boot record of a disk, saving a legitimate copy of the master boot record in a different location on the volume.
	Multipartite virus	Infects both the boot record and program files, making them especially difficult to repair. Successful removal requires that all instances of the virus be removed at once—on the boot records as well as all instances of files infected with the virus. Should any instance of the infection remain, the virus will infect the system again.
	Macro virus	Infects data files (such as word processing documents, spreadsheets, etc.), though newer versions now infect other program files as well. Computer users are advised to disable the automatic execution of macros on files they don't completely trust.

Viruses spread via a wide variety of applications and have even been found in legitimate shrink-wrapped software. In one case, a virus was inadvertently picked up at a trade show by a developer who unknowingly allowed it to infect the finished code of a completed commercial software package just before it was marketed. The package was quickly recalled.

In one bizarre example, a virus was distributed to tourists in the Middle East, embedded in part of an illegally copied (and illegally bought) software package. Reportedly, the sellers told authorities that they did it to teach the buyers a lesson in ethics.

A macro virus works by attaching itself to the template which, in turn, is attached to word processing documents. Once the template file is infected, every subsequent document created on that template is infected.

Worms

A **worm** is a memory-resident program that copies itself from one system to the next without requiring the aid of an infected program file. The immediate result of a worm is slower processing time of legitimate work because the worm siphons off processing time and memory space. Worms are especially destructive on networks, where they hoard critical system resources such as main memory and processor time.

Trojans

A **Trojan** (originally called a Trojan Horse) is a destructive program that's disguised as a legitimate or harmless program that sometimes carries within itself the means to allow the program's creator to secretly access the user's system. Intruders have been known to capture user passwords by using a Trojan to replace the standard login program on the computer with an identical fake login that captures keystrokes. Once it's installed, it works like this:

1. The user sees a login prompt and types in the user ID.
2. The user sees a password prompt and types in the password.
3. The rogue program records both the user ID and password and sends a typical login failure message to the user. Then the program stops running and returns control to the legitimate program.
4. Now, the user sees the legitimate login prompt and retypes the user ID.
5. The user sees the legitimate password prompt and retypes the password.
6. Finally, the user gains access to the system, unaware that the rogue program has stored the first attempt and recorded the user ID and password.

This series of events would look something like the dialog shown in Figure 11.3. A similar technique using simulated menu-driven screens is also easy to create.

Later, at a convenient time, the Trojan's creator retrieves the file with its list of valid user IDs and passwords, perhaps even a root password, which would allow access to sensitive administrative functions.

```
login: kat1422

password: ★★★★★★★

Error:login incorrect, please try again.

Login: kat1422

password: ★★★★★★★

Last login: Wed Nov 17 11:12:13
```

Rogue software doesn't need to be planted by someone outside the organization. In a California case, an employee planted a Trojan in his employer's system before quitting his job. The code was designed to erase a program he'd written on the job to track the availability and prices of parts for an orbital missile program. At its conclusion, the program was instructed to erase itself. Reportedly, the programmer hoped to become a consultant, and he planned to work for his former employer reconstructing the program he had written and then erased. The plan was foiled when another technician discovered the bad code and removed it before the scheduled date of operation. The rogue employee was indicted in federal court for his actions.

Bombs

A **logic bomb** is a destructive program with a fuse—a certain triggering event (such as a certain keystroke or connection with the Internet). A logic bomb often spreads unnoticed throughout a network until a predetermined event when it goes off and does its damage.

A **time bomb** is similar to a logic bomb but is triggered by a specific time, such as a day of the year. For example, the time bomb called the Michelangelo virus, first discovered in 1991, was one of the first logic bombs to prompt warnings to all computer users by the popular media. The code was designed to execute on the anniversary of the birth of the artist Michelangelo (March 6, 1475). The code was designed to execute when an infected computer was started up on the trigger date (March 6 of any year) and to overwrite the first 17 sectors on heads 0-3 of the first 256 tracks of the hard disk on the infected machine.

Blended Threats

A **blended threat** combines into one program the characteristics of other attacks, including a virus, a worm, a trojan, **spyware**, key loggers, and other malicious code. That is, this single program uses a variety of tools to attack systems and spread to others. Because the threat from these programs is so diverse, the only defense against them is a comprehensive security plan that includes multiple layers of protection. A blended threat shows the following characteristics:

- Harms the affected system. For example, it might launch a denial of service attack at a target IP address, deface a Web site, or plant Trojans for later execution.

- Spreads to other systems using multiple methods. For example, it might scan for vulnerabilities to compromise a system, such as embedding code in Web page files on a server, infect the systems of visitors who visit a compromised Web site, or send unauthorized e-mail from compromised servers with a worm attachment.

- Attacks other systems from multiple points. For example: inject malicious code into the .exe files on a system, raise the privilege level of an intruder's guest account, create world-readable and world-writeable access to private files, and add bogus script code to Web page files. (We discuss world access later in this chapter.)

- Propagates without human intervention. For example, it might continuously scan the Internet for vulnerable servers that are unpatched and open to attack.

- Exploits vulnerabilities of target systems. For example, it might take advantage of operating system problems (such as buffer overflows), Web page validation vulnerabilities on input screens, and commonly known default passwords to gain unauthorized access.

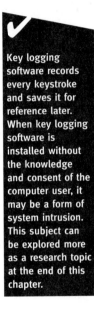

Key logging software records every keystroke and saves it for reference later. When key logging software is installed without the knowledge and consent of the computer user, it may be a form of system intrusion. This subject can be explored more as a research topic at the end of this chapter.

When the threat includes all or many of these characteristics, no single tool can protect a system. Only a combination of defenses in combination with regular patch management (discussed in Chapter 12) can hope to protect the system adequately.

System Protection

Threats can come from outsiders (those outside the organization) as well as from insiders (employees or others with access to the system) and can include theft of intellectual property or other confidential or sensitive information, fraud, and acts of system sabotage.

System protection is multifaceted. Four protection methods are discussed here: installing antivirus software (and running it regularly), using firewalls (and keeping them up-to-date), ensuring that only authorized individuals access the system, and taking advantage of encryption technology when the overhead required to implement it is mandated by the risk.

Antivirus Software

Antivirus software can be purchased to protect systems from attack by malicious software. The level of protection is usually in proportion to the importance of its data. Medical data should be highly protected. Student-written computer programs probably don't deserve the same level of security.

Software to combat viruses can be preventive or diagnostic, or both. Preventive programs may calculate a checksum for each production program, putting the values in a master file. Later, before a program is executed, its checksum is compared with the master. Generally, diagnostic software compares file sizes (checking for added code when none is expected), looks for replicating instructions, and searches for unusual file activity. Some software may look for certain specific instructions and monitor the way the programs execute. But remember: soon after these packages are marketed, system intruders start looking for ways to thwart them. Hence, only the most current software can be expected to uncover the latest viruses. In other words, old software will only find old viruses.

Information about current viruses is available from vendors and government agencies dedicated to system security, such as those listed in Table 11.5.

(table 11.5)

System security is a rapidly changing field. Current information can be found at these Web sites and many more. Sites are listed in alphabetical order.

Web Site	Organization
http://csrc.nist.gov	Computer Security Division of the National Institute of Standards and Technology
www.cert.org	CERT Coordination Center
www.mcafee.com	McAfee, Inc.
www.sans.org	SANS Institute
www.symantec.com	Symantec Corp.
www.us-cert.gov	U.S. Computer Emergency Readiness Team

While antivirus software (an example is shown in Figure 11.4) is capable of repairing files infected with a virus, it is generally unable to repair worms, Trojans, or blended threats because of the structural differences between viruses and worms or Trojans. A virus works by infecting an otherwise clean file. Therefore, antivirus software can sometimes remove the infection and leave the remainder intact. On the other hand, a worm or Trojan is malicious code in its entirety. That is, the entire body of the software code contained in a worm or Trojan is threatening and must be removed as a whole.

The only way to remove a Trojan is to remove the entire body of the malicious program. For example, if a computer game, available for free download over the Internet, is a worm that steals system IDs and passwords, there is no way to cleanse the game of the bad code and save the rest. The game must go.

Symantec.com › Business › Security Response › Threat Explorer › Threats

Threat Explorer

The Threat Explorer is a comprehensive resource for daily, accurate and up-to-date information on the latest threats, risks and vulnerabilities.

| Latest | **Threats** | Risks | Vulnerabilities | A - Z Threats and Risks | Search |

Threats

Severity	Name	Type	Protected*
‖‖‖	Downloader.Kuaiput	Trojan	09/28/2009
‖‖‖	Packed.Generic.254	Trojan, Virus, Worm	09/28/2009
‖‖‖	W32.SillyFDC.BCX	Worm	09/25/2009
‖‖‖	Suspicious.Zlob	Trojan	09/23/2009
‖‖‖	W32.Lafee	Virus	09/23/2009
‖‖‖	Trojan.Opachki	Trojan	09/22/2009
‖‖‖	Trojan.Bredolab!gen	Trojan	09/21/2009
‖‖‖	Trojan.Wampyrlinf	Trojan	09/21/2009
‖‖‖	Infostealer.Bzup.B	Trojan	09/20/2009
‖‖‖	W32.Xpaj.B	Virus, Worm	09/16/2009

(figure 11.4)

This screenshot from the Symantec.com Web site shows the threats (viruses, worms, and Trojans) as of September 2009.

Firewalls

Network assaults include compromised Web servers, circumvented firewalls, and FTP and Telnet sites accessed by unauthorized users, to name a few.

A **firewall** is a set of hardware and/or software designed to protect a system by disguising its IP address from outsiders who don't have authorization to access it or ask for information about it. A firewall sits between the Internet and the network, as shown in Figure 11.5, blocking curious inquiries and potentially dangerous intrusions from outside the system. The typical tasks of the firewall are to:

• log activities that access the Internet

• maintain **access control** based on the senders' or receivers' IP addresses

• maintain access control based on the services that are requested

• hide the internal network from unauthorized users requesting network information

• verify that virus protection is installed and being enforced

• perform authentication based on the source of a request from the Internet

The two fundamental mechanisms used by the firewall to perform these tasks are packet filtering and proxy servers. Using **packet filtering**, the firewall reviews the header information for incoming and outgoing Internet packets to verify that the source address, destination address, and protocol are all correct. For example, if a packet arrives from the Internet (outside the network) with an internal source address (which should be from inside the network), the firewall would be expected to refuse its entry.

(figure 11.5)

In this example of a university system, the firewall sits between the campus networks and the Internet, filtering requests for access.

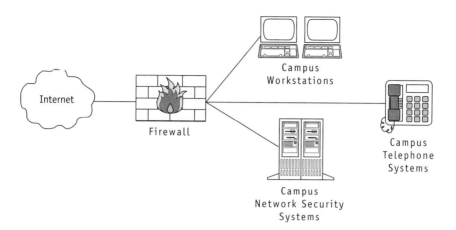

A **proxy server** hides important network information from outsiders by making the network server invisible. To do so, the proxy server intercepts the request for access to the network, decides if it is a valid request and, if so, then passes the request to the appropriate server that can fulfill the request—all without revealing the makeup of the network, the servers, or other information that might reside on them. Likewise, if information is to be passed from the network to the Internet, the proxy server relays the transmission but without revealing anything about the network. Proxy servers are invisible to the users but are critical to the success of the firewall.

Authentication

Authentication is verification that an individual trying to access a system is authorized to do so. One popular authentication tool is **Kerberos,** a network authentication protocol developed as part of the Athena Project at MIT. The name is taken from the three-headed dog of Greek mythology that guarded the gates of Hades.

To answer the need for password encryption to improve network security, Kerberos was designed to provide strong authentication for client/server applications. A free open-source implementation of this protocol (under copyright permissions) is available from MIT *(http://web.mit.edu/kerberos/)* or for purchase from numerous distributors.

The Kerberos protocol uses strong **cryptography** (the science of coding messages) so that a client can prove its identity to a server, and vice versa, across an insecure network connection. Then, once authentication is completed, both client and server can encrypt all of their subsequent communications to assure privacy and data integrity.

In simplest form, here's how Kerberos works, as shown in Figure 11.6:

1. When you (the client) want to access a server that requires a Kerberos ticket, you request authentication from the Kerberos Authentication Server, which creates a session key based on your password. This key also serves as your encryption key.

2. Next, you are sent to a Ticket Granting Server (this can be the same physical server but a different logical unit), which creates a ticket valid for access to the server.

3. Next, your ticket is sent to the server where it can be rejected or accepted. Once accepted, you are free to interact with the server for the specified period of time. The ticket is timestamped so you can make additional requests using the same ticket within a certain time period but must be reauthenticated after the time period ends. This design feature is to limit the likelihood that someone will later use your ticket without your knowledge.

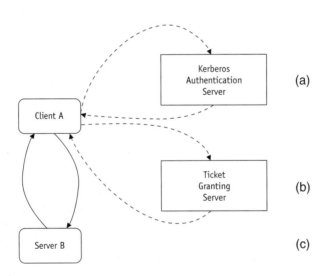

(figure 11.6)

Using Kerberos, when client A attempts to access server B, the user is authenticated (a) and receives a ticket for the session (b). Once the ticket is issued, client and server can communicate at will (c). Without the ticket, access is not granted.

Because the user gains access using a ticket, there's no need for the user's password to pass through the network, thus improving the protection of network passwords.

An essential part of maintaining a Kerberos protocol is the systematic revocation of access rights from clients who no longer deserve to have access. For this reason, the administrators of the Kerberos Authentication Server as well as the Ticket Granting Server must keep their databases updated and accurate. By keeping records of access revocation, the administrator can spot trends and anticipate the need for user education.

For example, if the organization hires new consultants in February of each year, which is followed by numerous calls of access revocation in March and April, as shown in Figure 11.7, then scheduling user education for new employees in February can be a proactive, cost effective move, thereby reducing the reason for revocation.

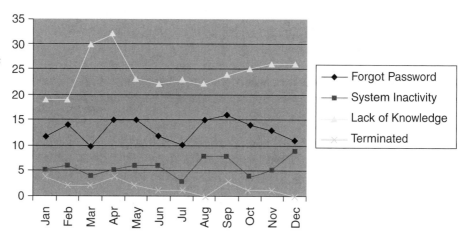

Access Revoked

Encryption

The most extreme protection for sensitive data is with **encryption**—putting it into a secret code. Total network encryption, also called communications encryption, is the most extreme form—that's when all communications with the system are encrypted. The system then decrypts them for processing. To communicate with another system, the data is encrypted, transmitted, decrypted, and processed.

Partial encryption is less extreme and may be used between a network's entry and exit points or other vulnerable parts of its communication system. Storage encryption means that the information is stored in encrypted form and decrypted before it's read or used.

There are two disadvantages to encryption. It increases the system's overhead and the system becomes totally dependent on the encryption process itself—if you lose the key, you've lost the data forever. But if the system must be kept secure, then this procedure might be warranted.

How Encryption Works

The way to understand cryptography is to first understand the role of a public key and a private key. The **private key** is a pair of two prime numbers (usually with 75 or more digits each) chosen by the person who wants to receive a private message. The two prime numbers are multiplied together, forming a third number with 150 or more digits. The person who creates this private key is the only one who knows which two prime numbers were used to create it. What are the chances that someone else can guess the two prime numbers? Very slim, because there is no known formula for factoring large numbers greater than 80 digits, and this product has at least 150 digits. Even with brute force computation on a supercomputer, the task would take decades (as of this writing, at least).

Once the message receiver has the product, known as the **public key**, it can be posted in any public place, even an online directory, for anyone to see, because the private key can't be decoded from the public key.

Then, anyone who wants to send a confidential message to the receiver uses encryption software and inserts the public key as a variable. The software then scrambles the message before it's sent to the receiver. Once received, the receiver uses the private key in the encryption software and the confidential message is revealed. Should someone else receive the encrypted message and attempt to open it with a private key that is incorrect, the resulting message would be scrambled, unreadable code.

Sniffers and Spoofing

If sensitive data is sent over a network or the Internet in **cleartext**, without encryption, it becomes vulnerable at numerous sites across the network. **Packet sniffers**, also called sniffers, are programs that reside on computers attached to the network.

They peruse data packets as they pass by, examine each one for specific information, and log copies of interesting packets for more detailed examination. Sniffing is particularly problematic in wireless networks. Anyone with a wireless device can detect a wireless network that's within range. If the network is passing cleartext packets, it's quite easy to intercept, read, modify, and resend them. The information sought ranges from passwords, Social Security numbers, and credit card numbers to industrial secrets and marketing information. This vulnerability is a fundamental shortcoming of cleartext transmission over the Internet.

Wireless security is a special area of system security that is too vast to cover here. Readers are encouraged to pursue the subject in the current literature for the latest research, tools, and best practices.

Spoofing is a security threat that relies on cleartext transmission whereby the assailant falsifies the IP addresses of an Internet server by changing the address recorded in packets it sends over the Internet. This technique is useful when unauthorized users want to disguise themselves as friendly sites. For example, to guard confidential information on an internal network (intranet), some Web servers allow access only to users from certain sites; however, by spoofing the IP address, the server could inadvertently admit unauthorized users.

Password Management

The most basic techniques used to protect hardware and software investments are good passwords and careful user training, but this is not as simple as it might appear. Passwords are forgettable, unlikely to be changed often, commonly shared, and considered bothersome by many people.

Password Construction

Passwords are one of the easiest and most effective protection schemes to implement, but only if they're used correctly. A good password is unusual, memorable, and changed often, usually every 30 to 90 days. Ideally, the password should be a combination of characters and numbers, something that's easy for the user to remember but difficult for someone else to guess. The password should be committed to memory, never written down, and not included in a script file to log on to a network.

Password files are normally stored in encrypted form so they are not readable by casual browsers. To verify a password, the system will accept the user's entry in cleartext, encrypt it, and compare the new sequence to the encrypted version stored in the password file for that user, as shown in Figure 11.8.

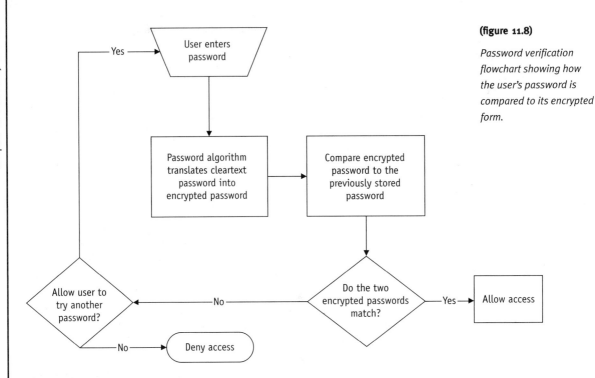

(figure 11.8)

Password verification flowchart showing how the user's password is compared to its encrypted form.

There are several reliable techniques for generating a good password:

- Using a minimum of eight characters, including numbers and nonalphanumeric characters
- Creating a misspelled word or joining bits of phrases into a word that's easy to remember
- Following a certain pattern on the keyboard, generating new passwords easily by starting your sequence with a different letter each time
- Creating acronyms from memorable sentences, such as MDWB4YOIA, which stands for: "My Dog Will Be 4 Years Old In April"
- If the operating system differentiates between upper- and lowercase characters (as UNIX and Linux do), users should take advantage of that feature by using both in the password: MDwb4YOia
- Avoiding any words that appear in any dictionary

The length of the password has a direct effect on the ability of the password to survive password cracking attempts. The longer passwords are, the better. For example, if the system administrator mandates that all passwords must be exactly eight characters long and contain any lowercase letters such as "abcdefgh," the possible combinations number 26^8. Likewise, if the policy mandates 10 characters of lowercase letters, the combinations total 26^{10}. However, if the rule allows eight characters from among 95 printable characters, the combinations jump to 95^8, as shown in Table 11.6.

	Length of Password in Characters					
	2	4	6	8	10	12
ASCII characters	128^2	128^4	128^6	128^8	128^{10}	128^{12}
Printable characters	95^2	95^4	95^6	95^8	95^{10}	95^{12}
Alphanumeric characters	62^2	62^4	62^6	62^8	62^{10}	62^{12}
Lowercase letters and numbers	36^2	36^4	36^6	36^8	36^{10}	36^{12}
Lowercase letters	26^2	26^4	26^6	26^8	26^{10}	26^{12}

Dictionary attack is the term used to describe a method of breaking encrypted passwords. Its requirements are simple: a copy of the encrypted password file and the algorithm used to encrypt the passwords. With these two tools, the intruder runs a software program that takes every word in the dictionary, runs it through the password encryption algorithm, and compares the encrypted result to the encrypted passwords contained in the file. If both encrypted versions match, then the intruder knows that this dictionary word was used as a legitimate password.

One technique used by some operating systems to make passwords harder to guess is to "salt" user passwords with extra random bits to make them less vulnerable to dictionary attacks. Here's how it works. The user enters the desired password, which is then encrypted. Then the system assigns the user a unique combination of bits (called the salt) that are tacked on the end of the encrypted password. That means, the stored combination of 0s and 1s contains the encrypted password combined with a unique salt. Therefore, if an intruder downloads the list of encrypted passwords, the intruder will need to guess not only the password but also the random salt. This is something that's much more difficult and time consuming to do than merely guessing obvious passwords.

Password Alternatives

As an alternative to passwords, some systems have integrated use of a **smart card**—a credit-card-sized calculator that requires both something you have and something you know. The smart card displays a constantly changing multidigit number that's synchronized with an identical number generator in the system. To enter the correct password, the user must type in the number that appears at that moment on the smart card. For added protection, the user then enters a secret code. The user is admitted to the system only if both number and code are validated. Using this scheme, an intruder needs more than either the card or the code because unless both are valid, entry is denied.

Another alternative is **biometrics**, the science and technology of identifying individuals based on the unique biological characteristics of each person. Current research focuses on analysis of the human face, fingerprints, hand measurements, iris/retina, and voice prints. Biometric devices often consist of a scanner or other device to gather the necessary data about the user, software to convert the data into a form that can be compared and stored, and a database to keep the stored information from all authorized users. One of the strengths of biometrics is that it positively identifies the person being scanned.

For example, a fingerprint has about 35 discriminators—factors that set one person's fingerprint apart from someone else's. Even better, the iris has about 260 discriminators and is unique from right eye to left. Not even identical twins have the same iris pattern. A critical factor with biometrics is reducing the margin of error so authorized users are rarely turned away and those who are not authorized are caught at the door. At this writing, the technology to implement biometric authentication is expensive, but there's every indication that it will become widespread in the years to come.

Another password alternative involves the use of graphics and a pattern of clicks using a mouse, stylus, touch screen, or other pointing device, as shown in Figure 11.9. With this technology, the user establishes a certain sequence of clicks on a photo or illustration and then repeats it to gain access. Because this system eliminates all keyboard entries, it is resistant to dictionary attacks (which involves testing every word in a dictionary to try to crack the targeted password). One of the research topics at the end of this chapter allows you to explore the latest developments in this evolving subject.

(figure 11.9)

A graphical password is created by clicking certain areas of the photo in a certain sequence.

Social Engineering

Historically, intruders gained access to systems by using innovative techniques to crack user passwords such as using default passwords, backdoor passwords, or trying words found in a file of dictionary terms. They also use a technique called **social engineering**, which means looking in and around the user's desk for a written reminder, trying the user logon ID as the password, searching logon scripts, and even telephoning friends and co-workers to learn the names of a user's family members, pets, vacation destinations, favorite hobbies, car model, etc.

It even works with military targets. One such instance involved a computer system in a remote location that was reported to be exceptionally secure. To test its security, a systems consultant was hired to try to break into the system. She started by opening an unprotected document that told her where the computer was located. Then she telephoned the base and learned the name of the base commanding officer. Then she learned the name of the commander's secretary. Then she called the data center, masquerading as the secretary, and informed them that the commander was having difficulty accessing the data. When the data center personnel were reluctant to help, the consultant got angry and demanded action. They responded with access so the "commander" could use the network. Soon the consultant was on the system with what appeared to be classified data. With that, the officers in charge of the exercise pulled the plug and sent the consultant on her way.

Phishing (pronounced "fishing") is a form of social engineering whereby an intruder pretends to be a legitimate entity and contacts unwary users asking them to reconfirm their personal and/or financial information. In 2003, many customers of eBay, Inc. received an e-mail saying that their account had been compromised and would be closed. Attached to the e-mail was a link to a page that looked like a genuine eBay Web page where they could reenter their credit card data, ATM personal identification numbers, Social Security number, date of birth, and their mother's maiden name. The owner of the site then had all the information required to steal the identity of the people who responded.

Default passwords pose unique vulnerabilities because they are widely known among system attackers but are a necessary tool for vendors. Default passwords are routinely shipped with hardware or software. They're convenient for the manufacturer because they give field service workers supervisor-level access to fix problem equipment on site or using a telecommunications connection. System intruders also find them useful because if they have not been changed, they allow powerful access to the system. Lists of default passwords are routinely passed from one hacker to the next, often serving as a starting point for an attack. To protect the system, managers should periodically identify and change all default passwords on their hardware and software.

Ethics

What is ethical behavior? In briefest form it is this: Be good. Do good.

Many professional associations have addressed the issue of **ethics**—the rules or standards of behavior that members of the computer-using community are expected to follow, demonstrating the principles of right and wrong. In 1992, the IEEE and the Association for Computing Machinery (ACM) issued a standard of ethics for the global computing community.

The apparent lack of ethics in computing is a significant departure from other professions. For example, we take for granted that our medical doctor will keep our records private, but many of us don't have the same confidence in the individuals working for companies that keep our credit records or the intruders who break into those systems. Although ethics is a subject that's not often addressed in computer science classes, the implications are so vast they can't be ignored by system administrators or users.

At issue are the seemingly conflicting needs of users: the individual's need for privacy, the organization's need to protect its proprietary information, and the public's right to know, as illustrated in freedom of information laws.

For the system's owner, ethical lapses by authorized or unauthorized users can have severe consequences:

• Illegally copied software can result in lawsuits and fines of several times the retail price of each product for each transgression. Several industry associations publish toll-free numbers encouraging disgruntled employees to turn in their employers who use illegal software.

• Plagiarism, the unauthorized copying of copyrighted work (including but not limited to music, movies, textbook material, databases), is illegal and punishable by law in the United States as well as in many other nations. When the original work is on paper, most users know the proper course of action, but when the original is in electronic form, some people don't recognize the ethical issues involved.

• Eavesdropping on e-mail, data, or voice communications is sometimes illegal and usually unwarranted, except under certain circumstances. If calls or messages must be monitored, the participants should always be notified before the monitoring begins.

• Cracking, sometimes called hacking, is gaining access to another computer system to monitor or change data, and it's seldom an ethical activity. Although it's seen as a sport by certain people, each break-in should cause the system's owner and users to question the validity of the system's data.

• Unethical use of technology, defined as unauthorized access to private or protected computer systems or electronic information, is a murky area of the law, but it's clearly the wrong thing to do. Legally, the justice system has great difficulty keeping up with each specific form of unauthorized access because the technology changes so quickly. Therefore, system owners can't rely on the law for guidance. Instead, they must aggressively teach their users about what is and is not ethical behavior.

How can users be taught to behave ethically? A continuing series of security awareness and ethics communications to computer users is more effective than a single announcement. Specific activities can include the following:

- Publish policies that clearly state which actions will and will not be condoned.
- Teach a regular seminar on the subject including real-life case histories.
- Conduct open discussions of ethical questions such as: Is it okay to read someone else's e-mail? Is it right for someone else to read your e-mail? Is it ethical for a competitor to read your data? Is it okay if someone scans your bank account? Is it right for someone to change the results of your medical test? Is it acceptable for someone to copy your software program and put it on the Internet? Is it acceptable for someone to copy a government document and put it on the Internet?

For a guide to ethical behavior, see excerpts from the ACM Code of Ethics and Professional Conduct in Appendix A of this book or visit *www.acm.org*.

Conclusion

The system is only as good as the integrity of the data that's stored on it. A single breach of security—whether catastrophic or not, whether accidental or not—damages the system's integrity. And damaged integrity threatens the viability of the best-designed system, its managers, its designers, and its users. Therefore, vigilant security precautions are essential.

So far in this text we've discussed each manager and each operating system function in isolation, but in reality, system performance depends on the combined effort of each piece. In the next chapter, we'll look at the system as a whole and examine how each piece contributes to, or detracts from, overall system performance.

Key Terms

access control: the control of user access to a network or computer system.

antivirus software: software that is designed to detect and recover from attacks by viruses and worms. It is usually part of a system protection software package.

authentication: the means by which a system verifies that the individual attempting to access the system is authorized to do so.

backup: the process of making long-term archival file storage copies of files on the system.

blended threat: a system threat that combines into one program the characteristics of other attacks, including a virus, a worm, Trojans, spyware, and other malicious code.

biometrics: the science and technology of identifying authorized users based on their biological characteristics.

browsing: a system security violation in which unauthorized users are allowed to search through secondary storage directories or files for information they should not have the privilege to read.

cleartext: in cryptography, a method of transmitting data without encryption, in text that is readable by anyone who sees it.

cryptography: the science of coding messages or text so unauthorized users cannot read them.

denial of service (DoS) attack: an attack on a network that makes it unavailable to perform the functions it was designed to do. This can be done by flooding the server with meaningless requests or information.

dictionary attack: the technique by which an intruder attempts to guess user passwords by trying words found in a dictionary.

encryption: translation of a message or data item from its original form to an encoded form, thus hiding its meaning and making it unintelligible without the key to decode it. Used to improve system security and data protection.

ethics: the rules or standards of behavior that individuals are expected to follow demonstrating the principles of right and wrong.

firewall: a set of hardware and software that disguises the internal network address of a computer or network to control how clients from outside can access the organization's internal servers.

Kerberos: an MIT-developed authentication system that allows network managers to administer and manage user authentication at the network level.

logic bomb: a virus with a trigger, usually an event, that causes it to execute.

packet filtering: reviewing incoming and outgoing Internet packets to verify that the source address, destination address, and protocol are correct. Usually a function of a firewall.

packet sniffer: software that intercepts Internet data packets sent in cleartext and searches them for information, such as passwords.

password: a user-defined access control method. Typically a word or character string that a user must specify in order to be allowed to log on to a computer system.

phishing: a technique used to trick consumers into revealing personal information by appearing as a legitimate entity.

private key: a tool that's used to decrypt a message that was encrypted using a public key.

proxy server: a server positioned between an internal network and an external network or the Internet to screen all requests for information and prevent unauthorized access to network resources.

public key: a tool that's used to encrypt a message, to be decoded later using a private key.

recovery: the steps that must be taken when a system is assaulted to recover system operability and, in the best case, recover any lost data.

smart card: a small, credit-card-sized device that uses cryptographic technology to control access to computers and computer networks. Each smart card has its own personal identifier, which is known only to the user, as well as its own stored and encrypted password.

social engineering: a technique whereby system intruders gain access to information about a legitimate user to learn active passwords, sometimes by calling the user and posing as a system technician.

spoofing: the creation of false IP addresses in the headers of data packets sent over the Internet, sometimes with the intent of gaining access when it would not otherwise be granted.

spyware: a blended threat that covertly collects data about system users and sends it to a designated repository.

system survivability: the capability of a system to fulfill its mission, in a timely manner, in the presence of attacks, failures, or accidents.

time bomb: a virus with a trigger linked to a certain year, month, day, or time that causes it to execute.

trapdoor: an unspecified and undocumented entry point to the system, which represents a significant security risk.

Trojan: a malicious computer program with unintended side effects that are not intended by the user who executes the program.

virus: a program that replicates itself by incorporating itself into other programs, including those in secondary storage, that are shared among other computer systems.

wiretapping: a system security violation in which unauthorized users monitor or modify a user's transmission.

worm: a computer program that replicates itself and is self-propagating in main memory.

Interesting Searches

- Network Security Tools
- Strong Password Security
- Encryption Practices
- Thwarting Insider Threats
- Legal Issues vs. Ethical Issues

Exercises

Research Topics

A. Research the practice of key logging in current literature. Describe what it is and explain why some people defend the practice while some others do not. Finally, give your own opinion and defend it. Cite your sources.

B. In current literature, research the use of graphics to replace typed passwords. Describe the historical milestones of the technology and list its significant advantages and disadvantages. Find at least two real world examples where this technology is used, citing your sources for each.

Exercises

1. Give three examples of excellent passwords and explain why each would be a good choice to protect a system from unauthorized users.

2. Give three advantages and disadvantages of password generator software. Would you recommend the use of such software for your own system? Explain why or why not.

3. System managers can't protect their resources without recognizing all threats and even learning to think like an intruder. Knowing that, and knowing that it's unethical to use a computer system without proper authorization, imagine that you are an unauthorized user who wants to break into your system. Describe how you might begin guessing the password of a legitimate user.

4. As a follow-up to the previous question, identify a friend who has chosen at least one computer password. On a piece of paper, list 20 possible passwords you might use if you were trying to access the friend's system. Then show the list to your friend and ask if any of your guesses were correct. You might try combinations of names of family members and friends, favorite hobbies, automobiles, pets, birthdays, slang terms, favorite sayings, etc.

5. Imagine that you are the manager of a small business computing center. List at least three reasons that you would use to convince a busy, reluctant staff member

to perform regular backups and manage your system's archives appropriately, and elaborate.

6. In the U.S., HIPAA (Health Insurance Portability and Accountability Act of 1996) legislation protects the privacy of patient medical data. Yet in an emergency, it's to your benefit if your caregivers have access to your history, medications, etc. Acknowledging the need for privacy as well as the need for accessibility, describe several advantages and disadvantages of maintaining strict patient data confidentiality.

7. Many users are required to log in to several networks and thus have multiple passwords, which are difficult to remember. Name three ways that a user can manage these password requirements, and compare the advantages and disadvantages of each. Finally, decide which one you would use and explain why.

Advanced Exercises

8. Describe the unique threats to a data center posed by disgruntled employees. Describe how you would identify such people, if possible, and how you would protect your system from these threats.

9. List 20 viruses discovered in the past 12 months and research three in detail, describing which files they infect, how they spread, and their intended effects.

10. Identify three sets of security parameters (one each for good, better, and best protection) for a computer that holds a university's registration information. Consider not only the operating system, but the protection software, access controls, and the room in which the computer is located. Then make a recommendation based on the need for security vs. the cost of that security.

11. Using information from the CERT Coordination Center *(www.cert.org)*, identify the latest vulnerability for an operating system of your choice. List the threat, the criticality of the threat, the potential impact, the suggested solution, the systems that are affected, and the actions you would take as a system administrator.

12. In the U.S., HIPAA legislation imposed stringent security requirements on the healthcare industry. Identify the requirements for data transmissions between networks and the role of encryption, if any, in those transmissions.

13. Wireless LANs pose unique challenges for system operators because of their accessibility. Imagine that you are the system administrator for a wireless network that is used in a scientific research setting. Identify the five biggest security challenges and how you would address each of them in spite of your limited budget.

14. With identity theft becoming widespread, many organizations have moved to secure the Social Security numbers of their customers, suppliers, and employees. Imagine that you are the system administrator for a college campus where the students' Social Security numbers are used as the key field to access student records (and realizing that you need to extend your protection to several decades of historical student records). Describe the steps you would follow to change the system. Make sure your solution also removes the student Social Security number on transcripts, course registration forms, student-accessible data screens, student ID cards, health center records, and other record-keeping systems. Finally, identify which individuals on campus would retain access to the Social Security numbers and explain why.

Chapter 12

System Management

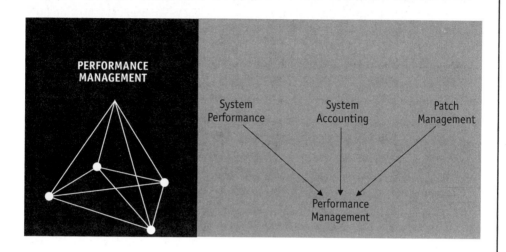

" There is no such thing as a single problem; ... all problems are interrelated. "

—Saul D. Alinsky (*1909–1972*)

Learning Objectives

After completing this chapter, you should be able to describe:

- The trade-offs to be considered when attempting to improve overall system performance
- The roles of system measurement tools such as positive and negative feedback loops
- Two system monitoring techniques
- The fundamentals of patch management
- The importance of sound accounting practices by system administrators

In Chapter 1 we introduced the overall operating system. In Chapters 2 through 8 we studied how each component works, and in Chapters 9 through 11 we discussed networking and security. In these chapters we examined each piece in isolation. In a real-life operating system, however, they don't work in isolation. Each component depends on the other components.

This chapter shows how they work together and how the system designer has to consider trade-offs to improve the system's overall efficiency. We begin by showing how the designer can improve the performance of one component, the cost of that improvement, and how it might affect the performance of the remainder of the system. We conclude with some methods used to monitor and measure system performance, including the need to keep the operating system patched correctly.

Evaluating an Operating System

Most operating systems were designed to work with a certain piece of hardware, a category of processors, or specific groups of users. Although most evolved over time to operate multiple systems, most still favor some users and some computing environments over others. For example, if the operating system was written for novice users to meet basic requirements, it might not satisfy the demands of those more knowledgeable. Conversely, if it was written for programmers, then a business office's computer operator might find its commands obscure. If it serves the needs of a multiuser computer center, it might be inappropriate for a small computing center. Or, if it's written to provide rapid response time, it might provide poor throughput.

To evaluate an operating system, you need to understand its design goals, its history, how it communicates with its users, how its resources are managed, and what trade-offs were made to achieve its goals. In other words, an operating system's strengths and weaknesses need to be weighed in relation to who will be using the operating system, on what hardware, and for what purpose.

Cooperation Among Components

The performance of any one resource depends on the performance of the other resources in the system. For example, memory management is intrinsically linked with device management when memory is used to buffer data between a very fast processor and slower secondary storage devices. Many other examples of interdependence have been shown throughout the preceding chapters.

If you managed an organization's computer system and were allocated money to upgrade it, where would you put the investment to best use? You might have several choices:

- more memory
- a faster CPU
- additional processors
- more disk drives
- a RAID system
- new file management software

Or, if you bought a new system, what characteristics would you look for that would make it more efficient than the old one?

Any system improvement can be made only after extensive analysis of the needs of the system's resources, requirements, managers, and users. But whenever changes are made to a system, often you're trading one set of problems for another. The key is to consider the performance of the entire system and not just the individual components.

Role of Memory Management

Memory management schemes were discussed in Chapters 2 and 3. If you increase memory or change to another memory allocation scheme, you must consider the actual operating environment in which the system will reside. There's a trade-off between memory use and CPU overhead.

For example, if the system will be running student programs exclusively and the average job is only three pages long, your decision to increase the size of virtual memory wouldn't speed up throughput because most jobs are too small to use virtual memory effectively. Remember, as the memory management algorithms grow more complex, the CPU overhead increases and overall performance can suffer. On the other hand, some operating systems perform remarkably better with additional memory.

Role of Processor Management

Processor management was covered in Chapters 4, 5, and 6. Let's say you decide to implement a multiprogramming system to increase your processor's utilization. If so, you'd have to remember that multiprogramming requires a great deal of synchronization between the Memory Manager, the Processor Manager, and the I/O devices. The trade-off: better use of the CPU versus increased overhead, slower response time, and decreased throughput.

There are several problems to watch for, among them:

• A system could reach a saturation point if the CPU is fully utilized but is allowed to accept additional jobs—this would result in higher overhead and less time to run programs.

• Under heavy loads, the CPU time required to manage I/O queues (which under normal circumstances don't require a great deal of time) could dramatically increase the time required to run the jobs.

• With long queues forming at the channels, control units, and I/O devices, the CPU could be idle waiting for processes to finish their I/O.

Likewise, increasing the number of processors necessarily increases the overhead required to manage multiple jobs among multiple processors. But under certain circumstances, the payoff can be faster turnaround time.

Role of Device Management

Device management, covered in Chapter 7, contains several ways to improve I/O device utilization including buffering, blocking, and rescheduling I/O requests to optimize access times. But there are trade-offs: each of these options also increases CPU overhead and uses additional memory space.

Blocking reduces the number of physical I/O requests, and that's good. But it's the CPU's responsibility to block and later deblock the records, and that's overhead.

Buffering helps the CPU match the slower speed of I/O devices, and vice versa, but it requires memory space for the buffers, either dedicated space or a temporarily allocated section of main memory, and this, in turn, reduces the level of processing that can take place. For example, if each buffer requires 64K of memory and the system requires two sets of double buffers, we've dedicated 256K of memory to the buffers. The trade-off is reduced multiprogramming versus better use of I/O devices.

Rescheduling requests is a technique that can help optimize I/O times; it's a queue reordering technique. But it's also an overhead function, so the speed of both the CPU and the I/O device must be weighed against the time it would take to execute the reordering algorithm. The following example illustrates this point. Figure 12.1 lists three different CPUs with the speed for executing 1,000 instructions and four disk drives with their average access speeds.

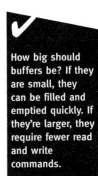

How big should buffers be? If they are small, they can be filled and emptied quickly. If they're larger, they require fewer read and write commands.

(figure 12.1)

*A system with three CPUs
and four disk drives of
different speeds.
Assuming the system
requires 1,000 instructions
to reorder I/O requests,
the advantages of
reordering vary depending
on the combination of CPU
and disk drive.*

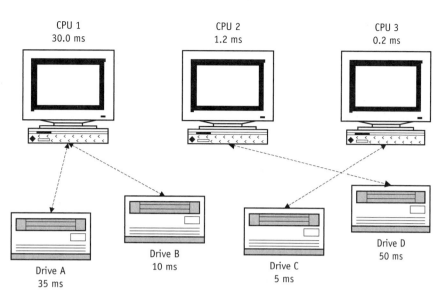

Using the data in Figure 12.1 and assuming that a typical reordering module consists of 1,000 instructions, which combinations of one CPU and one disk drive warrant a reordering module? To learn the answer, we need to compare disk access speeds before and after reordering.

For example, let's assume that a system consisting of CPU 1 and Disk Drive A has to access Track 1, Track 9, Track 1, and then Track 9, and that the arm is already located at Track 1. Without reordering, Drive A requires approximately 35 ms for each access: 35 + 35 + 35 = 105 ms, as shown in Figure 12.2.

(figure 12.2)

*Using the combination of
CPU 1 and Disk Drive A
without reordering, data
access requires 105 ms.*

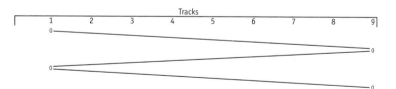

After reordering (which requires 30 ms), the arm can perform both accesses on Track 1 before traveling, in 35 ms, to Track 9 for the other two accesses, resulting in a speed nearly twice as fast: 30 + 35 = 65 ms, as shown in Figure 12.3. In this case, reordering would improve overall speed.

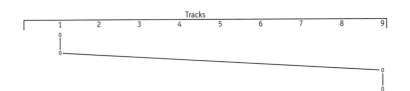

(figure 12.3)

Using CPU 1 and Disk Drive A after reordering (which takes 30 ms), data access takes 35 ms.

However, when the same situation is faced by CPU 1 and the much faster Disk Drive C, we find the disk will again begin at Track 1 and make all four accesses in 15 ms (5 + 5 + 5), but when it stops to reorder those accesses (which requires 30 ms), it takes 35 ms (30 + 5) to complete the task. Therefore, reordering requests isn't always warranted.

Remember that when the system is configured, the reordering algorithm is either always on or always off. It can't be changed by the systems operator without reconfiguration, so the initial setting, on or off, must be determined by evaluating the system based on average system performance.

Role of File Management

The discussion of file management in Chapter 8 looked at how secondary storage allocation schemes help the user organize and access the files on the system. Almost every factor discussed in that chapter can affect overall system performance.

For example, file organization is an important consideration. If a file is stored noncontiguously and has several sections residing in widely separated cylinders of a disk pack, sequentially accessing all of its records could be a time-consuming task. Such a case would suggest that the files should be compacted, also called defragmented, so each section of the file resides near the others. However, recompaction takes CPU time and makes the files unavailable to users while it's being done.

Another file management issue that could affect retrieval time is the location of a volume's directory. For instance, some systems read the directory into main memory and hold it there until the user terminates the session. If we return to our example in Figure 12.1 of the four disk drives of varying speeds, the first retrieval would take 35 ms when the system retrieves the directory for Drive A and loads it into memory. But every subsequent access would be performed at the CPU's much faster speed without the need to access the disk. Similar results would be achieved with each of the other disk drives, as shown in Table 12.1.

(table 12.1)	Disk Drive	Access Speed for First Retrieval	Subsequent Retrievals
A system with four disk drives of different speeds and a CPU speed of 1.2 ms. If the file's directory is loaded into memory, access speed affects only the initial retrieval and none of the subsequent retrievals.	A	35 ms	1.2 ms
	B	10 ms	1.2 ms
	C	5 ms	1.2 ms
	D	50 ms	1.2 ms

This poses a problem if the system crashes before any modifications have been recorded permanently in secondary storage. In such a case, the I/O time that was saved by not having to access secondary storage every time the user requested to see the directory would be negated by not having current information in the user's directory.

Similarly, the location of a volume's directory on the disk might make a significant difference in the time it takes to access it. For example, if directories are stored on the outermost track, then, on average, the disk drive arm has to travel farther to access each file than it would if the directories were kept in the center tracks.

Overall, file management is closely related to the device on which the files are stored and designers must consider both issues at the same time when evaluating or modifying computer systems. Different schemes offer different flexibility, but the trade-off for increased file flexibility is increased CPU overhead.

Role of Network Management

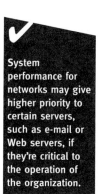

System performance for networks may give higher priority to certain servers, such as e-mail or Web servers, if they're critical to the operation of the organization.

The discussion of network management in Chapters 9 and 10 examined the impact of adding networking capability to the operating system and the overall effect on system performance. The Network Manager routinely synchronizes the load among remote processors, determines message priorities, and tries to select the most efficient communication paths over multiple data communication lines.

For example, when an application program requires data from a disk drive at a different location, the Network Manager attempts to provide this service seamlessly. When networked devices such as printers, plotters, or disk drives are required, the Network Manager has the responsibility of allocating and deallocating the required resources correctly.

In addition to the routine tasks handled by stand-alone operating systems, the Network Manager allows a network administrator to monitor the use of individual computers and shared hardware, and ensure compliance with software license agreements. The Network Manager also simplifies the process of updating data files and programs on networked computers by coordinating changes through a communications server instead of making the changes on each individual computer.

Measuring System Performance

Total system performance can be defined as the efficiency with which a computer system meets its goals—that is, how well it serves its users. However, system efficiency is not easily measured because it's affected by three major components: user programs, operating system programs, and hardware. In addition, system performance can be very subjective and difficult to quantify—how, for instance, can anyone objectively gauge ease of use? While some aspects of ease of use can be quantified—for example, time to log on—the overall concept is difficult to quantify.

Even when performance is quantifiable, such as the number of disk accesses per minute, it isn't an absolute measure but a relative one based on the interactions of the three components and the workload being handled by the system.

Measurement Tools

Most designers and analysts rely on certain measures of system performance: throughput, capacity, response time, turnaround time, resource utilization, availability, and reliability.

Throughput is a composite measure that indicates the productivity of the system as a whole; the term is often used by system managers. Throughput is usually measured under steady-state conditions and reflects quantities such as "the number of jobs processed per day" or "the number of online transactions handled per hour." Throughput can also be a measure of the volume of work handled by one unit of the computer system, an isolation that's useful when analysts are looking for bottlenecks in the system.

Bottlenecks tend to develop when resources reach their **capacity**, or maximum throughput level; the resource becomes saturated and the processes in the system aren't being passed along. Thrashing is a result of a saturated disk. Bottlenecks also occur when main memory has been overcommitted and the level of multiprogramming has reached a peak point. When this occurs, the working sets for the active jobs can't be kept in main memory, so the Memory Manager is continuously swapping pages between main memory and secondary storage. The CPU processes the jobs at a snail's pace because it's very busy flipping pages.

Throughput and capacity can be monitored by either hardware or software. Bottlenecks can be detected by monitoring the queues forming at each resource: when a queue starts to grow rapidly, this is an indication that the arrival rate is greater than, or close to, the service rate and the resource is saturated. These are called feedback loops, and we'll discuss them later in this chapter. Once a bottleneck is detected, the appropriate action can be taken to resolve the problem.

To online interactive users, **response time** is an important measure of system performance. Response time is the interval required to process a user's request: from when the user presses the key to send the message until the system indicates receipt of the message. For batch jobs, this is known as **turnaround time**—the time from the submission of the job until its output is returned to the user. Whether in an online or batch context, this measure depends on both the workload being handled by the system at the time of the request and the type of job or request being submitted. Some requests, for instance, are handled faster than others because they require fewer resources.

To be an accurate measure of the predictability of the system, measurement data showing response time and turnaround time should include not just their average values but also their variance.

Resource utilization is a measure of how much each unit is contributing to the overall operation. It's usually given as a percentage of time that a resource is actually in use. For example: Is the CPU busy 60 percent of the time? Is the line printer busy 90 percent of the time? How about each of the terminals? Or the seek mechanism on a disk? This data helps the analyst determine whether there is balance among the units of a system or whether a system is I/O-bound or CPU-bound.

Availability indicates the likelihood that a resource will be ready when a user needs it. For online users, it may mean the probability that a port is free or a terminal is available when they attempt to log on. For those already on the system, it may mean the probability that one or several specific resources, such as a plotter or a group of tape drives, will be ready when their programs make requests. Availability in its simplest form means that a unit will be operational and not out of service when a user needs it.

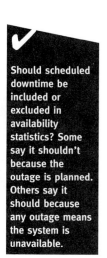

Should scheduled downtime be included or excluded in availability statistics? Some say it shouldn't because the outage is planned. Others say it should because any outage means the system is unavailable.

Availability is influenced by two factors: **mean time between failures (MTBF)** and **mean time to repair (MTTR)**. MTBF is the average time that a unit is operational before it breaks down, and MTTR is the average time needed to fix a failed unit and put it back in service. These values are calculated with simple arithmetic equations.

For example, if you buy a terminal with an MTBF of 4,000 hours (the number is given by the manufacturer), and you plan to use it for 4 hours a day for 20 days a month (or 80 hours per month), then you would expect it to fail once every 50 months (4000/80)—not bad. The MTTR is the average time it would take to have a piece of hardware repaired and would depend on several factors: the seriousness of the damage, the location of the repair shop, how quickly you need it back, how much you are willing to pay, and so on. This is usually an approximate figure. When calculating availability, make sure all your variables are in the same units (all are in hours, or all are in days, etc.).

The formula used to compute the unit's availability is:

$$\text{Availability} = \frac{\text{MTBF}}{\text{MTBF} + \text{MTTR}}$$

As indicated, availability is a ratio between the unit's MTBF and its total time (MTBF + MTTR). For our terminal, let's assume the MTTR is 2 hours; therefore:

$$\text{Availability} = \frac{4000}{4000 + 2} = 0.9995$$

So, on the average, this unit would be available 9,995 out of every 10,000 hours. In other words, you'd expect five failures out of 10,000 uses.

Reliability is similar to availability, but it measures the probability that a unit will not fail *during a given time period (t)*, and it's a function of MTBF. The formula introduced by Nickel in 1978 used to compute the unit's reliability (where *e* is the mathematical constant approximately equal to 2.71828) is:

$$Reliability(t) = e^{-(1/\text{MTBF})(t)}$$

To illustrate how this equation works, let's say you absolutely need to use the terminal for the 10 minutes before your upcoming deadline. With time expressed in hours, the unit's reliability is given by:

$$Reliability(t) = e^{-(1/4000)(10/60)}$$
$$= e^{-(1/24,000)}$$
$$= 0.9999584$$

This is the probability that it will be available (won't fail) during the critical 10-minute time period—and 0.9999584 is a very high number. Therefore, if the terminal was ready at the beginning of the transaction, it will probably remain in working order for the entire period of time.

These measures of performance can't be taken in isolation from the workload being handled by the system unless you're simply fine-tuning a specific portion of the system. Overall system performance varies from time to time, so it's important to define the actual working environment before making generalizations.

Feedback Loops

To prevent the processor from spending more time doing overhead than executing jobs, the operating system must continuously monitor the system and feed this information to the Job Scheduler. Then the Scheduler can either allow more jobs to enter the system or prevent new jobs from entering until some of the congestion has been relieved. This is called a **feedback loop** and it can be either negative or positive.

A **negative feedback loop** mechanism monitors the system and, when it becomes too congested, signals the Job Scheduler to slow down the arrival rate of the processes, as shown in Figure 12.4.

(figure 12.4)

A simple negative feedback loop. It monitors system activity and goes into action only when the system is too busy.

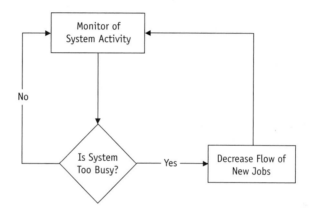

People on vacation use negative feedback loops all the time. For example, if you're looking for a gas station and the first one you find has too many cars waiting in line, you collect the data and you react negatively. Therefore, your processor suggests that you drive on to another station (assuming, of course, that you haven't procrastinated too long and are about to run out of gas).

In a computer system, a negative feedback loop monitoring I/O devices would inform the Device Manager that Printer 1 has too many jobs in its queue, causing the Device Manager to direct all newly arriving jobs to Printer 2, which isn't as busy. The negative feedback helps stabilize the system and keeps queue lengths close to expected mean values.

A **positive feedback loop** mechanism works in the opposite way: it monitors the system, and when the system becomes underutilized, the positive feedback loop causes the arrival rate to increase, as shown in Figure 12.5. Positive feedback loops are used in paged virtual memory systems, but they must be used cautiously because they're more difficult to implement than negative loops.

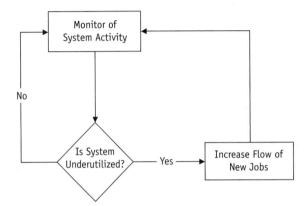

(figure 12.5)

A simple positive feedback loop. It monitors system activity and goes into action only when the system is not busy enough. System activity monitoring is critical here because the system can become unstable.

Here's how they work. The positive feedback loop monitoring the CPU informs the Job Scheduler that the CPU is underutilized, so the Scheduler allows more jobs to enter the system to give more work to the CPU. However, as more jobs enter, the amount of main memory allocated to each job decreases. If too many new jobs are allowed to enter the job stream, the result can be an increase in page faults. And this, in turn, may cause CPU utilization to deteriorate. In fact, if the operating system is poorly designed, positive feedback loops can actually put the system in an unstable mode of operation. Therefore, the monitoring mechanisms for positive feedback loops must be designed with great care.

As this example shows, an algorithm for a positive feedback loop should monitor the effect of new arrivals in two places: the Processor Manager's control of the CPU, and the Device Manager's read and write operations. That's because both areas experience the most dynamic changes, which can lead to unstable conditions. Such an algorithm should check to see whether the arrival produces the anticipated result and whether system performance is actually improved. If the arrival causes performance to deteriorate, then the monitoring algorithm could cause the operating system to adjust its allocation strategies until a stable mode of operation has been reached again.

Patch Management

Patch management is the systematic updating of the operating system and other system software. Typically, a **patch** is a piece of programming code that replaces or changes code that makes up the software. There are three primary reasons for the emphasis on software patches for sound system administration: the need for vigilant security precautions against constantly changing system threats; the need to assure system compliance with government regulations regarding privacy and financial accountability; and the need to keep systems running at peak efficiency.

Patches aren't new—they've been written and distributed since programming code was first created. However, the task of keeping computing systems patched correctly has become a challenge because of the complexity of the entire system (including the operating system, network, various platforms, and remote users), and the speed with which software vulnerabilities are exploited by worms, viruses, and other system assaults described in the last chapter.

According to the 2004 E-Crime Watch survey of security and law enforcement executives, manual and automatic patch management were among the eight technologies used most at their organizations, as shown in Table 12.2. The survey was conducted by CSO Online in cooperation with the U.S. Secret Service and the CERT Coordination Center.

(table 12.2)

Survey results show that patch management technologies were ranked by most respondents as being among the most effective tools used to detect and/or counter misuse or abuse of computer systems and networks (CSO Online, 2004).

Technologies in Use	Rank	Percentage
Firewalls	1	98.2%
Physical Security Systems	2	94.2%
Manual Patch Management	3	91.0%
Automated Patch Management	8	74.4%

Who has the overall responsibility of keeping an organization's software up-to-date? It depends on the organization. For many, overall responsibility lies with the chief information officer or chief security officer. For others, it falls on the shoulders of the network administrator or system security officer. In still others, individual users assume that role. Regardless of which individual owns this job, it is only through rigorous patching that the system's resources can reach top performance, and its information can be best protected.

Patching Fundamentals

While the installation of the patch is the most public event, there are several essential steps that take place before that happens:

1. Identify the required patch.
2. Verify the patch's source and integrity.
3. Test the patch in a safe environment.
4. Deploy the patch throughout the system.
5. Audit the system to gauge the success of the patch deployment.

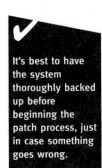

It's best to have the system thoroughly backed up before beginning the patch process, just in case something goes wrong.

Although this discussion is limited to managing operating system patches, all changes to the operating system or other critical system software must be undertaken in an environment that makes regular system backups, and tests the restoration from backups.

Patch Availability

Let's say you receive notification that a patch is available for an operating system on your network. Your first task is to identify the criticality of the patch, information that is available from the vendor. To be on the forefront of patch information, many system administrators enroll in automatic announcement services offered by government and industry groups or from software vendors.

If the patch is a critical one, it should be applied as soon as possible. Remember that with every patch announcement, system attackers are also armed with this critical information, and they will move quickly to compromise your system. If the patch is not critical in nature, you might choose to delay installation until a regular patch cycle begins. Patch cycles will be discussed later in this chapter.

Patch Integrity

Because software patches have authority to write over existing programming code, they can be especially damaging if they are not valid. Authentic patches will have a digital signature or validation tool. Before applying a patch, validate the digital signature used by the vendor to send the new software.

Patch Testing

Before installation on a live system, test the new patch on a sample system or an isolated machine to verify its worth. If a non-networked machine is not available, test the patch on a development system instead of the operational system.

First, test to see if the system restarts after the patch is installed. Then, check to see if the patched software performs its assigned tasks—whether it's warding off intruders or improving system performance. While it's often not feasible to test the patch on a duplicate system, the tested system should resemble the complexity of the target network as closely as possible.

This is also the time to make detailed plans for what you'll do if something goes terribly wrong during installation. Test your contingency plans to uninstall the patch and recover the old software should it become necessary to do so.

Patch Deployment

On a single-user computer, patch deployment is a simple task—install the software and restart the computer. However, on a multiplatform system with hundreds or thousands of users, the task becomes exceptionally complicated.

To assure success, maintain an accurate inventory of all hardware and software on those computers that need the patch. On a large network, this information can be gleaned from network mapping software that surveys the network and takes a detailed inventory of the system. This, in turn, assumes that all system hardware is connected to the network.

Finally, the deployment may be launched in stages so the help desk can cope with telephone calls. Often, because it's impossible to use the system during the patching process, it is scheduled for times when system use will be low, such as evenings or weekends.

Audit the Finished System

Before announcing the deployment's success, you will need to confirm that the resulting system meets your expectations by taking steps such as:

- verifying that all computers are patched correctly and perform fundamental tasks as expected
- verifying that no users had unexpected or unauthorized versions of software that may not accept the patch
- verifying that no users are left out of the deployment

The process should include documentation of the changes made to the system and the success or failure of each stage of the process. Keep a log of all system changes for future reference. Finally, get feedback from the users to verify the deployment's success.

Software Options

Patches can be installed manually, one at a time, or via software that's written to perform the task automatically. Organizations that choose software can decide to build their own deployment software or buy ready-made software to perform the task for them. Deployment software falls into two groups: those programs that require an agent (called agent-based software), and those that do not (agentless software).

If the deployment software uses an agent, which is software that assists in patch installation, then the agent must be installed on every target computer system before patches can be deployed. On a very large or dynamic system, this can be a daunting task. Therefore, for administrators of large, complex networks, agentless software may offer some time-saving efficiencies.

Timing the Patch Cycle

While critical system patches must be applied immediately, less-critical patches can be scheduled at the convenience of the systems group. These patch cycles can be based on calendar events or vendor events. For example, routine patches can be applied monthly or quarterly, or they can be timed to coincide with a vendor's **service pack** release. The advantage of having routine patch cycles is that they allow for thorough review of the patch and testing cycles before deployment.

System Monitoring

Several techniques for measuring the performance of a working system have been developed as computer systems have evolved, which can be implemented using either hardware or software components. Hardware monitors are more expensive but they have the advantage of having a minimum impact on the system because they're outside of it and attached electronically. They include hard-wired counters, clocks, and comparative elements.

> **Service pack is a term used by some vendors for operating system patches.**

Software monitors are relatively inexpensive; but because they become part of the system, they can distort the results of the analysis. After all, the software must use the resources it's trying to monitor. In addition, software tools must be developed for each specific system, so it's difficult to move them from system to system.

In early systems, performance was measured simply by timing the processing of specific instructions. The system analysts might have calculated the number of times an ADD instruction could be done in one second. Or they might have measured the processing time of a typical set of instructions (typical in the sense that they would represent the instructions common to the system). These measurements monitored only the CPU speed because in those days the CPU was the most important resource, so the remainder of the system was ignored.

Today, system measurements must include the other hardware units as well as the operating system, compilers, and other system software. Measurements are made in a variety of ways. Some are made using real programs, usually production programs that are used extensively by the users of the system, which are run with different configurations of CPUs, operating systems, and other components. The results are called **benchmarks** and are useful when comparing systems that have gone through extensive changes. Benchmarks are often used by vendors to demonstrate to prospective clients the specific advantages of a new CPU, operating system, compiler, or piece of hardware. A sample benchmark table is shown in Table 12.3.

Remember that benchmark results are highly dependent upon the system's workload, the system's design and implementation, as well as the specific requirements of the applications loaded on the system. Performance data is usually obtained in a rigorously controlled environment so results will probably differ in real-life operation. Still, benchmarks offer valuable comparison data—a place to begin a system evaluation.

If it's not advisable or possible to experiment with the system itself, a simulation model can be used to measure performance. This is typically the case when new hardware is being developed. A simulation model is a computerized abstraction of what is represented in reality. The amount of detail built into the model is dictated by time and money—the time needed to develop the model and the cost of running it.

Designers of simulation models must be careful to avoid the extremes of too much detail, which becomes too expensive to run, or of too little detail, which doesn't produce enough useful information. If you'd like to write a program that's an example of a simulation model, see the first programming exercise in Chapter 2.

Top 10 TPC-C by Performance (as of 22 Sep-2009)

Rank	Company	System	tpmC	Price/tpmC	System Availability	Database	Operating System	TP Monitor	Date Submitted	Cluster
1	IBM	IBM Power 595 Server Model 9119-FHA	6,085,166	2.81 USD	12/10/08	IBM DB2 9.5	IBM AIX 5L V5.3	Microsoft COM+	06/10/08	N
***	Bull	Bull Escala PL6460R	6,085,166	2.81 USD	12/15/08	IBM DB2 9.5	IBM AIX 5L V5.3	Microsoft COM+	06/15/08	N
2	HP	HP Integrity Superdome-Itanium2/ 1.6GHz/ 24MB iL3	4,092,799	2.93 USD	08/06/07	Oracle Database 10g R2 Enterprise Edt w/Partitioning	HP-UX 11i v3	BEA Tuxedo 8.0	02/27/07	N
3	IBM	IBM System p5 595	4,033,378	2.97 USD	01/22/07	IBM DB2 9	IBM AIX 5L V5.3	Microsoft COM+	01/22/07	N
4	IBM	IBM eServer p5 595	3,210,540	5.07 USD	05/14/05	IBM DB2 UDB 8.2	IBM AIX 5L V5.3	Microsoft COM+	11/18/04	N
5	Fujitsu	PRIMEQUEST 580A 32p/64c	2,382,032	3.76 USD	12/04/08	Oracle Database 10g R2 Enterprise Edt w/Partitioning	Red Hat Enterprise Linux 4 AS	BEA Tuxedo 8.1	12/04/08	N
6	Fujitsu	PRIMEQUEST 580 32p/64c	2,196,268	4.70 USD	04/30/08	Oracle 10g Enterprise Ed R2 w/ Partitioning	Red Hat Enterprise Linux 4 AS	BEA Tuxedo 8.1	10/30/07	N
7	IBM	IBM System p 570	1,616,162	3.54 USD	11/21/07	IBM DB2 Enterprise 9	IBM AIX 5L V5.3	Microsoft COM+	05/21/07	N
***	Bull	Bull Escala PL1660R	1,616,162	3.54 USD	12/16/07	IBM DB2 9.1	IBM AIX 5L V5.3	Microsoft COM+	12/17/07	N
8	IBM	IBM eServer p5 595	1,601,784	5.05 USD	04/20/05	Oracle Database 10g Enterprise Edition	IBM AIX 5L V5.3	Microsoft COM+	04/20/05	N
9	Fujitsu	PRIMEQUEST 540A 16p/32c	1,354,086	3.25 USD	11/22/08	Oracle Database 10g release2 Enterprise Edt	Red Hat Enterprise Linux 4 AS	BEA Tuxedo 8.1	11/22/08	N
10	NEC	NEC Express5800/ 1320Xf (16p/32c)	1,245,516	4.57 USD	04/30/08	Oracle Database 10g R2 Enterprise Edt w/Partitioning	Red Hat Enterprise Linux 4 AS	BEA Tuxedo 8.1	01/21/08	N

*** - Duplicate results are shown with an asterisk (*) in the *Rank* column.
Note 1: The TPC believes it is not valid to compare prices or price/performance of results in different currencies.

(table 12.3)

Benchmarking results published by the Transaction Processing Performance Council (TPC) on its Web site. This report includes transactions per minute (tpmC) as well as normalized price/performance ($/tpmC). This is only a sample report. For recent benchmark results and details of the testing conditions used to generate this report, please see the TPC Web site (www.tpc.org). Reprinted with permission of the Transaction Processing Performance Council.

Accounting

The accounting function of the operating system might seem a mundane subject, but it's not; it pays the bills and keeps the system financially operable. From a practical standpoint, it might be one of the most important elements of the system.

Most computer system resources are paid for by the users. In the simplest case, that of a single user, it's easy to calculate the cost of the system. But in a multiuser environment, computer costs are usually distributed among users based on how much each one uses the system's resources. To do this distribution, the operating system must be able to set up user accounts, assign passwords, identify which resources are available to each user, and define quotas for available resources, such as disk space or maximum CPU time allowed per job. At a university, for example, students are sometimes given quotas that include maximum pages per job, maximum logon time, and maximum number of jobs during a given period of time. To calculate the cost of the whole system, the accounting program must collect information on each active user.

Pricing policies vary from system to system. Typical measurements include some or all of the following:

- *Total amount of time* spent between job submission and completion. In interactive environments this is the time from logon to logoff, also known as connect time.
- *CPU time* is the time spent by the processor executing the job.
- *Main memory usage* is represented in units of time, bytes of storage, or bytes of storage multiplied by units of time—it all depends on the configuration of the operating system. For example, a job that requires 200K for 4 seconds followed by 120K for 2 seconds could be billed for 6 seconds of main memory usage, or 320K of memory usage or a combination of K/second of memory usage computed as follows:

$$[(200 * 4) + (120 * 2)] = 1040\text{K/second of memory usage}$$

- *Secondary storage used during program execution*, like main memory use, can be given in units of time or space or both.
- *Secondary storage used during the billing period* is usually given in terms of the number of disk tracks allocated.
- *Use of system software* includes utility packages, compilers, and/or databases.
- *Number of I/O operations* is usually grouped by device class: line printer, terminal, and disks.
- *Time spent waiting for I/O completion.*
- *Number of input records read*, usually grouped by type of input device.
- *Number of output records printed*, usually grouped by type of output device.
- *Number of page faults* is reported in paging systems.

Pricing policies are sometimes used as a way to achieve specific operational goals. By varying the price of system services, users can be convinced to distribute their workload to the system manager's advantage. For instance, by offering reduced rates during off-hours, some users might be persuaded to run long jobs in batch mode inexpensively overnight instead of interactively during peak hours. Pricing incentives can also be used to encourage users to access more plentiful and cheap resources rather than those that are scarce and expensive. For example, by putting a high price on printer output, users might be encouraged to order a minimum of printouts.

Should the system give each user billing information at the end of each job or at the end of each online session? The answer depends on the environment. Some systems only give information on resource usage. Other systems also calculate the price of the most costly items, such as CPU utilization, disk storage use, and supplies (i.e., paper used on the printer) at the end of every job. This gives the user an up-to-date report of expenses and, if appropriate, calculates how much is left in the user's account. Some universities use this technique to warn paying students of depleted resources.

The advantage of maintaining billing records online is that the status of each user can be checked before the user's job is allowed to enter the READY queue.

The disadvantage is overhead. When billing records are kept online and an accounting program is kept active, memory space is used and CPU processing is increased. One compromise is to defer the accounting program until off-hours, when the system is lightly loaded.

Conclusion

The operating system is more than the sum of its parts—it's the orchestrated cooperation of every piece of hardware and every piece of software. As we've shown, when one part of the system is favored, it's often at the expense of the others. So if a trade-off must be made, the system's managers must make sure they're using the appropriate measurement tools and techniques to verify the effectiveness of the system before and after modification, and then evaluate the degree of improvement.

With this chapter we conclude Part One of this book and we've seen how operating systems are alike. In Part Two we look at actual operating systems and show how they're different—and how each manages the components common to all operating systems. In other words, we see how close reality comes to the concepts learned so far.

Key Terms

availability: a resource measurement tool that indicates the likelihood that the resource will be ready when a user needs it. It's influenced by mean time between failures and mean time to repair.

benchmarks: a measurement tool used to objectively measure and evaluate a system's performance by running a set of jobs representative of the work normally done by a computer system.

capacity: the maximum throughput level of any one of the system's components.

feedback loop: a mechanism to monitor the system's resource utilization so adjustments can be made.

mean time between failures (MTBF): a resource measurement tool; the average time that a unit is operational before it breaks down.

mean time to repair (MTTR): a resource measurement tool; the average time needed to fix a failed unit and put it back in service.

negative feedback loop: a mechanism to monitor the system's resources and, when it becomes too congested, to signal the appropriate manager to slow down the arrival rate of the processes.

patch: executable software that repairs errors or omissions in another program or piece of software.

patch management: the timely installation of software patches to make repairs and keep the operating system software current.

positive feedback loop: a mechanism used to monitor the system. When the system becomes underutilized, the feedback causes the arrival rate to increase.

reliability: a standard that measures the probability that a unit will not fail during a given time period. It's a function of mean time between failures.

resource utilization: a measure of how much each unit is contributing to the overall operation of the system.

response time: a measure of an interactive system's efficiency that tracks the speed with which the system will respond to a user's command.

service pack: a term used by some vendors to describe an update to customer software to repair existing problems and/or deliver enhancements.

throughput: a composite measure of a system's efficiency that counts the number of jobs served in a given unit of time.

turnaround time: a measure of a system's efficiency that tracks the time required to execute a job and return output to the user.

Interesting Searches

- Performance Monitoring
- System Benchmarks
- Critical OS Patches
- MTBF and Reliability
- Computer System Auditing
- Memory Leaks

Exercises

Research Topics

A. Visit the Web site of a major operating system vendor and identify the patches that were issued in the last 12 months. For each patch, find its criticality and size. Then, as if you were assigned the task of installing these patches, decide the timing for their installation. How many would you install immediately and which ones could wait for the next patch cycle (assuming a four-per-year cycle)? Cite your sources.

B. Research the current literature to find availability statistics for a server farm or other collection of servers that supports a Web site. List the primary operating systems used and the calculated availability of the system as a whole. Mention whether planned outages are included (or not) in the availability statistics. Cite your sources.

Exercises

1. Describe how a bank manager might use a positive feedback loop to direct waiting customers to five loan officers, being careful to minimize waiting time for customers and maximize the speed of loan processing. Include a description of how you would monitor the system and measure its success.

2. Describe how you would use a negative feedback loop to manage your bank balance. Describe how you would do so with a positive feedback loop. Explain which you would prefer and why.

3. Remembering that there's a trade-off between memory use and CPU overhead, give an example where increasing the size of virtual memory will improve job throughput. Then give an example where doing so will cause throughput to suffer.

4. Imagine that you are managing a university system that becomes CPU-bound at the conclusion of each school semester. What effect on throughput would you expect if you were allowed to double the number of processors? If you could make one more change to the system, what would it be?

5. Imagine that you are managing the system for a consulting company that becomes I/O-bound at the end of each fiscal year. What effect on throughput

would you expect if you were allowed to double the number of processors? If you could make one more change to the system, what would it be?

6. Using the information given in Figure 12.1, calculate I/O access speed using CPU 1 and each of the four disk drives as they evaluate the following track requests in this order: 0, 31, 20, 15, 20, 31, 15. Then, in each case, calculate the access speeds after the track requests were reordered and rank the four disk drives before and after reordering.

7. Describe how you would convince a coworker to better manage a personal computer by performing regular backups and keep the system patches current.

8. Compare and contrast availability and reliability. In your opinion, which is more important to a system manager? Substantiate your answer.

9. Calculate the availability of a server with an MTBF of 80 hours and an MTTR of 3 days (72 hours).

10. Calculate the reliability of a hard disk drive with an MTBF of 1,050 hours during the last 40 hours of this month. Assume e = 2.71828 and use the formula:

$$Reliability(t) = e{-}(1/MTBF)(t)$$

Advanced Exercises

11. Calculate the availability of a hard disk drive with an MTBF of 1,050 hours and an MTTR of 8 hours.

12. Calculate the availability of a server with an MTBF of 28 weeks and an MTTR of 504 hours.

13. In this chapter, we described the trade-offs among all the managers in the operating system. Study a system to which you have access and, assuming you have sufficient funds to upgrade only one component for the system, explain which component you would choose to upgrade to improve overall system performance, and explain why.

14. Perform a software inventory of your computer system to identify all applications resident on the computer. If you have more than a dozen applications, choose 12 of them and check each for patches that are available for your software. For each vendor, identify how many patches are available for your software, the number of critical patches, and what patch cycle you would recommend for that vendor's patches: annual, quarterly, monthly, or weekly updates.

15. Perform an inventory of your computer system (similar to the one shown in Figure 12.6) to discover how many processes are active when it is connected to the Internet. What is the total number of processes currently running? For which processes can you identify the application? How many processes are linked to applications that you cannot identify? Discuss how the unidentifiable processes pose a challenge regarding effective system administration and what you would do to address this challenge.

Part Two

Operating Systems in Practice

Thus far in this text, we've explored how operating system software works in theory—the roles of the Memory Manager, Processor Manager, Device Manager, File Manager, and Network Manager. To do so, we've underplayed the intricate choreography required by all managers as they work together to accomplish even the simplest tasks. We've also described operating systems in their most basic form—operating systems running relatively simple hardware configurations.

In the second part of this book, we explore operating systems in practice by becoming acquainted with a few of the most popular operating systems. The following chapters each describe one operating system; the chapters are presented in the order in which the software was released. The four operating systems described here are all historically significant—three continue to be widely adopted.

For each chapter in Part Two, our discourse includes the history of the operating system's development; its design goals; the unique properties of its submanagers; and its user interface, the portion of the operating system that interacts with users. The user interface commands and formats vary from system to system, as shown in the examples presented in this section. The user interface is probably the most unique component of an operating system, which is why it hasn't been presented until now.

The history of an operating system's development often illustrates its intrinsic strengths and weaknesses. For instance, a system that evolved from a rudimentary single-user system to a multifunctional multiuser system might perform simple tasks well but struggle when trying to meet the needs of a large computing environment. On the other hand, an elegant mainframe system that was later scaled down might excel at complex tasks but prove overdesigned and cumbersome when executing tasks in the smaller environment.

Our discussion in this part cannot serve as an in-depth evaluation of any operating system, but it does present each system in a standard format to help you compare their relative strengths and weaknesses. To begin, Table 1 demonstrates a few of the significant events in operating system software during the past 50 years.

Operating System	Approximate Date	Significance
OS/PCP (IBM)	1964	Primary Control Program (PCP). Designed by IBM to run on the IBM 360 computer; it was a batch, single-task operating system.
OS/MVT (IBM)	1967	Multiprogramming with a variable number of tasks (MVT). Descendant of IBM's PCP; introduced spooling; used dynamic memory management.
UNIX	1969	Ken Thompson wrote first version of UNIX.
UNIX (AT&T)	1971	Based on MULTICS; introduced shell concept, written in assembly language to run on DEC's PDP-11 computer.
VM (IBM)	1973	IBM introduced the virtual machine (VM) concept. Built for the IBM 370 computer.
MVS (IBM)	1974	Multiple virtual storage system (MVS) for IBM computers.
CP/M	1975	Control Program/Microcomputer (CP/M). First operating system for small computers (PCs) sold commercially.
VMS (DEC)	1978	Written specifically for the VAX-11 computer to take best advantage of its architecture.
MS-DOS (Microsoft)	1981	First operating system for the IBM PC family of computers. Version 1 was CP/M compatible and supported only one directory.
UNIX System III (AT&T)	1981	First version of UNIX available for use on a mainframe.
Mac OS (Apple)	1984	The first widely distributed operating system with a graphical user interface. Also introduced was the mouse for home computers.
Windows 3.0 (Microsoft)	1990	First usable version of a Windows graphical user interface for the PC. Required MS-DOS operating system.
Linux	1991	Linus Torvalds released the Linux kernel.
OpenVMS Alpha (DEC)	1992	Introduced 64-bit addressing, multiple compilers, and networks for the Alpha system.
Novell UnixWare	1993	Novell's version of UNIX System V release 4, designed to work with NetWare.
FreeBSD 2 (UNIX) (freeBSD.org)	1994	A full 32-bit operating system for Intel chips: 386, 486, and Pentium class.

(table 1)

Selected operating systems and selected releases demonstrating the evolution of operating systems software.

Operating System	Approximate Date	Significance
Solaris (Sun Microsystems)	1994	Sun's version of UNIX designed to run on Sun workstations, derived from AT&T's UNIX System V, Release 4.
Linux 1.0 (Red Hat)	1995	First non-beta release of Linux by Red Hat.
Windows 95 (Microsoft)	1995	For PC users. The first true Windows operating system. Technically, Windows 95 was not related to Windows NT, which had networking capabilities.
Linux 3.0.3 (Red Hat)	1996	The first approximately concurrent multi-architecture release; it supported the Digital Alpha platform.
OS/390, ver 2 (IBM)	1997	Scalable transaction-processing capability, batch workload scheduler, firewall security, enhanced e-commerce capability.
OpenVMS Alpha, version 7 (DEC)	1997	Designed for very large memory applications on the Alpha system.
Windows 98	1998	For PC users. More extended hardware support and fully 32-bit. Not directly related to Windows NT.
Windows 2000	1999	For networks. The kernel contained 45 million lines of code, compared to 15 million for Windows NT. Not directly related to Windows 95 or Windows 98.
FreeBSD 4 (freeBSD.org)	2000	Improved file management system and security features.
Windows XP (Microsoft)	2001	**Home** version was successor to Windows 95 and Windows 98 for individual users. **Pro** version available in 32-bit and 64-bit versions.
Mac OS X 10.0 (Apple)	2001	Combined a UNIX-based core with Macintosh graphics and a new GUI.
Fedora Core 1	2003	Linux product based on Red Hat Linux 9; created by the Fedora Project in cooperation with Red Hat, Inc.
FreeBSD 6.0	2005	Multithreaded file system, expanded support for wireless technology.
FreeBSD 6.2	2007	Stability improvement, GUI updates.
Windows Vista (Microsoft)	2007	New security and new performance features.
Fedora 7	2007	New name. Allowed customization. Widened accessibility by contributors in Fedora community.

Operating System	Approximate Date	Significance
Mac OS X 10.5 (Apple)	2007	UNIX-based system allowing 64-bit processing with compatibility for existing 32-bit Mac OS X applications and drivers.
RHEL 5 (Red Hat)	2007	Improved performance, security, and flexibility, with storage virtualization.
FreeBSD 6.4	2008	Allows linear scalability to over eight CPU cores. Enhanced wireless support.
Fedora 11	2009	Fast boot-up (20 sec.) from power on to fully operational system. Can handle files up to 16TB.
Mac OS X 10.6 Server (Apple)	2009	The 64-bit kernel increases the total number of simultaneous system processes, threads, and network connections for the server to use. Supports the standard LP64 data model, so that code written for other 64-bit UNIX-based systems can be ported to Mac OS X Server.
Windows 7 (Microsoft)	2009	A 64-bit operating system with usability and networking improvements over Windows Vista.

Chapter 13 | UNIX Operating System

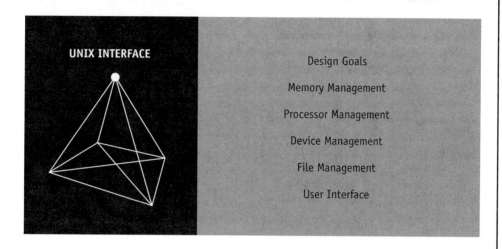

UNIX INTERFACE

Design Goals

Memory Management

Processor Management

Device Management

File Management

User Interface

"UNIX is simple. It just takes a genius to understand its simplicity."

—Dennis Ritchie

Learning Objectives

After completing this chapter, you should be able to describe:

- The goals of UNIX designers
- The significance of using files to manipulate devices
- The strengths and weaknesses of having competing versions of UNIX
- The advantages of command-driven user interfaces
- The roles of the Memory, Processor, Device, and File Managers in UNIX

Unlike many operating systems, UNIX isn't limited to specific computers using a particular microprocessor as a CPU. There are many versions of UNIX and they run on all sizes of computers using a wide range of microprocessors. In addition, current versions of many other operating systems have been revised to include the capability to run UNIX applications and connect smoothly with UNIX networks.

Linux (discussed in Chapter 16) and UNIX are different operating systems but they strongly resemble each other in many ways. And while UNIX was written several decades earlier, Linux and UNIX now compete as peers in almost every market. Since 2001 when Apple introduced the Macintosh OS X operating system, based on the FreeBSD version of UNIX, the company has advertised that its operating system is based on a proven and powerful UNIX foundation (Apple, 2009). The continuing competition and cooperation between these two operating systems are likely to play out in the marketplace for years to come.

Overview

UNIX (authored by Ken Thompson) has three major advantages: it is portable from large systems to small systems, it has very powerful utilities, and it provides a device independence to application programs. Its portability is attributed to the fact that most of it is written in a high-level language, C (authored by Dennis Ritchie), instead of assembly language. The utilities are brief, single-operation commands that can be combined in a single command line to achieve almost any desired result—a feature that many programmers find endearing. And it can be configured to operate virtually any type of device.

Throughout our discussion of UNIX we'll describe AT&T's version unless otherwise specified. Note: UNIX is case sensitive and strongly oriented toward lowercase characters, which are faster and easier to type. Therefore, throughout this chapter all filenames and commands are shown in lowercase.

History

The evolution of UNIX, summarized in Table 13.1, starts with a research project that began in 1965 as a joint venture between Bell Laboratories (the research and development group of AT&T), General Electric, and MIT (Massachusetts Institute of Technology).

When Bell Laboratories withdrew from the project in 1969, AT&T management decided not to undertake the development of any more operating systems—but that didn't stop two young veterans of the project, Ken Thompson and Dennis Ritchie. Some people say they needed a new operating system to support their favorite computer game. Regardless of their reasons for developing it, UNIX grew to become one of the most widely used operating systems in history.

(table 13.1)

The historical roots of UNIX and some of its features and modifications. For current information about the history of UNIX, see www.theopengroup.org.

✔

Berkeley UNIX isn't included in Table 13.1; it was originally developed from Version 7, although some features from the Berkeley version were later integrated into System V, such as the fast file system, demand paged memory management, networking, C shell, Vi, and others.

Year	Release	Features
1969	—	Ken Thompson wrote first version of UNIX
1971	UNIX V1	Based on MULTICS; introduced shell concept, written in assembly language
1975	UNIX V6	First version to become widely available to industry and academia
1980	UNIX System III	First version used in 16-bit microcomputers
1984	UNIX System V Release 2	Added features from Berkeley version: shared memory, more commands, vi editor, termcap database, flex filenames
1991	UNIX System V Release 4	Combined features from BSD, SunOS, and Xenix
1991	Solaris 1.0	Sun's version designed to run on Sun workstations, derived from AT&T's UNIX System V, Release 4
1994	Single UNIX Specification 1	Separates the UNIX trademark from actual code stream, opening the door to standardization
1997	Single UNIX Specification 2	Adds support for real-time processing, threads, and 64-bit processors
2000	FreeBSD 4	Improved file management system and security features
2001	Single UNIX Specification 3	Unites IEEE POSIX and industry efforts to standardize
2001	Mac OS X	Apple combined a UNIX-based core with Macintosh graphics and GUI
2003	ISO/IEC 9945	International standard approved for the core volumes of Single UNIX Specification Version 3
2005	FreeBSD 6.0	Multithreaded file system, expanded support for wireless technology
2007	Mac OS X 10.5	Allows 64-bit processing with compatibility for existing 32-bit Mac OS X applications and drivers
2008	FreeBSD 6.4	Allows linear scalability to over eight CPU cores; enhanced wireless support
2009	Mac OS X 10.6 Server	The 64-bit kernel increases the total number of simultaneous system processes, threads, and network connections for the server to use; supports the standard LP64 data model, so that code written for other 64-bit UNIX-based systems can be ported to Mac OS X Server

The Evolution of UNIX

Thompson and Ritchie originally wrote UNIX in assembly language for a Digital Equipment Corporation PDP-7 computer. It was named "UNIX" by a colleague, Brian Kernighan, as a play on words from MULTICS.

The first official version, presented in 1971 by Thompson and Ritchie, was designed to "do one thing well" and run on a popular DEC minicomputer. Before long, UNIX became known as a formidable operating system. For Version 3, Ritchie took the innovative step of developing a new programming language, called C, and wrote a compiler for the C language, which made it easier and faster for system designers to write code.

As UNIX grew in fame and popularity (see Figure 13.1 for an example), AT&T found itself in a difficult situation. At the time it was forbidden by U.S. federal government antitrust regulations to sell software—but it could, for a nominal fee, make the operating system available first to universities and later to independent developers who, in turn, transformed it into a commercial product. Between 1973 and 1975, several improved versions were developed—the most popular version was developed at the University of California at Berkeley and it became known as BSD. Its popularity in universities created a demand for it in business and industry.

(figure 13.1)

UNIX is a registered trademark of The Open Group. Graphic supplied courtesy of The Open Group.

AT&T entered the computer industry by offering a line of personal computers powered by UNIX System V—its version of UNIX with additional features from the Berkeley version. At that time, AT&T tried to promote its version of UNIX as the standard version, but by then UNIX had already been adopted and adapted by too many designers for too many computers. By 1990 there were about two dozen versions of UNIX, among them AT&T's UNIX System V; A/UX (UNIX System V for the Macintosh II); Ultrix (UNIX for DEC's VAX system); Microsoft's Xenix (a UNIX-based operating system for microcomputers using Intel processors); and the University of California at Berkeley's UNIX Versions 4.1 bsd, 4.2 bsd, and 4.3 bsd. Berkeley UNIX is an expanded version of AT&T's Version 7. It was designed originally to run on VAX computers and became quite popular in many academic circles. Although it was a UNIX derivative, in some areas, such as file system structure and network software, it was very different from AT&T's System V Release 1.

In 1991, IBM and Hewlett-Packard were among the companies that established The Open Group, which owns the trademark to the name UNIX, and created a standard version of the operating system.

By 1993 Berkeley released 4.4 bsd based on AT&T's UNIX, requiring customers to obtain licenses from AT&T to use it. Shortly thereafter, Novell acquired UNIX from AT&T and released its own version called UnixWare designed to interact with Novell's NetWare system.

The original "do one thing well" position of the early commands has been modified in current releases, and recent commands offer many options and controls. This factor has pros and cons—although some commands may be more difficult to use, they can be adapted to new situations with relative ease. In essence, the key features of the early systems, such as pipelines, have been preserved, while the potential of the commands has increased to meet new needs.

UNIX offers full support for local area networks and complies with international operating system standards. In addition, system security has been greatly improved and meets many of the U.S. government security requirements. Most UNIX systems feature a graphical user interface designed to give UNIX systems a standard look.

To resolve the issue of multiple standards, a problem that has plagued UNIX from its beginnings, the industry continues to try to standardize to improve portability of programs from one system to another. The release of ISO/IEC 9945:2003 was a big step in that direction, with more progress expected in the years to come.

✔

Some of the UNIX commands seem cryptic to users unfamiliar with the operating system. For example, *grep* is the command to find a specified string of characters in a file.

Design Goals

From the beginning, Thompson and Ritchie envisioned UNIX as an operating system created by programmers for programmers. It was to be fast, flexible, and easy to use.

The immediate goals were twofold: to develop an operating system that would support software development, and to keep its algorithms as simple as possible (without becoming rudimentary). To achieve their first goal, they included utilities in the operating system for which programmers at the time needed to write customized code. Each utility was designed for simplicity—to perform only one function but to perform it very well. These utilities were designed to be used in combination with each other so that programmers could select and combine any appropriate utilities that might be needed to carry out specific jobs. This concept of small manageable sections of code was a perfect fit with the second goal: to keep the operating system simple. To do this, Thompson and Ritchie selected the algorithms based on simplicity instead of speed or sophistication. As a result, UNIX can be mastered by experienced programmers in a matter of weeks.

The designers' long-term goal was to make the operating system, and any application software developed for it, portable from one computer to another. The obvious advantage of portability is that it reduces conversion costs and doesn't cause application packages to become obsolete with every change in hardware. This goal was finally achieved with UNIX Version 4 because it was **device independent**—an innovation at the time.

Numerous versions of UNIX meet the additional design element of conforming to the specifications for **Portable Operating System Interface for Computer Environments (POSIX)** (a registered trademark of the IEEE). POSIX is a family of IEEE standards that define a portable operating system interface to enhance the portability of programs from one operating system to another.

With POSIX, UNIX has developed into a powerful and flexible operating system for multiuser environments or single-user multiprogramming systems.

Memory Management

For multiprogramming systems, most UNIX operating systems use either swapping or demand paging (or both) memory management techniques. The best choice depends on the kind of applications that will run on the system: if most jobs are small then swapping could be the best choice, but if the system will be running many large jobs then demand paging is best.

Swapping requires that the entire program be in main memory before it can be executed, and this imposes a size restriction on programs. For example, if there is 256MB of memory and the operating system takes up half of it (125MB), then the size of the programs must be less than the remaining 125MB. Swapping uses a round robin policy—when a job's time slice is up, or when it generates an I/O interrupt, the entire job is swapped out to secondary storage to make room for other jobs waiting in the READY queue. That's fine when there are relatively few processes in the system, but when traffic is heavy this swapping back and forth can slow down the system.

Demand paging requires more complicated hardware configurations; it increases the system overhead and under heavy loads might lead to thrashing. But it has the advantage of implementing the concept of virtual memory.

Figure 13.2 shows the typical internal memory layout for a single user-memory part image. An image is an abstract concept that can be defined as a computer execution environment composed of a user-memory part (all of which is depicted in Figure 13.2), general register values, status of open files, and current **directory**. This image must remain in memory during execution of a process.

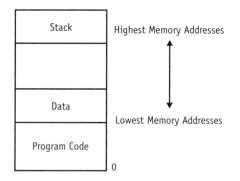

In Figure 13.2, the segment called program code is the sharable portion of the program. Because this code can be physically shared by several processes, it must be written in **reentrant code**. This means that the code is protected so that its instructions aren't modified in any way during its normal execution. In addition, all data references are made without the use of absolute physical addresses.

The Memory Manager gives the program code special treatment. Because several processes will be sharing it, the space allocated to the program code can't be released until all of the processes using it have completed their execution. UNIX uses a text table to keep track of which processes are using which program code, and the memory isn't released until the program code is no longer needed. The text table is explained in more detail in the next section on Processor Management.

The data segment shown in Figure 13.2 starts after the program code and grows toward higher memory locations as needed by the program. The stack segment starts at the highest memory address and grows downward as subroutine calls and interrupts add information to it. A stack is a section of main memory where process information is saved when a process is interrupted, or for temporary storage. The data and stack are nonsharable sections of memory, so when the original program terminates the memory, space is released.

The UNIX **kernel**, which permanently resides in memory, is the part of the operating system that implements the "system calls" to set up the memory boundaries so several processes can coexist in memory at the same time. The processes also use system calls to interact with the File Manager and to request I/O services.

The kernel is the set of programs that implements the most primitive of that system's functions, and it's the only part of the operating system to permanently reside in memory. The remaining sections of the operating system are handled in the same way as any large program. That is, pages of the operating system are brought into memory on demand, only when they're needed, and their memory space is released as other pages are called. UNIX uses the least recently used (LRU) page replacement algorithm.

Although we've directed this discussion to large multiuser computer systems, UNIX uses the same memory management concepts for networked computers and single-user systems. For example, a single computer with a UNIX operating system, using a demand paging scheme, can support multiple users in a true multitasking environment.

With the 64-bit addressing architecture in modern UNIX versions, including the Mac OS X, the operating system can make much faster system calls, which, in turn, improves the performance of I/O applications and network response. The 64-bit addressing scheme is one shared by most operating systems as of this writing.

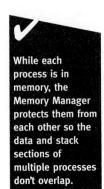

While each process is in memory, the Memory Manager protects them from each other so the data and stack sections of multiple processes don't overlap.

Process Management

The Processor Manager of a UNIX system kernel handles the allocation of the CPU, process scheduling, and the satisfaction of process requests. To perform these tasks, the kernel maintains several important tables to coordinate the execution of processes and the allocation of devices.

Using a predefined policy, the Process Scheduler selects a process from the READY queue and begins its execution for a given time slice. Remember, as we discussed in Chapter 4, the processes in a time-sharing environment can be in any of five states: HOLD, READY, WAITING, RUNNING, or FINISHED.

The process scheduling algorithm picks the process with the highest priority to be run first. Since one of the values used to compute the priority is accumulated CPU time, any processes that have used a lot of CPU time will get a lower priority than those that have not. The system updates the compute-to-total-time ratio for each job every second. This ratio divides the amount of CPU time that a process has used up by the total time the same process has spent in the system. A result close to 1 would indicate that the process is CPU-bound. If several processes have the same computed priority, they're handled round-robin (low-priority processes are preempted by high-priority processes). Interactive processes typically have a low compute-to-total-time ratio, so interactive response is maintained without any special policies.

The overall effect of this negative feedback is that the system balances **I/O-bound** jobs with **CPU-bound** jobs to keep the processor busy and to minimize the overhead for waiting processes.

When the Processor Manager is deciding which process from the READY queue will be loaded into memory to be run first, it chooses the process with the longest time spent on the secondary storage.

When the Processor Manager is deciding which process (currently in memory and waiting or ready to be run) will be moved out temporarily to make room for a new arrival, it chooses the process that's either waiting for disk I/O or that's currently idle. If there are several processes to choose from, the one that has been in memory the longest is moved out first.

If a process is waiting for the completion of an I/O request and isn't ready to run when it's selected, UNIX will dynamically recalculate all process priorities to determine which inactive but ready process will begin execution when the processor becomes available.

These policies seem to work well and don't impact the running processes. However, if a disk is used for secondary file storage as well as a "swapping area," then heavy traffic can significantly slow disk I/O because job swapping may take precedence over file storage.

Process management techniques described here refer to a pure swapping system such as that used in UNIX V 7.

Process Table Versus User Table

UNIX uses several tables to keep the system running smoothly, as shown in Figure 13.3. Information on simple processes, those with nonsharable code, is stored in two sets of tables: the process table, which always resides in memory, and the user table, which resides in memory only while the process is active. In Figure 13.3, Processes P3 and P4 show the same program code indicated in the text table by the number 2. Their data areas and user tables are kept separate while the code area is being shared. Process P5 isn't sharing its code with another process; therefore, it's not recorded in the text table, and its data and code area are kept together as a unit.

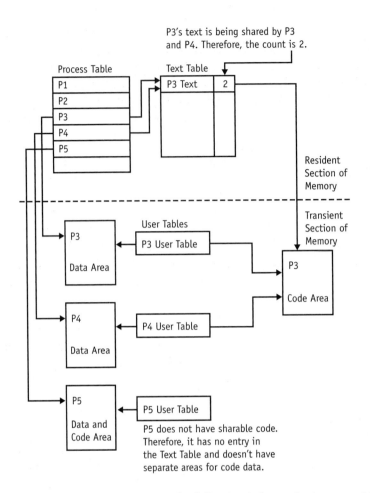

P3's text is being shared by P3 and P4. Therefore, the count is 2.

Process Table

Text Table

Resident Section of Memory

Transient Section of Memory

User Tables

P5 does not have sharable code. Therefore, it has no entry in the Text Table and doesn't have separate areas for code data.

(figure 13.3)

The process control structure showing how the process table and text table interact for processes with sharable code, as well as for those without sharable code.

Each entry in the process table contains the following information: process identification number, user identification number, process memory address or secondary storage address, size of the process, and scheduling information. This table is set up when the process is created and is deleted when the process terminates.

For processes with **sharable code**, the process table maintains a subtable, called the text table, which contains the following information: memory address or secondary storage address of the text segment (sharable code) and a count to keep track of the number of processes using this code. Every time a process starts using this code, the count is increased by 1; and every time a process stops using this code, the count is decreased by 1. When the count is equal to 0, the code is no longer needed and the table entry is released together with any memory locations that had been allocated to the code segment.

A user table is allocated to each active process. This table is kept in the transient area of memory as long as the process is active, and contains information that must be accessible when the process is running. This information includes: the user and group identification numbers to determine file access privileges, pointers to the system's file table for every file being used by the process, a pointer to the current directory, and a list of responses for various interrupts. This table, together with the process data segment and its code segment, can be swapped into or out of main memory as needed.

Synchronization

UNIX is a true multitasking operating system. It achieves process synchronization by requiring that processes wait for certain events. For example, if a process needs more memory, it's required to wait for an event associated with memory allocation. Later, when memory becomes available, the event is signaled and the process can continue. Each event is represented by integers that, by convention, are equal to the address of the table associated with the event.

A race may occur if an event happens during the process's transition between deciding to wait for the event and entering the WAIT state. In this case, the process is waiting for an event that has already occurred and may not recur.

fork

An unusual feature of UNIX is that it gives the user the capability of executing one program from another program using the fork command. This command gives the second program all the attributes of the first program, such as any open files, and saves the first program in its original form.

The system call fork splits a program into two copies, which are both running from the statement after the fork command. When fork is executed, a "process id" (called *pid* for short) is generated for the new process. This is done in a way that ensures that each process has its own unique ID number. Figure 13.4 shows what happens after the fork. The original process (Process 1) is called the **parent process** and the resulting process (Process 2) is the **child process**. A child inherits the parent's open files and runs asynchronously with it unless the parent has been instructed to wait for the termination of the child process.

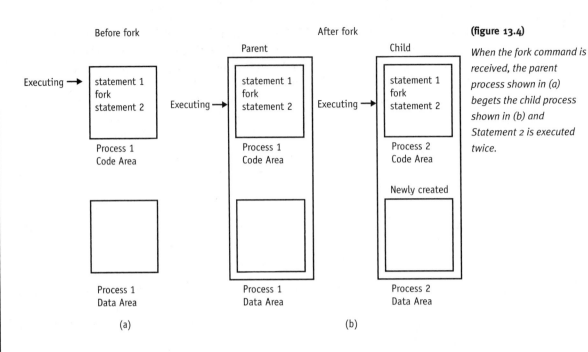

(figure 13.4)

When the fork command is received, the parent process shown in (a) begets the child process shown in (b) and Statement 2 is executed twice.

wait

A related command, wait, allows the programmer to synchronize process execution by suspending the parent until the child is finished, as shown in Figure 13.5.

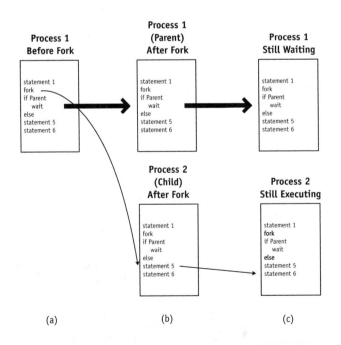

(figure 13.5)

The wait command used in conjunction with the fork command will synchronize the parent and child processes. In (a) the parent process is shown before the fork, (b) shows the parent and child after the fork, and (c) shows the parent and child during the wait.

In Figure 13.5, the IF-THEN-ELSE structure is controlled by the value assigned to the pid, which is returned by the fork system call. A pid greater than 0 indicates a parent process, a pid equal to 0 indicates a child process, and a negative pid indicates an error in the fork call.

exec

The exec family of commands—execl, execv, execle, execlp, and execvp—is used to start execution of a new program from another program. Unlike fork, which results in two processes running the same program being in memory, a successful exec call will lay the second program over the first, leaving only the second program in memory. The second program's code and data are now part of the original process whose pid does not change.

Notice that there's no return from a successful exec call; therefore, the concept of parent-child doesn't hold here. However, a programmer can use the fork, wait, and exec commands in this order to create a parent-child relationship and then have the child be overlaid by another program that, when finished, awakens the parent so that it can continue its execution, as shown in Figure 13.6.

(figure 13.6)

The exec command is used after the fork and wait combination. In (a) the parent is shown before the fork, (b) shows the parent and child after the fork, and (c) shows how the child process (Process 2) is overlaid by the ls program after the exec command.

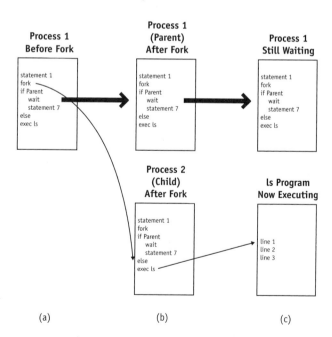

The ls command can generate a listing of the current directory. When the exec ls system call has been executed successfully, processing begins at the first line of the ls program. Once the ls program is finished in the child, control returns to the executable statement following wait in the parent process.

These system calls illustrate the flexibility of UNIX that programmers find extremely useful. For example, a child process can be created to execute a program by the parent process, as was done in Figure 13.6, without requiring the programmer to write code to load or find memory space for a separate program (in this case, the ls program).

Device Management

An innovative feature is the treatment of devices—UNIX is designed to provide device independence to the applications running under it. This is achieved by treating each I/O device as a special type of file. Every device that's installed in a UNIX system is assigned a name that's similar to the name given to any other file, which is given descriptors called iodes. These descriptors identify the devices, contain information about them, and are stored in the device directory. The subroutines that work with the operating system to supervise the transmission of data between main memory and a peripheral unit are called the **device drivers**.

If the computer system uses devices that are not supplied with the operating system, their device drivers must be written by an experienced programmer or obtained from a reliable source and installed on the operating system.

The actual incorporation of a device driver into the kernel is done during the system configuration. UNIX has a program called config that will automatically create a conf.c file for any given hardware configuration. This conf.c file contains the parameters that control resources such as the number of internal buffers for the kernel and the size of the swap space. In addition, the conf.c file contains two tables, bdevsw (short for *block device switch*) and cdevsw (short for *character device switch*), which provide the UNIX system kernel with the ability to adapt easily to different hardware configurations by installing different driver modules.

Device Classifications

The I/O system is divided into the block I/O system (sometimes called the structured I/O system) and the character I/O system (sometimes called the unstructured I/O system).

Each physical device is identified by a minor device number, a major device number, and a class—either block or character—as shown in Figure 13.7.

(figure 13.7)

When a process sends an I/O request, it goes to the UNIX kernel where the char and block device drivers reside.

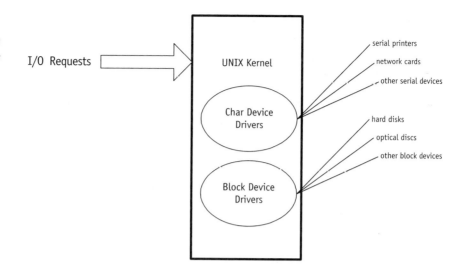

Each class has a Configuration Table that contains an array of entry points into the device drivers. This table is the only connection between the system code and the device drivers, and it's an important feature of the operating system. This table allows the system programmers to create new device drivers quickly to accommodate differently configured system. The major device number is used as an index to the array to access the appropriate code for a specific device driver.

The minor device number is passed to the device driver as an **argument** and is used to access one of several identical or similar physical devices controlled by the driver.

As its name implies, the block I/O system is used for devices that can be addressed as a sequence of identically sized blocks. This allows the Device Manager to use buffering to reduce the physical disk I/O. UNIX has from 10 to 70 buffers for I/O, and information related to these buffers is kept on a list.

Every time a read command is issued, the I/O buffer list is searched. If the requested data is already in a buffer, then it's made available to the requesting process. If not, then it's physically moved from secondary storage to a buffer. If a buffer is available, the move is made. If all buffers are busy, then one must be emptied out to make room for the new block. This is done by using a least recently used (LRU) policy, so the contents of frequently used buffers will be left intact, which, in turn, should reduce physical disk I/O.

Devices in the character class are handled by device drivers that implement character lists. Here's how it operates: a subroutine puts a character on the list, or queue, and another subroutine retrieves the character from the list.

A terminal is a typical character device that has two input queues and one output queue. The two input queues are labeled the raw queue and the canonical queue. It works like this: As the user types in each character, it's collected in the raw input queue. When the line is completed and the Enter key is pressed, the line is copied from the raw input queue to the canonical input queue, and the CPU interprets the line. Similarly, the section of the device driver that handles characters going to the output module of a terminal stores them in the output queue until it holds the maximum number of characters.

The I/O procedure is synchronized through hardware completion interrupts. Each time there's a completion interrupt, the device driver gets the next character from the queue and sends it to the hardware. This process continues until the queue is empty. Some devices can actually belong to both classes: block and character. For instance, disk drives and tape drives can be accessed in block mode using buffers or the system can bypass the buffers when accessing the devices in character mode.

Device Drivers

Each device has a special section in the kernel, called a device driver. Device drivers for disk drives use a seek strategy to minimize the arm movement, as explained in Chapter 7.

Device drivers are kept in a set of files that can be included as needed. When upgrades are made to peripherals, small changes to the device driver file can be linked into the kernel to keep the operating system apprised of the new features and capabilities. Although device files may be kept anywhere on the file system, by default and convention they are kept in the /dev directory. Keeping them in this directory clearly marks them as device files.

Each device driver includes all the instructions necessary for UNIX to communicate with the device.

The Mac OS X operating system has built-in support for RAID 0, RAID 1, RAID 01, and RAID 10, as shown in Figure 13.8.

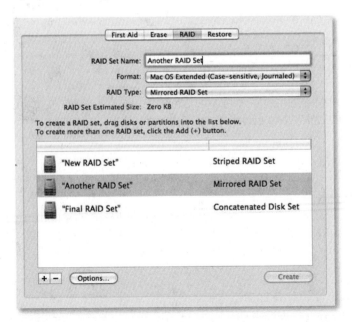

(figure 13.8)

Establishing a mirrored RAID set using Mac OS X.

File Management

UNIX has three types of files: directories, ordinary files, and special files. Each file enjoys certain privileges.

Directories are files used by the system to maintain the hierarchical structure of the file system. Users are allowed to read information in directory files, but only the system is allowed to modify directory files.

Ordinary files are those in which users store information. Their protection is based on a user's requests and related to the read, write, execute, and delete functions that can be performed on a file.

Special files are the device drivers that provide the interface to I/O hardware. Special files appear as entries in directories. They're part of the file system, and most of them reside in the /dev directory. The name of each special file indicates the type of device with which it's associated. Most users don't need to know much about special files, but system programmers should know where they are and how to use them.

UNIX stores files as sequences of bytes and doesn't impose any structure on them. Therefore, text files (those written using an editor) are strings of characters with lines delimited by the line feed, or new line, character. On the other hand, binary files (those containing executable code generated by a compiler or assembler) are sequences of binary digits grouped into words as they will appear in memory during execution of the program. Therefore, the structure of files is controlled by the programs that use them, not by the system.

The UNIX file management system organizes the disk into blocks of 512 bytes each and divides the disk into four basic regions:

- The first region (starting at address 0) is reserved for booting.
- The second region, called a superblock, contains information about the disk as a whole, such as its size and the boundaries of the other regions.
- The third region includes a list of file definitions, called the i-list, which is a list of file descriptors, one for each file. The descriptors are called i-nodes. The position of an i-node on the list is called an i-number, and it is this i-number that uniquely identifies a file.
- The fourth region holds the free blocks available for file storage. The free blocks are kept in a linked list where each block points to the next available empty block. Then, as files grow, noncontiguous blocks are linked to the already existing chain.

Whenever possible, files are stored in contiguous empty blocks. And since all disk allocation is based on fixed-size blocks, allocation is very simple and there's no need to compact the files.

Each entry in the i-list is called an i-node (also spelled *inode*) and contains 13 disk addresses. The first 10 addresses point to the first 10 blocks of a file. However, if a file is larger than 10 blocks, the eleventh address points to a block that contains the addresses of the next 128 blocks of the file. For larger files, the twelfth address points to another set of 128 blocks, each one pointing to 128 blocks. For files larger than 8 MB, there is a thirteenth address allowing for a maximum file size of over 1GB.

Each i-node contains information on a specific file, such as owner's identification, protection bits, physical address, file size, time of creation, last use and last update, number of links, and whether the file is a directory, an ordinary file, or a special file.

File Naming Conventions

Filenames are case sensitive so they recognize capital letters in filenames. For example, these are legitimate names for four different files in a single directory: FIREWALL, firewall, FireWall, and fireWALL.

Most versions of UNIX allow filenames to be up to 255 characters in length. Although the operating systems don't impose any naming conventions on files, some system programs, such as compilers, expect files to have specific suffixes (which are the same as extensions described in Chapter 8). For example, prog1.bas would indicate the file to be a BASIC program because of its suffix .bas, while the suffix in backup.sh would indicate the file to be a shell program.

UNIX supports a hierarchical tree directory structure. The root directory is identified by a slash (/); the names of other directories are preceded by the slash (/) symbol, which is used as a delimiter. A file is accessed by starting at a given point in the hierarchy and descending through the branches of the tree (subdirectories) until reaching the leaf (file). This path can become very long and it's sometimes advantageous to change directories before accessing a file. This can be done quickly by typing two periods ("..") if the file needed is one level up from the working directory in the hierarchy. Typing ../.. will move you up two branches toward the root in the tree structure.

To access the file `checks` in the system illustrated in Figure 13.9, the user can type the following:

```
/programs/pay/checks
```

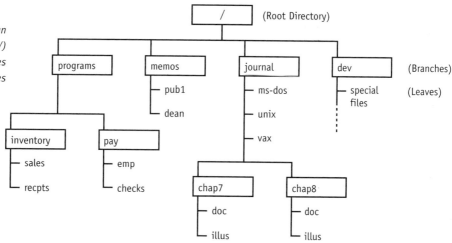

The first slash indicates that this is an absolute path name that starts at the root directory. On the other hand, a relative path name is one that doesn't start at the root directory. Two examples of relative path names from Figure 13.9 are:

```
pay/checks
journal/chap8/illus
```

A few rules apply to all path names:

- If the path name starts with a slash, the path starts at the root directory.
- A path name can be either one name or a list of names separated by slashes. The last name on the list is the name of the file requested.
- Using two periods (..) in a path name will move you upward in the hierarchy (closer to the root). This is the only way to go up the hierarchy; all other path names go down the tree.
- Spaces are not allowed within path names.

Directory Listings

As shown in Table 13.2, a "long listing" of files in a directory shows eight pieces of information for each file: the access control, the number of links, the name of the group and owner, the byte size of the file, the date and time of last modification, and, finally, the filename. Notice that the list is displayed in alphabetical order by filename.

(table 13.2)

This table shows the list of files stored in the directory journal from the system illustrated in Figure 13.9. The command ls -l (short for "listing-long") was used to generate this list.

Access Control	No. of Links	Group	Owner	No. of Bytes	Date	Time	Filename
drwxrwxr-x	2	journal	comp	128	Jan 10	19:32	chap7
drwxrwxr-x	2	journal	comp	128	Jan 15	09:59	chap8
-rwxr-xr-x	1	journal	comp	11904	Jan 6	11:38	ms-dos
-rwxr--r--	1	journal	comp	12556	Jan 20	18:08	unix
-rwx------	1	journal	comp	10362	Jan 17	07:32	vax

The first column shows the type of file and the access privileges for each file, as shown in Figure 13.10. The first character in the first column describes the nature of the file or directory; *d* indicates a directory and - indicates an ordinary file. Other codes that can be used are:

- *b* to indicate a block special file
- *c* to indicate a character special file
- *p* to indicate a named pipe file

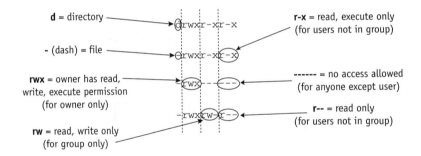

(figure 13.10)
Graphical depiction of a list of file and directory permissions in UNIX.

The next three characters (rwx) show the access privileges granted to the owner of the file: r stands for read, w stands for write, and x stands for execute. Therefore, if the list includes rwx, the user can read, write, and/or execute that program.

Likewise, the following three characters describe the access privileges granted to other members of the user's group. (In UNIX, a group is defined as a set of users who have something in common: the same project, same class, same department, etc.) Therefore, rwx for characters 5–7 means other users can also read, write, and/or execute that file. However, a hyphen - indicates that access is denied for that operation. In Table 13.2, r-- means that the file called unix can be read by other group members but can't be altered or executed.

Finally, the last three characters in column one describe the access privileges granted to users at large, those system-wide who are not the owner or part of the owner's group. Thus, at-large users can't modify the files listed in Table 13.2, nor can they modify or execute the file called unix. What's more, the vax file can't be read, modified, or executed by anyone other than the owner.

The second column in the directory listing indicates the number of links, also known as the number of aliases, that refer to the same physical file. Aliases are an important feature of UNIX; they support file sharing when several users work together on the same project. In this case, it's convenient for the shared files to appear in different directories belonging to different users even though only one central file descriptor (containing information on the file) exists for that file. The filename may be different from directory to directory since these names aren't kept in the file descriptor, but the numbers of links kept there is updated so the system knows how many users are sharing this file. Eventually this number will drop to 0 indicating that the file is no longer needed and can be deleted.

The next three columns show, respectively, the name of the group, the name of the owner, and the file size in bytes. The sixth and seventh columns show the date and time of the last modification, and the last column lists the filename.

Figure 13.11 shows that the Mac OS X uses an access control list to limit file access to certain users and groups.

(figure 13.11)

On the Mac OS X, the Finder uses an access control list to set permissions for file access.

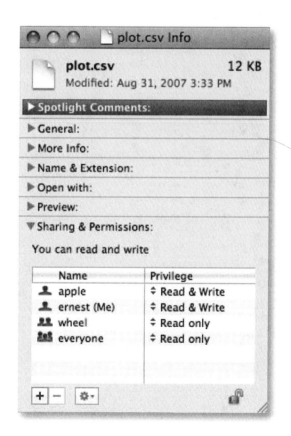

Data Structures

The information presented in the directory isn't all kept in the same location. UNIX divides the file information into parts, some in the directory entries and some in the i-nodes. Therefore, everything you see in Table 13.2, with the exception of the file-name and the addition of the device's physical addresses for the file contents, is kept in the i-node. All i-nodes are stored in a reserved part of the device where the directory resides, usually in Block 1. This structure is illustrated in Figure 13.12, which uses the directory memos from Figure 13.9 as an example.

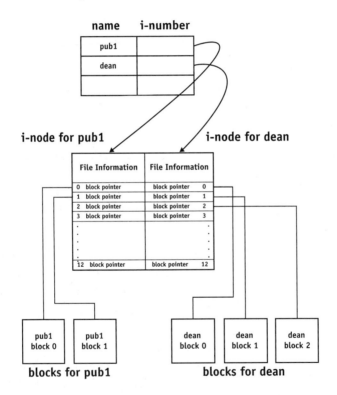

(figure 13.12)

Example of hierarchy for directories, i-nodes, and file blocks. Although the file blocks are represented here in physical serial order, they actually may be stored noncontiguously.

Each i-node has room for 13 pointers (0–12). The first 10 block numbers stored in the i-node list relate to the first 10 blocks of a file.

For the file called pub1 in Figure 13.12, only the first two entries have pointers to data blocks and all the others are zeros because this is a small file that occupies only two blocks of storage. If a file is larger than 10 blocks, then the eleventh entry points to a block that contains a list of the next 128 blocks in the file. Because it's an extra step in the path to the data, this block is called an indirect block.

For files larger than 138 blocks, the twelfth entry points to a block that contains a list of 128 indirect blocks (each one containing pointers to 128 file blocks). Because this block introduces two extra steps in the path to the data, it's called a double indirect block. Finally, for extremely large files of more than 16,522 blocks, the thirteenth entry points to a triple indirect block. This schema allows for 2,113,674 blocks to be allocated to a single file, for a total of 1,082,201,088 bytes.

Therefore, carrying this one step further, we can see that the bytes numbered below 5120 can be retrieved with a single disk access. Those in the range between 5120 and 70,656 require two disk accesses. Those in the range between 70,656 and 8,459,264 require three disk accesses, while bytes beyond 8,459,264 require four disk accesses. This would give very slow access to large data files but, in reality, the system maintains a rather complicated buffering mechanism that considerably reduces the number of I/O operations required to access a file.

When a file is created an i-node is allocated to it, and a directory entry with the filename and its i-node number is created. When a file is linked (which happens when another user begins sharing the same file), a directory entry is created with the new name and the original i-node number, and the link-count field in the i-node is incremented by 1.

When a shared file is deleted, the link-count field in the i-node is decremented by 1. And when the count reaches 0, the directory entry is erased and all disk blocks allocated to the file, along with its i-node entry in the disk i-list, are deallocated.

User Command Interface

UNIX was created as a command-driven system and its user commands (shown in Table 13.3) are very short: either one character (usually the first letter of the command) or a group of characters (an acronym of the words that make up the command). In command mode, the system prompt is very economical, often only one character, such as a dollar sign ($) or percent sign (%).

Command	Stands For	Action to be Performed
(filename)	Run File	Run/Execute the file with that name.
ls	List Directory	Show a listing of the filenames in directory.
ls -l	Long List	Show a comprehensive directory list.
cd	Change Directory	Change working directory.
cp	Copy	Copy a file into another file or directory.
rm	Remove	Remove/delete a file or directory.
mv	Move	Move or rename a file or directory.
more	Show More	Type the file's contents to the screen.
lpr	Print	Print out a file.
date	Date	Show date and time.
date -u	Universal Date/Time	Show date and time in universal format (in Greenwich Mean Time).
mkdir	Make Directory	Make a new directory.
grep	Global Regular Expression/Print	Find a specified string in a file.
cat	Concatenate	Concatenate files.
format	Format	Format a volume.
diff	Different	Compare two files.
pwd	Print Working Directory	Show name of working directory.

(table 13.3)

User commands can't be abbreviated or expanded and must be in the correct case (usually, commands must be entered only in lowercase letters). Many commands can be combined on a single line for additional power and flexibility. Check the technical documentation for your system for proper spelling and syntax.

The general syntax of commands is this:

```
command arguments file_name
```

The **command** is any legal operating system command, as shown in Figure 13.13. The **arguments** are required for some commands and optional for others. The `file_name` can be a relative or absolute path name. Commands are interpreted and executed by the shell, one of the two most widely used programs. The shell is technically known as the command line interpreter because that's its function. But it isn't only an interactive command interpreter; it's also the key to the coordination and combination of system programs. In fact, it's a sophisticated programming language in itself.

In this chapter, we discuss the command structures common to both UNIX and Linux. In Chapter 16, we discuss graphical user interfaces common to some versions of both operating systems.

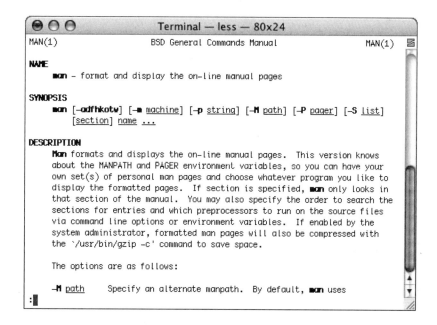

```
MAN(1)                    BSD General Commands Manual                    MAN(1)

NAME
     man - format and display the on-line manual pages

SYNOPSIS
     man [-adfhkotw] [-m machine] [-p string] [-M path] [-P pager] [-S list]
         [section] name ...

DESCRIPTION
     Man formats and displays the on-line manual pages.  This version knows
     about the MANPATH and PAGER environment variables, so you can have your
     own set(s) of personal man pages and choose whatever program you like to
     display the formatted pages.  If section is specified, man only looks in
     that section of the manual.  You may also specify the order to search the
     sections for entries and which preprocessors to run on the source files
     via command line options or environment variables.  If enabled by the
     system administrator, formatted man pages will also be compressed with
     the `/usr/bin/gzip -c' command to save space.

     The options are as follows:

     -M path      Specify an alternate manpath.  By default, man uses
:
```

Script Files

Command files, often called shell files or **script** files, can be used to automate repetitious tasks. Each line of the file is a valid command and the script file can be executed by simply typing sh and the name of the script file. Another way to execute it is to define the file as an executable command and simply type the filename at the system prompt.

Other common shells are csh (the C shell, which was originally developed to support C language development environments at Berkeley and NASA) and ksh (the Korn shell, which was developed after the Bourne and C shells). The Korn shell is usually available as an unbundled product.

Script files are used to automate repetitive tasks and to simplify complex procedures. Here is an example of a simple script file that's designed to configure the system for a certain user:

```
setenv DBPATH /u/lumber:.:/zdlf/product/central/db
setenv TERMCAP $INFODIR/etc/termcap
stty erase '^H'
set savehistory
set history=20
alias h history
alias 4gen infogen -f
setenv PATH /usr/info/bin:/etc
```

In this example, the working directory paths are set, the history is set to 20 lines, and it is given an alias of h (so the user can perform the history command simply by typing h). Similarly, 4gen is established as an alias for the command infogen-f. Finally, the path is defined as /usr/info/bin:/etc.

If this script file is included in the user's configuration file, it will be automatically executed every time the user logs on. The exact name of the user configuration file varies from system to system, but two common names are .profile and .login. See the documentation for your system for specifics.

Redirection

If you're an interactive user, most of the commands used to produce output will automatically send it to your screen and the editor will accept input from the keyboard. There are times when you may want to send output to a file or to another device. This is done by using the symbol > between the command and the destination to which the output should be directed. For example, to list the files in your current directory in the file named myfiles instead of listing them on the screen, use this command:

```
ls > myfiles
```

The following command will copy the contents of two files, chapt1 followed by chapt2, into a file named sectiona:

```
cat chapt1 chapt2 > sectiona
```

The command cat is short for "concatenate." If sectiona is a new file, then it's automatically created. If it already exists, the previous contents will be overwritten. (When cat is used with a single file and redirection is not indicated, then it displays the contents of that file on the screen.) Another way to achieve the same result is with the wild card symbol (*) like this:

```
cat chapt* > sectiona
```

The asterisk symbol (*) indicates that the command pertains to all files that begin with chapt—in this case, that means chapt1 and chapt2.

The symbol >> will append the new file to an existing file. Therefore, either of the following two commands will copy the contents of chapt1 and chapt2 onto the end of whatever already exists in the file called sectiona:

```
cat chapt1 chapt2 >> sectiona
cat chapt* >> sectiona
```

If sectiona doesn't exist, then the file will be created as an empty file and will then be filled with chapt1 and chapt2, in that order.

The reverse redirection is to take input for a program from an existing file instead of from the keyboard. For example, if you have written a memo and need to mail it to several people, the following command will send the contents of the file memo to the people listed between the command `mail` and the symbol `<`:

```
mail ann roger < memo
```

By combining the power of redirection with system commands, you can achieve results not possible otherwise. For example, the following command will store in the file called `temporary` the names of all users logged on to the system:

```
who > temporary
```

And the command sort will sort the list stored in `temporary` and display the sorted list on the screen as it's generated.

In each of these examples, it's important to note that the interpretation of `<` and `>` is done by the shell and not by the individual program (such as `mail`, `who`, or `sort`). This means that input and output redirection can be used with any program because the program isn't aware that anything unusual is happening. This is one instance of the power of UNIX—the flexibility that comes from combining many operations into a single brief command.

Pipes

Pipes and filters make it possible to redirect output or input to selected files or devices based on commands given to the command interpreter. UNIX does that by manipulating I/O devices as special files.

For the example just presented, we listed the number of users online into a file called temporary and we then sorted the file. There was no reason to create this file other than the fact that we needed it to complete the two-step operation required to see the list in alphabetical order on the screen. However, a pipe can do the same thing in a single step.

A pipe is the operating system's way to connect the output from one program to the input of another without the need for temporary or intermediate files. A pipe is a special type of file connecting two programs; information written to it by one program may be read immediately by the other, with synchronization, scheduling, and buffering handled automatically by the system. In other words, the programs are executing concurrently, not one after the other. By using a pipe, indicated by the vertical symbol (|), the last example can be rewritten as:

```
who | sort
```

As a result, a sorted list of all users logged on to the system will be displayed on the screen.

A pipeline is several programs simultaneously processing the same I/O stream. For example, the following command is a pipeline that takes the output from who (a list of all logged-on users), sorts it, and prints it out:

```
who | sort | lpr
```

Filters

UNIX has many programs that read some input, manipulate it in some way, and generate output; these programs are called filters. One example is wc, which stands for *word count* and counts the lines, words, and characters in a file. For example, the following command would execute the word count command on the file journal and send the output to the terminal:

```
wc journal
```

As a result, the system would respond with 10 140 700, meaning that the file journal has 10 lines, 140 words, and 700 characters. (A word is defined as a string of characters separated by blanks.) A shorter version (wc -1) counts just the number of lines in the file.

Another filter command is sort (the same command we used to demonstrate pipes). If a filename is given with the command, the contents of the file are sorted and displayed on the screen. If no filename is given with the command, sort accepts input from the keyboard and directs the output to the screen. When it's used with redirection, sort accepts input from a file and writes the output to another file. For example,

```
sort names>sortednames
```

will sort the contents of the file called names and send the output to the file sortednames. The data in names will be sorted in ASCII order, that is, using a standard collating sequence so lines with leading blanks come first (in sorted order), lines with lowercase characters follow, and lines beginning with uppercase characters come last. To sort the list in alphabetical order but ignore the case of letters, the command is:

```
sort -f names>sortednames
```

To obtain a numerical sort in ascending order, the command is:

```
sort -n names>sortednums
```

To obtain a numerical sort in descending order, the command is:

```
sort -nr names>sortednums
```

In every example presented here, sort uses each entire line of the file to conduct the sort. However, if the structure of the data stored in the file is known, then the sort can use other key fields.

For example, let's say a file called empl has data that follows the same column format: the ID numbers start in column 1, phone numbers start in column 10, and last names start in column 20. To sort the file by last name (the third field), the command would be:

```
sort +2f empl>sortedempl
```

In this example, the file empl will be sorted alphabetically by the third field and the output will be sent to the file called sortedempl. (A field is defined as a group of characters separated by at least one blank.) The +2 tells the sort command to skip the first two fields and the f says the list should be sorted in alphabetical order. The integrity of the file is preserved because the entire line is sorted—so each name keeps the correct phone and ID number.

Additional Commands

This section introduces several other commonly used commands.

man

This command displays the online manual supplied with the operating system. It's called with an argument that specifies which page of the online manual you are interested in seeing. For example, to display the page for the compare (cmp) command, the command would look like this:

```
man cmp
```

If the cmp entry appears more than once in the manual, all the pages are displayed, one after the other. You can redirect the output to a file, which can then be sent to a printer for future reference.

grep

One of the most-used commands is grep—it stands for *global regular expression and print* and it looks for specific patterns of characters. It's one of the most helpful (and oddly named) commands. It's the equivalent of the FIND and SEARCH commands used in other operating systems. When the desired pattern of characters is found, the line containing it is displayed on the screen.

Here's a simple example: If you need to retrieve the names and addresses of everyone with a Pittsburgh address from a large file called maillist, the command would look like this:

```
grep Pittsburgh maillist
```

As a result, you see on your screen the lines from maillist for entries that included Pittsburgh. And if you want the output sent to a file for future use, you can add the redirection command.

This grep command can also be used to list all the lines that do not contain a certain string of characters. Using the same example, the following command displays on the screen the names and addresses of all those who don't have a Pittsburgh address:

```
grep -v Pittsburgh maillist
```

Similarly, the following command counts all the people who live in Pittsburgh and displays that number on the screen without printing each line:

```
grep -c Pittsburgh maillist
```

As noted before, the power of this operating system comes from its ability to combine commands. Here's how the grep command can be combined with the who command. Suppose you want to see if your friend Sam is logged on. The command to display Sam's name, device, and the date and time he logged in would be:

```
who | grep sam
```

Combinations of commands, though effective, can appear confusing to the casual observer. For example, if you wanted a list of all the subdirectories (but not the files) found in the root directory, the command would be:

```
ls -l / | grep '^d'
```

This command is the combination of several simpler commands:

- ls for list directory
- -l, which is the long option of ls and includes the information shown in Table 13.3
- / to indicate the root directory
- | to establish a pipe
- grep to find
- '^d', which says that d is the character we're looking for (because we only want the directories), the ^ indicates that the d is at the beginning of each line, and the quotes are required because we used the symbol ^

nohup

If a program's execution is expected to take a long time, you can start its execution and then log off the system without having to wait for it to finish. This is done with the command nohup, which is short for "no hangup." Let's say, for example, you want to copy a very large file but you can't wait at the terminal until the job is finished. The command is:

```
nohup cp oldlargefile newlargefile &
```

The copy command (cp) will continue its execution copying oldlargefile to newlarge-file in the background even though you've logged off the system. For this example, we've indicated that execution should continue in the background; the ampersand (&) is the symbol for running the program in background mode.

nice

If your program uses a large number of resources and you are not in a hurry for the results, you can be "nice" to other processes by lowering its priority with the command nice. This command with a trailing & frees up your terminal for different work. For example, you want to copy oldlargefile to newlargefile and want to continue working on another project at the same time. To do that, use this command:

```
nice cp oldlargefile newlargefile &
```

However, you may not log off when using the nice command until the copy is finished because the program execution would be stopped.

The command nohup automatically activates nice by lowering the process's priority. It assumes that since you've logged off the system, you're not in a hurry for the output. The opposite isn't true—when nice is issued, it doesn't automatically activate nohup. Therefore, if you want to put a very long job in the background, work on some other jobs, and log out before the long job is finished, nohup with a trailing & is the command to use.

We've included only a few commands here. For a complete list of commands for a specific version of this operating system, their exact syntax, and more details about those we've discussed here, see a technical manual for the appropriate version.

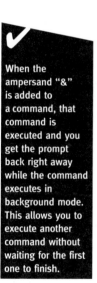

When the ampersand "&" is added to a command, that command is executed and you get the prompt back right away while the command executes in background mode. This allows you to execute another command without waiting for the first one to finish.

Conclusion

It is difficult to measure the impact that UNIX has had on the computing world. Since it was written in 1969, it has been a major force in the field of operating systems and is expected to remain so for many years to come.

UNIX began as a command-driven operating system written by and for programmers who became comfortable with this operating system's famously brief commands, but it has evolved into one of the most significant operating systems available. With the addition of a graphical user interface, UNIX has become an even more flexible operating system running computing hardware of every size and complexity, from telephones to super computers.

Since it was adopted by Apple for its Macintosh computers, UNIX has gained a new legion of users and is certain to grow in popularity in the years to come.

Key Terms

argument: in a command-driven operating system, a value or option placed in the command that modifies how the command is to be carried out.

child process: in UNIX-like operating systems, the subordinate processes that are created and controlled by a parent process.

CPU-bound: a job that will perform a great deal of nonstop processing before issuing an interrupt. A CPU-bound job can tie up the CPU for long periods of time.

device driver: a device-specific program module that handles the interrupts and controls a particular type of device.

device independent: programs that can work on a variety of computers and with a variety of devices.

directory: a logical storage unit that contains files.

I/O-bound: a job that requires a large number of input/output operations, resulting in much free time for the CPU.

kernel: the part of the operating system that resides in main memory at all times and performs the most essential tasks, such as managing memory and handling disk input and output.

parent process: in UNIX-like operating systems, a job that controls one or more child processes, which it created.

Portable Operating System Interface for Computer Environments (POSIX): a set of IEEE standards that defines the standard user and programming interfaces for operating systems so developers can port programs from one operating system to another.

reentrant code: code that can be used by two or more processes at the same time; each shares the same copy of the executable code but has separate data areas.

script: a series of executable commands written in plain text that can be executed by the operating system in sequence as a single procedure.

sharable code: executable code in the operating system that can be shared by several processes.

Interesting Searches

- UNIX for Supercomputers
- UNIX File Management
- Embedded UNIX
- History of UNIX and Linux
- Macintosh OS X

Exercises

Research Topics

A. Research current literature to discover the current state of IEEE POSIX Standards and list 10 UNIX operating systems that are currently 100 percent POSIX-compliant. Explain the significance of this compliance and why you think some popular operating systems might choose not to be compliant.

B. Explore the issues surrounding UNIX security. Specifically, identify major threats to systems running UNIX, and the steps system administrators must take to protect the system from unauthorized access. Compare the practical problems when balancing the need for accessibility with the need to restrict access, and suggest the first action you would take to secure a UNIX information system if you managed one.

Exercises

1. Describe the importance of hardware independence.

2. Early versions of UNIX were available only with a command-driven interface. In more recent years, graphical user interfaces became popular. Explain in your own words why these GUIs made an impact on the popularity of this operating system.

3. The role of the UNIX kernel is crucial. Explain why this is so and how it is treated differently from other parts of the operating system.

4. Explain how UNIX identifies CPU- and I/O-bound jobs and uses that information to keep the system balanced.

5. UNIX treats all devices as files. Explain why this was an innovative feature when it was first introduced and how it adds flexibility to this operating system.

6. In your own words, compare and contrast the three types of files: directories, ordinary files, and special files. Explain what would happen if a user modified a directory file.

7. Create an illustration showing how an i-node would track the disk addresses for a single file that's 1GB in size.

8. Describe at least one circumstance where you would want to run commands in background mode.

9. Explain why you might want to change the permissions on some of your directories to make them invisible to other users.

10. Compare and contrast block and character devices and how they are manipulated by the UNIX device manager.

Advanced Exercises

11. Describe in your own words how a parent and child are created from the fork command and why you think the child process will or will not continue if the parent process is terminated.

12. Using the command /dev, identify which devices are available and indicate which of these devices are character-oriented and which are block-oriented. Explain your reasoning.

13. If you were using a system and a system operator deleted the list (ls) command accidentally, can you think of another way to list all the files in a directory?

14. On your UNIX system, identify which of the following files systems are supported, and identify the format that is supported by each file system: FAT32, NTFS, ISO 9660, HFS+, UDF 2.5.

15. Compare and contrast the state of UNIX security in 1995 and in 2010 and describe any significant threats to UNIX-run systems at that time.

Chapter 14

MS-DOS Operating System

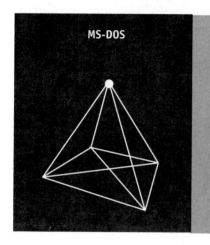

MS-DOS

Design Goals
Memory Management
Processor Management
Device Management
File Management
User Interface

"PCs gave the world a whole new way to work, play and communicate."

—Bill Gates

Learning Objectives

After completing this chapter, you should be able to describe:

- How to access MS-DOS emulators from other operating systems
- How MS-DOS provided a foundation for early Microsoft Windows releases
- The basics of command-driven systems and how to construct simple batch files
- How one processor can be shared among multiple processes
- The limitations of MS-DOS

MS-DOS, also known simply as DOS, was developed to run single-user, stand-alone desktop computers. When the personal computer market exploded in the 1980s, MS-DOS was the standard operating system delivered with millions of these machines.

This operating system is one of the simplest to understand. In many ways, MS-DOS exemplifies early operating systems because it manages jobs sequentially from a single user. Its advantages are its fundamental operation and its straightforward user commands. With only a few hours of instruction, a first-time user can learn to successfully manipulate a personal computer and its files and devices.

MS-DOS was written for a single family of microprocessors: the Intel 8086, 8088, 80186, and 80286 chips. When those microprocessors dominated the personal computer market, MS-DOS did too. When newer chips came along, MS-DOS lost its market advantage to more sophisticated operating systems. MS-DOS was the primary operating system for a generation of microcomputers and so it is included in this text as an example.

It's worth noting that early versions of Windows (versions 1.0 through 3.1) were merely graphical user interfaces that ran on top of the MS-DOS operating system. See Chapter 15 on Windows for more information.

✔
Do not confuse MS-DOS with software that goes by similar acronyms, such as "distributed operating systems" or a "disk operating system" sold by other vendors, such as IBM.

History

MS-DOS was the successor of the CP/M operating system. CP/M (for Control Program for Microcomputers) ran the first personal computers, 8-bit machines marketed by Apple Computer and Tandy Corporation. But when the 16-bit personal computers were developed in 1980, they required an operating system with more capability than CP/M, and many companies rushed to develop the operating system that would become the standard for the new generation of hardware.

IBM was the catalyst. When it searched for an operating system for its soon-to-be-released line of 16-bit personal computers, Digital Research offered the new CP/M-86 operating system. IBM looked carefully at both and began negotiations with Digital Research to buy the "new and improved CP/M" system. Meanwhile, Microsoft, a fledgling company started by Bill Gates and Paul Allen, discovered an innovative operating system, called 86-DOS, designed by Tim Paterson of Seattle Computer Products to run that company's line of 16-bit personal computers. Microsoft bought it, renamed it MS-DOS for Microsoft Disk Operating System, and made it available to IBM.

IBM chose MS-DOS in 1981, called it PC-DOS, and proclaimed it the standard for its line of personal computers. Eventually, with the weight of IBM's endorsement, MS-DOS became the standard operating system for most 16-bit personal computers in the 1980s.

This operating system went through many versions after its birth in Seattle. Some were needed to fix deficiencies, while others were made to accommodate major hardware changes, such as increased disk drive capabilities or different formats. Table 14.1 lists some of the major versions.

(table 14.1)

The evolution of MS-DOS.

Version No.	Release Date	Features
1.0	1981	CP/M compatible; supported only one directory
1.1	1982	Allowed double-sided 5¼ inch disks
2.0	1983	Eliminated some defects in earlier version
3.0	1984	Increased memory requirement to 36K, supported PC/AT
3.1	1984	First release to support networking
3.2	1986	Supported token ring and 3½ inch disks
3.3	1987	Supported the IBM PS/2 computer
4.0	1988	Supported hard disks larger than 32MB
5.0	1991	Better use of extended memory
6.0	1993	Better use of conventional memory
6.22	1994	Provided users with capabilities previously available only as third-party applications

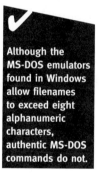

Although the MS-DOS emulators found in Windows allow filenames to exceed eight alphanumeric characters, authentic MS-DOS commands do not.

Each version of MS-DOS was a standard version, so later versions of MS-DOS were compatible with earlier versions. Therefore, programs written to run on Version 5.0 could also be run on Version 6.2. It also meant that, among different manufacturers, the same commands elicited the same response from the operating system regardless of who manufactured the hardware running it; this was a significant feature at the time.

Although MS-DOS is no longer widely used, many Windows operating systems offer a DOS emulator to allow anyone to enter some DOS-like commands. To find it in Windows, click the Start button, then All Programs, Accessories, Command Prompt to see a screen similar to Figure 14.1.

```
Command Prompt                                              _ □ ×

C:\Program Files>CD YAHOO!

C:\Program Files\Yahoo!>dir
 Volume in drive C is SQ004101P01
 Volume Serial Number is 001B-D93A

 Directory of C:\Program Files\Yahoo!

03/31/2007  10:00 AM    <DIR>          .
03/31/2007  10:00 AM    <DIR>          ..
03/31/2007  10:00 AM    <DIR>          Common
03/31/2007  10:00 AM    <DIR>          Installs
12/29/2005  04:20 PM    <DIR>          Shared
03/31/2007  10:00 AM    <DIR>          UPnP
03/31/2007  10:52 AM    <DIR>          Yahoo! Music Engine
               0 File(s)              0 bytes
               7 Dir(s)  62,579,499,008 bytes free

C:\Program Files\Yahoo!>
```

(figure 14.1)

The Command Prompt window opened from a Windows operating system. From the command prompt, users can enter selected MS-DOS commands.

Design Goals

MS-DOS was designed to accommodate a single novice user in a single-process environment, as shown in Figure 14.2. Its standard I/O support includes a keyboard, monitor, printer, and secondary storage unit. Its user commands are based on English words or phrases and are indicative of the action to be performed. Examples are shown in Appendix A. These commands are interpreted by the command processor, typically the only portion of the operating system with which most users interact.

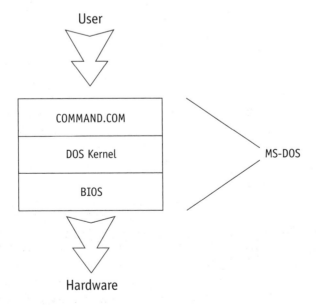

(figure 14.2)

The three layers of MS-DOS. The top layer is the command processor, a program called COMMAND.COM, which provides device independence. The DOS kernel software provides file management services. BIOS software provides device management services.

The layering approach is fundamental to the design of the whole MS-DOS system, which is to "protect" the user from having to work with the bits and bytes of the bare machine that make up the bottom layer—the hardware that includes the electrical circuits, registers, and other basic components of the computer. Each layer is built on the one that precedes it, starting from the bottom up.

The layer at the bottom of MS-DOS is **BIOS** (basic input/output system). This layer of the operating system interfaces directly with the various I/O devices such as printers, keyboards, and monitors. BIOS contains the **device drivers** that control the flow of data to and from each device except the disk drives. It receives status information about the success or failure of each I/O operation and passes it on to the processor. BIOS takes care of the small differences among I/O units so the user can purchase a printer from any manufacturer without having to write a device driver for it—BIOS makes it perform as it should.

The middle layer, the DOS kernel, contains the routines needed to interface with the disk drives. It's read into memory at initialization time from the MSDOS.SYS file residing in the boot disk. The DOS kernel is a proprietary program supplied by Microsoft Corporation that implements MS-DOS. It's accessed by application programs and provides a collection of hardware-independent services, such as memory management, and file and record management. These are called system functions. Like BIOS, the DOS kernel compensates for variations from manufacturer to manufacturer so all disk drives perform in the same way. In other words, the kernel makes disk file management transparent to the user so you don't have to remember in which tracks and sectors your files are stored—and which sectors of the disk are damaged and must be avoided. The kernel does that for you; it manages the storage and retrieval of files and dynamically allocates and deallocates secondary storage as it's needed.

The third layer, the command processor, is sometimes called the shell. This is the part of the system that sends prompts to the user, accepts the commands that are typed in, executes the commands, and issues the appropriate responses. The command processor resides in a file called COMMAND.COM, which consists of two parts stored in two different sections of main memory. Some users mistakenly believe the COMMAND.COM file is the entire operating system because it's the only part that appears on the public directory. Actually, it's only one of several programs that make up MS-DOS; the rest are hidden.

It's the command processor's job to carry out the user's commands entered from the **system prompt** without having to wait for device-specific instructions. For example, when a user issues a PRINT command, the command processor directs the output to the line printer via BIOS. Similarly, with a user command to TYPE a file, the command processor directs the output to the monitor. In these cases, the user doesn't need to compensate for the slow speed of the printer and the fast speed of the terminal; the user can interact with both devices and files in the same way.

The weakness of the command processor is that it isn't interpretive. That is, programmers can't take shortcuts by abbreviating the commands. New users must learn to enter each command completely and correctly. It's unforgiving to those who can't type, spell, or construct commands perfectly.

MS-DOS Version 4.0 introduced a menu-driven DOS shell to ease users' interaction with the system, but it was not widely accepted. When Version 5.0 was released, IBM and Microsoft also released a new operating system, OS/2, which was designed to replace MS-DOS. Although OS/2 offered several advantages over MS-DOS, such as using all available memory and supporting multiprogramming, it failed to generate the interest that both companies expected.

In its heyday, MS-DOS ran an enormous collection of software packages. Notable among these applications were Lotus 1-2-3 (a popular spreadsheet program at that time) and WordPerfect (a word processor). The widespread adoption of these two products helped novice users learn the power of a personal computer and spurred the growth of the industry.

Microsoft has continued to incorporate access to an MS-DOS emulator with a DOS prompt, a DOS-like command capability, on many of its Windows products (shown in Figure 14.1) even though MS-DOS has been officially withdrawn from the market.

Memory Management

The Memory Manager has a relatively simple job because it's managing a single job for a single user. To run a second job, the user must close or pause the first file before opening the second. The Memory Manager uses a **first-fit memory allocation** scheme. First-fit was selected for early DOS versions because it's the most efficient strategy in a single-user environment. (Some versions accommodate extended memory capabilities and **multitasking**, features that are available with add-on hardware and software; but to keep our discussion succinct, we won't include them here.)

Before we see how memory is allocated, let's see how it's structured. Main memory comes in two forms: read only memory (ROM) and random access memory (RAM).

ROM is usually very small in size and contains a program, a section of BIOS, with the sole task of starting up the system. The startup process is called **bootstrapping** because the system is effectively pulling itself up by its bootstraps. This program in ROM initializes the computer. It also retrieves the rest of the resident portion of the operating system from secondary storage and loads it into RAM.

RAM is the part of main memory where programs are loaded and executed. The RAM layout for a computer with 1 MB of memory is given in Figure 14.3.

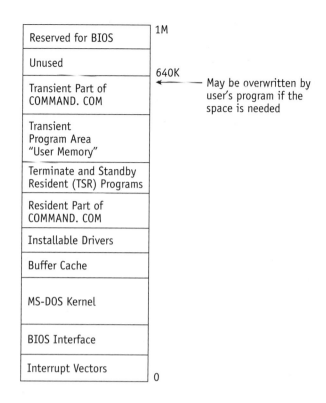

The lowest portion of RAM—known as low-addressable memory because this is where memory addressing starts: 0, 1, 2…—is occupied by 256 interrupt vectors and their tables. An interrupt vector specifies where the **interrupt handler** program for a specific interrupt type is located. The use of interrupt handlers was discussed in Chapter 4. This is followed by BIOS tables and DOS tables, and the DOS kernel with additional installable drivers, if any, which are specified in the system's configuration file called CONFIG.SYS. This is followed by the resident part of the COMMAND.COM command interpreter—the section that is required to run application programs.

Any user application programs can now be loaded into the transient program area (TPA). If a large program requires more space, the COMMAND.COM overlay area, located at the high-numbered memory location, can be used by the application program as well. The COMMAND.COM programs in this area are considered transient because they are used to execute commands, such as FORMAT, that can't be executed by the user when an application program is running, so they can be overlayed (or overwritten) by other programs.

Main Memory Allocation

The first versions of MS-DOS gave all available memory to the resident application program, but that proved insufficient because the simple contiguous memory allocation scheme didn't allow application programs to dynamically allocate and deallocate memory blocks. With Version 2.0, MS-DOS began supporting dynamic allocation, modification, and release of main memory blocks by application programs.

The amount of memory each application program actually owns depends on both the type of file from which the program is loaded and the size of the TPA.

Programs with the COM **extension** are given all of the TPA, whether or not they need it.

Programs with the EXE extension are only given the amount of memory they need. These files have a header that indicates the minimum and maximum amount of memory needed for the program to run. Ideally, MS-DOS gives the program the maximum amount of memory requested. If that isn't possible, it tries to satisfy the minimum requirement. If the minimum is more than the amount of main memory space available, then the program cannot be run.

Except for COM files, there can be any number of files in the TPA at one time. But this raises an interesting question: Why would a system have two programs in memory when it can run only one at a time? Answer: By having several files in memory at once, the user can quickly open one and work on it and close it before starting on the next. They can't both be open at the same time; but by alternately opening and closing them, the user can use two programs quickly and easily.

For example, a word-processing program might allow a user to display two files on the screen at once by opening a separate work area for each one. These work areas partition the screen into sections; in this example, one would show the active file and the other would show the dormant file. If the user indicates that work should begin on the second (dormant) file, then the first (active) file is quickly closed and the second file is activated.

Here's a second example: Let's say your word processor's main program includes the code required to compose and print a document; but if you want to check your spelling, the spell checker program has to be loaded from the disk. When that's done, the main portion of the word processor is kept in memory and the second program is added without erasing the first one already there. Now you have two programs in memory but only one of them is executing at any given time. This is discussed in the section on Process Management later in this chapter.

If a program that is already running needs more memory, such as for additional I/O buffers, the Memory Manager checks to see whether enough memory remains. If so, it allocates it to the program while updating the memory block allocation table for that program. If not, then an error message is returned to the user and the program is stopped. Although initial memory allocation is handled automatically by programs written in BASIC, Pascal, or any other language supported by MS-DOS, the shrinking and expanding of memory allocation during execution can be done only from programs written in either assembly language or C.

Memory Block Allocation

The Memory Manager allocates memory by using a first-fit algorithm and a linked list of memory blocks. But with Version 3.3 and beyond, a best-fit or last-fit strategy can be selected. When using last-fit, DOS allocates the highest addressable memory block big enough to satisfy the program's request.

The size of a block can vary from as small as 16 bytes (called a "paragraph") to as large as the maximum available memory. When a block is formed, its first five bytes contain the information shown in Table 14.2.

	Byte	Meaning
(table 14.2) *The first five bytes of a memory block define the block's structural characteristics.*	Byte 0	ASCII 90h if it's the last block, or ASCII 77h if it's not
	Bytes 1–2	Includes the number 0 to indicate a busy block and the pointer to the Program Segment Prefix (PSP) that is created by the EXEC function when the program is loaded
	Bytes 3–4	Gives the number of paragraphs contained in the block

Therefore, if a block contains four paragraphs and is the first of two blocks, then its code would be 7700000004h (as explained in Table 14.3). The letter *h* at the end indicates that the preceding value is in hexadecimal notation and is not recorded.

	Byte	Contents	Meaning
(table 14.3) *A sample memory block with the first five bytes containing 7700000004h.*	Byte 0	77	Indicates that this is *not* the last block
	Bytes 1–2	0000	Indicates that this is a busy block and its pointer to the PSP is 0
	Bytes 3–4	0004	Indicates that this block contains four paragraphs

Whenever a request for memory comes in, DOS looks through the free/busy block list, as shown in Figure 14.4, until it finds a free block that fits the request. If the list of blocks becomes disconnected, an error message is generated, and the system stops. To recover, the system must be rebooted.

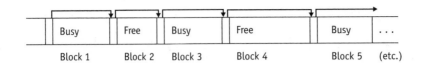

(figure 14.4)

The linked list of memory blocks.

A well-designed application program releases the memory block it no longer needs. If two free memory blocks are contiguous, they are merged immediately into one block and linked to the list. A program that isn't well designed, however, hoards its memory blocks until it stops running; only then can MS-DOS deallocate the memory blocks used by that program.

Processor Management

The Processor Manager has the relatively simple task of allocating the processor to the resident job when it's ready for execution.

Process Management

MS-DOS wasn't written in reentrant code, discussed in the section on Virtual Memory in Chapter 3, because it was designed for a single-user, single-task environment. Reentrant code is the basis for multitasking, and MS-DOS doesn't support it; therefore, programs can't break out of the middle of a DOS internal routine and then restart the routine from somewhere else.

In our word processing/spell checker example, the word processor's parent program called on the child spell checker program. The parent went to sleep, and remained asleep, while the child was running. There's no interleaving, so there's no need for sophisticated algorithms or policies to determine which job will run next or for how long. Each job runs in complete segments and is not interrupted midstream. In other words, there's no need to maintain a good job mix to balance system utilization.

However, although two jobs can't run together, some software programs give that illusion. Both Microsoft Windows and Borland's SideKick, for instance, appear to interrupt the parent program, change the screen displays, run unrelated programs, and then return to the parent—but this is not multitasking. (Multitasking is the microcomputer industry's synonym for multiprogramming.) These programs look and feel like multitasking operations because they retain their memory area and run executable programs, but they aren't both in the running state at the same time. In each case, the parent program goes to sleep while the child runs along on its own. This synchronization is possible because the interrupt handlers built into MS-DOS give programmers the capability to save all information about the parent program, which allows its proper restart after the child program has finished.

Interrupt Handlers

Interrupt handlers are a crucial part of the system. One might say they are responsible for synchronizing the processes. A personal computer has 256 interrupts and interrupt handlers, and they are accessed via the interrupt vector table residing in the lowest bytes of memory, as shown in Figure 14.3. Interrupts can be divided into three groups: internal hardware interrupts, external hardware interrupts, and software interrupts. Internal hardware interrupts are generated by certain events occurring during a program's execution, such as division by 0. The assignment of such events to specific interrupt numbers is electronically wired into the processor and isn't modifiable by software instructions.

External hardware interrupts are caused by peripheral device controllers or by coprocessors such as the 8087/80287. The assignment of the external devices to specific interrupt levels is done by the manufacturer of the computer system or the manufacturer of the peripheral device. These assignments can't be modified by software because they are hardwired—implemented as physical electrical connections.

Software interrupts are generated by system and application programs. They access DOS and BIOS functions, which, in turn, access the system resources.

Some software interrupts are used to activate specialized application programs that take over control of the computer. Borland's SideKick is one such program. This type of interrupt handler is called Terminate and Stay Resident (TSR). Its function is to terminate a process without releasing its memory, thus providing memory-resident programming facilities. The TSR is usually used by subroutine libraries that are called once from the MS-DOS command level and are then available to provide services to other applications through a software interrupt. When a TSR starts running, it sets up its memory tables and prepares for execution by connecting to a DOS interrupt; when all is ready, the program determines how much memory it needs to keep. Later, when the program exits, a return code is passed back to the parent.

How are these interrupts synchronized? When the CPU senses an interrupt, it does two things: (1) it puts on a stack the contents of the PSW (Program Status Word), the code segment register, and the instruction pointer register; and (2) it disables the interrupt system so that other interrupts will be put off until the current one has been resolved. The CPU uses the 8-bit number placed on the system bus by the interrupting device to get the address of the appropriate interrupt handler from the interrupt vector table and picks up execution at that address.

Finally, the interrupt handler reenables the interrupt system to allow higher-priority interrupts to occur, saves any register it needs to use, and processes the interrupt as quickly as possible.

Obviously, this is a delicate procedure. The synchronization of TSR activities with DOS functions already in progress must be carefully designed and implemented to avoid either modifying things that shouldn't be modified or crashing the system.

Device Management

The ability to reorder requests to optimize seek and search time is not a feature of MS-DOS because it's designed for a single-user environment. All requests are handled on a first-come, first-served basis. But, since Version 3.0, BIOS can support spooling allowing users to schedule several files to be printed one after the other. To do this, BIOS continuously transfers data from a specified memory buffer to the printer until the buffer is empty.

MS-DOS was written for simple systems that use a keyboard, monitor, printer, mouse, one or two serial ports, and maybe a second printer. For storage, most personal computer systems use direct access storage devices, usually floppy disks or hard disks. Some systems also support a magnetic tape sequential access archiving system. The MS-DOS Device Manager can work with all of them.

These systems use only one of each type of I/O device for each port, so device channels are not a part of MS-DOS. And because each device has its own dedicated control unit, the devices do not require special management from the operating system. Therefore, device drivers are the only items needed by the Device Manager to make the system work. A device driver is a software module that controls an I/O device but handles its interrupts. Each device has its own device driver. BIOS is the portion of the Device Manager that handles the device driver software.

BIOS is stored in both ROM and RAM. In many MS-DOS systems, the most primitive parts of the device drivers are located in ROM so they can be used by stand-alone applications, diagnostics, and the system's bootstrapping program. A second section is loaded from the disk into RAM and extends the capabilities of the basic functions stored in ROM so that BIOS can handle all of the system's input and output requests.

Normally, BIOS is provided by the system manufacturer adhering to Microsoft's specifications for MS-DOS and, because it's the link between the hardware and DOS, it uses standard operating system kernels regardless of the hardware. This means that programs with the standard DOS and BIOS interfaces for their system-dependent functions can be used on every DOS machine regardless of the manufacturer.

BIOS responds to interrupts generated by either hardware or software. For example, a hardware interrupt is generated when a user presses the Print Screen key—this causes BIOS to activate a routine that sends the ASCII contents of the screen to the printer.

Likewise, a software interrupt is generated when a program issues a command to read something from a disk file. This causes the CPU to tell BIOS to activate a routine to read data from the disk and gives it the following: the number of sectors to transfer, track number, sector number, head number, and drive number. After the operation has been successfully completed, it tells BIOS the number of sectors transferred and sends an all clear code. If an error should occur during the operation, an error code is returned so that BIOS can display the appropriate error message on the screen.

Most device drivers are part of standard MS-DOS. Of course, you can always write your own device driver. All you need is knowledge of assembly language, information about the hardware, and some patience. This option might be necessary if you're using a system with an unusual combination of devices. For instance, in its early years of commercial availability, there was not a high demand for interfacing a computer with a disc player—so its device drivers were not incorporated into BIOS. Therefore, users who wanted to use a disc as an I/O device had to write or buy their own device drivers and load them when the system was booted up. These device drivers are called installable because they can be incorporated into the operating system as needed without having to patch or change the existing operating system. Installable device drivers are a salient feature of MS-DOS design.

File Management

MS-DOS supports sequential, direct, and indexed sequential file organizations. Sequential files can have either variable- or fixed-length records. However, direct and indexed sequential files can only have fixed-length records.

Filename Conventions

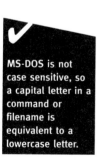

MS-DOS is not case sensitive, so a capital letter in a command or filename is equivalent to a lowercase letter.

A filename contains no spaces and consists of the drive designation, the directory, any subdirectory, a primary name, and an optional extension. (DOS isn't case sensitive so filenames and commands can be entered in uppercase, lowercase, or a combination of both.)

The drive name (usually A, B, C, or D) is followed by a colon (:). Directories or subdirectories can be from one to eight characters long and are preceded by a backslash (\). The primary filename can be from one to eight characters long and the extension from one to three characters long. The primary name and extension are separated by a period. A file's extension can have a special meaning to DOS—the user should be aware of the standard extensions and their uses.

If no directories or subdirectories are included in the name, it's assumed that the file is in the current **working directory.** If no drive is designated, it's assumed that the file is on the current drive. The root directory (see the next section, Managing Files, for a discussion of this) is called by a single backslash (\). The names of other directories are preceded by the backslash symbol. The backslash is also used as a delimiter between names.

A file's relative name consists of its primary name and extension, if used. A file's absolute name consists of its drive designation and directory location (called its **path**) followed by its relative name. When the user is working in a directory or subdirectory, it's called the working directory and any file in that directory can be accessed by its relative name. However, to access a file that's in another directory, the absolute name is required.

For example, if your working directory includes a file called JORDAN.DOC, then you can identify that file by typing:

```
JORDAN.DOC
```

However, if you changed to another working directory, then you would have to include the directory name when you called the file:

```
\JOURNAL\CHAP9\JORDAN.DOC
```

And if you changed to another drive, such as drive A, and wanted to call the file, you would have to include the drive designation as well:

```
C:\JOURNAL\CHAP9\JORDAN.DOC
```

DOS filenames can have no spaces within them. Therefore, to copy the file from drive C to drive B, the command would look like this:

```
COPY  C:\MEMO\DEAN.DOC  B:DEAN.DOC
```

A simpler way to access files is to select a working directory first and then access the files within that directory by their relative names. Later, when you're finished with one directory, you can issue the change directory command (see Table 14.4 later in this chapter) to move to another working directory.

Of course, there are many variations. For complete details, refer to a technical manual for your version of MS-DOS.

Managing Files

The earliest versions of MS-DOS kept every file in a single directory. This was slow and cumbersome, especially as users added more and more files. To retrieve a single file, the File Manager searched from the beginning of the list until either the file was found or the end of the list was reached. If a user forgot how the file was named, there was a good chance that it would never be seen again.

To solve this problem, Microsoft implemented a hierarchical directory structure in Version 2.0—an inverted tree directory structure. (It's inverted because the root is at the top and the leaves are on the bottom.)

When a disk is formatted (using the FORMAT command), its tracks are divided into sectors of 512 bytes each. (This corresponds to a buffer size of 512 bytes.) Single-sided disks have one recording surface, double-sided disks have two recording surfaces, and hard disks have from two to four platters, each with two recording surfaces. The concept of *cylinders*, presented in Chapter 7, applies to these hard disks because the read/write heads move in unison.

The sectors (from two to eight) are grouped into clusters and that's how the File Manager allocates space to files. When a file needs additional space, DOS allocates more clusters to it. Besides dividing up the disk space, FORMAT creates three special areas on the disk: the boot record, the root directory, and the **FAT**, which stands for **file allocation table**.

The *boot record* is the first sector of every logical disk, whether it's an entire physical unit (such as a floppy disk or hard disk) or only a virtual disk (such as a RAM disk). Beginning with Version 2.0, the boot record contains the disk boot program and a table of the disk's characteristics.

The *root directory* is where the system begins its interaction with the user when it's booted up. The root directory contains a list of the system's primary subdirectories and files, including any system-generated configuration files and any user-generated booting instructions that may be included in an AUTOEXEC.BAT file. This is a **batch file** containing a series of commands defined by the user. Every time the CPU is powered up or is reset, the commands in this file are executed automatically by the system. A sample AUTOEXEC.BAT file is discussed later in this chapter.

The information kept in the root directory is: (1) the filename, (2) the file extension, (3) the file size in bytes, (4) the date and time of the file's last modification, (5) the starting cluster number for the file, and (6) the file attribute codes. Of these six elements, the first four are displayed in response to the DIR command, as shown in Figure 14.5.

The number of entries in a root directory is fixed. For instance, only 512 entries are allowed for a 20 MB hard disk. The size of the root directory is limited because DOS needs to know where the disk's data area begins. Beginning with Version 2.0, users can avoid this limitation by creating subdirectories that have no size limit.

```
C:\WINDOWS\system32\cmd.exe                          _ □ ×

C:\DOCS>dir
 Volume in drive C is SQ004101P01
 Volume Serial Number is 001B-D93A

 Directory of C:\DOCS

05/23/2007  10:31 PM    <DIR>          .
05/23/2007  10:31 PM    <DIR>          ..
05/23/2007  10:31 PM    <DIR>          temp
04/27/2000  06:36 PM               766 UserGuide.ico
01/05/2006  01:49 PM         3,432,934 userguide.pdf
               2 File(s)      3,433,700 bytes
               3 Dir(s)  62,580,416,512 bytes free

C:\DOCS>
```

(figure 14.5)

A listing of the DOCS directory showing three subdirectories and two files.

The directory listing shown in Figure 14.5 was generated by the command DIR. Notice how the three subdirectories are distinguished from the two files. Notice, also, that the system maintains the date and time when it was most recently modified. Some software security programs use this data to detect any viruses or other unauthorized or unusual modifications of the system's software.

Each subdirectory can contain its own subdirectories and/or files, as shown in Figure 14.6.

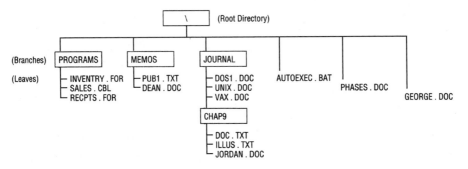

(figure 14.6)

The directory system: The root directory listing has six entries. The directory listing for JOURNAL has four entries: its three files and its subdirectory CHAP9. The directory listing for CHAP9 has three entries for its three files.

MS-DOS supports hidden files—files that are executable but not displayed in response to DIR commands. Some of MS-DOS's system files are hidden files; they're used to run the operating system but they don't show up on the directory listings. COMMAND.COM is the only system file that isn't hidden and so it's always displayed on public directories.

The FAT contains critical status information, including each sector's capability to be allocated or not, which may have resulted from formatting errors that rendered the sector unusable.

The directory notes the number of the first sector or cluster of the file—this number is recorded in the directory when the file is created. All successive sectors or clusters allocated to that file are recorded in the FAT, and are linked together to form a chain, with each FAT entry giving the sector/cluster number of the next entry. The last entry for each chain contains the hexadecimal value FF to indicate the end of the chain. As you can see in Figure 14.7, a file's sectors don't have to be contiguous.

(figure 14.7)

For each file, the directory includes the first sector/cluster location in the file allocation table so it can be accessed quickly. The FAT links every sector for each file. Notice that the sectors for the file PHASES.DOC are not contiguous (the arrows are a visual aid to show their linking).

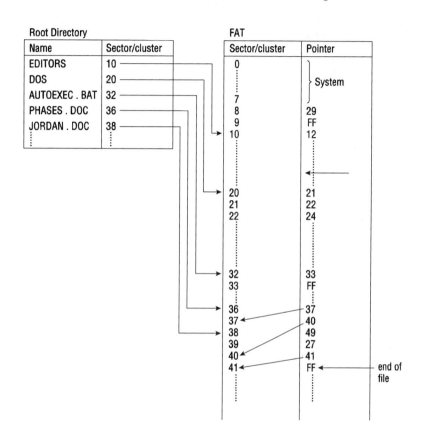

MS-DOS looks at data in a disk file as a continuous string of bytes. Therefore, I/O operations request data by relative byte (relative to the beginning of the file) rather than by relative sector. The transformation from physical sector (or cluster) to relative byte address is done by the File Manager so data on a disk appears to be accessed just like data in main memory.

As we mentioned a moment ago, MS-DOS supports noncontiguous file storage and dynamically allocates disk space to a file, provided there's enough room on the disk. Unfortunately, as files are added and deleted from the disk, a file may become quite fragmented, making it increasingly cumbersome and time consuming to retrieve.

Compaction became a feature of MS-DOS Version 6.0 with the inclusion of DEFRAG.EXE, a utility used to defragment a disk by picking up the fragments of a file and repositioning them as a single piece in a contiguous space.

Another command can be used to determine the need for compaction. Given CHKDSK (filename), the system responds with the number of noncontiguous blocks in which the file is stored. It's up to the user to compact the file, if necessary, so it's stored in as few noncontiguous blocks as possible to speed access time and reduce maintenance on the seek mechanism.

The ability to restrict user access to the computer system and its resources isn't built into MS-DOS. Add-on security software is available; but, for most users, data is kept secure by keeping the computer physically locked up or by removing the disks and keeping them in a safe place.

User Interface

MS-DOS uses a **command-driven interface**. Table 14.4 shows some of the most common commands. Users type in their commands at the system prompt. The default prompt is the drive indicator (such as C:) and the > character; therefore, C:> is the standard prompt for a hard drive system and A:> is the prompt for a computer with one floppy disk drive. The default prompt can be changed using the PROMPT command.

Command	Stands For	Action to Be Performed
DIR	Directory	List what's in this directory.
CD or CHDIR	Change Directory	Change the working directory.
COPY	Copy	Copy a file. Append one to another.
DEL or ERASE	Delete	Delete the following file or files.
RENAME	Rename	Rename a file.
TYPE	Type	Display the text file on the screen.
PRINT	Print	Print one or more files on printer.
DATE	Date	Display and/or change the system date.
TIME	Time	Display and/or change the system time.
MD or MKDIR	Make Directory	Create a new directory or subdirectory.
FIND	Find	Find a string. Search files for a string.
FORMAT	Format Disk	Logically prepare a disk for file storage.
CHKDSK	Check Disk	Check disk for disk/file/directory status.
PROMPT	System Prompt	Change the system prompt symbol.
DEFRAG	Defragment Disk	Compact fragmented files.
(filename)		Run (execute) the file.

(table 14.4)

Some common MS-DOS user commands. Commands can be entered in either upper- or lowercase characters; although in this text we use all capital letters to make the notation consistent. Check the technical documentation for your system for proper spelling and syntax.

When the user presses the Enter key, the shell called COMMAND.COM interprets the command and calls on the next lower-level routine to satisfy the request.

User commands include some or all of these elements in this order:

```
command     source-file     destination-file     switches
```

The command is any legal MS-DOS command. The source-file and destination-file are included when applicable and, depending on the current drive and directory, might need to include the file's complete pathname. The switches begin with a slash (i.e., /P /V /F) and are optional; they give specific details about how the command is to be carried out. Most commands require a space between each of their elements.

The commands are carried out by the COMMAND.COM file, which is part of MS-DOS, as shown in Figure 14.2. As we said before, when COMMAND.COM is loaded during the system's initialization, one section of it is stored in the low section of memory; this is the resident portion of the code. It contains the command interpreter and the routines needed to support an active program. In addition, it contains the routines needed to process CTRL-C, CTRL-BREAK, and critical errors.

The transient code, the second section of COMMAND.COM, is stored in the highest addresses of memory and can be overwritten by application programs if they need to use its memory space. Later, when the program terminates, the resident portion of COMMAND.COM checks to see if the transient code is still intact. If it isn't, it loads a new copy.

As a user types in a command, each character is stored in memory and displayed on the screen. When the Enter key is pressed, the operating system transfers control to the command interpreter portion of COMMAND.COM, which either accesses the routine that carries out the request or displays an error message. If the routine is residing in memory, then control is given to it directly. If the routine is residing on secondary storage, it's loaded into memory and then control is given to it.

Although we can't describe every command available in MS-DOS, some features are worth noting to show the flexibility of this operating system.

Batch Files

By creating customized batch files, users can quickly execute combinations of DOS commands to configure their systems, perform routine tasks, or make it easier for nontechnical users to run software.

For instance, if a user routinely checks the system date and time, loads a device driver for a mouse, moves to a certain subdirectory, and loads a program called MAIL.COM, then the program that performs each of these steps (called START.BAT), would perform each of those steps in turn as shown in Figure 14.8.

(figure 14.8)

Contents of the program START.BAT.

To run this program, the user needs only to type START at the system prompt. To have this program run automatically every time the system is restarted, then the file should be renamed AUTOEXEC.BAT and loaded into the system's root directory. By using batch files, any tedious combinations of keystrokes can be reduced to a few easily remembered customized commands.

Redirection

MS-DOS can redirect output from one standard input or output device to another. For example, the DATE command sends output directly to the screen; but by using the **redirection** symbol (>), the output is redirected to another device or file instead.

The syntax is:

```
command > destination
```

For example, if you want to send a directory listing to the printer, you would type DIR > PRN and the listing would appear on the printed page instead of the screen. Likewise, if you want the directory of the default drive to be redirected to a file on the disk in the B drive, you'd type DIR > B:DIRFILE and a new file called DIRFILE would be created on drive B and it would contain a listing of the directory.

You can redirect and append new output to an existing file by using the append symbol (>>). For example, if you've already created the file DIRFILE with the redirection command and you wanted to generate a listing of the directory and append it to the previously created DIRFILE, you would type:

```
DIR >> B:DIRFILE
```

Now DIRFILE contains two listings of the same directory.

Redirection works in the opposite manner as well. If you want to change the source to a specific device or file, use the < symbol. For example, let's say you have a program called INVENTRY.EXE under development that expects input from the keyboard, but for testing and debugging purposes you want it to accept input from a test data file. In this case, you would type:

```
INVENTRY < B:TEST.DAT
```

Filters

Filter commands accept input from the default device, manipulate the data in some fashion, and send the results to the default output device. A commonly used filter is SORT, which accepts input from the keyboard, sorts that data, and displays it on the screen. This filter command becomes even more useful if it can read data from a file and sort it to another file. This can be done by using the redirectional parameters. For example, if you wanted to sort a data file called STD.DAT and store it in another file called SORTSTD.DAT, then you'd type:

```
SORT <STD.DAT> SORTSTD.DAT
```

The sorted file would be in ascending order (numerically or alphabetically) starting with the first character in each line of the file. If you wanted the file sorted in reverse order, then you would type:

```
SORT /R  <STD.DAT> SORTSTD.DAT
```

You can sort the file by column. For example, let's say a file called EMPL has data that follows this format: the ID numbers start in Column 1, the phone numbers start in Column 6, and the last names start in Column 14. (A column is defined as characters delimited by one or more spaces.) To sort the file by last name, the command would be:

```
SORT /+14  <EMPL.DAT> SORTEMPL.DAT
```

The file would be sorted in ascending order by the field starting at Column 14.

Another common filter is MORE, which causes output to be displayed on the screen in groups of 24 lines, one screen at a time, and waits until the user presses the Enter key before displaying the next 24 lines.

Pipes

A **pipe** can cause the standard output from one command to be used as standard input to another command; its symbol is a vertical bar (|). You can alphabetically sort your directory and display the sorted list on the screen by typing:

```
DIR | SORT
```

You can combine pipes and other filters too. For example, to display on the screen the contents of the file INVENTRY.DAT one screen at a time, the command would be:

```
TYPE INVENTRY.DAT | MORE
```

You can achieve the same result using only redirection by typing:

```
MORE < INVENTRY.DAT
```

You can sort your directory and display it one screen at a time by using pipes with this command:

```
DIR | SORT | MORE
```

Or you can achieve the same result by using both pipes and filters with these two commands:

```
DIR | SORT > SORTFILE
```

```
MORE < SORTFILE
```

Additional Commands

Three additional commands often used in MS-DOS are FIND, PRINT, and TREE. Note that these are "traditional" MS-DOS commands, and some of the switches or options mentioned here might not work in Windows DOS-like emulators.

FIND

FIND is a filter command that searches for a specific string in a given file or files and displays all lines that contain the string from those files. The string must be enclosed in double quotes (" ") and must be typed exactly as it is to be searched; upper- and lowercase letters are taken as entered.

For example, the command to display all the lines in the file PAYROLL.COB that contain the string AMNT-PAID is this:

```
FIND "AMNT-PAID" PAYROLL.COB
```

The command to count the number of lines in the file PAYROLL.COB that contain the string AMNT-PAID and display the number on the screen is this:

```
FIND /C "AMNT-PAID" PAYROLL.COB
```

The command to display the relative line number, as well as the line in the file PAYROLL.COB that contains the string AMNT-PAID, is this:

```
FIND /N "AMNT-PAID" PAYROLL.COB
```

The command to display all of the lines in the file PAYROLL.COB that *do not* contain the string AMNT-PAID, is this:

```
FIND /V "AMNT-PAID" PAYROLL.COB
```

The command to display the names of all files on the disk in drive B that *do not* contain the string SYS is this:

```
DIR B: | FIND /V "SYS"
```

PRINT

The PRINT command allows the user to set up a series of files for printing while freeing up COMMAND.COM to accept other commands. In effect, it's a spooler. As the printer prints your files, you can type other commands and work on other applications. The PRINT command has many options; but to use the following two, they must be given the first time the PRINT command is used after booting the system:

- The command PRINT /B allows you to change the size of the internal buffer. Its default is 512 bytes, but increasing its value speeds up the PRINT process.
- The command PRINT /Q specifies the number of files allowed in the print queue. The minimum value for Q is 4 and the maximum is 32.

TREE

The TREE command displays directories and subdirectories in a hierarchical and indented list. It also has options that allow the user to delete files while the tree is being generated. The display starts with the current or specified directory, with the subdirectories indented under the directory that contains them. For example, if we issue the command TREE, the response would be similar to that shown in Figure 14.9.

(figure 14.9)

Sample results of the TREE command.

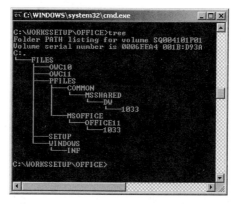

457

To display the names of the files in each directory, add the switch /F:

```
TREE /F
```

The TREE command can also be used to delete a file that's duplicated on several different directories. For example, to delete the file PAYROLL.COB anywhere on the disk, the command would be:

```
TREE PAYROLL.COB /D /Q
```

The system displays the tree as usual; but whenever it encounters a file called PAYROLL.COB, it pauses and asks if you want to delete it. If, you type Y, then it deletes the file and continues. If you type N, then it continues as before.

For illustrative purposes, we've included only a few MS-DOS commands here. For a complete list of commands, their exact syntax, and more details about those we've discussed here, see *www.microsoft.com*.

Conclusion

MS-DOS was written to serve users of 1980s personal computers, including the earliest IBM PCs. As such, it was a success but its limited flexibility made it unusable as computer hardware evolved.

MS-DOS is remembered as the first standard operating system to be adopted by many manufacturers of personal computing machines. As the standard, it also supported, and was supported by, legions of software design groups.

The weakness of MS-DOS was its single-user/single-task system design that couldn't support multitasking, networking, and other sophisticated applications required of computers of every size. Today it is a relic of times past, but its simple structure and user interface make it an accessible learning tool for operating system students.

Key Terms

batch file: a file that includes a series of commands that are executed in sequence without any input from the user. It contrasts with an interactive session.

BIOS: an acronym for basic input/output system, a set of programs that are hard-coded on a chip to load into ROM at startup.

bootstrapping: the process of starting an inactive computer by using a small initialization program to load other programs.

command-driven interface: an interface that accepts typed commands, one line at a time, from the user. It contrasts with a menu-driven interface.

compaction: the process of collecting fragments of available memory space into contiguous blocks by moving programs and data in a computer's memory or secondary storage.

device driver: a device-specific program module that handles the interrupts and controls a particular type of device.

extension: the part of the filename that indicates which compiler or software package is needed to run the files.

file allocation table (FAT): the table used to track segments of a file.

filter command: a command that directs input from a device or file, changes it, and then sends the result to a printer or display.

first-fit memory allocation: a main memory allocation scheme that searches from the beginning of the free block list and selects for allocation the first block of memory large enough to fulfill the request. It contrasts with *best-fit memory allocation.*

interrupt handler: the program that controls what action should be taken by the operating system when a sequence of events is interrupted.

multitasking: a synonym for multiprogramming, a technique that allows a single processor to process several programs residing simultaneously in main memory and interleaving their execution by overlapping I/O requests with CPU requests.

path: the sequence of directories and subdirectories the operating system must follow to find a specific file.

pipe: a symbol that directs the operating system to divert the output of one command so it becomes the input of another command. In MS-DOS, the pipe symbol is |.

redirection: an instruction that directs the operating system to send the results of a command to or from a file or a device other than a keyboard or monitor. In MS-DOS, the redirection symbols are < and >.

system prompt: the signal from the operating system that it is ready to accept a user's command, such as C:\> or C:\Documents>.

working directory: the directory or subdirectory that is currently the one being used as the home directory.

Interesting Searches

- MS-DOS Emulator
- Autoexec Batch File
- Basic Input/Output System (BIOS)

- Command-Driven User Interface
- MS-DOS Command Syntax

Exercises

Research Topics

A. Explore the computing world in the early 1980s and identify several reasons for the popularity of MS-DOS at that time. List competing operating systems and the brands of personal computers that were available. Cite your sources.

B. According to *www.microsoft.com*, the company still supports MS-DOS because this operating system is in use at sites around the world. Conduct your own research to find a site that is still running MS-DOS and explain in your own words why it is the operating system of choice there.

Exercises

1. Describe in your own words the purpose of all user interfaces, whether command- or menu-driven.

2. Name five advantages that a command-driven user interface has over a menu-driven user interface.

3. How is a legal MS-DOS filename constructed? Describe the maximum length and the roles of special characters, upper/lowercase, slashes, etc.

4. How do the sizes of system buffers and disk sectors compare? Which is larger? Explain why this is so.

5. Give examples of the CD, DIR, and TREE commands and explain why you would use each one.

6. Open the MS-DOS emulator from a Windows operating system (perhaps under the Accessories Menu and called "Command Prompt"). Change to a directory with several files and subdirectories and perform a DIR command. How is the resulting directory ordered (alphabetically, chronologically, or other)?

7. Open the MS-DOS emulator from a Windows operating system and perform a directory listing of the root directory (use the CD\ command and then the DIR command). Then using the Windows operating system, open the C folder. Compare the two listings and explain in your own words how they are similar and how they differ.

8. Open the MS-DOS emulator from a Windows operating system and perform a TREE command. Explain in your own words whether or not having access to this MS-DOS command could be valuable to a Windows user.

9. Describe in your own words the role of the file allocation table (FAT) and how it manages files.

10. How does the working directory described in this chapter compare to the working set described in Chapter 3?

Advanced Exercises

11. If you were configuring a small office with 10 personal computers running only MS-DOS, describe how you would network them and how many copies of the operating system you would need to purchase.

12. The FORMAT command wipes out any existing data on the disk being formatted or reformatted. Describe what safety features you would want to add to the system to prevent inadvertent use of this command.

13. Explain why a boot routine is a necessary element of all operating systems.

14. Describe how MS-DOS performs a cold boot and in what order its disk drives are accessed. Explain why this order does or does not make sense.

15. Describe how you would add control access to protect sensitive data in a computer running MS-DOS. Can you describe both hardware and software solutions? Describe any other features you would want to add to the system to make it more secure.

16. The boot routine is stored in the systems disk's first sector so that this routine can be the first software loaded into memory when the computer is powered on. Conduct your own research to discover the essential elements of the boot routine and describe why this software is needed to "boot up" the system.

Chapter 15 | Windows Operating Systems

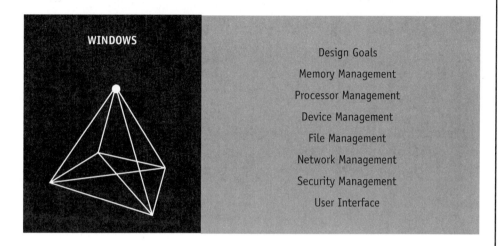

WINDOWS

Design Goals
Memory Management
Processor Management
Device Management
File Management
Network Management
Security Management
User Interface

> *" Windows has this exciting central position, a position that is used by thousands and thousands of companies to build their products. "*
>
> —Bill Gates

Learning Objectives

After completing this chapter, you should be able to describe:

- The design goals for Windows operating systems
- The role of MS-DOS in early Windows releases
- The role of the Memory Manager and Virtual Memory Manager
- The use of the Device, Processor, and Network Managers
- The system security challenges
- The Windows user interface

Windows 95 was the first full-featured operating system sold by Microsoft Corporation and each one since has been a financial success. Windows operating systems are now available for computing environments of all sizes.

Windows Development

The first Windows product used a **graphical user interface (GUI)** as its primary method of communication with the user and needed an underlying operating system so it could translate the users' requests into system commands.

Early Windows Products

Windows 1.0, introduced in 1985, ran on microcomputers with the MS-DOS operating system. That is, the first Windows application was not a true operating system. It was merely an interface between the actual MS-DOS operating system and the user. Even though this was a simple product (when compared to the complex operating systems of today), it was notable because it was the first menu-driven interface for desktop computers that were compatible with the IBM personal computer (PC).

Windows 1.0 was followed by increasingly sophisticated GUIs designed to run increasingly powerful desktop computers, as shown in Table 15.1. The first widely adopted Windows product, Windows 3.1, featured a standardized look and feel, similar to the one made popular by Apple's Macintosh computer. Windows 3.1 became the entry-level product for single-user installations or small-business environments.

Year	Product	Features
1985	Windows 1.0	First retail shipment of the first Windows product; required MS-DOS
1990	Windows 3.0	Improved performance and advanced ease-of-use; required MS-DOS
1992	Windows 3.1	Widely adopted, commercially successful GUI with more than 1,000 enhancements over 3.0; required MS-DOS
1992	Windows for Workgroups	GUI for small networks; required MS-DOS

(table 15.1)

Early Microsoft Windows GUI products ran "on top of" MS-DOS.

Notice in Table 15.1 that Windows for Workgroups was the first Windows product to accommodate the needs of network users by including programs and features for small LANs. For example, a Windows for Workgroups system could easily share directories, disks, and printers among several interconnected machines. It also allowed personal intercommunication through e-mail and chat programs. It was intended for small or mid-sized groups of PCs typically seen in small businesses or small departments of larger organizations.

Operating Systems for Home and Professional Users

Before the release of the Windows 95 operating system, all Windows products were built to run on top of the MS-DOS operating system. That is, MS-DOS was the true operating system but took its direction from the Windows program being run on it. However, this layering technique proved to be a disadvantage. Although it helped Windows gain market share among MS-DOS users, MS-DOS had little built-in security, couldn't perform multitasking, and had no interprocess communication capability. In addition, it was written to work closely with the microcomputer's hardware, making it difficult to move the operating system to other platforms.

To respond to these needs, Microsoft developed and released a succession of Windows operating systems (not mere GUIs) to appeal to home and office users, as shown in Table 15.2. (Parallel development of networking products is shown in Table 15.3.)

Each Windows product has a version number. For example, Windows XP is version 5.1, Windows Vista is version 6.0, and Windows 7 is version 6.1. To find the version number, press the Windows logo key and the *R* key together. Then type winver. Then click OK.

(table 15.2)			
The evolution of key Microsoft Windows operating systems for home and professional use.	1995	Windows 95	True operating system designed to replace Windows 3.x, Windows for Workgroups, and MS-DOS for single-user desktop computers.
	1998	Windows 98	For PC users. Implemented many bug fixes to Windows 95, had more extended hardware support, and was fully 32 bit. Not directly related to Windows NT.
	2000	Windows Millennium Edition (ME)	Last Windows operating system built on the Windows 95 code.
	2001	Windows XP Home	For PC users. A 32-bit operating system built to succeed Windows 95 and 98, but built on the Windows NT kernel.
	2001	Windows XP Professional	For networking and power users, built on the Windows NT kernel. The Professional Edition was available in 32-bit and 64-bit versions.
	2007	Windows Vista	Complex operating system with improved diagnostic and repair tools.
	2009	Windows 7	Available in six versions, most with 64-bit addressing. Designed to address the stability and response shortcomings of Windows Vista.

While Microsoft was courting the home and office environment with single-user operating systems, the company also began developing more powerful networking products, beginning with Windows NT (New Technology). Unlike the single-user operating systems, Windows NT never relied on MS-DOS for support.

Operating Systems for Networks

In the fall of 1988, Microsoft hired David Cutler to lead the development of the Windows NT operating system. As an experienced architect of minicomputer systems, Cutler identified the primary market requirements for this new product: portability, multiprocessing capabilities, distributed computing support, compliance with government procurement requirements, and government security certification. The finished product has evolved as shown in Table 15.3.

1993	Windows NT Advanced Server version 3.1	The first version of NT; featured true client/server operating system with support for Intel, RISC, and multiprocessor systems.
1994	Windows NT Server version 3.5	Introduced BackOffice applications suite, required 4MB less RAM, and offered tighter links to NetWare and UNIX networks through enhanced TCP/IP stack.
1996	Windows NT Server version 4.0	Added popular interface from Windows 95, included support for DCOM, and integrated support for e-mail and Internet connectivity.
1999	Windows 2000 Server	Introduced X.500-style directory services, Kerberos security, and improved Distributed Component Object Model (DCOM).
2003	Windows Server 2003	Available in Standard Edition, Web Edition, Enterprise Edition, and Datacenter Edition, this operating system was designed as a server platform for Microsoft's .NET initiative.
2009	Windows Server 2008 R2	Upgrade for Windows Server operating system.
2008	Windows Server 2008	Reduced power consumption, increased virtualization capabilities, supports up to 64 cores.

(table 15.3)

The evolution of key Microsoft Windows networking operating systems. All have evolved from Windows NT.

In 1999, Microsoft changed the operating system's name from Windows NT to Windows 2000, which was available in four packages: Windows 2000 Professional, Windows 2000 Server, Windows 2000 Advanced Server, and Windows 2000 Datacenter Server. The Datacenter Server was a new product designed for large data warehouses and other data-intensive business applications, and supported up to 64GB of physical memory. Likewise, Windows Server 2003 was also released with these same four packages plus a Web edition.

Windows Server 2008 Release 2 was launched in 2009 to coincide with the launch of Windows 7 and offered improved support for multiple cores, up to 64, reduced power consumption, and increased virtualization capabilities.

The rest of our discussion of Windows focuses primarily on the networking releases of this operating system.

Design Goals

For the operating system to fulfill its market requirements, certain features such as security had to be incorporated from the outset. Therefore, the designers of Windows assembled a set of software design goals to facilitate decision making as the coding process evolved. For example, if two design options conflicted, the design goals were used to help determine which was better.

When they were designed, Windows networking operating systems were influenced by several operating system models, using already-existing frameworks while introducing new features. They use an object model to manage operating system resources and to allocate them to users in a consistent manner. They use symmetric multiprocessing (SMP) to achieve maximum performance from multiprocessor computers.

To accommodate the various needs of its user community, and to optimize resources, the Windows team identified five design goals: extensibility, portability, reliability, compatibility, and performance—goals that Microsoft has met with varying levels of success.

Extensibility

Knowing that operating systems must change over time to support new hardware devices or new software technologies, the design team decided that the operating system had to be easily enhanced. This feature is called **extensibility**. In an effort to ensure the integrity of the Windows code, the designers separated operating system functions into two groups: a privileged executive process and a set of nonprivileged processes called protected subsystems. The term *privileged* refers to a processor's mode of operation. Most processors have a privileged mode (in which all machine instructions are allowed and system memory is accessible) and a nonprivileged mode (in which certain instructions are not allowed and system memory isn't accessible). In Windows terminology, the privileged processor mode is called **kernel mode** and the nonprivileged processor mode is called **user mode**.

Usually, operating systems execute in kernel mode only and application programs execute in user mode only, except when they call operating system services. In Windows, the protected subsystems execute in user mode as if they were applications, which allows protected subsystems to be modified or added without affecting the integrity of the executive process.

In addition to protected subsystems, Windows designers included several features to address extensibility issues:

- A modular structure so new components can be added to the executive process
- A group of abstract data types called objects that are manipulated by a special set of services, allowing system resources to be managed uniformly
- A remote procedure call that allows an application to call remote services regardless of their location on the network

Portability

Portability refers to the operating system's ability to operate on different machines that use different processors or configurations with a minimum amount of recoding. To address this goal, Windows system developers used a four-prong approach. First, they wrote it in a standardized, high-level language. Second, the system accommodated the hardware to which it was expected to be ported (32-bit, 64-bit, etc.). Third, code that interacted directly with the hardware was minimized to reduce incompatibility errors. Fourth, all hardware-dependent code was isolated into modules that could be modified more easily whenever the operating system was ported.

Windows is written for ease of porting to machines that use 32-bit or 64-bit linear addresses and provides virtual memory capabilities. Most Windows operating systems have shared the following features:

- The code is modular. That is, the code that must access processor-dependent data structures and registers is contained in small modules that can be replaced by similar modules for different processors.
- Much of Windows is written in C, a programming language that's standardized and readily available. The graphic component and some portions of the networking user interface are written in C++. Assembly language code (which generally is not portable) is used only for those parts of the system that must communicate directly with the hardware.
- Windows contains a hardware abstraction layer (HAL), a dynamic-link library that - provides isolation from hardware dependencies furnished by different vendors. The HAL abstracts hardware, such as caches, with a layer of low-level software so that higher-level code need not change when moving from one platform to another.

Reliability

Reliability refers to the robustness of a system—that is, its predictability in responding to error conditions, even those caused by hardware failures. It also refers to the operating system's ability to protect itself and its users from accidental or deliberate damage by user programs.

Structured exception handling is one way to capture error conditions and respond to them uniformly. Whenever such an event occurs, either the operating system or the processor issues an exception call, which automatically invokes the exception handling code that's appropriate to handle the condition, ensuring that no harm is done to either user programs or the system. In addition, the following features strengthen the system:

- A modular design that divides the executive process into individual system components that interact with each other through specified programming interfaces. For example, if it becomes necessary to replace the Memory Manager with a new one, then the new one will use the same interfaces.
- A file system called **NTFS (NT File System)**, which can recover from all types of errors including those that occur in critical disk sectors. To ensure recoverability, NTFS uses redundant storage and a transaction-based scheme for storing data.
- A security architecture that provides a variety of security mechanisms, such as user logon, resource quotas, and object protection.
- A virtual memory strategy that provides every program with a large set of memory addresses and prevents one user from reading or modifying memory that's occupied by another user unless the two are explicitly sharing memory.

Compatibility

Compatibility usually refers to an operating system's ability to execute programs written for other operating systems or for earlier versions of the same system. However, for Windows, compatibility is a more complicated topic.

Through the use of protected subsystems, Windows provides execution environments for applications that are different from its primary programming interface—the Win32 application programming interface (API). When running on Intel processors, the protected subsystems supply binary compatibility with existing Microsoft applications. Windows also provides source-level compatibility with POSIX applications that adhere to the POSIX operating system interfaces defined by the IEEE. (**POSIX** is the Portable Operating System Interface for UNIX, an operating system API that defines how a service is invoked through a software package. POSIX was developed by the IEEE to increase the portability of application software. [IEEE, 2004].

In addition to compatibility with programming interfaces, recent versions of Windows also support already-existing file systems, including the MS-DOS file allocation table (FAT), the CD-ROM file system (CDFS), and the NTFS.

Windows comes with built-in verification of important hardware and software. That is, the upgrade setup procedures include a check-only mode that examines the system's hardware and software for potential problems and produces a report that lists them. The procedure stops when it can't find drivers for critical devices, such as hard-disk controllers, bus extensions, and other items that are sometimes necessary for a successful upgrade.

Performance

The operating system should respond quickly to CPU-bound applications. To do so, Windows is built with the following features:

- System calls, page faults, and other crucial processes are designed to respond in a timely manner.
- A mechanism called the local procedure call (LPC) is incorporated into the operating system so that communication among the protected subsystems doesn't restrain performance.
- Critical elements of Windows' networking software are built into the privileged portion of the operating system to improve performance. In addition, these components can be loaded and unloaded from the system dynamically, if necessary.

That said, the response of some Windows operating systems slowed down as applications were installed and the computer was used over time. Even when these applications were uninstalled, performance remained slow and did not return to benchmarks the system achieved when the computer was new.

Memory Management

Every operating system uses its own view of physical memory and requires its application programs to access memory in specified ways. In the example shown in Figure 15.1, each process's virtual address space is 4GB, with 2GB each allocated to program storage and system storage. When physical memory becomes full, the Virtual Memory Manager pages some of the memory contents to disk, freeing physical memory for other processes.

The challenge for all Windows operating systems, especially those running in a network, is to run application programs written for Windows or POSIX without crashing into each other in memory. Each Windows environment subsystem provides a view of memory that matches what its applications expect. The executive process has its own memory structure, which the subsystems access by calling the operating system's inherent services.

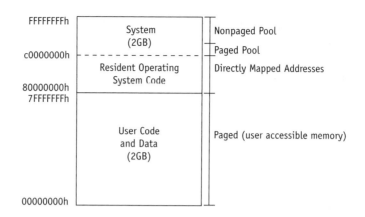

(figure 15.1)

Layout of Windows memory. This is a virtual memory system based on 32-bit addresses in a linear address space. The 64-bit versions use a similar model but on a much larger scale with 8TB for the user and 8TB for the kernel.

In recent versions of Windows, the operating system resides in high virtual memory and the user's code and data reside in low virtual memory, as shown in Figure 15.1. A user's process can't read or write to system memory directly. All user-accessible memory can be paged to disk, as can the segment of system memory labeled *paged pool*. However, the segment of system memory labeled *nonpaged pool* is never paged to disk because it's used to store critical objects, such as the code that does the paging, as well as major data structures.

User-Mode Features

The Virtual Memory (VM) Manager allows user-mode subsystems to share memory and provides a set of native services that a process can use to manage its virtual memory in the following ways:

• Allocate memory in two stages: first by reserving memory and then by committing memory, as needed. This two-step procedure allows a process to reserve a large section of virtual memory without being charged for it until it's actually needed.

• Provide read and/or write protection for virtual memory, allowing processes to share memory when needed.

• Lock virtual pages in physical memory. This ensures that a critical page won't be removed from memory while a process is using it. For example, a database application that uses a tree structure to update its data may lock the root of the tree in memory, thus minimizing page faults while accessing the database.

• Retrieve information about virtual pages.

• Protect virtual pages. Each virtual page has a set of flags associated with it that determines the types of access allowed in user mode. In addition, Windows provides object-based memory protection. Therefore, each time a process opens a section object, a block of memory that can be shared by two or more processes, the security reference monitor checks whether the process is allowed to access the object.

- Rewrite virtual pages to disk. If an application modifies a page, the VM Manager writes the changes back to the file during its normal paging operations.

Virtual Memory Implementation

The Virtual Memory Manager relies on address space management and paging techniques.

Address Space Management

As shown in Figure 15.1, the upper half of the virtual address space is accessible only to kernel-mode processes. Code in the lower part of this section, kernel code and data, is never paged out of memory. In addition, the addresses in this range are translated by the hardware, providing exceedingly fast data access. Therefore, the lower part of the resident operating system code is used for sections of the kernel that require maximum performance, such as the code that dispatches units of execution, called threads of execution, in a processor.

When users create a new process, they can specify that the VM Manager initialize their virtual address space by duplicating the virtual address space of another process. This allows environment subsystems to present their client processes with views of memory that don't correspond to the virtual address space of a native process.

Paging

The pager is the part of the VM Manager that transfers pages between page frames in memory and disk storage. As such, it's a complex combination of both software policies and hardware mechanisms. Software policies determine *when* to bring a page into memory and *where* to put it. Hardware mechanisms include the exact manner in which the VM Manager translates virtual addresses into physical addresses.

Because the hardware features of each system directly affect the success of the VM Manager, implementation of virtual memory varies from processor to processor. Therefore, this portion of the operating system isn't portable and must be modified for each new hardware platform. To make the transition easier, Windows keeps this code small and isolated. The processor chip that handles address translation and exception handling looks at each address generated by a program and translates it into a physical address. If the page containing the address isn't in memory, then the hardware generates a page fault and issues a call to the pager. The translation look-aside buffer (TLB) is a hardware array of associative memory used by the processor to speed memory access. As pages are brought into memory by the VM Manager, it creates entries for them in the TLB. If a virtual address isn't in the TLB, it may still be in memory. In that case, virtual software rather than hardware is used to find the address, resulting in slower access times.

Paging policies in a virtual memory system dictate *how* and *when* paging is done and are composed of fetch, placement, and replacement policies:

- The **fetch policy** determines when the pager copies a page from disk to memory. The VM Manager uses a demand paging algorithm with locality of reference, called clustering, to load pages into memory. This strategy attempts to minimize the number of page faults that a process encounters.

- The **placement policy** is the set of rules that determines where the virtual page is loaded in memory. If memory isn't full, the VM Manager selects the first page frame from a list of free page frames. This list is called the page frame database, and is an array of entries numbered from 0 through $n \times 1$, with n equaling the number of page frames of memory in the system. Each entry contains information about the corresponding page frame, which can be in one of six states at any given time: valid, zeroed, free, standby, modified, or bad. Valid and modified page frames are those currently in use. Those zeroed, free, or on standby represent available page frames; bad frames can't be used.

  Of the available page frames, the page frame database links together those that are in the same state, thus creating five separate homogeneous lists. Whenever the number of pages in the zeroed, free, and standby lists reaches a preset minimum, the modified page writer process is activated to write the contents of the modified pages to disk and link them to the standby list. On the other hand, if the modified page list becomes too short, the VM Manager shrinks each process's working set to its minimum working set size and adds the newly freed pages to the modified or standby lists to be reused.

- The **replacement policy** determines which virtual page must be removed from memory to make room for a new page. Of the replacement policies considered in Chapter 3, the VM Manager uses a local FIFO replacement policy and keeps track of the pages currently in memory for each process—the process's working set. The FIFO algorithm is local to each process, so that when a page fault occurs, only page frames owned by a process can be freed. When it's created, each process is assigned a minimum working-set size, which is the number of pages the process is guaranteed to have in memory while it's executing. If memory isn't very full, the VM Manager allows the process to have the pages it needs up to its working set maximum. If the process requires even more pages, the VM Manager removes one of the process's pages for each new page fault the process generates.

Certain parts of the VM Manager are dependent on the processor running the operating system and must be modified for each platform. These platform-specific features include page table entries, page size, page-based protection, and virtual address translation.

✔
We say pages are "removed" to indicate that these pages are no longer available in memory. However, these pages are not actually removed but marked for deletion and then overwritten by the incoming page.

Processor Management

In general, a process is the combination of an executable program, a private memory area, and system resources allocated by the operating system as the program executes. However, a process requires a fourth component before it can do any work: at least one thread of execution. A thread is the entity within a process that the kernel schedules for execution; it could be roughly equated to a task. Using multiple threads, also called multithreading, allows a programmer to break up a single process into several executable segments and also to take advantage of the extra CPU power available in computers with multiple processors. Windows Server 2008 Release 2 can coordinate processing among 64 cores.

Windows is a preemptive multitasking, multithreaded operating system. By default, a process contains one thread, which is composed of the following:

• A unique identifier
• The contents of a volatile set of registers indicating the processor's state
• Two stacks used during the thread's execution
• A private storage area used by subsystems and dynamic-link libraries

These components are called the thread's context; the actual data forming this context varies from one processor to another. The kernel schedules threads for execution on a processor. For example, when you use the mouse to double-click an icon in the Program Manager, the operating system creates a process, and that process has one thread that runs the code. The process is like a container for the global variables, the environment strings, the heap owned by the application, and the thread. The thread is what actually executes the code. Figure 15.2 shows a diagram of a process with a single thread.

Process

| Global Variables |
| Heap |
| Environment Strings |
| Thread Stack |
| Thread |

(figure 15.2)

Unitasking in Windows. Here's how a process with a single thread is scheduled for execution on a system with a single processor.

For systems with multiple processors, a process can have as many threads as there are CPUs available. The overhead incurred by a thread is minimal. In some cases, it's actually advantageous to split a single application into multiple threads because the entire program is then much easier to understand. The creation of threads isn't as complicated as it may seem. Although each thread has its own stack, all threads belonging to one process share its global variables, heap, and environment strings, as shown in Figure 15.3.

(figure 15.3)

Multitasking using multithreading. Here's how a process with four threads can be scheduled for execution on a system with four processors.

Process

Global Variables			
Heap			
Environment Strings			
Thread Stack	Thread Stack	Thread Stack	Thread Stack
Thread 1	Thread 2	Thread 3	Thread 4

(figure 15.3)

Multitasking using multithreading. Here's how a process with four threads can be scheduled for execution on a system with four processors.

Multiple threads can present problems because it's possible for several different threads to modify the same global variables independently of each other. To prevent this, Windows operating systems include synchronization mechanisms to give exclusive access to global variables as these multithreaded processes are executed.

For example, let's say the user is modifying a database application. When the user enters a series of records into the database, the cursor changes into a combination of hourglass and arrow pointer, indicating that a thread is writing the last record to the disk while another thread is accepting new data. Therefore, even as processing is going on, the user can perform other tasks. The concept of overlapped I/O is now occurring on the user's end, as well as on the computer's end.

Multithreading is advantageous when doing database searches because data is retrieved faster when the system has several threads of execution that are searching an array simultaneously, especially if each thread has its own CPU. Programs written to take advantage of these features must be designed very carefully to minimize contention, such as when two CPUs attempt to access the same memory location at the same time, or when two threads compete for single shared resources, such as a hard disk.

Client/server applications tend to be CPU-intensive for the server because, although queries on the database are received as requests from a client computer, the actual query is managed by the server's processor. A Windows multiprocessing environment can satisfy those requests by allocating additional CPU resources.

Device Management

The I/O system must accommodate the needs of existing devices—from a simple mouse and keyboard to printers, display terminals, disk drives, CD-ROM drives, multimedia devices, and networks. In addition, it must consider future storage and input technologies. The I/O system provides a uniform high-level interface for executive-level I/O operations and eliminates the need for applications to account for differences among physical devices. It shields the rest of the operating system from the details of device manipulation and thus minimizes and isolates hardware-dependent code.

The I/O system in Windows is designed to provide the following:
• Multiple installable file systems including FAT, the CD-ROM file system, and NTFS
• Services to make device-driver development as easy as possible yet workable on multiprocessor systems
• Ability for system administrators to add or remove drivers from the system dynamically
• Fast I/O processing while allowing drivers to be written in a high-level language
• Mapped file I/O capabilities for image activation, file caching, and application use

The I/O system is packet driven. That is, every I/O request is represented by an I/O request packet (IRP) as it moves from one I/O system component to another. An IRP is a data structure that controls how the I/O operation is processed at each step. The I/O Manager creates an IRP that represents each I/O operation, passes the IRP to the appropriate driver, and disposes of the packet when the operation is complete. On the other hand, when a driver receives the IRP, it performs the specified operation and then either passes it back to the I/O Manager or passes it through the I/O Manager to another driver for further processing.

In addition to creating and disposing of IRPs, the I/O Manager supplies code, common to different drivers, that it calls to carry out its I/O processing. It also manages buffers for I/O requests, provides time-out support for drivers, and records which installable file systems are loaded into the operating system. It provides flexible I/O facilities that allow subsystems such as POSIX to implement their respective I/O application programming interfaces. Finally, the I/O Manager allows device drivers and file systems, which it perceives as device drivers, to be loaded dynamically based on the needs of the user.

To make sure the operating system works with a wide range of hardware peripherals, Windows provides a device-independent model for I/O services. This model takes advantage of a concept called a multilayered device driver that's not found in operating systems, such as MS-DOS with monolithic device drivers. These multilayered drivers provide a large and complex set of services that are understood by an intermediate layer of the operating system.

Each device driver is made up of a standard set of routines including the following:

- Initialization routine, which creates system objects used by the I/O Manager to recognize and access the driver.

- Dispatch routine, which comprises functions performed by the driver, such as READ or WRITE. This is used by the I/O Manager to communicate with the driver when it generates an IRP after an I/O request.

- Start I/O routine, used by the driver to initiate data transfer to or from a device.

- Completion routine, used to notify a driver that a lower-level driver has finished processing an IRP.

- Unload routine, which releases any system resources used by the driver so that the I/O Manager can remove them from memory.

- Error logging routine, used when unexpected hardware errors occur such as a bad sector on a disk; the information is passed to the I/O Manager, which writes all this information to an error log file.

When a process needs to access a file, the I/O Manager determines from the file object's name which driver should be called to process the request, and it must be able to locate this information the next time a process uses the same file. This is accomplished by a driver object, which represents an individual driver in the system, and a device object, which represents a physical, logical, or virtual device on the system and describes its characteristics.

The I/O Manager creates a driver object when a driver is loaded into the system and then calls the driver's initialization routine, which records the driver entry points in the driver object and creates one device object for each device to be handled by this driver. An example showing how an application instruction results in disk access is shown in Table 15.4 and graphically illustrated in Figure 15.4.

(table 15.4)	Event	Result
Example showing how a device object is created from an instruction to read a file. The actual instruction is translated as illustrated in Figure 15.4.	Instruction: READ "MYFILE.TXT"	READ = FUNCTION CODE 1 "MYFILE.TXT" = DISK SECTOR 10
	Actions:	1. Access DRIVER OBJECT (1)
		2. Activate READ routine
		3. Access DISK SECTOR 10

Figure 15.4 illustrates how the last device object points back to its driver object, telling the I/O Manager which driver routine to call when it receives an I/O request. It works in the following manner: When a process requests access to a file, it uses a filename, which includes the device object where the file is stored. When the file is opened, the I/O Manager creates a file object and then returns a file handle to the process. Whenever the process uses the file handle, the I/O Manager can immediately find the device object, which points to the driver object representing the driver that services the device. Using the function code supplied in the original request, the I/O Manager indexes into the driver object and activates the appropriate routine because each function code corresponds to a driver routine entry point.

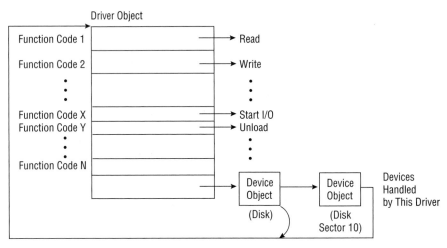

(figure 15.4)

The driver object from Table 15.4 is connected to several device objects. The last device object points back to the driver object.

A driver object may have multiple device objects connected to it. The list of device objects represents the physical, logical, and virtual devices that are controlled by the driver. For example, each sector of a hard disk has a separate device object with sector-specific information. However, the same hard disk driver is used to access all sectors. When a driver is unloaded from the system, the I/O Manager uses the queue of device objects to determine which devices will be affected by the removal of the driver.

Using objects to keep track of information about drivers frees the I/O Manager from having to know details about individual drivers—it just follows a pointer to locate a driver. This provides portability and allows new drivers to be easily loaded. Another advantage to representing devices and drivers with different objects is that it's easier to assign drivers to control additional or different devices if the system configuration changes.

Figure 15.5 shows how the I/O Manager interacts with a layered device driver to write data to a file on a hard disk by following these steps in order:

(figure 15.5)

Details of the layering of a file system driver and a disk driver first shown in Figure 15.4. These are the five steps that take place when the I/O Manager needs to access a secondary storage device to satisfy the user command shown here as number 1.

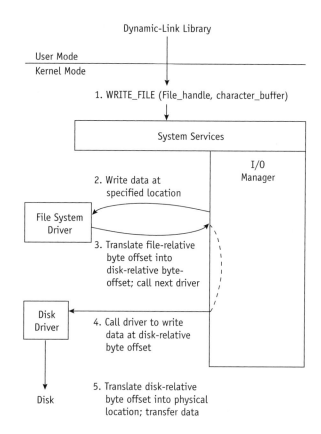

1. An application issues a command to write to a disk file at a specified byte off-set within the file.
2. The I/O Manager passes the file handle to the file system driver.
3. The I/O Manager translates the file-relative byte offset into a disk-relative byte offset and calls the next driver.
4. The function code and the disk-relative byte offset are passed to the disk driver.
5. The disk-relative byte offset is translated into the physical location and data is transferred.

This process parallels the discussion in Chapter 8 about levels in a file management system.

The I/O Manager knows nothing about the file system. The process described in this example works exactly the same if an NTFS driver is replaced by a FAT driver, a UNIX or Linux file system driver, a CD-ROM driver, a Macintosh file system driver, or any other.

Keep in mind that overhead is required for the I/O Manager to pass requests back and forth for information. So for simple devices, such as serial and parallel printer ports, the operating system provides a single-layer device driver approach in which the I/O Manager can communicate with the device driver, which, in turn, returns information directly. But for more complicated devices, particularly for devices such as hard drives that depend on a file system, a multilayered approach is a better choice.

Another device driver feature of recent Windows operating systems is that almost all low-level I/O operations are asynchronous. That means that when an application issues an I/O request, it doesn't have to wait for data to be transferred, but it can continue to perform other work while data transfer is taking place. Asynchronous I/O must be specified by the process when it opens a file handle. During asynchronous operations, the process must be careful not to access any data from the I/O operation until the device driver has finished data transfer. Asynchronous I/O is useful for operations that take a long time to complete or for which completion time is variable.

For example, the time it takes to list the files in a directory varies according to the number of files. Because Windows is a preemptive multitasking system that may be running many tasks at the same time, it's vital that the operating system not waste time waiting for a request to be filled if it can be doing something else. The various layers in the operating system use preemptive multitasking and multithreading to get more work done in the same amount of time.

File Management

Typically, an operating system is associated with the particular file structure that it uses for mass storage devices, such as hard disks. Therefore, we speak of a UNIX file system (i-nodes) or an MS-DOS file system (FAT). Although there is a resident NTFS, current versions of Windows are designed to be independent of the file system on which they operate.

The primary file handling concept in recent versions of Windows, first introduced in UNIX, is the virtual file—that's any I/O source or destination—and it's treated as if it were a file. In Windows, programs perform I/O on virtual files, manipulating them by using file handles. Although not a new concept, in Windows a file handle actually refers to an executive file object that represents all sources and destinations of I/O. Processes call native file object services such as those required to read from or write to a file. The I/O Manager directs these virtual file requests to real files, file directories, physical devices, or any other destination supported by the system. File objects have hierarchical names, are protected by object-based security, support synchronization, and are handled by object services.

When opening a file, a process supplies the file's name and the type of access required. This request moves to an environment subsystem that in turn calls a system service. The Object Manager starts an object name lookup and turns control over to the I/O Manager to find the file object. The I/O Manager checks the security subsystem to determine whether or not access can be granted. The I/O Manager also uses the file object to determine whether asynchronous I/O operations are requested.

The creation of file objects helps bridge the gap between the characteristics of physical devices and directory structures, file system structures, and data formats. File objects provide a memory-based representation of shareable physical resources. When a file is opened, the I/O Manager returns a handle to a file object. The Object Manager treats file objects like all other objects until the time comes to write to, or read from, a device, at which point the Object Manager calls the I/O Manager for assistance to access the device. Figure 15.6 illustrates the contents of file objects and the services that operate on them. Table 15.5 describes in detail the object body attributes.

(table 15.5)	Attribute	Purpose
	Filename	Identifies the physical file to which the file object refers
Description of the attributes shown in Figure 15.6.	Device type	Indicates the type of device on which the file resides
	Byte offset	Identifies the current location in the file (valid only for synchronous I/O)
	Share mode	Indicates whether other callers can open the file for read, write, or delete operations while this caller is using it
	Open mode	Indicates whether I/O is synchronous or asynchronous, cached or noncached, sequential or random, etc.
	File disposition	Indicates whether to delete the file after closing it

Let's make a distinction between a file object, a memory-based representation of a shareable resource that contains only data unique to an object handle, and the file itself, which contains the data to be shared. Each time a process opens a handle, a new file object is created with a new set of handle-specific attributes. For example, the attribute byte offset refers to the location in the file where the next READ or WRITE operation using that handle will occur. It might help if you think of file object attributes as being specific to a single handle.

Although a file handle is unique to a process, the physical resource isn't. Therefore, processes must synchronize their access to shareable files, directories, and devices. For example, if a process is writing to a file, it should specify exclusive write-access or lock portions of the file while writing to it, to prevent other processes from writing to that file at the same time.

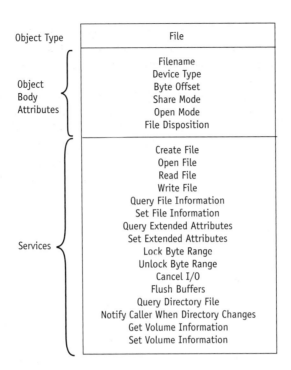

Object Type	File
Object Body Attributes	Filename Device Type Byte Offset Share Mode Open Mode File Disposition
Services	Create File Open File Read File Write File Query File Information Set File Information Query Extended Attributes Set Extended Attributes Lock Byte Range Unlock Byte Range Cancel I/O Flush Buffers Query Directory File Notify Caller When Directory Changes Get Volume Information Set Volume Information

(figure 15.6)

Illustration of a file object, its attributes, and the services that operate on them. The attributes are explained in Table 15.5.

Mapped file I/O is an important feature of the I/O system and is achieved through the cooperation of the I/O system and the VM Manager. At the operating system level, file mapping is typically used for file caching, loading, and running executable programs. The VM Manager allows user processes to have mapped file I/O capabilities through native services. Memory-mapped files exploit virtual memory capabilities by allowing an application to open a file of arbitrary size and treat it as a single contiguous array of memory locations without buffering data or performing disk I/O.

For example, a file of 100MB can be opened and treated as an array in a system with only 20MB of memory. At any one time, only a portion of the file data is physically present in memory—the rest is paged out to the disk. When the application requests data that's not currently stored in memory, the VM Manager uses its paging mechanism to load the correct page from the disk file. When the application writes to its virtual memory space, the VM Manager writes the changes back to the file as part of the normal paging. Because the VM Manager optimizes its disk accesses, applications that are I/O bound can speed up their execution by using mapped I/O—writing to memory is faster than writing to a secondary storage device.

A component of the I/O system called the **cache manager** uses mapped I/O to manage its memory-based cache. The cache expands or shrinks dynamically depending on the amount of memory available. Using normal working-set strategies, the VM Manager expands the size of the cache when there is memory available to accommodate the application's needs, and reduces the cache when it needs free pages. The cache manager takes advantage of the VM Manager's paging system, avoiding duplication of effort.

The file management system supports long filenames that can include spaces and special characters. Therefore, users can name a file *Spring 2005 Student Grades* instead of something cryptic like *S05STD.GRD*. Because the use of long filename could create compatibility problems with older operating systems that might reside on the network, the file system automatically converts a long filename to the standard eight-character filename and three-character extension required by MS-DOS and 16-bit Windows applications. The File Manager does this by keeping a table that lists each long filename and relates it to the corresponding short filename.

Network Management

In Windows operating systems, networking is an integral part of the operating system executive, providing services such as user accounts, resource security, and mechanisms used to implement communication between computers, such as with named pipes and mailslots. **Named pipes** provide a high-level interface for passing data between two processes regardless of their locations. **Mailslots** provide one-to-many and many-to-one communication mechanisms useful for broadcasting messages to any number of processes.

Microsoft Networks, informally known as MS-NET, became the model for the NT Network Manager. Three MS-NET components—the redirector, the server message block (SMB) protocol, and the network server—were extensively refurbished and incorporated into subsequent Windows operating systems.

The redirector, coded in the C programming language, is implemented as a loadable file system driver and isn't dependent on the system's hardware architecture. Its function is to direct an I/O request from a user or application to the remote server that has the appropriate file or resource needed to satisfy the request. A network can incorporate multiple redirectors, each of which directs I/O requests to remote file systems or devices. A typical remote I/O request might result in the following progression:

1. The user-mode software issues a remote I/O request by calling local I/O services.
2. After some initial processing, the I/O Manager creates an I/O request packet (IRP) and passes the request to the Windows redirector, which forwards the IRP to the transport drivers.
3. Finally, the transport drivers process the request and place it on the network. The reverse sequence is observed when the request reaches its destination.

The SMB protocol is a high-level specification for formatting messages to be sent across the network and correlates to the application layer (Layer 7), and the presentation layer (Layer 6) of the OSI model described in Chapter 9. An API called NetBIOS

To view server statistics, press the Windows logo key and the *R* key together. Then type CMD to open the command window. Then type net statistics server and press the Enter key. To view workstation statistics, from the command window, type net statistics workstation.

is used to pass I/O requests structured in the SMB format to a remote computer. Both the SMB protocols and the NetBIOS API were adopted in several networking products before appearing in Windows.

The Windows Server operating systems are written in C for complete compatibility with existing MS-NET and LAN Manager SMB protocols, are implemented as loadable file system drivers, and have no dependency on the hardware architecture on which the operating system is running.

Directory Services

The **Active Directory** database stores many types of information and serves as a general-purpose directory service for a heterogeneous network.

Microsoft built the Active Directory entirely around the **Domain Name Service or Domain Name System (DNS)** and **Lightweight Directory Access Protocol (LDAP)**. DNS is the hierarchical replicated naming service on which the Internet is built. However, although DNS is the backbone directory protocol for one of the largest data networks, it doesn't provide enough flexibility to act as an enterprise directory by itself. That is, DNS is primarily a service for mapping machine names to IP addresses, which is not enough for a full directory service, which must be able to map names of arbitrary objects (such as machines and applications) to any kind of information about those objects.

Active Directory groups machines into administrative units called domains, each of which gets a DNS domain name (such as pitt.edu). Each domain must have at least one domain controller that is a machine running the Active Directory server.

For improved fault tolerance and performance, a domain can have more than one domain controller with each holding a complete copy of that domain's directory database.

Current versions of Windows network operating systems eliminate the distinction between primary domain controllers and backup domain controllers, making the network simpler to administer because it doesn't have multiple hierarchies. Active Directory clients use standard DNS and LDAP protocols to locate objects on the network. As shown in Figure 15.7, here's how it works:

1. A client that needs to look up an Active Directory name first passes the DNS part of the name to a standard DNS server. The DNS server returns the network address of the domain controller responsible for that name.

2. Next, the client uses LDAP to query the domain controller to find the address of the system that holds the service the client needs.

3. Finally, the client establishes a direct connection with the requested service using the correct protocol required by that service.

(figure 15.7)

Active Directory clients use standard DNS and LDAP protocols to locate objects on the network.

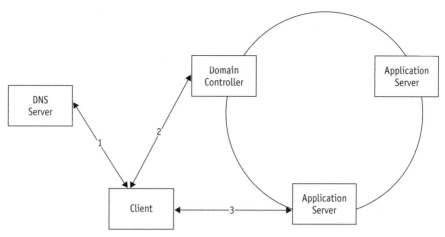

Security Management

Windows operating systems provide an object-based security model. That is, a security object can represent any resource in the system: a file, device, process, program, or user. This allows system administrators to give precise security access to specific objects in the system while allowing them to monitor and record how objects are used.

One of the biggest concerns about Windows operating systems is the need for aggressive patch management to combat the many viruses and worms that target these systems. Updates are available on *www.microsoft.com*, as shown in Figure 15.8.

(figure 15.8)

Operating system updates are available online.

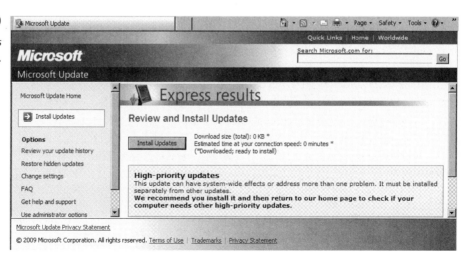

Security Basics

The U.S. Department of Defense has identified and categorized into seven levels of security certain features that make an operating system secure. Early versions of Windows targeted Class C2 level with a plan to evolve to Class B2 level—a more stringent level of security in which each user must be assigned a specific security level clearance and is thwarted from giving lower-level users access to protected resources.

To comply with the Class C2 level of security, Windows operating systems now include the following features:

- A secure logon facility requiring users to identify themselves by entering a unique logon identifier and a password before they're allowed access to the system
- Discretionary access control allowing the owner of a resource to determine who else can access the resource and what they can do to it
- Auditing ability to detect and record important security-related events or any attempt to create, access, or delete system resources
- Memory protection preventing anyone from reading information written by someone else after a data structure has been released back to the operating system

Password management is the first layer of security.

The second layer of security deals with file access security. At this level, the user can create a file and establish various combinations of individuals to have access to it because the operating system makes distinctions between owners and groups. The creator of a file is its owner. The owner can designate a set of users as belonging to a group and allow all the members of the group to have access to that file. Conversely, the owner could prevent some of the members from accessing that file.

In addition to determining who is allowed to access a file, users can decide what type of operations a person is allowed to perform on a file. For example, one may have read-only access, while another may have read-and-write privileges. As a final measure, the operating system gives the user auditing capabilities that automatically keep track of who uses files and how the files are used.

Security Terminology

The built-in security for recent Windows network operating systems is a necessary element for managers of Web servers and networks. Its directory service lets users find what they need and a communications protocol lets users interact with it. However, because not everyone should be able to find or interact with everything in the network, controlling access is the job of distributed security services.

Effective distributed security requires an authentication mechanism that allows a client to prove its identity to a server. Then the client needs to supply authorization information that the server uses to determine which specific access rights have been given to this client. Finally, it needs to provide data integrity using a variety of methods ranging from a cryptographic checksum for all transmitted data to completely encrypting all transmitted data.

Recent Windows operating systems provide this with **Kerberos** security, as described in Chapter 11. Kerberos provides authentication, data integrity, and data privacy. In addition, it provides mutual authentication, which means that both the client and server can verify the identity of the other. (Other security systems require only that the clients prove their identity. Servers are automatically authenticated.)

Each domain has its own Kerberos server, which shares the database used by Active Directory. This means that the Kerberos server must execute on the domain-controller machine and, like the Active Directory server, it can be replicated within a domain. Every user who wants to securely access remote services must log on to a Kerberos server. Figure 15.9 shows the path followed by a request from an application to a service provided on the network.

(figure 15.9)

Requests from an application flow through a series of security providers, as do the responses, from the network back to the application.

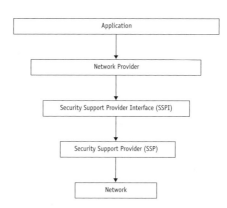

A successful login returns a **ticket granting ticket** to the user, which can be handed back to the Kerberos server to request tickets to specific application servers.

If the Kerberos server determines that a user is presenting a valid ticket, it returns the requested ticket to the user with no questions asked. The user sends this ticket to the remote application server, which can examine it to verify the user's identity and authenticate the user. All of these tickets are encrypted in different ways, and various keys are used to perform the encryption.

Different implementations of Kerberos send different authorization information. Microsoft has implemented the standard Kerberos protocol to make the product more compatible with other Kerberos implementations.

Different security protocols can have very different APIs, creating problems for applications that might want to use more than one of them. Microsoft has addressed this problem by separating the users of distributed security services from their providers, allowing support for many options without creating unusable complexity.

User Interface

Although a detailed description of the tools present on the desktop is beyond the scope of this chapter, we'll take a brief look at the Start Menu because it's the key application of the Windows desktop. Figure 15.10 shows a typical Start Menu.

(figure 15.10)

A typical Windows Start Menu divides functions into logical groups and lists the applications most frequently used.

The Start Menu organizes files and programs into logical groups. From here, users perform common functions including the following:

- *All Programs* goes to a list of many available applications. The applications shown in Table 15.10 were recently used. To open one again, click the icon.
- *Frequent* and *Recent* show applications and folders that are frequently or were recently used.
- *Search* initiates a searching routine.
- *Shut Down* with options for turning off the computer or hibernating.

The Windows Task Manager, opened by pressing and holding the Ctrl, Alt, and Delete keys, offers users the chance to view running applications and processes, and set the priorities of each, as shown in Figure 15.11. From this window, users can also view information about performance, networking, and other users logged in to the system.

(figure 15.11)

Priority management using the Task Manager.

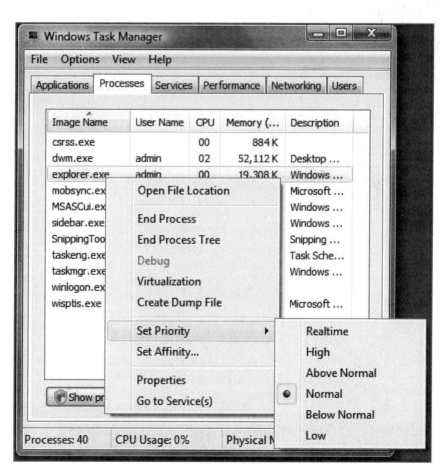

A standard utility program called Windows Explorer (not to be confused with the Web browser called Internet Explorer) contains directory and file display tools and a file finding tool, as shown in Figure 15.12.

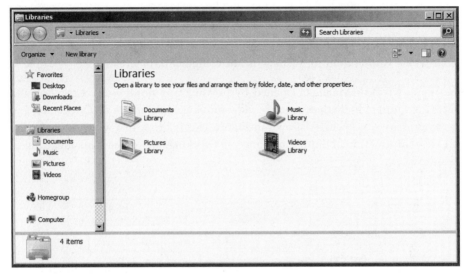

(figure 15.12)

Windows Explorer is a file management tool that displays directories (folders).

For networked systems, there are tools to help administrators identify and access network resources, such as folders, printers, and connections to other nodes. To find them, go to Network and Sharing Center and click View Computers and Devices, and then click the option to map a network drive, as shown in Figure 15.13.

A command interface that resembles that used for MS-DOS is available from most Windows desktops, as shown in Figure 15.14. Using this feature, one can try out MS-DOS commands from a computer running Windows.

For users who are faster with the keyboard than with a pointing device, Windows provides many keyboard shortcuts. For a guide, look for keyboard shortcuts on the pull-down menus, such as the one shown in Figure 15.15, which identifies ALT+TAB as the keyboard shortcut to switch to the next window.

A helpful Windows feature is its accommodation for users working in non-English languages. Windows has built-in input methods and fonts for many languages including double-byte languages such as Japanese. During installation, the system administrator can select one or several languages for the system, even adding different language support for specific individuals. For example, one user can work in Chinese while another can work in Hindi. Even better, the system's own resources also become multilingual, which means that the operating system changes its dialog boxes, prompts, and menus to support the user's preferred language.

(figure 15.13)

System administrators on a network can map a network drive to identify available resources.

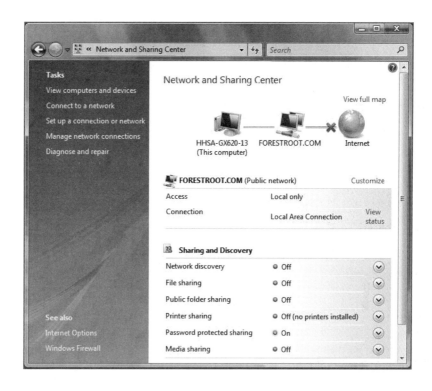

(figure 15.14)

Command window that allows users to run many MS-DOS commands.

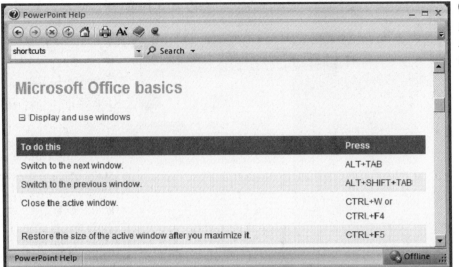

(figure 15.15)

Keyboard shortcuts are shown on the right next to the menu items.

For users who need enhanced accessibility options, or who have difficulty using a standard keyboard but need its functionality, Windows offers an on-screen keyboard, as shown in Figure 15.16. This and other tools (a magnifier, a narrator, speech recognition, and more) can be found from the Start button under Accessories, Ease of Access.

(figure 15.16)

From the Accessories folder, tools such as an on-screen keyboard are available to provide enhanced user interface tools.

Details about use of the system's hardware and software can be found from the Resource Monitor, as shown in Figure 15.17.

(figure 15.17)

The Resource Monitor, available from the Control Panel, can provide running statistics on use of system resources.

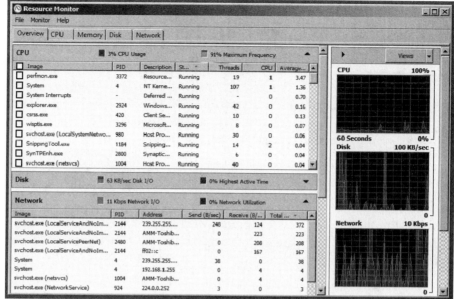

Conclusion

What started as a microcomputer operating system has grown to include complex multiplatform software that can be used to run computing systems of all sizes. Windows' commercial success is unquestioned, and its products have continued to evolve in complexity and scope to cover many global markets.

Windows products are ubiquitous, including Windows Embedded, Windows Automotive, and Windows Mobile, to name a few of the many specialty versions of this operating system. Microsoft offers technical support for operating systems that are no longer sold, including Windows NT and even MS-DOS.

A word of caution: The security vulnerabilities of Windows operating systems make them popular targets for programmers of malicious code. Whether these vulnerabilities are due to their enormous share of the market (making them enormously attractive) or coding errors on the part of Microsoft, the result is the same: There is a constant need for every system administrator and computer owner to proactively keep all Windows systems as secure as possible through vigilant access control and patch management.

Key Terms

Active Directory: Microsoft Windows directory service that offers centralized administration of application serving, authentication, and user registration for distributed networking systems.

cache manager: a component of the I/O system that manages the part of virtual memory known as cache. The cache expands or shrinks dynamically depending on the amount of memory available.

compatibility: the ability of an operating system to execute programs written for other operating systems or for earlier versions of the same system.

Domain Name Service or Domain Name System (DNS): a general-purpose, distributed, replicated, data query service. Its principal function is the resolution of Internet addresses based on fully qualified domain names such as .com (for commercial entity) or .edu (for educational institution).

extensibility: one of an operating system's design goals that allows it to be easily enhanced as market requirements change.

fetch policy: the rules used by the Virtual Memory Manager to determine when a page is copied from disk to memory.

graphical user interface (GUI): a user interface that allows the user to activate operating system commands by clicking on desktop icons or menus using a pointing device such as a mouse or touch screen. GUIs evolved from command-driven user interfaces.

Kerberos: MIT-developed authentication system that allows network managers to administer and manage user authentication at the network level.

kernel mode: name given to indicate that processes are granted privileged access to the processor. Therefore, all machine instructions are allowed and system memory is accessible. Contrasts with the more restrictive user mode.

Lightweight Directory Access Protocol (LDAP): a protocol that defines a method for creating searchable directories of resources on a network. It's called "lightweight" because it is a simplified and TCP/IP-enabled version of the X.500 directory protocol.

mailslots: a high-level network software interface for passing data among processes in a one-to-many and many-to-one communication mechanism. Mailslots are useful for broadcasting messages to any number of processes.

named pipes: a high-level software interface to NetBIOS, which represents the hardware in network applications as abstract objects. Named pipes are represented as file objects in Windows NT and later, and operate under the same security mechanisms as other executive objects.

NT File System (NTFS): the file system introduced with Windows NT that offers file management services, such as permission management, compression, transaction logs, and the ability to create a single volume spanning two or more physical disks.

placement policy: the rules used by the Virtual Memory Manager to determine where the virtual page is to be loaded in memory.

portability: the ability to move an entire operating system to a machine based on a different processor or configuration with as little recoding as possible.

POSIX: Portable Operating System Interface for UNIX; an operating system application program interface developed by the IEEE to increase the portability of application software.

reliability: the ability of an operating system to respond predictably to error conditions, even those caused by hardware failures; or the ability of an operating system to actively protect itself and its users from accidental or deliberate damage by user programs.

replacement policy: the rules used by the Virtual Memory Manager to determine which virtual page must be removed from memory to make room for a new page.

ticket granting ticket: a virtual "ticket" given by a Kerberos server indicating that the user holding the ticket can be granted access to specific application servers. The user sends this encrypted ticket to the remote application server, which can then examine it to verify the user's identity and authenticate the user.

user mode: name given to indicate that processes are not granted privileged access to the processor. Therefore, certain instructions are not allowed and system memory isn't accessible. Contrasts with the less restrictive kernel mode.

Interesting Searches

- Windows File System
- Embedded Windows Operating System
- Windows vs. Macintosh
- Windows Benchmarks
- Windows Patch Management

Exercises

Research Topics

A. Research current literature to discover the current state of IEEE POSIX Standards and find out if the version of Windows on the computer that you use is currently 100 percent POSIX-compliant. Explain the significance of this compliance and why you think some popular operating systems are not compliant.

B. Some Windows products do not allow the use of international characters in the username or password. These characters may be part of an international alphabet or Asian characters. Research the characters that are allowed in recent versions of Windows and cite your sources. Describe the advantages to the operating system of limiting the character set for usernames and passwords, and whether or not you suggest an alternative.

Exercises

1. If you wanted to add these four files to one Windows directory (october.doc, OCTober.doc, OCTOBER.doc, and OcTOBer.doc), how many new files would be displayed: one, two, three, or four? Explain why this is so. Do you think the answer is the same for all operating systems? Why or why not?

2. Explain the importance of monitoring system performance and why Windows makes this information available to the user.

3. In some Windows operating systems, the paging file is a hidden file on the computer's hard disk and its virtual memory is the combination of the paging file and the system's physical memory. (This is called pagefile.sys and the default size is equal to 1.5 times the system's total RAM.) Describe in your own words how the size of virtual memory might have an effect on system performance.

4. If the paging file is located where fragmentation is least likely to happen, performance may be improved. True or false? Explain in your own words.

5. When deploying Windows in a multilingual environment, administrators find that some languages require more hard-disk storage space than others. In your opinion, why is this the case?

6. The 64-bit version of Windows 7 can run all 32-bit applications with the help of an emulator, but it does not support 16-bit applications. Can you imagine a circumstance where someone might need support for a 16-bit application? Describe it.

7. Windows 7 features Kerberos authentication. Describe the role of the ticket granting ticket to authenticate users for network access.

8. Describe in your own words the role of the Active Directory in recent Windows operating systems.

9. The I/O system relies on an I/O request packet. Explain the role of this packet, when it is passed, and where it goes before disposal.

Advanced Exercises

10. Identify at least five major types of threats to systems running Windows and the policies that system administrators must take to protect the system from unauthorized access. Compare the practical problems when balancing the need

for accessibility with the need to restrict access, and suggest the first action you would take to secure a Windows computer or network if you managed one.

11. Windows Embedded is an operating system that is intended to run in real time. In your own words, describe the difference between hard real-time and soft real-time systems, and describe the benchmarks that you feel are most important in each type of system.

12-14 For these questions, refer to Table 15.6 (adapted from *www.microsoft.com*), which shows how the memory structures for a 64-bit Windows operating system using a 64-bit Intel processor compare with the 32-bit maximums on previous Windows operating systems.

(table 15.6)

Windows specifications for 32-bit and 64-bit systems adapted from www.microsoft.com.

Component	32-bit	64-bit
Virtual Memory	4GB	16TB
Paging File Size	16TB	256TB
System Cache	1GB	1TB
Hyperspace	4MB	8GB
Paged Pool	470MB	128GB
System PTEs	660MB	128GB

12. Hyperspace is used to map the working set pages for system process, to temporarily map other physical pages, and other duties. By increasing this space from 4MB to 8GB in 64-bit system, hyperspace helps Windows run faster. In your opinion, explain why this is so and describe other performance improvements that increased hyperspace may have on system performance. Can you quantify the speed increase from the information shown here? Explain your answer.

13. Paged pool is the part of virtual memory, created during system initialization, that can be paged in and out of the working set of the system process and is used by kernel-mode components to allocate system memory. If systems with one processor have two paged pools, and those with multiprocessors have four, discuss in your own words why having more than one paged pool reduces the frequency of system code blocking on simultaneous calls to pool routines.

14. System PTEs are a pool of system page table entries that are used to map system pages such as I/O space, kernel stacks, and memory descriptor lists. The 32-bit programs use a 4GB model and allocate half (2GB) to the user and half to the kernel. The 64-bit programs use a similar model but on a much larger scale with 8TB for the user and 8TB for the kernel. Given this structure, calculate how many exabytes a 64-bit pointer could address (one exabyte equals a billion gigabytes).

Chapter 16

Linux Operating System

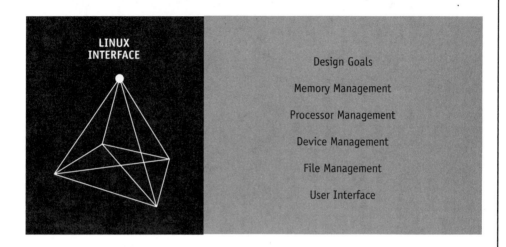

Design Goals

Memory Management

Processor Management

Device Management

File Management

User Interface

“ *I'm doing a (free) operating system ...* **”**

—Linus Torvalds

Learning Objectives

After completing this chapter, you should be able to describe:

- The design goals for the Linux operating system
- The flexibility offered by using files to manipulate devices
- The differences between command-driven and menu-driven interfaces
- The roles of the Memory, Device, File, Processor, and Network Managers
- Some strengths and weaknesses of Linux

Linux is not UNIX. Linux was based on a version of UNIX but capitalized on the lessons learned over the previous 20 years of UNIX development. Linux has unique features that set it apart from its predecessor and make it a global force in operating system development. What's more, Linux is not only powerful, but free or inexpensive to own.

Overview

Linux is POSIX-compliant (POSIX will be discussed shortly) and portable with versions available to run cell phones, supercomputers, and most computing systems in between. Unlike the other operating systems described in this book, its source code is freely available, allowing programmers to configure it to run any device and meet any specification. The frequent inclusion of several powerful desktop GUIs continues to attract users. It is also highly modular, allowing multiple modules to be loaded and unloaded on demand, making it a technically robust operating system.

Linux is an open source program, meaning that its source code is freely available to anyone for improvement. If someone sends a better program or coding sequence to Linus Torvalds, the author of Linux, and if it's accepted as a universal improvement to the operating system, then the new code is added to the next version made available to the computing world. Updates are scheduled every six months. In this way, Linux is under constant development by uncounted contributors around the world, most of whom have never met. The name *Linux* remains a registered trademark of Linus Torvalds.

✔ Linux is case sensitive. Throughout this text, we have followed the convention of expressing all filenames and commands in lowercase.

History

Linus Torvalds wanted to create an operating system that would greatly enhance the limited capabilities of the Intel 80386 microprocessor. He started with MINIX (a miniature UNIX system developed primarily by Andrew Tanenbaum) and rewrote certain parts to add more functionality. When he had a working operating system, he announced his achievement on an Internet usegroup with this message:

> Hello everybody out there using minix. I'm doing a (free) operating system (just a hobby, won't be big and profes-sional like gnu) for 386(486)AT clones.

It was August 1991, and Torvalds was a 21-year-old student at University of Helsinki, Finland. (The name *Linux* is a contraction of *Linus* and *UNIX* and, when pronounced, it rhymes with "mimics.") This new operating system, originally created to run a small microcomputer, was built with substantial flexibility, and it features many of the same functions found on expensive commercial operating systems. In effect, Linux brought much of the speed, efficiency, and flexibility of UNIX to small desktop computers.

The first Linux operating systems required typed and sometimes cryptic commands. Now users can enter commands using either a **command-driven interface** (terminal mode) or a **menu-driven interface** or **graphical user interface (GUI)**, greatly expanding the usability of the operating system. GUIs are discussed later in this chapter.

The first primary corporate supporter of Linux was Red Hat Linux, the world's leading Linux distributor until 2003. In September of that year, the company split its efforts in two directions, the Fedora Project to encourage continuation of open-source development of the Linux **kernel**, and Red Hat Enterprise Linux (RHEL) to meet the growing needs of organizations willing to pay for an enterprise-wide operating system and dedicated technical support.

As shown in Table 16.1, the Fedora Project issues updates free to the public about every six months. There are many other popular distributions of Linux, including Mandriva, Debian, and SUSE.

(table 16.1)

The major releases of Linux by Red Hat, Inc. RHL is an acronym for Red Hat Linux. RHEL is an acronym for Red Hat Enterprise Linux. Fedora is a trademark of Red Hat, Inc.

Year	Release	Features
1994	Beta versions	First Red Hat Linux product available to the public in a series of beta versions.
1995	RHL 1.0	First non-beta release of Red Hat Linux.
1995	RHL 2.0	Written in Perl for quick development.
1996	RHL 3.0.3	The first approximately concurrent multi-architecture release; supported the Digital Alpha platform.
1996	RHL 4.0	Based on the 2.0.18 kernel and the first release to include documentation freely available in electronic form.
1997	RHL 5.0	Named 1997 InfoWorld Product of the Year.
1999	RHL 6.0	Integrated GNOME desktop GUI.
2000	RHL 7.0	First release that supported Red Hat Network out of the box.
2001	RHL 7.0.90	Introduced the 2.4 kernel.
2002	RHEL 2.1 AS (Advanced Server)	Launch of Red Hat Enterprise Linux, the first commercial enterprise computing offering, based on RHL 7.2.
2002	RHL 8.0	Designed to provide a unified look across RHL and RHEL desktops.
2003	RHL 9	First release to include Native POSIX Thread Library (NPTL) support.
2003	RHEL 3	The first Red Hat product made to run on 7-chip architectures (by Intel, AMD, and IBM).

Year	Release	Features
2003	Fedora Core 1	Product based on RHL 9 for individual users; created by the Fedora Project in cooperation with Red Hat.
2004	Fedora Core 2	Introduced Security Enhanced Linux (SELinux), an implementation of Mandatory Access Control (MAC) in the kernel.
2004	Fedora Core 3	Supported the 2.6.9 Linux kernel, updated SELinux, and supported the latest popular GUIs, including KDE and Gnome.
2005	RHEL 4	Red Hat Enterprise Linux based on RHL 7.2.
2006	Fedora Core 5 & 6	Supported virtual machine technology.
2007	Fedora 7	New name (dropped Core). Allowed customization. Widened accessibility by contributors in Fedora community.
2007	RHEL 5	Improved performance, security, and flexibility, with storage virtualization.
2009	Fedora 11	Fast boot-up from power on to fully operational system. Handles files up to 16TB.

Because Linux is written and distributed under the GNU General Public License, its source code is freely distributed and available to the general public. As of this writing, the current GNU General Public License is Version 3. Everyone is permitted to copy and distribute verbatim copies of the license document, but changing it is not allowed. It can be found at: *www.gnu.org/licenses/gpl.html.*

Design Goals

Linux has three design goals: modularity, simplicity, and portability (personified in its mascot, shown in Figure 16.1). To achieve these goals, Linux administrators have

(figure 16.1)

The Linux mascot evolved from discussions with Linus Torvalds, who said, "Ok, so we should be thinking of a lovable, cuddly, stuffed penguin sitting down after having gorged itself on herring." More about the penguin can be found at www.linux.org.

access to numerous standard utilities, eliminating the need to write special code. Many of these utilities can be used in combination with each other so that users can select and combine appropriate utilities to carry out specific tasks. As shown in Table 16.2, Linux accommodates numerous functions.

(table 16.2)

Linux supports a wide variety of system functions.

Function	Purpose
Multiple processes and multiple processors	Linux can run more than one program or process at a time and can manage numerous processors.
Multiple platforms	Although it was originally developed to run on Intel's processors for microcomputers, it can now operate on almost any platform.
Multiple users	Linux allows multiple users to work on the same machine at the same time.
Inter-process communications	It supports pipes, sockets, etc.
Terminal management	Its terminal management conforms to POSIX standards, and it also supports pseudo-terminals as well as process control systems.
Peripheral devices	Linux supports a wide range of devices, including sound cards, graphics interfaces, networks, SCSI, USB, etc.
Buffer cache	Linux supports a memory area reserved to buffer the input and output from different processes.
Demand paging memory management	Linux loads pages into memory only when they're needed.
Dynamic and shared libraries	Dynamic libraries are loaded only when they're needed, and their code is shared if several applications are using them.
Disk partitions	Linux allows file partitions and disk partitions with different file formats.
Network protocol	It supports TCP/IP and other network protocols.

Linux conforms to the specifications for **Portable Operating System Interface** (**POSIX®**), a registered trademark of the IEEE. POSIX is an IEEE standard that defines operating system interfaces to enhance the portability of programs from one operating system to another (IEEE, 2004).

Memory Management

When Linux allocates memory space, it allocates 1GB of high-order memory to the kernel and 3GB of memory to executing processes. This 3GB address space is divided among: process code, process data, shared library data used by the process, and the stack used by the process.

When a process begins execution, its segments have a fixed size; but there are cases when a process has to handle variables with an unknown number and size. Therefore, Linux has system calls that change the size of the process data segment, either by expanding it to accommodate extra data values or reducing it when certain values positioned at the end of the data segment are no longer needed.

Linux offers memory protection based on the type of information stored in each region belonging to the address space of a process. If a process modifies access authorization assigned to a memory region, the kernel changes the protection information assigned to the corresponding memory pages.

When a process requests pages, Linux loads them into memory. When the kernel needs the memory space, the pages are released using a least recently used (LRU) algorithm. Linux maintains a dynamically managed area in memory, a page cache, where new pages requested by processes are inserted, and from which pages are deleted when they're no longer needed. If any pages marked for deletion have been modified, they're rewritten to the disk—a page corresponding to a file mapped into memory is rewritten to the file and a page corresponding to the data is saved on a swap device. The swap device could be a partition on the disk or it could be a normal file. Linux shows added flexibility with swap devices because, if necessary, Linux can deactivate them without having to reboot the system. When this takes place, all pages saved on that device are reloaded into memory.

To keep track of free and busy pages, Linux uses a system of page tables. With certain chip architectures, memory access is carried out using segments.

Virtual memory in Linux is managed using a multiple-level table hierarchy, which accommodates both 64- and 32-bit architectures. Table 16.3 shows how each virtual address is made up of four fields, which are used by the Memory Manager to locate the instruction or data requested.

Main Directory	Middle Directory	Page Table Directory	Page Frame
Page 1	Table 3	Page Table 2	Location of Line 214

(table 16.3)

The four fields that make up the virtual address for Line 214 in Figure 16.2.

Each page has its own entry in the main **directory**, which has pointers to each page's middle directory. A page's middle directory contains pointers to its corresponding page table directories. In turn, each page table directory has pointers to the actual page frame, as shown in Figure 16.2. Finally, the page offset field is used to locate the instruction or data within the requested page (in this example, it is Line 214).

(figure 16.2)

Virtual memory management uses three levels of tables (Main, Middle, and Page Table Directories) to locate the page frame with the requested instruction or data within a job.

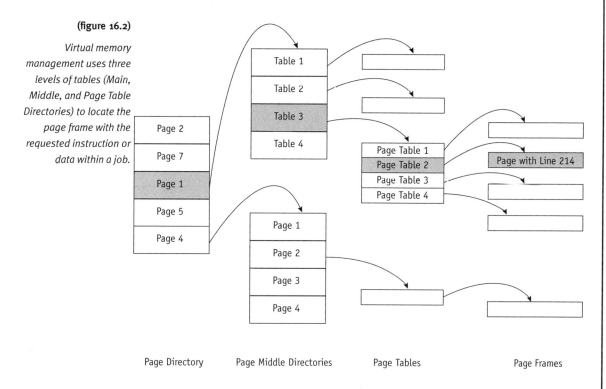

Page Directory   Page Middle Directories   Page Tables   Page Frames

Virtual memory is implemented in Linux through demand paging. Up to a total of 256MB of usable memory can be configured into equal-sized page frames, which can be grouped to give more contiguous space to a job. These groups can also be split to accommodate smaller jobs. This process of grouping and splitting is known as the **buddy algorithm,** and it works as follows.

Let's consider the case where main memory consists of 64 page frames and Job 1 requests 15 page frames. The buddy algorithm first rounds up the request to the next power of 2 (in this case, 15 is rounded up to 16, which is 2^4). Then the group of 64 page frames is divided into two groups of 32, and the lower section is then divided in half. Now there is a group of 16 page frames that can satisfy the request, so the job's 16 pages are copied into the page frames as shown in Figure 16.3 (a).

When the next job, Job 2, requests 8 page frames, the second group of 16 page frames is divided in two and the lower half with 8 page frames is given to Job 2, as shown in Figure 16.3 (b). Later, when Job 2 releases its page frames, they are combined with the upper 8 page frames to make a group of 16 page frames, as shown in Figure 16.3 (c).

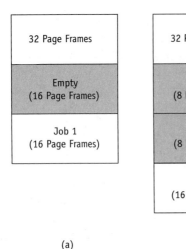
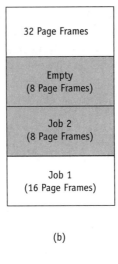
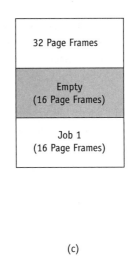

(a) (b) (c)

(figure 16.3)

Main memory is divided to accommodate jobs of different sizes. In (a), the original group of 32 page frames is divided to satisfy the request of Job 1 for 16 page frames. In (b), another group of 16 page frames is divided to accommodate Job 2, which needs eight page frames. In (c), after Job 2 finishes, the two groups of eight page frames each are recombined into a group of 16, while Job 1 continues processing.

The page replacement algorithm is an expanded version of the **clock page replacement policy** discussed in Chapter 3. Instead of using a single reference bit, Linux uses an 8-bit byte to keep track of a page's activity, which is referred to as its age. Each time a page is referenced, this age variable is incremented. Behind the scenes, at specific intervals, the Memory Manager checks each of these age variables and decreases their value by 1. As a result, if a page is not referenced frequently, then its age variable will drop to 0 and the page will become a candidate for replacement if a page swap is necessary. On the other hand, a page that is frequently used will have a high age value and will not be a good choice for swapping. Therefore, we can see that Linux uses a form of the least frequently used (LFU) replacement policy.

Processor Management

Linux uses the same parent-child process management design found in UNIX and described in Chapter 13, but it also supports the concept of "personality" to allow processes coming from other operating systems to be executed. This means that each process is assigned to an execution domain specifying the way in which system calls are carried out and the way in which messages are sent to processes.

Organization of Process Table

Each process is referenced by a descriptor, which contains approximately 70 fields describing the process attributes together with the information needed to manage the process. The kernel dynamically allocates these descriptors when processes begin execution. All process descriptors are organized in a doubly linked list, and the descriptors of processes that are ready or in execution are put in another doubly linked list with fields indicating "next run" and "previously run." There are several macro instructions used by the scheduler to manage and update these process descriptor lists as needed.

Process Synchronization

Linux provides wait queues and semaphores to allow two processes to synchronize with each other. A wait queue is a linked circular list of process descriptors. Semaphores, described in Chapter 6, are used to solve the problems of mutual exclusion and the problems of producers and consumers. In Linux the semaphore structure contains three fields: the semaphore counter, the number of waiting processes, and the list of processes waiting for the semaphore. The semaphore counter may contain only binary values, except when several units of one resource are available, and the semaphore counter then assumes the value of the number of units that are accessible concurrently.

Process Management

The Linux scheduler scans the list of processes in the READY state and, using predefined criteria, chooses which process to execute. The scheduler has three different scheduling types: two for real-time processes and one for normal processes. The combination of type (shown in Table 16.4) and priority is used by the scheduler to determine the scheduling policy used on processes in the READY queue.

(table 16.4) *Three process types with three different priority levels.*	Name	Priority Level	Process Type	Scheduling Policy
	SCHED_FIFO	Highest Priority	For non-preemptible real-time processes	First In First Out only
	SCHED_RR	Medium Priority	For preemptible real-time processes	Round Robin and Priority
	SCHED_OTHER	Lowest Priority	For normal processes	Priority only

From among the processes with the highest priority (SCHED_FIFO), the scheduler selects the process with the highest priority and executes it using the first in, first out algorithm. This process is normally not preemptible and runs to completion unless one of the following situations occurs:

• The process goes into the WAIT state (waiting for I/O, or another event, to finish).

• The process relinquishes the processor voluntarily, in which case the process is moved to a WAIT state and other processes are executed.

Only when all FIFO processes are completed does the scheduler proceed to execute processes of lower priority.

When executing a process of the second type (SCHED_RR), the scheduler chooses those from this group with the highest priority and uses a round robin algorithm with a small time quantum. Then, when the time quantum expires, other processes (such as a FIFO or another RR type with a higher priority) may be selected and executed before the first process is allowed to run to completion.

The third type of process (SCHED_OTHER) has the lowest priority and is executed only when there are no processes with higher priority in the READY queue. From among these processes, the scheduler selects processes in order after considering their dynamic priorities (which are set by the user using system calls and by a factor computed by the system). From among the SCHED_OTHER processes, the priorities of all processes that are **CPU-bound** are lowered during execution; therefore, they may earn a lower priority than processes that are not executing or those with a priority that has not been lowered.

Device Management

Linux is **device independent**, which improves its portability from one system to another. **Device drivers** supervise the transmission of data between main memory and the peripheral unit. Devices are assigned not only a name but also descriptors that further identify each device and are stored in the device directory, as shown in Figure 16.4.

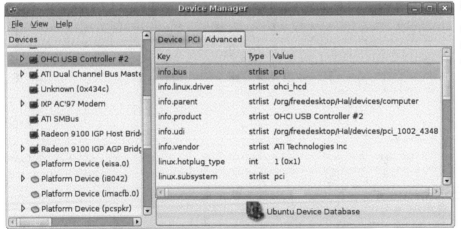

(figure 16.4)

Details about each device can be accessed via the Device Manager.

Device Classifications

Linux identifies each device by a minor device number and a major device number.

- The *minor device number* is passed to the device driver as an argument and is used to access one of several identical physical devices.
- The *major device number* is used as an index to the array to access the appropriate code for a specific device driver.

Each *class* has a Configuration Table that contains an array of entry points into the device drivers. This table is the only connection between the system code and the device drivers, and it's an important feature of the operating system because it allows the system programmers to create new device drivers quickly to accommodate differently configured systems.

Standard versions of Linux often provide a comprehensive collection of common device drivers; but if the computer system should include hardware or peripherals that are not on the standard list, their device drivers can be retrieved from another source and installed separately. Alternatively, a skilled programmer can write a device driver and install it for use.

Numerous device drivers are available for Linux operating systems at little or no cost. More information can be found at www.linux.org.

Device Drivers

Linux supports the standard classes of devices introduced by UNIX. In addition, Linux allows new device classes to support new technology. Device classes are not rigid in nature—programmers may choose to create large, complex device drivers to perform multiple functions, but such programming is discouraged for two reasons: (1) code can be shared among Linux users and there is a wider demand for several simple drivers than for a single complex one, and (2) modular code is better able to support Linux's goals of system scalability and extendibility. Therefore, programmers are urged to write device drivers that maximize the system's ability to use the device effectively—no more, no less.

A notable feature of Linux is its ability to accept new device drivers on the fly, while the system is up and running. That means administrators can give the kernel additional functionality by loading and testing new drivers without having to reboot each time to reconfigure the kernel. To understand the following discussion more fully, please remember that devices are treated in Linux in the same way all files are treated.

Open and Release

Two common functions of Linux device drivers are *open* and *release*, which essentially allocate and deallocate the appropriate device. For example, the operation to open a device should perform the following functions:

- Verify that the device is available and in working order
- Increase the usage counter for the device by 1, so the subsystem knows that the module cannot be unloaded until its file is appropriately closed
- Initialize the device so that old data is removed and the device is ready to accept new data
- Identify the minor number and update the appropriate pointer if necessary
- Allocate any appropriate data structure

Likewise, the *release* function (called device_close or device_release) performs these tasks:

- Deallocate any resources that were allocated with the *open* function
- Shut down the device
- Reduce the usage counter by 1 so the device can be released to another module

Modules can be closed without ever releasing the device. If this happens, the module is *not* deallocated.

Device Classes

The three standard classes of devices supported by Linux are character devices, block devices, and network devices, as shown in Figure 16.5.

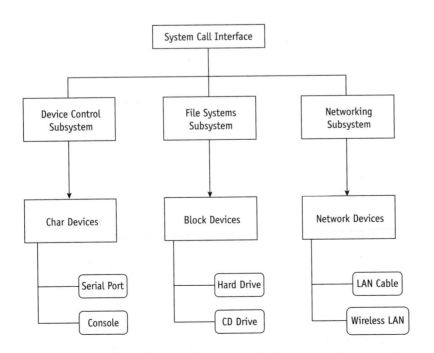

(figure 16.5)

This example of the three primary classes of device drivers shows how device drivers receive direction from different subsystems of Linux.

Char Devices

Character devices (also known as *char devices*) are those that can be accessed as a stream of bytes, such as a communications port, monitor, or other byte-stream-fed device. At a minimum, drivers for these devices usually implement the *open*, *release*, *read*, and *write* system calls although additional calls are often added. Char devices are accessed by way of file system nodes and, from a functional standpoint, these devices look like an ordinary data area. Their drivers are treated the same way as ordinary files with the exception that char device drivers are data channels that must be accessed sequentially.

Block Devices

Block devices are similar to char devices except that they can host a file system, such as a hard disk. (Char devices cannot host a file system.) Like char devices, block devices are accessed by file system nodes in the /dev directory, but these devices are transferred in blocks of data. Unlike most UNIX systems, data on a Linux system can be transferred in blocks of any size, from a few bytes to many. Like char device drivers, block device drivers appear as ordinary files with the exception that the block drivers can access a file system in connection with the device, something not possible with the char device.

Network Interfaces

Network interfaces are dissimilar from both char and block devices because their function is to send and receive packets of information as directed by the network subsystem of the kernel. So, instead of *read* and *write* calls, the network device functions relate to packet transmission.

Each system device is handled by a device driver that is, in turn, under the direction of a subsystem of Linux.

File Management

Data Structures

All Linux files are organized in directories that are connected to each other in a tree-like structure. Linux specifies five types of files, as shown in Table 16.5.

File Type	File Functions
Directory	A file that contains lists of filenames.
Ordinary file	A file containing data or programs belonging to users.
Symbolic link	A file that contains the path name of another file that it is linking to. (This is not a direct hard link. Rather it's information about how to locate a specific file and link it even if it's in the directories of different users. This is something that can't be done with hard links.)
Special file	A file that's assigned to a device controller located in the kernel. When this type of file is accessed, the physical device associated with it is activated and put into service.
Named pipe	A file that's used as a communication channel among several processes to exchange data. The creation of a named pipe is the same as the creation of any file.

(table 16.5)

The file type indicates how each file is to be used.

Filename Conventions

Filenames are case sensitive so Linux recognizes both uppercase and lowercase letters in filenames. For example, each of the following filenames are recognizable as four different files housed in a single directory: FIREWALL, firewall, FireWall, and fireWALL.

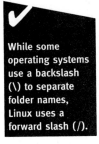

While some operating systems use a backslash (\) to separate folder names, Linux uses a forward slash (/).

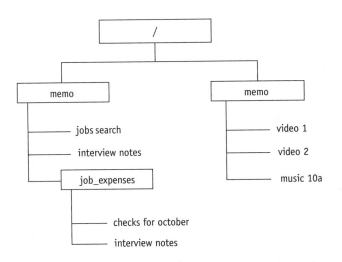

(figure 16.6)

A sample file hierarchy. The forward slash (/) represents the root directory.

Filenames can be up to 255 characters long and contain alphabetic characters, underscores, and numbers. File suffixes (similar to file extensions in Chapter 8) are optional. Filenames can include a space; however, this can cause complications if you're running programs from the command line because a program named *interview notes* would be viewed as a command to run two files: *interview* and *notes*. To avoid confusion, the two words can be enclosed in quotes: *"interview notes."* (This is important when using Linux in terminal mode by way of its command interpretive shell. From a Linux desktop GUI, users choose names from a list so there's seldom a need to type the filename.)

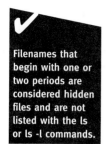

To copy the file called checks for october, illustrated in Figure 16.6, the user can type from any other folder:

```
cp/memo/job_expenses/checks for october
```

The first slash indicates that this is an absolute path name that starts at the root directory. If the file you are seeking is in a local directory, you can use a relative path name—one that doesn't start at the root directory. Two examples of relative path names from Figure 16.6 are:

```
Job_expenses/checks for october
memo/music 10a
```

A few rules apply to all path names:

1. If the path name starts with a slash, the path starts at the root directory.
2. A path name can be either one name or a list of names separated by slashes. The last name on the list is the name of the file requested. All names preceding the file's name must be directory names.
3. Using two periods (..) in a path name will move you upward in the hierarchy (closer to the root). This is the only way to go up the hierarchy; all other path names go down the tree.

Data Structures

To allow processes to access files in a consistent manner, the kernel has a layer of software that maintains an interface between system calls related to files and the file management code. This layer is known as the Virtual File System (VFS). Any process-initiated system call to files is directed to the VFS, which performs file operations independent of the format of the file system involved. The VFS then redirects the request to the module managing the file.

Directory Listings

While directory listings can be created from Terminal mode using typed commands (ls or ls -l), many Linux users find that the easiest way to list files in directories is from the GUI desktop. A typical listing shows the name of the file or directory, its size, and the date and time of modification. Information about file permissions shown in Figure 16.7 can be accessed from the View option on the menu bar.

(figure 16.7)

A sample list of files
stored in a directory,
including file permissions.

File	Edit	View	Go	Bookmarks	Tabs	Help			

Name	Size	Permissions	Type	Date Modifi
▽ 📁 6e 1st version to RTP	38 items	drwx------	folder	Tue 06 Oct 2
▽ 📁 archive	14 items	drwx------	folder	Tue 06 Oct 2
📄 AM C6471_Ch1.doc	637.5 KB	-rwx------	Word document	Mon 09 Feb
📄 AM Ch1 v01.doc	637.5 KB	-rwx------	Word document	Mon 09 Feb
📄 AM Ch1 v02.doc	5.0 MB	-rwx------	Word document	Wed 11 Feb
📄 AM Ch3 v01.pdf	726.8 KB	-rwx------	PDF document	Thu 19 Feb 2
📄 AM Ch05 v00.pdf	614.9 KB	-rwx------	PDF document	Fri 03 Jul 20(
📄 AM Ch05 v01.pdf	638.5 KB	-rwx------	PDF document	Fri 03 Jul 20(
📄 AM Ch07 v01.pdf	1.2 MB	-rwx------	PDF document	Tue 08 Sep 2

18 items, Free space: 370.9 MB

The Permissions column shows a code with the file's type and access privileges, as shown in Figure 16.8. To understand the specific kind of access granted, notice the order of letters in this column. (This same information is displayed if the directory listing is generated using the directory listing command in Terminal mode.)

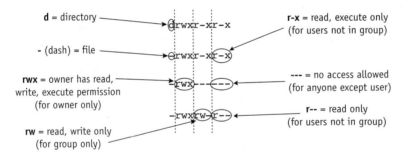

(figure 16.8)

Graphical depiction of a
list of file and directory
permissions in UNIX.

The first character in the column describes the nature of the folder entry:

- the dash (-) indicates a file
- d indicates a directory file
- l indicates a link
- b indicates a block special file
- c indicates a character special file

The next three characters (**rwx**) show the access privileges granted to the *owner* of the file:

- r indicates **read** access
- w indicates **write** access
- x indicates **execute** access

Likewise, the following three characters describe the access privileges granted to other members of the *user's group*. (A group is defined as a set of users, excluding the owner, who have something in common: the same project, same class, same department, etc.) Therefore, **rwx** for characters 5–7 means group users can also read, write, and/or execute that file, and a dash (-) indicates that access is denied for that operation.

Finally, the last three characters describe the access privileges granted to others, defined as users at large (but excluding the owner and members of the owner's group). This system-wide group of users is sometimes called world.

User Interface

Early versions of Linux required typed commands and a thorough knowledge of valid commands, as shown in Table 16.6. Although most current versions include the powerful and intuitive menu-driven interfaces described shortly that allow even novice users to successfully navigate the operating system, users can still use Terminal mode, shown in Figure 16.9, to type commands that are very similar to those used for UNIX, which can be helpful for those migrating from an operating system that's command-driven.

(table 16.6)

Sample user commands, which can be abbreviated and must be in the correct case (usually lowercase letters). Many commands can be combined on a single line for additional power and flexibility. Check the technical documentation for your system for proper spelling and syntax.

Command	Stands For	Action to Be Performed
(filename)	Run File	Run/Execute the file with that name.
ls	List Directory	Show a listing of the filenames in directory.
ls -l	Long List	Show a comprehensive directory list.
ls /bin	List /bin Directory	Show a list of valid commands.
cd	Change Directory	Change working directory.
chmod	Change Permissions	Change permissions on a file or directory.
cp	Copy	Copy a file into another file or directory.
mv	Move	Move a file or directory.
more	Show More	Type the file's contents to the screen.
lpr	Print	Print out a file.
date	Date	Show date and time.
mkdir	Make Directory	Make a new directory.
grep	Global Regular Expression/Print	Find a specified string in a file.
cat	Concatenate or Catenate	Concatenate the files and print the resulting file.
diff	Different	Compare two files.
pwd	Print Working Directory	Print the name of the working directory.

```
File  Edit  View  Terminal  Help
ann@ann-HP-laptop:/$ ls -l
total 84
drwxr-xr-x    2 root root  4096 2009-09-01 17:01 bin
drwxr-xr-x    3 root root  4096 2009-09-01 17:13 boot
lrwxrwxrwx    1 root root    11 2009-09-01 15:42 cdrom -> media/cdrom
drwxr-xr-x   16 root root  4160 2009-09-02 18:01 dev
drwxr-xr-x  124 root root 12288 2009-09-02 18:01 etc
drwxr-xr-x    3 root root  4096 2009-09-01 15:59 home
lrwxrwxrwx    1 root root    33 2009-09-01 17:05 initrd.img -> boot/initrd.img-2.
6.28-15-generic
lrwxrwxrwx    1 root root    33 2009-09-01 16:02 initrd.img.old -> boot/initrd.im
g-2.6.28-11-generic
drwxr-xr-x   19 root root  4096 2009-09-01 17:03 lib
drwx------    2 root root 16384 2009-09-01 15:41 lost+found
drwxr-xr-x    4 root root  4096 2009-09-02 18:01 media
drwxr-xr-x    2 root root  4096 2009-04-13 05:33 mnt
drwxr-xr-x    2 root root  4096 2009-04-20 09:59 opt
```

(figure 16.9)

In Terminal mode, users can run the operating system using commands instead of menu-driven GUI.

Command-Driven Interfaces

The general syntax for typed commands is this:

```
command arguments filename
```

• The `command` is any legal operating system command.

• The `arguments` are required for some commands and optional for others.

• The `filename` can be the name of a file and can include a relative or absolute path name.

Commands are interpreted and executed by the shell (such as the Bash shell). The shell is technically known as the command interpreter, but it isn't only an interactive command interpreter; it's also the key to the coordination and combination of system programs.

Graphical User Interfaces

Most Linux operating systems are delivered with multiple graphical user interfaces (often free of charge), allowing the end users to choose the GUI that best meets their needs or those of the organization. In fact, in certain environments, different GUIs can be used by different users on the same system. This flexibility has spurred the ever-widening acceptance of Linux and has helped it become more competitive.

In addition to GUIs, many Linux versions also come equipped with Windows-compatible word processors and spreadsheet and presentation applications— some at no cost. These software tools make it possible for Linux users to read and write documents that are generated, or read, by colleagues using proprietary software from competing operating system distributors. Because competing programs can cost hundreds of dollars, the availability of these affordable applications is one factor that has spurred the popularity of Linux.

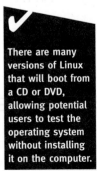

There are many versions of Linux that will boot from a CD or DVD, allowing potential users to test the operating system without installing it on the computer.

System Monitor

Information about the status of the system is available using the System Monitor window, shown in Figure 16.10, which shows the immediate history of CPU, memory, and network usage. Other information available from this window includes supported file systems and information about processes currently running.

(figure 16.10)

System Monitor displays historical information about CPU, memory, and network use.

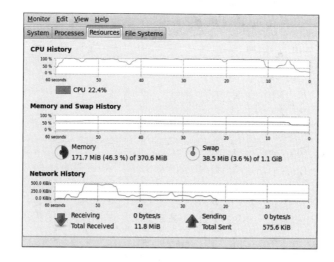

Service Settings

Depending on the Linux distribution, administrators can implement a variety of services to help manage the system. A sample list of services is shown in Figure 16.11, but options may vary from one system to another. See the documentation for your system for specifics.

(figure 16.11)

From the Services settings window, many applications are available for activation.

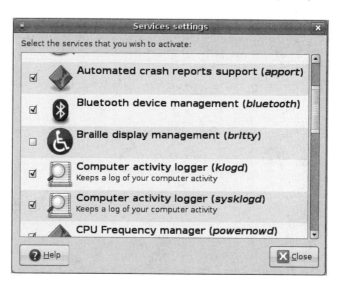

System Logs

Administrators use system logs that provide a detailed description of activity on the system. These logs are invaluable to administrators tracking the course of a system malfunction, firewall failure, disabled device, and more. These log files for some Linux operating systems can be found in the **/var/log** directory. A sample System Log Viewer is shown in Figure 16.12.

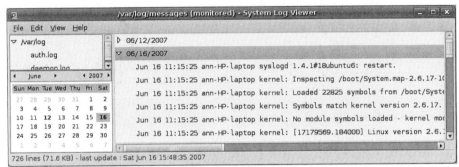

(figure 16.12)

Sample System Log Viewer.

There are numerous log files available for review (by someone with root access only) using any simple text editor. A few typical log files are listed in Table 16.7.

boot.log	Stores messages of which systems have successfully started up and shut down, as well as any that have failed to do so.
dmesg	A list of messages created by the kernel when the system starts up.
maillog	Stores the addresses that received and sent e-mail messages for detection of misuse of the e-mail system.
secure	Contains lists of all attempts to log in to the system, including the date, time, and duration of each access attempt.
xferlog	Lists the status of files that have been transferred using an FTP service.

(table 16.7)

Sample Linux log files. See the documentation for your system for specifics.

Keyboard Shortcuts

To allow users to switch easily from one task to another, Linux supports keyboard shortcuts (shown in Figure 16.13), many of which are identical to those commonly used on Windows operating systems, easing the transition from one operating system to the other. For example, CTRL-V is a quick way to issue a PASTE command in Linux, UNIX, and Windows.

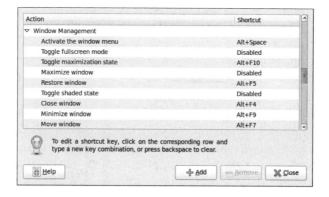

We've included here only a tiny sample of the many features available from a typical Linux desktop. Your system may have different windows, menus, tools, and options. For details about your Linux operating system, please see the help menu commonly available from the desktop or from your system menu.

System Management

All Linux operating systems are patched between version releases. These patches can be downloaded on request, or users can set up the system to check for available updates, as shown in Figure 16.14. **Patch management** is designed to replace or change

code that makes up the software. Three primary reasons motivate patches to the operating system: a greater need for security precautions against constantly changing system threats; the need to assure system compliance with government regulations regarding privacy and financial accountability; and the need to keep systems running at peak efficiency.

Every system manager, no matter the size of the system, should remain aware of security vulnerabilities that can be addressed with critical patches. After all, system intruders are looking for these same vulnerabilities and are targeting computing devices that are not yet patched.

When a patch becomes available, the user's first task is to identify the criticality of the patch. If it is important, it should be applied immediately. If the patch is not critical in nature, installation might be delayed until a regular patch cycle begins. Patch cycles were discussed in detail in Chapter 12.

Conclusion

What began as one man's effort to get more power from a 1990s microcomputer chip has evolved into a powerful, flexible operating system that can run supercomputers, cell phones, and many devices in between. Linux enjoys unparalleled popularity among programmers, who contribute enhancements and improvements to the standard code set. In addition, because there are a broad range of applications that are available for minimal cost and easy to install, Linux has found growing acceptance among those with minimal programming experience. For advocates in large organizations, commercial Linux products are available complete with extensive technical support and user help.

Linux is characterized by its power, flexibility, and constant maintenance by legions of programmers worldwide while maintaining careful adherence to industry standards. It is proving to be a viable player in the marketplace and is expected to grow in popularity for many years to come.

Key Terms

argument: in a command-driven operating system, a value or option placed in the command that modifies how the command is to be carried out.

buddy algorithm: a memory allocation technique that divides memory into halves to try to give a best fit and to fill memory requests as suitably as possible.

clock page replacement policy: a variation of the LRU policy that removes from main memory the pages that show the least amount of activity during recent clock cycles.

command: a directive to a computer program acting as an interpreter of some kind to perform a specific action.

command-driven interface: an interface that accepts typed commands, one line at a time, from the user. It is also called command line interface and contrasts with a menu-driven interface.

CPU-bound: a job that will perform a great deal of nonstop processing before issuing an interrupt. A CPU-bound job can tie up the CPU for long periods of time.

device driver: a device-specific program module that handles the interrupts and controls a particular type of device.

device independent: programs that can work on a variety of computers and with a variety of devices.

directory: a logical storage unit that contains files.

graphical user interface (GUI): allows the user to activate operating system commands by clicking on icons or symbols using a pointing device such as a mouse. It is also called a menu-driven interface.

kernel: the part of the operating system that resides in main memory at all times and performs the most essential tasks, such as managing memory and handling disk input and output.

menu-driven interface: an interface that accepts instructions that users choose from a menu of valid choices. It is also called a graphical user interface and contrasts with a command-driven interface.

patch management: the timely installation of software patches to make repairs and keep the operating system software current.

Portable Operating System Interface (POSIX): a set of IEEE standards that defines the standard user and programming interfaces for operating systems so developers can port programs from one operating system to another.

Interesting Searches

- Linux Kernel
- Open Source Software
- Linux Device Drivers
- Embedded Linux
- Linux for Supercomputers
- Linux vs. UNIX

Exercises

Research Topics

A. Research the similarities and differences between Linux and UNIX. List at least five major differences between the two operating systems and cite your sources. Describe in your own words which operating system you prefer and explain why.

B. Research the following statement: "Open source software is not free software." Explain whether or not the statement is true and describe the common misperceptions about open source software. Cite your sources.

Exercises

1. If you wanted to add these four files to one Linux directory (october.doc, OCTober.doc, OCTOBER.doc, and OcTOBer.doc), how many new files would be displayed: one, two, three, or four? Explain why this is so. Do you think the answer is the same for all operating systems? Why or why not?

2. Linux treats all devices as files. Explain why this feature adds flexibility to this operating system.

3. In Linux, devices are identified by a major or minor device number. List at least three types of devices that fall into each category and describe in your own words the differences between the two categories.

4. Explain why Linux makes system performance monitoring available to the user.

5. By examining permissions for each of the following files, identify if it is a file or directory, and describe the access allowed to the world, user, and group:

   a. -rwx---r-x

   b. drwx------

   c. -rwxrwxr--

   d. dr-x---r-x

   e. -rwx---rwx

6. Linux uses an LRU algorithm to manage memory. Suppose there is another page replacement algorithm called not frequently used (NFU) that gives each page its own counter that is incremented with each clock cycle. In this way, each counter tracks the frequency of page use, and the page with the lowest counter is swapped out when paging is necessary. In your opinion, how do these two algorithms (LRU and NFU) compare? Explain which one would work best under normal use, and define how you perceive "normal use."

7. There are many reasons why the system administrator would want to restrict access to areas of memory. Give the three reasons you believe are most important and rank them in order of importance.

8. Some versions of Linux place access control information among the page table entries. Explain why (or why not) this might be an efficient way to control access to files or directories.

9. With regard to virtual memory, decide if the following statement is true or false: If the paging file is located where fragmentation is least likely to happen, performance will be improved. Explain your answer.

Advanced Exercises

10. Compare and contrast block, character, and network devices, and how they are manipulated differently by the Linux device manager.

11. Describe the circumstance whereby a module would be closed but not released. What effect does this situation have on overall system performance? Describe the steps you would take to address the situation.

12. Security Enhanced Linux (SELinux) was designed and developed by a team from the U.S. National Security Agency and private industry. The resulting operating system, which began as a series of security patches, has since been included in the Linux kernel as of version 2.6. In your own words, explain why you think Linux was chosen as the base platform.

13. There are several ways to manage devices. The traditional way recognizes system devices in the order in which they are detected by the operating system. Another is dynamic device management, which calls for the creation and deletion of device files in the order that a user adds or removes devices. Compare and contrast the two methods and indicate the one you think is most effective, and explain why.

14. Device management also includes coordination with the Hardware Abstraction Layer (HAL). Describe which devices are managed by the HAL daemon and how duties are shared with the Linux device manager.

ACM Code of Ethics and Professional Conduct

The following passages are excerpted from the Code of Ethics and Professional Conduct adopted by the Association for Computing Machinery Council on October 16, 1992. They are reprinted here with permission. For the complete text, see *www.acm.org/about/code-of-ethics*.

Note: These imperatives are expressed in a general form to emphasize that ethical principles which apply to computer ethics are derived from more general ethical principles.

Preamble

Commitment to ethical professional conduct is expected of every member (voting members, associate members, and student members) of the Association for Computing Machinery (ACM).

This Code, consisting of 24 imperatives formulated as statements of personal responsibility, identifies the elements of such a commitment. It contains many, but not all, issues professionals are likely to face. Section 1 outlines fundamental ethical considerations, while Section 2 addresses additional, more specific considerations of professional conduct. Statements in Section 3 pertain more specifically to individuals who have a leadership role, whether in the workplace or in a volunteer capacity such as with organizations like ACM. Principles involving compliance with this Code are given in Section 4.

Section 1: GENERAL MORAL IMPERATIVES

As an ACM member I will ....

1.1 Contribute to society and human well-being.

This principle concerning the quality of life of all people affirms an obligation to protect fundamental human rights and to respect the diversity of all cultures. An essential aim of computing professionals is to minimize negative consequences of computing systems, including threats to health and safety. When designing or implementing systems, computing professionals must attempt to ensure that the products of their efforts will be used in socially responsible ways, will meet social needs, and will avoid harmful effects to health and welfare.

In addition to a safe social environment, human well-being includes a safe natural environment. Therefore, computing professionals who design and develop systems must be alert to, and make others aware of, any potential damage to the local or global environment.

1.2 Avoid harm to others.

"Harm" means injury or negative consequences, such as undesirable loss of information, loss of property, property damage, or unwanted environmental impacts. This principle prohibits use of computing technology in ways that result in harm to any of the following: users, the general public, employees, employers. Harmful actions include intentional destruction or modification of files and programs leading to serious loss of resources or unnecessary expenditure of human resources such as the time and effort required to purge systems of "computer viruses."

Well-intended actions, including those that accomplish assigned duties, may lead to harm unexpectedly. In such an event the responsible person or persons are obligated to undo or mitigate the negative consequences as much as possible. One way to avoid unintentional harm is to carefully consider potential impacts on all those affected by decisions made during design and implementation.

To minimize the possibility of indirectly harming others, computing professionals must minimize malfunctions by following generally accepted standards for system design and testing. Furthermore, it is often necessary to assess the social consequences of systems to project the likelihood of any serious harm to others. If system features are misrepresented to users, coworkers, or supervisors, the individual computing professional is responsible for any resulting injury.

In the work environment the computing professional has the additional obligation to report any signs of system dangers that might result in serious personal or social damage. If one's superiors do not act to curtail or mitigate such dangers, it may be necessary to "blow the whistle" to help correct the problem or reduce the risk. However, capricious or misguided reporting of violations can, itself, be harmful. Before reporting violations, all relevant aspects of the incident must be thoroughly assessed. In particular, the assessment of risk and responsibility must be credible. It is suggested that advice be sought from other computing professionals. See principle 2.5 regarding thorough evaluations.

1.3 Be honest and trustworthy.

Honesty is an essential component of trust. Without trust an organization cannot function effectively. The honest computing professional will not make deliberately false or deceptive claims about a system or system design, but will instead provide full disclosure of all pertinent system limitations and problems.

A computer professional has a duty to be honest about his or her own qualifications, and about any circumstances that might lead to conflicts of interest.

1.4 Be fair and take action not to discriminate.

The values of equality, tolerance, respect for others, and the principles of equal justice govern this imperative. Discrimination on the basis of race, sex, religion, age, disability, national origin, or other such factors is an explicit violation of ACM policy and will not be tolerated.

Inequities between different groups of people may result from the use or misuse of information and technology. In a fair society, all individuals would have equal opportunity to participate in, or benefit from, the use of computer resources regardless of race, sex, religion, age, disability, national origin or other similar factors. However, these ideals do not justify unauthorized use of computer resources nor do they provide an adequate basis for violation of any other ethical imperatives of this code.

1.5 Honor property rights including copyrights and patent.

Violation of copyrights, patents, trade secrets and the terms of license agreements is prohibited by law in most circumstances. Even when software is not so protected, such violations are contrary to professional behavior. Copies of software should be made only with proper authorization. Unauthorized duplication of materials must not be condoned.

1.6 Give proper credit for intellectual property.

Computing professionals are obligated to protect the integrity of intellectual property. Specifically, one must not take credit for other's ideas or work, even in cases where the work has not been explicitly protected by copyright, patent, etc.

1.7 Respect the privacy of others.

Computing and communication technology enables the collection and exchange of personal information on a scale unprecedented in the history of civilization. Thus, there is increased potential for violating the privacy of individuals and groups. It is the responsibility of professionals to maintain the privacy and integrity of data describing individuals. This includes taking precautions to ensure the accuracy of data, as well as protecting it from unauthorized access or accidental disclosure to inappropriate individuals. Furthermore, procedures must be established to allow individuals to review their records and correct inaccuracies.

This imperative implies that only the necessary amount of personal information be collected in a system, that retention and disposal periods for that information be clearly defined and enforced, and that personal information gathered for a specific purpose not be used for other purposes without consent of the individual(s). These principles apply to electronic communications, including electronic mail, and prohibit procedures that capture or monitor electronic user data, including messages, without the permission of users or bona fide authorization related to system operation and maintenance. User data observed during the normal duties of system operation and maintenance must be treated with strictest confidentiality, except in cases where it is evidence for the violation of law, organizational regulations, or this Code. In these cases, the nature or contents of that information must be disclosed only to proper authorities.

1.8 Honor confidentiality.

The principle of honesty extends to issues of confidentiality of information whenever one has made an explicit promise to honor confidentiality or, implicitly, when private information not directly related to the performance of one's duties becomes available. The ethical concern is to respect all obligations of confidentiality to employers, clients, and users unless discharged from such obligations by requirements of the law or other principles of this Code.

Glossary

absolute filename: a file's name, as given by the user, preceded by the directory (or directories) where the file is found and, when necessary, the specific device label.

access control: the control of user access to a network or computer system. See also *authentication*.

access control list: an access control method that lists each file, the names of the users who are allowed to access it, and the type of access each is permitted.

access control matrix: an access control method that uses a matrix with every file (listed in rows) and every user (listed in columns) and the type of access each user is permitted on each file, recorded in the cell at the intersection of that row and column.

access control verification module: the section of the File Manager that verifies which users are permitted to perform which operations with each file.

access time: the total time required to access data in secondary storage. For a direct access storage device with movable read/write heads, it is the sum of seek time (arm movement), search time (rotational delay), and transfer time (data transfer).

access token: an object that uniquely identifies a user who has logged on. An access token is appended to every process owned by the user. It contains the user's security identification, the names of the groups to which the user belongs, any privileges the user owns, the default owner of any objects the user's processes create, and the default access control list to be applied to any objects the user's processes create.

Active Directory: Microsoft Windows directory service that offers centralized administration of application serving, authentication, and user registration for distributed networking systems.

active multiprogramming: a term used to indicate that the operating system has more control over interrupts; designed to fairly distribute CPU utilization over several resident programs. It contrasts with *passive multiprogramming*.

address: a number that designates a particular memory location.

address resolution: the process of changing the address of an instruction or data item to the address in main memory at which it is to be loaded or relocated.

Advanced Research Projects Agency network (ARPAnet): a pioneering long-distance network funded by ARPA (now DARPA). It served as the basis for early networking research, as well as a central backbone during the development of the Internet. The ARPAnet consisted of individual packet switching computers interconnected by leased lines.

aging: a policy used to ensure that jobs that have been in the system for a long time in the lower level queues will eventually complete their execution.

algorithm: a set of step-by-step instructions used to solve a particular problem. It can be stated in any form, such as mathematical formulas, diagrams, or natural or programming languages.

allocation module: the section of the File Manager responsible for keeping track of unused areas in each storage device.

allocation scheme: the process of assigning specific resources to a job so it can execute.

anonymous FTP: a use of FTP that allows a user to retrieve documents, files, programs, and other data from anywhere on the Internet without having to establish a user ID and password. By using the special user ID of *anonymous* the network user is allowed to bypass local security checks and access publicly accessible files on the remote system.

antivirus software: software that is designed to detect and recover from attacks by viruses and worms. It is usually part of a system protection software package.

argument: in a command-driven operating system, a value or option placed in the command that modifies how the command is to be carried out.

arithmetic logic unit: The high-speed CPU circuit that is part of the processor core that performs all calculations and comparisons.

ARPAnet: see *Advanced Research Projects Agency network*.

assembler: a computer program that translates programs from assembly language to machine language.

assembly language: a programming language that allows users to write programs using mnemonic instructions that can be translated by an assembler. It is considered a low-level programming language and is very computer dependent.

associative memory: the name given to several registers, allocated to each active process, whose contents associate several of the process segments and page numbers with their main memory addresses.

authentication: the means by which a system verifies that the individual attempting to access the system is authorized to do so. Password protection is an authentication technique.

availability: a resource measurement tool that indicates the likelihood that the resource will be ready when a user needs it. It is influenced by mean time between failures and mean time to repair.

avoidance: the strategy of deadlock avoidance. It is a dynamic strategy, attempting to ensure that resources are never allocated in such a way as to place a system in an unsafe state.

backup: the process of making long-term archival file storage copies of files on the system.

batch system: a type of system developed for the earliest computers that used punched cards or tape for input. Each job was entered by assembling the cards together into a deck and several jobs were grouped, or *batched*, together before being sent through the card reader.

benchmarks: a measurement tool used to objectively measure and evaluate a system's performance by running a set of jobs representative of the work normally done by a computer system.

best-fit memory allocation: a main memory allocation scheme that considers all free blocks and selects for allocation the one that will result in the least amount of wasted space. It contrasts with the *first-fit memory allocation*.

biometrics: the science and technology of identifying authorized users based on their biological characteristics.

BIOS: an acronym for basic input output system, a set of programs that are hard-coded on a chip to load into ROM at startup.

blocking: a storage-saving and I/O-saving technique that groups individual records into a block that is stored and retrieved as a unit. The size of the block is often set to take advantage of the transfer rate.

bootstrapping: the process of starting an inactive computer by using a small initialization program to load other programs.

bounds register: a register used to store the highest location in memory legally accessible by each program. It contrasts with *relocation register*.

bridge: a data-link layer device used to interconnect multiple networks using the same protocol. A bridge is used to create an extended network so that several individual networks can appear to be part of one larger network.

browsing: a system security violation in which unauthorized users are allowed to search through secondary storage directories or files for information they should not have the privilege to read.

B-tree: a special case of a binary tree structure used to locate and retrieve records stored in disk files. The qualifications imposed on a B-tree structure reduce the amount of time it takes to search through the B-tree, making it an ideal file organization for large files.

buffers: the temporary storage areas residing in main memory, channels, and control units. They are used to store data read from an input device before it is needed by the processor and to store data that will be written to an output device.

bus: (1) the physical channel that links the hardware components and allows for transfer of data and electrical signals; or (2) a shared communication link onto which multiple nodes may connect.

bus topology: a network architecture in which elements are connected together along a single link.

busy waiting: a method by which processes, waiting for an event to occur, continuously test to see if the condition has changed and remain in unproductive, resource-consuming wait loops.

cache manager: a component of the I/O system that manages the part of virtual memory known as cache. The cache expands or shrinks dynamically depending on the amount of memory available.

cache memory: a small, fast memory used to hold selected data and to provide faster access than would otherwise be possible.

capability list: an access control method that lists every user, the files to which each has access, and the type of access allowed to those files.

capacity: the maximum throughput level of any one of the system's components.

Carrier Sense Multiple Access with Collision Avoidance (CSMA/CA): a method used to avoid transmission collision on shared media such as networks. It usually prevents collisions by requiring token acquisition.

Carrier Sense Multiple Access with Collision Detection (CSMA/CD): a method used to detect transmission collision on shared media such as networks. It requires that the affected stations stop transmitting immediately and try again after delaying a random amount of time.

CD-R: a compact disc storage medium that can be read many times but can be written to once.

CD-ROM: compact disc read-only memory; a direct access optical storage medium that can store data including graphics, audio, and video. Because it is read-only, the contents of the disc can't be modified.

CD-RW: a compact disc storage medium that can be read many times and written to many times.

central processing unit (CPU): the component with the circuitry, the *chips*, to control the interpretation and execution of instructions. In essence, it controls the operation of the entire computer system. All storage references, data manipulations, and I/O operations are initiated or performed by the CPU.

channel: see *I/O channel*.

channel program: see *I/O channel program*.

Channel Status Word (CSW): a data structure that contains information indicating the condition of the channel, including three bits for the three components of the I/O subsystem—one each for the channel, control unit, and device.

child process: in UNIX and Linux operating systems, the subordinate processes that are controlled by a parent process.

circuit switching: a communication model in which a dedicated communication path is established between two hosts, and on which all messages travel. The telephone system is an example of a circuit switched network.

circular wait: one of four conditions for deadlock through which each process involved is waiting for a resource being held by another; each process is blocked and can't continue, resulting in deadlock.

cleartext: in cryptography, a method of transmitting data without encryption, in text that is readable by anyone who sees it.

client: a user node that requests and makes use of various network services. A workstation requesting the contents of a file from a file server is a client of the file server.

clock cycle: the time span between two ticks of the computer's system clock.

clock policy: a variation of the LRU policy that removes from main memory the pages that show the least amount of activity during recent clock cycles.

C-LOOK: a scheduling strategy for direct access storage devices that is an optimization of C-SCAN.

COBEGIN: used with COEND to indicate to a multiprocessing compiler the beginning of a section where instructions can be processed concurrently.

COEND: used with COBEGIN to indicate to a multiprocessing compiler the end of a section where instructions can be processed concurrently.

collision: when a hashing algorithm generates the same logical address for two records with unique keys.

command-driven interface: an interface that accepts typed commands, one line at a time, from the user. It contrasts with a menu-driven interface.

compact disc: see *CD-R*.

compaction: the process of collecting fragments of available memory space into contiguous blocks by moving programs and data in a computer's memory or secondary storage.

compatibility: the ability of an operating system to execute programs written for other operating systems or for earlier versions of the same system.

compiler: a computer program that translates programs from a high-level programming language (such as FORTRAN, COBOL, Pascal, C, or Ada) into machine language.

complete filename: see *absolute filename*.

compression: see *data compression*.

concurrent processing: execution by a single processor of a set of processes in such a way that they appear to be happening at the same time. It is typically achieved by interleaved execution. Also called *multiprocessing*.

concurrent programming: a programming technique that allows a single processor to simultaneously execute multiple sets of instructions. Also called *multiprogramming* or *multitasking*.

connect time: in time-sharing, the amount of time that a user is connected to a computer system. It is usually measured by the time elapsed between log on and log off.

contention: a situation that arises on shared resources in which multiple data sources compete for access to the resource.

context switching: the acts of saving a job's processing information in its PCB so the job can be swapped out of memory, and of loading the processing information from the Process Control Block (PCB) of another job into the appropriate registers so the CPU can process it. Context switching occurs in all preemptive policies.

contiguous storage: a type of file storage in which all the information is stored in adjacent locations in a storage medium.

control cards: cards that define the exact nature of each program and its requirements. They contain information that direct the operating system to perform specific functions, such as initiating the execution of a particular job. See *job control language*.

control unit: see *I/O control unit*.

control word: a password given to a file by its creator.

core: The processing part of a CPU chip made up of the control unit and the arithmetic logic unit. The core does not include the cache.

C programming language: a general-purpose programming language developed by D. M. Ritchie. It combines high-level statements with low-level machine controls to generate software that is both easy to use and highly efficient.

CPU: see *central processing unit.*

CPU-bound: a job that will perform a great deal of nonstop processing before issuing an interrupt. A CPU-bound job can tie up the CPU for long periods of time. It contrasts with *I/O-bound.*

cracker: an individual who attempts to access computer systems without authorization. These individuals are often malicious, as opposed to *hackers*, and have several means at their disposal for breaking into a system.

critical region: the parts of a program that must complete execution before other processes can have access to the resources being used. It is called a critical region because its execution must be handled as a unit.

cryptography: the science of coding a message or text so an unauthorized user cannot read it.

C-SCAN: a scheduling strategy for direct access storage devices that is used to optimize seek time. It is an abbreviation for circular-SCAN.

CSMA/CA: see *Carrier Sense Multiple Access with Collision Avoidance.*

CSMA/CD: see *Carrier Sense Multiple Access with Collision Detection.*

current byte address (CBA): the address of the last byte read. It is used by the File Manager to access records in secondary storage and must be updated every time a record is accessed, such as when the READ command is executed.

current directory: the directory or subdirectory in which the user is working.

cylinder: for a disk or disk pack, it is when two or more read/write heads are positioned at the same track, at the same relative position, on their respective surfaces.

DASD: see *direct access storage device.*

database: a group of related files that are interconnected at various levels to give users flexibility of access to the data stored.

data compression: a procedure used to reduce the amount of space required to store data by reducing encoding or abbreviating repetitive terms or characters.

data file: a file that contains only data.

deadlock: a problem occurring when the resources needed by some jobs to finish execution are held by other jobs, which, in turn, are waiting for other resources to become available. The deadlock is complete if the remainder of the system comes to a standstill as a result of the hold the processes have on the resource allocation scheme. Also called *deadly embrace.*

deadly embrace: a colorful synonym for *deadlock.*

deallocation: the process of freeing an allocated resource, whether memory space, a device, a file, or a CPU.

dedicated device: a device that can be assigned to only one job at a time; it serves that job for the entire time the job is active.

demand paging: a memory allocation scheme that loads into memory a program's page at the time it is needed for processing.

denial of service (DoS) attack: an attack on a network that makes it unavailable to perform the functions it was designed to do. This can be done by flooding the server with meaningless requests or information.

detection: the process of examining the state of an operating system to determine whether a deadlock exists.

device: a computer's peripheral unit such as a printer, plotter, tape drive, disk drive, or terminal.

device driver: a device-specific program module that handles the interrupts and controls a particular type of device.

device independent: programs that can work on a variety of computers and with a variety of devices.

device interface module: transforms the block number supplied by the physical file system into the actual cylinder/surface/record combination needed to retrieve the information from a specific secondary storage device.

Device Manager: the section of the operating system responsible for controlling the use of devices. It monitors every device, channel, and control unit and chooses the most efficient way to allocate all of the system's devices.

dictionary attack: the technique by which an intruder attempts to guess user passwords by trying words found in a dictionary.

Dijkstra's algorithm: a graph theory algorithm that has been used in various link state routing protocols. This allows a router to step through an internetwork and find the best path to each destination.

direct access file: see *direct record organization.*

direct access storage device (DASD): any secondary storage device that can directly read or write to a specific place. Also called a *random access storage device.* It contrasts with a *sequential access medium.*

direct memory access (DMA): an I/O technique that allows a control unit to access main memory directly and transfer data without the intervention of the CPU.

direct record organization: files stored in a direct access storage device and organized to give users the flexibility of accessing any record at random regardless of its position in the file.

directed graphs: a graphic model representing various states of resource allocations. It consists of processes and resources connected by directed lines (lines with directional arrows).

directory: a logical storage unit that contains files.

disc: an optical storage medium such as CD or DVD.

disk pack: a removable stack of disks mounted on a common central spindle with spaces between each pair of platters so read/write heads can move between them.

displacement: in a paged or segmented memory allocation environment, it's the difference between a page's relative address and the actual machine language address. It is used to locate an instruction or data value within its page frame. Also called *offset.*

distributed operating system (DO/S): an operating system that provides control for a distributed computing system (two or more computers interconnected for a specific purpose), allowing its resources to be accessed in a unified way. See also *Network Operating System.*

distributed processing: a method of data processing in which files are stored at many different locations and in which processing takes place at different sites.

DNS: see *domain name service*.

Domain Name Service (DNS): a general-purpose, distributed, replicated, data query service. Its principal function is the resolution of Internet addresses based on fully qualified domain names such as .com (for commercial entity) or .edu (for educational institution).

DO/S: see *distributed operating system*.

double buffering: a technique used to speed I/O in which two buffers are present in main memory, channels, and control units.

DVD: digital video disc; a direct access optical storage medium that can store up to 17 gigabytes, enough to store a full-length movie.

dynamic partitions: a memory allocation scheme in which jobs are given as much memory as they request when they are loaded for processing, thus creating their own partitions in main memory. It contrasts with *static partitions,* or *fixed partitions*.

elevator algorithm: see *LOOK*.

embedded computer system: a dedicated computer system that often resides inside a larger physical system, such as jet aircraft or ships. It must be small and fast and work with real-time constraints, fail-safe execution, and nonstandard I/O devices. In some cases it must be able to manage concurrent activities, which requires parallel processing.

encryption: translation of a message or data item from its original form to an encoded form, thus hiding its meaning and making it unintelligible without the key to decode it. It is used to improve system security and data protection.

Ethernet: a 10-megabit, 100-megabit, 1-gigabit or more standard for LANs, initially developed by Xerox and later refined by Digital Equipment Corporation, Intel, and Xerox. All hosts are connected to a coaxial cable where they contend for network access.

ethics: the rules or standards of behavior that members of the computer-using community are expected to follow, demonstrating the principles of right and wrong.

explicit parallelism: a type of concurrent programming that requires that the programmer explicitly state which instructions can be executed in parallel. It contrasts with *implicit parallelism*.

extensibility: one of an operating system's design goals that allows it to be easily enhanced as market requirements change.

extension: in some operating systems, it is the part of the filename that indicates which compiler or software package is needed to run the files. UNIX and Linux call it a *suffix*.

extents: any remaining records, and all other additions to the file, that are stored in other sections of the disk. The extents of the file are linked together with pointers.

external fragmentation: a situation in which the dynamic allocation of memory creates unusable fragments of free memory between blocks of busy, or allocated, memory. It contrasts with *internal fragmentation*.

external interrupts: interrupts that occur outside the normal flow of a program's execution. They are used in preemptive scheduling policies to ensure a fair use of the CPU in multiprogramming environments.

FCFS: see *first come first served.*

feedback loop: a mechanism to monitor the system's resource utilization so adjustments can be made.

fetch policy: the rules used by the virtual memory manager to determine when a page is copied from disk to memory.

field: a group of related bytes that can be identified by the user with a name, type, and size. A record is made up of fields.

FIFO: see *first-in first-out.*

FIFO anomaly: an unusual circumstance through which adding more page frames causes an increase in page interrupts when using a FIFO page replacement policy.

file: a group of related records that contains information to be used by specific application programs to generate reports.

file allocation table (FAT): a table used to track noncontiguous segments of a file.

file descriptor: information kept in the directory to describe a file or file extent. It contains the file's name, location, and attributes.

File Manager: the section of the operating system responsible for controlling the use of files. It tracks every file in the system including data files, assemblers, compilers, and application programs. By using predetermined access policies, it enforces access restrictions on each file.

file server: a dedicated network node that provides mass data storage for other nodes on the network.

File Transfer Protocol (FTP): a protocol that allows a user on one host to access and transfer files to or from another host over a TCP/IP network.

filter command: a command that directs input from a device or file, changes it, and then sends the result to a printer or display.

FINISHED: a job status that means that execution of the job has been completed.

firewall: a set of hardware and software that disguises the internal network address of a computer or network to control how clients from outside can access the organization's internal servers.

firmware: software instructions or data that are stored in a fixed or *firm* way, usually implemented on *read only memory* (ROM). Firmware is built into the computer to make its operation simpler for the user to understand.

first come first served (FCFS): (1) the simplest scheduling algorithm for direct access storage devices that satisfies track requests in the order in which they are received; (2) a nonpreemptive process scheduling policy (or algorithm) that handles jobs according to their arrival time; the first job in the READY queue will be processed first by the CPU.

first-fit memory allocation: a main memory allocation scheme that searches from the beginning of the free block list and selects for allocation the first block of memory large enough to fulfill the request. It contrasts with *best-fit memory allocation.*

first generation (1940–1955): the era of the first computers, characterized by their use of vacuum tubes and their very large physical size.

first-in first-out (FIFO) policy: a page replacement policy that removes from main memory the pages that were brought in first. It is based on the assumption that these pages are the least likely to be used again in the near future.

fixed-length record: a record that always contains the same number of characters. It contrasts with *variable-length record*.

fixed partitions: a memory allocation scheme in which main memory is sectioned off, with portions assigned to each user. Also called *static partitions*. It contrasts with *dynamic partitions*.

flash memory: a type of nonvolatile memory used as a secondary storage device that can be erased and reprogrammed in blocks of data.

FLOP: a measure of processing speed meaning floating point operations per second (FLOP). See *megaflop, gigaflop, teraflop*.

floppy disk: a removable flexible disk for low-cost, direct access secondary storage.

fragmentation: a condition in main memory where wasted memory space exists within partitions, called *internal fragmentation*, or between partitions, called *external fragmentation*.

FTP: the name of the program a user invokes to execute the File Transfer Protocol.

gateway: a communications device or program that passes data between networks having similar functions but different protocols. A gateway is used to create an extended network so that several individual networks appear to be part of one larger network.

gigabit: a measurement of data transmission speed equal to 1,073,741,824 bits per second.

gigabyte (GB): a unit of memory or storage space equal to 1,073,741,824 bytes or 2^{30} bytes. One gigabyte is approximately 1 billion bytes.

gigaflop: a benchmark used to measure processing speed. One gigaflop equals 1 billion floating point operations per second.

graphical user interface (GUI): a user interface that allows the user to activate operating system commands by clicking on icons or symbols using a pointing device such as a mouse.

group: a property of operating systems that enables system administrators to create sets of users who share the same privileges. A group can share files or programs without allowing all system users access to those resources.

groupware: software applications that support cooperative work over a network. Groupware systems must support communications between users and information processing. For example, a system providing a shared editor must support not only the collective amendment of documents, but also discussions between the participants about what is to be amended and why.

hacker: a person who delights in having an intimate understanding of the internal workings of a system—computers and computer networks in particular. The term is often misused in a pejorative context, where *cracker* would be the correct term.

Hamming code: an error-detecting and error-correcting code that greatly improves the reliability of data, named after mathematician Richard Hamming.

hard disk: a direct access secondary storage device for personal computer systems. It is generally a high-density, nonremovable device.

hardware: the physical machine and its components, including main memory, I/O devices, I/O channels, direct access storage devices, and the central processing unit.

hashing algorithm: the set of instructions used to perform a key-to-address transformation in which a record's key field determines its location. See also *logical address*.

high-level scheduler: another term for the *Job Scheduler.*

HOLD: one of the process states. It is assigned to processes waiting to be let into the READY queue.

hop: a node network through which a packet passes on the path between the packet's source and destination nodes.

host: (1) the Internet term for a network node that is capable of communicating at the application layer. Each Internet host has a unique IP address. (2) a networked computer with centralized program or data files that makes them available to other computers on the network.

hybrid system: a computer system that supports both batch and interactive processes. It appears to be interactive because individual users can access the system via terminals and get fast responses, but it accepts and runs batch programs in the background when the interactive load is light.

hybrid topology: a network architecture that combines other types of network topologies, such as tree and star, to accommodate particular operating characteristics or traffic volumes.

impersonation: in Windows, the ability of a thread in one process to take on the security identity of a thread in another process and perform operations on that thread's behalf. Used by environment subsystems and network services when accessing remote resources for client applications.

implicit parallelism: a type of concurrent programming in which the compiler automatically detects which instructions can be performed in parallel. It contrasts with *explicit parallelism.*

indefinite postponement: means that a job's execution is delayed indefinitely because it is repeatedly preempted so other jobs can be processed.

index block: a data structure used with indexed storage allocation. It contains the addresses of each disk sector used by that file.

indexed sequential record organization: a way of organizing data in a direct access storage device. An index is created to show where the data records are stored. Any data record can be retrieved by consulting the index first.

indexed storage: the way in which the File Manager physically allocates space to an indexed sequentially organized file.

interactive system: a system that allows each user to interact directly with the operating system via commands entered from a keyboard. Also called *time-sharing system.*

interblock gap (IBG): an unused space between blocks of records on a magnetic tape.

internal fragmentation: a situation in which a fixed partition is only partially used by the program. The remaining space within the partition is unavailable to any other job and is therefore wasted. It contrasts with *external fragmentation.*

internal interrupts: also called *synchronous interrupts,* they occur as a direct result of the arithmetic operation or job instruction currently being processed. They contrast with *external interrupts.*

internal memory: see *main memory.*

International Organization for Standardization (ISO): a voluntary, non-treaty organization founded in 1946 that is responsible for creating international standards in many areas, including computers and communications. Its members are the national standards organizations of the 89 member countries, including ANSI for the United States.

Internet: the largest collection of networks interconnected with routers. The Internet is a multiprotocol internetwork.

Internet Protocol (IP): the network-layer protocol used to route data from one network to another. It was developed by the United States Department of Defense.

interrecord gap (IRG): an unused space between records on a magnetic tape. It facilitates the tape's start/stop operations.

interrupt: a hardware signal that suspends execution of a program and activates the execution of a special program known as the interrupt handler. It breaks the normal flow of the program being executed.

interrupt handler: the program that controls what action should be taken by the operating system when a sequence of events is interrupted.

inverted file: a file generated from full document databases. Each record in an inverted file contains a key subject and the document numbers where that subject is found. A book's index is an inverted file.

I/O-bound: a job that requires a large number of input/output operations, resulting in much free time for the CPU. It contrasts with *CPU-bound.*

I/O channel: a specialized programmable unit placed between the CPU and the control units. Its job is to synchronize the fast speed of the CPU with the slow speed of the I/O device and vice versa, making it possible to overlap I/O operations with CPU operations. I/O channels provide a path for the transmission of data between control units and main memory, and they control that transmission.

I/O channel program: the program that controls the channels. Each channel program specifies the action to be performed by the devices and controls the transmission of data between main memory and the control units.

I/O control unit: the hardware unit containing the electronic components common to one type of I/O device, such as a disk drive. It is used to control the operation of several I/O devices of the same type.

I/O device: any peripheral unit that allows communication with the CPU by users or programs, including terminals, line printers, plotters, card readers, tape drives, and direct access storage devices.

I/O device handler: the module that processes the I/O interrupts, handles error conditions, and provides detailed scheduling algorithms that are extremely device dependent. Each type of I/O device has its own device handler algorithm.

I/O scheduler: one of the modules of the I/O subsystem that allocates the devices, control units, and channels.

I/O subsystem: a collection of modules within the operating system that controls all I/O requests.

I/O traffic controller: one of the modules of the I/O subsystem that monitors the status of every device, control unit, and channel.

IP: see *Internet Protocol*.

ISO: see *International Organization for Standardization*.

Java: a cross-platform programming language, developed by Sun Microsystems, that closely resembles C++ and runs on any computer capable of running the Java interpreter.

job: a unit of work submitted by a user to an operating system.

job control language (JCL): a command language used in several computer systems to direct the operating system in the performance of its functions by identifying the users and their jobs and specifying the resources required to execute a job. The JCL helps the operating system better coordinate and manage the system's resources.

Job Scheduler: the high-level scheduler of the Processor Manager that selects jobs from a queue of incoming jobs based on each job's characteristics. The Job Scheduler's goal is to sequence the jobs in the READY queue so that the system's resources will be used efficiently.

job status: the condition of a job as it moves through the system from the beginning to the end of its execution: HOLD, READY, RUNNING, WAITING, or FINISHED.

job step: units of work executed sequentially by the operating system to satisfy the user's total request. A common example of three job steps is the compilation, linking, and execution of a user's program.

Job Table (JT): a table in main memory that contains two entries for each active job—the size of the job and the memory location where its page map table is stored. It is used for paged memory allocation schemes.

Kerberos: an MIT-developed authentication system that allows network managers to administer and manage user authentication at the network level.

kernel: the part of the operating system that resides in main memory at all times and performs the most essential tasks, such as managing memory and handling disk input and output.

kernel level: in an object-based distributed operating system, it provides the basic mechanisms for dynamically building the operating system by creating, managing, scheduling, synchronizing, and deleting objects.

kernel mode: the name given to indicate that processes are granted privileged access to the processor. Therefore, all machine instructions are allowed and system memory is accessible. Contrasts with the more restrictive *user mode*.

key field: (1) a unique field or combination of fields in a record that uniquely identifies that record; (2) the field that determines the position of a record in a sorted sequence.

kilobyte (K): a unit of memory or storage space equal to 1,024 bytes or 2^{10} bytes.

LAN: see *local area network*.

lands: flat surface areas on the reflective layer of a CD or DVD. Each land is interpreted as a 1. Contrasts with *pits*, which are interpreted as 0s.

leased line: a dedicated telephone circuit for which a subscriber pays a monthly fee, regardless of actual use.

least-frequently-used (LFU): a page-removal algorithm that removes from memory the least-frequently-used page.

least-recently-used (LRU) policy: a page-replacement policy that removes from main memory the pages that show the least amount of recent activity. It is based on the assumption that these pages are the least likely to be used again in the immediate future.

LFU: see *least-frequently-used*.

Lightweight Directory Access Protocol (LDAP): a protocol that defines a method for creating searchable directories of resources on a network. It is called *lightweight* because it is a simplified and TCP/IP-enabled version of the X.500 directory protocol.

link: a generic term for any data communications medium to which a network node is attached.

livelock: a locked system whereby two or more processes continually block the forward progress of the others without making any forward progress itself. It is similar to a deadlock except that neither process is blocked or waiting; they are both in a continuous state of change.

local area network (LAN): a data network intended to serve an area covering only a few square kilometers or less.

local station: the network node to which a user is attached.

locality of reference: behavior observed in many executing programs in which memory locations recently referenced, and those near them, are likely to be referenced in the near future.

locking: a technique used to guarantee the integrity of the data in a database through which the user locks out all other users while working with the database.

lockword: a sequence of letters and/or numbers provided by users to prevent unauthorized tampering with their files. The lockword serves as a secret *password* in that the system will deny access to the protected file unless the user supplies the correct lockword when accessing the file.

logic bomb: a virus with a trigger, usually an event, that causes it to execute.

logical address: the result of a key-to-address transformation. See also *hashing algorithm*.

LOOK: a scheduling strategy for direct access storage devices that is used to optimize seek time. Sometimes known as the elevator algorithm.

loosely coupled configuration: a multiprocessing configuration in which each processor has a copy of the operating system and controls its own resources.

low-level scheduler: a synonym for *process scheduler.*

LRU: see *least-recently-used.*

magnetic tape: a linear secondary storage medium that was first developed for early computer systems. It allows only for sequential retrieval and storage of records.

magneto-optical (MO) disk drive: a data storage drive that uses a laser beam to read and/or write information recorded on magneto-optical disks.

mailslots: a high-level network software interface for passing data among processes in a one-to-many and many-to-one communication mechanism. Mail slots are useful for broadcasting messages to any number of processes.

main memory: the memory unit that works directly with the CPU and in which the data and instructions must reside in order to be processed. Also called *random access memory (RAM), primary storage,* or *internal memory.*

mainframe: the historical name given to a large computer system characterized by its large size, high cost, and high performance.

MAN: see *metropolitan area network.*

master file directory (MFD): a file stored immediately after the volume descriptor. It lists the names and characteristics of every file contained in that volume.

master/slave configuration: an asymmetric multiprocessing configuration consisting of a single processor system connected to *slave* processors, each of which is managed by the primary *master* processor, which provides the scheduling functions and jobs.

mean time between failures (MTBF): a resource measurement tool; the average time that a unit is operational before it breaks down.

mean time to repair (MTTR): a resource measurement tool; the average time needed to fix a failed unit and put it back in service.

megabyte (MB): a unit of memory or storage space equal to 1,048,576 bytes or 2^{20} bytes.

megaflop: a benchmark used to measure processing speed. One megaflop equals 1 million floating point operations per second.

megahertz (MHz): a speed measurement used to compare the clock speed of computers. One megahertz is equal to 1 million electrical cycles per second.

Memory Manager: the section of the operating system responsible for controlling the use of memory. It checks the validity of each request for memory space and, if it is a legal request, allocates the amount of memory needed to execute the job.

Memory Map Table (MMT): a table in main memory that contains as many entries as there are page frames and lists the location and free/busy status for each one.

menu-driven interface: an interface that accepts instructions that users choose from a menu of valid choices. It contrasts with a *command-driven interface.*

metropolitan area network (MAN): a data network intended to serve an area approximating that of a large city.

microcomputer: a small computer equipped with all the hardware and software necessary to perform one or more tasks.

middle-level scheduler: a scheduler used by the Processor Manager to manage processes that have been interrupted because they have exceeded their allocated CPU time slice. It is used in some highly interactive environments.

midrange computer: a small to medium-sized computer system developed to meet the needs of smaller institutions. It was originally developed for sites with only a few dozen users. Also called *minicomputer*.

minicomputer: see *midrange computer*.

MIPS: a measure of processor speed that stands for a million instructions per second. A mainframe system running at 100 MIPS can execute 100,000,000 instructions per second.

module: a logical section of a program. A program may be divided into a number of logically self-contained modules that may be written and tested by a number of programmers.

monoprogramming system: a single-user computer system.

most-recently-used (MRU): a page-removal algorithm that removes from memory the most-recently-used page.

MTBF: see *mean time between failures*.

MTTR: see *mean time to repair*.

multiple-level queues: a process-scheduling scheme (used with other scheduling algorithms) that groups jobs according to a common characteristic. The processor is then allocated to serve the jobs in these queues in a predetermined manner.

multiprocessing: when two or more CPUs share the same main memory, most I/O devices, and the same control program routines. They service the same job stream and execute distinct processing programs concurrently.

multiprogramming: a technique that allows a single processor to process several programs residing simultaneously in main memory and interleaving their execution by overlapping I/O requests with CPU requests. Also called *concurrent programming* or *multitasking*.

multitasking: a synonym for *multiprogramming*.

mutex: a condition that specifies that only one process may update (modify) a shared resource at a time to ensure correct operation and results.

mutual exclusion: one of four conditions for deadlock in which only one process is allowed to have access to a resource. It is typically shortened to *mutex* in algorithms describing synchronization between processes.

named pipes: a high-level software interface to NetBIOS, which represents the hardware in network applications as abstract objects. Named pipes are represented as file objects in Windows and operate under the same security mechanisms as other executive objects.

natural wait: common term used to identify an I/O request from a program in a multiprogramming environment that would cause a process to wait naturally before resuming execution.

negative feedback loop: a mechanism to monitor the system's resources and, when it becomes too congested, to signal the appropriate manager to slow down the arrival rate of the processes.

NetBIOS interface: a programming interface that allows I/O requests to be sent to and received from a remote computer. It hides networking hardware from applications.

network: a system of interconnected computer systems and peripheral devices that exchange information with one another.

Network Manager: the section of the operating system responsible for controlling the access to, and use of, networked resources.

network operating system (NOS): the software that manages network resources for a node on a network and may provide security and access control. These resources may include electronic mail, file servers, and print servers. See also *distributed operating system.*

no preemption: one of four conditions for deadlock in which a process is allowed to hold on to resources while it is waiting for other resources to finish execution.

noncontiguous storage: a type of file storage in which the information is stored in nonadjacent locations in a storage medium. Data records can be accessed directly by computing their relative addresses.

nonpreemptive scheduling policy: a job scheduling strategy that functions without external interrupts so that, once a job captures the processor and begins execution, it remains in the RUNNING state uninterrupted until it issues an I/O request or it is finished.

NOS: see *network operating system.*

N-step SCAN: a variation of the SCAN scheduling strategy for direct access storage devices that is used to optimize seek times.

NT file system (NTFS): The file system introduced with Windows NT that offers file management services, such as permission management, compression, transaction logs, and the ability to create a single volume spanning two or more physical disks.

null entry: an empty entry in a list. It assumes different meanings based on the list's application.

object: any one of the many entities that constitute a computer system, such as CPUs, terminals, disk drives, files, or databases. Each object is called by a unique name and has a set of operations that can be carried out on it.

object-based DO/S: a view of distributed operating systems where each hardware unit is bundled with its required operational software, forming a discrete object to be handled as an entity.

object-oriented: a programming philosophy whereby programs consist of self-contained, reusable modules called objects, each of which supports a specific function, but which are categorized into classes of objects that share the same function.

offset: in a paged or segmented memory allocation environment, it is the difference between a page's address and the actual machine language address. It is used to locate an instruction or data value within its page frame. Also called *displacement.*

open shortest path first (OSPF): a protocol designed for use in Internet Protocol networks, it is concerned with tracking the operational state of every network interface. Any changes to the state of an interface will trigger a routing update message.

open systems interconnection (OSI) reference model: a seven-layer structure designed to describe computer network architectures and the ways in which data passes through them. This model was developed by the ISO in 1978 to clearly define the interfaces and protocols for multi-vendor networks, and to provide users of those networks with conceptual guidelines in the construction of such networks.

operating system: the software that manages all the resources of a computer system.

optical disc: a secondary storage device on which information is stored in the form of tiny holes called *pits* laid out in a spiral track (instead of a concentric track as for a magnetic disk). The data is read by focusing a laser beam onto the track.

optical disc drive: a drive that uses a laser beam to read and/or write information recorded on compact optical discs.

order of operations: the algebraic convention that dictates the order in which elements of a formula are calculated.

OSI reference model: see *open systems interconnection reference model*.

OSPF: see *open shortest path first*.

overlay: a technique used to increase the apparent size of main memory. This is accomplished by keeping in main memory only the programs or data that are currently active; the rest are kept in secondary storage. Overlay occurs when segments of a program are transferred from secondary storage to main memory for execution, so that two or more segments occupy the same storage locations at different times.

owner: one of the three types of users allowed to access a file. The owner is the one who created the file originally. The other two types are *group* and *everyone else*, also known as *world* in some systems.

P: an operation performed on a semaphore, which may cause the calling process to wait. It stands for the Dutch word *proberen,* meaning *to test*, and it is part of the P and V operations to test and increment.

packet: a unit of data sent across a network. *Packet* is a generic term used to describe units of data at all layers of the protocol stack, but it is most correctly used to describe application data units.

packet sniffer: software that intercepts network data packets sent in cleartext and searches them for information, such as passwords.

packet switching: a communication model in which messages are individually routed between hosts, with no previously established communication path.

page: a fixed-size section of a user's job that corresponds to page frames in main memory.

page fault: a type of hardware interrupt caused by a reference to a page not residing in memory. The effect is to move a page out of main memory and into secondary storage so another page can be moved into memory.

page fault handler: part of the Memory Manager that determines if there are empty page frames in memory so that the requested page can immediately be copied from secondary storage, or determines which page must be swapped out if all page frames are busy.

page frame: individual sections of main memory of uniform size into which a single page may be loaded.

Page Map Table (PMT): a table in main memory with the vital information for each page including the page number and its corresponding page frame memory address.

page replacement policy: an algorithm used by virtual memory systems to decide which page or segment to remove from main memory when a page frame is needed and memory is full. Two examples are FIFO and LRU.

page swap: the process of moving a page out of main memory and into secondary storage so another page can be moved into memory in its place.

paged memory allocation: a memory allocation scheme based on the concept of dividing a user's job into sections of equal size to allow for noncontiguous program storage during execution. This was implemented to further increase the level of multiprogramming. It contrasts with *segmented memory allocation.*

parallel processing: the process of operating two or more CPUs in parallel: that is, more than one CPU executing instructions simultaneously.

parent process: In UNIX and Linux operating systems, a job that controls one or more child processes, which are subordinate to it.

parity bit: an extra bit added to a character, word, or other data unit and used for error checking. It is set to either 0 or 1 so that the sum of the 1 bits in the data unit is always even, for even parity, or odd for odd parity, according to the logic of the system.

partition: a section of hard disk storage of arbitrary size. Partitions can be static or dynamic.

passive multiprogramming: a term used to indicate that the operating system doesn't control the amount of time the CPU is allocated to each job, but waits for each job to end an execution sequence before issuing an interrupt releasing the CPU and making it available to other jobs. It contrasts with *active multiprogramming.*

pass-through security: used to perform remote-validation activities in Windows 95. Logon information is passed to the appropriate networking protocol for processing that enables Windows 95 to use existing network hardware and software with all the security that is built into these external network servers.

password: a user-defined access control method. Typically a word or character string that a user must specify in order to be allowed to log on to a computer system.

patch: executable software that repairs errors or omissions in another program or piece of software.

patch management: the rigorous application of software patches to make repairs and keep the operating system software up to the latest standard.

path: (1) the sequence of routers and links through which a packet passes on its way from source to destination node; (2) the sequence of directories and subdirectories the operating system must follow to find a specific file.

PCB: see *process control block.*

peer (hardware): a node on a network that is at the same level as other nodes on that network. For example, all nodes on a local area network are peers.

peer (software): a process that is communicating to another process residing at the same layer in the protocol stack on another node. For example, if the processes are application processes, they are said to be application-layer peers.

performance: the ability of an operating system to give users good response times under heavy loads and when using CPU-bound applications such as graphic and financial analysis packages, both of which require rapid processing.

phishing: a technique used to trick consumers into revealing personal information by appearing as a legitimate entity.

pipe: a symbol that directs the operating system to divert the output of one command so it becomes the input of another command.

pirated software: illegally obtained software.

pits: tiny depressions on the reflective layer of a CD or DVD. Each pit is interpreted as a 0. Contrasts with *lands*, which are interpreted as 1s.

placement policy: the rules used by the virtual memory manager to determine where the virtual page is to be loaded in memory.

pointer: an address or other indicator of location.

polling: a software mechanism used to test the flag, which indicates when a device, control unit, or path is available.

portability: the ability to move an entire operating system to a machine based on a different processor or configuration with as little recoding as possible.

positive feedback loop: a mechanism used to monitor the system. When the system becomes underutilized, the feedback causes the arrival rate to increase.

POSIX: Portable Operating System Interface is a set of IEEE standards that defines the standard user and programming interfaces for operating systems so developers can port programs from one operating system to another.

preemptive scheduling policy: any process scheduling strategy that, based on predetermined policies, interrupts the processing of a job and transfers the CPU to another job. It is widely used in time-sharing environments.

prevention: a design strategy for an operating system where resources are managed in such a way that some of the necessary conditions for deadlock do not hold.

primary storage: see *main memory.*

primitives: well-defined, predictable, low-level operating system mechanisms that allow higher-level operating system components to perform their functions without considering direct hardware manipulation.

priority scheduling: a nonpreemptive process scheduling policy (or algorithm) that allows for the execution of high-priority jobs before low-priority jobs.

process: an instance of execution of a program that is identifiable and controllable by the operating system.

process control block (PCB): a data structure that contains information about the current status and characteristics of a process. Every process has a PCB.

process identification: a user-supplied unique identifier of the process and a pointer connecting it to its descriptor, which is stored in the PCB.

process scheduler: the low-level scheduler of the Processor Manager that sets up the order in which processes in the READY queue will be served by the CPU.

process scheduling algorithm: an algorithm used by the Job Scheduler to allocate the CPU and move jobs through the system. Examples are FCFS, SJN, priority, and round robin scheduling policies.

process scheduling policy: any policy used by the Processor Manager to select the order in which incoming jobs will be executed.

process state: information stored in the job's PCB that indicates the current condition of the process being executed.

process status: information stored in the job's PCB that indicates the current position of the job and the resources responsible for that status.

Process Status Word (PSW): information stored in a special CPU register including the current instruction counter and register contents. It is saved in the job's PCB when it isn't running but is on HOLD, READY, or WAITING.

process synchronization: (1) the need for algorithms to resolve conflicts between processors in a multiprocessing environment; (2) the need to ensure that events occur in the proper order even if they are carried out by several processes.

process-based DO/S: a view of distributed operating systems that encompasses all the system's processes and resources. Process management is provided through the use of client/server processes.

processor: (1) another term for the CPU (central processing unit); (2) any component in a computing system capable of performing a sequence of activities. It controls the interpretation and execution of instructions.

Processor Manager: a composite of two submanagers, the Job Scheduler and the Process Scheduler. It decides how to allocate the CPU, monitors whether it is executing a process or waiting, and controls job entry to ensure balanced use of resources.

producers and consumers: a classic problem in which a process produces data that will be consumed, or used, by another process. It exhibits the need for process cooperation.

program: a sequence of instructions that provides a solution to a problem and directs the computer's actions. In an operating systems environment it can be equated with a job.

program file: a file that contains instructions for the computer.

protocol: a set of rules to control the flow of messages through a network.

proxy server: a server positioned between an internal network and an external network or the Internet to screen all requests for information and prevent unauthorized access to network resources.

PSW: see *Process Status Word*.

queue: a linked list of PCBs that indicates the order in which jobs or processes will be serviced.

race: a synchronization problem between two processes vying for the same resource. In some cases it may result in data corruption because the order in which the processes will finish executing cannot be controlled.

RAID: redundant arrays of independent disks. A group of hard disks controlled in such a way that they speed read access of data on secondary storage devices and aid data recovery.

random access memory (RAM): see *main memory.*

random access storage device: see *direct access storage device.*

read only memory (ROM): a type of primary storage in which programs and data are stored once by the manufacturer and later retrieved as many times as necessary. ROM does not allow storage of new programs or data.

readers and writers: a problem that arises when two types of processes need to access a shared resource such as a file or a database. Their access must be controlled to preserve data integrity.

read/write head: a small electromagnet used to read or write data on a magnetic storage medium, such as disk or tape.

READY: a job status that means the job is ready to run but is waiting for the CPU.

real-time system: the computing system used in time-critical environments that require guaranteed response times, such as navigation systems, rapid transit systems, and industrial control systems.

record: a group of related fields treated as a unit. A file is a group of related records.

recovery: (1) when a deadlock is detected, the steps that must be taken to break the deadlock by breaking the circle of waiting processes; (2) when a system is assaulted, the steps that must be taken to recover system operability and, in the best case, recover any lost data.

redirection: a symbol that directs the operating system to send the results of a command to or from a file or device other than a keyboard or monitor.

reentrant code: code that can be used by two or more processes at the same time; each shares the same copy of the executable code but has separate data areas.

register: a hardware storage unit used in the CPU for temporary storage of a single data item.

relative address: in a direct organization environment, it indicates the position of a record relative to the beginning of the file.

relative filename: a file's simple name and extension as given by the user. It contrasts with *absolute filename.*

reliability: (1) a standard that measures the probability that a unit will not fail during a given time period—it is a function of MTBF; (2) the ability of an operating system to respond predictably to error conditions, even those caused by hardware failures; (3) the ability of an operating system to actively protect itself and its users from accidental or deliberate damage by user programs.

relocatable dynamic partitions: a memory allocation scheme in which the system relocates programs in memory to gather together all of the empty blocks and compact them to make one block of memory that is large enough to accommodate some or all of the jobs waiting for memory.

relocation: (1) the process of moving a program from one area of memory to another; (2) the process of adjusting address references in a program, by either software or hardware means, to allow the program to execute correctly when loaded in different sections of memory.

relocation register: a register that contains the value that must be added to each address referenced in the program so that it will be able to access the correct memory addresses after relocation. If the program hasn't been relocated, the value stored in the program's relocation register is 0. It contrasts with *bounds register.*

remote login: the ability to operate on a remote computer using a protocol over a computer network as though locally attached.

remote station: the node at the distant end of a network connection.

repeated trials: repeated guessing of a user's password by an unauthorized user. It is a method used to illegally enter systems that rely on passwords.

replacement policy: the rules used by the virtual memory manager to determine which virtual page must be removed from memory to make room for a new page.

resource holding: one of four conditions for deadlock in which each process refuses to relinquish the resources it holds until its execution is completed, even though it isn't using them because it is waiting for other resources. It is the opposite of *resource sharing.*

resource sharing: the use of a resource by two or more processes either at the same time or at different times.

resource utilization: a measure of how much each unit is contributing to the overall operation of the system. It is usually given as a percentage of time that a resource is actually in use.

response time: a measure of an interactive system's efficiency that tracks the speed with which the system will respond to a user's command.

ring topology: a network topology in which each node is connected to two adjacent nodes. Ring networks have the advantage of not needing routing because all packets are simply passed to a node's upstream neighbor.

RIP: see *Routing Information Protocol.*

root directory: (1) for a disk, it is the directory accessed by default when booting up the computer; (2) for a hierarchical directory structure, it is the first directory accessed by a user.

rotational delay: a synonym for *search time.*

rotational ordering: an algorithm used to reorder record requests within tracks to optimize search time.

round robin: a preemptive process scheduling policy (or algorithm) that allocates to each job one unit of processing time per turn to ensure that the CPU is equally shared among all active processes and isn't monopolized by any one job. It is used extensively in interactive systems.

router: a device that forwards traffic between networks. The routing decision is based on network-layer information and routing tables, often constructed by routing protocols.

routing: the process of selecting the correct interface and next hop for a packet being forwarded.

Routing Information Protocol (RIP): a routing protocol used by IP. It is based on a distance-vector algorithm.

RUNNING: a job status that means that the job is executing.

safe state: the situation in which the system has enough available resources to guarantee the completion of at least one job running on the system.

SCAN: a scheduling strategy for direct access storage devices that is used to optimize seek time. The most common variations are *N-step SCAN* and *C-SCAN*.

scheduling algorithm: see *process scheduling algorithm.*

script file: A series of executable commands written in plain text and executed by the operating system in sequence as a procedure.

search strategies: algorithms used to optimize search time in direct access storage devices. See also *rotational ordering.*

search time: the time it takes to rotate the drum or disk from the moment an I/O command is issued until the requested record is moved under the read/write head. Also called *rotational delay.*

second generation (1955–1965): the second era of technological development of computers, when the transistor replaced the vacuum tube. Computers were smaller and faster and had larger storage capacity than first-generation computers and were developed to meet the needs of the business market.

sector: a division in a disk's track. Sometimes called a *block*. The tracks are divided into sectors during the formatting process.

security descriptor: a Windows data structure appended to an object that protects the object from unauthorized access. It contains an access control list and controls auditing.

seek strategy: a predetermined policy used by the I/O device handler to optimize seek times.

seek time: the time required to position the read/write head on the proper track from the time the I/O request is issued.

segment: a variable-size section of a user's job that contains a logical grouping of code. It contrasts with *page*.

Segment Map Table (SMT): a table in main memory with the vital information for each segment including the segment number and its corresponding memory address.

segmented memory allocation: a memory allocation scheme based on the concept of dividing a user's job into logical groupings of code to allow for noncontiguous program storage during execution. It contrasts with *paged memory allocation.*

segmented/demand paged memory allocation: a memory allocation scheme based on the concept of dividing a user's job into logical groupings of code and loading them into memory as needed.

semaphore: a type of shared data item that may contain either binary or nonnegative integer values and is used to provide mutual exclusion.

sequential access medium: any medium that stores records only in a sequential manner, one after the other, such as magnetic tape. It contrasts with *direct access storage device.*

sequential record organization: the organization of records in a specific sequence. Records in a sequential file must be processed one after another.

server: a node that provides to clients various network services such as file retrieval, printing, or database access services.

server process: a logical unit composed of one or more device drivers, a device manager, and a network server module; needed to control clusters or similar devices, such as printers or disk drives, in a process-based distributed operating system environment.

service pack: a term used by some vendors to describe an update to customer software to repair existing problems and/or deliver enhancements.

sharable code: executable code in the operating system that can be shared by several processes.

shared device: a device that can be assigned to several active processes at the same time.

shortest job first (SJF): see *shortest job next.*

shortest job next (SJN): a nonpreemptive process scheduling policy (or algorithm) that selects the waiting job with the shortest CPU cycle time. Also called *shortest job first.*

shortest remaining time (SRT): a preemptive process scheduling policy (or algorithm), similar to the SJN algorithm, that allocates the processor to the job closest to completion.

shortest seek time first (SSTF): a scheduling strategy for direct access storage devices that is used to optimize seek time. The track requests are ordered so the one closest to the currently active track is satisfied first and the ones farthest away are made to wait.

site: a specific location on a network containing one or more computer systems.

SJF: see *shortest job first.*

SJN: see *shortest job next.*

smart card: a small, credit-card-sized device that uses cryptographic technology to control access to computers and computer networks. Each smart card has its own personal identifier, which is known only to the user, as well as its own stored and encrypted password.

sniffer: see *packet sniffer.*

social engineering: a technique whereby system intruders gain access to information about a legitimate user to learn active passwords, sometimes by calling the user and posing as a system technician.

socket: abstract communication interfaces that allow applications to communicate while hiding the actual communications from the applications.

software: a collection of programs used to perform certain tasks. They fall into three main categories: operating system programs, compilers and assemblers, and application programs.

spin lock: a Windows synchronization mechanism used by the kernel and parts of the executive that guarantees mutually exclusive access to a global system data structure across multiple processors.

spoofing: the creation of false IP addresses in the headers of data packets sent over the Internet, sometimes with the intent of gaining access when it would not otherwise be granted.

spooling: a technique developed to speed I/O by collecting in a disk file either input received from slow input devices or output going to slow output devices such as printers. Spooling minimizes the waiting done by the processes performing the I/O.

SRT: see *shortest remaining time.*

SSTF: see *shortest seek time first.*

stack: a sequential list kept in main memory. The items in the stack are retrieved from the top using a last-in first-out (LIFO) algorithm.

stack algorithm: an algorithm for which it can be shown that the set of pages in memory for *n* page frames is always a subset of the set of pages that would be in memory with *n* + 1 page frames. Therefore, increasing the number of page frames will not bring about Belady's anomaly.

star topology: a network topology in which multiple network nodes are connected through a single, central node. The central node is a device that manages the network. This topology has the disadvantage of depending on a central node, the failure of which would bring down the network.

starvation: the result of conservative allocation of resources in which a single job is prevented from execution because it is kept waiting for resources that never become available. It is an extreme case of *indefinite postponement.*

static partitions: another term for *fixed partitions.*

station: any device that can receive and transmit messages on a network.

storage: the place where data is stored in the computer system. Primary storage is main memory. Secondary storage is nonvolatile media, such as disks and flash memory.

store-and-forward: a network operational mode in which messages are received in their entirety before being transmitted to their destination, or to their next hop in the path to their destination.

stripe: a set of consecutive strips across disks; the strips contain data bits and sometimes parity bits depending on the RAID level.

subdirectory: a directory created by the user within the boundaries of an existing directory. Some operating systems call this a folder.

subroutine: also called a *subprogram,* a segment of a program that can perform a specific function. Subroutines can reduce programming time when a specific function is required at more than one point in a program.

subsystem: see *I/O subsystem.*

suffix: see *extension.*

supercomputers: the fastest, most sophisticated computers made, used for complex calculations at the fastest speed permitted by current technology.

symmetric configuration: a multiprocessing configuration in which processor scheduling is decentralized and each processor is of the same type. A single copy of the operating system and a global table listing each process and its status is stored in a common area of memory so every processor has access to it. Each processor uses the same scheduling algorithm to select which process it will run next.

synchronous interrupts: another term for *internal interrupts.*

system prompt: the signal from the operating system that it is ready to accept a user's command, such as C:\ >.

system survivability: the capability of a system to fulfill its mission, in a timely manner, in the presence of attacks, failures, or accidents.

task: (1) the term used to describe a process; (2) the basic unit of concurrent programming languages that defines a sequence of instructions that may be executed in parallel with other similar units.

TCP/IP reference model: a common acronym for the suite of transport-layer and application-layer protocols that operate over the Internet Protocol.

terabyte (TB): a unit of memory or storage space equal to 1,099,511,627,776 bytes or 2^{40} bytes. One terabyte equals approximately 1 trillion bytes.

teraflop: a benchmark used to measure processing speed. One teraflop equals 1 trillion floating point operations per second.

test-and-set: an indivisible machine instruction known simply as *TS,* which is executed in a single machine cycle and was first introduced by IBM for its multiprocessing System 360/370 computers to determine whether the processor was available.

third generation: the era of computer development beginning in the mid-1960s that introduced integrated circuits and miniaturization of components to replace transistors, reduce costs, work faster, and increase reliability.

thrashing: a phenomenon in a virtual memory system where an excessive amount of page swapping back and forth between main memory and secondary storage results in higher overhead and little useful work.

thread: a portion of a program that can run independently of other portions. Multithreaded application programs can have several threads running at one time with the same or different priorities.

Thread Control Block (TCB): a data structure that contains information about the current status and characteristics of a thread.

throughput: a composite measure of a system's efficiency that counts the number of jobs served in a given unit of time.

ticket granting ticket: a virtual *ticket* given by a Kerberos server indicating that the user holding the ticket can be granted access to specific application servers. The user sends this encrypted ticket to the remote application server, which can then examine it to verify the user's identity and authenticate the user.

time bomb: a virus with a trigger linked to a certain year, month, day, or time that causes it to execute.

time quantum: a period of time assigned to a process for execution. When it expires the resource is preempted, and the process is assigned another time quantum for use in the future.

time-sharing system: a system that allows each user to interact directly with the operating system via commands entered from a keyboard. Also called *interactive system*.

time slice: another term for *time quantum*.

token: a unique bit pattern that all stations on the LAN recognize as a permission to transmit indicator.

token bus: a type of local area network with nodes connected to a common cable using a CSMA/CA protocol.

token ring: a type of local area network with stations wired into a ring network. Each station constantly passes a token on to the next. Only the station with the token may send a message.

track: a path along which data is recorded on a magnetic medium such as tape or disk.

transfer rate: the rate with which data is transferred from sequential access media. For magnetic tape, it is equal to the product of the tape's density and its transport speed.

transfer time: the time required for data to be transferred between secondary storage and main memory.

transport speed: the speed that magnetic tape must reach before data is either written to or read from it. A typical transport speed is 200 inches per second.

trap door: an unspecified and nondocumented entry point to the system. It represents a significant security risk.

Trojan: a malicious computer program with side effects that are not intended by the user who executes the program. Also called a *Trojan horse*.

turnaround time: a measure of a system's efficiency that tracks the time required to execute a job and return output to the user.

universal serial bus (USB) controller: the interface between the operating system, device drivers, and applications that read and write to devices connected to the computer through the USB port. Each USB port can accommodate up to 127 different devices.

unsafe state: a situation in which the system has too few available resources to guarantee the completion of at least one job running on the system. It can lead to deadlock.

user: anyone who requires the services of a computer system.

user mode: name given to indicate that processes are not granted privileged access to the processor. Therefore, certain instructions are not allowed and system memory isn't accessible. Contrasts with the less restrictive *kernel mode*.

V: an operation performed on a semaphore that may cause a waiting process to continue. It stands for the Dutch word *verhogen*, meaning *to increment*, and it is part of the P and V operations to test and increment.

variable-length record: a record that isn't of uniform length, doesn't leave empty storage space, and doesn't truncate any characters, thus eliminating the two disadvantages of fixed-length records. It contrasts with a *fixed-length record.*

verification: the process of making sure that an access request is valid.

version control: the tracking and updating of a specific release of a piece of hardware or software.

victim: an expendable job that is selected for removal from a deadlocked system to provide more resources to the waiting jobs and resolve the deadlock.

virtual device: a dedicated device that has been transformed into a shared device through the use of spooling techniques.

virtual memory: a technique that allows programs to be executed even though they are not stored entirely in memory. It gives the user the illusion that a large amount of main memory is available when, in fact, it is not.

virtualization: the creation of a virtual version of hardware or software. Operating system virtualization allows a single CPU to run multiple operating system images at the same time.

virus: a program that replicates itself on a computer system by incorporating itself into other programs, including those in secondary storage, that are shared among other computer systems.

volume: any secondary storage unit, such as hard disks, disk packs, CDs, DVDs, removable disks, or tapes. When a volume contains several files it is called a *multifile volume.* When a file is extremely large and contained in several volumes it is called a *multivolume file.*

WAIT and SIGNAL: a modification of the test-and-set synchronization mechanism that is designed to remove busy waiting.

WAITING: a job status that means that the job can't continue until a specific resource is allocated or an I/O operation has finished.

waiting time: the amount of time a process spends waiting for resources, primarily I/O devices. It affects throughput and utilization.

warm boot: a feature that allows the I/O system to recover I/O operations that were in progress when a power failure occurred.

wide area network (WAN): a network usually constructed with long-distance, point-to-point lines, covering a large geographic area.

wire tapping: a system security violation in which unauthorized users monitor or modify a user's transmission.

working directory: the directory or subdirectory in which the user is currently working.

working set: a collection of pages to be kept in main memory for each active process in a virtual memory environment.

workstation: a desktop computer attached to a local area network that serves as an access point to that network.

worm: a computer program that replicates itself and is self-propagating in main memory. Worms, as opposed to viruses, are meant to spawn in network environments.

Bibliography

Anderson, R. E. (1991). ACM code of ethics and professional conduct: *Communications of the ACM. 35* (5), 94–99.

Apple (2009). *Technology brief: Mac OS X for UNIX users.* www.apple.com/macosx retrieved 11/5/2009.

Barnes, J. G. P. (1980). An overview of Ada. Software Practice and Experience, 10, 85187.

Belady, L. A., Nelson, R. A., & Shelder, G. S. (1969, June). An anomaly in space-time characteristics of certain programs running in a paging environment. *CACM, 12*(6), 349–353.

Ben-Ari, M. (1982). *Principles of concurrent programming.* Englewood Cliffs, NJ: Prentice-Hall.

Bhargava, R. (1995). *Open VMS: architecture, use, and migration.* New York: McGraw-Hill.

Bic, L. & Shaw, A. C. (1988). *The logical design of operating systems* (2nd ed.). Englewood Cliffs, NJ: Prentice-Hall.

Bic, L. & Shaw, A. C. (2003). *Operating systems principles.* Upper Saddle River, NJ: Pearson Education, Inc.

Bourne, S. R. (1987). *The UNIX system V environment.* Reading, MA: Addison-Wesley.

Brain, M. (1994). *Win32 system services. The heart of Windows NT.* Englewood Cliffs, NJ: Prentice-Hall.

Calingaert, P. (1982). *Operating system elements: A user perspective.* Englewood Cliffs, NJ: Prentice-Hall.

Christian, K. (1983). *The UNIX operating system.* New York: Wiley.

Columbus, L. & Simpson, N. (1995). *Windows NT for the technical professional.* Santa Fe: OnWord Press.

Courtois, P. J., Heymans, F. & Parnas, D. L. (1971, October). Concurrent control with readers and writers. *CACM, 14*(10), 667–668.

CSO Online (2004, May). 2004 E-Crime Watch SURVEY., www.csoonline.com.

Custer, H. (1993). *Inside Windows NT.* Redmond, WA: Microsoft Press.

Davis, W. S. & Rajkumar, T.M. (2001). *Operating systems: A systematic view* (5th ed.). Reading, MA: Addison-Wesley.

Deitel, H., Deitel, P., & Choffnes, D. (2004). *Operating systems* (3rd ed.). Upper Saddle River, NJ: Pearson Education, Inc.

Denning, D.E. (1999). *Information warfare and security.* Reading, MA: Addison-Wesley.

Dettmann, T. R. (1988). *DOS programmer's reference.* Indianapolis, IN: Que Corporation.

Dijkstra, E. W. (1965). *Cooperating sequential processes*. Technical Report EWD-123, Technological University, Eindhoven, The Netherlands. Reprinted in Genuys (1968), 43–112.

Dijkstra, E. W. (1968, May). The structure of the T.H.E. multiprogramming system. *CACM, 11*(5), 341–346.

Dougherty, E.R. & Laplante, P.S. (1995). *Introduction to real-time imaging, Understanding Science & Technology Series*. New York: IEEE Press.

Dukkipati, N., Ganjali, Y., & Zhang-Shen, R. (2005). *Typical versus Worst Case Design in Networking*, Fourth Workshop on Hot Topics in Networks (HotNets-IV), College Park.

Fitzgerald, J. (1993). *Business data communications. Basic concepts, security, and design* (4th ed.). New York: Wiley.

Frank, L. R. (Ed.). (2001). *Quotationary*. New York: Random House.

Gal, E. & Toledo, S. (2005). *Algorithms and data structures for flash memories*. (Author Abstract). In ACM Computing Surveys, 37, 138(26).

Gollmann, D. (1999). *Computer security*. Chichester, England: Wiley.

Gosling, J. & McGilton, H. (1996). *The Java language environment: Contents*. Sun Microsystems, Inc., http://java.sun.com/docs/white/langenv/.

Harvey, M.S. & Szubowicz, L.S. (1996). Extending OpenVMS for 64-bit addressable virtual memory. *Digital Technical Journal, 8*(2), 57–70.

Havender, J. W. (1968). Avoiding deadlocks in multitasking systems. *IBMSJ, 7*(2), 74–84.

Haviland, K. & Salama, B. (1987). *UNIX system programming*. Reading, MA: Addison-Wesley.

Horvath, D. B. (1998). *UNIX for the mainframer* (2nd ed.). Upper Saddle River, NJ: Prentice-Hall PTR.

Howell, M.A. & Palmer, J.M. (1996). Integrating the Spiralog file system into the OpenVMS operating system. *Digital Technical Journal, 8*(2), 46–56.

Hugo, I. (1993). *Practical open systems. A guide for managers* (2nd ed.). Oxford, England: NCC Blackwell Ltd.

IEEE. (2004). *Standard for Information Technology — Portable Operating System Interface (POSIX) 1003.1-2001/Cor 2-2004*. IEEE Computer Society.

Intel. (1999). *What is Moore's Law?*, http://www.pentium.de/intel/museum/25anniv/hof/moore.htm.

Johnson, J.E. & Laing, W.A. (1996). Overview of the Spiralog file system. *Digital Technical Journal, 8*(2), 5–14.

Lai, S.K. (2008). Flash memories: successes and challenges, IBM Journal Research & Development. 52(4/5), 529–535.

Lewis, T. (1999). Mainframes are dead, long live mainframes. *Computer, 32*(8), 102–104.

Linger, R.C. et al. (2002). Life-cycle models for survivable systems. (CMU/SEI-2002-TR-026). Pittsburgh, PA: Software Engineering Institute, Carnegie Mellon University.

Negus, C. et al. (2007). *Linux Bible 2007 Edition*. Indianapolis, IN: Wiley Publishing.

Otellini, P. (2006). Paul Otellini Keynote. http://www.intel.com/pressroom/kits/events/idffall_2006/pdf/idf 09-26-06 paul otellini keynote transcript.pdf.

Pase, D.M. & Eckl, M.A. (2005). *A comparison of single-core and dual-core Opteron processor performance for HPC.* http://www-03.ibm.com/servers/eserver/opteron/pdf/IBM_dualcore.pdf.

Petersen, R. (1998). *Linux: the complete reference* (2nd ed.). Berkeley, CA: Osborne/McGraw-Hill.

Pfaffenberger, B. (Ed.). (2001). *Webster's new world computer dictionary (9th ed.).* New York: Hungry Minds.

Pinkert, J. R. & Wear, L. L. (1989). *Operating systems: concepts, policies, and mechanisms.* Englewood Cliffs, NJ: Prentice-Hall.

Ritchie, D. M. & Thompson, K. (1978, July–August). The UNIX time-sharing system. *The Bell Systems Technical Journal, 57*(6), 1905–1929.

Rubini, A. & Corbet, J. (2001). *Linux Device Drivers* (2nd ed.). Sebastopol, CA: O'Reilly.

Ruley, J. D., et al. (1994). *Networking Windows NT.* New York: Wiley.

Shoch, J. F. & Hupp, J. A. (1982, March). The "worm" programs—early experience with a distributed computation. *Communications of the ACM, 25*(3), 172–180.

Stair, R.M. & Reynolds, G.W. (1999). *Principles of Information Systems* (4th ed.). Cambridge, MA: Course Technology-ITP.

Stallings, W. (1994). *Data and computer communications* (4th ed.). New York: Macmillan.

Swabey, M., Beeby, S., Brown, A., & Chad, J. (2004). "Using Otoacoustic Emissions as a Biometric," *Proceedings of the First International Conference on Biometric Authentication, Hong Kong, China,* July 2004, 600–606.

The Open Group, (2009). The History of the Single UNIX® Specification Poster. www.unix.org/Posters/ Retrieved: 11/5/2009.

Thompson, K. (1978, July–August). UNIX implementation. *The Bell Systems Technical Journal, 57*(6), 1905–1929.

Wall, K., Watson, M., & Whitis, M. (1999). *Linux programming unleashed.* Indianapolis, IN: Sams Publishing.

Index